Education Law

Third Edition

ANTHONY F. BROWN
LL.B., LL.M., M.Ed.

MARVIN A. ZUKER
B.A., LL.B., M.Ed.
JUSTICE OF THE ONTARIO COURT
OF JUSTICE

© 2002 Thomson Canada Limited

All rights reserved. No part of this publication may be reproduced, stored in a retrieval system, or transmitted, in any form or by any means, electronic, mechanical, photocopying, recording, or otherwise, without the prior written permission of the publisher.

The publisher is not engaged in rendering legal, accounting or other professional advice. If legal advice or other expert assistance is required, the services of a competent professional should be sought. The analysis contained herein represents the opinions of the authors and should in no way be construed as being official or unofficial policy of any governmental body.

Canadian Cataloguing in Publication Data

Brown, Anthony F., 1953–
   Education law/Anthony F. Brown, Marvin A. Zuker. — 3rd ed.

Includes bibliographical references and index.
ISBN 0-459-24035-8

   1. Educational law and legislation — Canada. I. Zuker, Marvin A. II. Title.

KE3805.B76 2002   344.71'07   C2002-903555-4
KF4119.B76 2002

The paper used in this publication meets the minimum requirements of the American National Standard for Information Sciences — Permanence of Paper for Printed Library Materials, ANSI X39.48-1984.

THOMSON
★ ™
CARSWELL

One Corporate Plaza, 2075 Kennedy Road, Toronto, Ontario M1T 3V4
Customer Service:
Toronto: 1-416-609-3800
Elsewhere in Canada/U.S. 1-800-387-5164
Fax 1-416-298-5094

Dedicated To

Rebecca Brooke Zuker

and

Sebastian Étienne-Pascal Maoming Brown

Preface to the Third Edition

Education law will always be important to those of us who are interested in children. In fact, the seemingly endless proliferation of new statutes, regulations, case law and government memoranda speak of the need to be ever vigilant of how new laws affect education. The challenge for lawyers and educators, then, is to harness the knowledge in this ever-growing field so that we can all make our schools better places for all children. Education law is a dynamic, invigorating and intellectually stimulating discipline because it is constantly evolving. That evolution is reflected in the changes to this edition of *Education Law*.

This edition discusses recent developments in the area of school boards' vicarious liability and fiduciary responsibility in respect of sexual assaults committed by staff against students. We also explain Ontario's new provisions in the *Education Act* about suspension and expulsion of pupils and we discuss the potential impact of the new "zero tolerance" approach to student discipline, which appears headed for the same extreme and unfortunate results precipitated by similar policies in the United States. We discuss the recent Ontario court decision upholding the constitutionality of section 43 of the *Criminal Code* which permits corrective force to be used on a child. In addition, the chapter on special education has been updated to reflect important regulatory changes providing for enhanced parental participation in the identification and placement of exceptional pupils.

The education community has not seen, at the time of writing, the final judicial word on the ability of school boards to limit teachers' and students' *Charter* freedoms both within and outside the school. Moreover, the Constitutional rights of Roman Catholics continue to be the subject of litigation, as examined in Chapter One. Indeed, an Ontario court recently held that a separate school board could not prohibit a gay student from attending a school prom with his partner.

The evolution of education law is also seen in the centralization of government control over education that impinges on the traditional local autonomy of elected trustees, particularly in curriculum and financing. Of course, this trend is not unique to Ontario or, indeed, to Canada. On the other hand, some jurisdictions have delegated significant power to parent councils. Although some would argue that centralization is necessary to deal with inconsistent educational standards and inequality of opportunity, only time will tell whether centralized curriculum and testing policy, including testing, evaluation and upgrading of teachers, will improve the quality and accountability of the education system over the long term. We note, further, that Ontario has taken steps to ensure that certain safeguards are put in place against sexual misconduct by teachers. In particular, the

Student Protection Act, 2002 was passed in June, 2002 in response to an important report by Mr. Justice Sydney L. Robins on sexual misconduct in schools.

It is an underlying premise of this book that legal issues in education are better understood in the context of other, related areas of law, such as family law and young offenders law. To that end, we have included information about matters such as custody, access, separation and divorce, and we have included a summary of the changes brought about by the *Youth Criminal Justice Act*, which (when proclaimed) will replace the *Young Offenders Act*. Making streets safer has as much to do with literacy as it does with law, with the strength of families as with the length of sentences, with early intervention as with mandatory supervision. Crime prevention means recognizing connections between the crime rate and the unemployment rate, between how a child behaves at school and whether that child has had a hot meal that day.

Changes to our schools should not be driven by myths or by attempts at fiscal restraint masquerading as educational reform. Improvements must be based on principles that have to do with the kind of education we want for our children. If we view education as a commodity or a product, as opposed to a process, we run the risk of losing control over our own future. The responsibility for educating our young people is a collective responsibility. We all have an interest, and a say, in seeing that our schools reflect our society's values. Values and motivation are at the core of educational achievement. Kids do well in school when their internal value system encourages achievement, when their parents and teachers demand it and when their peers reinforce it.

The message from many teachers is that children today come with more emotional baggage than ever before. Many teachers feel they need more time and training to meet their many daily challenges. Teaching our young people has always been a demanding and exhausting job. It can be rewarding and even exhilarating. However, when children with increasingly complex needs are put into larger schools with larger classes teachers feel overworked, overstressed and burned out. Teachers today not only teach, but also act as counsellor, social worker, administrator, and marketing director, bringing in everything from art therapy to conflict resolution and anger management programs.

The legal issues in education reflect that all of the constituent elements of the education system must work collaboratively. Parents hold the responsibility for supporting their child's efforts to succeed, and teachers hold the professional responsibility to apply effective pedagogy and to challenge their students to reach their full potential. However, an effective system depends on the role of the larger community in ensuring student success. What happens to a child outside the classroom, whether it is nurturing and supportive or abusive and neglectful, clearly affects the ability of a teacher to teach that child. Without family literacy support services, without tutors and mentors, without after-school, weekend enrichment and recreational programs, and without childcare and pre-school services, it is difficult to provide healthy relationships and environments conducive to fostering a real sense of community belonging and to reducing school misconduct and crime.

We hope that this edition will assist the reader in understanding and reflecting upon the legal issues that continue to confront educators, lawyers and courts, and to appreciate how the law has evolved to this point. Where appropriate, we have set out the law in a contextual discussion that shows why the issues are important to the health and well-being of children, and of society in general.

Justice Marvin A. Zuker
Anthony F. Brown

July 2002

Acknowledgments

The authors wish to acknowledge our heartfelt appreciation to our respective spouses, Catherine Sim and Brenda Zuker. As many of us increasingly discover, life sometimes seems too full to get everything done, but Catherine and Brenda helped us find the time for writing, and supported us with both encouragement and suggestions. We are also indebted to our Product Development Manager at Carswell, Fred Glady, who provided highly professional assistance to us, along with gentle prodding to keep us to deadlines. He is a pleasure to work with.

Contents

Preface v
Acknowledgements ix
Table of Cases xiii
Chapter 1 **School Boards** 1
Chapter 2 **Civil Liability of School Boards and Their Employees** 77
Chapter 3 **The Family** 149
Chapter 4 **Pupils and the Law** 203
Chapter 5 **Special Education** 291
Chapter 6 **Teachers** 305
Appendix **Canadian Charter of Rights and Freedoms** 373
               Young Offenders Act 383
Index 393

Table of Cases

A.(C.) v. C.(J.W.) (1998), 196 D.L.R. (4th) 475 (B.C.C.A.) 140
A.(L.L.) v. B.(A.) (1995), 103 C.C.C. (3d) 92 (S.C.C.) 279
Abbey v. Essex (County) Board of Education (1999), 42 O.R. (3d) 481
 (C.A.) 25
Abbotsford School Dist. 34 v. Shewan (1987), 21 B.C.L.R. (2d) 93 at 97
 (C.A.) 317
Adler v. Ontario, [1996] 3 S.C.R. 609, 140 D.L.R. (4th) 407 .... 6, 7, 8
Agostini v. Felton, 65 U.S.L.W. 4524 (1997) 209
Aguilar v. Felton, 473 U.S. 402 (1985) 209
Alabama & Coushatta Tribes v. Big Sandy School Dist., 817 F. Supp 1319 (E.D.
 Tex. 1993) 249
Albach v. Odle, 531 F. 2d 983 (10th Cir. 1976) 206
Anderson v. Twin Rivers School Division No. 65 (1994), 19 Alta. L.R. (3d) 408
 (Q.B.) 40
Anderson v. Vansittart (1849), 5 U.C.Q.B. 335 (C.A.) 70
Aragona v. Elegant Lamp Co. (1982), 3 C.H.R.R. D/1109 (Bd. Of Inquiry) .. 331
Archbishop Walsh High School v. Section VI of New York State Public High
 School Athletic Assn. 88 N.Y. 2d 131, 666 N.E. 2d 521, 643 N.Y.S. 2d 928
 (1996) 209
Arsenault-Cameron v. Prince Edward Island, [2000] 1 S.C.R. 3 .... 26, 27, 28
Avery v. Homewood City Bd. of Education, 674 F. 337 (1982) 344
B.(J.) v. B.(A.W.), [1958] O.R. 281 (C.A.) 167
B.(P.A.) v. Curry (1997), 146 D.L.R. (4th) 72 (B.C.C.A.), additional reasons 1997
 CarswellBC 1169 (C.A.), leave to appeal allowed (1997), 104 B.C.A.C. 239
 (S.C.C.), affirmed (1999), 62 B.C.L.R. (3d) 173 (S.C.C) 125, 126, 127,
 129, 130, 135
B.(R.) v. Children's Aid Society of Metropolitan Toronto, [1995] 1 S.C.R.
 315 .... 185, 186, 189
B.(S.M.) v. B.(K.R.) (1997), CarswellOnt 3050 (Ont. Gen. Div.) 174
Bain v. Calgary Board of Education, [1994] 2 W.W.R. 468 (Alta. Q.B.) 90, 92
Bains v. Hill (1992), 93 D.L.R. (4th) 117 (B.C.C.A.) 120
Baker v. Canada (Minister of Citizenship & Immigration), [1999] 2 S.CF.R.
 417 .... 40, 196, 229
Bal v. Ontario (Attorney General) (1994), 121 D.L.R. (4th) 96 (Ont. Gen.
 Div.) 15
Baldwin v. Lyons (1961), 29 D.L.R. (2d) 290 (Ont. C.A.), affirmed (1962), 36
 D.L.R. (2d) 244 (S.C.C.) 101
Bales v. Central Okanagan (Board of School Trustees, School District 23) (1984),
 54 B.C.L.R. 203 (B.C.S.C.) 297
Bareham v. London (Bd. of Education) (1984), 46 O.R. (2d) 705 (C.A.) 60
Barnes v. Hampshire County Council, [1969] 3 All E.R. 746 (H.L.) 101, 103

Beauparlent v. Bd. of Trustees of Separate School Section No. 1 of Appleby, [1955] 4 D.L.R. 558 (Ont. H.C.) 79
Becker v. Pettkus, [1980] 2 S.C.R. 834 (S.C.C.) 155
Bell v. Ladas (1980), 1 C.H.R.R. D/155 at D/156 (Bd. Of Inquiry) 331, 332
Benn v. Lozinski (1982), 37 O.R. (2d) 607 (Co. Ct.) 49
Berardinelli v. Ontario Housing Corp. (1978), 90 D.L.R. (3d) 48 (S.C.C.) 112
Bethel School Dist. No. 403 v. Fraser, 478 U.S. 675, 106 S.Ct. 3159, 92 L.E.2d 549 (1986) 238, 241, 251
Bezaire v. Bezaire (1980), 20 R.F.L. (2d) 358 (Ont. C.A.) 163
Bezaire (Litigation Guardian of) v. Windsor (Roman Catholic Separate School Board) (1992), 9 O.R. (3d) 737 (Div. Ct.) 59, 60
Black v. Metropolitan Separate School Board (1988), 65 O.R. (2d) 598 (Div. Ct.) 16, 344
Blore v. Halifax (Dist. School Bd.) (1991), 105 N.S.R. (2d) 414, 284 A.P.R. 414 (T.D.) 59
Board of Education v. Ingels, 394 N.E. 2d 69 (1979) 358
Board of Education for the City of London and O.S.S.T.F. (1993), E.R.C. 504 356
Board of Education of City of Chicago v. Box, 547 N.E. 2d 627 (Ill. App. Dist. 1989) 322
Boryszko v. Toronto (City Board of Education, [1962] O.R. 600 (H.C.), reversed [1963] 1 O.R. 1 (C.A.) 120
Bradstreet v. Sobol, 225 A.D. 2d 175, 650 N.Y.S. 2d 402 (N.Y. App. 1996) .. 208
Brown v. Bd. of Education of Topeka, 347 U.S. 483 at 493 (1954) 204
Brown v. Essex (County) Roman Catholic Separate School Board (1990), Action No. 453/85 (Ont. H.C.) 97, 106, 110
Bundy v. Jackson, 641 F. 2d 934 (1981) 332
Burgis v. Brampton (City) Public Library Board (1994), 110 D.L.R. (4th) 210 (Ont. Div. Ct.) 41
Burk v. Burk, [1991] O.J. No. 1443, 1991 CarswellOnt 293 (Ont. U.F.C.) 172
Burke v. Yeshiva Beit Yitzchak of Hamilton (1996) 90 O.A.C. 81 (Div. Ct.) .. 74, 229
Butterworth v. Ottawa (Collegiate Institute Board), [1940] 3 D.L.R. 466 (Ont. H.C.) 94, 95, 106
C., Re (1999), 181 D.L.R. (4th) 300 (Alta. Q.B.) 162
Calder v. Calder (1974), 15 R.F.L. 265 (Ont. H.C.) 167, 768
Caldwell v. Stuart (1985), 15 D.L.R. (4th) 1 (S.C.C.) 15, 344
Callon v. Callon (1999), 68 C.R.R. (3d) 350, [1990] O.J. No. 3108 (Ont. Div. Ct.) 184
Campbell v. Bd. of Education of New Milford, 475 A. 2d 289 (Conn. 1984)   239
Canada v. Sask. Wheat Pool, [1983] 1 S.C.R. 205 (S.C.C.) 142
Canada (Director of Investigation & Research, Combines Investigation Branch) v. Southam Inc., [1984] 2 S.C.R. 145 (S.C.C.) 219
Canadian Foundation for Children, Youth & the Law v. Canada (Attorney General) (2000), 49 O.R. (3d) 662, [2000] O.J. No. 2535, 2000 CarswellOnt 2409 (S.C.J.), additional reasons 2001 CarswellOnt 935 (Ont. S.C.J.), affirmed 207 D.L.R. (4th) 632 (Ont C.A.) 192, 193, 194

Capital Cities Communications Inc. v. Canada (Radio-Television &
  Telecommunications Commission) [1978] 2 S.C.R. 141 236
Cardinal v. Kent Institution (1985), 24 D.L.R. (4th) 44 (S.C.C.) 38
Carruthers v. College of Nurses of Ontario (1996), 31 O.R. (3d) 377 (Div.
  Ct.) 321
Casagrande v. Hinton (R.C. Separate School Dist. No.155) (1987), 51 Alta. L.R.
  (2d) 349 (Q.B.) 16, 344
Cashin v. C.B.C. (No. 2) (1990), 12 C.H.R.R. D/222 (Cdn. Human Rights
  Trib) 333
Catherwood (Guardian ad litem of) v. Heinrichs, [1996] B.C.J. No. 1373, 1996
  CarswellBC 1411 (B.C.S.C.) 87
Cdn. Civil Liberties Assn. v. Ontario (Min. of Education) (1990), 71 O.R. (2d)
  341 (C.A.) 55
Cdn. National Ry. Co. v. Canada (Cdn. Human Rights Commn.) (1987), 8
  C.H.R.R. D/4210 .... 333, 334
Centurion Investigations Ltd. v. Villemaire (1979), 23 O.R. (2d) 371 (Div.
  Ct.) 233
Chabot v. Manitoba (Horse Racing Commission), [1987] 1 W.W.R. 149 (Man.
  C.A.), leave to appeal refused (1987), 50 Man. R. (2d) 79n (S.C.C.) 233
Chalifoux v. New Cancy Independent School District, 976 F. Supp. 659 (1997)
  243
Chamberlain v. Surrey School District No. 36 (1998), 168 D.L.R (4th) 222
  (B.C.S.C [in Chambers]), reversed (2000), 191 D.L.R (4th) 128 (B.C.C.A),
  additional reasons at (2001), 2001 CarswellBc 2146 (C.A.), leave to appeal
  allowed (2001), 2001 CarswellBC 2121 (S.C.C.) 34
Cirillo v. Milwaukee, 150 N.W 2d 460 (Wis. 1967) 94
Clark v. Monmouthshire County Council (1954), 52 L.G.R. 246 93
Clark (Litigation Guardian of) v. Ontario Federation of School Athletic Assn.,
  [1997] O.J. No. 94, 1997 CarswellOnt 397 (Gen. Div) 208
Cloutier c. Lasglois, [1990] 1 S.C.R. 158 (S.C.C.) 370
Colby v. Schmidt (1986), 37 C.C.L.T 1 (B.C.S.C) 133
Committee for the Commonwealth of Canada (1991), 4 C.R.R. (2d) 60
  (S.C.C) 53
Conseil des ecoles séparées catholiques romaines de Dufferin & Peel v. Ontario
  (Ministre de l'éducation & de la formation) (1996), 30 O.R. (3d) 681(Div.
  Ct.), leave to appeal allowed (1996), 30 O.R. (3d) 681n (C.A.) 25
Cook v. Dufferin-Peel (R.C. Separate School Bd.) (1983), 34 C.P.C. 178 (Ont.
  Master) 277
Cox v. Dardenelle, 790 F. 2d 668 (1986) 355
Crawford v. Ottawa (Bd. of Education), [1971] 1 O.R. 267 (H.C.), affirmed
  [1971] 2 O.R. 179 (C.A.) 60
Crocker v. Sundance Northwest Resorts Ltd. (1988), 51 D.L.R. (4th) 321
  (S.C.C.) 120
Cromer v. B.C.T.F. (1986), 29 D.L.R. (4th) 641 (B.C. C.A.). 355
Crosby v. Crosby (1971), 6 R.F.L. 8 (Ont. H.C.) 170
Crouch v. Essex County Council (1966), 64 L.G.R. 240 100
D.(C.) (Litigation Guardian of) v. Ridley College (1996), 138 D.L.R (4th) 176
  (Ont. Gen. Div.) 72, 73, 229

Dalli v. Bd. of Education, 267 N.E. 2d 219 (Mass. 1971) 210
Daly v. Ontario (Attorney General) (1987), 38 O.R. (3d) 37, 154 D.L.R. (4th) 464
   (Gen. Div.); affirmed (1999), 172 D.L.R. (4th) 241 (Ont. C.A.) 20, 21
Dao (Guardian ad litem of) v. Sabatino (1993), 16 C.C.L.I. (2d) 235
   (B.C.S.C.) 102
Davidson v. Winston-Salem, 303 S.E. 2d 202 350
Davis v. Munroe County Bd. of Education, 74 F.3d 118 Cat 1193 (U.S. 11th Cir.,
   1996) 357
Des Champs v. Prescott-Russell (Conseil des écoles séparées catholiques de
   langue française) (1997), 1997 CarswellOnt 11 (C.A.) leave to appeal
   allowed (1997), 108 O.A.C. 159n (S.C.C.); leave to appeal allowed (1997),
   109 O.A.C. 200n, reversed 117 D.L.R. (4th) 23, [1999] 3 S.C.R. 343 70,
                                                                                                            112, 115
Devita v. Coburn (1997), 15 O.R. (2d) 769 (Co. Ct.) 50
Dhillon v. F.W. Woolworth Co. (1982), 3 C.A.R.R. D/743 (Bd. of Inquiry)   332
Dobson (Litigation Guardian of) v. Dobson (1999), 45 C.C.L.T. (2d) 217 (S.C.C)
   188
Doe v. Koger, 480 F. Supp. 255 (N. d. Ind. 1979) 293
Dolphin Delivery Ltd. v. R.W.E.S.U. Local 580 (1986), 38 C.C.L.T 184
   (S.C.C.) 187
Dolyny v. Fort Frances-Rainy River Board of Education (July 27, 1995), Fort
   Francis 885/95 (Ont. Gen. Div.) 60
Donohue v. Copiague Union Free School District, 407 N.Y.S. 2d 874, 64 A.D. 2d
   29 (1978) 143, 144, 145
Doucet v. Doucet (1974), 4 O.R. (2d) 27 (Co. Ct.) 171
Douglas/Kwantlen Faculty Association v. Douglas College, [1990] 3 S.C.R. 570
   (S.C.C.) 364, 367
Droit de la famille - 1150, [1993] 4 S.C.R. 141 (S.C.C.) 189, 190
Dubé v. Labar (1986), 27 D.L.R. (4th) 653 (S.C.C.) 120
Durham Board of Education and O.S.S.T.F., Re (1990), E.R.C. 118 355
Dustin W. Seal v. Knox County Board of Education, 2000 U.S. App. Lexis 24939
   (2000) 236
Dziwenka v. R., [1972] S.C.R. 419 .... 84, 95
Eaton v. Brant County Board of Education, [1977] 1 S.C.R. 241 (S.C.C.) 289,
                                                                                                            297, 298
Eckman v. Bd. of Hawthorne School Dist., 636 F. Supp. 1214 (1986) 344
Eddington v. Kent County (Board of Education) (1986), 56 O.R. (2d) 403 at 406
   (Ont. Div. Ct.) 112
Edmondson v. Moose Jaw (Bd. of Trustees) (1920), 55 D.L.R. 563 (Sask.
   C.A.) 101
Einarson v. Einarson, [1971] 5 W.W.R. 478 (B.C.S.C.) 170
Eisel v. Board of Education of Montgomery, 597 A. 2d 454 (1991) 254
Elliott v. Burin School District No. 7 (1998), 13 Admin. L.R. (3d) 91 (Nfld.
   C.A.) 62
Eshome v. Board of Education of School District of the State of Nebraska, 364
   N.W. (2d) 7 (1985). 351
Essex County (Roman Catholic Separate School Board) v. Porter (1978), 21 O.R.
   (2d) 255 (C.A.) 15

TABLE OF CASES xvii

Essex County (Roman Catholic Separate School Board) v. Tremblay-Webster (1984), 45 O.R. (2d) 83 (C.A.) 16, 344
Essex (County) Roman Catholoic Separate School Board v. Porter (1977), 78 D.L.R. (3d) 417 (Ont. Div. Ct.) 344
Eston-Elrose (School Division No. 33) v. Stoneouse (1988), 65 Sask. R. 216 (Q.B.) 353
Etobicoke Board of Education v. O.S.S.T.F. (1981), 2 L.A.C. (3d) 265 (Ont.) 356
Evans v. Milton (1979), 24 O.R. (2d) 181 (C.A.), leave to appeal refused (1979), 28 N.R. 86 (note) (S.C.C.) 233
FCC v. Pacifica, 438 U.S. 726, 98 S.Ct. 3026, 57 L.Ed.2d 1073 (1978) 238
Finot v. Pasadena City Bd. of Education, 58 Cal. Rptr. 520 (1967) 343
Fisher v. Burkburnett Independent School Dist., 419 F. Supp. 1200 (N.D. Tex. 1976) 239
Fisher Park Residents Assn. Inc. v. Ottawa (Bd. of Education) (1986), 57 O.R. (2d) 486 (H.C.) 59, 61
Fleetwood v. Board of Educ., 252 N.E. 2d 318 (U.S. Ohio, 1969) 225
Fogel v. Fogel (1976), 24 R.F.L. 18 (Ont. H.C.), affirmed (1979), 9 R.F.L. (2d) 55 (Ont. C.A.) 169
Forrester v. Saliba, [2000] O.J. No. 3018, 2000 CarswellOnt 2835 (C.J.) 163
Forster v. Forster, [1955] 4 D.L.R. 710 (Ont. C.A.) 169
Frame v. Smith (1987), 42 D.L.R. (4th) 81 (S.C.C.) 135, 136
Frank v. Orleans Parish School Bd., 195 So. 2d 451 (1967) 132
Fraser v. Campbell River (Board of School Trustees of School District No. 72) (1987), 5 A.C.W.S. (3d) 300 (B.C.S.C.) 100
Fraser v. Canada (Public Service Staff Relations Board), [1985] 2 S.C.R. 455 (S.C.C.) 343
Funk v. Wellington County Roman Catholic Separate School Board (1994), 71 O.A.C. 321 (Div. Ct.) 60
Furey v. Conception Bay Centre (R.C. School Bd.) (1993), 104 D.L.R. (4th) 455 (Nfld. C.A.) 59, 63
G.(C.E.), Re, [1995] O.J. No. 4072, [1995] CarswellOnt 612 (Gen. Div.) 162
G.C.(E.D) v. Hammer, [2001] B.C.J. No 585, 2001 CarswellBC 721 (C.A.) 137, 138
Galbraith v. Galbraith (1969), 69 W.W.R. 390 (Man. C.A.) 167
Gard v. Duncan (Bd. of School Trustees) [1946] 2 D.L.R. 441 (B.C.C.A.) 85
Garrod v. Rhema Christian School (1991), 15 C.H.R.R. D/477 (Ont. Bd. of Inquiry) 16
George v. Port Alberni (Bd. of Trustees, School Dist. 70) (1986), 3 A.C.W.S. (3d) 361 (B.C.S.C.) 101
Gianfrancesco v. Junior Academy Inc., [2001] O.J. No. 2730, 201 CarswellOnt 2383 (S.C.J.), additional reasons 2001 CarswellOnt 4536 (S.C.J.) 229
Gibbs v. Jalbert (1996), 18 B.C.L.R. (3d) 351 (C.A.) 122
Ginsberg v. New York, 390 U.S. 629, 88 S.Ct. 1274, 20 L.Ed.2d 195 (1968) 238
Giouvanoudis v. Golden Fleece Restaurant (1984), 5 C.H.R.R. D/1967 (Bd. of Inquiry) 332

xviii EDUCATION LAW

Goodwin c. Laurenval (Commn. scolaire) (1991), 8 C.C.L.T. (2d) 267 (S.C. Qué.) 79
Gordon v. Goertz, [1996] 2 S.C.R. 27, 19 R.F.L. (4th) 177, 134 D.L.R. (4th) 321 (S.C.C.) 175, 191
Gould v. Regina (East) School Division No. 77 (1996), 151 Sask. R. 189 141
Graesser v. Porto (1983), 4 C.H.R.R. D/1569 (Bd. of Inquiry Q.B.) 331
Greenway v. Seven Oaks School Division No. 10 (1990), 70 Man. R. (2d) 2 (C.A.), leave to appeal refused [1991] 1 S.C.R. ix. 315
Guerin v. R. (1984), 13 D.L.R. (4th) 321 (S.C.C.) 135, 136
Hagerty v. State Tenure Commn., 445 N.W. 2d 178 (Mich. App. 1989). 353
Hall v. Powers, [2002] O.J. No. 1803 22
Hamilton (City of) Board of Education and O.P.S.T.F., Re (1985), E.R.C. 260 355
Harrison v. University of British Columbia, [1990] 3 S.C.R. 451 (S.C.C.) 364
Hatch v. London (Bd. of Education) (1979), 25 O.R. (2d) 481 (H.C.) 60
Hayes v. Phoenix-Talent School Dist., 893 F. 2d 235 (1990) 350
Haynes (Guardian ad litem of) v. Llleres (1997), Doc. Vancouver 369025, [1997] B.C.J. No. 1202 (B.C. Prov. Ct.) 141, 142
Hazelwood School Dist. v. Kuhlmeier, 484 U.S. 260, 108 S.Ct. 562, 98 L.E.2d 592 (1988) 238, 241, 242, 251
Hearst (Town) v. Ontario North East District School Board, [2000] O.J. No. 3419, 2000 CarswellOnt 3219 (Ont. S.C.J.) 67
Hegener v. Bd of Ed. of the City of Chicago (1991), 567 N.E. 2d 566 321
Herman v. Herman (1969), 1 R.F.L. 41 (N.S.T.D.) 167
Hickman v. Valley Local School Dist. Bd. of Education, 619 F. 2d 606 (1980). 362
Hicks v. Etobicoke (City) Board of Education (1988), Doc. 306622/87, [1988] O.J. No. 1000 (Ont. Dist. Ct.) 142
Hill v. Church of Scientology of Toronto (1995), 126 D.L.R. (4th) 129 (S.C.C.) 187
Hill (Guardian ad litem of) v. Langley School District No. 35, [2000] B.C.J. No. 474, 2000 CarsewllBC 504 (S.C. [in Chambers]) 93
Hoar v. Nanaimo (Board of School Trustees, District 68), [1984] 6 W.W.R. 143 (B.C.C.A.) 98
Homex Realty & Development Co. v. Wyoming (Village), [1980] 2 S.C.R. 1011 64
Homer v. Board of Education, 383 N.E. 2d (1978) 239
Hothi v. R., [1985] 3 W.W.R. 256 at 256 (headnote) (Man. Q.B.), affirmed [1986] 3 W.W.R. 671 (Man. C.A.), leave to appeal to S.C.C. refused (1986), 43 Man. R. (2d) 240 (note) (S.C.C.). 248
Hornepayne Board of Education and O.S.S.T.F., Re (1992), E.R.C. 456 355
Howard v. Lemoignan (1987), 3 C.H.R.R. D/1150 (Bd. of Inquiry) 332
Hughes v. Lord Advocate, [1963] A.C. 837 (H.L.) 98
Hunter v. Montgomery County (Bd. of Education), 439 A. 2d 582 (1982) 145
Hyde v. Hyde (1866), L.R. 1 P. & D. 130 (Eng. P.D.A.) 159
Hyde v. Wellpinit School District No. 495, 611 P. 2d 1388 (1980), cert. denied 648 P. 2d 892 (1982) 360

Indian Head School Div. No. 19 v. Knight (1990), 69 D.L.R. (4th) 489
(S.C.C.) 38, 39
Ins. Corp. of B.C. v. Heerspink, [1982] 2 S.C.R. 145. 335
Islamic Schools Federation of Ontario v. Ottawa Board of Education (1997), 99
O.A.C. 127, 145 D.L.R. (4th) 659, 43 C.R.R. (2d) 151 (Ont. Gen. Div.),
leave to appeal refused (1997), Doc. CA M20514 (Ont. C.A.) 249
Iven v. Hazelwood School District, 710 S.W. 2d 462 (Mo. App. 1986) 361
J. (L.A.) v. J.(H.) (1993), 102 D.L.R. (4th) 177 (Ont. Gen. Div.) 137
Jacobi v. Newell No. 4 (County) (1994), 112 D.L.R. (4th) 229 (Alta. Q.B.) 7
Janzen v. Platy Enterprises Ltd., [1989] 1.S.C.R. 1252 330
Jaworski v. Jaworski, [1973] 2 O.R. 420 (H.C.) 170
Johnson v. Horace Mann Mutual Ins. Co., 241 So. 2d 588 (1970) 132
Johnson (Litigation Guardian of) v. Ontario Federation of School Athletic
Association, [2000] O.J. No. 4994, 2000 CarswellOnt 4986 (S.C.J.) 207
Jonson v. Ponoka County (Board of Education) (No. 3) (1998), 88 A.R. 31
(Q.B.) 38
K.(K.M.) v. Ackerman (1996), 15 O.T.C. 16 (Gen. Div.) 137
K., Re (1995), 23 O.R. (3d) 679 (Prov. Div.) 162, 163
Kane v. Univ. of B.C. (1980), 110 D.L.R. (3d) 311 (S.C.C.) 38, 41
Kaptein v. Conrad School Dist., 1997 WL 51724 (U.S. Mont. 1997) 206, 208
Keefe v. Geanakos, 418 F. 2d 359 (1st Cir. 1969) 342
Kennedy v. Waterloo (County) Board of Education (1999), 45 O.R. (3d) 1 (Ont.
C.A.), leave to appeal refused (2000), 254 N.R. 199n (S.C.C.) 117
Kirkland Lake Board of Education and O.S.S.T.F., Re (1994), E.R.C. 543 354
Knight v. Board, 348 N.E. 2d 299 (1976) 239
Knight v. Indian Head School Division No. 19, [1990] 1 S.C.R. 653 229
Knoll v. Knoll, [1970] 2 O.R. 169 (C.A.) 169
Korach v. Moore (1991), 42 O.A.C. 248, leave to appeal to S.C.C. refused (1991),
3 O.R. (3d) xi (S.C.C.) 122
Kraychy v. Edmonton Public School District No. 7 (1990), 73 Alta. L.R. (2d)
69 315
Kudasik v. Board of Directors, Port Alleghany School, 455 A. 2d 261 (Pa.
1983) 353
LAC Minerals Ltd. v. International Corona Resources Ltd. (1989), 61 D.L.R.
(4th) 14 (S.C.C.) 136
Lacarte v. Toronto (Bd. of Education), [1954] O.R. 435 (C.A.), affirmed [1955] 5
D.L.R. 369 (S.C.C.) 111
Ladson v. Bd. of Education Union Free Sch. Dist. #9, 323 N.Y.S. (2d) 545
(1971) 239
LaFrentz v. Gallagher, 462 P. 2d) 804 (1970) 132
Lanark, Leeds & Grenville) Roman Catholic Separate School Board v. Ontario
(Human Rights Commission) (1987), 60 O.R. (2d) 441 (Div. Ct.) affirmed
(1989), 67 O.R. (2d) 479 (C.A.) 287
Lataille v. Farnham (Commissaires d'Écolés de la Municipalité Scolaire) (1975),
9 N.R. 368 (S.C.C.) 103
Lavigne v. O.P.S.E.U., [1991] 2 S.C.R. 211 .... 364, 368
Lawes v. New York (Bd. of Education), 213 N.E. 2d 667, 266 N.Y.S. 2d 364, 16
N.Y. (2d) 302 (1965) 103

Lemenson v. Lemenson and Draho (1969), 1 R.F.L. 206 (Man. Q.B.) 169
Leshner v. Ontario (1992), 16 C.H.R.R. D/184 (Ont. Bd. Inquiry) 158
Lewis (Next Friend of) v. York Region Board of Education (1996) 27 C.H.R.R.
    D/261 (Ont. Bd. of Inquiry) 282
Lincoln County Roman Catholic Separate School Board and O.E.C.T.A., Re
    (1993), E.R.C. 488 355
Lister & Others v. Hesley Hall Ltd., [2001] 2 All E.R. 769 (H.L.) 131
Lussier v. Windsor-Essex Catholic District School Board, [1999] O.J. No. 4303,
    1999 CarswellOnt 3632 (Div. Ct.) 70
Lutes (Litigation Guardian of) v. Prairie View School Division No. 74 (1992),
    101 Sask. R. 232 (Sask. Q.B.) 242
Lyth v. Dagg (1988), 46 C.C.L.T. 25 (B.C.S.C.) 104, 133
M. v. H. (1999), 171 D.L.R. (4th) 577 (S.C.C.) 159, 162, 163, 189
M. (A.) v. Ryan (1997), 143 D.L.R. (4th) 1 (S.C.C.) 256
M.(K.) v. M.(H.) (1992), 96 D.L.R. (4th) 289 (S.C.C.) ... 124, 134, 135, 136, 137
MacCabe v. Westlock Roman Catholic Separate School District No. 110, [2001]
    A.J. No. 1278, 2001 CarswellAlta 1364 (C.A.) 91
MacDonald v. Lambton County (Bd. of Education) (1982), 37 O.R. (2d) 221
    (H.C.) 60
MacDonald v. MacDonald (1991), Doc. Ottawa 11D-016, [1991] O.J. No. 1274
    (Ont. Gen. Div.) 173
MacDougall v. MacDougall (1970), 3 R.F.L. 175 (C.A.) 170
MacDougall v. Ontario Federation of School Athletic Assns. [1987] O.J. No.
    1728, 1987 CarswellOnt 577 (Ont. Dist. Ct.) 207
MacPherson v. MacPherson (1977), 13 O.R. (2d) 233 (Ont. C.A.) 171
Magnusson v. Nipawin Board (1975), 60 D.L.R. (3d) 372 (S.C.C.) 94
Mahe v. Alberta (1990), 68 D.L.R. (4th) 69 (S.C.C.) 23, 24, 25
Mainville v. Ottawa (Board of Education) (1990), 75 O.R. (2d) 315 (Prov.
    Ct.) 94
Mangano v. Moscoe (1991), 4 O.R. (3d) 469 (Gen. Div.) 47
Margolis v. Brown (1991), Supreme Court of BC No. 11468 (B.C.S.C.) 50
Martineau v. Matsqui Institution Disciplinary Bd. (No. 2) (1980), 106 D.L.R. (3d)
    385 (S.C.C.) 38
Martinez v. School Bd. of Hillsborough County Fla., 861 F. 2d 1502 (11th Cir.
    1988), on remand, 711 F. Supp. 1066 (M.D. Fla. 1989) 211
Mattinson v. Wonnacott (1975), 8 O.R. (2d) 654 (H.C.) 101
Mayberry v. Mayberry, [1971], 2 O.R. 378 (C.A.) 167
McCue v. Etobicoke (Board of Education) (1982), 18 A.C.W.S. (2d) 128 (Ont.
    H.C.) 100
McDonald v. Interlake School Division No. 21 (1995), 131 D.L.R. (4th) 312
    (Man. C.A.), leave to appeal refused (1996), 137 D.L.R. (4th) vi
    (S.C.C.) 33
McEllistrum v. Etches, [1956] S.C.R. 787 108
McEvay v. Torry (1988), 46 C.C.L.T. 85 (B.C.S.C.) 102
McInerney v. MacDonald (1992), 93 D.L.R. (4th) 415 (S.C.C.) 136
McIntire v. Bethel Independent School District No. 3, 804 F. Supp. 1415 (U.S.
    W.D. Okla. 1992) 242

McKay v. Bd. of Govan School Unit No. 29 of Sask. (1968), 68 D.L.R. (2d) 519
  (S.C.C.) 84, 95, 96
McKerron v. Marshall, [1999] O.J. No. 4048, 1999 CarswellOnt 3432
  (S.C.J.) 122
McKinney v. University of Guelph, [1990] 3 S.C.R. 229 (S.C.C.)   364, 365, 369
McMurdy v. McMurdy (1975), 22 R.F.L. 312 (Ont. H.C.) 169
Metropolitan Community Church of Toronto v. Attorney General of Canada et al.
  (2001), No. 39/2001, 2002 CarswellOnt 2309 (Ont. S.C.J.) 160
Metropolitan Toronto Separate School Board v. O.E.C.T.A. (1994), 41 L.A.C.
  (4th) 353 .... 16, 343
Miles v. Denver Public Schools, 944 F. 2d 773 (1991) 355
Milne v. Nipissing District Secondary School Athletic Association, [1998] O.J.
  No. 4687, 1998 CarswellOnt 4377 (Div. Ct.) 207
Miron v. Trudel (1995), 124 D.L.R. (4th) 693 (S.C.C.) 157, 163, 189
Misir v. Children's Rehabilitation Centre of Essex County, [1989] O.J. No. 1653
  (Ont. Dist. Ct.) 92
Mitchell v. Louisiana High School Athletic Assn., 430 F. 2d 1155 (5th Cir.
  1970) 206
Moddejonge v. Huron County (Board of Education), [1972] 2 O.R. 437
  (H.C.) 99
Moffat v. Dufferin County (Bd. of Education), [1973] 1 O.R. 351 (C.A.) 111
Moll v. Fisher (1979), 23 O.R. (2d) 609 (Div. Ct.) 48
Mongitore v. Regas, 520 N.Y.S. 2d 194 (1987) 350
Montreal Tramways Co. v. Leveille, [1933] S.C.R. 456 (S.C.C.) 188
Moore v. Hampshire County Council (1982), 80 L.G.R. 481 (C.A.) 89
Murphy v. Welsh, [1993] 2 S.C.R. 1069 .... 110, 111
Murray v. Belleville (Bd. of Education), [1943] 1 D.L.R. 494 (Ont H.C.) 87
Murray v. Montrose County School District, 51 3d Cir 921 (U.S. 10th Cir., 1995),
  certiori denied 116 S. Ct. 1418 (1996) 282
Myers v. Peel County (Board of Education) (1981), 123 D.L.R. (3d) 1
  (S.C.C.) 85, 86, 89, 92, 106
N.(F.), Re, [2000] 1 S.C.R. 880 (S.C.C.) 265
N. (R). v. Edmonton Public School District No. 7 (1994), 118 D.L.R. (4th) 519
  (Alta. C.A.) 40
Nanaimo (City) v. Rascal Trucking Ltd., [2000] 1 S.C.R. 342 35
Nevels v. Board of Education, 822 S.W. 2d 898 (Mo. App. 1991)
New Jersey v. T.L.O., 469 U.S. 325 (U.S. N.J., 1985) 216, 218
New York State Assn. v. Carey, 466 F. Supp. 479 (E.D.N.Y. 1978), and see 612
  F. 2d 644 (1979) 210
Nicholson v. Haldimand-Norfolk (Regional Municipality) Cmmrs. of Police
  (1978), 88 D.L.R. (3d) 671, [1979] 1 S.C.R. 311 (S.C.C.) 38, 229
Nishri v. North York Board of Education (1994), Doc. No. 2117/87 (Ont. Gen.
  Div.) 141
Norberg v. Wynrib, [1992] 2 S.C.R. 226, additional reasons [1992] 2 S.C.R.
  318 133
O (Y.) v. Belleville (City) Chief of Police (1993), 12 O.R. (3d) 618 (Div.
  Ct.) 264

O'Brien v. Procureur General de la province de Que., [1961] S.C.R. 184 94
O'Connell High School v. Virginia High School League, 581 F. 2d 81 (4th Cir.
    1978), cert. denied 440 U.S. 996 (1979) 209
Oklahoma High School Athletic Assn. v. Bray, 321 F. 2d 269 (10th Cir.
    1963) 206
Oglesby v. Seminole County Bd. of Public Instruction, 328 So. 2d 515
    (1976) 103
Ont. English Catholic Teachers Assn. v. Essex County (R.C. Separate School Bd.)
    (1987), 58 O.R. (2d) 545 (Div. Ct.); leave to appeal to S.C.C. refused (1988),
    65 O.R. (2d) x (note) (S.C.C.) 38
Ontario (Human Rights Commission) v. Simpsons Sears Ltd. (1986), 7 C.H.R.R.
    D/3102 (S.C.C.) 332, 333
Ontario (Police Complaints Commissioner) v. Dunlop (1995), 26 O.R. (3d) 582
    (Div. Ct.) 328, 329
O.E.C.T.A. v. Dufferin-Peel Roman Catholic Separate School Board (1999), 172
    D.L.R. (4th) 260 (Ont. Gen. Div.) 16, 20, 21
O.E.C.T.A. v. Ontario (Attorney General), [2001] 1 S.C.R. 470 ..... 2, 7, 8, 14, 64
Orth v. Phoenix Union High School System, 613 P. 2d 311 (Ariz. App.
    1980) 360
Ottawa Electric Light Co. v. Ottawa (1906), 12 O.L.R. 290 (C.A.) 38
Pandori v. Peel (Bd. of Education) (1990), 12 C.H.R.R. D/364 (Ont. Bd. of
    Inquiry), affirmed (1991), 47 O.A.C. 234 (*sub nom. Ontario (Human Rights
    Commn.) v. Peel (Bd. of Education)*) (Div. Ct.), leave to appeal to Ont. C.A.
    refused (1991), 3 O.R. (3d) 531n (C.A.) 245, 297
Papamonolopoulos v. Toronto (Board of Education) (1986), 56 O.R. (2d) 1
    (C.A.), leave to appeal to S.C.C. refused (1987), 58 O.R. (2d) 528n 110
Peel Board of Education v. Ontario Human Rights Commission (1990), 72 O.R.
    (2d) 593 (Div. Ct.) 32, 245
Pepin v. Lincoln County (Bd. of Education) (1983), 22 A.C.W.S. (2d) 302 (Ont.
    H.C.) 94
Perry Education Assn. v. Perry Local Educators' Assn., 460 U.S. 37 (U.S. Ind.
    1983) 251
Peter v. Beblow (1993), 44 R.F.L. (3d) 329 (S.C.C.) 155
Phelps v. Scarborough Bd. of Education (1993), Doc. 350779/89, [1993] O.J. No.
    1318 (Ont. Gen. Div.) 112
Phoenix Elementary Sch. Dist. No. 1 v. Green, 943 P. 2d 836, 120 Educ. L. Rep.
    1170 (U.S. Ariz. Ct. App. 1997) 242
Pickering v. Bd. of Education, 391 U.S. 563 (1968) 343
Pierce v. Society of Sisters of the Holy Names of Jesus and Mary, 268 U.S. STO
    (1925) 205
Piszel v. Etobicoke (Bd. of Education) (1977), 16 O.R. (2d) 22 (C.A.) 78
Plumb (Guardian ad litem of) v. Cowichan School District No. 65, [1993] B.C.J.
    No. 1936, 1993 CarswellBC 239 (C.A.) 87
Plumley v. North York Board of Education, [2000] O.J. No. 2636, 2000
    CarswellOnt 2439 (S.C.J.) 98
Pottgen v. Missouri State High School Activities Association, 40 F. 3d 926 (8th
    Cir. 1994) 206
Powell v. Powell (1971), 5 R.F.L. 194 (Sask. C.A.) 170

TABLE OF CASES xxiii

Prete v. Ontario (1994), 16 O.R. (3d) 161 (C.A.) 111
Provincial Schools Authority and Provincial Schools Authority Teachers (1984),
    E.R.C. 228 356
Public School Boards' Assn. (Alberta) v. Alberta (Attorney General), [2000] 2
    S.C.R. 409 .... 2, 3, 4, 5
Québec (Commission des droits de la personne) v. St-Jean-Sur-Richelieu
    (Commission scolaire) (1994), 117 D.L.R. (4th) 67 (Que. C.A.) 303, 304
Queen (The) v. Jones, [1986] 2 S.C.R. 284 32
R. v. Araujo, [2000] 2 S.C.R. 992 (S.C.C.) 370
R. v. Atkinson, [1994] 9 W.W.R. 485 (Man. Prov. Ct.) 197
R. v. Audet, [1996] 2 S.C.R. 171 (S.C.C.) 317, 319
R. v. B. (A.) (1986), 26 C.C.C. (3d) 17 (Ont. C.A.) 268, 270
R. v. Bernshaw (1993), 85 C.C.C. (3d) 404 (B.C.C.A.), reversed (1994), 8 M.V.R.
    (3d) 75 (S.C.C.) 329
R. v. Butler, [1992] 1 S.C.R. 452 (S.C.C.) 187
R. v. Collins, [1987] 1 S.C.R. 265 (S.C.C.) 370
R. v. D.(D.), [2000] 2 S.C.R. 275 (S.C.C.) 327
R. v. Debot, [1989] 2 S.C.R. 1140 (S.C.C.) 370
R. v. Dyment, [1988] 2 S.C.R. 417 (S.C.C.) 255
R. v. G. (T.F.) (1992), 11 C.R. (4th) 211 (Ont. C.A.), leave to appeal refused 145
    N.R. 391n (S.C.C.) 318, 322
R. v. G. (J.M.) (1986), 56 O.R. (2d) 705 (C.A.), leave to appeal refused (1987), 54
    C.R. (3d) 380n (S.C.C.) 215, 216, 218, 248
R. v. Grant (1991), 67 C.C.C. (3d) 268 (S.C.C.) 329
R. v. Greenbaum (1993), 100 D.L.R. (4th) 183 (S.C.C.) 37
R. v. Gruenke, [1991] 3 S.C.R. 263 (S.C.C.) 255
R. v. Hann (No. 2) (1990), 86 Nfld. & P.E.I.R. 33, 268 A.P.R. 33 (Nfld.T.D.),
    affirmed 15 C.R. (4th) 355 (Nfld. C.A.) 322
R. v. J. (J.T.), [1990] 2 S.C.R. 755 (S.C.C.) 270
R. v. Jones (1983), 49 A.R. 135 (Prov. Ct.), reversed (1984), 57 A.R. 266 (C.A.),
    affirmed [1986] 2 S.C.R. 284 (S.C.C.) 204
R. v. Kalin, [1987] B.C.J. No. 2580 (B.C. Co. Ct.) 371
R. v. Keegstra, [1990] 3 S.C.R. 697 (S.C.C.) 187
R. v. Keukens (1995), 23 O.R. (3d) 582 (Gen. Div.) 277
R. v. King, [1999] O.J. No. 565 (Ont. Gen. Div.) 371
R. v. Laporte (1972), 8 C.C.C. (2d) 343 (Que. Q.B.) 370
R. v. Lasecki (1994), 163 A.R. 354 (Q.B.). 319
R. v. Lavellee [1990] 1 S.C.R. 852, 55 C.C.C. (3d) 97 (S.C.C.) 177
R. v. Leon (1992), 44 Q.A.C. 143 320
R. v. M. (J.J.), [1993] 2 S.C.R. 421 (S.C.C.) 271
R. v. M. (M.A.), [1998] S.C.J. No. 12, 1998 CarswellOnt 419 (S.C.C.) 177
R. v. M. (M.R.), [1998] 2 S.C.R. 393 (S.C.C.) 215, 216, 217, 220
R. v. Miller, [1993] B.C.J. No. 1613 (B.C.S.C.) 371
R. v. Mills (1999), 139 C.C.C. (3d) 321 (S.C.C.) 187
R. v. N. (R.O.) (1986), 6 B.C.L.R. (2d) 306 (S.C.), affirmed 22 B.C.L.R. (2d) 45
    (C.A.), leave to appeal refused 27 B.C.L.R. (2d) xxxv (S.C.C.) 322
R. v. Nelson (1989), 51 C.C.C. (3d) 150 (Ont. N.C.). 322
R. v. O'Connor (1996), 103 C.C.C. (3d) 1 (S.C.C.) 279

R. v. O'Connor, [1995] 4 S.C.R. 411 (S.C.C.) 256
R. v. Ogg-Moss, [1984] 2 S.C.R. 173, 14 C.C.C. (3d) 116 (S.C.C.) 193
R. v. Palmer (1990), Doc. No. 362-89 (Ont. Dist. Ct.) 136
R. v. Profit (1993), 85 C.C.C. (3d) 232 (S.C.C.). 322
R. v. S. (K.D.) (1990), 65 Man. R. (2d) 301 (Q.B.) 371
R. v. Smith, [1991] 1 S.C.R. 714 (S.C.C.) 268
R. v. Stillman, [1997] 1 S.C.R. 607 (S.C.C.) 370
R. v. Stott, [1997] O.J. No. 5449, 1997 CarswellOnt 5443 (Prov. Div.) 371
R. v. Swain (1991), 63 C.C.C. (3d) 481 (S.C.C.) 274
R. v. V. (K.B.) (1992), 71 C.C.C. (3d) 65 (Ont. C.A.), affirmed [1993] 2 S.C.R. 857 322
R. v. W.(J.) (1997), S.C.R. (5th) 248, 115 C.C.C. (3d) 18 (Ont. C.A.) 275
R. v. Z. (D.A.) (1992), 76 C.C.C. (3d) 97 (S.C.C.) 270
R.W.D.S.U. v. Dolphin Delivery Ltd., [1986] 2 S.C.R. 573 364
Radio CHUM 1050 Ltd. v. Toronto (Bd. of Education), [1964] 2 O.R. 207 (C.A.) 68
Rahn v. Prescott-Russell County Board of Education, 53 A.C.W.S. (3d) 73 (Ont. Div. Ct.) 41
Ramsden v. Hamilton (Bd. of Education), [1942] 1 D.L.R. 770 (H.C.) 85, 94, 95, 106
Raney v. Raney (1973), 1 O.R. (2d) 491 (S.C.) 170
Rathwell v. Rathwell, [1978] 2 S.C.R. 436 (S.C.C.) 154
Rawluk v. Rawluk (1990), 23 R.F.L. (3d) 337 (S.C.C.) 154
Reaves v. Mills, 904 F. Supp. 120 (U.S. W.D. N.Y., 1995) 206
Reference re an Act to Amend the Education Act (Ont.) (1987), 40 D.L.R. (4th) 18 (S.C.C.) 7
Renaud v. Renaud (1989), 22 R.F.L. (2d) 366 (Ont. Dist. Ct.) 172
Reynen v. Antonenko (1975), 20 C.C.C. (2d) 342 (Alta. T.D.) 370
Robichaud v. Canada (Treasury Bd.) (1987), 8 C.H.R.R. D/4326 333
Rochon v. Spirit River School District No. 47 (1994), 111 D.L.R. (4th) 452 (Alta. C.A.) 40
Roman Catholic Separate School Board of Sudbury and A.E.F.O (1993), E.R.C. 477 356
Ross v. Avon Maitland District School Board, [2000] O.J. No. 1714, 2000 CarswellOnt 1701 (S.C.C.) 62, 63
Ross v. New Brunswick District No. 15, [1996] 1 S.C.R. 825 .... 314, 317
Rousell v. Rousell (1969), 69 W.W.R. 568 (Sask. Q.B.) 167
Rowett v. York Region (Bd. of Education) (1988), 63 O.R. (2d) 767 (H.C) reversed (1989), 69 O.R. (2d) 543 (C.A.). 292
Rowett v. York Region (Bd. of Education) (1988), 63 O.R. (2d) 767 (H.C.) .. 296
Rumley v. British Columbia, [2001] S.C.J. No. 39, 2001 CarswellBC 1223 (S.C.C.), additional reasons 205 D.L.R. (4th) 39 (S.C.C.) 124
Rushton v. Rushton (1968), 66 W.W.R. 764 (B.C.S.C.) 167
S-1 v. Turlington, 635 F.2d 342 (U.S. 5th Cir. 1981) 293
Sable Communications v. FCC, 492 U.S. 115, 109 S.Ct. 2829, 106 L.Ed.2d 93 (1989) 238
Sacco v. Ontario (A.G.) (1991), 77 D.L.R. (4th) 764 (Ont. Gen. Div.), additional reasons (Feb. 13, 1991), Doc. No. RE 1079/89 (Ont. Gen. Div.) 66

Sandison v. Michigan High School Athletic Association, Inc., 64 F.3d 1026 (U.S. 6th Cir., 1995) 206
Sask. Human Rights Commn. v. Cdn. Odeon Theatres Ltd. (1985), 18 D.L.R. (4th) 93 at 115 (Sack. C.A.). 296
Sauter v. Mount Vernon School District (1990), 791 P. 2d 549 321
Savidant v. MacLeod (1992), 40 R.F.L. (3d) 443 (P.E.I.C.A.) 172
Scott v. Thompson, 363 N.E. 2d 295 (1977) 101
Segerman v. Jones, 259 A. 2d 794 (Md. 1969) 94
Seminuk v. Seminuk (1969), 68 W.W.R. 249 (Sask. Q.B.), reversed on other grounds (1970), 72 W.W.R. 304 (Sask. C.A.) 167
Shell Canada Products Ltd. v. Vancouver (City) (1994), 110 D.L.R. (4th) 1, 20 M.P.L.R. (2d) 1 (S.C.C.) 34, 38
Shumila v. Shumila, [1975] 5 W.W.R. 697 (Man. C.A.) 170
Silano v. Sag Harbour Union Free School District Board, 42 F. 3d 719 (2d Cir. 1994) 342
Simms v. School Dist. No. 1, Multnomah County, 508 P. 2d 236 (1973) 132
Simpson v. Ottawa-Carleton District School Board, [1999] O.J. No. 1563, 1999 CarswellOnt 1279 (Div. Ct.) 61
Slade v. New Hanover County Board of Education, 178 S.E. 2d 316, 10 N.C. App. 287 (1971) 101
Slocum v. Holton Bd. of Education, 429 N.W. 2d 607 (Mich. Ct. App. 1988) 239
Smith v. Ontario Federation of School Athletic Assns. (Jan. 15, 1992) (Ont. Gen. Div.) 207
Smith v. Smith, [1952] 2 S.C.R. 312 (S.C.C.) 169
Southam Inc. v. Hamilton-Wentworth (Reg. Mun.) Economic Development Committee (1988), 56 O.R. (2d) 213 (C.A.); leave to appeal to S.C.C. refused (1989), 102 N.R. 238 (S.C.C.) 44
Southam Inc. v. R. (1984), 48 O.R. (2d) 678 .... 264, 265
Southam Inc. v. Ottawa (City) (1992), 5 O.R. (3d) 726 (Div. Ct.) 45
St. Louis Teacher's Union, Loc. 420 v. St. Louis Bd. of Education, 652 F. Supp. 425 (E.D. Mo. 1987). 360
Stack v. St. John's (R.C. School Bd.) (1979), 99 D.L.R. (3d) 278 (Nfld. T.D.) 344
Stathopoulos v. McKinlay Door Sales & Installation Ltd. (1993), 12 O.R. (3d) 790 (Gen. Div.) 111
Stephenson v. Davenport Community School District, 110 Fed. 1308 (1997) 243
Stewart v. Lincoln County (Bd. of Education) (1976), 8 O.R. (2d) 168 (H.C.) 111
Stillman v. Stillman, [1991] N.S.I. No. 200, 1991 CarswellNS 407 (N.S.T.D.) 171
Stoddard v. Watson, [1993] 2 S.C.R. 1069 .... 110, 111
Stoffman v. Vancouver General Hospital, [1990] 3 S.C.R. 483 (S.C.C.) 364, 366
Storr v. Storr (1974), 14 R.F.L. 346 (N.S.C.A.) 169
Symes v. The Queen, [1993] 4 S.C.R. 695 (S.C.C.) 189

Syndicat des employés de production du Qué. de l'Acadie v. Canada (Cdn.
  Human Rights Commn.) (1989), 62 D.L.R. (4th) 385 (S.C.C.) 38, 39, 40
T.(G.) v. Griffiths, [1999] 2 S.C.R. 570 .... 130, 131, 137, 140
Tarasoff v. Regents of Univ. of California, 551 P.2d 334 (Cal. 1976) 255
Tardif v. Quinn, 545 F. 2d 761 (1976) 343
Taylor v. Patterson's Administrator, 114 S.W. 2d 488 (1938) 101
Taylor v. Taylor (1978), 6 R.F.L. (2d) 341 (Ont. U.F.C.) 171
Termination of James E. Johnson, Re, 451 N.W. 2d 343 (Minn. 1990) 351
Thibaudeau v. R., [1995] 2 S.C.R. 627 (S.C.C.) 189
Thomas v. Atascadero Unified School Dist., 662 F. Supp. 376 (C.D. Cal.
  1987) 211
Thomas v. Hamilton (City Board of Education) (Feb. 8, 1990) Action Nos. 2754/
  83, 5794/88 (Ont. H.C.), affirmed 20 O.R. (3d) 598 (C.A.)   88, 89, 108, 110
Thornton v. Board of School Trustees of School District No. 57 (Prince
  George) 85, 86, 89
Tinker v. Des Moines Independent Community School District, 393 U.S. 503, 89
  S. Ct. 733 (1969) 237, 241, 242, 243
Titus v. Lindberg, 228 A. 2d 65 (1967) 103
Tomen v. F.W.T.A.O. (1987), 29 Admin. L.R. 1 (Ont. H.C.) 368, 369
Toronto (Board of Education) v. Higgs (1960), 22 D.L.R. (2d) 49 (S.C.C.) 93,
    97, 110
Toronto (City) Board of Education v. O.S.S.T.F., District 15 (1997), 144 D.L.R.
  (4th) 385 (S.C.C.) 315, 316
Trinity Western University v. College of Teachers (British Columbia), [2001] 1
  S.C.R. 772 (S.C.C.) 307
Torres v. Royalty Kitchenware Ltd. (1982), 3 C.H.R.R. D/858 333
Trofimenkoff v. Saskatchewan (Minister of Education), [1991] 6 W.W.R. 97
  (Sask. C.A.) 297
Trimboli v. Board of Education of Wayne County, 280 S.E. 2d 686 (1981) ... 361
Tuli v. St. Albert (Professional Bd. of Education) (1985), 8 C.H.R.R. D/
  3736 247
Urzi v. North York (Bd. of Education) (1980), 30 O.R. (2d) 300 (H.C.); affirmed
  (1981), 127 D.L.R. (3d) 768 (C.A.) 111
Van Schyndel v. Harrell (1991), 4 O.R. (3d) 474 (Gen. Div.) 47
Van Schyndel v. Harrell (1991), 6 O.R. (3d) 335 (Div. Ct.); leave to appeal to
  C.A. refused (1992), 6 O.R. (3d) 335n (C.A.) 48
Vaughan School Section No. 24 v. Scott (1932), 41 O.W.N. 149 (H.C.) 69
Vanderkloet v. Leeds & Grenville County (Board of Education) (1985), 51 O.R.
  (2d) 377 (C.A.), leave to appeal to S.C.C. refused (1986), 54 O.R. (2d)
  352n 43, 44, 60
Vecchiarelli v. Toronto Catholic District School Board, [2002] O.J. No. 2458
  (Ont. S.C.) 63
Venneri v. Bascom (1996), 28 O.R. (3d) 281 (Gen. Div.) 122
W. (Peter) v. San Francisco Unified School District 60 Cal. App. 3d 314, 131 Cal.
  Rptr. 854 (1976) 141, 142, 143, 144, 145
Wagner v. Lim (1994), 22 Alta. L.R. (3d) 109 (Q.B.) 122
Waldick v. Malcolm (1991), 83 D.L.R. (4th) 114 (S.C.C.) 107, 120
Walsh v. Buchanan, [1995] O.J. No. 64 (Ont. Gen. Div.) 124

Walsh v. Newfoundland (Treasury Bd.) (1988), 71 Nfld. & P.E.I.R. 21 (Nfld. C.A.) 16, 344
Warkentin v. Sault Ste. Marie Board of Education (1985), 49 C.P.C. 31 (Ont. Dist. Ct.) 207
Watson v. State Bd. of Education, 99 Cal. Rptr. 468 (1971) 318
Wellington Board of Education v. O.S.S.T.F. (1991), 24 L.A.C. (4th) 110 356
Whaton v. Flin Flon School Division No. 46 (1980), 4 Man. R. (2d) 420 (C.A.) 343
Williams v. Eady (1893), 10 T.L.R. 41 (C.A.) 84, 85, 96, 100, 109
Windsor Roman Catholic Separate School Board and O.E.C.T.A., Re 355
Winnipeg Child & Family Services (Central Area) v. W. (K.L.) (2000), 10 R.F.L. (5th) 122 (S.C.C.). 326
Wisconsin v. Yoder, 406 U.S. 205 (1972) 205
Wittstock v. Wittstock, [1971] 2 O.R. 472 (C.A.) 170
Wynja v. Halsey-Brandt (1993), 102 D.L.R. (4th) 393 (B.C. C.A.) 50, 51
Young v. Young (1989), 19 R.F.L. (3d) 227 (Ont. H.C.), additional reasons (1989), 19 R.F.L. (3d) 227 (Ont. H.C.) 172, 189, 190, 196
Zaba v. Saskatchewan Institute of Applied Science & Technology [1996] 1 W.W.R. 534 (Sask. Q.B.), reversed (1997), 152 Sask. R. 245 (C.A.) 91
Zobrest v. Catalina Foothills Sch. Dist., 509 U.S. 1 (1993) 209
Zylberberg v. Sudbury (Bd. of Education) (1989), 65 O.R. (2d) 641 (C.A.) 55

1

School Boards

1. INTRODUCTION 2
2. PROVINCIAL JURISDICTION OVER EDUCATION 2
   (a) Denominational Rights 6
   (b) Funding Private Schools 12
   (c) Hiring by Separate School Boards 15
   (d) Minority Language Education Rights 22
   (e) Native Education 28
   (f) School Councils 30
   (g) Pupil Representation 30
3. THE EXERCISE OF PROVINCIAL POWER OVER EDUCATION 31
4. THE EXERCISE OF DELEGATED POWER BY SCHOOL BOARDS 31
   (a) Collective Action 31
   (b) Mandatory and Discretionary Powers 36
5. PROCEDURAL FAIRNESS AND NATURAL JUSTICE 38
6. PUBLIC ACCESS TO BOARD MEETINGS 42
   (a) Exclusion from Meetings 43
   (b) Retreats and *In Camera* Meetings 43
7. CONFLICT OF INTEREST 46
8. ACCESS TO INFORMATION 51
   (a) Board Books 51
   (b) Freedom of Information and Protection of Privacy 51
9. THE BOARD AND ITS PROPERTY 53
   (a) Public Access 53
   (b) Trespassers 55
   (c) School Closure 58
10. ELECTION AND ORGANIZATION OF THE BOARD 64
    (a) Qualification and Disqualification of Board Members 64
    (b) Vacancies on the Board 67
    (c) Meeting Procedures 67
    (d) Appointment of Secretary and Treasurer 68
    (e) Offences under the *Education Act* (Ontario) 69
    (f) Personal Liability of Board Members 70
11. PRIVATE SCHOOLS 71
12. CONCLUSION 74

1. INTRODUCTION

In this chapter, we examine school boards in their corporate capacity. What are school boards? What are some of their primary legal concerns? How is their conduct governed? It is not the purpose of this chapter to cover the hundreds of provisions pertaining to board powers under provincial legislation. More important is an understanding of how boards acquire and exercise their powers and responsibilities. We examine the important components of the constitutional, statutory and common law framework which governs or affects the jurisdiction and actions of school boards. These components include denominational education, minority language education, freedom of information, property ownership, closure of schools, copyright, conflict of interest, and the duty to ensure procedural fairness.

2. PROVINCIAL JURISDICTION OVER EDUCATION

Section 93 of the *Constitution Act, 1867*[1] gives provinces exclusive jurisdiction to enact laws governing education. In addition to this plenary power over education, the *Constitution Act, 1867* and the *Canadian Charter of Rights and Freedoms*[2] contain specific rights to denominational education and to minority language education.

In discussing the constitutional status of school boards, Mr. Justice Campbell stated in *Ontario Public School Boards' Assn. v. Ontario (Attorney General)*[3]:

> Subject to any school rights that might be protected by s. 93 of the *Constitution Act, 1867*, there is no constitutionally protected right to effective representation through municipal institutions or local school boards. Under our constitutional arrangements the federal and provincial governments and their constituent electoral systems are constitutionally protected, but not municipalities or school boards, subject to any argument arising out of s. 93.
>
> . . .
>
> Municipal governments and special purpose municipal institutions such as school boards are creatures of the provincial government. Subject to the constitutional limits of s. 93 . . . these institutions have no constitutional status or independent autonomy and the province has absolute and unfettered legal power to do with them as it wills.

The Supreme Court of Canada confirmed this approach in *Public School Boards' Assn. (Alberta) v. Alberta (Attorney General)*[4] in which public

---
1 (30 & 31 Vict.), c. 3.
2 Being Part I of the *Constitution Act, 1982* [en. by the *Canada Act, 1982* (U.K.), c. 11, s. 1].
3 (1997), 151 D.L.R. (4th) 346 at 361 (Ont. Gen. Div.), reversed (1999), 175 D.L.R. (4th) 609 (Ont. C.A.), leave to appeal refused (1999), 249 N.R. 400 (note) (S.C.C.)..
4 [2000] 2 S.C.R. 409.

school boards unsuccessfully argued that the *Constitution Act, 1867* and s.17 of the *Alberta Act* allows them reasonable autonomy. The Court stated:

> The appellants' submission that ss. 92(8) and 93 of the *Constitution Act, 1867* and s. 17 of the *Alberta Act* provide a legal basis for reasonable autonomy fails. I agree with the PSBAA [the public school boards] that school boards are a form of municipal institution. However, municipal institutions take various forms and are not identical. Although their characteristics and historical backgrounds differ, all municipal institutions are delegates of provincial jurisdiction under s. 92(8) of the *Constitution Act, 1867*. See *Godbout v. Longueuil (City)*, [1997] 3 S.C.R. 844, at paras. 51-52; *R. v. Greenbaum*, [1993] 1 S.C.R. 674; *R. v. Sharma*, [1993] 1 S.C.R. 650, at p. 668; and *Nanaimo (City) v. Rascal Trucking Ltd.*, [2000] 1 S.C.R. 342, 2000 SCC 13, at para. 31.

> Municipal institutions do not have an independent constitutional status. School boards are somewhat unique, however, as they represent the vehicles through which the constitutionally entrenched denominational rights of individuals are realized. Yet that is not to say that the institutions themselves are entrenched or must remain mired in their historical form to fulfill these constitutional guarantees.

> The proposition that educational institutions are malleable and subject to legislative reform is sound. The introductory language of s. 93 has been found to confer upon the provinces a plenary jurisdiction over education. See *Reference Re Bill 30, An Act to Amend the Education Act (Ont.)*, [1987] 1 S.C.R. 1148, at p. 1169, *per* Wilson J., and at p. 1202, *per* Estey J.; *Reference Re Education Act (Que.)*, [1993] 2 S.C.R. 511, at pp. 530-31, 541-42 and 564-65. *Per* Gonthier J., at pp. 541-42:

>> What s. 93 of the Constitution guarantees . . . is the right to dissent itself, not the form of the institutions which have made it possible to exercise that right since 1867. This means, for example, that while the right of dissent obviously includes the means and framework in which it is exercised, the latter are not in themselves constitutionally guaranteed. The framers of the Constitution were wise enough not to determine finally the form of institutions, as it is those very institutions which must be capable of change in order to adapt to the varying social and economic conditions of society.

> This conclusion is applicable to public schools. See *Adler v. Ontario*, [1996] 3 S.C.R. 609, at paras. 47-48, *per* Iacobucci J.:

>> ...public school rights are not themselves constitutionally entrenched. It is the province's plenary power to legislate with regard to public schools, which are open to all members of society, without distinction, that is constitutionally entrenched...

>> One thing should, however, be made clear. The province remains free to exercise its plenary power with regard to education in whatever way it sees fit, subject to the restrictions relating to separate schools imposed by s. 93(1).

A claim to an institutional sphere of reasonable autonomy is inconsistent with, and would impair, this plenary power. Section 17 of the *Alberta Act* does not alter this position. The Province of Alberta may alter educational institutions within its borders as it sees fit, subject only to those rights afforded through the combined effect of s. 93 and s. 17. Whether the impugned provisions infringe these rights in respect of public schools in Alberta is the subject matter of the following two constitutional questions in this appeal.[5]

In *Public School Boards'*, the applicants also argued that the government's funding model was discriminatory in that it permitted separate school boards to opt to raise funds through local taxation, but did not permit public boards this option. The funding scheme did not allow the separate school boards to raise and retain more through local taxation than they would have obtained through the province. The Court found that the funding scheme was not discriminatory:

> In this sense, s. 17(2) [of the Alberta Act] carries forward a principle of proportionality which this Court has described as a constitutional right embodied in s. 93(1). In *Ontario Home Builders' Association v. York Region Board of Education*, [1996] 2 S.C.R. 929, this Court had the opportunity to describe the proportionality principle as applicable to s. 20 of *An Act to restore to Roman Catholics in Upper Canada certain rights in respect to Separate Schools*, S. Prov. C. 1863, 26 Vict., c. 5 ("*Scott Act*"). See Iacobucci J., at para. 73:
>
>> In my view, when one reviews the history and purpose of s. 93(1), the principle of proportionality can be seen for what it really is, namely, the means to a constitutional end which is equality of educational opportunity.... While the notion of proportionality contained in s. 20 of the *Scott Act* is a constitutional right embodied in s. 93(1), the substantive purpose of this notion must be borne in mind: the achievement of an educational system that distributes provincial funds in a fair and non-discriminatory manner to common and separate schools alike.... As the Court *per* Gonthier J. stated in *Reference re Education Act (Que.)*, [1993] 2 S.C.R. 511, at p. 567:
>>
>>> When we speak of equality, this must be understood in the sense of equivalence and not that of strict quantitative identity, as Chouinard J. noted in *Greater Hull, supra*, at p. 591:
>>>
>>>> Proportionality is more significant. Whether on the basis of total population or that of school attendance, the principle of a *fair and non-discriminatory* distribution is recognized. [Emphasis added by Gonthier J.]
>
> Section 17(2) is equally intended to guarantee proportionality between the educational opportunities of separate and public school supporters. It does so by imposing a standard of fairness upon the distribution by the Government of monies for the support of schools. There are two significant limits, however, on the content of this notion of fairness. First, it does not prohibit all distinctions

---

5 *Ibid.*, at paras. 34-37.

in funding, as it does not guarantee absolute or formalistic equality but rather a general concept of fairness. Second, it does not deal with distinctions in the distribution of rights, but only with a general fairness in the distribution of monies.

It follows that it is unnecessary to ascertain the scope of separate school rights under s. 17(1) in adjudicating whether the impugned funding scheme meets a standard of fairness under s. 17(2). Equally, the unique ability of separate schools to opt out of the scheme cannot be a source of discrimination under s. 17(2).[6]

The Court went on to reject the public school boards' "mirror argument" to the effect that section 17 of the *Alberta Act* entitled public boards to what the separate boards were guaranteed under the Act. The Court stated:

> Only the second portion of s. 17(1) refers to public schools:
>
>> Nothing in any such law shall prejudicially affect any right or privilege with respect to ... *religious instruction in any public or separate school* as provided for in the said ordinances. [Emphasis added.]
>
> This interpretation follows the jurisprudence stating that s. 17(1) is primarily separate school protective legislation which affords only limited and non-equivalent protection to public schools. With respect to the identical s. 17(1) of the *Saskatchewan Act*, see *Gratton, supra*, at p. 600, *per* Fitzpatrick C.J. dissenting, and at p. 621, *per* Anglin J. dissenting. With respect to the *Alberta Act*, see *Reference Re s. 17 of the Alberta Act*, [1927] S.C.R. 364, at p. 373, and *Calgary Board of Education, supra*, at p. 355, *per* Stevenson J.:
>
>> I come to the conclusion that subs. [17](1) is protective legislation. It guarantees certain rights to the minority residents and the boards established by them and it does not lie in the mouth of the public board to attack legislation on the basis that its rights are prejudiced.
>
> This position was affirmed on appeal. See McDermid J.A., at pp. 191-92:
>
>> In any event, the clear purpose of s. 93(1), and the section substituted for it in respect of Alberta, is to give constitutional protection to the rights of certain minorities, rights which had already been yielded by the majority, and not to give constitutional protection against these minority rights.
>
> In addition, this Court has stated that public school rights are not constitutionally entrenched under s. 93(1). See *Adler, supra*, at p. 648, *per* Iacobucci J. This is relevant because the Court has also stated that given the clear similarities in language between s. 93 and s. 17(1), the jurisprudence of the former is relevant in interpreting the latter. See *Mahe v. Alberta*, [1990] 1 S.C.R. 342, at p. 381.
>
> In the same manner as s. 93(1), s. 17(1) "fr[eezes] in time" the rights and privileges of separate schools and the rights to religious instruction of both

---

6 *Ibid.*, at paras. 47-49.

public and separate schools as they existed in 1905. See *Greater Montreal Protestant School Board v. Quebec (Attorney General)*, [1989] 1 S.C.R. 377, at p. 400. Subject to constitutionalization of then existing rights and the continuing effect of s. 17(2), separate and public schools were free to evolve independently after 1905 under the plenary jurisdiction of the Province. Section 17(1) was not intended to be a basis for a "continuous mirroring" of the rights and privileges of separate and public schools.[7]

Moreover, the Court in *Public School Boards'* agreed with Sopinka J. in *Adler v. Ontario*[8] that denominational rights are not a "benchmark" for public school rights.

(a) Denominational Rights

The term "denominational rights" is commonly used to refer to the constitutional right of Roman Catholics or Protestants to have their own, denominational school systems.

Section 93 of the *Constitution Act, 1867*, states:

> In and for each Province the Legislature may exclusively make Laws in relation to Education, subject and according to the following Provisions:—
>
> (1) Nothing in any such Law shall prejudicially affect any Right or Privilege with respect to Denominational Schools which any Class of Persons have by Law in the Province at the Union:
>
> (2) All the Powers, Privileges, and Duties at the Union by Law conferred and imposed in Upper Canada on the Separate Schools and School Trustees of the Queen's Roman Catholic Subjects shall be and the same are hereby extended to the Dissentient Schools of the Queen's Protestant and Roman Catholic Subjects in Quebec:
>
> (3) Where in any Province a System of Separate or Dissentient Schools exists by Law at the Union or is thereafter established by the Legislature of the Province, an Appeal shall lie to the Governor General in Council from any Act or Decision of Any Provincial Authority affecting any Right or Privilege of the Protestant or Roman Catholic Minority of the Queen's Subjects in relation to Education:
>
> (4) In case any such Provincial Law as from Time to Time seems to the Governor General in Council requisite for the due Execution of the Provisions of this Section is not made, or in case any Decision of the Governor General in Council on any Appeal under this Section is not duly executed by the proper Provincial Authority in that Behalf, then and in every such Case, and as far only as the Circumstances of each Case require, the Parliament of Canada may make remedial Laws for the due Execution of the Provisions of this Section and of any Decision of the Governor General in Council under this Section.

---

7 *Ibid.*, at paras. 60-64.
8 [1996] 3 S.C.R. 609, 140 D.L.R. (4th) 407.

Provincial laws about education may not prejudicially affect the rights to denominational schools that were in effect at the time of Confederation. Accordingly, these rights are different in each province depending on the laws in effect at the time they joined Confederation.

As the Supreme Court of Canada explained in *O.E.C.T.A. v. Ontario (Attorney General)*:

> Section 93 applies directly to Ontario, Nova Scotia, New Brunswick, Prince Edward Island, and British Columbia. However, only Ontario had denominational education rights conferred "by law" at the relevant time, and so the guarantees provided by s. 93(1) are of no importance in Nova Scotia, New Brunswick, Prince Edward Island, and British Columbia. A modified version of s. 93 applies to the western provinces of Manitoba, Saskatchewan and Alberta: s. 22 of the *Manitoba Act, 1870*, S.C. 1870, c. 3; s. 17 of the *Saskatchewan Act*, S.C. 1905, c. 42, and s. 17 of the *Alberta Act*, S.C. 1905, c. 3. As a result of recent constitutional amendments, Quebec and Newfoundland have new constitutional frameworks for education rights. Quebec has removed the protection of denominational education rights altogether, by amending the Constitution so that ss. 93(1) through (4) no longer apply to Quebec: *Constitution Amendment, 1997 (Québec)*, SI/97-141; s. 93A of the *Constitution Act, 1867*. Newfoundland no longer has denominational schools, but instead guarantees the provision of courses in religion that are not specific to a religious denomination and guarantees that religious observances shall be permitted in a public school where requested by parents: *Constitution Amendment, 1998 (Newfoundland Act)*, SI/98-25.[9]

Section 29 of the *Canadian Charter of Rights and Freedoms* states specifically that section 93 rights are not abrogated or derogated by the *Charter*. In the *Bill 30 Reference* case,[10] the Supreme Court of Canada was asked to consider whether Ontario's extension of funding for the Roman Catholic school system was constitutional. In upholding the extension of funding, the Court decided that the funding of denominational education for Roman Catholics in Ontario is immune from review under the *Charter*. Therefore, the equality rights in section 15 cannot be used to strike down the rights contained in section 93. This was confirmed by the Supreme Court of Canada in *Adler v. Ontario*[11] in holding that the funding of denominational schools, as required by section 93, does not mean that Ontario is obligated to fund religious private schools on the basis of section 15(1) equality rights.

In *Jacobi v. Newell No. 4 (County)*[12] a separate school district in Alberta was found not to come within the constitutional protection that applies to separate schools because the school district did not in fact operate a school.

---

9 [2001] 1 S.C.R. 470 at para. 4.
10 *Reference re an Act to Amend the Education Act (Ont.)* (1987), 40 D.L.R. (4th) 18 (S.C.C.).
11 Above, note 8.
12 (1994), 112 D.L.R. (4th) 229 (Alta. Q.B.).

Instead, it purchased services from the neighbouring public board. The court found that for the constitutional protection to apply, the district would have to provide its students with a denominational education adhering to some minimum standard.

In 1997, the Ontario legislature passed extensive amendments to the *Education Act* which, among other things, revised the funding model for school boards and removed the right of school boards to set property tax rates. The changes were summarized in *O.E.C.T.A. v. Ontario* as follows:

> In 1997, the Ontario government, represented on this appeal by the respondent Attorney General for Ontario, passed Bill 160, the *Education Quality Improvement Act, 1997*, S.O. 1997, c. 31 (*"EQIA"*). The *EQIA* amended the *Education Act*, R.S.O. 1990, c. E.2, to create a new governance and funding model for all school boards in Ontario, including both public and separate (denominational) boards. To address a disparity of revenues between school boards, both between urban and rural boards and between separate and public boards, the *EQIA* allocates funds on a per-pupil basis. It also removes the ability of school boards to set property tax rates for education purposes, and centralizes this taxation power in the hands of the Minister of Finance. At the same time, the *EQIA* limits the power of school boards to control their budgets and expenditures, although it guarantees local control over denominational expenditures. Finally, the *EQIA* allows the Minister of Education and Training to take control of a school board temporarily if financial problems arise, again subject to certain protections, which are set out below.[13]

The legislation was challenged by separate school supporters and by public school supporters on a number of grounds as being unconstitutional. At the trial level, in Divisional Court, Cumming J. held that Roman Catholics in Ontario are constitutionally guaranteed the right to finance a Catholic education system from within their own community. He therefore declared the *Education Quality Improvement Act* to be of no force and effect insofar as it interferes with the right to raise money by taxation. Cumming J. rejected the remaining arguments of the appellants. He upheld the legal validity of the new powers conferred on the Minister in respect of the supervision of school and he rejected the public boards' "mirror equality" argument that a right to tax must also exist for public school supporters. He agreed with Campbell J. in *Ontario Public School Boards' Assn. v. Ontario (Attorney General)*[14] that *Adler*,[15] a leading case on this issue, "is a shield to protect the public school system against *Charter* challenges . . . not a sword to win denominational rights for public schools". Cumming J. also rejected the assertion that that there is a constitutional convention protecting the design of the public education system in Ontario and held that, even if there was,

---

13 Above, note 9, at para. 6.
14 Above, note 3.
15 Above, note 8.

a constitutional convention cannot be used to invalidate express legislation. Cumming J. also held that the delegation of taxing power in the *Education Act* did not violate sections 53 and 54 of the *Constitution Act, 1867*.

The Ontario Court of Appeal disagreed with Cumming J. about the right to tax, holding that the right to tax is a non-denominational aspect of denominational schools, and that section 93(1) guarantees only the funding of denominational schools, not a right of separate school boards to tax their supporters. The Court agreed with Cumming J. that the other challenges against the legislation should fail. The Court held that the new funding model limits the spending power of trustees only in relation to matters that are entirely non-denominational, and therefore did not have a prejudicial effect on the rights guaranteed by section 93(1). The supervisory powers given to the Minister of Education are also constitutional. Having rejected the separate school supporters' claim to a right to tax and a right of independent management and control, the court rejected the mirror equality claim by public school boards, along with their argument regarding a constitutional "convention". The Court of Appeal also agreed that the delegation of the setting of property tax rates for education purposes to the Minister of Finance did not contravene section 53 of the *Constitution Act, 1867*.

The same constitutional issues came before the Supreme Court of Canada, and that Court agreed with the Ontario Court of Appeal. The Court summarized its "purposive approach" to section 93 as follows:

> Instead, this Court employs "a purposive approach to s. 93": see the *Reference Re Bill 30, supra*, at p. 1175, *per* Wilson J. Such an approach gives provincial legislatures the flexibility to use the plenary power granted to them in s. 93 to alter their education systems. At the same time, the jurisprudence reveals that care has been exercised to avoid using the purposive approach to expand the original purpose of s. 93. Beetz J., for a majority of this Court in *G.M.P.S.B., supra*, at p. 401, rejected an approach to s. 93(1) that would "improperly amplify the provision's purpose" and thereby transform s. 93(1) into "a blanket affirmation of freedom of religion or freedom of conscience". Using the properly confined purposive approach, Beetz J. concluded, at p. 402, that "the law in force 'at the Union' cannot on its own set the content of the constitutional right in s. 93(1)". In other words, the rights guaranteed by s. 93(1) do not replicate the law word-for-word as it stood in 1867. It is the broader purpose of the laws in force which continues to be protected. Therefore, s. 93(1) should be viewed as protecting the denominational aspects of education, as well as those non-denominational aspects necessary to deliver the denominational elements. As Beetz J. stated in *G.M.P.S.B.*, at p. 411:
>
>> In other words, constitutional protection "with respect to Denominational Schools" has both denominational and non-denominational components. This approach is commonly referred to as the "aspects analysis" or the "aspects approach".

Dickson C.J. summarized the aspects approach in *Mahe, supra*, at p. 382:

[Subsection 93(1)] protects powers over denominational aspects of education and those non-denominational aspects which are related to denominational concerns which were enjoyed at the time of Confederation. The phrase does not support the protection of powers enjoyed in respect of non-denominational aspects of education except in so far as is necessary to give effect to denominational concerns. [Emphasis deleted.][16]

The Supreme Court held that the *Education Quality Improvement Act, 1997* (EQIA):

affects only secular aspects of education, and does not prejudicially affect denominational aspects of education or any non-denominational aspects required to deliver the protected denominational elements. In this respect, it is constitutional. As Meredith C.J.C.P. stated in *Ottawa Separate School Trustees v. City of Ottawa, supra,* at p. 630, "[e]ducational methods and machinery may and must change, but separation, and equal rights regarding public schools, must remain as long as provincial public schools last". The *EQIA* brings change to the financial management and control of separate schools in Ontario, but it treats all school boards equally and preserves the denominational aspects of separate schools.[17]

The Court was also satisfied that the power of the Minister to supervise school boards is constitutional because the Minister is not permitted to interfere with denominational aspects of a separate school board:

I also find constitutional the Division D provisions that, under certain conditions, empower the Minister of Education and Training to take over the financial control of a school board. Similar legislation was successfully challenged in *Ottawa Separate Schools Trustees v. Ottawa Corporation, supra.* However, the legislation held to be *ultra vires* in that case allowed the Lieutenant Governor in Council to take over *all* of the powers of a school board for an indefinite period of time. Lord Buckmaster L.C. struck down the legislation because of the sweeping, open-ended nature of the interference with rights protected by s. 93(1) (at p. 81):

> The case before their Lordships is not that of a mere interference with a right or privilege, but of a provision which enables it to be withdrawn in toto for an indefinite time. Their Lordships have no doubt that the power so given would be exercised with wisdom and moderation, but it is the creation of the power and not its exercise that is subject to objection, and the objection would not be removed even though the powers conferred were never exercised at all.

The Ontario government responded by passing new legislation, which was held to be constitutional by the Ontario Supreme Court, Appellate Division in *Re Ottawa Separate Schools, supra.* Meredith C.J.O. distinguished the new legislation from the failed legislation on the following grounds: (1) control over

---

16 Above, note 9, at paras. 32-33.
17 *Ibid.,* at para. 430.

a board could be vested in a provincial body only under certain circumstances and had to be revested by the Minister of Education once it appeared that the schools would be conducted by the Board according to law; and (2) any dispute over whether the criteria for vesting or revesting had been met was to be resolved on summary application to the courts. He held that those safeguards were sufficient to meet the requirements of s. 93(1).

In my opinion, the *EQIA* provides greater protection to denominational rights than the legislation upheld in *Re Ottawa Separate Schools, supra*. Section 257.52(1) of the new *Education Act* specifically forbids the Minister from interfering with the denominational aspects of a Roman Catholic school board. Whether such an interference has occurred can be reviewed by the courts, pursuant to s. 257.40(5). As will be examined below, a province is free to deal with public school boards as it sees fit. The constitutional concern with financial supervision only relates to separate school boards, and then only in relation to the denominational aspects of those boards. The protection provided by s. 257.52(1) is sufficient on its own to meet the requirements of s. 93(1) of the *Constitution Act, 1867*. Unlike *Ottawa Separate School Trustees v. City of Ottawa, supra*, the *EQIA* does not interfere with *all* the powers of a denominational school board, but only with the non-denominational powers of a school board. If the Minister interferes in any way with the denominational aspects of a separate school, even if the interference results from the exercise of a non-denominational power, an interested party can ask the courts to remedy the interference. The protections provided by ss. 257.52(1) and 257.40(5) therefore result in Division D of the new *Education Act* meeting the requirements of s. 93(1).[18]

The Supreme Court then addressed the issue of local taxation, the sole issue upon which the separate school supporters had succeeded at trial. The Supreme Court rejected the idea that, although separate school supporters had the right of local taxation at the time of Confederation, the province was powerless to alter the way in which separate boards were funded:

It is beyond question that Roman Catholic school boards in Ontario had the legal right to tax their supporters in 1867. Section 7 of the *Scott Act* explicitly conferred this right. It states, in part, that separate school trustees "shall have the power to impose, levy and collect School rates or subscriptions, upon and from persons sending children to, or subscribing towards the support of such Schools". The political reality at the time was that education could only be paid for out of funds raised locally, and so all school boards in the province were given the power to tax their supporters. As the Court of Appeal noted, at p. 16, "[c]omplete provincial responsibility for the financing of education was simply outside the experience of the founders of Confederation". Local funds were supplemented by provincial grants, but moneys raised through local taxation remained the dominant component of education funding in the province up until the enactment of the *EQIA* in 1997.

---

18 *Ibid.*, at paras. 44-46.

However, the fact that the right to tax existed in 1867 does not mean that it is automatically protected by s. 93(1). Section 93(1) only protects rights or privileges "with respect to Denominational Schools". This threshold requirement to access the protections of s. 93(1) is the genesis of the aspects approach, which has long been applied by the courts. The aspects approach to s. 93(1) requires that the right in question be related to a denominational aspect of education, or to a non-denominational aspect necessary to deliver the protected denominational elements. I agree with the Court of Appeal that the authority to tax supporters is not a right or privilege "with respect to Denominational Schools". Section 93(1) protects the right to funding for denominational education, not the specific mechanism through which that funding is delivered. As Gonthier J. stated in the *Quebec Education Reference, supra*, at p. 590:

> ...fundamentally what matters is having the financial and physical resources to operate school boards. The taxing power is only one possible means of attaining this end. If it can be done otherwise, such as by an equal, or at least appropriate and equitable, allocation of financing sources, it is hard to speak of a prejudicial effect.
>
> The *Scott Act* includes two funding mechanisms for denominational schools in Ontario: local taxation (s. 7) and provincial grants (s. 20). The province is generally free to alter the funding allocation between these sources as it sees fit, provided that the source relied on provides sufficient funds to operate a denominational education system which is equivalent to the public education system in place at the time. The animating principle is equality of educational opportunity. I need not decide the constitutionality of removing the local tax base altogether, as the *EQIA* does not attempt to do so. While it removes the ability of school boards to set the rate that is to be applied to raise funds through local taxation, it does not remove the funding mechanism of property taxation.[19]

The Court went on to deal with the challenges to the legislation brought by the public school boards, and agreed with the result reached by the Court of Appeal.

(b) Funding Private Schools

While section 93 imposes obligations on the provinces with respect to denominational education, provinces have the discretionary power to provide funding to schools of all religious denominations. Many provinces, such as British Columbia and Alberta, do fund private schools, either wholly or partially. In Ontario, no private schools are directly funded by the province. In *Adler*, the Supreme Court of Canada held that the *Charter* is not infringed by reason of the failure of the province to fund religious private schools under the *Education Act*. The applicants represented members of the Jewish and Christian faiths who send their children to private schools

---

19 *Ibid.*, at paras. 48-50.

for religious reasons. They asserted that sending their children to the secular public school system would be contrary to their beliefs.

They argued their case on two main points, as summarized by Iacobucci, J.: "The first is that s. 2(a)'s guarantee of freedom of religion requires the Province of Ontario to provide public funding for independent religious schools. The second is that, by funding Roman Catholic separate schools and secular public schools at the same time as it denies funding to independent religious schools, the province is discriminating against the appellants on the basis of religion contrary to s. 15(1)."[20]

As stated above, the Court rejected the applicants' argument that Ontario must fund religious private or independent schools because it funds denominational schools established under section 93 of the *Constitution Act, 1867*. In Mr. Justice Iacobucci's view, section 93 is "a comprehensive code with respect to denominational school rights",[21] much in the same way that section 23 of the Charter is a comprehensive code with respect of minority language education rights. Section 2(a) (freedom of religion) cannot be used to enlarge this comprehensive code. Furthermore, an argument based on section 15(1) (equality rights) fails because the government has no choice but to fund Roman Catholic separate schools.

With respect to the argument based on equality with the public schools, Iacobucci J. stated:

> In my view, this argument is mistaken in supposing that public schools are not contemplated by the terms of s. 93, as it applies to Ontario. On the contrary, the public school system is an integral part of the s. 93 scheme. When the province funds public schools, it is, in the words of Wilson J. in *Reference re Bill 30*, at p. 1198, legislating 'pursuant to the plenary power in relation to education granted to the provincial legislatures as part of the Confederation compromise'.[22]

In Iacobucci's view,

> the public school system is an integral part of the Confederation compromise and consequently, receives a protection against constitutional or Charter attack.

> This protection exists despite the fact that the public school rights are not themselves constitutionally entrenched. It is the province's plenary power to legislate with regard to public schools, which are open to all members of society, without distinction, that is constitutionally entrenched. This is what creates the immunity from Charter scrutiny.[23]

Although Sopinka J. also rejected the applicants' claim in *Adler*, he disagreed with Iacobucci J.'s analysis with respect to whether or not section 93

---

20 Above, note 8, at 400.
21 *Ibid.*, at 402.
22 *Ibid.*, at 404.
23 *Ibid.*, at 406-407.

is a "comprehensive code" that protects the funding of public schools from *Charter* scrutiny. He stated:

> I note at the outset that this proposition erroneously assumes that because certain rights and privileges of the Protestant majoritarian schools are relevant in identifying the rights and privileges of separate schools, the former are *ipso facto* given constitutional protection. My colleague says that 'public schools are part and parcel of s. 93's comprehensive Code.' But, the rights and privileges of public schools are merely the benchmarks for ascertaining the rights and privileges of separate schools. Certain provisions of pre-Confederation statutes gave separate schools the same rights as enjoyed by public schools. While the terms of those statutes are relevant to ascertain what these rights and privileges were, the statutes themselves are not given constitutional status. Only the rights and privileges of separate schools were given constitutional protection.[24]

Sopinka J. expanded upon this argument at some considerable length. In his view, legislation about the public school system involves the exercise of the plenary power found in the introduction of section 93, much like the exercise of any other provincial plenary power. If public schools are somehow protected as part of section 93, this could seriously restrict the ability of a province to change or even eliminate the system. Sopinka J. took great pains to send a message to potential litigants that public school rights are not entrenched:

> Inasmuch as it has not been suggested in the past that changes to the public school system may infringe s. 93, a decision to this effect would likely produce a flurry of litigation as many of the past changes to the public school system are challenged on the basis of their departure from the Confederation benchmark.[25]

Having found that the funding of public schools, as opposed to separate denominational schools, is not protected from *Charter* scrutiny, Sopinka J. held that there was no infringement of sections 2(a) or 15 of the *Charter*.

> The appellants cannot, however, complain that the Ontario *Education Act* prevents them from exercising this aspect [i.e. religious education] of their freedom of religion since it allows for the provision of education within a religious school or at home. The statute does not compel the appellants to act in any way that infringes their freedom of religion . . . Thus with or without s. 21 of the *Education Act*, the appellants would act in the same manner, thereby eliminating any potentially coercive aspect of the legislation.[26]

---

24 *Ibid.*, at 435.
25 See *OPSBA v. Ontario (Attorney General)*, above, note 3, in which the court stated: "What *Adler* says is that the public school system does not enjoy denominational school rights."
26 Above, note 8, at 444-445.

In examining whether the *Education Act* has the effect of imposing a different burden on different religions vis-à-vis non-observers, Sopinka J. stated:

> The legislation is not the source of any distinction amongst all the groups whose exercise of their religious freedom involves an economic cost . . . In addition, the failure to act in order to facilitate the practice of religion cannot be considered state interference with freedom of religion.[27]

Sopinka J. also confirmed that the public school system is to be secular:

> The reason why the public school system is not acceptable to the appellants lies in its secular nature. This secular nature is itself mandated by s. 2(a) of the Charter as held by several courts in this country.[28]

In *Bal v. Ontario (Attorney General)*[29] the applicants appealed a decision of Winkler J. in Ontario Court (General Division)[30] holding that Ontario has no legal obligation to permit "alternative religious schools" to be established within the public school system. In the face of *Charter* court decisions that effectively require public schools to be secular, and in the face of *Adler* (in which the *Bal* applicants intervened) the Ontario Court of Appeal had little difficulty agreeing with Winkler J. and it held that the province was not required to fund alternative religious schools.

(c) Hiring by Separate School Boards

The courts have been asked to consider whether the right to denominational schools under section 93 of the *Constitution Act, 1867*, includes the right to employ only teachers who adhere to the Catholic or Protestant faith, as the case may be. Catholic-only hiring practices of denominational school boards have been considered by the courts, in relation to section 93 and human rights legislation. In addition, religious private schools have successfully defended their right to hire teachers of certain faiths, as a *bona fide* occupational requirement under provincial human rights legislation.

The Supreme Court of Canada, in *Caldwell v. Stuart*[31] decided that conformity to Roman Catholic religious practices is a *bona fide* requirement of teachers in a Roman Catholic school. In this case, a British Columbia teacher married a divorced man in a civil ceremony. In *Essex County (Roman Catholic Separate School Board) v. Porter*,[32] the Ontario Court of Appeal decided that two teachers, who entered into civil marriages and were dis-

---

27 *Ibid.*, at 446.
28 *Ibid.*, at 448.
29 (1997), 34 O.R. (3d) 484 (Ont. C.A.), leave to appeal refused (1998), 49 C.R.R. (2d) 188 (note) (S.C.C.).
30 *Bal v. Ontario (Attorney General)* (1994), 121 D.L.R. (4th) 96 (Ont. Gen. Div.).
31 (1985), 15 D.L.R. (4th) 1 (S.C.C.).
32 (1978), 21 O.R. (2d) 255 (C.A.).

missed for denominational cause, had no right to a Board of Reference because the right of separate school boards to dismiss teachers for denominational cause was a right or privilege existing in 1867 and is therefore protected by section 93(1). In *Essex County (Roman Catholic Separate School Board) v. Tremblay-Webster*,[33] the Ontario Court of Appeal decided that the *Porter* decision does not prevent a teacher from grieving a dismissal under a collective agreement. In *Essex County*, the teacher had married outside the requirements of the Roman Catholic religion. The Ontario Divisional Court in *Black v. Metropolitan Separate School Board*,[34] decided that the separate school board's termination of a teacher's contract because she did not direct her education taxes to the separate board did not contravene sections 2(a), 7 or 15(1) of the *Charter*.[35]

The issue of whether or not a board may discriminate against non-Catholic teachers in its promotion policy has been considered in the Ontario Court (General Division) in *O.E.C.T.A. v. Dufferin-Peel Roman Catholic Separate School Board*.[36] In this case, the applicant sought judicial review of an arbitration award that found the right to apply a denominational promotion policy was protected by section 93(1) of the Constitution as part of the right of separate school boards in Ontario to maintain the denominational character of their schools. The Board of Arbitration concluded that the school boards was not required to justify its promotion policy as a *bona fide* occupational qualification (BFOQ) pursuant to section 24(1)(a) of the *Human Rights Code*. The Board concluded the *Code* did not prohibit the promotion policy.

Upon an application for judicial review, the Divisional Court quashed the arbitration award, stating that the operation of section 24(1)(a) of the *Code* does not prejudicially affect the school board's right to operate denominational schools. The matter was remitted to a differently constituted board of arbitration to consider the matter in light of the court decision.

---

33 (1984), 45 O.R. (2d) 83 (C.A.).
34 (1988), 65 O.R. (2d) 598 (Div. Ct.).
35 See also *Casagrande v. Hinton (R.C. Separate School Dist. No.155)* (1987), 51 Alta. L.R. (2d) 349 (Q.B.) - pre-marital sex was valid denominational cause for termination; *Walsh v. Newfoundland (Treasury Bd.)* (1988), 71 Nfld. & P.E.I.R. 21 (Nfld. C.A.). Leave to appeal to S.C.C. refused (1989), 76 Nfld. & P.E.I.R. 191 (note) (S.C.C.) - marriage outside the Roman Catholic church; *Garrod v. Rhema Christian School* (1991), 15 C.H.R.R. D/477 (Ont. Bd. of Inquiry) - private school teacher dismissed for contravening the rules of the denomination which operated the school (*bona fide* occupational requirement under the *Ontario Human Rights Code*); *Metropolitan Separate School Board v. O.E.C.T.A.* (1994), 41 L.A.C. (4th) 353 - teacher successfully grieved separate school board's decision to disallow her from teaching religion because of the way the teacher described herself in controversial published articles - board's discipline was for political, not denominational, reasons.
36 (1999), 172 D.L.R. (4th) 260.

The decision was appealed to the Ontario Court of Appeal, which upheld the decision in Divisional Court and provided a thorough analysis of denominational rights in the employment context. The Court stated (at paras 19-32):

> The Board's position in this appeal is that the right to manage the schools within its jurisdiction, including the right to adopt a policy that only Catholics may be promoted, is a right which is protected by s. 93(1) of the Constitution. The imposition of an obligation to justify its policy as a bona fide occupational requirement pursuant to s. 24(1) of the Human Rights Code, it says, prejudicially affects this right and cannot stand.
>
> The opening words of s. 93 of the *Constitution Act, 1867* clearly grant to the province the power to make laws in relation to education. That basic power is subject to the limitation that the law cannot violate any right or privilege pertaining to denominational schools existing at the time of Confederation: *Hirsch v. Protestant Board of School Commissioners of Montreal*, [1928] 1 D.L.R. 1041 (J.C.P.C.) at 1052. There are two stages to the constitutional analysis of the interpretation of s. 93(1). Initially, one must determine whether there was a right or privilege enjoyed by a particular class of persons by law at the time of Confederation. If so, one must go on to the second stage of the analysis which is to determine whether the legislation at issue prejudicially affects this right or privilege: *Quebec Association of Protestant School Boards v. Attorney-General of Quebec* (1993), 105 D.L.R. (4th) 266 (S.C.C.) at 306-307. Within the first stage of the analysis concerning s. 93(1) one must answer two questions. First, what was the extent of the power of the Trustees at the time of Confederation? Second, in what measure is this power a "Right or Privilege with respect to Denominational Schools": *Greater Montreal Protestant School Board v. Quebec (Attorney General)*, [1989] 1 S.C.R. 377 at 405.
>
> Beginning with the first stage of the analysis, the power of the Trustees at the time of Confederation is not in issue in this appeal. It is not disputed that Catholics had, at the time of Confederation, the right by law to employ teachers and the right to manage their separate schools and that this right would include the right to promote teachers. See, for example, *Reference re Act to Amend the Education Act (Ont.)* (1987), 40 D.L.R. (4th) 18 (S.C.C.) (the Bill 30 Reference). The question here is the extent to which the power to promote teachers is a "Right or Privilege with respect to Denominational Schools".
>
> As stated in Greater Montreal Protestant School Board, supra, at 402, cited with approval by Iacobucci J. in *Ontario Home Builders' Association v. York Region Board of Education* (1996), 137 D.L.R. (4th) 449 (S.C.C.) at 489:
>
>> The approach courts have taken to the interpretation of the expression "with respect to Denominational Schools" in cases such as [Attorney General of Quebec v. Greater Hull School Board, [1984] 2 S.C.R. 575] ... demonstrates that the law in force "at the Union" cannot on its own set the content of the constitutional rights in s. 93(1).

The constitutional guarantee in s. 93(1) has both denominational and non-denominational aspects: Greater Montreal Protestant School Board, supra, at 410 citing the decision of Chouinard J. in *Attorney General of Quebec v. Greater Hull School Board*, supra, at 584. The aim of s. 93(1) was to ensure equality of educational opportunity for Roman Catholics: Ontario Home Builders' Association, supra, at 489. At the same time the ultimate aim of the section is also a religious one: Greater Montreal Protestant School Board, supra, at 411 citing with approval the text of Professors Chevrette, Marx and Tremblay, Les problemes constitutionnels poses par la restructuration scolaire de l'ile de Montreal (Quebec: Ministere de l'Education, 1972). A number of means to ensure that the denominational status of education is respected are also protected by s. 93(1). The following translated passage from the text of Professors Chevrette, Marx and Tremblay was cited with approval by both Beetz J. in *Greater Montreal Protestant School Board*, supra, at 410-411 and by Gonthier J. in Reference Re: Education Act (Quebec), [1993] 2 S.C.R. 511 at 541:

> It should be noted that in themselves, and viewed in isolation, these means are not necessarily religious in nature, for they may include financial powers, the power to hire teachers and so on: however, such means should still be related to the denominational status of education directly and connected directly with maintaining it. [Emphasis added.]

In other words one of the means of ensuring the denominational status of education is through the power to hire teachers. In this regard, see the reasons of this Court in *Daly v. The Ontario Secondary School Teachers' Federation*, released concurrently with these reasons. The constitutional protection in s. 93(1) applies to the power to hire teachers and, inferentially, the power to promote teachers to the extent that such power is related to maintaining the denominational character of Catholic schools and education. The power to promote teachersh as been entrenched only in so far as this power is necessary to maintain the denominational status of education. While the right and privilege of Catholics to a denominational education in s. 93 obviously includes the means and framework in which the right is exercised, the means to achieve that end are not themselves constitutionally guaranteed. Gonthier J. made this clear when he stated in *Reference re: Education Act (Quebec)*, supra, at 541-542 and at 579:

> I note that in G.M.P.S.B., supra, this Court has already held that rights of ownership, powers to hire staff and powers to use material resources are incidental rights that are only protected to the extent that they are necessary to preserve the denomination character of education. [Emphasis added.]

The Board of Arbitration ruled that the Board's promotion policy was constitutionally protected. It did so without considering whether the policy was in fact justified under the Human Rights Code. However, in reaching its conclusion the Board did not consider the second question within the first stage of the constitutional analysis, namely, the extent to which the power was a right or privilege with respect to denominational schools. The Board of Arbitration ought to have considered that the promotion policy was a means to an end, namely a denominational system of education. As a means, the promotion policy is constitutionally protected only insofar as it is necessary to maintain or achieve that end. As a result, the Board of Arbitration failed to correctly interpret s. 93(1) of the *Constitution Act, 1867*.

> 2. Was the Divisional Court correct in concluding that the Board of Arbitration erred because it failed to apply s. 24 of the Human Rights Code?

In the first part of my reasons I concluded that the Trustees' right to promote teachers was constitutionally protected only insofar as it was necessary to maintain a denominational system of education. It is now appropriate to go on to the second stage of the analysis concerning s. 93(1) and determine whether s. 24 of the Code prejudicially affects the rights or privileges guaranteed at the time of Confederation.

The Board of Arbitration held that the right of the Separate School Board to manage separate schools to preserve their denominational character was not subject to any review under the Human Rights Code. In reaching this conclusion the Board of Arbitration erred. The province has the power to pass laws and to regulate certain aspects of Catholic education so long as that power is exercised in conformity with s. 93(1): *Reference re Act to Amend the Education Act (Ont.)* (1987), 40 D.L.R. (4th) 18 (S.C.C.) per Wilson J. at p. 55. It does not follow from the fact that the power to promote teachers existed at Confederation that the equality provisions of the Human Rights Code automatically have no application. The Board should have inquired whether the application of s. 24 of the Code prejudicially affected a right or privilege guaranteed by s. 93(1).

As stated in Re Ontario Human Rights Code 1961-62 and Gore, supra, cited by McMurtry C.J.O.C. with approval, at p. 184 of the reasons below:

> Section 93(1) could not have been intended, therefore, to prevent the legislature from enacting any law which affects the rights and powers of Separate School Boards . . . it could not be argued that the province could not today apply, for example, collective bargaining or trade union legislation to the separate schools merely because in 1867 such legislation did not exist. If recognition of trade unions or teachers' associations can now be made applicable to school boards, despite the fact that there could be an argument that school boards were free to ignore such associations in 1867, then surely the province could decide to apply the Ontario Human Rights Code to schools unless the discrimination practised by the school board is such as can be described as being a "reasonable occupational qualification".

The appellant Board submits that the application of the bona fide occupational requirement standard should only be applied if its right to pursue its promotion policy is not protected by s. 93(1). I have already determined that the policy itself is not protected. Rather, it is only to the extent that the policy is necessary to preserve the denominational aspect of the school that the policy is protected.

Section 24 of the Human Rights Code provides an objective means by which to measure the extent to which the policy in this case is necessary to maintain the denominational aspect. If the policy is a bona fide occupational requirement, it surely can be said to be necessary to the preservation of denominational education. Hence the application of s. 24 to the policy does not prejudicially affect the denominational guarantee in s. 93(1); on the contrary, it is consistent with it.

In *Re Caldwell, et al. v. Stuart et al.* (1984), 15 D.L.R. (4th) 1 at 17 (S.C.C.), McIntyre J. was dealing with the application of the equality provision of the Human Rights Code in the context of a dismissal for denominational cause. The contract of a teacher at a Roman Catholic school was not renewed because she married a divorced person in a civil ceremony. In his reasons, McIntyre J. noted that he had had occasion to consider the nature of a bona fide occupational requirement in *Ontario Human Rights Com'n et al. v. Borough of Etobicoke* (1982), 132 D.L.R. (3d) (S.C.C.) 14 under different statutory provisions. He held, at 16-17, that the test of a bona fide occupational requirement has two branches. The first is subjective. It is whether the limitation has been imposed honestly and in good faith. There is no issue here as to the Board's good faith. The second branch, as adapted to the circumstances of dismissal for denominational cause, was phrased as follows:

> Is the requirement of religious conformance by Catholic teachers, objectively viewed, reasonably necessary to assure the accomplishment of the objectives of the Church in operating a Catholic school with its distinct characteristics for the purposes of providing a Catholic education to its students?

A similar test is appropriate in the present case. The essence of the test may be phrased in this way: "Is the policy of prohibiting certain non-Catholic teachers from promotion, objectively viewed, reasonably necessary to preserve the Catholic nature of the schools?" If so, the policy would be a reasonable and bona fide employment qualification within the meaning of s. 24 of the Code.

The Divisional Court was correct in concluding that the Board of Arbitration erred because it failed to apply s. 24 of the Human Rights Code. I would accordingly confirm the order of the Divisional Court remitting the issue to a differently constituted Board of Arbitration.[37]

In *Daly v. Ontario (Attorney General)*[38] the applicant asserted that subsection 136(2) of the *Education Act* infringed the denominational rights of separate schools to prefer Roman Catholic teachers in respect of hiring, employment, advancement and promotion. The case was heard concurrently

---

37 *O.E.C.T.A. (Branch Affiliates) v. Dufferin-Peel Roman Catholic Separate School Board.* Above, note 36, at paras. 19-32.
38 (1997), 38 O.R. (3d) 37, 154 D.L.R. (4th) 464 (Gen. Div.), affirmed (1999), 172 D.L.R. (4th) 241 (Ont. C.A.), additional reasons at (1999), 124 O.A.C. 152 (C.A.), leave to appeal refused (1999), 249 N.R. 396 (note) (S.C.C.), additional reasons at (2001), 2001 CarswellOnt 491 (S.C.J.).

with the *Dufferin-Peel* case quoted above, although the *Daly* case was not connected to a review of an arbitration decision or to a specific promotion policy. Section 136 arose when Ontario extended the separate school funding into Grades 11, 12 and 13. It came into force in the 11th year after a Roman Catholic separate board commenced performing the duties of a secondary school board. Most separate boards elected to "extend" in September 1985. Subsection 136(2) of the *Education Act* required separate school boards to comply with section 5 of the *Human Rights Code* with respect to its employees. Section 5 prohibits discrimination with respect to employment on the basis of certain grounds, namely, race, ancestry, place of origin, colour, ethnic origin, citizenship, creed, sex, sexual orientation, age, record of offences, marital status, same-sex partnership status, family status or handicap. Section 136 meant that if a teacher agreed to respect the philosophy of a separate school, a Roman Catholic school board could take into consideration the religion of the teacher in making employment decisions.

The Divisional Court (Sharpe J.) found section 136 to be of no force and effect because it violates the denominational guarantee contained in section 93(1) of the *Constitution Act, 1867*. The Ontario Court of Appeal agreed. After a detailed review of the relevant history of section 93 denominational rights in Ontario, the Court found, first, that Sharpe J. "correctly concluded that, at the time of Confederation, Roman Catholic separate school trustees did have the implicit legal right to prefer persons of the Roman Catholic faith when making employment decisions relating to teachers. The second issue for the Court was whether section 136 prejudicially affected the section 93 guarantee. The Court stated that it did. The Court did not accept the argument that the right to hire and to promote is in and of itself a denominational guarantee and is protected from scrutiny—a view that would make it unnecessary to justify the right to preferentially hire or promote a teacher for a Catholic high school. However, the Court concluded that:

> [t]he evidence does support the conclusion of Sharpe J. that the ability to hire preferentially on the basis of religion will be necessary to preserve the Catholic character of Roman Catholic Separate Schools in many cases. Section 136 prejudicially affects the denominational guarantee because it prohibits any consideration of religion when exercising the power to employ, advance and promote teachers within a separate school system even when such consideration is necessary to achieve the denominational guarantee in s. 93 of the *Constitution Act*.

There are two approaches one can use to arrive at this conclusion. One is that the guarantee under s. 93(1) is a nondenominational, or administrative, "aspect" of the right to a Catholic education. On this view the right to preferentially hire and promote is protected insofar as it is necessary to give effect to the denominational guarantee of the Catholicity of the school: *Greater Montreal Prot-*

estant School Board, supra, per Beetz J at p. 415. The other approach is that s. 136(2) violates s. 93(1) of the Constitution Act because it prohibits the preference of Roman Catholic teachers even where it can be established by objective and cogent evidence that such preference is a bona fide occupational requirement under the Human Rights Code. The two approaches are not mutually exclusive and the adoption of the one or the other may depend on the manner in which the issue arose.

Under either approach, the evidence before Sharpe J. justified his conclusion that s. 136 infringes the constitutional guarantee under s. 93(1) because it takes away the right to even consider whether a teacher is Catholic or not in making employment decisions in Roman Catholic Separate Schools.

In a recent Ontario decision, a court was called upon to weigh a student's individual rights against those of a separate school board. In *Hall v. Powers*[39] MacKinnon J. of the Ontario Superior Court of Justice dealt with a request by a 17-year-old secondary school student for an interlocutory injunction against the defendant school principal employed by a Roman Catholic separate school board. The student was refused permission to bring his same-sex partner to the school prom. The school board felt that granting permission would be contrary to its understanding of Catholic beliefs. The Court granted an interlocutory injunction and also found that allowing the student to attend the prom did not prejudicially affect rights with respect to denominational schools under section 93(1). The specific right in question was not in effect at the time of the Union in 1867 and, moreover, it could not be said that the conduct in question went to the essential denominational nature of the school.

(d) Minority Language Education Rights

The educational rights of the French-speaking or English-speaking linguistic minority in a province are guaranteed by s. 23 of the *Constitution Act, 1982*, which states:

23.(1) Citizens of Canada

(a) whose first language learned and still understood is that of the English or French linguistic minority population of the province in which they reside, or
(b) who have received their primary school instruction in Canada in English or French and reside in a province where the language in which they received that instruction is the language of the English or French linguistic minority population of the province,

have the right to have their children receive primary and secondary school instruction in that language in that province.

---

39 [2002] O.J. No. 1803.

(2) Citizens of Canada of whom any child has received or is receiving primary or secondary school instruction in English or French in Canada, have the right to have all their children receive primary and secondary school instruction in the same language.

(3) The right of citizens of Canada under subsections 1 and 2 to have their children receive primary and secondary school instruction in the language of English or French linguistic minority population of a province

(a) applies wherever in the province the number of children of citizens who have such a right is sufficient to warrant the provision to them out of public funds of minority language instruction; and
(b) includes, where the number of those children so warrants, the right to have them receive that instruction in minority language educational facilities provided out of public funds.

Section 23 has generated a considerable amount of litigation about the nature of the rights contained in the section and the measures which a province must take to give effect to those rights.

In 1990, the Supreme Court of Canada, in *Mahe v. Alberta*,[40] attempted to define the rights provided by section 23. The general questions for the *Mahe* Court to decide were (1) whether section 23 mandates a right to management and control over education by the linguistic minority, depending on the number of students; and (2) whether the number of students in Edmonton was sufficient to invoke this right. The chief findings of the Court are summarized below.

The Court found that any broad guarantee of language rights, especially in the context of education, cannot be separated from a concern for the culture associated with the language. "Language is more than a mere means of communication, it is part and parcel of the identity and culture of the people speaking it."[41] Schools "provide needed locations where the minority community can meet and facilities which they can use to express their culture."[42] Section 23 is a remedial provision. It does not merely preserve the status quo; rather, it confers "a right which places positive obligations on government to alter or develop major institutional structures."[43]

Section 23 should be viewed as encompassing a "sliding scale". Section 23 guarantees whatever type and level of rights and services are appropriate in order to provide minority language instruction for the particular number of students involved.[44] There is a general right of minority language instruction. The general right is qualified by paragraphs (a) and (b) of subsection (3). The right is guaranteed only if the "number of children" warrants. The

---

40 (1990), 68 D.L.R. (4th) 69 (S.C.C.).
41 *Ibid.*, at 82.
42 *Ibid.*, at 83.
43 *Ibid.*, at 85.
44 *Ibid.*

right is further qualified by saying that, where numbers warrant, it includes the right to minority language educational facilities. The provision of facilities represents the upper range of requirements under section 23, although a province may provide greater rights if it wishes. The lower end of the scale is "instruction"; instruction is the minimum guaranteed right. The province must ensure that the minority group receives the full amount of protection that its numbers warrant.

The scale has outer limits. At the minimum level, it would be difficult to provide minority language instruction to a very small number of students, and section 23 does not require that programs be put in place. The court did not define the minimum number of students at which instruction must be provided. It simply conveyed the idea that there are obvious practical limitations to providing a program of instruction when there are very few students involved. At the upper end of the sliding scale, the Court held that section 23(3)(b) requires a measure of management and control by the minority group of education facilities. The use of the term "facilities" does not refer only to physical structures. The right to "manage and control" does not always mean that a separate school board must be established, although in some instances a board may be necessary to meet the purpose of section 23. Other approaches may be appropriate depending on the number of students. For example, giving the minority exclusive authority within an existing board structure may be appropriate.[45]

Completely separate boards "are not necessarily the best means of fulfilling the purpose of s. 23".[46] Even where a separate board or district is created, the right to tax is not "essential to satisfy the concerns of s. 23 with linguistic and cultural security," provided that public funds are provided.[47] Funding must be, on a per pupil basis, equal to that of the majority. The minority must have equality with the majority. Special start-up funds for the minority may be necessary, as well.

> Imposing a specific form of educational system in the multitude of different circumstances which exist across Canada would be unrealistic and self-defeating.... At this stage of early development of s. 23 jurisprudence, the appropriate response for the courts is to describe in general terms the requirements mandated. It is up to the public authorities to satisfy these general requirements.[48]

The "numbers warrant" provision refers to the number of students who may eventually take advantage of a contemplated program or facility. In determining what section 23 demands, there are pedagogical and financial

---

45 The nature of management and control to be exercised by the minority component of an existing board is described at page 94 (above, note 40) of the *Mahe* decision.
46 *Mahe*, above, note 40, at 92-93.
47 Above, note 40, at 93.
48 *Ibid.*

considerations. Section 23 does not create an absolute right, and a rigid formula for implementing the section should be avoided.[49]

In *Mahe*, the Court was also asked to consider the effect of section 23 rights upon the right to a denominational school system. The Court concluded that the "transfer of powers in respect of management and control thus amounts to the *regulation* of a non-denominational aspect of education, namely, the language of instruction, a form of regulation which the courts have long held to be valid".[50] The Alberta regulation under consideration in *Mahe* did not alter the denominational character of the board. However, denominational rights could affect the number of students who comprise a minority language group because the students could be split between two different boards. In this way, section 93 rights affect the ability of the minority language group to have its own school, or board.

Although *Mahe* provides guidance and direction, issues about minority language education are still very much alive in Canada. For example, in *Conseil des écoles séparées catholiques romaines de Dufferin et Peel v. Ontario (Ministre de l'éducation et de la formation)*, Hawkins J. found that the ministry's across-the-board moratorium on capital projects infringed the section 23 *Charter* rights of certain citizens residing in the jurisdiction of the board. He stated that "the open-ended delay in funding the construction of Ecole Secondaire Sainte-Famille after seven years of temporary and inadequate facilities does constitute an infringement of the applicant's rights under section 23 of the Charter."[51] The province was ordered to restore the school's funding in accordance with its capital grant process.

In *Abbey v. Essex (County) Board of Education*[52] the Ontario Court of Appeal was asked to determine whether the right under section 23(2) of the *Charter* (which gives Canadian citizens the right to have all of their children receive either French or English language instruction if any of their children has received it) extends to a parent whose first language is not that of the linguistic minority population of the province in which that parent lives. The Abbeys wished to enrol their child in a French language school. One of their children had previously been admitted to a French language school in Essex County, and all three children attended French language schools when the family moved to London. However, when the family moved back to Windsor, the public board denied the parents' request to pay tuition fees for the children to attend a French language school operated by the local separate school board. The Divisional Court agreed with the school board.

---

49 *Mahe*, above, note 40, at 100-101.
50 Above, note 40, at 98 [*Emphasis in original*].
51 *Conseil des ecoles séparées catholiques romaines de Dufferin & Peel v. Ontario (Ministre de l'éducation & de la formation)* (1996), 30 O.R. (3d) 681 at 685 (Div. Ct.), leave to appeal allowed (1996), 30 O.R. (3d) 681n (C.A.).
52 (1999), 42 O.R. (3d) 481 (C.A.), on appeal from (June 10, 1997), Doc. 97/97, [1997] O.J. No. 2379 (Ont. Gen. Div.).

It found that subsection 23(2) is available only to provide continuity of language instruction to those who qualify under section 23(1), namely, citizens whose first language is that of the linguistic minority population of the province in which they live and "does not provide the anglophone community in Ontario with the right to have their children educated in French", whether or not they have already received their education in the French language. However, in 1999, the Court of Appeal disagreed:

> [I]t is my view that s. 23(1) and (2) set out separate entitlements which are conceptually related, but independent from each other. Minority language educational rights are not merely those of children of citizens whose first language is that of the English or French linguistic minority population of the province in which they reside, or who received their primary school education in that language: s. 23(1). These educational rights are also available to all the children of a Canadian citizen if any of that citizen's children has received primary or secondary school instruction in English or French in Canada. Not only do children who have received - or are receiving - their education in the language of the linguistic minority have the right to continue receiving their primary and secondary school education in that language, their siblings enjoy the same continuous right.
>
> For purposes of s. 23(2), it does not matter whether this prior language instruction originated in another province, another part of a province, or through the kind of admissions committee contemplated by the Education Act. However it originated, it is the fact of it having occurred which attracts the protection of s. 23(2).[53]

In *Arsenault-Cameron v. Prince Edward Island*,[54] the Supreme Court of Canada considered whether section 23 of the *Charter* includes the right to instruction in an education facility in a specific location. A group of parents who held section 23 rights requested the establishment of a French-language school for Grades 1 to 6, in Summerside, Prince Edward Island. The Minister of Education conceded that the parents of children in question were entitled to French language instruction and that the number of children warranted such instruction. However, the Minister's response to the parents was to offer to transport the children to another locality having an existing French-language school. This required an average school bus ride of 57 minutes. The parents went to court seeking a declaration of their rights under the *Charter*. The main issue before the Supreme Court of Canada was the delineation of the right of management and control exercised by the French Language Board with regard to the location of minority language schools and the discretion of the Minister to approve of the decisions of the Board in that regard.

---

53 *Ibid.*, at paras. 24-25.
54 [2000] 1 S.C.R. 3.

The Supreme Court of Canada overturned the P.E.I. Court of Appeal and decided that the parents had the right to send their children to a primary school in Summerside. The Court began its analysis by focusing on the "remedial purpose" of section 23 of the *Charter*, and observed:

> As this Court recently observed in *R. v. Beaulac*, [1999] 1 S.C.R. 768, at para. 24, the fact that constitutional language rights resulted from a political compromise is not unique to language rights and does not affect their scope. Like other provisions of the *Charter*, s. 23 has a remedial aspect; see *Mahe, supra*, at p. 364. It is therefore important to understand the historical and social context of the situation to be redressed, including the reasons why the system of education was not responsive to the actual needs of the official language minority in 1982 and why it may still not be responsive today. It is clearly necessary to take into account the importance of language and culture in the context of instruction as well as the importance of official language minority schools to the development of the official language community when examining the actions of the government in dealing with the request for services in Summerside. As this Court recently explained in *Beaulac*, at para. 25, "[l]anguage rights must *in all cases* be interpreted purposively, in a manner consistent with the preservation and development of official language communities in Canada" (emphasis in original). A purposive interpretation of s. 23 rights is based on the true purpose of redressing past injustices and providing the official language minority with equal access to high quality education in its own language, in circumstances where community development will be enhanced.[55]

The Court found that the Minister of Education:

> [f]ailed to give proper weight to the promotion and preservation of minority language culture and to the role of the French Language Board in balancing the pedagogical and cultural considerations. This was essential to giving full regard to the remedial purpose of the right. The approach adopted by the Minister therefore increased the probability that his decision would fail to satisfy constitutional review by the courts.[56]

In respect of the role of the French language school board, the Court stated:

> [T]he Appeal Division failed to take into account the minority language children's specific circumstances and the importance of the French Language Board in deciding matters that affect the linguistic and cultural development of the community. The French Language Board has the exclusive power to decide how it will provide services to the minority in the Summerside area, within the legitimate constraints set out by the province, its decisions also being subject to the rights of individual beneficiaries under s. 23.[57]

---

55 *Ibid.*, at para. 27.
56 *Ibid.*, at para. 30.
57 *Ibid.*, at para. 62.

The decision is of particular interest in respect of its attempt to weigh the role of the French language school board against the role of the Minister:

> This is not to say that the Minister's role is not important. In *Mahe, supra*, Dickson C.J. accepted, at p. 393, that "the government should have the widest possible discretion in selecting the institutional means by which its s. 23 obligations are to be met". This discretion is however subject to the positive obligation on government to alter or develop "major institutional structures" to effectively ensure the provision of minority language instruction and facilities and parental control on the scale warranted by the relevant number of children of the minority (see *Mahe*, at p. 365).
>
> The province has a legitimate interest in the content and qualitative standards of educational programs for the official language communities and it can impose appropriate programs in so far as they do not interfere with the legitimate linguistic and cultural concerns of the minority. School size, facilities, transportation and assembly of students can be regulated, but all have an effect on language and culture and must be regulated with regard to the specific circumstances of the minority and the purposes of s. 23.
>
> In the present case, the French Language Board had the obligation, pursuant to s. 6.07 of the Regulations, to offer French language instruction where numbers warrant and, pursuant to s. 128(2) of the Act, to determine the location of the required classes or facilities, subject to the approval of the Minister. The Minister accepted that, according to the Regulations and s. 23 factors, numbers warranted instruction, but objected to it being offered in Summerside. The Minister's decision is unconstitutional because the offer of classes or a facility came within the exclusive right of management of the minority and met with all provincial and constitutional requirements. The Minister's discretion was limited to verifying whether the Board had met provincial requirements. There were no pedagogical or financial parameters that were not met by the Board. Indeed, the Minister confirmed on the appeal as he had throughout the litigation that there were no financial impediments. The Minister had no power to impose his own criteria as a substitute. Nor could the Minister substitute his decision for that of the Board simply because he was of the view that the decision of the Board was not a good one.[58]

(e) Native Education

Provincial laws are subject to the *Constitution Act, 1867* and the *Canadian Charter of Rights and Freedoms* and they may not encroach upon areas of exclusive Federal jurisdiction. The Federal government has exclusive legislative authority in relation to "Indians, and Lands reserved for Indians".[59] The Federal government uses this constitutional authority to exercise jurisdiction over the education of some of Canada's aboriginal

---

58 *Ibid.*, at paras. 52-53, 55.
59 *Constitution Act, 1867*, s. 91(24).

peoples. Section 4(3) of the *Indian Act*[60] states that section 114-122 of the Act, which deal with the education of Indians, "do not apply to or in respect of any Indian who does not ordinarily reside on a reserve or on lands belonging to . . . Canada or a province." The Federal government also has treaty obligations in relation to the education of members of various bands.[61] The Federal government and aboriginal peoples have made, and continue to work toward, arrangements which give the latter various degrees of self-government over education. For instance, the *Cree-Naskapi (of Quebec) Act (1984)* and the *Sechelt Indian Band Self-Government Act (1986)* provide significant measures of self-government for the bands involved. The vast majority of Federal schools for Indian pupils have been "devolved" to Indian bands (*i.e.*, First Nations), so that children are now educated on a reserve by a band-controlled school, or they attend a school operated by the local school board under an agreement between the board and the band.

In Ontario, aboriginal peoples who do not reside on reserves or Federal or Provincial Crown land are covered by education laws of general application in the province. As noted above, Indian pupils who reside on a reserve may attend a school operated by a school board, pursuant to an agreement between the board and a band, band council or education authority.[62]

Where an agreement is entered into between a band, band council or education authority (or the Federal Crown) as provided in section 188 of the *Education Act*, O. Reg. 462/97 provides that the council of the band (or councils of the bands, where there is more than one agreement) may appoint a person to represent on the school board "the interests of the Indian pupils". Where the enrolment of Indian pupils exceeds 25 per cent of the board's average daily enrolment, two representatives may be named. A representative named to serve on a Roman Catholic board shall be Roman Catholic, and a representative named to serve on a French-language district school board must be a French-language rights holder. A representative must be at least 18 years old. There is no obligation, under the *Education Act*, to appoint a representative who has native ancestry.

First Nations have consistently expressed dissatisfaction with the level of representation that they are provided on school boards where there are one or more section 188 agreements in place. The appointment of a single representative to represent all of the bands or band councils that send their children to the board assumes that the bands or councils all have the same priorities and can all speak through one voice. On the other hand, appointing a representative for each band or band council could result in a level of

---

60 R.S.C. 1985, c. I-5.
61 For an excellent report on the legal, constitutional and treaty aspects of Indian education see the MacPherson Report on Traditional and Education: Towards a Vision of our Future, September 1991, by James C. MacPherson.
62 *Education Act*, s. 188.

representation far out of proportion to the number of Indian children being served by the board. The relevant legal provisions are now contained in O. Reg. 462/97, rather than the *Education Act* itself, and this may provide greater flexibility to address these issues in the years to come because it obviates the need to pass new legislation. However, genuine responsiveness exhibited by school board to the First Nations' education concerns is likely more important than a mere head count at the board table.

(f) School Councils

Section 170.1 of the *Education Act* provides that the Lieutenant Governor in Council may make regulations respecting school councils. Section 170(1)[17.1] states that the school board must establish a school council for each school operated by the board in accordance with the regulations. Ontario Reg. 612/00 deals with the purpose, composition, election, term of office, filling of vacancies and other aspects of school councils. Section 2 of the regulation states:

> 2.(1) The purpose of school councils is, through the active participation of parents, to improve pupil achievement and to enhance the accountability of the education system to parents.
>
> (2) A school council's primary means of achieving its purpose is by making recommendations in accordance with this Regulation to the principal of the school and the board that established the council.

Section 19 of the regulation lists several topics about which a school board must consult its school councils, including codes of conduct, dress codes for pupils, fundraising, and implementation of new education initiatives. Section 5 sets out the composition of school councils. Members must include parents, the principal, a teacher and other staff members, pupil representative(s) and community representative(s). The regulation provides the details as to how the exact composition is to be arrived at.[63]

(g) Pupil Representation

Every board in Ontario is required by O. Reg. 461/97 to develop and implement a policy providing for the representation of the interests of pupils from grade 7 and higher. A pupil representative has no voting rights on the board, is not a member of the board, and may not attend closed meetings. Generally, the pupil may "participate" fully in board meetings. A board must have at least one pupil representative. The board policy must set out how the pupil representative is appointed or elected, the extent and type of

---

[63] In addition to Reg. 612/00, regard should be had to Reg. 298 concerning a principal's duties and to the Ministry of Education publication "School Councils: A Guide for Members", published in 2001.

participation, how vacancies are to be filled and various other operational matters mentioned in the regulation.

3. THE EXERCISE OF PROVINCIAL POWER OVER EDUCATION

The exercise of provincial power over education is achieved by means of legislation, regulations, guidelines and policies. No legally enforceable regulation, policy or guideline may be made without the statutory authority to do so.[64] In many cases, the provisions which are of the most direct and practical relevance to teachers and pupils are found in regulations and policies. For example, the different means by which teachers may become qualified to teach are found in O. Reg. 184/97 made under the *Ontario College of Teachers Act, 1996*. The contents of the "Ontario Student Record" are prescribed in a mandatory "OSR Guideline" issued under the authority of the *Education Act*. Ontario's diploma requirements are prescribed by policy. In addition to legislation, regulations and policies on education, school boards must comply with other legislation, such as the *Occupiers' Liability Act*[65] and the *Occupational Health and Safety Act*,[66] unless exempted by the statute. There are, therefore, many non-education statutes, both federal[67] and provincial, which directly or indirectly govern or determine the conduct of school boards.

4. THE EXERCISE OF DELEGATED POWER BY SCHOOL BOARDS

(a) Collective Action

School boards are "creatures of statute". They are created by or under provincial statute and their power and jurisdiction is limited to that conferred by or under statute. They have no "inherent" power of their own. Moreover, they are corporations and must make decisions as a body. Individual trustees have no legal authority to act on behalf of a school board merely by reason of their office as trustee.[68]

Committees of boards report their recommendations to the board. They do not finally decide matters on behalf of the board in the absence of specific statutory authority to make such a sub-delegation. For example, there is statutory authority for a board to delegate to a committee its power to

---

64 Ontario education statutes include, for example, the *Education Act*, R.S.O. 1990, c. E.2; the *Teaching Profession Act*, R.S.O. 1990, c. T.2; and the *Teachers' Pension Act*, R.S.O. 1990, c. T.1.
65 R.S.O. 1990, c. O.2.
66 R.S.O. 1990, c. O.1.
67 *Young Offenders Act*, R.S.C. 1985, c. Y-1, for example.
68 For example, boards in Ontario are specifically referred to as corporations in the *Education Act*.

conduct suspension appeals and expulsion hearings, and, in doing so, the board may impose "conditions" on such a committee.[69]

Because board members have no individual decision-making power, education statutes provide little guidance as to their role or how they should interact with board staff. While some board members seemingly take little interest in the day-to-day operation of the board, others far exceed the traditional role and can become quite meddlesome in the administration of the board and the schools. Board members have no individual authority to direct staff, discipline pupils, or tell the school principal how to manage the school. Administration is the responsibility of the Chief Executive Officer of the board, who in turn delegates power to subordinates. Requests by board members for information or staff reports should be made through the Chief Executive Officer. Reports prepared by staff for the board should be forwarded through senior management to the board.

When a board exceeds its legal jurisdiction, its actions are said to be *ultra vires* and can be attacked on this ground by any person, such as a ratepayer, having legal standing to bring an application for judicial review. Courts will strike down a policy made by a school board if the policy is *ultra vires*, made in bad faith, or contrary to the *Charter* or *Human Rights Code*.[70]

This was made clear by the Supreme Court of Canada in *The Queen v. Jones*,[71] a decision dealing with the issue of whether compulsory education laws in Alberta violated the freedom of religion (in section 2 of the *Charter*) or the right to liberty and security (section 7). Jones was charged with truancy on the part of his children when he refused to send them to public school or to seek the alternatives of applying for government approval of his own religious private school or applying for exemption under which his children would be certified as attending school at "home or elsewhere". This scheme relied upon the "educational authorities" to enforce it, thus involving both the province and the Calgary Board of Education. Three judges found that the freedom of religion was contravened by the provincial legislation but was saved by section 1 of the *Charter*. Two other members of the panel found no violation of section 2. All but one member of the panel found that section 7 had not been violated. (Wilson J. in dissent found that section 7 was violated and was not saved by section 1.) *Jones* is an interesting case from a constitutional law perspective, but the Court (LaForest J.) also commented on the circumstances in which a policy will be reviewed by a court. LaForest J. did not agree with Mr. Jones that the

---

69 *Education Act*, R.S.O. 1990, c. E.2, ss. 308(7) and 309(13).
770 See, e.g., *Peel Board Of Education v. Ontario Human Rights Commission* (1990), 72 O.R. (2d) 593 (Div. Ct.).
71 [1986] 2 S.C.R. 284.

process of "certifying instruction" by a school district was in the nature of a "judicial hearing". However, he stated:

> I have no doubt that if in exercising their functions the school authorities sought to impose arbitrary standards, i.e. standards extraneous to the educational policy under the Act, or if they in other respects acted in a manner that was fundamentally unfair, such as failing to examine the facts or to fairly consider the appellant's representations, the courts could intervene."[72]

LaForest J. had no difficulty with the legislative scheme that delegated power to the school district "to spell out the details in order to meet the variegated needs through the province". He stated:

> The province may, if it chooses, deal with educational policy in the Act itself or by means of regulations or by designating officials to particularize the requirements within the general confines of the Act. In a word, the school authorities are participating in the elucidation of an educational policy the province has a compelling interest in carrying out. Of course, these authorities have a vested interest in the system. But it seems normal enough to refer a question of efficient instruction within the meaning of the *School Act* to a school inspector or a Superintendent of Schools who is knowledgeable of the requirements and workings of the educational system under the *School Act*.
>
> It is true that some provinces have adopted another method of doing this, by having the issue determined by a court. There are, no doubt, some advantages to the latter approach but there are disadvantages too. It creates a more cumbersome administrative structure. If the decision-maker is more detached, he is also less knowledgeable and sensitive to the needs of the educational system. I do not think such a system can be imposed on the province in the present context. Some pragmatism is involved in balancing fairness and efficiency. The provinces must be given room to make choices regarding the type of administrative structure that will suit their needs unless the use of such structure is in itself so manifestly unfair, having regard to the decisions it is called upon to make, as to violate the principles of fundamental justice.[73]

The Manitoba Court of Appeal in *McDonald v. Interlake School Division No. 21*,[74] was asked to intervene when a parent applied for an order of *mandamus* to require a school board to offer French immersion after the board had decided to cut the program. Having been unsuccessful at trial, the parent appealed. The appellate court examined the nature of the board's duty to offer programs to its pupils and determined that the board had met its obligation under the Manitoba *Public Schools Act*. It found no evidence of bad faith on the part of the board. The Court observed: "Unless the decision of an elected body is shown to be made in bad faith, or contrary to

---

72 *Ibid.*, at para. 39.
73 *Ibid.*
74 (1995), 131 D.L.R. (4th) 312 (Man. C.A.), leave to appeal refused (1996), 137 D.L.R. (4th) vi (S.C.C.).

due process, the courts will not interfere."[75] In other words, if the correct procedure is followed in making the policy, the policy itself will not be questioned. The Court stated:

> School boards are required to make decisions balancing students' needs, parents' requests, economic and education factors and staff and space requirements, to name just some of the considerations for each decision. The passage of time brings about changes in demographics, in demands and in the supply of professionals. A board is not tied to an earlier decision if the factors which once justified that decision no longer exist.[76]

As indicated above, a school board's policy can be challenged on the ground that the board lacks jurisdiction to make the policy. Court decisions involving allegations that policies are *ultra vires* are rare in respect of school boards. However, in *Chamberlain v. Surrey School District No. 36*,[77] the court declared *ultra vires* a school board resolution indicating that educational resources from gay and lesbian groups for use in schools was not approved by the board. The court held that the board had jurisdiction to determine the resource material used in classrooms by teachers delivering curriculum to students, but did not have jurisdiction under the British Columbia *Schools Act* to approve other materials for use in the library or as resources for teachers.

As a form of local government, school boards are in many respects comparable to municipalities and for that reason the decision of the Supreme Court of Canada in *Shell Canada Products Ltd. v. Vancouver (City)*[78] is of interest. The issue in *Shell Canada* was whether a resolution by Vancouver City Council *not* to contract with Shell Canada because it was doing business in South Africa was made pursuant to a "municipal purpose". The decision of the majority was written by Sopinka J., for Cory, Iacobucci and Major JJ. and there was a strong dissent by Madame Justice McLachlin (now Chief Justice), supported by Lamer, then C.J., L'Heureux-Dubé, and Gonthier, JJ. The majority held that the resolution was *ultra vires*. In arriving at this decision, the Court stated that the exercise of City Council's "business or corporate powers" was not immune from judicial review. Sopinka J. stated:

> The authorities referred to in argument do not support the contention that the exercise of business or corporate powers is immune from review.
>
> Moreover, there does not appear to be any valid policy ground for providing such immunity. There is good reason to encourage municipalities to act within

---

75 *Ibid.*, at 317.
76 (1995), 131 D.L.R. (4th) 312 at 315 (Man. C.A.).
77 (1998), 168 D.L.R. (4th) 222 (B.C. S.C. [In Chambers]), reversed (2000), 191 D.L.R. (4th) 128 (B.C. C.A.), additional reasons at (2001), 2001 CarswellBC 2146 (C.A.), leave to appeal allowed (2001), 2001 CarswellBC 2121 (S.C.C.).
78 (1994), 110 D.L.R. (4th) 1 (S.C.C.).

their statutory powers. An absence of judicial review would leave some ratepayers without an effective remedy. The suggestion that the only remedy is at the polls is of no value to the minority who would be left with no remedy and Council could continue to enlarge its statutory powers as long as it was able to retain its majority support. The public policy in favour of restricting a municipality to its statutory powers exists as much for the minority as for the majority.[79]

McLaughlin J., (now C.J.) in dissent, agreed that municipal procurement powers are not immune from judicial review:

> If a municipality's power to spend public money is exercised for improper purposes or in an improper manner, the conduct of the municipality should be subject to judicial review.[80]

However, she took a more deferential approach to the right of City Council to make its resolution about Shell Canada. In her view:

> Recent commentary suggests an emerging consensus that courts must respect the responsibility of elected municipal bodies to serve the people who elected them and exercise caution to avoid substituting their views of what is best for the citizens for those of municipal councils. Barring clear demonstration that a municipal decision was beyond its powers, courts should not so hold. In cases where powers are not expressly conferred but may be implied, courts must be prepared to adopt the "benevolent construction" which this Court referred to in *Greenbaum*, and confer the powers by reasonable implication. Whatever rules of construction are applied, they must not be used to usurp the legitimate role of municipal bodies as community representatives.[81]

McLaughlin J. [now C.J.] criticized courts that,

> under the guise of vague doctrinal terms such as "irrelevant considerations," "improper purpose," "reasonableness," or "bad faith," have not infrequently arrogated to themselves a wide and sweeping power to substitute their views for those of the elected representatives of municipalities.[82]

In a more recent case, *Nanaimo (City) v. Rascal Trucking Ltd.*,[83] the Supreme Court had occasion to consider *Shell Canada*, although the municipal resolutions in the two cases were quite different. The City of Nanaimo had ordered Rascal Trucking to remove a large pile of dirt from a vacant lot. The first issue was whether the City had jurisdiction to make such an order under the British Columbia *Municipal Act*. The Court favoured a "broad and purposive" approach to interpreting the Act and found, on a standard of correctness, that the City had jurisdiction. The issue then became

---

79 *Ibid.*
80 *Ibid.*
81 *Ibid.*
82 *Ibid.*
83 [2000] 1 S.C.R. 342.

what standard of review should apply to an *intra vires* decision of a municipality. The Court found that the standard was one of "patent unreasonableness". It characterized the decision to make the order against Rascal Trucking as "adjudicative" (as distinct from "policy"), and confirmed that the "pragmatic and functional" approach to judicial review can be applied "harmoniously" to decisions of municipal councils. Having determined that the decision was *intra vires*, the Court stated:

> The fact that municipal councils are elected representatives of their community, and accountable to their constituents, is relevant in scrutinizing *intra vires* decisions. The reality that municipalities often balance complex and divergent interests in arriving at decisions in the public interest is of similar importance. In short, these considerations warrant that the *intra vires* decision of municipalities be reviewed upon a deferential standard.[84]

The Court then referred to *Shell Canada* and appeared to adopt the more deferential minority position in that case.

(b) Mandatory and Discretionary Powers

Legislation gives boards mandatory duties and discretionary powers. In Ontario, boards have numerous mandatory duties. For example, they must appoint a secretary, hold meetings, have a head office, provide instruction for pupils, keep buildings in proper repair, and appoint an adequate number of teachers. There is a broadly stated duty to ensure that every school under its charge is conducted in accordance with the *Education Act* and regulations. A board is also required to do anything that it is required to do by the Minister of Education exercising his or her powers under the *Education Act*. The Act contains only limited means by which a board can be forced to comply with its statutory obligations. However, the provincial government, a ratepayer, or other person with legal standing, can bring an application for judicial review in Ontario Court (General Division) seeking a declaration that a board has not complied with its legal obligations and an order instructing the board as to what it must do (or cease doing) to remedy the situation.

"Division D" of the *Education Act* contains extensive powers under which the Minister of Education may supervise the financial affairs of school boards. The Minister may order an investigation into the financial affairs of a board if the board has incurred a deficit, has failed to pay debentures or other instruments, has failed to pay any of its other debts or liabilities when due (as a result of its financial difficulties) or if "the Minister has concerns about the board's ability to meet its financial difficulties".[85] An investigator may require the production of board records, examine and copy records and

---

84 *Ibid.*, at para. 35.
85 *Education Act*, s. 257.30.

summons persons so to appear before him or her to give evidence. The investigator's report is transmitted to the Minister, who must give a copy to the secretary of the school board. If the investigator discovers that the board is in financial difficulty, he or she may recommend that control and charge over the administration of the affairs of the board be vested in the Minister. If the Minister wishes to be vested with this power, the Minister is required to seek a vesting order from the Lieutenant Governor in Council. "Division D" states the specific powers that may be exercised by the Minister under a vesting order. The vesting order is revoked by the Lieutenant Governor in Council when it is satisfied that the order is no longer needed or if the board's audited financial statements no longer show a deficit.

It is important to note that section 257.52 of the *Education Act* prohibits the Minister from interfering with or controlling the denominational aspects of a Roman Catholic board or Protestant separate school, or the linguistic or cultural aspects of a French-language district school board. Moreover, the powers exercised under "Division D" must be exercised "in a manner that is consistent" with the denominational aspects of a Roman Catholic board or Protestant separate school, or the linguistic or cultural aspects of a French-language district school board.

Discretionary board powers are those which a board may exercise if it deems it necessary or appropriate to do so. In Ontario, for example, a board may provide continuing education programs, borrow and invest funds, close schools, operate playgrounds, and determine school attendance areas. In many cases, such as closing schools and borrowing funds, the government prescribes conditions which must be fulfilled by the board in the exercise of its discretion.

Powers of school boards may be either express or implied. Express powers, as one might expect, are provided for by express language in legislation or regulations. Powers may also be implied from the language of the legislation or regulation. There are some actions which a board must be able to take in order to function, even though these actions are not specifically authorized by statute. For instance, it is obvious that school boards must be able to retain lawyers for a variety of purposes, although the legislation provides no general statutory authority to do so.

The Supreme Court of Canada in *R. v. Greenbaum*[86] has quoted Stanley Makuch's *Canadian Municipal and Planning Law*[87] explanation of municipal government powers, which are comparable in this context to those of school boards:

> The courts, as a result of this inferior position [of municipalities], have traditionally interpreted narrowly statutes respecting grants of powers to municipalities. This approach may be described as "Dillon's rule", which states that

---

86 (1993), 100 D.L.R. (4th) 183 (S.C.C.).
87 (Toronto: Carswell, 1983), at 115.

a municipality may exercise only those powers expressly conferred by statute, those powers necessarily or fairly implied by the expressed power in the statute, and those indispensable powers essential and not merely convenient to the effectuation of the purposes of the corporation.[88]

5. PROCEDURAL FAIRNESS AND NATURAL JUSTICE

In some circumstances, school boards are required to be procedurally fair in making their decisions. "Fairness" is a universal, albeit highly subjective, concept. Teachers set examinations, mark papers, and apply discipline as fairly as they can. Parents know instinctively that they must get "both sides of the story" before resolving disputes between their children. School boards try to strike a fair balance between competing interests among ratepayers. All of these involve elements of fairness.

One must, however, distinguish between moral fairness and procedural fairness. Procedural fairness does not mean that everyone must believe that a board's decision was right. It refers to the procedure used to arrive at the board's decision.[89] The statutory power invested in boards to make decisions which affect the rights of others carries with it a heavy responsibility to ensure that those decisions cannot be successfully challenged in court on the basis of lack of procedural fairness, or on the grounds of "bias", "lack of jurisdiction", or "error of law". Many decisions of a school board are purely administrative in nature. In such instances, the board is not acting as a "tribunal" which must deliberate and decide upon the rights of others, and the common law does not require procedural fairness. For example, if a board resolves to hire a purchasing manager, or to select one brand of classroom computer over another, or to hold a staff conference, it has no common law obligation to be procedurally fair, although it must act within the scope of its powers, and must avoid bias and conflict of interest. The board is not required to seek submissions or hold a hearing about whether to hold a professional development conference, how much to spend on the conference, the conference location, or the selection of workshops. However, a decision to close a school, expel a student, uphold a student suspen-

---

88 See also: *Jonson v. Ponoka County (Board of Education) (No. 3)* (1998), 88 A.R. 31 (Q.B.) and *Shell Canada Products Ltd. v. Vancouver (City)* (1994), 20 M.P.L.R. (2d) 1 (S.C.C.) and *Ottawa Electric Light Co. v. Ottawa* (1906), 12 O.L.R. 290 (C.A.).

89 For a discussion of procedural fairness, see generally: *Nicholson v. Haldimand-Norfolk (Regional Municipality) Cmmrs. of Police* (1978), 88 D.L.R. (3d) 671 (S.C.C.); *Kane v. Univ. of B.C.* (1980), 110 D.L.R. (3d) 311 (S.C.C.); *Martineau v. Matsqui Institution Disciplinary Bd. (No. 2)* (1980), 106 D.L.R. (3d) 385 (S.C.C.); *Cardinal v. Kent Institution* (1985), 24 D.L.R. (4th) 44 (S.C.C.); *Ont. English Catholic Teachers Assn. v. Essex County (R.C. Separate School Bd.)* (1987), 58 O.R. (2d) 545 (Div. Ct.); leave to appeal to S.C.C. refused (1988), 65 O.R. (2d) x (note) (S.C.C.); *Syndicat des employés de production du Qué. de l'Acadie v. Canada (Cdn. Human Rights Commn.)* (1989), 62 D.L.R. (4th) 385 (S.C.C.); *Indian Head School Div. No. 19 v. Knight* (1990), 69 D.L.R. (4th) 489 (S.C.C.).

sion, or terminate a teacher may be declared null and void by a court if it is not made in accordance with the board's duty of procedural fairness.[90]

Not all employees are entitled under the common law to procedural fairness upon termination of employment. In some circumstances, a contract of employment may be terminated without the necessity of being procedurally fair. However, the employment relationship between school boards and teachers, supervisory officers, and officers of the board (*e.g.*, treasurer) is governed in various degrees by statute and regulation across Canada. They are not merely "master and servant" relationships. Boards have a duty of procedural fairness in respect of teachers, supervisory officers, and officers of the board when considering their suspension (disciplinary) or dismissal for cause.[91]

In *Indian Head School Division No. 19 v. Knight*, the Supreme Court of Canada considered the dismissal of the director of education of a school district. L'Heureux-Dubé J. commented on the circumstances giving rise to the duty of fairness:

> The existence of a general duty to act fairly will depend on the consideration of three factors: (i) the nature of the decision to be made by the administrative body: (ii) the relationship existing between that body and the individual; and (iii) the effect of that decision on the individual's rights.[90]

The common law duty of fairness does not mean that a school board must act like a court of law. Procedural and evidentiary rules before a board are generally much less formal than those used in a court or quasi-judicial tribunal. The rules of natural justice differ according to the tribunal and the circumstances. In *Knight*, L'Heureux-Dubé J. stated:

> There is no longer a need, except perhaps where the statute mandates it, to distinguish between judicial, *quasi*-judicial and administrative decisions. Such a distinction may have been necessary before the decision of this court in *Nicholson v. Haldimand-Norfolk Regional Board of Commissioners of Police* (1978), 88 D.L.R. (3d) 671 ... Prior to this case, the "duty to act judicially" was thought to apply only to tribunals rendering decisions of a judicial or *quasi*-judicial nature, to the exclusion of those of an administrative nature. Following *Nicholson*, that distinction became less important and was found to be of little utility since both the duty to act fairly and the duty to act judicially have their roots in the same general principles of natural justice ...[93]

---

90 The termination and dismissal of teachers is discussed in detail in chapter 6. It is discussed here to illustrate the concepts which apply to all board decisions where there is a duty of procedural fairness.
91 See *Indian Head School Div. No. 19 v. Knight* (1990), 69 D.L.R. (4th) 489 at 506 (S.C.C.).
92 *Ibid.*, at 500.
93 Above, note 91, at 500.

L'Heureux-Dubé J. quoted the decision of Sopinka J. in the Supreme Court of Canada in *Syndicat des employés de production du Québec de l'Acadie v. Canada (Canadian Human Rights Commission)*:

> Both the rules of natural justice and the duty of fairness are variable standards. Their content will depend on the circumstances of the case, the statutory provisions and the nature of the matter to be decided.[94]

While the duty of fairness is firmly established in Canadian common law, procedural rights are also conferred by legislation, such as Ontario's *Statutory Powers Procedure Act*.[95] However, the issue of whether or not a decision is supported by the facts (i.e., has merit) is different from the question of whether the board used a fair procedure.[96]

In *Baker v. Canada (Minister of Citizenship & Immigration)*[97], the Court described the essence of what is meant by the "duty of fairness":

> Although the duty of fairness is flexible and variable, and depends on an appreciation of the context of the particular statute and the rights affected, it is helpful to review the criteria that should be used in determining what procedural rights the duty of fairness requires in a given set of circumstances. I emphasize that underlying all these factors is the notion that the purpose of the participatory rights contained within the duty of procedural fairness is to ensure that administrative decisions are made using a fair and open procedure, appropriate to the decision being made and its statutory, institutional, and social context, with an opportunity for those affected by the decision to put forward their views and evidence fully and have them considered by the decision-maker.[98]

In *Rochon v. Spirit River School District No. 47*,[99] the court applied the *Knight* test for procedural fairness and stated "a superintendent of schools is a holder of public office. He is entitled to notice and to the reasons for his termination. The fact that he may have, by his behaviour, created reasons for his termination does not deny him the right to attend and address the board on the very issues underlying the problems that exist."[100] In *Anderson v. Twin Rivers School Division No. 65*[101] the court quashed two resolutions of the board of trustees suspending and later terminating the employment

---

94 (1989), 62 D.L.R. (4th) 385 at 425 (S.C.C.).
95 R.S.O. 1990, c. S.22.
96 See *N. (R.) v. Edmonton Public School District No. 7* (1994), 118 D.L.R. (4th) 519 (Alta. C.A.) for a discussion of the standard of proof required in civil proceedings in cases where there is an allegation of conduct that constitutes a criminal offence. The burden of proof is proof on a balance of probabilities. However, "the degree of probability within the civil standard varies with the seriousness of the allegation and the potential consequences thereof upon the offender." (at p. 523)
97 [1999] 2 S.C.R. 817.
98 *Ibid.*, at para. 22.
99 (1994), 111 D.L.R. (4th) 452 (Alta. C.A.).
100 *Ibid.*, at 456.
101 (1994), 19 Alta. L.R. (3d) 408 (Q.B.).

contracts of two superintendents. The applicants were not given a reasonable opportunity to be heard by the board; there was also evidence leading to a reasonable apprehension of bias on the part of some board members. In *Rahn v. Prescott-Russell County Board of Education*,[102] the Ontario Divisional Court quashed a decision of the board suspending its director of education where he had not been given reasonable information, was refused an opportunity to make submissions to the board, and was not given reasons for the suspension. He was awarded costs on a solicitor and client basis.

The common law duty of procedural fairness requires, at a minimum, that a person must be informed in advance that the board is intending to consider a matter which may affect his or her individual rights. The person must be given a reasonable opportunity to make oral or written submissions to the board on the matter before it. He or she is entitled to be informed of and to respond to all information before the board having any bearing on its decision.[103] The person must also be told the reasons for the decision of the board.

The right "to be heard" does not always equate to a right to a "hearing". L'Heureux-Dubé J., in *Knight*, stated:

> It must not be forgotten that every administrative body is the master of its own procedure and need not assume the trappings of a court. The object is not to import into administrative proceedings the rigidity of all the requirements of natural justice that must be observed by a court, but rather to allow administrative bodies to work out a system that is flexible, adapted to their needs and fair. As pointed out by de Smith (*Judicial Review of Administraive Action*, 4th ed. (1980), at p. 240), the aim is not to create "procedural perfection" but to achieve a certain balance between the need for fairness, efficiency and predictability of outcome. Hence, in the case at bar, if it can be found that the respondent indeed had knowledge of the reasons for his dismissal and had an opportunity to be heard by the board, the requirement of procedural fairness will be satisfied even if there was no structured "hearing" in the judicial meaning of the word.[104]

A board may offer the opportunity to have a hearing if it believes that this would be the best way of ensuring that a person is fairly treated. A formal "hearing" involves the right to appear personally before the tribunal, to be represented by counsel, to introduce evidence and call witnesses, and to cross-examine witnesses under oath.

---

102 53 A.C.W.S. (3d) 73.
103 See *Kane v. Univ. of B.C.* (1980), 110 D.L.R. (3d) 311 at 322 (S.C.C.).
104 Above, note 91 at 512. See also *Kane, ibid.*, at 321. See also *Burgis v. Brampton (City) Public Library Board* (1994), 110 D.L.R. (4th) 210 (Ont. Div. Ct.) in which a librarian, whose appointment was "at pleasure" was reinstated to his position by the court because his employer did not tell him why his services were no longer required and he was given no opportunity to respond.

In some circumstances a school board may be required to hold a hearing. For example, the *Education Act* in Ontario requires that a hearing be held by a school board (or committee) in order for the board to expel a student. The *Statutory Powers Procedure Act* requires that a tribunal which is exercising a "statutory power of decision" must hold a "hearing". An expulsion hearing is the exercise of a "statutory power of decision" as defined in the Act. The board must comply with the process outlined in the Act which states how the proceedings are to be conducted, including such aspects as the giving of notice, summons to witnesses, legal representation, presence or exclusion of the public, *etc.* Although boards in Ontario are not expressly required to hold a formal "hearing" in order to terminate a teacher, supervisory officer or officer of the board, they frequently offer the opportunity of a hearing to the employee to ensure that the employee has every reasonable opportunity to make submissions, and to hear and respond to the submissions of management.

6. PUBLIC ACCESS TO BOARD MEETINGS

Meetings of school boards in Ontario are open to the public.[105] This means that the board itself may not go *in camera*. It must resolve to go into Committee of the Whole Board and then may hold its meeting *in camera* if the subject-matter of the meeting is permitted or required by statute to be considered in private. Meetings of committees of the board, including committee of the whole board, are open to the public, except that they may be closed to the public when the subject-matter under consideration involves:

(a) the security of the property of the board;
(b) the disclosure of intimate, personal or financial information in respect of a member of the board or committee, an employee or prospective employee of the board or pupil or his or her parent or guardian;
(c) the acquisition or disposal of a school site;
(d) decisions in respect of negotiations with employees of the board; or
(e) litigation affecting the board.[106]

Section 208.1 of the *Education Act* permits the Lieutenant Governor in Council to make regulations respecting the use of electronic means for the holding of meetings of a district school board and of board committees. A board member who attends such an "electronic" meeting is deemed to be present at the meeting. However, section 229 of the *Education Act* requires (despite section 208.1) that a board member be physically present at at least three regular meetings of the board in each 12-month period commencing December 1. Ontario Reg. 463/97 requires every district school board to

---

105 *Education Act*, s. 207 (1).
106 *Ibid.*, s. 207 (2).

develop and implement a policy providing for the use of electronic means for the holding of meetings of the board and committees of the board. Such a policy could provide that board members be physically present at more than three meetings of the board. The regulation deals with a number of matters that flow from the holding of electronic meetings. For example, pupil representatives on the board must not be electronically present for matters that are closed to the public, and trustees' "conflict of interest" provisions must be complied with (such as being absent during discussions). The board's policy must also deal with how the general public is to have access to the open portions of the board and committee meetings.

(a) Exclusion from Meetings

The board may expel or exclude from *any* meeting *any* person who has been guilty of improper conduct at the meeting.[107] A person who disrupts or endeavours to disturb or interrupt a meeting after having been expelled or excluded from the meeting is guilty of an offence and is subject to a fine upon conviction of not more that $200.[108]

(b) Retreats and *In Camera* Meetings

School boards are accustomed to holding retreats or workshops in which trustees and usually a limited number of staff discuss matters in an informal environment, away from the public eye. Sometimes the workshops are primarily for providing information to trustees, without any discussion of issues. For example, trustees may which to learn more about the budgetary process, or about the impact of new legislation. In some cases, however, boards have debated or discussed issues which were squarely within the realm of board business, and should have been discussed at a duly constituted meeting of the board or one of its committees. The public and the media have the right to inquire into whether a retreat or workshop was in fact a meeting of the board. Several court decisions provide guidance as to what is considered to be a "meeting".

Vanderkloet v. Leeds & Grenville County (Board of Education)[109] is a 1985 decision of the Ontario Court of Appeal which dealt with a situation where the board decided *in camera* to reorganize three elementary schools under its jurisdiction. The board held an informal dinner meeting to consider a report of the projected enrolment for the three schools. Eleven days later, it held a board meeting *in camera* to discuss what to do with the schools in question. On the same day, the board met in public and passed the resolution

---

107 *Ibid.*, s. 207 (3).
108 *Ibid.*, s. 212 (3).
109 (1985), 51 O.R. (2d) 577 (C.A.). Leave to appeal to S.C.C. refused (1986), 54 O.R. (2d) 352 (note) (S.C.C.).

to which the ratepayers objected. No members of the public were present and the item was not noted on the agenda for the meeting. At the next regular meeting of the board, the matter was reconsidered after hearing from delegations from the affected schools. The board confirmed its prior decision.

One of the issues on the appeal was whether or not the board had breached its statutory duty to hold its meetings in public. The Court held that the board had not breached this duty. Dubin J.A. (as he then was) stated:

> With respect, I do not think that the requirement that the meetings of the Board should be open to the public precludes informal discussions among board members, either alone or with the assistance of their staff. Nor does the statute require that the Board prepare an agenda to be distributed to the public in advance of a board meeting.[110]

In 1988, a similar issue came before the Ontario Court of Appeal in *Southam Inc. v. Hamilton-Wentworth (Regional Municipality) Economic Development Committee*.[111] The Economic Development Committee of the municipality held a workshop from which it excluded the public and media. A by-law of the Regional Municipality required that its meetings be held in public unless they involved consideration of various matters listed in the by-law, none of which applied to the topics discussed in the workshop. The question, therefore, was whether or not the workshop was in fact a meeting of the committee.

The Court (Grange J.A. for the majority) had no difficulty finding that the workshop was a meeting of the committee. After considering the definition of "meeting" in *Black's Law Dictionary* (5th Ed.), the Court stated:

> In the context of a statutory committee, "meeting" should be interpreted as any gathering to which all members of the committee are invited to discuss matters within their jurisdiction . . . . No matter how the meeting might be disguised by the use of terms such as "workshop", or the failure to make a formal report, the committee members were meeting to discuss matters within their jurisdiction.[112]

The Court distinguished *Vanderloet v. Leeds & Grenville County (Board of Education)*, stating that *Vanderkloet* does not stand "for the proposition that a committee, bound to hold its meetings in public, can convert a scheduled meeting into an informal discussion and thus avoid the necessity of public foreclosure."[113] The Court also stated that:

> There is no doubt that members of a committee, meeting informally, can discuss questions within the jurisdiction of the committee privately, but when all

---

110 *Ibid.*, at 586-587.
111 (1988), 66 O.R. (2d) 213 (C.A.); leave to appeal to S.C.C. refused (1989), 102 N.R. 238 (S.C.C.).
112 *Ibid.*, at 217-218.
113 *Ibid.*, at 219.

members are summoned to a regularly scheduled meeting and there attempt to proceed *in camera*, they are defeating the intent and purpose of council's by-law which governs their procedure.[114]

In a strong dissent, Lacourcière J.A., stated that the right of the press to gather information:

> ... is not an absolute freedom and it is limited in this case by the common law rule expressed in the *Vanderkloet* case which recognizes the benefit to the public of informal discussions, provided that, as contemplated in this case, the actual resolutions or decisions are made in public.[115]

In *Southam Inc. v. Ottawa (City)*,[116] the Ontario Court, General Division considered whether a "retreat" held by Ottawa City Council was in fact a meeting, which as such should have been open to the public. The Court found that the detailed, structured agenda for the retreat dealt with many items which would ordinarily be the subject of Council business. The Court considered both the *Vanderkloet* and *Southam Inc. v. Hamilton-Wentworth* decisions, and noted that the *Municipal Act*[117] provisions respecting open meetings are materially similar to the *Education Act* provisions. Farley J. examined at some length the meaning of the word "meeting" and stated:

> However, it would appear that this is rather a question of looking at the essence of the events. Clearly, it is not a question of whether all or any of the ritual trappings of a formal meeting of council are observed: for example, the prayer to commence the meeting or the seating of councillors at a U-shaped table. . . . The key would appear to be whether the councillors are requested to attend (or do, in fact, attend without summons) a function at which matters which would ordinarily form the basis of Council's business are dealt with in such a way as to move them materially along the way in the overall spectrum of a Council decision. In other words, is the public being deprived of the opportunity to observe a material part of the decision-making process?[118]

The Court concluded on the evidence of what was discussed at the retreat that Council had in fact held meetings, contrary to its by-laws and the *Municipal Act*. It is noteworthy that, in both the *Hamilton-Wentworth* and *Ottawa (City)* cases, the Court commented upon the lack of evidence as to what actually transpired at the closed meetings. In *Vanderkloet*, on the other hand, the board was forthcoming about what had transpired. What is clear from these cases, is that the Court, in the absence of evidence, may

---

114 *Ibid.*, at 219.
115 *Ibid.*, at 225.
116 (1992), 5 O.R. (3d) 726 (Div. Ct.).
117 R.S.O. 1990, c. M.45.
118 Above, note 116, at 731.

draw a negative inference and conclude that a meeting, rather than a mere information session, had occurred.[119]

7. CONFLICT OF INTEREST

Board members are required by statute to disclose when they have a conflict of interest with respect to a matter under consideration by the board. In Ontario, the conflict of interest provisions for members of school boards are in the *Municipal Conflict of Interest Act*.[120]

Section 5(1) provides:

> (1) Where a member, either on his or her own behalf or while acting for, by, with or through another, has any pecuniary interest, direct or indirect, in any matter and is present at a meeting of the council or local board at which the matter is the subject of consideration, the member,
> (a) shall, prior to any consideration of the matter at the meeting, disclose the interest and the general nature thereof;
> (b) shall not take part in the discussion of, or vote on any question in respect of the matter; and
> (c) shall not attempt in any way whether before, during or after the meeting to influence the voting on any such question.

If the meeting is closed, the board member is also required to leave the meeting or the part of the meeting during which the matter is under consideration.[121] If a member misses a meeting at which he or she would have had to declare a conflict of interest under subsection 5(1), the member must declare the conflict at the next meeting of the council or board that he or she attends.[122] The minutes of the board must record the declaration of interest and its general nature. If the meeting was closed, however, the minutes of the closed meeting which are brought forward into a subsequent open meeting, are not required to disclose the general nature of the conflict of interest.[123]

Section 4 of the *Municipal Conflict of Interest Act* lists the types of pecuniary interest that do not have to be declared. For instance, an interest which the member has "in common with electors generally"[124] is excluded. A pecuniary interest does not have to be declared if it is "so remote or

---

119 For a United States perspective, see H.C. Hudgins, Jr. and Richard S. Vacca, *Law and Education: Contemporary Issues and Court Decisions*, 3rd ed. (Charlottesville, Virginia: The Michie Co., 1991), at pp. 66-69.
120 R.S.O. 1990, c. M.50.
121 *Ibid.*, s. 5(2).
122 *Ibid.*, s. 5(3).
123 *Ibid.*, s. 6.
124 Defined by s. 1 of the Act.

insignificant in its nature that it cannot reasonably be regarded as likely to influence the member".[125]

The definition of "indirect pecuniary interest" permits a piercing of the corporate veil. Under some circumstances, the interest of a corporation or a "body" is regarded as the member's interest.[126] The Act also provides that "the pecuniary interest, direct or indirect, of a parent or the spouse or any child of the member shall, if known to the member, be deemed to be also the pecuniary interest of the member."[127]

Where declarations of interest result in a loss of quorum, section 7 deems the remaining number of members to constitute a quorum, provided such number is not less than two. Where it is reduced to less than two, the board may apply to a judge for a declaration that section 5 (duty to declare) does not apply in respect of the matter under consideration. The judge may permit the members to proceed as if there were no conflict, subject to such conditions and directions as the judge may consider appropriate.[128] This section has practical significance in the case of very small school boards, which may be comprised of only three trustees.

A frequent criticism of the *Municipal Conflict of Interest Act* is that it is up to "an elector" to initiate an application to court to determine whether or not a board member has failed to declare an interest. The elector has six weeks to commence the application, from the time he or she became aware of the contravention. Few electors have the time or financial resources to pursue such an action. It is also arguable that it should not be necessary for a judge to hear the application.[129]

Under section 10, the judge, upon finding that a member has contravened section 5, shall declare the member's seat vacant. The judge may also disqualify the member or former member from being a member for up to seven years. Where there has been personal financial gain, the judge may order restitution. The judge has no authority to suspend a member. However, if the judge finds that the contravention was committed through inadvertence or by reason of an error in judgement, the seat will not be declared vacant and the member or former member will not be disqualified. An order of a judge under section 10 may be appealed to Ontario Superior Court

---

125 *Municipal Conflict of Interest Act*, s. 4(k). See *Mangano v. Moscoe* (1991), 4 O.R. (3d) 469 (Gen. Div.) — the Act does not apply to a sub-committee of a municipal council. See also *Van Schyndel v. Harrell* (1991), 4 O.R. (3d) 474 (Gen. Div.) — standing committees of city council (except committee of the whole) are not included within the definitions in the Act.
126 *Municipal Conflict of Interest Act*, s. 2.
127 *Ibid.*, s. 3.
128 *Ibid.*, s. 7(3).
129 See "Report of the Municipal Conflict of Interest Consultation Committee to the Minister of Municipal Affairs", July 1991 (Queen's Printer), which suggests the establishment of a Commission to deal with matters under the Act.

Division (Divisional Court). However, if the judge does not make an order under section 10, *i.e.*, the judge determines that the member did not have a conflict of interest, then there is no right of appeal.[130]

The failure of a member to declare an interest in a matter does not invalidate the board's proceedings in respect of the matter, but the matter is voidable at the instance of the board unless this would adversely affect the rights of any person who acquired rights as a result of the proceedings and who was acting in good faith and without actual notice of the member's contravention.[131]

While there are relatively few court decisions on conflict of interest of school board members, courts have dealt with circumstances in which a board member has been alleged to have a pecuniary benefit arising from his or her material connection with the teaching profession. In *Moll v. Fisher*,[132] the Ontario Divisional Court dealt with a situation in which two school board members were both married to elementary school teachers employed by the board. They voted on a proposed collective agreement with the board's secondary teachers. In addition, one of the trustees chaired a board sub-committee on collective agreement policy and both of the trustees voted upon a report by the sub-committee.

The Divisional Court agreed with the lower court that the evidence showed a real connection between the elementary and secondary collective agreements of the board. For instance, for 20 years, the two groups had parity between their salary grids. Mr. Justice Robins, speaking for the Court, stated:

> In my view, on any realistic and objective appraisal of the continuing bargaining process in which this Board is engaged with its teachers, it can hardly be said that the terms negotiated with secondary teachers in regard to items such as salary, job security, fringe benefits, and the like, would not have a direct and significant bearing on the terms of a contract shortly to be agreed upon with another group holding similar professional standing and constituting part of the same educational system.[133]

The Court found that the two trustees had a pecuniary interest in voting on the secondary collective agreement because it would influence the outcome of the elementary negotiations. The direct interest of their spouses in the elementary contract was a pecuniary interest, under the Act, of the trustees. Robins J. stated:

---

130 *Van Schyndel v. Harrell* (1991), 6 O.R. (3d) 335 (Div. Ct.); leave to appeal to C.A. refused (1992), 6 O.R. (3d) 335n (C.A.) (*note:* this is *not* the *Van Schyndel* decision cited above).
131 *Municipal Conflict of Interest Act*, s. 12.
132 (1979), 23 O.R. (2d) 609 (Div. Ct.).
133 *Ibid.*, at 618.

In essence, the appellants have placed themselves on both sides of the bargaining table. Their family purse is in conflict with their public duty. Trustees, like Caesar's wife, must be, and appear to be, beyond temptation and reproach. The law sets a high objective standard of conduct.[134]

The Court made *obiter* comments that the trustee's participation on the collective bargaining policy committee placed him in a "difficult position with respect to the [*Municipal Conflict of Interest*] Act, one, indeed, fraught with the probability of conflict situations.[135]

In another Ontario case, *Benn v. Lozinski*,[136] a trustee of the Windsor Roman Catholic Separate School Board voted upon a proposed collective agreement between the board and its teachers. The trustee was also a secondary school teacher employed by the coterminous public board, the Board of Education for the City of Windsor. The trustee had obtained legal advice that there was no conflict of interest. Upon application by a ratepayer under the *Municipal Conflict of Interest Act*, the Court found that the trustee had an indirect pecuniary interest in the matter. Because the separate school contract would expire a year before the public, secondary contract would expire, the outcome of the vote would have little or no effect on the trustee's own collective agreement as a teacher and the respondent therefore had no direct or indirect pecuniary interest in the outcome of the vote. The Court noted that its finding would have been different had the separate school contract been in effect while the respondent's secondary school contract was being negotiated. However, the Court found that the trustee had an indirect pecuniary interest by virtue of being a member of the Ontario Teachers' Federation. The Court found the Federation to be "vitally interested in practically all matters in which the local board is concerned" and that the Federation derives its fees from members in accordance with their salaries. The court also found as a matter of evidence that:

> [G]enerally a collective bargaining agreement with one class of teachers will invariably affect a subsequent agreement with another class of teachers. The agreement invariably is used as a negotiating lever likely to influence financial and other terms in collective bargaining agreements. I am therefore prepared to find that the respondent was in conflict by reason of being in the employment of a body that has an interest in a contract reasonably likely to be affected by a decision of the local board.[137]

Because the trustee had sought legal advice, and had voted on similar matters previously, the Court found that he contravened the Act by reason of a *bona fide* error in judgment, and he was therefore not disqualified or required to vacate his seat. The Court did not find that the trustee's interest

---
134 *Ibid.*, at 621.
135 *Ibid.*, at 620.
136 (1982), 37 O.R. (2d) 607 (Co. Ct.).
137 *Ibid.*, at 615.

was remote or insignificant. The Court noted the effect of its decision upon teacher/trustees generally:

> Because the *Municipal Conflict of Interest Act* has far-reaching application the teacher/trustee will find it exceedingly difficult to add his or her considerable expertise and knowledge and to exercise his or her vote on many matters which come up for consideration before the board without running the risk of breaching the conflict of interest provisions in the Act.[138]

In British Columbia, the *School Act*[139] contains provisions for school trustees similar, although not identical, to Ontario's *Municipal Conflict of Interest Act*.[140] In *Margolis v. Brown*,[141] the British Columbia Supreme Court considered the case of a trustee who was married to a teacher who was employed by the school board. The teachers were on strike. The trustee voted on a resolution which dealt with how much money the board's negotiators were authorized to negotiate with. The Court found that the trustee had a conflict of interest because of the pecuniary interest of his spouse in reaching an agreement and having the strike come to an end. The Court also found that the contravention was not inadvertent or a result of an error in judgment.

Another British Columbia Court decision, *Wynja v. Halsey-Brandt*,[142] dealt with a situation in which two school trustees were employed as teachers by another school board. The trustees had voted upon ratification of the board's collective agreement with its teachers. The Court held that this was a contravention of the *School Act*. The Court found that there was a close relationship among the collective agreements of the local teachers' associations, not just locally, but across the province. The trustees should not have voted upon a collective agreement which might have influenced what they themselves received under the collective agreement in a neighbouring board.

On appeal, Wood J.A. (for the Court) agreed:

> I am satisfied that the specific terms of that relationship, [between the British Columbia Teachers' Federation and its locals] as formally recognized in the Constitution and by-laws of the various associations and in the members guide to the BCTF, are a manifestation of the fact that all teachers throughout the province share a common interest in establishing consistent working conditions and terms of employment, a fact which by itself leads inexorably to the very

---

138 *Ibid.*, at 617. See also *Devita v. Coburn* (1997), 15 O.R. (2d) 769 (Co. Ct.), decided before the *Municipal Conflict of Interest Act* was passed.
139 S.B.C. 1989, c. 61 [now R.S.B.C. 1996, c. 412].
140 See Judith A. Clark, "School Trustees and Conflict of Interest: The B.C. Experience", paper presented at CAPSLE 1992; and J.L. Dixon and S. Radke, "Statutory Conflict of Interest Provisions, Common Law Bias and Local Government In Alberta", paper presented at CAPSLE 1991.
141 (1991), Supreme Court of B.C. No. 11468, Nanaimo Registry, July 15, 1991, Gow J. (B.C.S.C.).
142 (1991), 62 B.C.L.R. (2d) 22 (S.C.), affirmed (1993), 102 D.L.R. (4th) 393 (C.A.).

conclusions reached by the trial judge. I am not persuaded that he misconstrued the evidence before him or that the conclusions he reached are unreasonable. Indeed, they seem to me to be a matter of common sense.[143]

8. ACCESS TO INFORMATION

(a) Board Books

Under the *Education Act*, any person may at all reasonable hours inspect the minute book, the audited financial report and the current accounts of a board. A person may request certified copies of these documents or extracts and the board may charge up to 25 cents for every 100 words. This provision does not entitle a person to request copies of all the board's financial records; it refers to "current accounts".[144]

(b) Freedom of Information and Protection of Privacy

In Ontario, the *Municipal Freedom of Information and Protection of Privacy Act*[145] governs the use, collection and storage of personal information by municipalities, school boards and many other agencies. It is based upon two fundamental principles. The first is that the public has the right to have access to records. The second is that personal information should be protected to ensure privacy.

The right to see public records is subject to a list of specific exemptions. These include:

- records of meetings which are authorized by law to be upheld in private
- advice or recommendations to the board
- law enforcement records
- information received in confidence from another government
- information from a third party containing trade secrets or scientific, technical, commercial, financial or labour relations information
- information which might prejudice the economic, financial, competitive, or negotiating interests of an institution
- information covered by solicitor-client privilege
- information which, if made public, may seriously threaten the safety or health of an individual
- personal information

This list contains only the major exemptions, many of which are subject to various conditions.[146] Certain of the exemptions do not apply if there is a

---

143 *Wynja v. Halsey-Brandt* (1993), 102 D.L.R. (4th) 393 at 400 (B.C. C.A.).
144 *Education Act*, s. 207(4).
145 R.S.O. 1990, c. M.56.
146 See *ibid.*, ss. 6-15.

compelling public interest in disclosure of the record.[147] Most of the information that a board would normally want to keep confidential can be kept confidential under the *Municipal Freedom of Information and Protection of Privacy Act*. Disputes over whether information should be disclosed can be referred to the Information and Privacy Commissioner.

The Act defines "record" as follows:

> "record" means any record of information however recorded, whether in printed form, on film, by electronic means or otherwise, and includes,
>
> (a) correspondence, a memorandum, a book, a plan, a map, a drawing, a diagram, a pictorial or graphic work, a photograph, a film, a microfilm, a sound recording, a videotape, a machine readable record, any other documentary material, regardless of physical form or characteristics, and any copy thereof, and
> (b) subject to the regulations, any record that is capable of being produced from a machine readable record under the control of an institution by means of computer hardware and software or any other information storage equipment and technical expertise normally used by the institution;[148]

The definition of "record" includes notes made by interviewers at a job interview. Great care should be taken that only necessary information is recorded during the interview. Job applicants are entitled to see what was written about them by interviewers. Seemingly harmless written remarks may cause legal difficulties if the interview process is later challenged (*e.g.*, in a complaint to a human rights tribunal) and the remarks have no bearing on the purpose of the interview.

The Act defines "personal information" as follows:

> "personal information" means recorded information about an identifiable individual, including,
>
> (a) information relating to the race, national or ethnic origin, colour, religion, age, sex, sexual orientation or marital or family status of the individual,
> (b) infomation relating to the education or the medical, psychiatric, psychological, criminal or employment history of the individual or information relating to financial transactions in which the individual has been involved,
> (c) any identifying number, symbol, or other particular assigned to the individual,
> (d) the address, telephone number, fingerprints or blood type of the individual,
> (e) the personal opinions or views of the individual except if they relate to another individual,
> (f) correspondence sent to an institution by the individual that is implicitly or

---

147 *Ibid.*, s. 16.
148 *Ibid.*, s. 2.

explicitly of a private or confidential nature, and replies to that correspondence that would reveal the contents of the original correspondence,

(g) the views or opinions of another individual about the individual, and

(h) the individual's name if it appears with other personal information relating to the individual or where the disclosure of the name would reveal other personal information about the individual;[149]

The legislation restricts how personal information can be collected, used and disclosed by the collecting institution. As indicated in Chapter 4, provisions in the *Education Act*, along with mandatory "Ontario Student Record Guidelines", address the confidentiality of student records. The *Municipal Freedom of Information and Protection of Privacy Act* applies to student records but it does not obviate the need to comply with the *Education Act*. Unless there is a valid consent to the release of student records, or a statute authorizes the release without consent, the board cannot release the information in the absence of a court order (for example, at a criminal trial). The provisions of the *Education Act* with respect to the retention of student records also apply in conjunction with retention and storage provisions in the *Municipal Freedom of Information and Protection of Privacy Act*. Boards must comply with both statutes.

9. THE BOARD AND ITS PROPERTY

(a) Public Access

School board property is owned by school boards and the public has no unrestricted right of access to the property. Issues may arise as to the extent to which members of the public have the right to use board property to exercise their freedom of expression under section 2(*b*) of the *Canadian Charter of Rights and Freedoms*. For example, do religious groups have the right to hold religious meetings on the school lawn? May pro- or anti-abortion groups hold demonstrations on school property? One view is that schools are different from such places as streets, parks, and post offices, and there is no *Charter* right of members of the general public to use board property to exercise freedom of expression. Schools exist for specific purposes. Generally speaking, a person has a right to enter the property for a reason which is consistent with those purposes, provided that the person has not been legally barred from having access. Others would assert that the right of access is a broad one, perhaps attempting to rely upon the case of *Committee for the Commonwealth of Canada v. Canada*.[150]

The *Commonwealth* case dealt with Federal regulations which purported to restrict the respondents from distributing pamphlets at Dorval

---

149 *Ibid.*
150 (1991), 4 C.R.R. (2d) 60 (S.C.C.). Application for rehearing refused (May 8, 1991), Doc. 20334 (S.C.C.).

Airport in Montreal. The respondents claimed that the regulation infringed their section 2(*b*) right to freedom of expression under the *Charter*. The Supreme Court of Canada examined at length the meaning of "public property". Although the members of the Court arrived at the decision by different routes, they decided that using the thoroughfare of the airport terminal to distribute pamphlets was not incompatible with the use of the airport and that the broad restriction imposed by the regulation infringed the *Charter* and was not demonstrably justified in a free and democratic society. The court also cited examples of "public property", such as libraries, where the use by the public would be much more curtailed. Lamer C.J.C. stated:

> In my opinion, the "freedom" which an individual may have to communicate in a place owned by the government must necessarily be circumscribed by the interests of the latter and of the citizens as a whole: the individual will only be free to communicate in a place owned by the state if the form of expression he uses is compatible with the principal function or intended purpose of that place.[151]

L'Heureux-Dubé J. echoed this view:

> [T]he *Charter*'s framers did not intend internal government offices, air traffic control towers, prison cells and judge's chambers to be made available to leafleting or demonstrations. It is evident that the right to freedom of expression under s. 2(b) of the *Charter* does not provide a right to access to all property whether public or private.[152]

McLachlin J. (as she then was) was the only member of the Court to mention schools specifically:

> Conversely, as abhorrent as arbitrary or unfair content-related limitations may be, it must be conceded that when carefully tailored they may be integrally tied to important government purposes outweighing any interest a speaker may have in communicating a conflicting message. Restrictions on content may be capable of being justified on the basis that certain messages are incompatible with the purpose of (sic) function of a particular government institution. Pornography or literature promoting drug use, for example, might be legitimately banned at a school or a children's festival in a government park. The point is that generalizations are of little assistance. What is essential is that the court in each case undertake the process of balancing and weighing the true interests at stake with a view to determining whether the limit on free expression in question is "reasonable" and "demonstrably justified in a free and democratic society".[153]

School board property is often viewed as being "public" because it is paid for by the public and the public may be accustomed to using the school as a formal or informal community gathering place. It is submitted, however,

---

151 *Ibid.*, at 72-73.
152 *Ibid.*, at 103.
153 *Ibid.*, at 139.

that there is no *Charter* right to use the property for indoctrinal religious exercises or services. It is clear from the *Zylberberg*[154] and *Elgin County*[155] decisions in the Ontario Court of Appeal that public schools must be free of indoctrinal religious influences (at least to the extent that the imposition upon pupils of religious exercises or instruction is found to infringe the *Charter*). The board may permit religious groups to operate on board property outside school hours, but such groups have no *Charter* right to use board property to spread their religious beliefs. This is especially true if pupils are on site at the time. Whether individuals who are associated with other kinds of groups, of a non-religious nature, have a *Charter* right to exercise freedom of expression on board property will depend on the circumstances in each case.

(b) Trespassers

School boards in Ontario are "occupiers", as defined under the *Trespass to Property Act*,[156] in respect of school sites. In the *Education Act*, "school site" means "land or premises or an interest in land or premises required by a board for a school, school playground, school garden, teacher's residence, caretaker's residence, gymnasium, school offices, parking areas or for any other school purpose"[157] Trespassing is an offence under the *Trespass to Property Act*. Entry to premises may be prohibited by notice to that effect. The notice may permit entry only for specific activities, with all other activities being prohibited. Alternatively, if a board prohibits only certain activities by notice, all other lawful activities would be permitted. Notice that entry to premises is prohibited may be made orally or in writing, or by means of posted signs or markings as prescribed under the Act. A trespasser may be arrested without warrant, on reasonable grounds, by the police, the occupier, or a person, such as a school principal, authorized by the occupier. If the arresting person is not a police officer, the trespasser must be promptly placed into the custody of a police officer, who shall then be deemed to have made the arrest for the purposes of the *Provincial Offences Act*[158] as it relates to release, bail and continued detention. While principals or other employees may be authorized by the board to arrest trespassers, it is recommended that the police be called in order to perfom this function. This will help ensure that the trespasser's rights under the *Charter of Rights and Freedoms* are not inadvertently violated. Once the person is off the premises, only a police officer may make the arrest.

---

154 *Zylberberg v. Sudbury (Bd. of Education)* (1989), 65 O.R. (2d) 641 (C.A.).
155 *Cdn. Civil Liberties Assn. v. Ontario (Min. of Education)* (1990), 71 O.R. (2d) 341 (C.A.).
156 R.S.O. 1990, c. T.21.
157 *Education Act*, s. 1(1).
158 R.S.O. 1990, c. P.33.

The *Criminal Code of Canada*[159] gives an occupier the right to eject trespassers from property, provided no more force is used than is necessary. A trespassers who resists an attempt by an occupier to prevent his or her entry or to remove him or her from the property is deemed to have committed an assault without justification or provocation.

Access by the public to board property for other than "school" purposes is normally allowed by boards if a permit has been granted by the board. Permits generally specify the intended use of the building or school grounds, the permitted hours of access, cost, insurance coverage requirements and caretaking obligations. The public often uses school playgrounds and playground equipment during off-hours or weekends on an informal basis, without specific permission. Boards do not normally try to prevent this kind of casual use provided that it does not interfere with the board's use of the property and that the activities being carried on are not unlawful or dangerous. Therefore, while the *Trespass to Property Act* permits boards considerable latitude in controlling access by the public to school sites, boards may choose to post signs prohibiting only certain activities. For example, softball may be allowed but baseball prohibited.

If a pupil has been suspended or expelled, the pupil may be notified that if he or she comes onto board property, he or she may be charged with trespassing. This advance notice is usually provided in writing. A copy of the letter may be sent to the local police so that they will not have questions about whether the pupil has been put on notice.

School principals in Ontario must maintain a visitor's book, when so determined by a board. This requirement is perhaps more important now than ever, given the problems that some schools are having with strangers entering board property with the intent to threaten or harm staff members and students, or to sell drugs. Under the *Education Act*,[160] members of the school board, members of the clergy, members of the Assembly, parents and legal guardians have certain specific rights to visit schools. A school principal may exclude persons from the school under the *Education Act*,[161] subject to an appeal to the board. This discretionary power must not be exercised in an unreasonable or arbitrary manner. The power to refuse admittance applies in respect of "persons" and does not exclude any particular category of persons, such as pupils or parents. However, if a pupil has been expelled or is under suspension and has been put on notice not to come onto board property, he or she should be dealt with by the police under the *Trespass to Property Act*.

If a pupil is not expelled or suspended, he or she has a right to attend the school and cannot be considered a trespasser. That right is subject to his

---

159 R.S.C. 1985, c. C-46. See, *e.g.*, s. 38 - defence of personal property.
160 *Education Act*, ss. 50 and 53.
161 *Ibid.*, s. 265(1)(m).

or her presence not being detrimental to the well-being of other pupils. In appropriate circumstances, a principal could conceivably prohibit a pupil from coming onto school property, but this power should be used with caution and not as a "back door" means of suspending or expelling pupils. Parents who are otherwise entitled to visit the school may have their visitation rights restricted under this section where their presence would be detrimental to the well-being of the pupils.

Section 305 was added to the *Education Act* in the year 2000 and it deals with access to school property. It permits the Minister of Education to make regulations governing access to school premises and it prohibits persons from entering or remaining on school premises unless allowed to be there under the regulation. Section 305 also prohibits persons from being or remaining on school premises contrary to a board policy. A principal of a school may direct a person to leave the school premises if the principal believes that the person is prohibited by regulation or under a board policy from being there.

Ontario Regulation 474/00 was made pursuant to the power in section 305. It states as follows:

Access to School Premises

1. This Regulation governs access to school premises under section 305 of the Act.

2.(1) The following persons are permitted to be on school premises on any day and at any time:

   1. A person enrolled as a pupil in the school.
   2. A parent or guardian of such a pupil.
   3. A person employed or retained by the board.
   4. A person who is otherwise on the premises for a lawful purpose.

(2) A person who is invited to attend an event, a class or a meeting on school premises is permitted to be on the premises for that purpose.

(3) A person who is invited onto school premises for a particular purpose by the principal, a vice-principal or another person authorized by board policy to do so is permitted to be on the premises for that purpose.

(4) Subsection (1), (2) or (3) does not entitle a person to have access to all areas of the school premises.

(5) Subsection (1) does not restrict the right of the board to lock the school premises when the premises are not being used for a purpose authorized by the board.

3.(1) A person is not permitted to remain on school premises if his or her presence is detrimental to the safety or well-being of a person on the premises, in the judgment of the principal, a vice-principal or another person authorized by the board to make such a determination.

(2) A person is not permitted to remain on school premises if a policy of the board requires the person to report his or her presence on the premises in a specified manner and the person fails to do so.

As Roderick C. Flynn has remarked[162] it is difficult to see how section 305 and O. Reg. 474/00 add anything of substance to the existing legal framework comprised of section 265(1)(m) and the *Trespass to Property Act*. In essence, the regulation says that if a person is a pupil, parent, employee or other authorized person, he or she is allowed to be on school premises. All others can be on school premises for a particular purpose. Arguably, however, the regulation is a useful tool for school principals who will now have something specific that they can point to when dealing with people who have no business being on school property. The regulation also enables the board to be very specific in terms of limiting the *purpose* of a person's visit.

(c) School Closure

Schools or classes may be closed temporarily because of the failure of transportation arrangements or because of inclement weather, fire, flood, breakdown of the heating plant, failure of an essential utility or a similar emergency.[163] However, schools may also be closed permanently or for indefinite periods of time. The fact that a school is closed does not necessarily mean that the board will dispose of it. The permanent or long-term closure of a school is often a difficult decision for board members, and is often met with considerable opposition from the community. The school inevitably contains memories for all those who have passed through it, and it may function as a community focal point. Board members who are considering a school closure know that they are usually in for a long and emotional battle. They can win the battle if the process used is open and fair.

To ensure fairness, boards in Ontario are required to file with the Ministry of Education and Training a policy on school closures. The policy must contain components prescribed by the Minister which ensure that members of the public are consulted early in the process and are given the time and opportunity to express their views. The board must consider the effects of the closure on the community's activities of a social, educational, cultural or recreational nature at the school, the effect on attendance areas, including busing, program implications and financial effects, and possible alternative uses or disposition if the school is closed.

---

162 *The 2002 Annotated Education Act* (Carswell), at 485.
163 *Education Act*, s. 19.

The issue of school closures in Ontario has been considered in several court cases,[164] including *Bezaire (Litigation Guardian of) v. Windsor (Roman Catholic Separate School Board)*.[165] In this case, the school board closed nine schools without undertaking any meaningful public consultation. The first issue addressed by the Court was whether or not the school board's decision to close the schools was subject to judicial review. The Court held that it had jurisdiction to review the decision of a board where the board has breached its statutory duties or where it has breached its duty to act fairly.

The Court was asked to decide whether or not a school closure decision was a "statutory power of decision" under the *Statutory Powers Procedure Act* and the *Judicial Review Procedure Act*. If the board's decision was made under a "statutory power of decision", then a hearing would have been required by the *Statutory Powers Procedure Act*. However, the Court said that it was not necessary to determine this point because the case could be decided on the basis of procedural fairness. Another issue considered by the Court was whether or not boards are compelled to conform to the Ministry's guideline on school closure, which requires that boards develop closure policies. The Court decided that boards must follow their closure policies and that those policies must substantially conform to the ministry's guidelines.

The Court was also asked to determine whether or not the board had a duty of fairness towards the public in making its decision to close the schools. The Court concluded that the board had failed to follow its own policy on school closure and had not met the expectations outlined in the ministry's guidelines, which included a requirement for public consultation:

> There was no input into the [consultant's] report by parents or community representatives and the operative decision [was] made without any knowledge of the so-called policy.
>
> There was a complete disregard of the consultative process which the board espoused and the Ministry of Education required.[166]

---

164 For *e.g., Fisher Park Residents Assn. Inc. v. Ottawa (Bd. of Education)* (1986), 57 O.R. (2d) 486 (H.C.). See also *Furey v. Conception Bay Centre (R.C. School Bd.)* (1993), 104 D.L.R. (4th) 455 (Nfld. C.A.), which examines the doctrine of legitimate expectation in relation to school closure. See also *Blore v. Halifax (Dist. School Bd.)* (1991), 105 N.S.R. (2d) 414, 284 A.P.R. 414 (T.D.) - no right of pupil to attend specific school. Legislation in Nova Scotia did not create statutory duty of procedural fairness, although general duty of fairness exists at common law; see EduLaw School Newsletter, Vol. 3, No. 10, June 1992.
165 (1992), 9 O.R. (3d) 737 (Div. Ct.).
166 *Ibid.*, at 753-754.

In the result, the board's decision was declared void and of no force and effect.[167]

The *Bezaire* Court commented upon the case of *Vanderkloet v. Leeds & Grenville County (Board of Education)*.[168] *Vanderkloet* dealt, *inter alia*, with the issue of a school board's power to determine its school attendance areas. Dubin J.A. (as he then was) stated:

> In my opinion, a board acting in good faith within its statutory authority has complete power over reallocation of students within a district and, in so doing, is not affecting the legal rights of any person.
>
> I am not satisfied that the principles of procedural fairness are applicable to a board of education, an elected public body, who, in good faith and within the jurisdiction assigned to it by the Legislature, resolve to reallocate the student body within its school district.[169]

The Court in *Bezaire* noted that the statutory power to determine attendance areas is different from the power to close schools. The closure of schools is subject to ministry guidelines requiring public input, whereas there are no guidelines for establishing attendance areas. The Court in *Vanderkloet* refused to overturn a board's decision about attendance areas.[170] In addition, this matter is distinguishable from the provisions in the *Education Act* which provide that an elementary or secondary pupil has the right to attend school in a neighbouring board if it is "more accessible" to the student, provided that the neighbouring board can accommodate the student.[171]

In *Dolyny v Fort Frances-Rainy River Board of Education*,[172] the Ontario Court (General Division) dealt with a situation in which the school board resolved to consolidate two campuses of a high school into one facility. This would involve the eventual closure of the "downtown" campus building. The applicant argued that this was in fact a "school closure" and that the province's mandatory closure policies had not been followed, con-

---

167 See also *Funk v. Wellington County Roman Catholic Separate School Board* (1994), 71 O.A.C. 321 (Div. Ct.) in which the late disclosure of information, during the public hearing process, about the elimination of the board's deficit was held not to invalidate a recommendation for the closure of a school.
168 (1985), 51 O.R. (2d) 577 (C.A.), leave to appeal to S.C.C. refused (1986), 54 O.R. (2d) 352 (note) (S.C.C.).
169 *Ibid.*, at 585 (C.A.).
170 See also *Crawford v. Ottawa (Bd. of Education)*, [1971] 1 O.R. 267 (H.C.), affirmed [1971] 2 O.R. 179 (C.A.); and *MacDonald v. Lambton County (Bd. of Education)* (1982), 37 O.R. (2d) 221 (H.C.); *Hatch v. London (Bd. of Education)* (1979), 25 O.R. (2d) 481 (H.C.).
171 *Education Act* also enables secondary students to go to the neighbouring board for program reasons. See *Bareham v. London (Bd. of Education)* (1984), 46 O.R. (2d) 705 (C.A.) as to the meaning of "more accessible".
172 (July 27, 1995), Fort Francis 885/95 (Ont. Gen. Div.).

trary to the *Education Act*. The board argued that consolidation of two school campuses belonging to one school is not a school closure.

The board maintained that a "school" consists of more than a building; it is also comprised of a body of pupils and the school staff. The pupils, staff, attendance areas, and other indicia of the "school" would not change under the proposed plan. The issue was whether the closure of the downtown campus building itself would attract the requirements of the closure policy. The court held that the board's proposed plan did amount to a school closure, when one considers all the factors about the importance of a school building within the local community.

In *Simpson v. Ottawa-Carleton District School Board*[173] the applicant sought judicial review of the board's decision to close four elementary schools. The board had developed school closing guidelines as it was required to do under the *Education Act*. The issue in this case was not whether there had been public consultation but whether the board had followed its guidelines in reaching its decision. The applicant asserted that the guidelines required the board to have an impact study. The Court (Chadwick J.) was satisfied that the guidelines did not require an impact study, and that "all interested parties affected by the impact of the decision had proper notice and procedural avenues in which to address their concerns. The decision of the board was reached after a great deal of consultation and input from the public and did address the guidelines and followed their own policy." Chadwick J. adopted the approach in *Fisher Park Residents Assn. Ltd. v. Ottawa (City) Board of Education*[174] in which Eberle J. stated:

> The guidelines as they existed then and as continued call for a policy on procedures. I think it is reasonable to infer therefore that the underlying aim of the Legislature was to ensure that the closure decision was taken according to certain procedural norms, allowing for reasonable time for an adequate input from the electorate. These matters were to be dealt with by each board in accordance with its own view of what was appropriate for it and its constituents. Accordingly, it appears to be that the policy developed by an individual board is not to be regarded nor scrutinized in the same way as a legislative enactment would be. In my view, the amendments envision a board's policy as a means of obtaining a fair procedure for the closing of schools. Thus, the substance of what is done is crucial rather than the technicalities. It must always be borne in mind that we are dealing with an administrative or management function and not with a judicial function, nor quasi-judicial function.

> Accordingly, a crucial central consideration is whether or not the plaintiffs have been treated fairly or unfairly. To this I think the plain answer is they have not been treated unfairly. I hasten to say, though perhaps it is unnecessary to do so, that we are not at all concerned with whether the decision to close

---

173 [1999] O.J. No. 1563, 1999 CarswellOnt 1279 (Div. Ct.).
174 (1986), 57 O.R. (2d) 468 at 477 (H.C.).

62 EDUCATION LAW

Fisher Park School was right or wrong, reasonable or unreasonable, the best decision or the worst decision, or somewhere in between. Those questions relate to the merits of the case. The merits or otherwise of the closure of Fisher Park School are not open for my consideration. It is solely the Board of Education which is given that obligation.

In *Ross v. Avon Maitland District School Board*,[175] the Court (Heeney J.) considered an application for interim relief prohibiting a school board from implementing a school closure decision pending the hearing of an application for judicial review. As part of the analysis, Heeney J. was required to determine if the applicants had a strong *prima facie* case. The applicants contended that the school board's school closure policy did not comply with the Minister's school guidelines. The Court stated:

> It is the closure policy established by the Board, and not the ad hoc procedure followed in any given case, that is of paramount importance, because it is through those policies that the statutory power to close schools is derived. The Board only has the power to close schools in accordance with the policies established by the Board. If, as I have found, those policies did not comply with Ministry guidelines, it follows that the Board lacked the statutory authority to close the school in question, and I so conclude.[176]

The Court went on to consider whether the Board's decision was procedurally unfair, and stated: "Fairness demands that each interested party be given an equal opportunity to participate in the decision-making process and influence the decision to be made."[177]

Heeney J. stated:

> The content and degree of the duty of fairness must be proportionate to the impact of the decision on those affected by it. In the case before me, the impact of the Board's decision so dramatically affects the people of Seaforth that a high degree of fairness is called for.[178]

The Court found that the school board's approach to arriving at its decision did not afford procedural fairness to the parents of Seaforth. The Court also found that the "right to be heard includes the right to the reasonable disclosure of information and documentation that will enable the affected party to fully develop and present the viewpoint that he or she wishes to be heard."[179] This accords with the decision of the Newfoundland Court of Appeal in *Elliott v. Burin School District No. 7*[180] which considered a school closing and held that the duty of fairness requires consultation that

---

175 [2000] O.J. No. 1714, 2000 CarswellOnt 1701 (S.C.J.).
176 *Ibid.*, at para. 37.
177 *Ibid.*, at para. 41.
178 *Ibid.*, at para. 45.
179 *Ibid.*, at para. 57.
180 (1998), 13 Admin. L.R. (3d) 91 (Nfld. C.A.).

is "meaningful and realistic, designed to ensure that there is a real opportunity for persons affected to take reasonable steps to influence the decision", and there must be disclosure of sufficient information and material "so that the persons affected will have a context in which to make their input".[181]

Although the Court refused to grant interim relief in *Avon Maitland*, the school board's decision was later quashed by the Divisional Court when the application for judicial review was heard.[182]

In *Vecchiarelli v. Toronto Catholic District School Board*[183] the Ontario Superior Court of Justice dealt with an application for judicial review of a school closure decision affecting 10 schools. The initial vote by the school trustees was preceded by a debate among them in the presence of approximately 200 members of the public, who made their views known in a very vocal manner. The trustees voted to close eight schools. There was a motion for reconsideration. Because of the disruption by the public gallery, the board felt compelled to recess to a private room, and when they returned twenty or thirty minutes later they voted on the motion for reconsideration and decided to close all ten schools, consistent with the original motion placed before the board. The Court held that observers of these events could reasonably conclude that some arrangement had been made while the trustees and staff were out of public view, and that "the heart of the decision-making had therefore not taken place at a public meeting as required by the *Education Act*". The appearance of fairness was therefore compromised. The application for judicial review was granted and the matter was remitted to the school board for its further consideration.

In *Furey v. Conception Bay Centre Roman Catholic School Board*[184] the Newfoundland Supreme Court found that the decision to close an elementary school was "an administrative decision, and not in any sense legislative" although ultimately the closure was the board's decision to make, and not the court's. Wells J. found that the consultative process and the communications to parents by the board raised a reasonable expectation in the minds of the parents that there would be procedural fairness by adhering to some form of guidelines before closing the school. For Wells J., the distinction between a legislative and administrative decision was that "legislative decisions are usually general decisions of broad application" whereas "administrative decisions usually deal with specifics". In *Furey*, Wells J. appears to have drawn a distinction similar to that used by the Supreme Court of Canada in *Homex Realty & Development Co. v. Wyoming*

---

181 *Ibid.*, at 106.
182 [2000] O.J. No. 1716 (May 19, 2000), Doc. 1121, [2000] O.J. No. 1716 (Ont. S.C.J.).
183 [2002] O.J. No. 2458.
184 (1991), 2 Admin. L.R. (2d) 263 (Nfld. T.D.), reversed (1993), 108 Nfld. & P.E.I.R. 328 (Nfld. C.A.).

(Village)[185] where the Court held that when a by-law affects a particular individual, its decision is administrative in nature rather than legislative, and its exercise of power is therefore subject to the duty of procedural fairness.

10. ELECTION AND ORGANIZATION OF THE BOARD

(a) Qualification and Disqualification of Board Members

The qualifications of board members in Ontario are prescribed by the *Education Act*. A person is qualified to be elected a member of a board (a term which includes both district school boards and school authorities) if the person is qualified to vote for members of that board and is resident in its area of jurisdiction. The person can run in any part of the board's geographical jurisdiction.

Under section 219(4) of the *Education Act*, a person is not qualified to be elected or to act as a member of a district school board or school authority if the person is:

(a) an employee of a district school board or school authority;
(b) the spouse or same-sex partner of a person mentioned in clause (a). This provision has been struck down by the courts (see below);
(c) the clerk or treasurer or deputy clerk or deputy treasurer of a county or municipality, including a regional municipality, the County of Oxford and the District Municipality of Muskoka, all or part of which is included in the area of jurisdiction of the district school board or the school authority;
(d) a member of the Assembly or of the Senate or House of Commons of Canada; or
(e) otherwise ineligible or disqualified under the *Education Act* or any other Act.

However, a board employee may become eligible to run if the person applies to his or her employer for an unpaid leave of absence beginning no later than nomination day and ending on voting day. The persons mentioned in paragraph (c) may also apply for an unpaid leave in order to be eligible to run for a position on the board. If the person is elected, he or she is deemed to have resigned from employement.

The prohibition against running for office as a board member if one's spouse or same-sex partner is a school board employee was struck down as being unconstitutional, in *Ontario Public School Boards' Assn. v. Ontario (Attorney General)*[186] In that case, the Court determined that the prohibition

---

185 [1980] 2 S.C.R. 1011.
186 (1999), 175 D.L.R. (4th) 609 (Ont. C.A.), leave to appeal refused (1999), 249 N.R. 400 (note) (S.C.C.).

infringed section 15(1) of the *Charter*, and that it was not justified as a "reasonable limit in a free and democratic society" under section 1 of the *Charter*. Abella J.A. for the majority stated:

> In the case before us, individuals are being disadvantaged because they are spouses, and are therefore being disadvantaged based on their marital status, an analogous ground.
>
> The effect of the disqualification based on marital status is to withhold a benefit from spouses of board employees; namely, the right to seek election to district school boards. This right is a benefit denied in a manner which reflects and perpetuates an assumption that spouses, unlike others in society, are incapable of independent decision-making. There is no doubt that the interests of spouses are in many ways inter-related, but a blanket exclusion of all spouses reflects the unrealistic view that spouses always share in common all interests and opinions with their partners. It thereby attributes a stereotypical quality to spouses, namely, that their decision-making abilities are in a state of perpetual conflict with their capacity to decide issues of a public nature.
>
> The distinction based on marital status is accordingly discriminatory since it arbitrarily disadvantages, based on personal and presumed group characteristics, individuals who are spouses, by restricting their right to public office and thereby restricting their right to participate in the democratic process: see also *Brossard (Town) v. Quebec (Commission des Droits de la Personne)*, [1988] 2 S.C.R. 279 and *Cashin v. C.B.C.* (1988), 86 N.R. 24 (Fed. C.A.).
>
> Accordingly, s. 219(4)(b) violates s. 15(1) of the Charter.[187]

In addressing the section 1 *Charter* argument, the Court stated:

> The stated objective of the exclusion in s. 219(4)(b) is to reduce the possibility of conflicts of interest. But as Campbell J. observed, at p. 369, the evidence of spousal conflicts in this case is "anecdotal", and he himself questioned whether the problem was a serious one.
>
> There is, in fact, no evidence that spousal conflicts of interest represent a problem at all, let alone a pressing or substantial one. A district school board, like any workplace, undoubtedly has a variety of employees performing a variety of jobs, but there is no evidence before us about what the range of employee categories is in this case, or, for that matter, what range of work those employees perform. There is, therefore, no way to assess how being an employee's spouse relates to the potential for conflict, let alone to assess whether that potential justifies the outright exclusion of all spouses of all employees.
>
> . . .
>
> Moreover, there is already legislation to deal with conflicts of interest. The *Municipal Conflict of Interest Act*, R.S.O. 1990, c. M.50 states that trustees

---

187 *Ibid.*, at paras. 24-27.

attending a meeting who have a direct or indirect pecuniary interest in a matter under consideration, are obliged to disclose their interest and refrain from participating in the discussion or vote. Pursuant to s. 7 of that Act, the remaining trustees are deemed to constitute a quorum despite any other general or special Act, permitting the school board to continue its decision-making duties. To the extent that there may be a problem arising from potential conflicts, there is a statutory solution in place.[188]

In *Sacco v. Ontario (A.G.)*,[189] the provisions of the *Education Act* that restricted a school board employee from running for or serving on the board that employs him or her were found not to infringe sections 2(d) or 15 of the *Canadian Charter of Rights and Freedoms*. Madame Justice Weiler found that there is no constitutionally protected right to run for school trustee, thus no right to "freedom of association" as a trustee could be infringed.

The section 15 argument failed because "to constitute discrimination, the distinction [between the treatment of groups and individuals] must relate to some personal characteristic of the individual group and impose a disadvantage or limit not suffered by others. These distinctions identify, 'discreet and insular minorities' who suffer social, political or legal disadvantage or vulnerability."[190] Schoolteachers were found to be "a heterogeneous group linked together only by their profession or occupation and as such are not a 'discreet insular minority' having a personal characteristic in a larger social, political or legal context. . . ."[191]

A person may not run for election to more than one board.[192] A person who is already a member of a board cannot run during a by-election for another board if the person's term of office has at least two months to run, unless the person has filed a resignation from the other school board, council or local board.[193] Similar provisions apply to restrict a board member from running for a county or municipal council or "local board" that shares all or part of the area of jurisdiction of the school board.

The members of a board shall remain in office until their successors are elected and the new board is organized. A board does not cease to exist by reason only of the lack of members.[194]

A member of a board cannot resign without the consent of a majority of the members present at a meeting at which a resignation is tendered. A

---

188 *Ibid.*, at paras. 29-30, 34.
189 (1991), 77 D.L.R. (4th) 764 (Ont. Gen. Div.), additional reasons at (February 13, 1991), Doc. No. RE 1079/89 (Ont. Gen. Div.).
190 *Ibid.*, at 768.
191 *Ibid.*
192 *Education Act*, s. 219(10).
193 *Ibid.*, s. 219(7).
194 *Ibid.*, s. 220.

member may not resign if the resignation will reduce the number of members on the board to less than a quorum: section 220(3).[195]

(b) Vacancies on the Board

A vacancy on a board occurs when,

(a) a member is convicted of an indictable offence. In this case, the vacancy shall not be filled until the time for taking an appeal from the conviction has elapsed or until the final determination of the appeal. If the conviction is quashed, the vacancy is deemed not to have occurred.
(b) a member absents himself or herself without being authorized by resolution entered in the minutes, from three consecutive regular meetings of the board.
(c) the member ceases to hold the qualifications required to act as a member of the board. For example, the member is elected to the House of Commons.
(d) the member becomes disqualified under subsection 219(4). For example, the member is hired as an employee of the board.
(e) the member fails to meet the requirements of section 229 (requirement to be physically present at a minimum number of board meetings).

Sections 221 to 225 of the *Education Act* provide for how a board is to replace a vacant member. Subject to specific exceptions, the board may appoint a new member for the remainder of the term or may hold a by-election.

(c) Meeting Procedures

In Ontario, the first meeting of the board is to be held not later than seven days after the day on which the term of office of the members commences.[196] Otherwise, it must be held on the first Wednesday following the commencement of the term of office. A majority of members may petition the appropriate supervisory officer to call the first meeting at some other time and date. The board chair is elected annually at the first meeting in December of each year. The Chief Executive Officer of the board presides over the first meeting in December of each year until the chair is elected. Where there is a tie vote for chair or vice-chair, the candidates for the position draw lots.

---

195 See also *Hearst (Town) v. Ontario North East District School Board* (2000), [2000] O.J. No. 3419, 2000 CarswellOnt 3219 (Ont. S.C.J.) where, in the context of litigation, a solicitor acting for a client in a case against a school board was prevented from dealing directly with an individual board member as a witness.
196 *Ibid.*, s. 208(2).

The board may elect a vice-chair, who presides in the absence of the chair. There is no requirement to elect a vice-chair at the first meeting although this is the usual practice. Subsequent meetings of the board are held at the times and places that the board considers expedient. When neither the chair nor the vice-chair is present at a meeting, the board members may elect one of themselves as chair for that meeting. A presence of a majority of all the members constituting the board is necessary to form a quorum. A tie vote on any motion means the motion is lost. The chair may vote with the other board members on board motions. Special meetings may be called by the chair.

A board may establish the procedures by which it will conduct its meetings.[197] Meeting procedures include the order of business, arrangements for the hearing of public delegations, and rules of order. Boards may vary their internal procedures for meetings, provided that this is not motivated by bad faith or fraudulent intent.[198]

> The general rule of law is that, in the absence of controlling statutes and rules, strict adherence to technical rules of procedure is not required. The reason for this is that it is not so important to have a board comprised of strict parliamentarians or to be the best possible adherent to Robert's Rules of Order, but rather to have an orderly system for the transaction of business. Thus, a board has considerable autonomy in determining the extent to which it wishes to be formal or informal, rigid or flexible.[199]

(d) Appointment of Secretary and Treasurer

A board shall appoint a secretary and treasurer or a secretary-treasurer.[200] The secretary of a board is responsible for keeping a full and complete record of the proceedings of every board meeting in the board's minute book, and for ensuring that the minutes are properly signed. The secretary also transmits copies of reports to the Ministry, gives notice of meetings to board members, calls special meetings at the request of a majority of board members, and performs such other duties as required by the board or the *Education Act* and regulations.[201] In the absence of a secretary from a meeting, the chair or other member presiding may appoint any member or other person to act as secretary for that meeting. It is fairly

---

197 *Radio CHUM 1050 Ltd. v. Toronto (Bd. of Education)*, [1964] 2 O.R. 207 (C.A.). The "Trustees' 2000 Handbook", available on the Ministry of Education website http://www.trustees2000.com/handbook.html, contains useful suggestions about Rules of Order at board meetings, at pages 45-46.
198 See *Canadian Encyclopedic Digest (Ontario)*, 3rd ed., Vol. 22, Title 98, "Municipal Corporations" (Toronto: Carswell), at p. 98-126.
199 H.C. Hudgins, Jr. and Richard S. Vacca, *Law and Education: Contemporary Issues and Court Decisions*, 3rd ed. (Charlottesville, Virginia: The Michie Co., 1991), at p. 69.
200 *Education Act*, s. 170(1) [1].
201 *Ibid.*, s. 198.

common for a board to appoint its director of education as secretary of the board. This does not prevent the board from excluding the director from *in camera* meetings where the board believes the director should not be present, usually because the topic of discussion is the director or the director's salary.

(e) Offences under the *Education Act* (Ontario)

Every treasurer must give security, by bond, for the faithful performance of his or her duties and if a board refuses or neglects to take security from the treasurer or other person to whom it entrusts its money, every member of the board is personally liable if money is lost as a result of such refusal or neglect.[202]

Section 217 of the *Education Act* prohibits teachers and other employees from selling or promoting certain kinds of products to boards and to pupils. This is, in effect, a "conflict of interest" provision. For example, the section would clearly prevent a teacher from selling magazine subscriptions for personal gain to his or her pupils. However, the section only lists tangibles such as materials and equipment. It seems unlikely that section 217 would, for example, prohibit a teacher from offering for sale tutorial *services* to students after school. The section does specifically accommodate educators who write school textbooks, by allowing them to collect a fee or royalty. More problematic might be a situation where an employee has written software for use by school boards if the software is a "teaching or learning material". Is software a "material" and when is it considered to be for teaching or learning? Would school time-tabling software come within section 217? Section 217 states:

> 217 (1) No teacher, supervisory officer or other employee of a board or of the Ministry shall, for compensation of any kind other than his or her salary as such employee, promote, offer for sale or sell, directly or indirectly, any book or other teaching or learning materials, equipment, furniture, stationery or other article to any board, provincial school or teachers' college, or to any pupil enrolled therein.
>
> (2) Subsection (1) does not apply to a teacher, supervisory officer or any other employee in respect of a book or other teaching or learning materials of which he or she is an author where the only compensation that he or she receives in respect thereof is a fee or royalty thereon.
>
> (3) No person or organization or agent thereof shall employ a teacher, supervisory officer or other employee of a board or of the Ministry to promote, offer for sale or sell, directly or indirectly, any book or other teaching or learning materials, equipment, furniture, stationery or other article to any board, pro-

---

202 *Education Act*, s. 198. See *Vaughan School Section No. 24 v. Scott* (1932), 41 O.W.N. 149 (H.C.).

vincial school or teachers' college, or to any pupil enrolled therein, or shall, directly or indirectly, give or pay compensation to any such teacher, supervisory officer or employee for such purpose.

(4) Every person who contravenes any provision of subsection (1) or (3) is guilty of an offence and on conviction is liable to a fine of not more than $1,000.

(f) Personal Liability of Board Members

It is very rare for a school board member to be found personally liable for actions taken in his or her capacity as a board member. However, trustees may be held personally liable if they act in bad faith, or if they willfully (as opposed to inadvertently) act outside the scope of their authority.

The Ontario Divisional Court (Desmarais J.) held in *Deschamps v. Conseil des écoles séparées catholiques de langue française de Prescott-Russell* that school trustees were not personally liable where a superintendent was declared redundant and transferred to a lesser position. The Court adopted the principle as stated under "Education" in 10 C.E.D. (Ont. 3rd), Title 52, para. 133:

> Where school trustees are constituted as a corporation with capacity to sue and be sued, in carrying out their statutory duties, acting in their public corporate capacity and within the scope of their authority, it is only in that character that they are liable and not in their private individual capacity. Hence no action will lie against trustees individually for acts done in their corporate capacity.[203]

Desmarais J. noted that trustees can be held individually liable where it can be shown they acted in bad faith. In the case before him, he found insufficient evidence to conclude that the individual trustee defendants had acted in bad faith.

The *Deschamps* case was appealed to the Ontario Court of Appeal and Supreme Court of Canada. However, those courts dealt with the main issue in the case, that is, the application of the *Public Authorities Protection Act*. These courts did not vary the trial court's comments on the general principles respecting the personal liability of trustees.

In *Lussier v. Windsor-Essex Catholic District School Board*[204] a former director of education sued the school board for breach of contract and added a claim against individual trustees for the torts of conspiracy and defamation, based upon the participation of the trustees in the decision-making process which led to the alleged breach of contract. The school board responded that where trustees were acting in good faith in their participation and capacity within the decision-making process, they are protected from per-

---

203 (1993), 16 O.R. (3d) 278 (Gen. Div.). See also *Anderson v. Vansittart* (1849), 5 U.C.Q.B. 335 (C.A.).
204 [1999] O.J. No. 4303, 1999 CarswellOnt 3632 (Div. Ct.).

sonal liability unless it can be shown that their actions are themselves tortious or separate from that of the school board. The defendant asked the Ontario Superior Court of Justice (Divisional Court) to strike the plaintiff's pleadings against the individual trustees (on appeal from a decision of a single judge refusing to strike). The Divisional Court stated:

> The Ontario Court of Appeal has held that officers or employees of limited companies are protected from personal liability unless it can be shown that their actions are themselves tortious or exhibit a separate identity from that of the company so as to make the act or conduct complained of their own.[205]

The Court found:

> The defendant Windsor-Essex Catholic District School Board being an inanimate entity, the court can only assess its liability by assessing the conduct of those persons (the trustees) who caused the Board to act the way it did.
>
> The individual defendants in this case were acting within the scope of their authority as the agents or operating mind of the defendant Board. They had no interests other than the interest of the Board in pursuing the actions that took place. It cannot be said that the procedures that followed were outside the scope of their employment.[206]

Section 230.12(3) of the *Education Act* states that if a board that is subject to an order under section 230.3(2) (i.e. an order by the Lieutenant Governor in Council to vest in the Ministry of Education control and charge over the administration of the affairs of the board), applies any of its funds otherwise than as ordered or authorized by the Minister, the members of the board who voted for the application are jointly and severally liable for the amount so applied. The school board is not permitted to indemnify the board members for any such liability. In addition, section 198(4) provides that a board member may be held personally liable for losses if the board fails to take proper security from its treasurer.

11. PRIVATE SCHOOLS

A brief overview of private schools in Ontario is included at this point for comparison with school boards. Because school boards control the expenditure of public money, they are heavily regulated. In some provinces, the degree of provincial regulation of private schools depends on the amount of public money they receive.[207] In Ontario, private schools receive no direct funding from the province or local ratepayer.

If parents desire to opt out of the public school system, they are obligated, under compulsory school attendance laws, to ensure that their child

---

205 *Ibid.*, at para. 17.
206 *Ibid.*, at paras. 23-24.
207 British Columbia provides one example of this.

receives instruction elsewhere. In Ontario, if a child of compulsory school age is not enrolled in school,[208] the parent or guardian must show that the child is legally excused from attendance. This usually means that the child is receiving "satisfactory instruction at home or elsewhere". If the child is being educated at home, school board officials visit the home in order to ascertain if the instruction being provided is satisfactory. There is no definition of "satisfactory instruction" in the *Education Act*. Boards may provide the child with learning materials, but are not obligated to do so. If the parent or guardian indicates to the board that the child is enrolled in a private school, the board ceases to be involved with the child's education unless the child subsequently ceases to be enrolled in the private school.

Private schools in Ontario must file an annual "Notice of Intention to Operate". Upon receipt of this document, the provincial ministry places the name of the private school on a list of private schools. Ministry officials visit the private school when the Notice of Intention is first filed, but do not conduct regular inspections of private schools to ensure that they are providing satisfactory instruction. The ministry has the statutory power to conduct inspections of private schools, but only exercises this power in response to allegations that pupils may be at risk because of safety concerns or where other serious concerns have been raised about the school's practices. The ministry will also inspect private secondary schools, at the schools' request and expense, in order to ensure compliance with curriculum guidelines. This enables the pupils to obtain secondary school credits toward the provincial secondary school diploma. The inspection of the standard of instruction does not necessarily include an assessment or evaluation of school's safety procedures, the effectiveness of school administration, or the competence of the teachers.

Private schools are not required to hire teachers who are members of the Ontario College of Teachers. The governing bodies of private schools are not elected by enumerated "school supporters", and are not required by law to hold public meetings. They cannot levy taxes. They are not required to hire supervisory officers. Unlike school boards, they may teach indoctrinal religious education. They may charge a fee for admission to the school. Their relationship to parents and pupils is primarily contractual. A private school may refuse to admit a pupil.

A duty of fairness may arise in some circumstances in respect of private schools. For example, in *D. (C.) (Litigation Guardian of) v. Ridley College*[209] Mr. Justice Quinn quashed a decision of Ridley College expelling a student for alleged involvement in drugs. Ridley College is a private school in St.

---

208 "School" is defined in the *Education Act*, and does not include "private school", which is also defined.
209 (1996), 138 D.L.R. (4th) 176 (Ont. Gen. Div.).

Catherines, Ontario, governed by the *Ridley College Act*.[210] In an earlier application for leave to bring an application for judicial review, for an interim injunction and for an order to re-admit the student[211] Quinn, J. found that the expulsion decision of the College was made in the exercise of a statutory power of decision, and therefore subject to judicial review.

The court rejected the argument that the fact that Ridley College is a private school means that the *Judicial Review Procedure Act (JRPA)* does not apply. Quinn J. found that the College is providing a "public service" and that it is in the public interest that private schools operate within principles of natural justice when it comes to expulsion of students. He also found that the fact that the College has certain powers of land expropriation renders it a "quasi" public entity sufficient to allow the applicants to invoke the protection of the *JRPA*. Quinn J. also stated:

> Although it is undoubtedly correct that part of the relationship between the applicants and Ridley is governed by the law of contract, I do not consider that the issues facing this court are a matter of contract. However, even if they are, I would grant relief to the applicants in the form of a declaration that the contract contains an implied term of procedural fairness as a condition precedent to the right of expulsion. I would regard such a term reasonably to have been within the contemplation of the parties at the time C.D. was enrolled at Ridley. As a result, I would grant an interim interim mandatory order requiring Ridley to re-admit C.D. pending the hearing of the within application.[212]

The College was found by the court to have acted in a "very high-handed and callous manner towards [the student]. The summary nature of the expulsion is quite shocking."[213] The student's parents had not been notified of the expulsion hearing and the student was not afforded the opportunity to be represented by a legal or other representative.

In his July 9, 1996 decision following the granting of the interim interim injunction against Ridley, Quinn J. quashed Ridley's decision to expel the student. He stated that he was guided by the following considerations and legal principles in respect of natural justice:

1. Denial of natural justice is an error that vitiates the whole proceedings. The tribunal is bound to start afresh to cure the defect.
2. Even without express statutory authority, a tribunal's power of rehearing is to be implied in circumstances where natural justice has failed.
3. A retrospective operation is not to be given to a statute so as to impair an existing right or obligation, otherwise than as regards matters of procedure.

---

210 S.O. 1924, c. 145.
211 (1996), 140 D.L.R. (4th) 696 (Ont. Gen. Div.).
212 *Ibid.*, at 708.
213 *Ibid.*, at 705.

4. It is of fundamental importance that justice should not only be done but should manifestly and undoubtedly be seen to be done.
5. If there is to be a rehearing it must take place before a body not comprised of [the student's] adversaries and there is, unfortunately, an abundance of evidence that Ridley has assumed that mantle.
6. An adjudicative body should not have an interest in the result of the adjudication [as this would create a reasonable apprehension of bias].

In the result, the original decision to expel the student was quashed and a rehearing was ordered before neutral individuals.

In *Burke v. Yeshiva Beit Yitzchak of Hamilton*,[214] the Ontario Court (General Division) dealt with an application by a student and his parents for judicial review in respect of the expulsion from a Yeshiva school. The Court (White, MacFarland and Feldman JJ.) granted the application and quashed the expulsion. White J. (for the Court) found that the Court had jurisdiction to hear the matter.

> [b]ecause notwithstanding that the school is a private one supported entirely from private funds, it is required to comply with the *Education Act* R.S.O., c. E.2 in providing for the secular education of its students. There is a public law component involved when the education of a pupil is interfered with by the drastic punishment of expulsion sufficient to merit this court's review of the process leading to expulsion.
>
> We are satisfied that the process in the case at bar was faulty in (i) not giving David Burke's parents sufficient detailed notice of the grounds proposed for his expulsion and (ii) not giving the parents an opportunity to be heard on the merits of the expulsion.

The pupil was permitted to complete the academic year.

Private schools may be denominational or non-denominational. Many are founded because a religious community wants to combine religious instruction with other subjects. As noted above, if a private school wishes to grant secondary school credits toward the Ontario Secondary School Diploma, it must comply with the province's curriculum and student transcript requirements. If it does not wish to grant credits, there is no requirement for compliance with provincial guidelines, provided that the instruction is "satisfactory".

12. CONCLUSION

This chapter discusses the complex constitutional and statutory framework that governs and directs the delivery of public education generally, with specific reference to Ontario. Those who are new to the "education system" are invariably amazed at the complex interaction of the many

---

214 (1996), 90 O.A.C. 81 (Div. Ct.).

different laws and regulations which directly affect the operation of a school board. It is important to understand where those laws come from, and how the *Charter* may affect them. When called upon, it is incumbent upon legal counsel to provide advice to board members to help them understand their role, their responsibility to ensure procedural fairness, the need to keep the decision-making process as open as possible, and the legal basis for the members' actions.

2

Civil Liability of School Boards and Their Employees

1. INTRODUCTION   78
   (a) Provincial Role   78
   (b) Vicarious Liability   79
   (c) Burden of Proof   79
2. NEGLIGENCE   79
   (a) Introduction   79
   (b) Duty of Care   80
       (i) Statutory Duty of Care   80
       (ii) *Education Act* and Regulations (Ontario)   81
       (iii) Common Law Duty of Care   84
   (c) The Standard of Care   84
       (i) General Principles   84
       (ii) Absence of the Supervisor   92
       (iii) Modified Standards of Care   95
       (iv) Proximate Cause and Foreseeability   99
       (v) Transportation of Pupils   100
       (vi) Negligence Outside School Hours   102
       (vii) Negligence and Sexual Misconduct   103
   (d) Defences to Negligence Claims   105
       (i) Contributory Negligence   106
       (ii) Voluntary Assumption of Risk   107
   (e) Negligence Involving Minors   107
   (f) Consent to Participate   108
   (g) Commentary on School Negligence   109
3. LIMITATION PERIODS   110
4. OCCUPIERS' LIABILITY   116
5. INTENTIONAL TORTS   121
   (a) Introduction   121
   (b) Assault and Battery   123
   (c) Sexual Misconduct   124
   (d) Corporal Punishment and Physical Restraint   132
   (e) Defences to Intentional Tort Actions   133
6. FIDUCIARY DUTY   134
7. EDUCATIONAL MALPRACTICE   141
8. RISK MANAGEMENT   145

1. INTRODUCTION

Tort law consists of the body of statutory and case law dealing with civil liability for negligent or intentional acts or omissions which have caused a legally recognized loss or injury. There are hundreds of reported cases about the liability of school boards and their employees for negligence or intentional torts. This chapter discusses the leading cases and the statutory basis for civil liability of educators and school boards.

Despite the large number of reported and unreported cases, it can still be stated that school boards and their employees have been remarkably successful in ensuring the safety and well-being of pupils and others who use school property, given the huge number of pupils being taught, and the number of properties which are owned by boards. Thousands of minor incidents are reported to boards' insurance companies each year, yet very few result in a civil action actually being commenced. Risk management and proper precautions will reduce the number of injuries; this is discussed in detail later in the chapter.

A tort is a civil wrong which is recognized at law. A tort is not a crime, although tortious conduct, such as assault, may also lead to a criminal conviction. A tort must also be distinguished from breach of contract, infringement of the *Canadian Charter of Rights and Freedoms*[1], and infringement of the "rules of natural justice". While a court may provide a remedy for these wrongs, they are not torts. Although many of our comments and examples in this chapter refer to teachers as being the defendants in a lawsuit, several defendants are usually named in the plaintiff's statement of claim, including the school principal and the board itself. School boards or districts are corporate entities, created by statute. They are legally distinct from the provincial government. They can sue and be sued in their own name and are liable for torts committed in their corporate capacity. For example, failure to have an adequate playground supervision policy could result in a finding of negligence against the board where the failure results in an accident.[2]

(a) Provincial Role

Barring any statutory provision to the contrary, provincial governments are not legally responsible for torts which take place in public or private schools. For example, although a province determines, through its legislation and regulations, how a teacher may become legally qualified to teach, it does not hire, dismiss, evaluate or supervise teachers or other staff em-

---

1 Being Part I of the *Constitution Act, 1982* [en. by the *Canada Act, 1982* (U.K.) c. 11, s. 1].
2 *Piszel v. Etobicoke (Bd. of Education)* (1977), 16 O.R. (2d) 22 (C.A.). The board's "perimeter system" of ensuring that wrestling mats would not separate during competition was found to be inadequate.

ployed at the local level, and therefore should not be held legally responsible for their actions. The responsibility for pupil safety under statutory and common law falls squarely at the door of the school board and its staff.

(b) Vicarious Liability

Where an employee of a school board is found liable in tort, the school board may be found vicariously liable for the employee's conduct.[3] This is examined in greater detail below. Vicarious liability is distinct from a school board being found liable for its own actions as a corporate entity. A board which is held vicariously liable may seek indemnity from its employee, although this is rarely done. A board may also be vicariously liable for the tortious conduct of volunteers in the school.

(c) Burden of Proof

Generally speaking, the burden of proof in tort cases is on the plaintiff, who must prove his or her case on a "balance of probabilities". The court does not have to be convinced beyond a reasonable doubt, as it would in order to find an accused guilty in a criminal case. Once the plaintiff has led sufficient evidence to tip the balance of probabilities in the plaintiff's favour, the onus shifts to the defendant to lead evidence against the plaintiff's case. At the end of the trial, a finding of civil liability requires that "the plaintiff establish by relevant evidence that it is more likely than not that the defendant was to blame for the plaintiff's injury. If the evidence shows only that the defendant *may* have been at fault, the plaintiff will fail:"[4]

2. NEGLIGENCE

(a) Introduction

Schools are, by their very nature, fertile ground for accidents to occur. It is impossible to contain a large number of young people within a relatively confined space and expect that injuries or other losses will not occur. This is particularly true if the pupils are engaged in activities which have an element of heightened or inherent danger, such as sports, technical shops, and science labs.

---

3 See *Beauparlent v. Bd. of Trustees of Separate School Section No. 1 of Appleby*, [1955] 4 D.L.R. 558 (Ont. H.C.); but see *Goodwin c. Laurenval (Commn. scolaire)* (1991), 8 C.C.L.T. (2d) 267 (S.C. Qué.) janitor fondled pupil's buttock, causing her to injure herself when rushing from the building — janitor not acting in course of his duties — board not liable.

4 Allen Linden, *Canadian Tort Law*, 7th ed. (Toronto: Butterworths, 2001), p. 234. Linden also notes on page 234 that there are circumstances when the initial burden of proof may shift to the defendant. This shift is rare in school negligence cases.

The elements of negligence are normally identified by making the following kinds of inquiries, although their order may vary from case to case and the distinctions between them may be blurred:

1. Did the defendant have a duty of care toward the plaintiff?
2. Did the defendant breach the duty of care? That is, did the defendant's conduct toward the plaintiff meet the required standard of care?
3. Was there actual loss or injury to the plaintiff?
4. Did the loss or injury result from the breach of care? That is, was there a sufficient causal connection between the loss or injury and the defendant's conduct?
5. Did the plaintiff contribute to his or her own loss or injury?

(b) Duty of Care

In negligence cases, the court must first determine if the defendant owed a duty of care toward the plaintiff. Where there is no statutory or common law duty to ensure the safety or well-being of another person, there cannot be a finding of liability in negligence if the person is injured. However, the imposition of a duty of care upon boards and teachers to ensure the safety and well-being of students has been well-established in both common law and statute for over one hundred years. Therefore, most reported cases on school negligence focus, not on arguments as to whether a duty of care exists, but on the nature of the duty in a given fact situation, whether the defendant has failed to discharge that duty, and whether the injury or loss was reasonably foreseeable.

(i) *Statutory Duty of Care*

The following commentary by McMurrich and Roberts, on the Ontario *Public Schools Act, 1891,*[5] outlines the duties of school trustees a century ago:

> Trustees should, for convenience, appoint one of their number, or the secretary-treasurer, or other responsible person, and give him the authority, as well as make it his duty, to keep the schoolhouse in good repair. He should also see that the windows are properly fitted with glass; and that, at a proper season, the stove and pipes are in a fit condition, and suitable wood provided; that the desks and seats are in good repair; that the outhouses are properly provided with doors and are frequently cleaned; that the blackboards are painted, the water supply abundant, and everything provided necessary for the comfort of the pupils and the efficiency of the school.[6]

---

5 1891, c. 55.
6 William B. McMurrich and Henry N. Roberts, *The School Law of Ontario* (Toronto: The Goodwin Law Book & Publishing Co., 1894), p. 53.

Section 131(3) of the *Public Schools Act, 1891*, stated:

> It shall be the duty of every teacher of a Public School:
>
> To maintain proper order and discipline in his school, according to the prescribed regulations.

Subsections 7(7) and (8) of Departmental Regulations under the *Public Schools Act, 1891* stated:

> In addition to the duties prescribed by the School Act, the following shall be the duties of every teacher in a Public School:
>
> . . . .
>
> (7) To give strict attention to the proper ventilation and cleanliness of the schoolhouse; to make and enforce such rules as will ensure the keeping of the school grounds and outbuildings in a neat and tidy condition.
>
> (8) To see that the school grounds, sheds, and water-closets are kept in proper order; that no damage is done to the furniture, fences, outbuildings, or other school property; to give notice in writing to the Trustees of any necessary repairs or supplies.

Historically, society's concerns for a safe and healthy learning environment have always accompanied concerns about teaching methodology and curriculum.

Education statutes across Canada reflect concern for the health and welfare of pupils. Although provincial statutes and regulations usually impose express duties to supervise pupils, ensure cleanliness, provide ventilation, inspect equipment, *etc.*, the absence of such specific provisions will not absolve the board or teachers of their statutory duty of care. The statutory obligation may simply require the principal or teacher to maintain "order and discipline" in the school. This requirement alone is sufficient to establish a statutory duty of care.

(ii) *Education Act and Regulations (Ontario)*

In Ontario, the *Education Act*[7] and regulations contain the following obligations upon boards and teachers to ensure pupils' safety:

Education Act — Section 170(1)

Every board shall,

. . . .

8. keep the school buildings and premises in proper repair and in a proper sanitary condition, provide suitable furniture and equipment and keep it in proper repair, and protect the property of the board;

9. make provision for insuring adequately the buildings and equipment of

---

7 R.S.O. 1990, c. E-2.

the board and for insuring the board and its employees and volunteers who are assigned duties by the principal against claims in respect of accidents incurred by pupils while under the jurisdiction or supervision of the board;

Section 264(1)

It is the duty of a teacher and a temporary teacher,

(a) to teach diligently and faithfully the classes or subjects assigned to the teacher by the principal;

. . . .

(e) to maintain, under the direction of the principal, proper order and discipline in the teacher's classroom and while on duty in the school and on the school ground;

Section 265(1)

It is the duty of a principal of a school, in addition to the principal's duties as a teacher,

(a) to maintain proper order and discipline in the school;

. . . .

(j) to give assiduous attention to the health and comfort of the pupils, to the cleanliness, temperature and ventilation of the school, to the care of all teaching materials and other school property, and to the condition and appearance of the school buildings and grounds;

Regulation 298[8] — Section 11(1)

The principal of a school, subject to the authority of the appropriate supervisory officer, is in charge of,

(a) the instruction and the discipline of pupils in the school; and

(b) the organization and management of the school.

Section 11(3)

In addition to the duties under the Act and those assigned by the board, the principal of a school shall, except where the principal has arranged otherwise under subsection 26(3),

. . . .

(e) provide for the supervision of pupils during the period of time during each school day when the school buildings and playgrounds are open to the pupils;

(f) provide for the supervision of and the conducting of any school activity authorized by the board;

---

8 *Operation of Schools – General*, R.R.O. 1990, Reg. 298.

. . . .

(k) provide for the instruction of pupils in the care of the school premises;

(l) inspect the school premises at least weekly and report forthwith to the board,
   (i) any repairs to the school that are required, in the opinion of the principal,
   (ii) any lack of attention on the part of the building maintenance staff of the school, and
   (iii) where a parent of a pupil has been requested to compensate the board for damage to or destruction, loss or misappropriation of school property by the pupil and the parent has not done so, that the parent of the pupil has not compensated the board;

Section 20

In addition to the duties assigned to the teacher under the Act and by the board, a teacher shall,

(a) be responsible for effective instruction, training and evaluation of the progress of pupils in the subjects assigned to the teacher and for the management of the class or classes, and report to the principal on the progress of pupils on request;

(b) carry out the supervisory duties and instructional program assigned to the teacher by the principal and supply such information related thereto as the principal may require;

. . . .

(g) ensure that all reasonable safety procedures are carried out in courses and activities for which the teacher is responsible; and

(h) co-operate with the principal and other teachers to establish and maintain consistent disciplinary practices in the school.

Breach of a statutory duty is not negligence *per se,* although a court may consider a breach of statutory duty as part of the evidence by which the plaintiff may prove negligence. Therefore, the breach of one or more of the provisions in the *Education Act* dealing with the safety and well-being of pupils is not automatically proof of negligence, and the imposition of a statutory duty arguably does not make more burdensome the common law prudent parent standard of care.[9]

---

9 See John Bell, "Liability Issues Affecting Boards of Education, Their Trustees, Servants, Agents and Employees" in *Education Law – After the ABC's,* a Canadian Bar Association of Ontario publication (1988), p. 16.

(iii) *Common Law Duty of Care*

Across Canada, the common law clearly establishes that teachers have a duty of care toward pupils in their care. The duty derives from the special relationship that exists between a teacher and his or her pupil. Parents entrust their children to the care of teachers and other board employees. Unless parents opt for home schooling, they must send their children, of compulsory school age, to private or public school. In return, they are entitled to expect at least three things for their children: the opportunity to acquire knowledge and skills, fair and equitable discipline, and a safe learning environment.

(c) The Standard of Care

(i) *General Principles*

Given that there is a statutory and common law duty of care upon a school board and its employees in respect of pupils, the issue for the court becomes whether there was a breach of the duty, *i.e.*, whether the required standard of care was met. Within certain parameters, the courts will modify the standard of care to meet the individual facts of a case.

The following kinds of allegations are typically found in a plaintiff's statement of claim against boards and teachers:[10]

1. lack of adequate supervision by a teacher or other staff member;
2. improper, inadequate or defective equipment;
3. failure to warn pupils of specific dangers in doing an activity;
4. failure to train pupils in the proper use of equipment or in safety procedures;
5. failure to take reasonable precautions against injury or loss;
6. failure to hire competent staff and to provide them with necessary training;
7. failure to properly treat an injury.

The standard of care owed by teachers toward their pupils has been compared in numerous cases to that of a "careful or prudent parent". In 1893, the standard was established in *Williams v. Eady*[11] and it has served as the implicit or explicit starting point for virtually all Canadian school negligence cases since:[12]

> [T]he schoolmaster was bound to take such care of his boys as a careful father would take of his boys, and there could not be a better definition of the duty of a schoolmaster. Then he was bound to take notice of the ordinary nature of

---

10 These do not apply in occupiers' liability cases: slip and fall cases are a major cause of insurance claims against school boards.
11 (1893), 10 T.L.R. 41 at 42 (C.A.).
12 See, *e.g.*, *Dziwenka v. R.*, [1972] S.C.R. 419, and *McKay v. Bd.* of *Govan School Unit No. 29 of Sask.* (1968), 68 D.L.R. (2d) 519 (S.C.C.).

young boys, their tendency to do mischievous acts, and their propensity to meddle with anything that came in their way.[13]

In so stating, the Court found that the schoolmaster was negligent in leaving a bottle of phosphorus about the conservatory. This enabled some school boys to find it, and light it with a match. The resulting flash fire severely burned one of the students.

The standard of care imposed upon boards and teachers does not require them to take precautions against accidents which are unforeseeable. "Human prudence would be taxed beyond reason, were it to endeavour to foresee every possibility of human ingenuity, or boyish mischievousness, in its search for opportunities to get into trouble, in even the remotest and most unlikely corners, nooks, or crannies."[14] It is also well-established that the mere possibility of an injury resulting from an activity does not mean that it is negligent to permit students to participate in the activity."[15]

In 1981, the Supreme Court of Canada in *Myers v. Peel County (Board of Education)*[16] applied the *Williams v. Eady* prudent parent standard of care. *Myers* dealt with a claim on behalf of a 15-year-old boy who broke his neck after attempting a straddle dismount from a gymnastic rings apparatus. A teacher was not present in the room at the time of the accident, and the plaintiff's spotter had moved away from the apparatus by the time the plaintiff attempted the dismount.

In addressing the issue of supervision by the teacher, the Court stated:

> The standard of care to be exercised by school authorities in providing for the supervision and protection of students for whom they are responsible is that of the careful or prudent parent, described in *Williams v. Eady* (1893), 10 T.L.R. 41. It has, no doubt, become somewhat qualified in modern times because of the greater variety of activities conducted in schools, with probably larger groups of students using more complicated and more dangerous equipment than formerly: see *McKay et al. v. The Board of Govan School Unit No. 29 of Saskatchewan et. al.* (1968), 68 D.L.R. (2d) *519*. . . , but with the qualification expressed in the *McKay* case and noted by Carrothers J.A. in *Thornton supra,* it remains the appropriate standard for such cases. It is not, however, a standard which can be applied in the same manner and to the same extent in every case. Its application will vary from case to case and will depend upon the number of students being supervised at any given time, the nature of the exercise or activity in progress, the age and the degree of skill and training which the students may have received in connection with such activity, the nature and condition of the equipment in use at the time, the competency and capacity of the students involved, and a host of other matters which may be

---

13 *Williams v. Eady*, above, note 11, at 42.
14 *Ramsden v. Hamilton (Bd. of Education)*, [1942] 1 D.L.R. 770 at 773 (Ont. H.C.).
15 See *Thornton,* below, note 19 (B.C. C.A.) and *Gard v. Duncan (Bd. of School Trustees)*, [1946] 2 D.L.R. 441 (B.C. C.A.).
16 (1981), 123 D.L.R. (3d) 1 (S.C.C.).

widely varied but which, in a given case, may affect the application of the prudent-parent standard to the conduct of the school authority in the circumstances.[17]

After considering the evidence as to what procedures and equipment were in use leading up to the plaintiff's accident, the Court (McIntyre J.) stated:

> Against this background I am unable to conclude that a prudent parent would be content to provide as protective matting only the two and one-half inch compressed slab mats when other and more protective mats could be obtained. I am also unable to conclude that, considering the nature of the activity which was contemplated in the gymnastics course, a prudent parent would have been content to have his son permitted to depart from the gymnasium into a room where there would be no adult supervision to practice gymnastic manoeuvres on the rings which could involve the straddle dismount with its potential dangers.[18]

Prior to the *Myers* case, the Supreme Court of Canada considered an appeal from the British Columbia Court of Appeal in the case of *Thornton v. Prince George (Board of School Trustees of School District No. 57).*[19] In the Supreme Court of Canada, the Court dealt with the question of assessment of damages; there was no appeal as to the finding of liability. However, the analysis by Carrothers J. in the British Columbia Court of Appeal as to the standard of care was accepted by the Supreme Court of Canada in *Myers*. The test used by Carrothers J. has become the definitive guide to courts across Canada for assessing liability in similar fact situations.

Like the *Myers* case, *Thornton* dealt with a claim by a 15-year-old pupil who was very seriously injured in gymnastics class. As far as could be determined or inferred from the testimony at trial, the plaintiff jumped off a vaulting box onto a springboard and attempted an aerial somersault. He overshot the landing pit and landed on his head on a thinner mat on the periphery of the pit. The trial judge found the physical education instructor liable, and found the school board vicariously liable for the negligence of the instructor.

The British Columbia Court of Appeal provided an important analysis of negligence law as it relates to activities, such as gymnastics, where there is an element of inherent danger:

1. There is an element of risk or danger in gymnastics which was known to the plaintiff and the school authorities.
2. The plaintiff participated in the aerial somersault of his own free will,

---

17 *Ibid.,* at 10.
18 *Ibid.,* at 10-11.
19 (1975), 57 D.L.R. (3d) 438 (B.C. S.C.), varied on other grounds (1976), 73 D.L.R. (3d) 35 (B.C. C.A.), which was varied on other grounds (1978), 83 D.L.R. (3d) 480 (S.C.C.).

although this did not mean that he exclusively assumed the risk of the activity.
3. The school authorities had a common law duty to take care of the plaintiff during this activity in the manner of a reasonable and careful parent. This must take into account "the judicial modification of the reasonable-and-careful-parent test to allow for the larger-than-family size of the physical education class and the supraparental expertise commanded of a gymnastics instructor".[20]
4. The school authorities are not "strictly or absolutely liable for any consequential injury however occurring to any pupil in respect of whom the school authorities had accepted the responsibility of care and control".[21] It was not negligent to permit a student to perform an aerial front somersault.
5. Students may be permitted to participate in gymnastic activities provided that the following component criteria of the standard of care are adhered to:
   (a) the activity must be suitable to the pupil's age and mental and physical condition;
   (b) the pupil must be progressively trained and coached to do the activity properly and avoid the danger;
   (c) the equipment must be adequate and suitably arranged; and
   (d) the performance of the activity must be properly supervised.

These criteria are equally applicable to any similar activity by students in which there is an element of inherent danger. The inherent danger enhances the foreseeability that an accident may happen and demands greater caution on the part of school authorities. However, giving students permission to participate in dangerous activities is not negligence in and of itself.[22]

---

20 *Ibid.*, at 57 (B.C. C.A.).
21 *Ibid.*
22 *Murray v. Belleville (Bd. of Education)*, [1943] 1 D.L.R. 494 (Ont. H.C.). A 12-year-old was injured when the students formed a human pyramid. They had been properly trained and coached. There was no negligence. The mere element of danger did not mean that the school authorities were negligent. See also *Plumb (Guardian ad litem of) v. Cowichan School District No. 65* (B.C.C.A.), [1993] B.C.J. No. 1936, 1993 CarswellBC 239 (C.A.), in which the Court found that the school board was not negligent in circumstances where a child was hurt by a "mis-thrown" ball during a game of catch. The activity was not inherently dangerous and there was no reckless disregard for the safety of others. And see *Catherwood (Guardian ad litem of) v. Heinrichs*, [1996] B.C.J. No. 1373, 1996 CarswellBC 1411 (B.C.S.C.) in which the 16-year-old plaintiff was injured as a result of falling from a tree that he had climbed while waiting for his turn at baseball. The Court held that the incident could not possibly have been foreseen. The Court found that the plaintiff was not prone to climbing trees and was old enough to know better.

In the case of *Thomas v. Hamilton (City Board of Education)*,[23] the Court dealt with a claim arising out of a serious and tragic accident during a school sponsored football game. The plaintiff was, at the time of the accident, a Grade 11 student who was very athletic and an accomplished football player. The plaintiff executed a tackle and unintentionally hit the ball carrier on the thigh with his head down. The Court found that the plaintiff's helmet had become slightly dislodged as a result of the accident, and was removed by attendants prior to the plaintiff being moved onto a spinal board. Despite quick and expert medical attention, the plaintiff's injuries were such that he was rendered a quadriplegic.

The plaintiff alleged that the defendants should have warned him and his parents of the risk of playing football. It was alleged that he was not properly trained how to tackle, and that he was allowed to play although fatigued and not in proper physical condition. It was also alleged that the defendants should have known that the plaintiff's alleged "long, lean, swan neck" rendered him more susceptible to injury and that he should not have been permitted to play the position that he did.

The Court found that football is commonly known to be a dangerous sport which results in many injuries. The issue was whether, in addition to its duty as a careful or prudent parent, the board was obliged to warn the plaintiff and his mother of the additional risks involved in the plaintiff playing football. Much emphasis was placed by the plaintiff upon the theory that the board should have taken extra precautions because his long neck allegedly made him more susceptible to injury. The Court stated:

> A careful and prudent parent is not the perfect parent who explores every specialist theory. The board was in a position that it might know or have access to more information than an actual parent. However, there was no obligation upon it to be the perfect parent and explore every theory when there was no obvious reason for it to do so.[24]

The Court found that there was no evidence that the board or its coaches should have been aware of the long, swan neck theory, and they had no reason to warn the plaintiff or his parents of any additional risk by reason of the length of his neck. The Court also found that there was no evidence that the plaintiff was particularly fatigued before the accident, or that he was not in proper physical condition. It also found that the school board's standard of coaching complied with reasonable standards for junior high school football.

The evidence showed that the plaintiff and his mother knew that football is a dangerous sport and the Court found that "[t]he careful and prudent

---

23 (February 8, 1990), Steele J., Action Nos. 2754/83 and 5794/88 (Ont. H.C.); affirmed 20 O.R. (3d) 598 (C.A.).
24 *Ibid.*

parent would assume the normal risk of injury which could include an injury as serious as [the plaintiff's]." The plaintiff's mother had signed a consent for him to participate in school athletics and the plaintiff had obtained a medical certificate stating that he was fit to participate. While the consent was evidence that the mother was aware of the risks of the game and had the opportunity to refuse permission to participate, the Court noted that:

> The consent in itself does not absolve the Board because if the Board knew of, or had reason to believe that there were dangers involved that a reasonable parent would not know, or that Jeff was the subject of particular risk, then as a prudent and careful parent itself it should not have permitted him to participate in the sport.[25]

The Ontario Court of Appeal upheld the decision of the trial court.[26] After a careful review of the evidence, the first issue examined by Osborne J.A. (for the court) was the standard of care owed to the plaintiff by the school board and coaches. The appellant contended that the trial judge should not have applied a "careful or prudent parent" standard of care, but rather should have resorted to a "supraparental" standard of care. The appellant referred to comments by McIntyre J. in *Myers v. Peel County Board of Education*[27] in which McIntyre J. referred to comments about a "supraparental standard" made by Carrothers J.A. in *Thornton v. Board of School Trustees of School District No. 57 (Prince George)*.

Osborne J.A. rejected the argument that Mr. Justice Steele should have applied a higher, supraparental standard of care:

> I take McIntyre J.'s comments in *Myers* to mean no more than that the careful or prudent parent standard of care applies, but that it must be adjusted to the circumstances where, for example, in a school setting the particular expertise expected of the school authorities — those responsible for a given group of students— may extend beyond the expertise which may be provided by a careful or prudent parent.
>
> The trial judge was alert to the "qualifications" imposed upon the "careful or prudent parent" standard of care to which he resorted. I see no error in his characterization and application of the standard of care.[28]

Osborne J.A. examined in considerable detail the evidence about the "long, lean swan neck" theory asserted by the appellant. He concluded:

> In summary, the evidence supports the trial judge's findings that the long, lean swan neck theory was not widely known, particularly to coaches, and that there

---

25 *Ibid.* See also *Moore v. Hampshire County Council* (1982), 80 L.G.R. 481 (C.A.) regarding the need to check with parents as to whether a student should participate in gym activity.
26 *Thomas v. Hamilton (City) Board of Education* (1994), 20 O.R. (3d) 598 (C.A.).
27 Above, note 16.
28 Above, note 26, at 607.

was no reason why the Board should have undertaken a search of the sports medicine literature concerning serious neck injuries.[29]

Osborne J.A. also agreed with the trial judge that the evidence did not support the view that the plaintiff/appellant did, in fact, have a long, lean swan neck. He also found that "there is no evidence which provides a basis for concluding that there is a correlation between serious axial loading neck injuries and the athlete's neck configuration.[30]

In dealing with the issue of "consent" to injury, Osborne J.A. found:

> The appellant was appropriately and progressively coached. He was an excellent athlete who excelled in a number of sports, including football. His equipment was adequate. The injury he sustained occurred during a routine play and, although the consequences of his injury were, and continue to be, devastating, the injury came within the ambit of those risks inherent in a contact sport such as football. He did not, of course, give a consent which would overcome negligent conduct on the part of the Board or his coaches. However, I agree with the trial judge that neither the Board nor the coaches were negligent and that the appellant and his mother "consented to the normal risks of the game". I am not prepared to say that the trial judge was wrong in reaching that conclusion.[31]

In *Bain v. Calgary Board of Education*,[32] the Alberta Queen's Bench (Virtue J.) considered a case in which the 19-year-old plaintiff had been injured on a hike. The plaintiff was a Grade 11 student at a vocational school for the learning disabled. He was participating in a school-sponsored tour. On the evening of the accident, the students were scheduled to watch a movie. Instead, they decided that they wanted to climb a nearby mountain. Although he initially refused them permission, the defendant teacher ultimately drove them to the starting point of the climb just after 6:00 p.m., but did not accompany the students on the climb. The boys were dressed in shorts, had not eaten and took no food, water, watches or flashlights with them. When they reached a rock face and got into climbing difficulty, the plaintiff lost his grip and fell off the cliff head first onto a protruding rock. He sustained very serious permanent injuries.

Virtue J. stated:

> The fact that a student may be an adult does not detract from the fact that the student-parent relationship is one which creates a duty of care. The basis for this is that the teacher is vested with an element of control over the student, which carries with it a corresponding duty to take care for the safety of and to properly supervise the student.

---

29 *Ibid.*, at 616.
30 *Ibid.*, at 618.
31 *Ibid.*, at 619.
32 [1994] 2 W.W.R. 468 (Alta. Q.B.).

. . . .

The forestry tour was an extension of the classroom, occurring during the school year, with the specific authorization of the school board and subject to its rules and regulations. The defendant teacher remained in control of the students to the same extent as if they were in the classroom, and he owed them the same, or a higher duty of care .... The defendant teacher could have avoided the injury simply by following the agenda authorized by the school board and approved by the parents for that evening's activities. The risk of harm was reasonably foreseeable.[33]

The court held that the plaintiff had not voluntarily assumed the risk of being injured on the climb. However, the plaintiff did fail to "take proper steps for his own safety"[34] and was held 25 per cent contributorily liable.[35]

In *MacCabe v. Westlock Roman Catholic Separate School District No. 110*,[36] the Alberta Court of Appeal considered whether a school board should be held liable for injuries suffered by a 16-year-old student who was rendered quadriplegic as a result of a gymnasium accident on a box horse. The trial judge found the board liable but did not find the plaintiff contributorily negligent. The Appeal Court determined that the trial judge had followed the proper steps in her analysis of liability:

As the law required, she first determined whether a duty of care was owed by Romaniuk [the physical education teacher] to MacCabe; second, what standard of care was owed and whether that standard was met; third, if the standard of care was breached, whether that breach cause the harm suffered; and finally, whether MacCabe voluntarily accepted the risk or whether she was contributorily negligent.[37]

The Court had no difficulty in finding that a duty of care was owed to the student. As to the standard of care, the Court agreed with the trial judge that the appropriate standard of care was a modified standard, namely that of "a prudent and careful parent having the supra-parental expertise that is demanded of a gymnastics instructor", a standard formulated in *Myers*.[38]

The school board attempted to defend the action by saying that the manoeuvre by the plaintiff on the box horse (a partial back salto) was not

---

33 *Ibid.*, at 470.
34 *Ibid.*, at 471.
35 See also, *Zaba v. Saskatchewan Institute of Applied Science & Technology* (1995), [1996] 1 W.W.R. 534 (Sask. Q.B.), reversed (1997), 152 Sask. R. 245 (C.A.) where a 35 year-old nursing student was successful in a claim for damages for injuries caused when she incorrectly lifted a patient. She was held 70% contributorily negligent for not informing her instructor that she had pre-existing back problems.
36 [2001] A.J. No. 1278, 2001 CarswellAlta 1364 (C.A.).
37 *Ibid.*, para. 23.
38 Above, note 16.

an authorized manoeuvre and the criteria in *Thornton*[39] should not apply. The Court rejected this argument:

> Saying back saltos off the box horse were neither included in Romaniuk's instruction nor demonstrated, and saying the manoeuvre was expressly forbidden and the students knew they were not to attempt such a move, is not the same thing.[40]

The Court then considered whether the teacher's failure to supervise the student's activities on the box horse caused the injuries. The plaintiff was not required to show that the teacher's failure to supervise was the sole cause. The Court noted that two tests are used to determine causation, depending on the facts. One test is whether the defendant's act or omission "materially contributed" to the cause of the accident. This test was used in *Myers*.[41] The other test is the "but for test". The Court was satisfied that "but for" the teacher's lack of instruction and failure to clearly tell the students not to perform such a manoeuvre on the box horse, "but for" his failure to stop them, "but for" the presence of a crash mat, and "but for" the pressure on the students to be "creative", the plaintiff would not have attempted the partial salto. Finally, the Court had to determine if the plaintiff was contributorily negligent, and stated that the proper question to ask is whether the plaintiff took reasonable care of herself in the circumstances. The Court found that MacCabe knew or ought to have known that she might be incapable of performing the partial back salto, and knew or ought to have realized that harm was reasonably foreseeable. She was aware of the dangers of the manoeuvre and could have chosen a less hazardous one. She was found 25 per cent responsible. The Court cited *Bain v. Board of Education*[42] with approval.

(ii) *Absence of the Supervisor*

The standard of care does not require the presence of a teacher or other responsible person in the classroom or area of activity at all times.[43] For the presence of the teacher to be relevant, it must be shown on the evidence that it might have prevented the accident. The lack of supervision must be causally connected to the events giving rise to the loss or injury.

---

39 Above, note 19.
40 *Ibid.*, para. 34.
41 Above, note 16.
42 Above, note 32.
43 See, e.g., *Misir v. Children's Rehabilitation Centre of Essex county* (September 8, 1989), Doc. 2624/86, [1989] O.J. No. 1653 (Ont. Dist. Ct.), in which a teacher was not found negligent when he stepped out of his classroom for three minutes, during which an 8 year-old student managed to injure the 13 year-old plaintiff.

In *Myers,* in response to the argument by the defendant that there was no causal connection between the absence of the teacher and the accident, the Court stated:

> In my opinion, it cannot be said that the presence of a teacher among six to eight students in the exercise room would not have had a restraining effect upon the students which could have influenced the course of events and prevented the accident.[44]

In *Toronto (Board of Education) v. Higgs,* Mr. Justice Ritchie of the Supreme Court of Canada stated:

> The duty of supervision which a school authority owes to its pupils while they are at play must of necessity vary from school to school and even from day to day, and it is, therefore, not possible to elicit from the decided cases any guiding principle for the exact measurement of the degree of care to which any particular set of circumstances may give rise.[45]

The Court adopted the statement of Laidlaw J.A. in the Court below:

> It is not the duty of school authorities to keep pupils under supervision during every moment while they are in attendance at school.[46]

The Court also agreed with Morris L.J. in *Clark v. Monmouthshire County Council* who stated:

> It is not shown that this accident might not have happened whether they had been there or not. It was the sort of accident which might have happened suddenly and unexpectedly and be all over before anyone could intervene.[47]

In *Hill (Guardian ad litem of) v. Langley School District No. 35,*[48] the British Columbia Supreme Court, (Burnyeat J.) considered whether a school board was liable for injuries suffered by a student who was struck by a vehicle in the school parking lot. The plaintiff alleged that, among other things, the board did not meet the standard of care required of it in its supervision of the students as they exited the school building and site at the end of the school day. The board did in fact supervise the entrance and exit to the parking lot because it was concerned about safety. A street owned by the local municipality had essentially become an extension of the school site, and the Court found that:

> With the advent of field trips and off-site athletic events and of factors such as students and more teachers driving to school, it can no longer be said that the duty of care and supervision extends only within the strict confines of the legal

---

44 Above, note 16, at 13.
45 (1960), 22 D.L.R. (2d) 49 at 55 (S.C.C.).
46 *Ibid.,* at 58.
47 (1954), 52 L.G.R. 246 at 250.
48 [2000] B.C.J. No. 474, 2000 CarswellBC 504 (S.C. [In Chambers]).

description of what constitutes the site of a school. Rather, the "zone over which the school authorities exercise supervision" [quoting *Pearson v. Vancouver Board of School Trustees et al.*, [1941] 3 W.W.R. 874] will include areas so adjacent and so associated with the school as to be incorporated into the boundary of what would be referred to as the school grounds and areas adjacent to the school over which school authorities have undertaken supervisory authority.[49]

The Court found that the appropriate standard of care was that of a careful or prudent parent and that the amount of supervision provided by the school was inadequate. "One teacher and an indefinite and unscheduled number of administrative staff" were on duty to supervise the entire school grounds of a school holding 1200 pupils. The issue then became whether the lack of proper supervision caused the accident. Citing *Mainville v. Ottawa (Board of Education)*[50] the Court held that no amount of supervision or surveillance would have prevented the accident. Moreover, the school had taken steps to educate its students about traffic safety. The Court dismissed the claim. (The liability of the driver who was alleged to have hit the plaintiff had not been determined.)

In *Ramsden v. Hamilton (Board of Education)*,[51] a 16-year-old student injured himself by flicking a chisel into a revolving sander. In finding the plaintiff solely responsible for the accident, the Ontario High Court found that the presence or absence of the teacher in the room "had nothing to do with the accident."[52] In *Butterworth v. Ottawa (Collegiate Institute Board)*,[53] the Court was faced with a lack of evidence as to how the 14-year-old plaintiff injured his elbow while vaulting a horse in gymnastics class. Two senior boys were left in charge and the teacher was not present at the time of the accident. The Court was unable to determine the exact cause of the accident and was therefore not satisfied that the absence of the teacher was causally connected to the accident. The plaintiff was held to be responsible for the accident because he knew he was clumsy and he knew that he should have had spotters. Knowing the danger, he voluntarily assumed the risk of vaulting the horse. It is probable that, in view of *Thornton,* a court today would likely find the defendant liable on the same facts.[54]

---

49 *Ibid.*
50 (1990), 75 O.R. (2d) 315 (Prov. Ct.).
51 Above, note 14.
52 Above, note 14, at 772.
53 [1940] 3 D.L.R. 466 (Ont. H.C.).
54 See also *Pepin v. Lincoln County (Bd. of Education)* (1983), 22 A.C.W.S. (2d) 302 (Ont. H.C.); *Cirillo v. Milwaukee,* 150 N.W. 2d 460 (Wis. 1967); *Segerman v. Jones,* 259 A. 2d 794 (Md. 1969); and *O'Brien v. Procureur General de la province de Que.,* [1961] S.C.R. 184; *Magnusson v. Nipawin Board* (1975), 60 D.L.R. (3d) 572, (board not liable when pupil injured by broken glass on nearby fairground during recess).

Earlier reported cases such as *Butterworth* and *Ramsden* often reflect the fact that school boards did not carry liability insurance to the extent that they do now. It is apparent that some courts believed that, for social policy reasons, the school ratepayers should not be burdened with large damage awards. The cases also reflect a judicial attitude toward students which is considered old-fashioned today — that if they hurt themselves it was their own fault or it was "to be expected".

(iii) *Modified Standards of Care*

Courts will vary or modify the required standard of care, according to the individual circumstances of each case. The imposition of a higher duty of care where students are involved in inherently dangerous activities reflects the fact that a reasonably prudent parent would take extra precautions and that teachers should do likewise. The continuum envisaged in *Myers* simply reflects the fact that different situations call for different precautions and responses. For instance, this was clearly the case in *Dziwenka v. R.*[55] where the Supreme Court of Canada stated that a teacher should have been especially vigilant when teaching woodworking to a class of learning disabled (hearing impaired) students.

In *McKay v. Board of Govan School Unit No. 29 of Saskatchewan*,[56] the Supreme Court of Canada dealt specifically with the issue of whether a physical education instructor had a higher duty of care toward pupils than the traditional prudent parent standard. In this case, a high school student was severely injured when he attempted a dismount from the parallel bars apparatus in gymnastics. There were 12 to 18 students in the group under the supervision of the instructor at the time. The evidence showed that the plaintiff had minimal experience on the parallel bars and that the instructor had not demonstrated the dismount. The spotters were not in a position to assist the plaintiff when he fell.

The trial judge had instructed the jury that the appropriate duty of care was that which a careful father of a large family owed to his children. On appeal, the Saskatchewan Court of Appeal said that the "careful father" standard, while it might apply in other situations, did not apply to the facts of this case. Mr Justice Woods of the Court of Appeal stated:

> A physical training instructor in directing or supervising an evolution or exercise is bound to exercise the skill and competence of an ordinarily competent instructor in the field. The standard of the careful parent does not fit a responsibility which demands special training and expertise.[57]

---

55 Above, note 12.
56 Above, note 12.
57 *McKay*, above, note 12, at 523.

The Supreme Court of Canada considered whether the Saskatchewan Court of Appeal was correct in stating that the trial judge had misdirected the jury as to the standard of care. In considering the trial judge's application of the "careful father" test, as originally expounded in *Williams v. Eady*,[58] Mr. Justice Ritchie stated:

> While I am not satisfied that this definition is of universal application, particularly in cases where a schoolmaster is required to instruct or supervise the activities of a great number of pupils at one time, I am nevertheless of the opinion that a small group, such as that which [the instructor] had in his charge in the improvised gymnasium, is one to which Lord Escher's words do apply.[59]

Although the *Williams v. Eady* standard was held to apply to the facts of the *McKay* case, there was also judicial recognition that some situations may require a higher standard of care than that of the "careful parent". Both *Myers*[60] and *Thornton*[61] agreed with *McKay* that the careful parent test could be modified in light of the expertise and training required to teach and supervise students in dangerous activities.

On the facts of the *McKay* case, Ritchie J. was satisfied that the trial judge had not misdirected the jury. He also noted that the trial judge, in applying the standard of a "careful parent", rather than a "physical training instructor", had applied a lower standard of care — one which the defendant school board would be able to meet more easily. The board was therefore hardly in a position to complain that it should have been held to the higher standard.

Other court decisions, while acknowledging the existence of the prudent parent standard, have in fact applied a "reasonably prudent teacher" standard. In *Higgs*,[62] the Court had to consider whether the school's practice of having four teachers on school yard supervision was negligent. Whereas in the Court below, Laidlaw J.A. had applied the "careful father" standard, Ritchie J. distinguished between the duty which applies to teachers and that which applies to school authorities:

> [I]t seems to me that the analogy between the duty of a school master to his pupils and that of a parent to his children, while it applies with some force to the duty which the individual master owes to children under his care, cannot be related with the same validity to the responsibilities of organization and administration which rested on Mr. Macpherson as principal of a school with an enrolment of 750 pupils.[63]

---

58 Above, note 11.
59 Above, note 12, at 523.
60 Above, note 16.
61 Above, note 19 (B.C. C.A.).
62 Above, note 45.
63 Above, note 45, at 55-56.

The relevant question was what "standard of organization the law required of the school authority."[64] While a school board may be held vicariously liable for the negligence of its employees for actions done in the course of their duties, the board may also be held liable of its own accord. The *Higgs* case raises the argument that a different standard of care may apply to the board as a corporate entity, as compared to the standard which applies to individual employees. Thus, a policy of using four supervisors to supervise the playground may or may not meet the required standard of care, and the Court in *Higgs* found that the prudent parent standard was not particularly useful in deciding this issue.

On the facts, the Court decided that the system of supervision used by the principal was reasonably safe, having regard to the number and age of the children. The prevailing winter conditions did not "indicate a condition which would cause a *prudent school principal* to anticipate danger to his pupils . . . ."[65] As an implementer of school policies and procedures, the principal was not judged against the standard of a prudent parent, but rather against the standard of a prudent principal. The board was ultimately found to be liable in *Higgs,* but only because its employees failed to treat the plaintiff's injuries with due care after the accident occurred.

The case of *Brown v. Essex (County) Roman Catholic Separate School Board,*[66] involved an accident in a sewing class. The plaintiff was in a Grade 8 cooking and sewing class comprised of 13 students, five of whom were doing sewing activities at the time of the accident. The teacher had demonstrated and instructed sewing activities prior to the day of the accident. Students had practised sewing on paper, but not on cloth. They had not been instructed on what to do if the cloth "bunched". Bunching causes the needle to stay in one spot, creating a knot which the needle eventually cannot penetrate. This causes the bottom part of the needle to break. The plaintiff did not stop the sewing machine when the cloth bunched, and the needle broke into three pieces. One piece became imbedded in his right eye, resulting in some permanent impairment of his vision.

The major issue in this case was whether or not the injury was reasonably foreseeable. Testimony of sewing teachers and sewing machine experts revealed that they had never heard of an eye injury from a broken sewing machine needle, although other types of injury were not unknown. The question was not whether it was reasonably foreseeable that a needle might break but whether the manner of breaking and the injury to the eye were reasonably foreseeable. Mr. Justice Ewaschuk found that "the plaintiff's injury was of the type or kind which a prudent parent or teacher might have

---

64 Above, note 45, at 56.
65 Above, note 45, at 57 [emphasis added].
66 (August 10, 1990), Ewaschuk J., Action No. 453/85 (Ont. H.C.) (as reported in LEXUS 209).

foreseen."[67] He cited the case of *Hughes v. Lord Advocate* to establish that liability is incurred even though "the danger actually materialising is not identical with the danger reasonably foreseen and guarded against."[68]

In addressing the liability of the sewing teacher, the Court found that she "did not act as would a careful or prudent parent with her background in and knowledge of sewing."[69] From this it appears that her experience as a sewing teacher was held to be an integral element which determined what standard of conduct the plaintiff had a right to expect of her. The Court went on to state: "In the end, I find that a *reasonably prudent sewing teacher* owed students the duty of care to have warned them of the particular dangers involved in sewing on the spot."[70] Thus, after duly acknowledging the prudent parent standard, the Court went one step further and created an additional standard: the "reasonably prudent sewing teacher".

The decision of the British Columbia Court of Appeal in *Hoar v. Nanaimo (Board of School Trustees, District 68)*[71] indicates that some courts will hold teachers to a very high standard of care. In this case, a 17-year-old boy injured himself on a wood jointer. He had missed five demonstration lessons on the use of the jointer. In finding the teacher 50 per cent liable, the Court said that the teacher should have known that the plaintiff was absent for the demonstration lessons, and should have held a make-up lesson for him. This places a fairly stringent, and at times impractical, burden upon the classroom teacher. Students who are in courses where the classroom activities have a high degree of risk are entitled to full and complete instruction, no matter what the practical difficulties.

In *Plumley v. North York Board of Education*,[72] the plaintiff was injured during a swimming class. She alleged that she suffered an injury to her shoulder when an instructional assistant pulled her part-way out of the pool by her right arm in an effort to demonstrate a pool rescue technique called "resecuring". The trial judge (Garton J.) found that the force applied by the assistant was in fact excessive and the manner in which she performed the resecuring manoeuvre was unreasonable. The Court held that the assistant "did not act in the circumstances as would a careful or prudent parent with her background in and knowledge of swimming and lifeguarding techniques."[73] After reviewing the medical evidence about the injury to the plaintiff's shoulder, the Court was satisfied that the injury was in fact caused by the assistant pulling the plaintiff part-way out of the water in a forceful manner, and that the *injury* was reasonably foreseeable by someone with

---

67 *Ibid.*, LEXUS 209, at p. 5.
68 [1963] A.C. 837 at 850 (H.L.).
69 *Brown*, above, note 57, LEXUS 209, at p. 5.
70 *Ibid. [emphasis added]*.
71 [1984] 6 W.W.R. 143 (B.C. C.A.).
72 [2000] O.J. No. 2636, 2000 CarswellOnt 2439 (S.C.J.).
73 *Ibid.*, para. 79.

the assistant's "training and experience in swimming and lifeguarding techniques".[74]

The classroom teacher was also held liable for lack of instruction:

> It was almost inevitable and certainly foreseeable in the circumstances that while practicing [sic] the method, a rescuer would lose her grip on a victim. The lack of instruction in this regard laid the groundwork for, or gave rise to, the circumstances in which the plaintiff was injured. By failing to have Greenhough [the assistant] advise the students on what to do in this situation, Ruprecht [the teacher] failed to meet the instructional component inherent in the standard of care expected of a prudent parent with her expertise in swimming.[75]

The school board was held vicariously liable for the negligence of the teacher and assistant.

(iv) *Proximate Cause and Foreseeability*

There must be a link or relationship between the defendant's conduct and the plaintiff's injury. Courts often use what is known as the "but-for" test in determining the issue: would the accident have occurred but for the defendant's negligence?

After being satisfied that the defendant breached his or her duty of care toward the plaintiff, and that there was a link between the defendant's conduct and the injury, the court must still be satisfied that the defendant's conduct was the proximate cause of the injury. In other words, the injury must not be too remote in relation to what the defendant has been found to have done. Courts have applied a number of different tests to determine the issue of remoteness. Generally speaking, a defendant will not be held liable for injury or loss which, although they can be traced to the defendant's conduct, were completely unpredictable or which occurred after unforeseeable intervening events or intervening negligence on the part of another person.

In *Moddejonge v. Huron County (Board of Education)*,[76] the Ontario High Court dealt with a claim arising from a tragic drowning accident. On a field trip, an outdoor education instructor permitted a small number of students to go swimming in a reservoir. The instructor indicated to the students where there was a drop-off under the water and told them not to go beyond that point. However, the drop-off line was irregular and was not indicated by buoys. A breeze came up and apparently pushed one of students, who could not swim, beyond the drop-off. Another student drowned while unsuccessfully attempting to rescue the first.

---

74 *Ibid.*, para. 127.
75 *Ibid.*, para. 80.
76 [1972] 2 O.R. 437 (H.C.).

The Court applied the *Williams v. Eady* prudent parent test, and stated: "It was the duty of [the instructor] to guard, in the same manner as a reasonably prudent parent would guard, against foreseeable risks to which [the plaintiff] was exposed under the circumstances:"[77] A number of factors led to the conclusion that the instructor was liable. He had permitted the students to go into water where there was a dangerous drop-off. He did not swim and had not ensured that life-saving equipment was readily available. When a breeze came up, he had not taken steps to guard against the foreseeable risk which it posed to the students. The Court also found him liable for the death of the student who had tried to rescue the other plaintiff, as this was a foreseeable response to the emergency which had been created through his negligence.

The cases show that the issue of whether or not an accident was foreseeable is often determined by looking at the age and capacity of the pupils involved. If the class is boisterous or excitable, the foreseeability of an accident happening is increased. Therefore, it is important for the defendant to show that the class or activity was being conducted in a reasonably controlled and disciplined manner. In *Fraser v. Campbell River (Board of School Trustees of School District No. 72)*,[78] students were playing in the snow on a school ground when one of the students injured himself by diving into the snow. The plaintiff had not been behaving in a manner which would have made his action reasonably foreseeable by the teacher, and the teacher was not found liable for his injuries.

In *McCue v. Etobicoke (Board of Education)*,[79] a high school student was injured when hit in the eye with a paper clip fired by another student. The incident took place before class began, when no teacher was present, and the Court found that there was no reason to anticipate that the paper clip shooting would take place. In *Crouch v. Essex County Council*,[80] the Court considered an incident which took place during a science lesson comprised of 15-year-old students. A student was deliberately sprayed with caustic soda by another student. The Court was satisfied that the teacher had maintained a reasonable standard of discipline in the class and that, on the whole, the class was being well-behaved. The students were warned about the dangers of using caustic soda and it was not foreseeable that a student would deliberately spray another with the chemical.

(v) *Transportation of Pupils*

When a school board provides for the transportation of pupils to and from school, or on school trips, it has an obligation to take reasonable steps

---

77 *Ibid.*, at 442-443. *Williams v. Eady* (1893), 10 T.L.R. 41 (C.A.).
78 (1987), 5 A.C.W.S. (3d) 300 (B.C. S.C.).
79 (1982), 18 A.C.W.S. (2d) 128 (Ont. H.C.).
80 (1966), 64 L. G. R. 240.

to ensure the safety of the pupils against foreseeable risk of harm. Transportation may be provided directly by the board, using board-owned buses and board employee-drivers. A board may also enter into a contract with a bus company to provide the transportation. In the latter case, issues may arise as to whether the school board or the bus company should bear the legal responsibility for an accident arising out of negligent transportation. The bus company will be held liable in negligence if it was an independent contractor whose operations were not controlled by the school board.[81] However, if the bus company was required to follow practices or procedures prescribed by the board, thus giving the board meaningful control over the bus company's operations, a court will be more inclined to hold the board legally responsible.[82]

The board and bus company may also be held jointly and severally liable. The plaintiff may also take the position that, even where the bus company is an independent contractor, the school board should be found liable for hiring an incompetent bus company, or for ignoring previous reports of unsafe mechanical condition or unsafe operation of the buses. Where children are transported by taxi, the board may be held liable for not ensuring that the driver was competent, even though the taxi driver would normally be considered an independent contractor.

In *Scott v. Thompson*,[83] a bus driver was found liable for an accident which arose because he left the children on the bus unsupervised while he went for a cup of coffee. The plaintiff student left the bus and was hit while crossing the street. In another case, *Slade v. New Hanover County Board of Education*,[84] the school system was held liable when a child was run over after departing a school bus. The bus route had been changed, and the child was not accustomed to crossing the street to his house after being let off. In *Taylor v. Patterson's Administrator*,[85] the bus driver failed to operate the stop sign on the bus when a pupil was being discharged. In holding the driver negligent, the Court said that the duty of care for a child's safety was

---

81 *Baldwin v. Lyons* (1961), 29 D.L.R. (2d) 290 (Ont. C.A.), affirmed (1962), 36 D.L.R. (2d) 244 *(sub nom. Baldwin v. Erin (Dist. High School Bd.); McKinney v. Erin (Dist. High School Bd.))* (S.C.C.).
82 *Mattinson v. Wonnacott* (1975), 8 O.R. (2d) 654 (H.C.) — kindergarten child hit by car; let off bus at wrong location; driver, bus company, board and driver of vehicle that struck child all held liable. *George v. Port Alberni (Bd. of Trustees, School Dist. 70)* (1986), 3 A.C.W.S. (3d) 361 (B.C. S.C.); *Barnes v. Hampshire County Council*, [1969] 3 All E.R. 746 (H.L.) — five-year-old child let out early; hit when crossing the road alone; defendant found liable. *Edmondson v. Moose Jaw (Bd. of Trustees)* (1920), 55 D.L.R. 563 (Sask. C.A.) — no liability when 8-year-old child injured while watching other students jumping over a cross-pole; accident occurred five minutes after school dismissed: "It was out of school hours; his duty was to go home." Per Elwood J.A. at 573.
83 363 N.E. 2d 295 (1977).
84 178 S.E. 2d 316, 10 N.C. App. 287 (1971).
85 114 S.W. 2d 488, 272 Ky. 415 (1938).

owed until the child got to the side of the street where the child's home was located. Clearly, the duty of the bus driver goes beyond the duty to drive safely. The driver and the driver's employer have a duty to supervise the pupils on the bus, to supervise them during boarding, to provide safe pick-up areas, and to discharge at safe locations.

McEvay v. Torry[86] was an action against a transit bus driver. The infant plaintiff, aged 6, had missed the school bus and the bus driver agreed to a request by the plaintiff's mother to drive him to school. The plaintiff ignored the driver's instructions to cross the road carefully at a point behind the bus. Instead, he crossed in front of the bus and was injured by a car. The Court held that the driver was not negligent.

> It would be asking too much of the defendant bus driver to expect him to get out of the bus and help this child across the road . . . . That he had omitted specifically to alert the boy to approaching traffic, which might have been seen at the material time in his rear-view mirror, was likewise no evidence of negligence, since his attention was required to various other matters.

In *Dao (Guardian ad litem of) v. Sabatino*[87] the six year-old plaintiff was severely injured when he ran into traffic while returning home from school at mid-day. The Vancouver school district (District 39) was made a defendant and it was alleged that the board had been negligent in failing to implement a crossing guard program, to instruct children in coping with traffic, or otherwise in supervising or monitoring the street crossing behaviour of the children in its charge. The claim against the board was dismissed. The school followed a detailed and repetitive practice of continuing education of children and of their parents in respect of traffic safety. Traffic rules were posted and reinforced in classes and with individual pupils. Outside agencies and police workers visited the school to help instill traffic awareness. The school district had met the standard of care required of it.

(vi) *Negligence Outside School Hours*

The school's duty of care applies in relation to students during school hours and during school-related activities outside normal school hours. These activities include field trips and extra-curricular activities. Students participate in these activities as students, not as members of the general public, and the "prudent parent" standard applies.

Issues arise as to the board's legal responsibility when a student is injured on board property before or after school hours while not participating in a school-related activity. The classic example occurs when a child shows up too early for school, or does not leave in a timely fashion after school. When does a person change from "child" to "student"? The court must

---

86 (1988), 46 C.C.L.T. 85 (B.C. S.C.).
87 (1993), 16 C.C.L.T. (2d) 235 (B.C. S.C.).

determine what the child was doing on the property outside school hours, and what the expectations of the child, the parents and the school were in relation to the provision of supervision and other safety measures.

If a child is not participating in a school-related activity, and is using the property outside regular school hours, then the child is owed the same duty of care which applies to any young member of the public using the property.[88] School opening and closing times must be clearly communicated to parents and children. There is a strong obligation upon parents to respect the designated school hours and not to presume that schools will automatically provide supervision outside those hours. There is also a strong obligation upon schools to be consistent in their practices. Otherwise, children, parents and staff will not know when the supervision actually starts and finishes. Legislation or regulation may prescribe the maximum length of the school day, or the time at which the school must be open to the pupils.[89] However, in a civil suit, the actual opening or closing times of the school are more relevant: in other words, at what times would the parent or child expect school supervision to be in effect?

Another obligation upon schools is to avoid sending younger pupils into a situation of danger off school property.[90] If a child is stranded at school due to an emergency, or must unexpectedly go home early, it is not sufficient for schools to say that they owe no legal duty to the child after the child leaves the property. Common sense precautions must be taken, even if it means driving the child home or calling a taxi. In addition, keeping pupils after school for detentions may give rise to safety and transportation concerns, depending on their age and the distance they must travel.[91]

(vii) *Negligence and Sexual Misconduct*

Elsewhere in this chapter, we indicate that sexual misconduct may, like other forms of unwanted conduct, comprise the intentional tort of either "assault" or "battery", or both. The intentional action of a staff member or student in sexually abusing, attacking or molesting a student is not negli-

---

88 See section on occupiers' liability, below. See also *Lataille v. Farnham (Commissaires d'Écolés de la Municipalité Scolaire)* (1975), 9 N.R. 368 (S.C.C.) regarding use of school property outside school hours.
89 See *e.g.*, R.R.O. 1990, Reg. 298, ss. 3 and 20(d).
90 *Barnes v. Hampshire County Council*, above, note 82— early release of child led to her death; school held liable. See also *Titus v. Lindberg*, 228 A. 2d 65 (1967)—liability toward student who arrived early; *Lawes v. New York (Bd. of Education)*, 213 N.E. 2d 667, 266 N.Y.S 2d 364, 16 N.Y. 2d 302 (1965) — board not liable for injury to student caused by snowball throwing on the way to school. See also *Oglesby v. Seminole County Bd. of Public Instruction*, 328 So. 2d 515 (1976) — board not liable for injuries due to assault between students while walking home.
91 Eugene T. Connors, *Educational Tort Liability and Malpractice* (Bloomington, Ind.: Phi Delta Kappa, 1981), at p. 67.

gence. However, under some circumstances, teachers, administrators and the board itself may be found liable for negligently permitting such misconduct to occur or continue to occur.

In his examination of the legal implications of child abuse in schools, William Foster maintains that teachers may be found liable if they fail to respond appropriately when a student is being abused at school or if they fail to identify or recognize situations of abuse.[92]

This overriding duty means that, quite apart from their statutory duty to report abuse, school administrators cannot afford to ignore information which comes to them, from whatever source, in relation to possible abuse of pupils by staff, visitors or fellow pupils. Comprehensive documentation must be maintained in order to be in a position to prove to a court that oral or written reports of abuse were dealt with quickly and appropriately by those who had the authority to act.

Provided that the elements of negligence are proved by the plaintiff, the board itself may incur liability for negligence where its pupils have been sexually assaulted or abused.[93] Although a board is not the absolute insurer of the safety of its pupils, it has a clear legal obligation to take reasonable steps to ensure their safety from foreseeable harm. This includes taking appropriate steps to ensure that board employees do not pose a risk to the pupils. This obligation involves proper screening during the hiring process, checking of references, investigating properly whenever suspicions are reported, and ensuring that substantiated incidents are properly dealt with through dismissal or other disciplinary measures.

The board must also take reasonable steps to ensure pupils' safety from the sexual misconduct of other students and of visitors to the school. For instance, if a student is known, from prior incidents, to have a propensity to engage in sexually inappropriate conduct with other students, extra supervision on the part of the school is required, and the school may ultimately need to separate the dangerous pupil from potential victims, or consider expulsion of the pupil.

On June 27, 2002, the *Student Protection Act, 2002*[94] received Royal Assent and will come into force on proclamation. The Act amends the *Education Act*, the *Ontario College of Teachers Act, 1996* and the *Teaching Profession Act*. The amendments require a school board that has become aware of a teacher employed by it who has been charged with or convicted of certain *Criminal Code* offences to ensure that the teacher performs no

---

92 William F. Foster, "Child Abuse in Schools: The Statutory and Common Law Obligations of Educators", (1993) 4 E.L.J. 1.
93 *Lyth v. Dagg* (1988), 46 C.C.L.T. 25 (B.C. S.C.), in which the Court held a teacher liable in tort for causing a pupil emotional trauma caused by the teacher's sexual misconduct. The board and vice-principal were found to have a duty of care toward the student, but the facts indicated that they had discharged that duty and they were not found liable.
94 S.O. 2000, c. 7.

duties involving contact with pupils. It adds a definition of "sexual abuse" to the *Ontario College of Teachers Act, 1996*, and provides that "professional misconduct" as defined under that Act includes sexual abuse of a student by a member of the College.

The amendments require an employer of a member of the Ontario College of Teachers to report to the College where the employer terminates the member's employment or restricts the member's duties for reasons of professional misconduct. An employer of a member must report to the College if the employer intended to terminate the member's employment or restrict the member's duties for reasons of professional misconduct but did not do so because the member resigned. The employer is required to report to the College if the member resigns while the employer is engaged in an investigation into allegations of an act or omission by the member that would, if proven, have caused the employer to terminate the member's employment or to impose restrictions on the member's duties for reasons of professional misconduct. Employers must report to the College when they become aware that a member employee has been charged with or convicted of certain offences under the *Criminal Code*, or has engaged in conduct that, in the opinion of the employer, should be reviewed by a committee of the College. Section 12 of the *Teaching Profession Act* has been amended to provide that a member of the Ontario Teachers' Federation who makes an adverse report about another member of the Federation respecting suspected sexual abuse of a student by that other member need not advise the other member of the report.

It is arguable that a board could be found liable for injuries sustained by a pupil who is enrolled elsewhere, if it failed to advise subsequent employers of the misconduct of its former employee upon being called for references, or if it failed to advise the appropriate provincial authorities.[95] However, the plaintiff may have difficulty establishing a sufficient connection between a board's failure to provide information about its former employee and the injury sustained by a pupil who is not even within its jurisdiction. In addition, the fact that an employee has been convicted of a sexual offence and has been dismissed by a prior employer, does not automatically mean that he or she will repeat this behaviour.

(d) Defences to Negligence Claims

The defendant in a negligence action will attempt to show that the elements of negligence have not been proved by the plaintiff. Even if this is unsuccessful, it is still open to the defendant to try to defeat the claim on the basis that the plaintiff was contributorily negligent, or that the plaintiff voluntarily assumed the risk of injury.

---

95 Foster, above, note 81, at p. 51.

(i) *Contributory Negligence*

Students have a duty to act with reasonable care for their own safety. Therefore, it is open to the defendant in a school negligence lawsuit to attempt to prove that the plaintiff-student breached this duty, and thereby caused or contributed to his or her own injury or loss. There are many cases where students have been found to have been contributorily negligent. The student's conduct will be judged according to a variety of considerations, including the age of the student, whether the student ignored warnings, and whether the student should have realized that he or she was not sufficiently trained, fit or knowledgeable to do the activity.

In *Myers v. Peel County (Board of Education)*,[96] the plaintiff was held to be partly responsible for injuries sustained in dismounting gymnastic rings. In the Supreme Court of Canada, McIntyre J. adopted the statement of Brooks J.A. in the Court of Appeal:

> In my opinion, the learned trial Judge correctly found that there was contributory negligence on the part of [the plaintiff] in performing a difficult manoeuvre, fraught with danger, without announcing his move and without the presence of a spotter in position to break his fall.[97]

The risky nature of gymnastics imposes a higher standard of care on the plaintiff, as well as the defendant.

In *Ramsden v. Hamilton (Board of Education)*,[98] the plaintiff was held to be completely at fault for injuries sustained by flicking a chisel into a rotating sanding wheel during woodworking class. In *Butterworth v. Ottawa (Collegiate Institute Board),* the Court held the plaintiff responsible for his own injuries sustained on a vaulting horse, stating:

> Notwithstanding that it was the duty of the defendant to anticipate that boys using a gymnasium equipped with gymnastic apparatus would have a tendency to use that apparatus, and also that it may very well be that it was the duty of the defendant to recognize that the use of gymnastic apparatus, such as a vaulting horse, involves the risk of injury, I am of the opinion that boys of 14 years of age are capable of and indeed should be held to exercise reasonable intelligence and care for their own safety.[99]

In *Brown v. Essex (County) Roman Catholic Separate School Board,* where a broken sewing needle caused partial impairment of the plaintiff's eye, Mr. Justice Ewashuk applied the standard of a "reasonably prudent and intelligent student" in considering the issue of contributory negligence:

---

96 (1981), 123 D.L.R. (3d) 1 (S.C.C.).
97 *Ibid.,* at 14.
98 [1942] 1 D.L.R. 770 (Ont. H.C.).
99 [1940] 3 D.L.R. 466 at 472 (Ont. H.C.).

The standard to be applied to the plaintiff is that of the reasonably prudent and intelligent student in Grade 8. The question then is whether that student would be at fault in acting in like circumstances as the plaintiff did.[100]

The Court found the plaintiff to have been 10 per cent contributorily negligent, "given his young age and the novel event he experienced."[101]

The Ontario *Negligence Act*[102] provides that a court may apportion liability against the plaintiff if fault or negligence is found on the part of the plaintiff that contributed to the damages. Section 4 of the Act provides that:

> If it is not practicable to determine the respective degree of fault or negligence as between any parties to an action, such parties shall be deemed to be equally at fault or negligent.

(ii) *Voluntary Assumption of Risk*

A defendant to a negligence suit may defend it on the basis that the plaintiff voluntarily assumed the risk that he or she would suffer injury or loss. Risk may be voluntarily assumed by the express act of the plaintiff, or voluntary assumption may be implied from the plaintiff's actions. Knowledge by the plaintiff that an activity is risky is not enough to establish the defence. There must be a voluntary express or implied agreement by the plaintiff to waive the right to claim damages for any injury which might occur as a result of the defendant's breach of the duty of care.[103]

For boards and teachers, the concept of voluntary assumption of risk is most relevant in the area of sports. Participation in many sports involves an implied consent by the participants to accidental injuries that arise in the normal course of the activity. Players will not be held liable for actions that might constitute negligence outside the sports activity. However, implied consent only extends to normal risk. The courts will draw the line at injuries that result from deliberate attempts to cause severe injury, and they will not imply consent to dangers that are not obvious to the plaintiff or are not a necessary part of the activity.

(e) Negligence Involving Minors

Injuries to students or staff members may result from a student's conduct. For example, a student who accidentally injures another student with a snowball during recess may be sued by the injured student.[104] The issue arises, therefore, as to what circumstances permit a court to find a young

---

100 (August 10, 1990), Ewaschuk J., Action No. 453/85 (Ont. H.C.) (as reported in LEXUS 209, at p. 3).
101 *Ibid.*, LEXUS 209, at p. 4.
102 R.S.O. 1990, c. N.1.
103 *Waldick v. Malcolm* (1991), 83 D.L.R. (4th) 114 (S.C.C.).
104 *Mainville v. Ottawa (Bd. of Education)* (1990), 75 O.R. (2d) 315 (Prov. Ct., Civ. Div.).

person negligent, or contributorily negligent.[105] Some basic principles can be derived from the cases:

- Minors of "tender age" cannot be found negligent or contributorily negligent. Although there is no firm rule, "tender age" appears to be under 6 years.[106]
- Minors between tender age and adulthood may be found negligent but the standard of care which is applied depends on a number of variables. The court will ask whether the child "exercised the care to be expected from a child of like age, intelligence and experience."[107] One can imagine the difficulties inherent in attempting to establish a relatively objective basis for determining the standard of care which should apply to a minor in a given fact situation. Reasonably careful children are prone to doing unusual or mischievous acts as part of their normal behaviour. How does one not penalize the defendant child for being a child, while striving for some reasonable standard of care? Incorporating elements of intelligence and experience, rather than using age as the sole criterion, makes the standard of care partially subjective; it allows to some extent for the nature of the particular defendant.
- When a child is engaged in an activity which is considered to be an adult activity, such as driving an automobile, the child will generally be held to the same standard of care as would be expected of a reasonable adult. One might conclude from this that the practice of placing senior students as volunteer supervisors in charge of younger pupils may result in a senior student being held to the careful parent standard of care if an accident occurs, despite the fact that the student may be lacking the knowledge and experience of an adult supervisor. This could attract personal liability on the part of the student supervisor. The board could be held liable for using the student as a supervisor, and vicariously liable for the student's actions.

(f) Consent to Participate

The written consent of parents should be obtained in order for pupils who are legally minors to participate in any activity which is either unusual or outside the regular classroom routine.[108] This includes field trips, sports, extracurricular clubs, and helping to supervise younger children. The consent may be useful in helping to show a court that the school was not negligent in permitting the child to participate in the activity. It is essential

---

105 For a full discussion of the issues, see Linden, *Canadian Tort Law* (Butterworths Toronto: 2001) at 140-146.
106 Linden, above, at 140.
107 *McEllistrum v. Etches*, [1956] S.C.R. 787 at 793.
108 See *Thomas v. Hamilton (City) Board of Education*, above, note 26.

that the parent understand what the consent is for. In other words, the proposed activity must be thoroughly outlined in writing in order for the parent to be able to judge whether or not the student should participate. For example, permission to participate in "sports" is inadequate; the individual sports must be named. In the case of sports activities, if the student is sufficiently mature, it is recommended that the student also be asked to sign a form acknowledging that he or she wants to participate despite the potential risk of injury. Legal advice should be obtained when drafting parental and student consent forms. A waiver or release of legal rights is distinct from a consent or permission to participate. A parent may not waive a child's legal right to sue for negligence.

(g) Commentary on School Negligence

The application of the careful or prudent parent standard of care to boards and teachers continues to be the subject of debate and commentary.[109] Although originally expounded when teachers, like parents, received the deference and respect of the children in their care, the *Williams v. Eady*[110] standard remains essentially intact. Its endurance is attributable to the fact that it is both fundamentally sensible and sufficiently adaptable. What it amounts to is a reflection of society's expectation that anyone who has responsibility for the safety of a child must take that responsibility very seriously, whether a parent of the child or not.

What is evident from the cases is that there is some recognition of a "reasonably prudent teacher" standard of care. Counsel for the plaintiff, and for the defendant, should lead evidence on both the "reasonably careful parent" standard and the "reasonably careful teacher" standard. The disadvantage of adhering solely to the former is that courts are not only willing to modify the standard when appropriate, but they may find it increasingly difficult to know what a reasonable parent is or does.

In litigation about the professional negligence of doctors or lawyers, the Court will examine the conduct of the defendant in light of what a reasonably competent doctor or lawyer of average ability[111] would have done in similar circumstances. In doing so, the Court may examine the customary practices of the profession. The mere fact that a practice is customary does not mean that it is not a negligent practice, but evidence of custom is often useful and persuasive. If, in the case of teachers, a court used a "reasonably careful teacher" standard, it could then examine the relevant customary practices of teachers as part of the evidence. As some

---

109 See, *e.g.*, comments in A. Wayne MacKay and Lyle I. Sutherland, *Teachers and the Law: A Practical Guide for Educators* (Toronto: Emond Montgomery Publications, 1992).
110 (1893), 10 T.L.R. 41 (C.A.).
111 A specialist may be held to a higher standard.

cases reveal,[112] the courts have been willing to look at how reasonable principals, teachers or coaches would have conducted themselves. This may include a consideration of customs. In the *Thomas* case, for instance, the normal training and background of junior football coaches was an important part of the evidence.

Parental "customs" are imbedded in culture, and parents from different cultural backgrounds do not have the same practices, procedures and expectations as to the discipline, supervision and behaviour of their children. One cannot consider parental customs in the same way that one might consider the customs of professions such as doctors, lawyers, dentists, and teachers. This has forced courts to recognize, implicitly or explicitly, that the careful parent standard has limitations, and that the facts may require a look at what a reasonably careful teacher would have done in the circumstances.

3. LIMITATION PERIODS

Most common law jurisdictions impose statutory limitation periods which govern the amount of time a person has in which to commence his or her legal action to recover damages. Statutes of limitations cover many different kinds of actions, including breach of contract, defamation, and negligence. Within the negligence category, different kinds of actions may have specific limitation periods, such as claims involving motor vehicle accidents, hospitals, and public authorities. The periods may be prescribed within a general statute of limitations or within a specific statute such as the *Libel and Slander Act*,[113] and the *Municipal Act*.[114]

The rationale for statutes of limitations is three-fold.[115] First, the potential defendant is entitled to know at some point that he or she will not be held accountable for ancient obligations. Secondly, evidence relating to the potential cause of action will eventually grow stale and it is reasonable not to have to preserve it indefinitely. Thirdly, plaintiffs are expected to bring suit in a timely fashion. On the other hand, limitation periods should not commence until the plaintiff has discovered, or ought reasonably to have discovered, that a cause of action exists.

The Ontario Court of Appeal in *Papamonolopoulos v. Toronto (Board of Education)*[116] had to decide upon the relationship between the 6-month limitation period in Ontario's *Public Authorities Protection Act*[117] and sec-

---

112 *E.g., Higgs,* above, note 45; *Thomas,* above, note 23; and *Brown,* above, note 100.
113 R.S.O. 1990, c. L.12.
114 R.S.O. 1990, c. M.45.
115 See *Murphy v. Welsh; Stoddard v. Watson,* [1993] 2 S.C.R. 1069.
116 (1986), 56 O.R. (2d) 1 (C.A.); leave to appeal to S.C.C. refused (1987), 58 O.R. (2d) 528 (note) (S.C.C.).
117 R.S.O. 1990, c. P.38.

tion 47 of the *Limitations Act*[118] which states that a limitation period does not run against a minor until he or she reaches the age of majority. The Court decided that the commencement of the 6-month limitation period was subject to section 47 of the *Limitations Act*. Therefore, the plaintiff who was injured at the age of 16 had 6 months from the age of majority in which to commence his action.

Similarly, the Supreme Court of Canada found, in *Murphy v. Welsh; Stoddard v. Watson*,[119] that the 2-year limitation period in Ontario's *Highway Traffic Act* is postponed by section 47 of the *Limitations Act*. However, if a minor is represented by a guardian *ad litem,* statutes of limitation will run against the minor. In addition, a derivative claim by a minor under Ontario's *Family Law Act*[120] will be subject to a limitation period which applies to the main action. If the main action is out of time, so, too, will the minor's derivative action.[121]

Section 7(1) of the *Public Authorities Protection Act* states:

> No action, prosecution or other proceeding lies or shall be instituted against any person for an act done in pursuance or execution or intended execution of any statutory or other public duty or authority, or in respect of any alleged neglect or default in the execution of any such duty or authority, unless it is commenced within six months next after the cause of action arose, or, in the case of continuance of injury or damage, within six months after the ceasing thereof.

This limitation period applies to actions against school boards and to members and employees of school boards who are acting within their statutory authority.[122]

The *Public Authorities Protection Act* section 11(1) limitation period does not, however, bar an action for damages as a remedy under section 24(1) of the *Canadian Charter of Rights and Freedoms*.[123]

Courts are reluctant to deny a plaintiff's claim upon the technical ground of being statute-barred. In the case of the *Public Authorities Protection Act,* if the actions of a defendant cannot clearly be characterized as the perfor-

---

118 R.S.O. 1990, c. L.15.
119 Above, note 116.
120 R. S.O. 1990, c. F.3.
121 However, see *Stathopoulos v. McKinlay Door Sales & Installation Ltd.* (1993), 12 O.R. (3d) 790 (Gen. Div.), which permitted a defendant to be added to an action although the limitation period had expired; the original action was commenced within the proper period.
122 See, *e.g., Stewart v. Lincoln County (Bd. of Education)* (1976), 8 O.R. (2d) 168 (H.C.); *Moffat v. Dufferin County (Bd. of Education),* [1973] 1 O.R. 351 (C.A.); *Urzi v. North York (Bd. of Education)* (1980), 30 O.R. (2d) 300 (H.C.), affirmed (1981), 127 D.L.R. (3d) 768 (C.A.); *Lacarte v. Toronto (Bd. of Education),* [1954] O.R. 435 (C.A.), affirmed [1955] 5 D.L.R. 369 (S.C.C.).
123 *Prete v. Ontario* (1994), 16 O.R. (3d) 161 (C.A.).

mance of a statutory or other public duty, a court may resolve the ambiguity in favour of the plaintiff. In *Berardinelli v. Ontario Housing Corporation*,[124] the failure to remove snow and ice from the premises of an Ontario Housing Complex was found by the Supreme Court of Canada to be "subordinate" or "private" in nature and was not one of the primary duties of the housing corporation. The claim was not barred by the *Public Authorities Protection Act*. However, in *Eddington v. Kent County (Board of Education)*, the plaintiff's claim, alleging negligent supervision of a physical education class, was found by Campell J. to be statute-barred under the same Act:

> In my view, there is nothing subordinate or incidental to the duties being performed by the defendants allegedly in a negligent manner. They were doing precisely what they were authorized and obliged to do under the provisions of the *Education Act* and the regulations.[125]

In *Des Champs v. Prescott-Russell (Conseil des écoles séparées catholiques de langue française)*[126] the Ontario Court of Appeal considered whether or not the six-month limitation period in section 7(1) of the *Public Authorities Protection Act* barred two actions against school boards in respect of their reassignment of superintendents under the redundancy provisions in Regulation 309 made under the *Education Act*. In each case, the plaintiff commenced his action after the six-month limitation period had expired.

The Appeal Court held that the *Public Authorities Protection Act* applies when a board declares the position of superintendent redundant and transfers the person to another position pursuant to Regulation 309. This action is not a subordinate act to the public duty and the plaintiffs were persons for whose benefit Regulation 309 was passed. The Court noted that even a strict construction of the statute would lead it to the same conclusion. The limitation period began to run when the board passed its resolution declaring the redundancy, or at the latest, on the date when the plaintiffs were advised of their new position. In either case, it had expired.

However, these decisions were reversed by the Supreme Court of Canada.[127] The Court's analysis is found in the *DesChamps* decision, where the

---

124 (1978), 90 D.L.R. (3d) 481 (S.C.C.).
125 (1986), 56 O.R. (2d) 403 at 406 (Ont. Dist. Ct.). But see *Phelps v. Scarborough Bd. of Education* (June 18, 1993), Doc. 350779/89, [1993] O.J. No. 1318 (Ont. Gen. Div.), where the Court held that the duty to maintain a baseball field is not of a public character and therefore not barred by the *Public Authorities Protection Act*.
126 (1997), 1997 CarwsellOnt 111 (C.A.), leave to appeal allowed (1997), 108 O.A.C. 159 (note) (S.C.C.), leave to appeal allowed (1997), (*sub nom. Abouchar v. Conseil scolaire de langue française d'Ottawa-Carleton*) 109 O.A.C. 200 (note) (S.C.C.), reversed (1999), 177 D.L.R. (4th) 23 (S.C.C.), reversed [1999] 3 S.C.R. 343.
127 *Des Champs* [1999] 3 S.C.R. 281 and *Abouchar*, [1999] 3 S.C.R. 343.

Court (Binnie J.) began by stating the general principles of the legislation and discussing the different interpretations of section 7 in case precedents:

> A few general observations should be stated at the outset. The wording of s. 7 of the Act indicates that the legislature did not intend to throw the protective net of s. 7 around public authorities in Ontario as a matter of status. The reference to the "intended execution of any statutory or other public duty or authority" (emphasis added) limits the protection to public duties and powers and confirms inferentially that a public authority may well have other duties and powers that are essentially of a private nature. In drawing the line between the public aspects and private aspects, the general principle is that the wording of s. 7 is to be read narrowly and against the party seeking its special protection. This produces an inevitable line drawing exercise that requires the court to examine the nature of the statutory power or duty imposed on the defendant public authority as well as the character of the particular conduct about which the plaintiff complains. The School Board, to take this case, is required to provide educational services to the public. In order to carry out its program, it has to build schools and hire teachers. If the Board were sued by an injured child for operating an unsafe school, or by parents for wrongly refusing to admit their child to classes, the claims would properly engage the public duties of the school, and be covered by the special limitation. On the other hand, a claim by a disgruntled builder under a school construction contract, or an unpaid caterer who had provided food services, would stand on a different footing. Although the subject matter of their claim clearly relates to the execution by the school of its public mandate, it is incidental thereto. The builder or caterer would be asserting private rights under private contracts. Their claims would not be within the intended scope of the disability imposed by the special limitation period.
>
> For purposes of this analysis, it does not matter whether the claim arises in contract or in tort. The analysis is directed to whether the claim, whatever it is, "correlates" to a public power or duty exercised or owed by the authority.
>
> These observations follow from a consideration of the decided cases, not all of which are readily reconcilable. Arnup J.A. has traced the roots of the Ontario legislation back to a 1609 English statute entitled An Acte for ease in pleading against troublesome and contencious Suites prosecuted against Justices of the Peace, Maiors, Constables and certain other his Majestie's Officers, for the lawfull execucion of their Office, 7 Jas. 1, c. 5 (see *Re Colledge and Niagara Regional Police Commission* (1983), 44 O.R. (2d) 289 (C.A.), at pp. 294 et seq., and the historical appendix starting at p. 312). As Aylesworth J.A. noted in *Lacarte v. Board of Education of Toronto*, [1954] O.R. 435 (C.A.), at p. 451: "Many eminent judges have given eloquent expression to the difficulty of determining precisely what acts or classes of act are excluded by the statute."
>
> At least three different views emerge from the case law about the proper scope of s. 7 of the Act:
>
> (i) The first, and most expansive, view is that the limitation applies whenever the cause of action relates to the exercise or failure to exercise a statutory or

prerogative power. As most public authorities are creatures of statute, this view includes within the limitation almost everything done by the public authority. The acts of a public authority, on this view, must of necessity be for a public purpose and in furtherance of a public policy (see, e.g., Henry J. in *Berardinelli v. Ontario Housing Corp.* (1976), 71 D.L.R. (3d) 56 (Ont. H.C.), at p. 59). Some support for variants of this view is found in the decision of the Ontario Court of Appeal, in *Lacarte, supra,* and in the majority decision of the British Columbia Court of Appeal in *Riddle v. University of Victoria* (1979), 95 D.L.R. (3d) 193, and in their progeny.

(ii) A second more restrictive view is that the limitation applies only where the act complained of relates to duties owed to that "public" which the general operations of the public authority were intended to benefit (or burden), as opposed to acts which are indistinguishable in substance from transactions in the private sector (such as breach of a contract between a government ministry and its supplier). Judicial support for this more limited view is found in *Clarke v. Ottawa Board of Education* (1975), 54 D.L.R. (3d) 321 (Ont. Co. Ct.); *Re Beauchamp and Town of Espanola* (1981), 122 D.L.R. (3d) 149 (Ont. Div. Ct.), aff'd (1981), 128 D.L.R. (3d) 766 (Ont. C.A.), per MacKinnon A.C.J.O.; the dissenting judgment of Taggart J.A. in *Riddle*, supra; as well as trial level judgments in *Collier v. Lake Superior Board of Education* (1986), 14 C.C.E.L. 183 (Ont. Dist. Ct.); and *Molloy v. Ontario (Human Rights Commission)* (1992), 41 C.C.E.L. 101 (Ont. Ct. (Gen. Div.)).

(iii) A third and even more restrictive view holds that not only is the limitation confined to the "direct performance" of statutory powers and duties owed to the public, but it excludes acts in furtherance of that performance which are of an internal or operational nature, having a predominantly private aspect. This view has been endorsed by this Court over the years, notably in *McGonegal v. Gray,* [1952] 2 S.C.R. 274, and especially in *Berardinelli, supra,* where Estey J. said, at p. 280, that s. 7 (formerly s. 11) "... attracts a strict interpretation and any ambiguity found upon the application of the proper principles of statutory interpretation should be resolved in favour of the person whose right of action is being truncated". Estey J. went on to observe: "There is little doubt about the presence of ambiguity and uncertainty of meaning in the section". On a policy level, Estey J. held at p. 284 that a broader interpretation in that case would have created an objectionable double standard, i.e., "different conditions of owner liability for two apparently similar housing facilities".

One might have expected that in a well-ordered system of justice the third and narrowest view, having on at least two occasions been endorsed by this Court, would have prevailed. What seems to have happened, however, is that in the mid-1950s a series of wrongful dismissal "teacher cases" became detached from the main body of jurisprudence under s. 7 of the Act and related statutes. I do not share Major J.'s view that the "teacher cases" are of no consequence to the case at bar. They established a contrary line of jurisprudence which led directly to the decision in appeal: the court below, relying solely on *Gallant, supra,* summarily found that the acts complained of were "not subordinate acts to the public duty". The disposition of the present appeal requires a review of the correctness of these authorities.[128]

The Court (Major J. dissenting) concluded that:

> My view is that Regulation 309 is a piece of indoor management which, to use Estey J.'s expression in *Berardinelli*, has predominantly a "private connotation". It is a regulatory document that governs the private relationship between the Board and its superintendents created by an employment contract. It consists of two parts. The first part sets out a certification procedure including academic and professional qualifications and related provisions governing individuals seeking that type of employment. The second part addresses the transfer and dismissal of such supervisory officers. The contents would not be out of place in an *Employment Standards Act* directed to private employers, or duplicated in the human resources manual of a comparably bureaucratic private corporation. The only reason it appears in the form of a regulation is that we are dealing here with a public sector employer.
>
> I acknowledge that the duties laid on the Board in favour of supervisory personnel are expressed in obligatory terms ("shall") and that some of the earlier cases drew a distinction between mandatory conduct (which was thought to be covered by the limitation) and discretionary activity (which possibly might not be); see, e.g., *Compton v. Council of the County Borough of West Ham*, [1939] Ch. 771, and *McManus v. Bowes*, [1938] 1 K.B. 98 (C.A.). In this case, as in *Berardinelli*, the mandatory nature of the obligation does not save it from being "more of an internal or operational nature having a predominantly private aspect" (p. 284 (underlining added; italics deleted)). The appellant's complaint is that his selection for reassignment was contrary to the Board's own internal rules of seniority because it based its decision on the appellant's seniority as a superintendent rather than on his seniority as a Board employee. Having improperly singled out the appellant, the Board then compounded its fault (the appellant says) by assigning him to a position for which he was overqualified, and which required him to teach 30 percent of his time instead of being allowed to administer all of his time. With due respect for the contrary view, these actions by the Board were not the inevitable consequence of the decision to downsize its complement of superintendents, and the illustration of back-to-work legislation is not comparable, even supposing such legislation could give rise to litigation. The appellant's basic point is that downsizing in the public interest could and ought to have been implemented without actionable wrong to any of the employees. I am aware that in *Riddle, supra*, the majority distinguished between contract problems with teachers and the "more mundane function of providing maintenance staff" (*per* Hinkson J.A., at p. 228), but in either case, it seems to me, the teaching of *Berardinelli, supra*, is [page318] to avoid subjecting such routine problems of management and mundane labour relations to a double limitation standard depending on whether they happen to arise with a private employer or a public employer.[129]

---

128 *Des Champs Ibid.*, at paras. 12-19.
129 *Ibid.*, paras. 57-58.

This case is important, not only because of its extensive review of the often-conflicting case law, but also because it provides a recommended approach (at paragraph 50) as to how courts should deal with issues around section 7 of the *Public Authorities Protection Act* and similar legislation.

4. OCCUPIERS' LIABILITY

School boards own a considerable amount of real estate. Their property is used by students, staff, parents and the general public. This results in a large number of "slip and fall" cases, in which plaintiffs usually have slipped on snow, ice or water, or have tripped over something. It is essential that boards understand their obligations as "occupiers" and ensure that they comply with their statutory duty to make their property safe.

The common law of occupiers' liability developed over a long series of cases in which courts dealt with the standard of care which occupiers of land or premises owed to those who came onto the land or premises. Distinctions were drawn between the duty owed to trespassers and that owed to those who were invited onto the property. Distinctions were also drawn between invitees and licensees. Much time was spent by courts in determining the "status" of the plaintiff, that is whether the plaintiff was a trespasser, licensee or invitee.

"Occupiers' liability" legislation codified and simplified the common law. Ontario's *Occupiers' Liability Act*,[130] section 3, states that an occupier of premises (which is defined to include land and structures) owes a duty,

> ... to take such care as in all the circumstances of the case is reasonable to see that persons entering on the premises, and the property brought on the premises by those persons are reasonably safe while on the premises.

The duty of care applies both to the condition of the premises and to the activity being carried on. The duty does not apply to risks willingly assumed by the person who enters the premises.[131] However, even if a person voluntarily assumes risks, the occupier must not create a danger with the deliberate intent of doing harm or damage to the person or his or her property, and must not act with reckless disregard for the presence of the person or his or her property. Persons on the property with the intent to commit a criminal act, and persons who are trespassing, are still owed this basic level of care although they are considered to have willingly assumed the risks of entering the premises. Property owners may not set traps which might harm trespassers.

---

130 R.S.O. 1990, c. O.2.
131 *Ibid.*, s. 4.

In *Kennedy v. Waterloo (County) Board of Education*,[132] the Ontario Court of Appeal considered a case in which the plaintiff asserted that the school board failed to fulfil its duty of care under section 3 of the *Occupiers' Liability Act*. The plaintiff exited a school parking lot on his motorcycle at high speed, left the roadway and crashed. He was very seriously injured when he flew off the motorcycle and hit his head on a bollard on school property. The bollard consisted of a corrugated steel pipe that had been filled with cement. The school had previously removed some chains that ran between the bollards, but did not remove the bollards themselves. The trial judge found the school board was not liable because the decision not to remove the bollards was a "policy" decision, not an "operational" one, and secondly that the board was not negligent.

The Court of Appeal disagreed. The Court referred to the principles behind the policy/operational distinction, as follows:

> In *Just*, the court held that where a government authority owes a duty of care because of a relationship of sufficient proximity with the plaintiff, the government authority may be exempted from that duty of care and from any liability from what would have been a breach of that duty in two circumstances: the first is where it has made a true policy decision as to how and to what extent it will devote resources to fulfilling that duty, as opposed to an operational decision implementing the policy decision: "True policy decisions should be exempt from tortious claims so that governments are not restricted in making decisions based upon social, political or economic factors. However, the implementation of those decisions may well be subject to claims in tort." (p. 705). The second circumstance is where there is an express statutory exemption.

Cory J. for the majority summarized the applicable principles in the following way at pp.708-9:

> It may be convenient at this stage to summarize what I consider to be the principles applicable and the manner of proceeding in cases of this kind. As a general rule, the traditional tort law duty of care will apply to a government agency in the same way that it will apply to an individual. In determining whether a duty of care exists, the first question to be resolved is whether the parties are in a relationship of sufficient proximity to warrant the imposition of such a duty. In the case of a government agency, exemption from this imposition of duty may occur as a result of an explicit statutory exemption. Alternatively, the exemption may arise as a result of the nature of the decision made by the government agency. That is, a government agency will be exempt from the imposition of a duty of care in situations which arise from its pure policy decisions.
>
> In determining what constitutes such a policy decision, it should be borne in mind that such decisions are generally made by persons of a high level

---

132 (1999), 45 O.R (3d) 1 (Ont. C.A.), leave to appeal refused (2000), 254 N.R. 199 (note) (S.C.C.).

of authority in the agency, but may also properly be made by persons of a lower level of authority. The characterization of such a decision rests on the nature of the decision and not on the identity of the actors. As a general rule, decisions concerning budgetary allotments for departments or government agencies will be classified as policy decisions. Further, it must be recalled that a policy decision is open to challenge on the basis that it is not made in the bona fide exercise of discretion. If after due consideration it is found that a duty of care is owed by the government agency and no exemption by way of statute or policy decision-making is found to exist, a traditional torts analysis ensues and the issue of standard of care required of the government agency must next be considered.

The manner and quality of an inspection system is clearly part of the operational aspect of a governmental activity and falls to be assessed in the consideration of the standard of care issue. At this stage, the requisite standard of care to be applied to the particular operation must be assessed in light of all the surrounding circumstances including, for example, budgetary restraints and the availability of qualified personnel and equipment.

One issue which was not specifically addressed in the three cases is whether the policy/operational analysis can have any application where the duty of care on the government agency does not arise as a result of a relationship of proximity, but where it is imposed by statute. In such a case, can there be room for a policy decision to be made which would in any way exempt the government agency from its statutory duty? In effect, the legislature has already made its policy decision by mandating the statutory duty.[133]

The Ontario Court of Appeal found that the trial judge erred in applying the policy/operational distinction in a case such as this, where the school board had a statutory duty under section 3 of the *Occupiers' Liability Act*. There is a distinction between a statutory *power* and a statutory *duty*, and the school board could not absolve itself of liability by characterizing its decision not to remove the bollards as a "policy" decision. The Court went on to examine whether the board had met its standard of care under the *Occupiers' Liability Act*. It stated:

> It has been clear since the decision of the Supreme Court of Canada in *Waldick v. Malcolm* (1991), 83 D.L.R. (4th) 114 that s. 3(1) of the *Occupiers' Liability Act* places an affirmative duty on occupiers to take reasonable care for the safety of those whom they permit onto their premises. Furthermore, as Iacobucci J. said at p. 124:
>
>> The statutory duty on occupiers...is to take reasonable care in the circumstances to make the premises safe. That duty does not change but the factors which are relevant to an assessment of what constitutes reasonable

---

133 *Ibid.*, paras. 17-19.

care will necessarily be very specific to each fact situation – thus the proviso 'such care as in all the circumstances of the case is reasonable'.[134]

The Court was satisfied that the school board did not meet the standard of care and should have removed the bollards in order to make the premises reasonably safe for students. It stated:

> In this case, the first circumstance is that the premises in question are a school and the occupier is the school Board. Under s. 236 [now s. 265] of the *Education Act* the principal, an employee of the Board, has a duty to give assiduous attention to the health and comfort of the pupils and to the condition of the school grounds. Both principals who testified, as well as Mr. Hearn, acknowledged that a paramount concern of the school Board is the safety of the students, and it was acknowledged by the witnesses with expertise and experience in school construction that safety for the students is a major factor in school design and construction.
>
> At this location there was a known history of vehicles driving onto the playground. In fact, Mr. Hearn testified that they had had "every kind of incident happen" which was why he believed in 1977 they put a complete line of bollards and chains all the way from the street to the school building in order to block access to the playing field to vehicles.[135]

The Court stated what it considered to be the relevant factors in determining whether reasonable care was taken:

> The following factors are relevant to the criteria for reasonable care highlighted by Lord Denning and approved by Dickson J. in *Veinot, supra*: the gravity of the potential injury from an accident involving contact with the bollards was high; the roadway was curved; the property was a school used by teenage students with limited driving experience which raised the likelihood that they might be less cautious and capable than adults; the history of the property before the barrier was erected was of vehicles which would go off the road and onto the playing field.
>
> Although these factors point to the danger of leaving the bollards in place, the likelihood of an accident where a student motorcyclist travelling on the road would go out of control, and the driver get thrown off and hit a bollard was not contemplated by the Board because it had not happened. Was it therefore reasonable for the possibility of such an accident not to be contemplated by the Board? In most cases the event which occurs and causes the injury such as a slip and fall on ice: *Waldick, supra*; *Preston v. Canadian Legion, Kingsway Branch*, No. 175 (1981), 123 D.L.R. (3d) 645 (Alta. C.A.), a student's fall through a glass skylight accessible to students: *Leblond v. Ottawa Board of Education*, [1984] O.J. No. 1150 (H.C.) (Q.L.), or a fall off a bridge with no railings: *Chretien v. Jensen* (1998), 116 B.C.A.C. 81, is reasonably foreseeable,

---

134 *Ibid.*, para 33.
135 *Ibid.*, at paras. 80-81.

and the issue is did the occupier of the premises do enough in all the circumstances to make the premises safe by taking steps to prevent the accident itself.

In this case, the risk of serious injury was reasonably foreseeable if the bollards were not removed and if there was an accident. The issue is was an accident involving contact with the bollards reasonably foreseeable, obliging the Board to take the necessary steps to remove the danger of injury and thereby make the premises reasonably safe in the event of such an accident?[136]

The school board was found negligent because it contributed to the severity of the injuries by failing to make the premises reasonably safe. Its responsibility was apportioned at 75 per cent. The plaintiff was found not to have voluntarily assumed the risk of his actions, but he was found 25 per cent contributorily negligent.

In the case of *Waldick v. Malcolm*,[137] the Supreme Court of Canada decided that the defence of "voluntary assumption of risk" must be given a narrow interpretation. In order for a visitor to premises to have voluntarily assumed the risk of injury they must have assumed the physical risk and legal risk involved in coming onto the premises. For instance, it is not a defence to say that a person voluntarily assumed the risk of walking across an icy parking lot unless the defendant can show that the plaintiff also expressly or impliedly assumed the legal risks of doing so. The occupier has a positive duty to make sure the premises are safe. If the occupier wants to restrict, modify or exclude its duty of care as an occupier, it may do so, provided that it takes reasonable steps to bring the restrictions, modifications or exclusions to the person to whom the duty is owed. The effectiveness of such restrictions, in a legal sense, often depends upon whether the plaintiff was properly made aware of them.[138]

The *Occupiers' Liability Act* does not reduce the high standard of care owed by a school board in respect of its pupils. The Act establishes the duty of care owed to visitors and trespassers. It also applies to persons who may be enrolled as pupils, when they are on school property for reasons other than instruction or school authorized activities.[139]

---

136 *Ibid.*, at paras. 85-87.
137 (1991), 83 D.L.R. (4th) 114 (S.C.C.).
138 See also *Bains v. Hill* (1992), 93 D.L.R. (4th) 117 (B.C. C.A.); *Crocker v. Sundance Northwest Resorts Ltd.* (1988), 51 D.L.R. (4th) 321 (S.C.C.); *Dubé v. Labar* (1986), 27 D.L.R. (4th) 653 (S.C.C.).
139 See *Boryszko v. Toronto (City Board of Education* [1962] O.R. 600 (H.C.), reversed, [1963] 1 O.R. 1 (C.A.), a case decided prior to the *Occupiers' Liability Act*, under the common law of occupiers' liability, in which the Court found it foreseeable that a child would be injured by playing *after school hours* around a pile of cement blocks that had been left on the school yard by a construction company. The decision contains an interesting discussion of what constitutes a "warning" to young children. The Court found that "a warning to heedless children by teachers [during school hours] could not be expected to carry its force in the evening when those children return, not supervised

5. INTENTIONAL TORTS

(a) Introduction

Tort law provides that where a person intentionally inflicts harm upon another, he or she may be found liable and may be required to pay damages to compensate for the resulting loss or injury. Intentional torts include assault, battery, false imprisonment, defamation, nuisance, and deliberate infliction of mental suffering. In determining liability, the Court must examine what the defendant did, what he or she intended to do, and what actually resulted from the defendant's actions.

The defendant's actions must be voluntary in order for there to be a finding of liability for an intentional tort. However, a court may treat conduct as intentional even though the defendant's intended result was not exactly what actually occurred. In such a case, the results of the defendant's actions may be "imputed" to the defendant.[140] Conduct may also be intentional even though the defendant's actions were mistaken, provided that they were voluntary, as opposed to accidental.[141] The classic example of this is the act of trespassing on someone else's land, believing it to be your own. Intent may also be "transferred". If the defendant intended to harm A but instead harmed B, the court may regard the defendant as having intended to harm B.

The intentional torts most commonly found in schools are "assault" and "battery". The stress of school work upon pupils, the stress of teaching, the high level of activity, and the concentration of persons within the school, are all factors which contribute to the occurrence of assault and battery. Assault and battery may take place between staff members, between students, and between staff and students. In addition, visitors to the school may be involved. Other intentional torts, such as defamation, may occur in schools. Intentional, false statements about a student, teacher, or administrator, such that his or her reputation is damaged, may result in a finding of defamation. Legitimate criticism is not defamation. Therefore, a school administrator's report about a teacher's performance, written in conjunction with the carrying out of the administrator's responsibilities, will not be defamatory (in the absence of malice) even though it contains critical com-

---

by teachers, to play in the school yard." The injury was actually caused by another boy who dropped a cement block on the plaintiff's foot. However, the Court did not find this to be an intervening act that would let the board off the hook. The school board should have foreseen what would happen if cement blocks remained unguarded in the school yard.

140 Allen Linden, *Canadian Tort Law,* 7th ed. (Toronto: Butterworths, 2001), p. 34.
141 *Ibid.*

ments, because there is a "qualified privilege" to make the comments."[142] Critical comments by a teacher in a student's report card are not defamation, assuming that they are statements of fact or *bona fide* professional observations.

In *McKerron v. Marshall*,[143] a decision of Reilly J. in Ontario Superior Court of Justice, a parent was found guilty of defamation as a result of his campaign against an elementary school teacher in order to remove her from the classroom. The Court had no difficulty finding that the defendant had published statements that were libelous of the plaintiff. One of the libelous statements published by the defendant Marshall was a large banner. The display of the banner at a school did not give rise to a qualified privilege because Marshall had no right or duty to publish his comments about the teacher to the world at large. The Court then considered whether certain other communications by Marshall were protected by "qualified privilege". The Court stated:

> [A] parent has a right and arguably a duty to report concerns about a teacher to the teacher's principal, superintendent or to the school board. This communication will be protected by a qualified privilege even if the statements contained therein prove to be untrue. It is the circumstance of the communication however, not the communication itself which gives rise to the privilege. This privilege may be lost if the privilege is exceeded or if the plaintiff can prove malice on the part of the defendant. Such malice may be established by intrinsic or extrinsic evidence.
>
> . . .
>
> In the usual case, the falsity of the libel is presumed together with malice. The onus is on the defendant to prove justification or truth of the libelous statements. In circumstances of qualified privilege however, as long as the defendant honestly believes that the words published are true, (even if such belief) is unreasonable), there shall be no liability for defamation. In these circumstances the onus is on the plaintiff to remove the "cloak" of qualified privilege by proving malice on the part of the defendant. If the "cloak" of qualified privilege

---

142 *Korach v. Moore* (1991), 42 O.A.C. 248 — libel suit by occasional teacher against vice-principal and school board; defence of "qualified privilege" analyzed (leave to appeal to S.C.C. refused (1991), 3 O.R. (3d) xii (note) (S.C.C.)). See also, *Wagner v. Lim* (1994), 22 Alta. L.R. (3d) 109 (Q.B.) as summarized in *School Law Commentary* March, 1995 Vol. 9, No. 7 (successful defamation suit against parents of student); *Gibbs v. Jalbert* (1996), 18 B.C.L.R. (3d) 351 (C.A.) (parents permitted to use defence of qualified privilege); *Venneri v. Bascom* (1996), 28 O.R. (3d) 281 (Gen. Div.) (Ontario Court — General Division dismissed action against high school principal that claimed principal's letter about plaintiff's job performance was defamatory. Court held that, as an employment related matter, the complaint about the letter should have been dealt with through arbitration under the collective agreement; the application was dismissed as an abuse of process).
143 [1999] O.J. No. 4048, 1999 CarswellOnt 3432 (S.C.J.).

is removed by evidence of malice then the defendant must once again prove justification or truth of the alleged defamation.[144]

The Court found that the evidence of malice on the part of Marshall was "overwhelming", and that he had made and frequently repeated defamatory statements that he knew were false. Marshall was found liable for defamation, and for a pattern of conduct amounting to harassment and intentional infliction of mental suffering.

False imprisonment occurs where a person has been detained wrongfully or without authority, within fixed boundaries.[145] The statutory authority to discipline students may legitimately be used to detain them after class or during recess. However, arbitrary or capricious detention of students against their will, within the school, may constitute false imprisonment.

Intentional torts are civil wrongs; they are not criminal acts, although the same set of facts may give rise to criminal proceedings. A criminal prosecution is commenced by the state to preserve law and order. A conviction will result in a sentence against the accused, often comprising a fine or imprisonment. The civil courts, on the other hand, are the forum for seeking damages.[146]

Children may be held liable for intentional torts where they are capable of forming the necessary intention to commit the tortious act. Children who fight their teachers or other students, or who engage in pranks, should be aware that they can be found liable for such intentional actions. This is distinct from the liability of minors in negligence, which involves such issues as whether or not the child ought reasonably to have foreseen the consequences of his or her actions. Intention to cause harm or loss is necessary in intentional torts, whereas it is not an ingredient in negligence.

(b) Assault and Battery

Assault comprises an intentional act which causes a person to believe that he or she is about to be harmed. While the perception or apprehension of imminent harm is a necessary ingredient, no actual contact is required for an assault to occur. Provided that there is an apprehension of imminent harm or unwanted contact, many actions in a school setting may constitute assault. Assaults may be verbal, or by means of threatening gestures. Threats by means of such actions as bullying, surrounding a pupil, or blocking the path of a teacher, may all be assaults even though there is no actual physical contact. Even though the plaintiff may not have suffered significant injury

---

144 *Ibid.* paras. 90 and 92.
145 Linden, above, note 140, at p. 49.
146 Restitution orders may be made by criminal courts in appropriate circumstances, *e.g.*, under the *Young Offenders Act*.

by reason of being assaulted, he or she may still be entitled to nominal damages.

Battery involves offensive or hostile contact with the plaintiff, or something directly connected to the plaintiff, such as clothing. Actions which may constitute battery include spitting, striking, pushing, tripping, burning, and shooting. No actual harm is necessary; an insult or indignity to a person by way of physical contact is sufficient. While the defendant's actions must have been intentional, the existence of motive or malice is not relevant, except as to damages.[147]

(c) Sexual Misconduct

Intentional, unwanted sexual contact is battery. In schools, a person, whether student, staff member or visitor, who engages in sexual misconduct or abuse may be found liable in civil court.[148] While such conduct may also result in criminal charges being laid, a conviction does not result in compensation to the plaintiff-victim. As can be seen from recent cases involving victims of abuse at the hands of parents,[149] doctors and spouses, people are now more willing to seek damages in civil court as a result of being sexually victimized. Teachers who prey sexually upon students may not be deterred by the criminal law because of the difficulty of obtaining criminal convictions for sexual assault, exploitation or touching. However, the prospect of being sued in civil court, where the burden of proof is less onerous, may ultimately prove to be the most effective means of conveying the "hands off" message to those who would victimize vulnerable and impressionable young people.

Because sexual misconduct does not occur in the normal course of an employee's duties, one would think that it is unlikely that a board would be found vicariously liable for the employee's intentional misconduct. However, the case law now suggests the "normal course of employment test" is not always applicable in the context of sexual misconduct, and that a board could be held vicariously liable for the sexual misconduct of an employee

---

147 Margaret Brazier, *The Law of Torts, (Street on Torts)* 8th ed. (London: Butterworths, 1988), at p. 22. See *Walsh v. Buchanan* [1995] O.J. No. 64 (January 10, 1994) Hamilton 8787/87 (Ont. Gen. Div.) in which the plaintiff sought damages for injuries (severe depression and post-traumatic stress disorder) occurring as a result of a fight with the defendant after a floor hockey game in high school. The school staff were found not to have been negligent. Although the plaintiff picked the fight, the defendant (a trained boxer) was found 50% liable for using excessive force in retaliation.
148 See *Rumley v. British Columbia* [2001], S.C.J. No. 39, 2001 CarswellBC 1223 (S.C.C.), additional reasons at (2001), 205 D.L.R. (4th) 39 (S.C.C.), for a decision as to whether a class action by former residents of a residential school for deaf children for damages for sexual, physical and emotional abuse should be permitted to proceed as a class action under the *Class Proceedings Act*, R.S.B.C. 1996, c. 50, s. 4.
149 *E.g., M.(K.) v. M.(H.)* (1992), 96 D.L.R. (4th) 289 at 299 (S.C.C.).

if the employment enables the employee to exercise parental control over the victim.

In *B. (P.A.) v. Curry*[150] the British Columbia Court of Appeal considered the question of whether the Children's Foundation was vicariously liable for the intentional misconduct of its employee, Mr. Curry. The Court was not asked to consider any issues of negligence. The Foundation provides residential care for children between the ages of six and twelve. The Court (Huddart J.) found as a fact that the Foundation "exercised the same control over the respondent that a parent would exercise over a 10 to 12 year old."[151]

Mr. Curry was employed by the Foundation as a childcare counsellor. He was expected to fulfil the role of a parent to the children in the group homes. He abused the respondent and was convicted of various criminal offences. Was the Foundation vicariously liable for his acts of sexual misconduct?

The Court stated that the test of considering whether or not the employee's actions were within the normal course of his or her duties may have some usefulness in a negligence action, but "is of no use at all when the responsibility of an employer for the intentional tort of sexual assault by an employee placed in a position of control over the victim comes to be considered, as it has in the case at bar."[152]

The decision contains an exhaustive review of the case law on vicarious liability. The Court concluded that Mr. Curry's conduct was a "breach of trust", and "primarily a breach of employer-created authority".[153]

> Without the power given to Mr. Curry by the appellant [Foundation], the breach could not have occurred. The appellant did not merely provide the opportunity for seduction to take place and a wrong to occur, it made the wrong significantly more probable by conferring parental power over the respondent, then a young and vulnerable child, and permitting that power to be exercised in the absence of any other person.[154]

The Court noted that these facts were distinguishable from some other kinds of assault cases:

> The assault cases cited by the appellant do not deal with a situation like the one before us where parental authority has been conferred over a child. Teachers, police officers, bouncers or priests who abuse in non-residential settings do not have the same degree of control over every aspect of a child's emotional and physical well-being as a parental figure does.

---

150 (1997), 146 D.L.R. (4th) 72 (B.C. C.A.), additional reasons at (1997), 1997 CarswellBC 1169 (C.A.), leave to appeal allowed (1997), (sub nom. *P.A.B. v. Children's Foundation*) 104 B.C.A.C. 239 (note) (S.C.C.), affirmed (1999), 62 B.C.L.R. (3d) 173 (S.C.C.).
151 *Ibid.*, at 76.
152 *Ibid.*, at 83.
153 *Ibid*, at 100.
154 *Ibid.*, at 100.

The decision was appealed to the Supreme Court of Canada,[155] which defined the issue before it as follows:

> Both parties agree that the answer to this question is governed by the Salmond test, which posits that employers are vicariously liable for (1) employee acts authorized by the employer; or (2) unauthorized acts so connected with authorized acts that they may be regarded as modes (albeit improper modes) of doing an authorized act. Both parties also agree that we are here concerned with the second branch of the test. They diverge, however, on what the second branch of the test means.[156]

After considering the legal precedents, the Court identified three "classes" of cases in which employers have been found vicariously liable:

> Looking at these three general classes of cases in which employers have been held vicariously liable for employees' unauthorized torts, one sees a progression from accidents, to accident-like intentional torts, to torts that bear no relationship to either agency-like conduct or accident. In search of a unifying principle, one asks what the three classes of cases have in common. At first glance, it may seem little. Yet with the benefit of hindsight it is possible to posit one common feature: in each case it can be said that the employer's enterprise had created the risk that produced the tortious act. The language of "furtherance of the employer's aims" and the employer's creation of "a situation of friction" may be seen as limited formulations of the concept of enterprise risk that underlies the dishonest employee cases. The common theme resides in the idea that where the employee's conduct is closely tied to a risk that the employer's enterprise has placed in the community, the employer may justly be held vicariously liable for the employee's wrong.[157]

The Court also closely examined the policy rationale behind holding employers vicariously liable, and concluded from its analysis that:

> Underlying the cases holding employers vicariously liable for the unauthorized acts of employees is the idea that employers may justly be held liable where the act falls within the ambit of the risk that the employer's enterprise creates or exacerbates. Similarly, the policy purposes underlying the imposition of vicarious liability on employers are served only where the wrong is so connected with the employment that it can be said that the employer has introduced the risk of the wrong (and is thereby fairly and usefully charged with its management and minimization). The question in each case is whether there is a connection or nexus between the employment enterprise and that wrong that justifies imposition of vicarious liability on the employer for the wrong, in terms of fair allocation of the consequences of the risk and/or deterrence.[158]

However, the Court cautioned that:

---

155 *B.(P.A.) v. Curry*, [1999] 2 S.C.R. 534.
156 *Ibid.*, para. 10.
157 *Ibid.*, para. 22.
158 *Ibid.*, para. 37.

[O]ne must not confuse the relevance of foreseeability in this sense with its usual function on a negligence issue. We are not here concerned with attributing fault to the master for failing to provide against foreseeable harm (for example in consequence of employing an incompetent servant), but with the measure of risks that may fairly be regarded as typical of the enterprise in question. *The inquiry is directed not at foreseeability of risks from specific conduct, but at foreseeability of the broad risks incident to a whole enterprise.* [Emphasis added.]

On the other hand, this analysis's focus on what might be called "general cause", while broader than specific foreseeability, in no way implies a simple "but-for" test: but for the enterprise and employment, this harm would not have happened. This is because reduced to formalistic premises, *any* employment can be seen to provide the causation of an employee's tort. Therefore, "mere opportunity" to commit a tort, in the common "but-for" understanding of that phrase, does not suffice: *Morris v. C. W. Martin & Sons Ltd.*, [1966] 1 Q.B. 716 (C.A.) (*per* Diplock L.J.). The enterprise and employment must not only provide the locale or the bare opportunity for the employee to commit his or her wrong, it must *materially* enhance the risk, in the sense of significantly contributing to it, before it is fair to hold the employer vicariously liable.[159]

The Court recognized the importance of giving lower courts across Canada some guidance in this area of law and offered the following principles (at paras 41-46):

Reviewing the jurisprudence, and considering the policy issues involved, I conclude that in determining whether an employer is vicariously liable for an employee's unauthorized, intentional wrong in cases where precedent is inconclusive, courts should be guided by the following principles:

(1) They should openly confront the question of whether liability should lie against the employer, rather than obscuring the decision beneath semantic discussions of "scope of employment" and "mode of conduct".

(2) The fundamental question is whether the wrongful act is *sufficiently related* to conduct authorized by the employer to justify the imposition of vicarious liability. Vicarious liability is generally appropriate where there is a significant connection between the *creation or enhancement of a risk* and the wrong that accrues therefrom, even if unrelated to the employer's desires. Where this is so, vicarious liability will serve the policy considerations of provision of an adequate and just remedy and deterrence. Incidental connections to the employment enterprise, like time and place (without more), will not suffice. Once engaged in a particular business, it is fair that an employer be made to pay the generally foreseeable costs of that business. In contrast, to impose liability for costs unrelated to the risk would effectively make the employer an involuntary insurer.

(3) In determining the sufficiency of the connection between *the employer's creation or enhancement of the risk* and the wrong complained of, subsidiary factors may be considered. These may vary with the nature of the case. When

---

159 *Ibid.*, paras. 39-40.

related to intentional torts, the relevant factors may include, but are not limited to, the following:
(a) the opportunity that the enterprise afforded the employee to abuse his or her power;
(b) the extent to which the wrongful act may have furthered the employer's aims (and hence be more likely to have been committed by the employee);
(c) the extent to which the wrongful act was related to friction, confrontation or intimacy inherent in the employer's enterprise;
(d) the extent of power conferred on the employee in relation to the victim;
(e) the vulnerability of potential victims to wrongful exercise of the employee's power.

Applying these general considerations to sexual abuse by employees, there must be a strong connection between what the employer was asking the employee to do (the risk created by the employer's enterprise) and the wrongful act. It must be possible to say that the employer *significantly* increased the risk of the harm by putting the employee in his or her position and requiring him to perform the assigned tasks. The policy considerations that justify imposition of vicarious liability for an employee's sexual misconduct are unlikely to be satisfied by incidental considerations of time and place. For example, an incidental or random attack by an employee that merely happens to take place on the employer's premises during working hours will scarcely justify holding the employer liable. Such an attack is unlikely to be related to the business the employer is conducting or what the employee was asked to do and, hence, to any risk that was created. Nor is the imposition of liability likely to have a significant deterrent effect; short of closing the premises or discharging all employees, little can be done to avoid the random wrong. Nor is foreseeability of harm used in negligence law the test. What is required is a material increase in the risk as a consequence of the employer's enterprise and the duties he entrusted to the employee, mindful of the policies behind vicarious liability.

What factors are relevant to whether an employer's enterprise has introduced or significantly exacerbated a risk of sexual abuse by an employee? (Again, I speak generally, supplementing the factors suggested above.) It is obvious that the risk of an employee sexually abusing a child may be materially enhanced by giving the employee an opportunity to commit the abuse. There are many kinds of opportunity and the nature of the opportunity in a particular case must be carefully evaluated in determining whether it has, in fact, materially increased the risk of the harm that ensued. If an employee is permitted or required to be with children for brief periods of time, there may be a small risk of such harm — perhaps not much greater than if the employee were a stranger. If an employee is permitted or required to be alone with a child for extended periods of time, the opportunity for abuse may be greater. If in addition to being permitted to be alone with a child for extended periods, the employee is expected to supervise the child in intimate activities like bathing or toiletting, the opportunity for abuse becomes greater still. As the opportunity for abuse becomes greater, so the risk of harm increases.

The risk of harm may also be enhanced by the nature of the relationship the employment establishes between the employee and the child. Employment that puts the employee in a position of intimacy and power over the child (i.e., a parent-like, role-model relationship) may enhance the risk of the employee feeling that he or she is able to take advantage of the child and the child submitting without effective complaint. The more the employer encourages the employee to stand in a position of respect and suggests that the child should emulate and obey the employee, the more the risk may be enhanced. In other words, the more an enterprise requires the exercise of power or authority for its successful operation, the more materially likely it is that an abuse of that power relationship can be fairly ascribed to the employer. See *Boothman v. Canada, supra*.

Other factors may be important too, depending on the nature of the case. To require or permit an employee to touch the client in intimate body zones may enhance the risk of sexual touching, just as permitting an employee to handle large sums of money may enhance the risk of embezzlement or conversion. This is the common sense core of the "mode of conduct" argument accepted by the trial judge in this case. (The same factor might of course be analyzed in terms of enhanced opportunity.) Time and place arguments may also be relevant in particular cases. The mere fact that the wrong occurred during working hours or on the jobsite may not, standing alone, be of much importance; the assessment of material increase in risk cannot be resolved by the mechanical application of spatial and temporal factors. This said, spatial and temporal factors may tend to *negate* the suggestion of materially enhanced risk of harm, insofar as they suggest that the conduct was essentially unrelated to the employment and any enhanced risk it may have created (for example, the employee's tort occurred offsite and after hours). The policy considerations of fair compensation and deterrence upon which vicarious liability is premised may be attenuated or completely eliminated in such circumstances.

In summary, the test for vicarious liability for an employee's sexual abuse of a client should focus on whether the employer's enterprise and empowerment of the employee materially increased the risk of the sexual assault and hence the harm. The test must not be applied mechanically, but with a sensitive view to the policy considerations that justify the imposition of vicarious liability — fair and efficient compensation for wrong and deterrence. This requires trial judges to investigate the employee's specific duties and determine whether they gave rise to special opportunities for wrongdoing. Because of the peculiar exercises of power and trust that pervade cases such as child abuse, special attention should be paid to the existence of a power or dependency relationship, which on its own often creates a considerable risk of wrongdoing.[160]

The Court agreed with the lower courts that the Children's Foundation should be held vicariously liable for the intentional torts committed by Curry:

---

160 *Ibid.*, paras. 41-46.

Applying these considerations to the facts in the case at bar, the Foundation is vicariously liable for the sexual misconduct of Curry. The opportunity for intimate private control and the parental relationship and power required by the terms of employment created the special environment that nurtured and brought to fruition Curry's sexual abuse. The employer's enterprise created and fostered the risk that led to the ultimate harm. The abuse was not a mere accident of time and place, but the product of the special relationship of intimacy and respect the employer fostered, as well as the special opportunities for exploitation of that relationship it furnished. Indeed, it is difficult to imagine a job with a greater risk for child sexual abuse. This is not to suggest that future cases must rise to the same level to impose vicarious liability. Fairness and the need for deterrence in this critical area of human conduct — the care of vulnerable children — suggest that as between the Foundation that created and managed the risk and the innocent victim, the Foundation should bear the loss.[161]

The Supreme Court of Canada released its decision in *T.(G.) v. Griffiths*[162] at the same time as *B.(P.A.) v. Curry*. In *T.(G.)*, the issue was whether a Boys' and Girls' Club should be held vicariously liable for sexual assaults committed by an employee. The Court split 4-3, with the majority holding that the defendant club was not vicariously liable. The majority applied the principles and analysis set forth in *B.(P.A.)*, but found the facts in the two cases to be significantly different:

> The Club did not confer any meaningful "power" over the appellants. They were free to walk out of the Club at any time. They went home to their mother every night. In the circumstances I agree with the point made by Newbury J.A. in the British Columbia Court of Appeal in the *Children's Foundation* case (1997), 30 B.C.L.R. (3d) 1 (*sub nom. B. (P.A.) v. Curry*), at pp. 39-40:
>
>> Where, for example, a teacher uses his or her authority to develop a relationship with a pupil in his or her class and then abuses that relationship by approaching the child at a park during the summer holidays, it may be said that by employing the teacher and giving him or her some authority (albeit not parental authority) over the child, the teacher's employer "made the wrong more probable". But it is likely vicarious liability would not be imposed on the employer given the absence of a close connection between the teacher's duties and his or her wrongful acts. To put the matter another way, *the fact that the teacher took advantage of his opportunity at the school to develop a relationship with the child is not enough: something more is required — a close connection between the teacher's duties and his or her wrongful acts — to render the school board liable without proof of negligence or other fault on its part.* [Emphasis added.]
>
> Griffiths took advantage of the opportunity the Club afforded him to make friends with the children. His manipulation of those friendships is both despi-

---

161 *Ibid.*, para. 58.
162 [1999] 2 S.C.R. 570.

cable and criminal, but whatever power Griffiths used to accomplish his criminal purpose for personal gratification was neither conferred by the Club nor was it characteristic of the type of enterprise which the respondent put into the community. That being the case, I do not think the one act of sexual touching which occurred on the Club van, given that it was a minor and incidental part of Griffiths' ongoing campaign of sexual predation outside Club facilities and outside Club hours, was sufficient to trigger no-fault liability. As McLachlin J. pointed out in *Children's Foundation* at para. 45, the mechanical application of time and place criteria obscures the more fundamental analysis.[163]

T.(G.) provides a useful summary of both Canadian and United States case law in respect of employer liability for sexual abuse. For example, one such case related to the conduct of a school janitor:

> [I]n *Goodwin c. Commission scolaire Laurenval*, [1991] R.R.A. 673, 8 C.C.L.T. (2d) 267 (Que. S.C.), Forget J. found that a janitor of a school in that case had been told that if he let students into the locked school after hours, he was to follow them to ensure that they did not wander in the school without supervision. A young girl who had asked the janitor to use the washroom facilities at a time when the school was closed was subjected to an episode of sexual touching by the janitor. Forget J. found that the school board was not liable because even though the Board had conferred some child-related responsibilities (i.e., supervision to and from the washroom), the assault was insufficiently connected to the janitor's duty to supervise (at p. 679 R.R.A.):
>
>> [TRANSLATION] Applying these criteria, it becomes clear that Mr. Cheng was not acting in the performance of his duties when he engaged in the alleged conduct. What Mr. Cheng said and what he did were not in any way connected with a supervisory activity. The situation would be entirely different if, for example, the janitor had struck the children because they refused to leave the school or obey his instructions; but that is not the case.[164]

The Court in *T.(G.)* was asked only to consider the issue of vicarious liability, which it described as a form of "no-fault" liability. The Court remitted the case back to trial court for a determination as to whether the Club was liable under a fault-based cause of action, i.e., negligence or breach of fiduciary duty.[165]

---

163 *Ibid.*, para 83-84.
164 *Ibid.*, para. 47.
165 For an analysis of the British law in this area, see *Lister & Others v. Hesley Hall Ltd.*, [2001] 2 All E.R. 769, [2001] UKHL 22 (H.L.) and a Case Note on *Lister* by Peter Williams in Australia & New Zealand Journal of Law & Education, Volume 6, No 1 & 2, 2001, pp. 101-106.

(d) Corporal Punishment and Physical Restraint

Assault and battery litigation involving principals and teachers usually arises out of their attempts to physically restrain students or to administer corporal punishment. The administration of corporal punishment may be permitted or prohibited by legislation or regulation, or by local board policies. The common law itself does not prohibit corporal punishment. However, excessive corporal punishment may amount to a civil wrong, as well as criminal conduct or child abuse.

There is no exact point at which the administration of corporal punishment will constitute an intentional tort. Each case will be decided upon its individual facts. Corporal punishment must not be unreasonable or malicious, and it is invariably subject to specific restrictions, either in legislation or local policy. For instance, it is often only the principal or vice-principal who is permitted to administer corporal punishment, and it is usually allowed only as a last resort.

Physical contact between a teacher and student also occurs in situations which do not involve corporal punishment. Corporal punishment is a disciplinary measure which involves intentionally creating discomfort or pain in the student by physical means. However, where a teacher restrains a student from harming the teacher or another student, the teacher is not administering corporal punishment. The teacher is acting in self-defence or safe-guarding the safety of the student and those near the student.

Breaking up a student fight is a proper exercise of the statutory and common law duty to maintain order and to ensure the safety of students. Failure to do so may result in an action based upon negligent supervision. Physical restraint may be required where the student has behavioural difficulties and is unable to control his or her actions. Local boards should establish what types of physical restraint are permissible and should provide training to teachers and instructional aides in the application of restraint techniques. The simple act of guiding a student down the hall by his arm would be battery unless justified by the carrying out by the teacher of professional responsibilities to maintain order or ensure safety. The application of physical force, whether to defend oneself, maintain order, or restrain a student is subject to many of the same limitations that apply to corporal punishment: the teacher's actions must not be excessive, malicious, arbitrary, or unreasonable.[166]

When an employee is found liable for assault or battery because of excessive or unreasonable corporal punishment or physical restraint, the board may be found vicariously liable for the employee's actions.

---

166 See the following United States cases: *Johnson v. Horace Mann Mutual Ins. Co.*, 241 So. 2d 588 (1970); *Simms v. School Dist. No. 1, Multnomah County*, 508 P. 2d 236 (1973); *LaFrentz v. Gallagher*, 462 P. 2d 804 (1970); *Frank v. Orleans Parish School Bd.*, 195 So. 2d 451 (1967).

(e) Defences to Intentional Tort Actions

Generally speaking, when a person consents to an activity which otherwise might amount to a tort, that person is precluded from suing for injuries which may result from the activity. Consent may be express or implied and it may be manifested orally or in writing. The defendant who alleges consent must prove it. Participants in sports that permit physical contact are assumed to have impliedly or expressly consented to the type and amount of contact which might be expected within the ordinary standards of the game or which is permitted by the rules.[167] The consent of the plaintiff must be genuine. It may not be obtained under duress, by deceit, or by fraud. The court may find consent to be lacking where the defendant has exploited the weakness of the plaintiff. In *Norberg v. Wynrib*,[168] a relationship of dependency was held by the Supreme Court of Canada to exist between the defendant doctor and the plaintiff patient. Being in a vulnerable position, the plaintiff could not be said to have consented to sexual relations with the doctor. Likewise, in *Lyth v. Dagg*,[169] the Court held that the defendant teacher exercised power and control over a student and that the student did not consent to the initial sexual encounter between them.

A person giving a consent must have the legal capacity to do so. In other words, the consent of someone who, by reason of age, impairment or mental incapacity cannot understand the nature of what he or she is consenting to, is not valid. As noted elsewhere in this chapter in relation to negligence, written consent for students to participate in sports, field trips and extra-curricular activities should be obtained from parents. While a court may recognize the validity of a consent given by an older student, the fact that the student is under the legal age of majority will make it that much harder for the defendant to prove consent. Written consents should be obtained from parents and older students.

Self-defence is a valid defence against a claim based on intentional tort. Persons are permitted to defend themselves against harm or perceived imminent harm. Actions taken in self-defence must be reasonable and proportionate to what is required to defend oneself under the circumstances. Teachers who are being threatened or attacked by other persons in the school, whether students, staff, strangers or irate parents, may defend themselves against harm.

The law also recognizes that a person may use reasonable force in protecting other persons from harm. Clearly it is reasonable to expect teachers to defend fellow teachers or their students from harm at school. Teachers may intervene in school fights in order, not only to maintain order and

---

167 *Colby v. Schmidt* (1986), 37 C.C.L.T. 1 (B.C. S.C.).
168 [1992] 2 S.C.R. 226, additional reasons at [1992] 2 S.C.R. 318.
169 (1988), 46 C.C.L.T. 25 (B.C. S.C.).

discipline, but also to protect one participant from harm at the hands of the other. Only a reasonable level of force may be used in rendering assistance to another. While the *Criminal Code of Canada*[170] provides a defence to teachers who have been charged as a result of disciplining a student, it does not enable teachers to claim that their use of physical force was legally *authorized* by law. This is distinct from statutory provisions which specifically permit persons to act in a manner which would otherwise be tortious conduct.

Reasonable force may also be used to protect personal or real property. Where a principal is authorized to remove trespassers from school property, reasonable force may be used. In addition, teachers may use reasonable force to protect their personal property from damage by students or others.

Just as a plaintiff in a negligence action may be held to have been contributorily negligent, a court may allocate a portion of liability to a plaintiff in an action based on intentional tort. Therefore, a plaintiff may recover only a portion of his or her total damages if the court holds him or her partially liable for the harm which occurred, assuming that this apportionment is not barred by the statutory or common law of the particular jurisdiction.

6. FIDUCIARY DUTY

One of the most significant legal developments in recent years, and one which has profound implications for school boards, involves the law of "fiduciary duty". The case of *M. (K.) v M. (H.)*,[171] decided by the Supreme Court of Canada in 1992, may provide the foundation for the expansion of this concept into the relationship between teacher and student. In particular, it may be another legal means of holding teachers accountable for their sexual misconduct in relation to students. Fiduciary duty is not based on the law of tort.

M.(K.) v. M.(H.) was a civil action by a woman against her father in which she claimed damages arising from her father's incestuous conduct. She based her claim in tort and in breach of fiduciary duty. Two key issues were dealt with.[172] The first was the question of when the limitation period started to run against the plaintiff with respect to her tort claim for assault and battery. The Court confirmed that incest is an intentional tort:

> [I]ncest constitutes an assault and battery, which can be compendiously defined as causing another person to apprehend the infliction of immediate harmful or

---

170 R.S.C. 1985, c. C-46, s. 43.
171 Above, note 149.
172 Aside from an examination of the doctrine of fraudulent concealment which was not part of the ratio of the case because it was not argued in the lower courts.

offensive force on her person coupled with actual infliction of that harmful or offensive force . . . .[173]

After an exhaustive analysis of evidence about the psychological damage and recovery process of incest victims, the Court decided that the statutory limitation period did not start to run against the plaintiff until she was "fully cognizant of who bears the responsibility for her childhood abuse, for it is then that she realizes the nature of the wrong done to her."[174] It was found on the facts that the plaintiff only became fully cognizant after she had received therapy, and accordingly, her tort action was within the limitation period.

The second issue was whether or not the incestuous conduct of the father was a breach of a fiduciary duty toward his daughter. The plaintiff argued that the Ontario *Limitations Act* does not apply to an action based upon breach of fiduciary duty, which is based in equity, and the limitations period could not, therefore, be raised as a defence. The Court agreed that incest is "a breach of both common law and equitable duties, and the latter claim is not foreclosed by the [Limitations] Act."[175]

The Court had little difficulty characterizing the relationship of parent and child as fiduciary in nature:

> It is intuitively apparent that the relationship between parent and child is fiduciary in nature, and that the sexual assault of one's child is a grievous breach of the obligations arising from that relationship. Indeed, I can think of few cases that are clearer than this. For obvious reasons society has imposed upon parents the obligation to care for, protect and rear their children. The act of incest is a heinous violation of that obligation. Equity has imposed fiduciary obligations on parents in contexts other than incest, and I see no barrier to the extension of a father's fiduciary obligation to include a duty to refrain from incestuous assaults on his daughter.[176]

La Forest J., for the majority, examined in detail a line of cases in which the meaning of the concept of "fiduciary duty" was developed and expanded. In *Guerin v. R.*,[177] which dealt with the fiduciary duty of the federal government toward aboriginal peoples, the Supreme Court of Canada rejected the notion that fiduciary duty was limited to the standard categories of agent, trustee, partner, director or similar positions. In *Frame v. Smith*,[178] Wilson J. of the Supreme Court of Canada (in a minority opinion later adopted by

---

173 Above, note 149, at 299.
174 Above, note 149, at 312.
175 Above, note 149, at 321-322.
176 Above, note 150, at 323.
177 (1984), 13 D.L.R. (4th) 321 (S.C.C.).
178 (1987), 42 D.L.R. (4th) 81 (S.C.C.).

the Supreme Court of Canada in *LAC Minerals Ltd. v. International Corona Resources Ltd.*[179]), identified fiduciary relationships as follows:

> Relationships in which a fiduciary obligation have been imposed seem to possess three general characteristics:
>
> (1) The fiduciary has scope for the exercise of some discretion or power.
> (2) The fiduciary can unilaterally exercise that power or discretion so as to affect the beneficiary's legal or practical interests.
> (3) The beneficiary is peculiarly vulnerable to or at the mercy of the fiduciary holding the discretion or power.[180]

After considering *Guerin, Frame* and LAC *Minerals,* La Forest J. stated that:

> [T]he substance of the fiduciary obligation in any given case is not derived from some immutable list of duties attached to a category of relationships. In other words, the duty is not determined by analogy with the "established" heads of fiduciary duty. Rather, the nature of the obligation will vary depending on the factual context of the relationship in which it arises.[181]

La Forest J. also referred to *McInerney v. MacDonald,*[182] in which His Lordship decided that a doctor-patient relationship could be described as "fiduciary", although each set of facts would shape the nature and extent of the fiduciary obligation.

Clearly, the Supreme Court of Canada does not feel constrained by traditional categories of fiduciary duty. The field of education law is replete with comparisons and analogies between "parent-child" and "teacher-student" relationships. The term *"in loco parentis"* is often used to describe a teacher's relationship with his or her students. Section 43 of the *Criminal Code* permits "every schoolteacher, parent or person standing in the place of the parent" to use reasonable force by way of correction. Teachers have been held to be in a position of trust over their pupils, under section 153 of the *Criminal Code.*[183] Ontario school children must accept such discipline as would be exercised by a "kind, firm and judicious parent".[184] The law of negligence in relation to teachers is founded upon the "careful or prudent parent" standard of care.

On the basis of *M.(K.) v. M.(H.),* some fact situations may give rise to a fiduciary relationship between a teacher and a student, and damages could be claimed for breach of that duty. Teachers who prey sexually upon students

---

179 (1989), 61 D.L.R. (4th) 14 (S.C.C.).
180 Above, note 178, at 99.
181 Above, note 149, at 326.
182 (1992), 93 D.L.R. (4th) 415 (S.C.C.).
183 *E.g.*, see *R. v. Palmer* (January 10, 1990), Doc. No. 362-89, Cosgrove D.C.J. (Ont. Dist. Ct.).
184 R.R.O. 1990, Reg. 298, s. 23.

often choose those who are particularly vulnerable by reason of their family background, or their psychological profile. By intentionally building up a relationship of trust with a student, the teacher is able to initiate sexual activity and the victim may not be fully aware that the teacher's conduct is improper. Some student victims have physical or mental disabilities which may make it particularly difficult for them to understand what is happening to them, or to respond appropriately. Children in residential settings may feel particularly isolated from their families. Therefore, a relationship between teacher and student could in some instances be considered fiduciary in nature. This possibility was recognized in *K.(K.M.) v. Ackerman*[185] in which Somers J. refused, in Motions Court, to strike a Statement of Claim that, *inter alia,* alleged breach of fiduciary duty by a school board in respect of a pupil. Although Somers J. expressed doubt as to whether such a claim could ultimately succeed against a school board, he felt it would be premature to strike the claim at an early point in the litigation.

In 1993, the *M.(K.) v. M.(H.)* case was applied by Rutherford J. in *J. (L.A.) v. J.(H.),*[186] in the Ontario Court (General Division). This case concerned a claim for damages based upon breach of fiduciary duty, arising out of incest by an uncle who was regarded by the plaintiff as her father. On the facts, the Court had no difficulty finding a breach of fiduciary duty. However, it also held the plaintiff's mother liable on the basis that the mother had failed to protect her daughter against the father's abuse, of which the mother was aware.

In *G.C.(E.D) v. Hammer,*[187] the British Columbia Court of Appeal considered a case in which the plaintiff sued a school board for damages as a result of a series of sexual assaults perpetrated against her in an elementary school by a janitor employed by the board. The Court dismissed the plaintiff's assertion of breach of fiduciary duty because "there was no basis for finding that the Board took advantage of a relationship of trust or confidence for its own direct or indirect personal advantage; nor is there any taint of disloyalty or dishonesty on the part of the Board."[188] The claim based on negligence was abandoned at trial as a result of the Supreme Court's decision in *T.(G.).* The central issue remaining on appeal was whether or not the plaintiff's claim could succeed against the board as a claim for breach of "non-delegable duty". The issue was therefore whether the school board owed a direct, non-delegable duty to children to ensure that reasonable care is taken of them while they are attending school, and whether that duty extends to protecting those children from intentional torts perpetrated upon

---

185 (1996), 15 O.T.C. 16 (Gen. Div.).
186 (1993), 102 D.L.R. (4th) 177 (Ont. Gen. Div.).
187 [2001] B.C.J. No. 585, 2001 CarswellBC 721 (C.A.), leave to appeal allowed (2001), 2001 CarswellBC 2756 (S.C.C.). Also at (2001), 151 BCAC 34.
188 *Ibid.*, para. 23.

them by individuals employed by the Board which occur on school property during school hours. This is a direct duty to the child, as distinct from vicarious liability resulting from the board's status as an employer. Prowse J.A., in dissent, found that the school board should be held liable on the basis of non-delegable duty toward its pupils. However, the majority took a narrower view of the circumstances in which a "breach of non-delegable duty" may occur, and found that the claim should fail:

> [I]f a claim for vicarious liability must fail because, in the traditional language, the employee's tort was outside the course and scope of his employment then any claim for breach of non-delegable duty of the employer equally must fail.[189]

This case has been appealed to the Supreme Court of Canada, and has enormous potential implications for school boards if that Court agrees with Prowse J.A.'s dissenting view that:

> [I]t is reasonable to conclude that where the legislature gives a Board de facto supervisory powers over the school in its district, including the power to hire and fire support staff, and where children within the district are statutorily compelled to attend these schools and abide by the directions of their teachers while there, the Board has a non-delegable duty to ensure that reasonable care is taken for the safety of those children while on school premises. Absent statutory language indicating a contrary intent, this duty would exist whether the claim against the Board arose in negligence or as a result of an intentional tort on the part of one of its employees.[190]

The decision of the Alberta Court of Queen's Bench (McMahon J.) in *H.(S.G.) v. Gorsline*[191] was issued in the same month as the above referenced British Columbia appellate decision in *G.(E.D.) v. Hammer*. In *Gorsline*, the plaintiff was sexually abused by a teacher. In respect of the teacher himself, the Court found that Gorsline was liable for the intentional torts of assault and battery, and, in addition, for breach of his fiduciary relationship as a teacher toward the plaintiff. The plaintiff asserted that the school board should be held vicariously liable for the teacher's conduct, and directly negligent for its own breach of duty. In considering the issue of vicarious liability, the Court had the benefit of the guidelines offered by the Supreme Court of Canada in *B.(P.A.)*, referred to above. In reviewing the case precedents, the Court found that none of them provided unambiguous precedents for determining the issue of vicarious liability for sexual assault in a non-residential school setting. The Court held that the school board should not be held vicariously liable for the teacher's actions. Unlike the facts in

---

189 *Ibid.*, para. 75.
190 *Ibid.*, para. 50.
191 [2001] A.J. No. 263, 2001 CarswellAlta 277 (Q.B.), additional reasons at (2001), 96 Alta. L.R. (3d) 88 (Q.B.).

B.(P.A.), the teacher's duties did not require him to be alone with the plaintiff for extended periods or to have any form of intimate contact with her.

> It was not his job to transport a student alone, after hours, to and from a private track club or to competitions, or to his own home for babysitting. Yet he used all of these occasions to advance his agenda.[192]

Moreover, "teachers are not "substitute" parents when the parents retain their presence and authority."[193]

The Court then considered whether the school board should be held negligent for its failure to observe and respond to Gorsline's conduct; for permitting an atmosphere in the school which tolerated inappropriate behaviour; or for its failure to initiate programs of awareness and protection against abuse. The issue therefore was whether the board's employees knew or ought to have known about his conduct. The evidence was that although students knew of Gorsline's reputation for inappropriate conduct, none of the staff or parents seemed to have been aware of his propensities. The Court found that:

> The evidence is persuasive that Gorsline was successful in hiding his sexual abuse of the plaintiff. None of his teaching colleagues who testified harboured any suspicion.[194]

The Court was not satisfied that the board permitted an atmosphere that tolerated inappropriate conduct that would encourage sexual assault or prevent its disclosure. As for the need for policies to prevent sexual abuse, the Court held that there was no evidence that in 1978-79, the time of the offence, the board knew or ought to have known of the need for such policies, or that the absence of such policies was causally connected to the harm inflicted.

The Court went on to consider whether the school board had a fiduciary relationship to the student, and found that such a relationship did exist:

> There was a significant power imbalance between the student on the one hand and the combined forces of the teachers, principals and administrators on the other, combined with the legislative authority of the School Board. In those circumstances and at her age the student was particularly vulnerable.[195]

The Court found that there was no breach of the fiduciary relationship. This was not a case of failure of the board to act upon disclosure. The Court stated:

---

192 *Ibid.*, para. 74.
193 *Ibid.*, para. 76.
194 *Ibid.*, para. 102.
195 *Ibid.*, para. 113.

[There was no] evidence against the School Board of personal wrongdoings beyond negligence, nor any element of dishonesty, disloyalty or personal advantage as described in *A.(C.) v. C.(J.W.), supra.*

I have concluded that there is not even evidence of simple negligence on the part of the School Board. A breach of fiduciary duty is a greater wrong. it is conduct which is offensive. It is a wrongful advantage taken of a position of trust.[196]

The Court also rejected the plaintiff's assertion that the board had a non-delegable duty: "I conclude that this form of strict liability should also not be imposed upon a School Board except by a legislature."[197]

Comment

Although not dealing with non-residential school settings, the decisions in *B.(P.A.)* and *T.(G.)* will guide lower courts in determining the circumstances in which a school board may be found vicariously liable for abuse committed by an employee. The facts in *Gorsline*[198] illustrate the difference between the opportunities for abuse created in a residential setting, where employees of the institution are afforded opportunity for constant and close contact with potential victims, contrasted with a non-residential setting where a teacher must typically create an "aura of secrecy and intimacy" in the words of MacMahon J. in *Gorsline*. However, non-residential school settings operate in different ways and afford different opportunities to staff members to perpetrate harm. Some facts could give rise to a finding of vicarious liability on the part of a school board for employee sexual assault. The *Gorsline* decision is also interesting because it found that the *school board* had a fiduciary relationship with the student, even though there was no breach of the relationship. This expands what is considered to be a fiduciary relationship and it remains to be seen whether a consistent picture will emerge in courts across Canada. In *A.(C.) v. C.(J.W.)*,[199] for example, the British Columbia Court of Appeal held that the provincial Crown was not liable for breach of fiduciary duty where it had placed the plaintiff in an abusive foster home. The Court commented at some length about the expansion of the concept of fiduciary relationship and argued in favour of an approach that would "confine recovery based on fiduciary duties to cases of the kind where, in addition to other usual requirements such as vulnerability and the exercise of a discretion, the defendant personally takes advantage of a relationship of trust or confidence for his or her direct or indirect personal advantage." (*C.(J.W.)*, at page 500). In addition, as we mentioned above, the question raised in *G.(E.D.) v. Hammer* about whether school

---

196 *Ibid.*, paras. 116-117.
197 *Ibid.*, para. 120.
198 *Above*, note 191.
199 (1998), 166 D.L.R. (4th) 475 (B.C. C.A.).

boards have a statutory non-delegable duty of care toward students is before the Supreme Court at time of writing, and has the potential to significantly expand the exposure of school boards to findings of liability.

7. EDUCATIONAL MALPRACTICE

We stated previously that parents expect at least three things for their children: the opportunity to acquire knowledge and skills, the administration of fair and equitable discipline, and a safe learning environment. Failure to provide a safe learning environment or to apply fair discipline both invite tort actions. Both concern "educational malpractice" in the broader sense. However, the term "educational malpractice" usually refers to the alleged failure to impart knowledge or to teach practical skills. In particular, a legal claim of "educational malpractice" usually alleges that a school system has failed to provide the plaintiff with the academic skills necessary to undertake the most rudimentary tasks involved in coping with adult life. Inability to complete a job application, despite the acquisition of a diploma, is one example.[200]

Plaintiffs alleging educational malpractice have met with little success in the courts. There is, as yet, no definitive decision by a Canadian appellate court on educational malpractice. Lower Canadian courts, on the rare occasion when they have addressed the issue, have followed the American lead, as established in the leading case of *Peter W. v. San Francisco Unified School District*.[201] At issue is not the obligation upon school authorities to provide education; that is, after all, why they exist.[202] The issue is whether

---

200 Michael W. La Morte, *School Law: Cases and Concepts,* 4th ed. (Needham Heights: Allyn & Bacon, 1993), p. 412.
201 60 Cal. App. 3d 814, 131 Cal. Rptr. 854 (1976). See for example *Nishri v. North York Board of Education* (April 27, 1994) Doc. No. 2117/87 (Ont. Div. Ct.) in which the defendant board successfully moved for summary judgment dismissing the plaintiff's claim that the public school system failed him in terms of "the normal socialization process" — that is, it did not teach him properly in terms of human relations. The claim was dismissed on the basis that it was filed beyond the limitation period in the *Public Authorities Protection Act* (Ontario). However, MacPherson J., also indicated that summary judgment dismissing the claim would be justified even if the claim were filed within the limitation period. The plaintiff had in fact graduated from secondary school and obtained a university degree. There was no evidence that the board was responsible for the alleged failure in respect of the plaintiff's socialization. See also, *Haynes (Guardian ad litem of) v. Llleres* (B.C. Prov. Ct.) (March 10, 1997), Doc. Vancouver 969025, [1997] B.C.J. No. 1202 (B.C. Prov. Ct.) and *Gould v. Regina (East) School Division No. 77* (1996), 151 Sask. R. 189 (Q.B.), (actions for educational malpractice dismissed).
202 In Ontario, for instance, a board shall "provide instruction and adequate accommodation during each school year for the pupils who have a right to attend a school under the jurisdiction of the board." *(Education Act,* s. 170(1), para. 6.) Teachers have a legal obligation to "teach diligently and faithfully" (s. 264 (1)(a)) and to "encourage pupils in the pursuit of learning" (s. 264(1)(b)). Failure to provide an education, while a failure to comply with statutory responsibilities does not automatically mean that a board may be

or not the plaintiff has a cause of action based on negligence against the school authority which the courts are prepared to recognize. In other words, assuming that the plaintiff can prove that he or she failed to learn, will the courts recognize the existence of a tort action based on educational malpractice? Educational malpractice suits based on lack of competency are distinguishable from special education litigation dealing with the interpretation of the rights of exceptional children under education or human rights legislation, or under the *Canadian Charter of Rights and Freedoms*.[203]

For example, in *Haynes (Guardian ad litem of) v. Lleres*,[204] the British Columbia Provincial Court dismissed a civil action against a teacher, superintendent and school board asserting that they were negligent in the manner in which they instructed a component of the plaintiff's French immersion Grade 9 social studies class. The judge (Moss J.) held that the claim could only be characterized as educational malpractice and that such a claim was not recognized in Canadian or American law as an actionable tort, and that the individual teacher must have "broad discretion to teach according to his/her perception of the class dynamics." In *Hicks v. Etobicoke (City) Board of Education*[205] the plaintiff student and his mother claimed that the defendants owed a duty of care to the infant plaintiff which they breached by failing to provide proper education and corrective instruction to the infant plaintiff in accordance with their obligations under the *Education Act*. The plaintiffs' complaint was not only with the identification or placement of the child but with the actions taken and the procedures followed by the Board in its dealings with the child, in that they did not fulfil the Board's statutory obligation to provide the child with proper instruction. That is, the plaintiff alleged that the Board breached its statutory duty of care because of the special duty that exists between the Board and its pupils, that being a professional relationship. The Court dismissed the claim as failing to disclose a reasonable cause of action.

In *Peter W.*, the California Court of Appeals considered the plaintiff's allegations that the school system was negligent in that it failed to apprehend his reading disabilities; assigned him to classes in which he could not read the materials; permitted him to advance grade levels without the necessary knowledge or skills; assigned unqualified instructors; and permitted him to graduate from high school although unable to read above the grade 8 level. By permitting him to graduate, the school system was alleged to have deprived him of the right to receive additional instruction which he needed.

---

sued in negligence or that it has in fact been negligent. However, if the tort of malpractice were recognized, non-compliance with statutory requirements could be adduced as evidence of negligence. See *Canada v. Sask. Wheat Pool*, [1983] 1 S.C.R. 205.
203 See Chapter 5, on Special Education.
204 (March 10, 1997), Doc. Vancouver 969025, [1997] B.C.J. No. 1202 (B.C. Prov. Ct.).
205 (November 23, 1988), Doc. 306622/87, [1988] O.J. No. 1900 (Ont. Dist. Ct.).

The California Court of Appeals affirmed the decision of the lower courts in dismissing the action. In order for the action to succeed, the plaintiff was required to satisfy the Court that the elements of negligence were present. The Court relied upon public policy arguments in holding that there was no "duty of care" toward the plaintiff:

> Few of our institutions, if any, have aroused the controversies, or incurred the public dissatisfaction, which have attended the operation of the public schools during the last few decades. Rightly or wrongly, but widely, they are charged with outright failure in the achievement of their educational objectives; according to some critics, they bear responsibility for many of the social and moral problems of our society at large. Their public plight in these respects is attested in the daily media, in bitter governing board elections, in wholesale rejections of school bond proposals, and in survey upon survey. To hold them to an actionable "duty of care," in the discharge of their academic functions, would expose them to the tort claims — real or imagined — of disaffected students and parents in countless numbers.[206]

The Court also held that recognition of this type of tort would be, in a legal sense, unmanageable:

> Unlike the activity of the highway or the marketplace, classroom methodology affords no readily acceptable standards of care, or cause, or injury. The science of pedagogy itself is fraught with different and conflicting theories of how or what a child should be taught, and any layman might — and commonly does — have his own emphatic views on the subject. The "injury" claimed here is the plaintiff's inability to read and write. Substantial professional authority attests that the achievement of literacy in the schools, or its failure, is influenced by a host of factors which affect the pupil subjectively, from outside the formal teaching process, and beyond the control of its ministers. They may be physical, neurological, emotional, cultural, environmental; they may be present but not perceived, recognized but not identified.[207]

The Court found that there was no misrepresentation of the plaintiff's academic progress, and that, in any event, for public policy reasons, there can be no cause of action in negligence based on the misrepresentation alleged.

The second leading case on educational malpractice was decided by the New York Supreme Court, Appellate Division in *Donohue v. Copiague Union Free School District*.[208] In this case, the plaintiff alleged that the school system failed in virtually all of its responsibilities to educate the plaintiff, including failure to ascertain his learning ability, properly test him, teach him the required subjects, supervise him, and to provide adequate facilities, teachers, administrators, psychologists and other personnel. It was

---

206 Above, note 201, at 825.
207 *Ibid.*
208 407 N.Y.S. 2d 874, 64 A.D. 2d 29 (1978).

also alleged that there was a failure to keep parents properly advised of the plaintiff's difficulties.

The Court agreed with the California Court of Appeals in *Peter W.* that public policy runs against the involvement of the judiciary in matters of education. It also stated that the failure to learn was not necessarily the fault of the teacher. Even though the plaintiff had received some failing grades, neither he nor his parents requested special assistance. There was no evidence that the plaintiff's classmates also failed to learn. The *Donohue* case differs from the *Peter W.* case in that, in *Donohue*, the Court recognized that a plaintiff could theoretically satisfy the elements of a negligence case. However, the Court said that it would take an extreme case to overcome the public policy considerations leading to non-involvement by the judiciary:

> This determination does not mean that educators are not ethically and legally responsible for providing a meaningful public education for the youth of our State. Quite the contrary, all teachers and other officials of our schools bear an important public trust and may be held to answer for the failure to faithfully perform their duties. It does mean, however, that they may not be sued for damages by an individual student for an alleged failure to reach certain educational objectives.[209]

One might speculate from these comments that a class action claim alleging systemic incompetency in a class or school might overcome the public policy hurdle. The increased use of standardized testing across Canada will establish educational benchmarks for assessing the progress of students. This testing is not designed to evaluate the competence of teachers. An attempt to use testing scores in court to show professional incompetence, even if ultimately unsuccessful, would likely have a chilling effect upon those who teach, and who administer and mark the tests.

Where standardized tests, unlike "benchmarks", are used to evaluate the suitability of students for graduation or entrance to college or university, the pupil's score may have a more tangible impact upon the student, and may certainly affect his or her future prospects and economic well-being. If test scores in an entire school, or in classes taught by a certain teacher, are below average, would this provide the evidentiary basis for a court action? Given the many variables affecting student achievement, it would be difficult to establish what evidentiary weight should be given to such a statistical occurrence and whether the lack of achievement was caused by incompetence on the part of the teacher or school administration, or by other factors. However, a pattern of underachievement may help to isolate some of the other variables affecting student performance and may assist counsel in establishing liability. It is clear from the present case law, however, that courts will continue to rely upon the public policy argument against edu-

---

209 *Ibid.*

cational malpractice actions, except perhaps where there has been a gross violation by the school system of its responsibilities to educate students.

It has been suggested[210] that, had *Peter W.* and *Donohue* been decided on stronger facts, the results may have been different. It is only a matter of time before a higher Canadian court will be asked to rule upon the issue of educational malpractice. It is not difficult to imagine a movement away from the American precedents. Incompetent teaching damages children. It reduces their self-esteem and destroys career prospects. It causes mental anxiety. It deprives children of the knowledge and skills that they will need to survive. Teachers are therefore normally required to have a university education, specialized courses, and regular classroom performance evaluations. It is arguable that public policy should not prevent a malpractice action where a teacher whose performance is known by a board to be unsatisfactory is nevertheless permitted to teach, and where it is proved that the plaintiff student was in some meaningful way "injured". Because of the variables which affect learning, courts are understandably reluctant to recognize claims for damages based on allegations that the plaintiff should have learned more. However, the obligation to teach goes beyond imparting knowledge. Teachers may cause considerable stress among pupils by failing to properly manage the classroom, by yelling at or ridiculing pupils, or even by failing to mark papers properly and promptly. Is negligent infliction of mental stress a form of educational malpractice? It will become increasingly difficult for courts to distinguish between educational malpractice and those torts which presently have judicial recognition.[211]

8. RISK MANAGEMENT

In addition to understanding the fundamentals of tort law, educators, school administrators and board members must be committed to minimizing the occurrence of accidents. "Risk management" means taking steps to prevent situations from occurring which may lead to legal liability. The term is normally used in a liability insurance context, to refer to minimizing exposure to successful negligence claims. However, preventative measures can embrace training for staff and students in the area of conflict resolution

---

210 *E.g.*, see Michael Hines, "Malpractice in Education" 1991 CAPSLE Conference materials.

211 *E.g.*, the Court in *Hunter v. Montgomery County (Bd. of Education)*, 439 A.2d 582 (Md. 1982), acknowledged that parents of a disabled child could maintain an action against a school system alleging intentional acts which resulted in injury to the child, although the burden of proof would be onerous. The Court rejected a malpractice claim based upon the board's unintentional actions. See comments in Martha M. McCarthy and Nelda H. Cambron-McCabe, *Public School Law: Teachers' and Students' Rights*, 2nd ed. (Needham Heights, Mass.: Allyn & Bacon, 1987), at pp. 91-92. See also, Joanna Holloway "The Liability of the Local Education Authority to Pupils Who Receive a Defective Education" [1996, 7 E.L.J. No. 2, page 95].

in order to reduce violent incidents and potential lawsuits arising from assault and battery.

Risk management has at least two benefits for school boards and their employees. First, the number of accidents is decreased through attention to safety and training. Secondly, when an accident does occur, it is easier to defend a lawsuit when the defendant can show that reasonable safety measures and training were in effect at the time.

Statistically, relatively few accidents take place in the regular classroom. Playgrounds and sports activities have predictably high rates of accident occurrence. Slip-and-fall accidents on board property are also a major concern.

Numerous measures can be taken to reduce the risk of an accident, or to ensure that proper steps are taken after an accident occurs. School boards should:

1. Systematically identify potential dangers to students, staff and visitors. Insurance companies and other organizations can provide "risk surveys" or "safety audits" of schools which help to spot potential trouble areas.
2. Ensure that teachers and coaches have current training. The cost of training courses is far less than the human cost of injuries or the monetary cost of defending a lawsuit and paying damages.
3. Ensure that staff are trained in first aid and Cardiac Pulmonary Resuscitation. Failure to provide adequate first aid is negligence.
4. Provide adequate first aid kits.
5. Provide equipment which is reasonably current and which is maintained on a fixed schedule. Records of regular equipment maintenance are essential in defending a lawsuit where there are allegations of defective equipment.
6. Ensure that science laboratories and technical shops have safe, up-to-date equipment and that staff and students know how to use the equipment properly. Staff and students must also know what to do if an accident happens. This involves first aid, eye wash procedures, emergency burn treatment, and evacuation due to fire or noxious fumes. Safety training must be a constant process throughout the students' program of study.
7. Ensure that transportation of pupils during school activities is safe. Board policy should be clear as to what form of transportation is permitted and as to whose insurance coverage applies.
8. Ensure that adequate staff/pupil supervision ratios are established for playgrounds and for school activities such as field trips. It is not sufficient merely to select any adult or senior student as a supervisor. The supervisor must be a sensible, competent person: the kind of person to whom a parent would entrust a child. Supervisors must be trained how

to supervise, and how to respond when an accident or other incident occurs. The number of supervisors required depends on the type and location of the activity, and the age and competency of the pupils. Because of these variables, there is no single standard which can be used as a benchmark, although it is useful to know the supervision ratios used by other school boards. Ontario does not prescribe specific supervision standards in the *Education Act* or the regulations.
9. Ensure that the staff member who is responsible for a student activity knows how to contact parents and the appropriate authorities (medical, fire, police) if an injury occurs. Staff should know in advance who is responsible for what action. Students who participate in school sports or who go on school trips must be asked to provide emergency phone numbers, medical information (*e.g.*, on allergies and medication), parental permission forms, and medical certificates of fitness for the activity.
10. Ensure that records are kept of the time, date and nature of all inspections of property, hallways, sidewalks and equipment. Slip and fall accidents due to water, snow or ice on floors, parking lots and sidewalks can often be successfully defended if records are kept to prove that adequate safety measures were taken in a timely fashion.
11. Ensure that emergency and fire drills are conducted in accordance with provincial legislation or regulations (as a minimum).
12. Provide seminars for staff and coaches on negligence law and risk management. Understanding the problem is a first step toward preventing it.
13. Appoint a staff person to be responsible for risk management for the school board.

After the Fact

After an incident has occurred which involves actual or possible injury to a student or staff member, there are several important things for staff to remember:
1. Report the matter to senior management and to the insurance company in the prescribed manner.
2. Inform parents at the earliest possible moment.
3. Senior management must keep school trustees informed; they do not like to hear about accidents through the local newspaper.
4. If possible, preserve evidence of what has happened. Make written notes about the incident as to time; weather conditions; what the student or staff member was doing just before the accident; what warnings had been given; what kind of footwear or equipment was being used; what evidence of injury was noticed; what first aid was applied; what was done to assist the injured; and what statements were made after the

accident. These notes will be invaluable if the staff member is called as a witness in a civil lawsuit, often many years after the accident occurred.
5. No statements should be made to the press, other than by senior management or the board's press officer.
6. No written or oral statements should be given to parents or to their representatives, without the prior approval of senior management. These statements may make it difficult to defend a subsequent lawsuit, particularly if they contain admissions. This does not mean that school staff should not contact parents to see how an injured pupil is progressing. There is sometimes a fine line between a human expression of concern for the student and a statement which could affect a lawsuit.
7. School staff must cooperate with the insurance adjuster and legal counsel who are acting for the board. They should never discuss an accident or legal case with an adjuster or legal counsel representing a plaintiff or potential plaintiff without first obtaining the approval of senior management.

3

The Family

1. INTRODUCTION   150
2. MARRIAGE   150
   (a) Marriage and the Family   150
   (b) Spousal Rights   154
   (c) Cohabitation   156
   (d) Same Sex Relationships   157
   (e) The Marriage of Gays and Lesbians   158
   (f) Registered Domestic Partnerships   160
   (g) Custody, Access and Adoption by Gays and Lesbians   163
3. DIVORCE   165
   (a) Proceedings under the Divorce Act   165
   (b) Separation   166
   (c) Adultery and Cruelty   168
   (d) Reconciliation and Condonation   170
   (e) Taking Violent Conduct into Account   171
4. CUSTODY AND ACCESS   174
5. DOMESTIC VIOLENCE AND SPOUSAL ABUSE   177
   (a) The Cycle of Violence   178
   (b) Domestic Violence Defined   179
   (c) Myths About Domestic Violence   179
   (d) Some Sobering Facts   181
   (e) Police Protocols   182
   (f) The Domestic Violence Protection Act, 2000   183
   (g) Effect of Family Violence upon Children   184
6. PARENTAL AUTHORITY   185
   (a) The Family and the Canadian Charter of Rights and Freedoms   185
   (b) Corporal Punishment   191
   (c) Home Schooling   197
   (d) School Councils   198

1. INTRODUCTION

Schools do not exist in a vacuum, nor does education law. As a field of study, education law brings in elements of administrative, tort, corporate, criminal, constitutional and family law. Trends and developments in education law often mirror or shadow developments that happen in society at large and may reflect what is happening to the "family". Moreover, the breakdown of family relationships has ramifications in respect of how schools cope with the effects of broken families and domestic violence. Family breakdown also spills over into the ability of individual children to learn when caught up in the breakdown. This chapter provides a "family" context for education law. It includes a brief overview of the huge area of family law, including some key provisions in the *Family Law Act* (Ontario) and the *Divorce Act*, as well as recent changes affecting the rights of gays and lesbians. It discusses spousal abuse and the effect of domestic abuse on children in the home. Corporal punishment is also discussed in this chapter, because it is a family issue as well as a school issue. Although school councils are briefly discussed in Chapter 1, we look at some of the issues and implications of these councils, which are essentially a vehicle for families to have a voice in local school operations.

2. MARRIAGE

(a) Marriage and the Family

Sir Winston Churchill was probably typical of others in the first half of the 20th century, in his attitude towards the family, women, and women's rights. He had been brought up to believe that women ran the household, gave birth, and looked after the children. Family life and motherhood, he once claimed: "must be the fountain spring of present happiness and future survival". His pronouncement: "You must have four children. One for Mother, one for Father, one for Accidents and one for Increase" has a very Victorian ring to it – although it could have been uttered tongue-in-cheek. Times have certainly changed. With the 21st century upon us, no social institution is under greater pressure than marriage and the family. The 21st century began with no greater challenge than to align current reality with livable law and rediscover necessary social understandings. The family, once the corollary of marriage and the institution that constituted the basis of civilized societies, has been shaken by the widespread abandonment of fundamental traditional social understandings and the failure of visible alternatives for ongoing social functions and needs. Things are not what they used to be, even while popular perception continues to wrap "marriage" and "family" in an irrational, sentimental cocoon that has clouded logical discussion and intelligent debate. Most family law reform has responded, in common law fashion, to specific situations and circumstances, often haphazardly. Will reason have much say in an area as emotionally contested as family behaviour and its regulation?[1]

Today, society offers a broad variety of lifestyles for sexual partners. We still see the traditional model of marriage with children, in which one spouse takes on primary responsibility for the raising of the children, thereby sacrificing earnings and career prospects, and the other is freed to build a career, but the economic risks of divorce make "role division" even less attractive. The downside of traditional marriage is that one partner, typically the woman, has sacrificed earnings and career to raise children and, on divorce, has little property and limited employment prospects. The risk is often mutual in that the earning partner, typically the husband, faces increased responsibilities after divorce. Increasingly, one sees the modern variant of traditional marriage with minor children where both parents participate in the job market and the child-care function is at least in part delegated to extended family, day-care, nursery schools, kindergarten, the school system, or, if a second income makes that financially possible, to a "nanny" or "babysitter". One also sees childless relationships, married or unmarried, heterosexual or of the same sex, in which partners pursue their individual careers and, along with their sexual relationship, set up housekeeping together. Indeed, modern divorce law and practice result in (serial) polygamy in the form of multiple marriages or relationships of persons who have continuing legal, financial, and social ties to prior partners and children – responsibilities many cannot meet and many others shirk.

The *Constitution Act, 1867*, provides that legislative jurisdiction with respect to marriage is shared between the federal and provincial governments. Parliament has exclusive jurisdiction concerning "marriage and divorce" (see section 91(26)) and the provincial Legislatures have exclusive jurisdiction concerning "solemnization of marriage in the province (see section 92(12)) and "property and civil rights in the province" (see section 92(13)). The Constitution provides for overlapping legislative authority. Parliament has legislative authority with respect to the capacity to marry, that is, who can or cannot marry. Parliament has enacted legislation prohibiting certain persons who are related by blood or adoption from marrying. Moreover, a decree of nullity must be distinguished from a divorce. A divorce puts an end to a valid marriage, whereas nullity rectifies the status of the parties as a result of some defect or disability at the time of the marriage ceremony. The ground of annulment is one which renders the marriage voidable, whereas the decree of nullity annuls it, at common law, with retroactive effect.

---

[1] See Harry D. Karuse, "Marriage for the New Millennium: Heterosexual Same Sex – or Not at All?", 34 F. L.Q. 271 (2000).

In order to have a marriage that is unquestionably valid, the parties must have capacity (essential validity) to marry according to the law of their domiciles at the time of marriage and must comply with the solemnization requirements of the place where the marriage is celebrated. In Ontario, the *Marriage Act*[2] sets out who may perform marriages, when a licence is required, where and from whom that licence may be obtained, and who may obtain one. If there has been a breach of the formal requirements pursuant to the *Marriage Act*, the marriage will generally be regarded as invalid unless the defect is cured and the marriage is validated. Marriages will not be invalidated for breach of the Act if the parties went through the marriage in good faith and cohabited as husband and wife. A marriage licence cannot be issued to a minor without the written consent of both parents. Obtaining the consent of parents is to be regarded as a matter of the formalities requisite for marriage; it is, accordingly, a matter regulated by the law of the place where the marriage is celebrated. If a marriage has been entered into in a country where no formalities are required other than an agreement to marry followed by cohabitation, that marriage will be, with respect to formalities, regarded as valid in Ontario. The case law definition of marriage may be stated as "...the voluntary union for life of one man and one woman, to the exclusion of all others". Marriage is a relationship of heterosexual monogamy. No person is entitled to undergo a second form of marriage while the first marriage remains valid and subsisting. A marriage will be void if one of the parties does not have the capacity to understand the basic nature of a marriage and its obligations. An operative lack of understanding may result from a lack of mental capacity or such non-inherent factors as being under the influence of drugs or alcohol. Duress of such a kind as to negate consent invalidates a marriage. In order to establish duress it is necessary to prove three factors: (1) the person must be sufficiently afraid to remove the element of consent to marriage; (2) the fear must be reasonably entertained; and (3) the fear must arise from some external circumstances for which the applicant is not personally responsible.

The rules of Cannon Law banning marriages between people too closely related by blood or marriage form the basis for the common law rules rendering marriages within the prohibited degrees of consanguinity and affinity void *ab initio*. All of the prohibitions in Canadian law against marriage based on the parties being related are contained in the *Marriage (Prohibited Degrees) Act*[3], section 4, or see the *Marriage Act*, section 19, Form 1. The relevant provisions of the *Marriage (Prohibited Degrees) Act*, are as follows:

---

[2] R.S.O. 1990, c. M.3.
[3] S.C. 1990, c. 46.

2. No prohibition. — (1) Subject to subsection (2), persons related by consanguinity, affinity or adoption are not prohibited from marrying each other by reason only of their relationship.

(2) Prohibition. — No person shall marry another person if they are related

(a) lineally by consanguinity or adoption;
(b) as brother and sister by consanguinity, whether by the whole blood or by the half-blood; or
(c) as brother and sister by adoption

Marriage not valid. — (1) Subject to subsection (2), a marriage between persons related by consanguinity, affinity or adoption is not invalid by reason only of their relationship.

(2) Marriage void. – A marriage between persons who are related in the manner described in paragraph 2(2)(a), (b) or (c) is void.

Consanguinity is used throughout the *Marriage Act*, with respect to the "Form" that appears as an appendix to the Act. The "Form" provides:

Degrees of consanguinity which, under the *Marriage (Prohibited Degrees) Act*, (Canada), bar the lawful solemnization of marriage.

A man may not marry his
1. Grandmother
2. Mother
3. Daughter
4. Sister
5. Granddaughter

A woman may not marry her
1. Grandfather
2. Father
3. Son
4. Brother
5. Grandson

The relationships set forth in this table include all such relationships, whether by the whole or half-blood or by order of adoption.

A marriage is voidable if one of the parties was unable to consummate the marriage at the time of the ceremony. A marriage is consummated when ordinary and complete sexual intercourse takes place between the spouses after the marriage ceremony. Accordingly, the use of contraceptives, sterility or capricious refusal to engage in sexual intercourse does not amount to an inability to consummate. The parties to a void marriage are in the same position as a man and a woman who are living together as unmarried. A voidable marriage is a valid subsisting marriage until annulled and all the normal consequences of marriage flow. Once a decree of nullity is pronounced, it is as if the marriage never took place.

(b) Spousal Rights

In Ontario, for the purposes of the *Family Law Act*, the definition of a "spouse" includes either a man and woman who have together entered into a marriage that is voidable or void, in good faith on the part of the person asserting a right under the Act. Parties to a void or voidable marriage are therefore clearly covered by Part I (Family Property) provided they have gone through a form of marriage and the person asserting a right under the Act has acted in good faith. Part III of the *Family Law Act* imposes mutual obligations on "spouses" to support each other. The definition of "spouses" in section 1(1) continues to apply. There is a duty on parents to support their children and no distinction is drawn between children born in void, voidable or valid marriages. In defining the rights of children, the law in Ontario no longer distinguishes between children born within or outside of the marriage unless paternity is an issue.

In the early 1960s, cohabitants were largely ignored by the legal system, but since that time enormous strides have been made in recognizing extra-marital relationships. In Ontario the developments have been so far-reaching that there are few remaining legal differences between married and cohabiting couples. During the 1970s and 1980s the Supreme Court of Canada developed unjust enrichment principles in the context of property disputes between cohabitants. Initially these developments occurred in the context of matrimonial property disputes,[4] but legislative reforms largely superseded the use of unjust enrichment and trust doctrines in that context.[5] However, Part I of the *Family Law Act*, which deals with equalizing claims between married spouses, does not cover cohabitants.

What does the word "family" mean? There is no official meaning at common law or statute law for the word "family". When confronted with the need for a definition, judges acknowledge that it is an extremely fluid concept and a function of ongoing social processes.[6] Although various aspects of law and social policy encourage the creation and strengthening of the "family", the "family" has no legal standing under any Western legal regime or of any legal system derived from Roman civil law with its emphasis on individual rights and responsibilities. A family is not a corporation and has no collective rights or liabilities as such. (In non-Western systems, the clan or the family was able to assert territorial rights and other privileges, usually through the voice of the clan patriarch. Under those regimes, modern "family law" as we would know it could scarcely exist.)

The *Family Law Act* has several definitions of "spouse". For the purposes of Parts I and II (which deal with the matrimonial home) "spouse"

---

4 See *Rathwell v. Rathwell*, [1978] 2 S.C.R. 436 (S.C.C.).

5 see *Rawluk v. Rawluk* (1990), 23 R.F.L. (3d) 337 (S.C.C.).

6 Dubler discusses the ongoing contest between legal doctrine and social norms. See *A Legal History of Acting Married*, 100 Columbia Law Review 957 (2000).

refers to spouses in a valid marriage, and extends to void and voidable marriages if the marriage was entered into in good faith on the part of the person asserting a right under the Act. Although cohabitants do not have rights under Part I of the *Family Law Act*, they do enjoy access to common law remedies, which are in fact available to everyone, irrespective of the type of relationship involved. Thus, cohabitants may claim an interest in property by using resulting trust principles, or more commonly, by resort to the doctrine of unjust enrichment. The court has a choice of remedy: use of the constructive trust to award a beneficial interest in the property or monetary compensation.

Becker v. Pettkus[7] was the first Supreme Court of Canada decision to unequivocally adopt the concept of the constructive trust and the Court first laid down the three-part test for unjust enrichment that has been used in all subsequent decisions. The requisites are:

1. an enrichment of the defendant
2. a deprivation suffered by the plaintiff; and
3. the absence of a juristic reason for the enrichment.

The Supreme Court had a further opportunity to refine unjust enrichment principles in *Peter v. Beblow*.[8] In the early 1970s, B asked P to live with him. P moved in with her children and became stepmother to B's children. For the next 12 years P performed a number of tasks including domestic work, gardening, general maintenance of the property and child care. In an action based in unjust enrichment P was awarded title to the property. McLachlin J. for the majority indicated that a straightforward economic approach should be taken to both enrichment and deprivation and that the more complex value judgments should be addressed under the third criterion for unjust enrichment (*i.e.*, the absence of a juristic reason for the enrichment). It is at that point that the court should consider whether the enrichment and deprivation are "unjust". It has been argued that homemaking and child care services should not be seen as giving rise to equitable claims against the other partner, an argument forcefully rejected by McLachlin J.

Although unjust enrichment principles have proved very useful in resolving property disputes between cohabitants, there are significant differences between the situation of married spouses under Part I of the *Family Law Act* and the situation of cohabitants. Perhaps the most important distinction is that whereas the onus is on a cohabitant to establish unjust enrichment, under Part I equal contributions are assumed, entitling a married spouse to a share of a wide range of assets acquired during the relevant

---

7 [1980] 2 S.C.R. 834 (S.C.C.).
8 (1993), 44 R.F.L. (3d) 329 (S.C.C.).

period. It is certainly more difficult for a cohabitant to access "non-family type" assets acquired during the relationship.

In Ontario, the right of possession to the matrimonial home arises under Part II of the *Family Law Act*. However, that right is currently restricted to married persons, as the definition of "spouse" is the same in Part I and in Part II. There has not yet been a decided case on whether this provision is discriminatory on the basis of section 15 of the *Charter* to common law opposite sex partners or same sex couples. There does not appear to be any rational basis for excluding an opposite or same sex common law partner from asserting that he or she is entitled to exclusive possession of the home. In Ontario, although common law and same sex couples are still excluded from the property division scheme set out in Parts 1 and 11 of the *Family Law Act*, those persons are entitled to make a claim for exclusive possession as part of a claim for support pursuant to section 34(1)(d).

(c) Cohabitation

Ever since the passage of the Ontario *Family Law Reform Act, 1978*, cohabitants have been covered under the provincial statutory support provisions. All that has changed is the length of cohabitation required to trigger the provisions. Section 29 of the *Family Law Act* defines a "spouse" for the purposes of Part III of the Act as including

> . . . either of a man and woman who are not married to each other and have cohabited,
>
> (a) continuously for a period of no less than three years, or
> (b) in a relationship of some permanence, if they are the natural or adoptive parents of a child.

In this area there is no distinction between cohabitants and married spouses, and both have the full range of remedies, including orders for compensatory support. The term "cohabit" is defined in section1(1) of the *Family Law Act*: "to live together in a conjugal relationship, whether within or outside marriage". There have been several decisions accepting that there can be cohabitation even where the parties maintained separate residences. The cohabitation must be for a continuous period of three years and, there are potential difficulties when the couple separates – perhaps for a trial separation. Alternatively, there must be cohabitation "in a relationship of some permanence" if the parties are the parents of a child, whether natural or adopted. In general, this has proved to involve a low threshold, once cohabitation is established.

Part II of *the Family Law Act* sets out specific rights and responsibilities in regard to the matrimonial home. Cohabitants cannot inherit under the intestacy provisions in the *Succession Law Reform Act*. However, a cohabitant may apply for support under Part V of that Act if he or she was a "dependant". Cohabitants can, of course, provide for each other by will. Since the 1970s, cohabitation agreements have been expressly provided for in provincial legislation dealing with domestic contracts. The current sections are sections 53 (cohabitation agreements) and 54 (separation agreements) of the *Family Law Act*. Under the latter, but not under the former, the couple may provide for the custody of children (subject always to the overriding jurisdiction of the Court under section 56(1)). Since cohabitants are not covered under Part II of the *Family Law Act*, they are not subject to the restrictions dealing with the family home which are imposed on married spouses in the context of marriage contracts (under s. 52(2)). The *Canada Pension Plan*,[9] section 2 extends spousal benefits to cohabitants who have cohabited for at least one year. In Ontario the *Pension Benefits Act* includes cohabitants as defined in Part III of the *Family Law Act*. In Ontario, following the coming into force of section15(1) of the *Charter* in April 1985, a large number of statutes were amended to include heterosexual cohabitants within the definition of spouse because it was assumed that marital status would be found to be an analogous ground of discrimination. In *Miron v. Trudel*,[10] the Supreme Court of Canada held (by a 5-4 majority) that marital status is an analogous ground of discrimination under section15(1) of the *Charter* and that exclusion of heterosexual partners from accident benefits available to married spouses violated section 15(1) and was not saved under section 1 of the *Charter*. This is the first occasion on which the Supreme Court of Canada has had the opportunity to address the *Charter* rights of heterosexual cohabitants, and the ruling in *Miron v. Trudel* represents a major step in the recognition of the rights of heterosexual cohabitants.

(d) Same Sex Relationships

Over the past several decades there has been increasing recognition of heterosexual cohabitation but greater resistance to the recognition of same-sex relationships. However, in recent years, there is a tremendous acceleration in the recognition of such relationships. Anecdotally, we know that in recent years gay and lesbian couples have become more visible in schools, neighbourhoods and workplaces. But what of the children? How many children are being raised in gay and lesbian families? One American study concluded that "there are between 3 and 8 million gay and lesbian parents in the United States, raising between 6 and 14 million children.[11] Canadian scholars have assumed that the same percentages apply, that is, as much as

---

9   R.S.C. 1985, c. C-8.
10 (1995), 124 D.L.R (4th) 693 (S.C.C.).
11 See April Martin, *The Gay and Lesbian Parenting Handbook: Creating and Raising Our Families* (New York: HarperCollins, 1993) at 6, citing Charlotte Patterson, "Children of Lesbian and Gay Parents," *Child Development* 63,5 (1992).

5 per cent of the population is comprised of children who are being raised in same-sex families.[12]

A survey conducted in April 2001 showed that 55 per cent of Canadians supported allowing lesbian and gay couples to marry, and another in June 2001 concluded that 65 per cent supported same-sex marriage.[13] The 2001 census in Canada, for the first time, asked people whether they lived with a common-law partner of the same sex and explicitly stated that children of a person's common law same-sex partner should be considered that person's children as well. Some argue that continuing discrimination against lesbians and gay men will result in under-reporting of lesbian and gay families.[14]

The most significant developments in the recognition of same-sex unions have occurred under provincial human rights legislation and the *Charter*. Under the former, the gains have occurred in employment situations.[15] Those developments occurred because sexual orientation is a prohibited ground of discrimination under many human rights statutes, including the Ontario *Human Rights Code*. Sexual orientation is not one of the enumerated heads of discrimination within section 15(1) of the *Charter* but it has been almost universally accepted that it constitutes an analogous ground of discrimination. However, the mere recognition of sexual orientation as an analogous ground of discrimination within section 15(1) does not by any means guarantee that exclusion of same-sex couples from particular benefits will be found to be discriminatory. While most recent gains for same-sex couples have come in the area of employment law, there are several recent family law decisions that have extended rights to gay and lesbian couples.

(e) The Marriage of Gays and Lesbians

In Canada, gays and lesbians are recognized in a variety of legislative schemes as spouses or quasi-spouses but cannot choose marriage. Presently eight Ontario couples, one Quebec couple and five British Columbia couples have commenced court actions that seek to end what they feel is discrimination. They seek a court order that they be granted licences and a declaration that any law, practice or policy of government that restricts otherwise lawful marriages between two persons of the same sex is contrary to the *Charter of Rights* and is therefore of no force and effect. As already indi-

---

12 See Katherine Arnup, *Lesbian Parenting: Living with Pride and Prejudice* (Charlottetown: Gynergy, 1995; 1997).
13 Environics Research Group, "Most Canadians Favour Gay Marriage; Approval of Homosexuality Continues to Increase" (May 10, 2001), online: http://erg.environics.net/news/.
14 See EGALE Canada, "2001 Census Kit" (May 2001), online: www.egale.ca/documetns.census-kit-e.htm.
15 See *Leshner v. Ontario* (1992), 16 C.H.R.R. D/184 (Ont. Bd. of Inquiry) which resulted in an extension of pension survivor benefits to gay and lesbian partners of Ontario government employees.

cated, the federal government has jurisdiction over capacity to marry. The province has jurisdiction over the solemnization of marriages. Ontario legislation does not require that a couple be of the opposite sex in order to marry (nor does any province except Quebec). The statute does contain language that presumes that the parties are heterosexual (the vows must include the words "husband" and "wife", for example), but no specific opposite-sex requirement exists.

When Parliament, in 2000, enacted the *Modernization of Benefits and Obligations Act*[16] in response to *M. v. H.*,[17] it included in section 1.1 of that Act, under the title "interpretation", the following:

> For greater certainty, the amendments made by this Act do not affect the meaning of the word "marriage", that is, the lawful union of one man and one woman to the exclusion of all others.

(This definition is from *Hyde v. Hyde* [18]; except that the words "for life" have been omitted, no doubt because of the modern prevalence of divorce.)

Between 1999 and 2001, British Columbia, Manitoba, Ontario, Québec, Nova Scotia, Saskatchewan and the federal government all enacted omnibus legislation to recognize same-sex partners. The Netherlands became, in 2001, the first country in the world to extend legal marriage to same-sex partners at exactly the same basis as afforded opposite-sex partners. The Vermont Legislature, in 2000, enacted legislation which created a new legal status, "civil union", available to same-sex couples only, and which provided that "[p]arties to a civil union shall have all the benefits, protections and responsibilities under law, whether they derive from statute, administrative or court rule, policy, common law or any other source of civil law, as are granted to spouses in a marriage".[19]

In the last several years, same-sex partners in Nova Scotia, Québec, Ontario and British Columbia have applied for marriage licences.[20] In 2001, two same-sex couples were married in the Metropolitan Community Church of Toronto, after the Church had complied with a provision in the *Ontario Marriage Act* permitting the reading of banns as an alternative to obtaining a marriage licence. However, when the Church applied to register these marriages under the *Ontario Vital Statistics Act,* the Ontario Attorney General refused to allow the registration. The Church applied to the Ontario

---

16 S.C. 2000, c. 12.
17 (1999), 171 D.L.R. (4th) 577 (S.C.C.), reconsideration refused (2000), 2000 CarswellOnt 1913 (S.C.C.).
18 (1866), L.R. 1 P. & D. 130 (Eng. P.D.A.).
19 See an *Act Relating to Civil Unions*, H.847.
20 See EGALE Canada, Press Release: "EGALE Board Member Applies for Marriage Licence, Calls for Full Legal Equality for Same-Sex Couples" (26 May 2000) online: www.egale.ca/pressrel/.

Divisional Court for judicial review of this refusal in November, 2001 and a decision was rendered on July 12, 2002.[21]

The conclusions of the Court were as follows:

(a) that there is no statutory impediment to the issuance of marriage licences to same-sex couples who otherwise meet the requiste criteria, or to the registration of their church marriages pursuant to the publication of banns of marriage.

(b) that there is a common law rule – as the common law presently stands – which is an impediment to same-sex marriages;

(c) that the existing common law rule is inconsistent with constitutional values in modern Canadian society, and offends the equality rights of gays and lesbians under s. 15(1) of the Charter;

(d) that the inconsistency and infringement of s. 15(1) cannot be demonstrably justified in a free and democratic society, and therefore cannot be saved by a s. 1 analysis under the Charter, to the extent that such an analysis may be necessary when dealing with a common law provision.

(e) that the existing common law rule does not infringe the s. 2(a), s. 2(b) or s. 7 Charter rights of the Applicant Couples or the Metropolitan Community Church of Toronto; and

(f) that the argrument to the effect that any change in the word "marriage", as found in the division of powers in s. 91 and s. 92 of the Constitution Act 1867, requires a constitutional amendment, cannot succeed.

At time of writing, the Federal Government had signaled that it would appeal this decision.

(f) Registered Domestic Partnerships

Numerous jurisdictions have instituted Registered Domestic Partnership schemes ("RDPS"), including Denmark (the first, in 1989), the Netherlands, Norway, Sweden, Hungary, France, Iceland, and Spain.[22] Sweden's *Registered Partnership (Family Law) Act*, for example, allows for the registration of parties of the same sex, who are not required to be gay or lesbian, in a process similar to a marriage ceremony.[23] The registration must be conducted in the presence of witnesses, the parties must provide individual

---

21 see *Metropolitan Community Church of Toronto v. Attorney General of Canada et al.,* Ontario Superior Court of Justice (Divisional Court), No. 39/2001, 2002 CarswellOnt 2309.
22 See James D. Wilets, *"International Human Rights Law and Sexual Orientation"*, 18:1 Hastings Int'l & Comp. L. Rev. 1 (1994)at 96. M. Bailey, *"Hawaii's Same Sex Marriage Initiatives: Implications for Canada"*, 15 Can. J. Fam. L. 153 (1988).
23 See the Hon. Dr. Peter Nygh, "Homosexual Partnerships in Sweden", 11 *Australian Journal of Family Law* 11 (1977).

consent in response to a question from an authorized celebrant, and the authorized celebrant must declare them to be registered partners.

Children who grow up in a society where gays and lesbians are banished from a normal practice in which most people engage are not only likely but casually determined to believe, at the very least as children, that gays and lesbians lack, or at least are considered by society (and the Courts) to lack, the properties deemed necessary for marrying.

I know a four-year-old, Reilly, whose parents are lesbians. Reilly notices that, like Gary and me, her parents love each other dearly. She knows that, like Gary and me, her parents live together, have sex together, have a long-standing relationship, make future plans together, share their resources, etc., etc. The *only* differences Reilly can perceive between her parents' relationship and mine are (1) that we are allowed to be married but they are not, and (2) that we are heterosexual and they are not.

Children are phenomenally curious and constantly at work building theories about the world. Inevitably, Reilly will form a hypothesis as to why it is that Gary and I can be married but her parents cannot (*regardless* of whatever else they can do). Professor Stainton would have us think that a four-year-old growing up in this environment should end up explaining to herself that her parents are not married because of some feature of *the meaning of the word 'marriage'*. ("Oh, I get it. The *word* marriage *means* a union of a man and a woman. So *that's* why my parents can't marry. Ah, no big deal".) There are undoubtedly philosophically super-precious children somewhere who are capable of formulating to themselves such a meta-linguistic thought, but most four-year-olds who use words don't read dictionaries and even fewer explicitly reflect on the essential semantic features of the words they use. (I do that for a living, and I only learned to do it sensically after fourteen years of graduate school.) I maintain that it is empirically far more plausible that a four-year-old would explain the situation herself as due to *the fact that her parents are lesbians*.

Now children know that marriage is generally considered to be a good thing. They are also not perfect but pretty good reasoners. So Reilly is bound to reason that, since marriage is a good thing, but her parents are barred from it because they are lesbians, there must be something not-so-good about being lesbian.

It is completely disingenuous to maintain that no harm is done when Reilly, who loves her parents, is led to the conclusion that there is something not-so-good about them. It is even more disingenuous to expect no harm to accrue to gays and lesbians when other children, who do not have Reilly's mitigating exposure to loving and decent lesbians, reach the same conclusions and grow up to be adults with various abilities to impose their view of the world, including by influencing the attitudes of the next generation.

To claim that we need confirmation from Cognitive Science before we can trust our sense of reality about this is to deify science outrageously and to mock human wisdom even more so.[24]

In the area of adoption rights, the decision in *K., Re*[25] is important.[26] Dealing with a preliminary constitutional challenge by four lesbian couples seeking the right to jointly adopt children born by artificial insemination to the other partner, Nevins Prov. J. held that the provision of the Ontario *Child and Family Services Act*[27], which does not permit adoption in such circumstances, was contrary to section 15(1) and was not saved under section 1 of the *Charter*.[28]

The exclusion of same-sex couples from the *Family Law Act* was challenged in *M. v. H,*[29]. M and H were two women who lived together and were business associates for ten years. After the relationship broke down, M sued H for interim and permanent support under Part III of the *Family Law Act*. The Supreme Court (Gonthier J. dissenting) held section 29 to be unconstitutional and declared it to be of no force or effect. Both the appeal and cross-appeal were dismissed but the remedy was modified so that the declaration of invalidity was suspended for a period of six months. The exclusion of such couples from section 29 promoted the view that same sex couples were less worthy of recognition and protection and such exclusion violated section 15(1) of the *Charter*.

The Supreme Court of Canada considered the meaning of "conjugal" in the process of determining that the extended definition of "spouse" in the Ontario *Family Law Act* infringed section 15(1) of the *Canadian Charter of Rights and Freedoms* and was not saved by section 1. *Per* Cory J.:

> *Molodowich v. Penttinen* (1980), 17 R.F.L. (2d) 376 (Ont. Dist. Ct.) sets out the generally accepted characteristics of a conjugal relationship. They include shared shelter, sexual and personal behaviour, services, social activities, economic support and children, as well as the societal perception of the couple. However, it was recognized that these elements may be present in varying degrees and not all are necessary for the relationship to be found to be conjugal. While it is true that there may not be any consensus as to the societal perception of same-sex couples, there is agreement that same-sex couples share many other 'conjugal' characteristics. In order to come within the definition, neither

---

24 (See affidavit of Dr. Adele Mercier, sworn June 6, 2001, Expert Report filed in the Ontario Freedom to Marry Case, *Halpern et al v. Canada et al*. Superior Court of Justice (Divisional Court), Court File No. 684/00, hearings commenced November 5, 2001).
25 (1995), 23 O.R. (3d) 679 (Prov. Div.).
26 See also *Re G.(C.E.)*, (1995), [1995] O.J. No. 4072, 1995 CarswellOnt 612 (Gen. Div.) and [1995] O.J. No. 4073, 1995 CarswellOnt 611 (Gen. Div.).
27 R.S.C. 1990, c. C.11, s. 136(1).
28 See also *Re C.* (1999), 181 D.L.R. (4th) 300 (Alta. Q.B.) as to the private adoption provisions in the *Child Welfare Act*, S. A. 1984, c. C-8.1.
29 Above, note 17.

opposite-sex couples, nor same-sex couples are required to fit precisely the traditional marital model to demonstrate that the relationship is 'conjugal'.

Certainly an opposite-sex couple may, after many years together, be considered to be in a conjugal relationship although they have neither children nor sexual relations. Obviously the weight to be accorded the various elements or factors to be considered in determining whether an opposite-sex couple is in a conjugal relationship will vary widely and almost infinitely. The same must hold true of same-sex couples. Courts have wisely determined that the approach to determining whether a relationship is conjugal must be flexible. This must be so, for the relationship of all couples will vary widely. In these circumstances, the Court of Appeal correctly concluded that there is nothing to suggest that same-sex couples do not meet the legal definition of 'conjugal'.[30]

Charter jurisprudence suggests that same-sex spouses are entitled to receive equal treatment to married spouses under the law. Although some distinctions continue to exist in the treatment of same-sex spouses in Ontario, these are vulnerable to constitutional challenge as discrimination on the basis of sexual orientation. Reading *M. v. H.* together with *Miron*[31] strongly suggests that there must be equal treatment for all spouses, whether married or unmarried, opposite-sex or same-sex.

(g) Custody, Access and Adoption by Gays and Lesbians

In litigation between a deceased's co-parenting same-sex spouse and the surviving biological parent, the decision of *Bezaire v. Bezaire*,[32] establishes that sexual orientation is irrelevant except insofar as it affects the best interests of the child. Query whether anyone would suggest that heterosexuality is "irrelevant except as insofar as it affects the best interests of the child"? The better view is that sexual orientation without more, is irrelevant. This approach is articulated, in the context of gender identity, in the decision of *Forrester v. Saliba*.[33] The inability of same-sex couples to register the births of their children with both parents has led many couples to pursue a joint application for adoption. Prior to the decision of Justice Nevins in *Re K.*,[34] the step-parent provisions of the *Child and Family Services Act* were restricted to opposite sex spouses. In *Re K.*, Justice Nevins read in to the definition of spouse such that spouse "means the person to whom a person of the opposite sex is married or *with whom a person of the same or opposite sex is living in a conjugal relationship outside marriage.*" When the Ontario government passed "*An Act to Amend Certain Statutes Because of the Supreme Court of Canada Decision in M. v. H.*", the amendments did not

---

30 Above, note 17, para. 91.
31 Above, note 10.
32 (1980), 20 R.F.L. (2d) 358 (Ont. C.A.).
33 [2000] O.J. No. 3018, 2000 CarswellOnt 2835 (C.J.).
34 Above, note 25.

include the extension of the definition of same-sex partners to the adoption provisions of the *Child and Family Services Act*. Instead, the Act amended section 146(4) to allow "any other individuals that the court may allow, having regard to the best interests of the child" to apply to adopt.

Persons of either sex, in any sexual or non-sexual relationship, who are emotionally attached to each other can fill all their spiritual needs by undergoing religious or secular ceremonies of their choice. In addition, they may contractually assume vis-à-vis each other any obligations they choose – short of offending what social norms remain to be offended. Whatever the changes in lifestyles, the real purpose of giving special legal status to marriage and family remains what it has always been: the provision of a first-choice setting for the procreation and raising of children. Social stability depends on a legal system that balances modern "family facts" and society's legitimate needs. There may be plenty of room to disagree on particulars, but there also are areas in which we can reach broad agreement regarding a rational definition of modern society's legitimate interests in children and parents, in the family, and appropriate regulation.

A child-oriented restructuring of our family and social laws would redefine the scope of individual parental authority over children as well as family-based financial obligations (parent to child and child to parent). The active, supportive role of the state, through agencies and appropriate intervention, needs to be rethought. "Neutrality" is always an attractive concept, but applied here it turns into a misleading slogan. No matter how "neutrality" is defined, it favours one side or the other. If "neutrality" spells non-intervention when intervention is needed – to protect a child, for instance – "neutrality" favours the person harming the child. In short, whatever the definition of "neutrality", it must not mean inattention. The task is to devise welfare or social security legislation that will affect family behaviour "positively", pragmatically defined in terms of enabling "familial" associations to fulfill appropriate social functions.

It is important to distinguish religious marriage from civil marriage. Only the latter is in issue in the same-sex marriage claims currently before the courts. Legally extending civil marriage to same-sex partners would not require religious congregations, contrary to their beliefs, to marry same-sex partners. The *Charter*'s guarantee of freedom of religion would presumably protect religious congregations from any legislative attempt to compel them to perform same-sex marriages. While human rights legislation prohibits discrimination on the basis of sexual orientation with respect to access to services customarily available to the public, it is doubtful whether marriage in any particular religious congregation would ever be held to be a service customarily available to the public. Therefore, same-sex partners could not legally compel a religious organization to marry them.

Rational and radical reform is needed. A "post-modern" social contract must eschew "neutrality" and accept some value judgments. Pragmatic value judgments to be sure, but value judgments all the same. The task is in identifying which way the association in question serves legitimate public and social purposes, purposes that can rationally justify whatever financial or other privileges society accords to, or duties that it imposes on, persons in specific associational circumstances. We must identify and define social and economic incentives and disincentives affecting child-related family behaviour – all in the light of a rational, tolerant, and forward-looking redefinition of the kind of constructive family behaviour society needs and should seek.[35]

3. DIVORCE

(a) Proceedings under the Divorce Act

The *Divorce Act* came into force on June 1, 1986, and replaced the earlier *Divorce Act* which had been law since 1968. The Act is federal in nature and applies throughout Canada. Unlike the law relating to the division of property after marriage, the law of divorce is the same from province to province. A husband and wife, no matter the province or territory where they live, will experience the same law of divorce. Matters of property are local with each province or territory having its own legislation and sometimes its own approach to principle or detail. This is not so in the area of divorce.

There are three kinds or proceedings permitted by the Act:

(1) divorce, with or without corollary relief, ss. 2(1), 8 and 15
(2) corollary relief (support or custody or both), section 15 and 16; and
(3) variation of a previous order for corollary relief, section 17.

A proceeding for divorce with or without a claim for other relief, is brought to the Superior Court of Justice in Ontario or the Unified Family Court in Ontario. A judge of a Superior Court has jurisdiction to entertain a divorce proceeding if,

(a) no other proceeding has been commenced on an earlier or the same day in the court of another province: sections 2 and 3; and
(b) either spouse has been ordinarily resident in the province for at least

---

[35] The following references may be of interest: W. Holland, *"Intimate Relationships in the New Millennium: The Assimilation of Marriage and Cohabitation?"* 17 Can. J. Fam. L. 113 (1999); McCarthy, Martha and Joanne L. Radbord, *"Family Law for Same Sex Couples; Chart(er)ing the Course"*, 15 Can. J. Fam. L. No. 2 (1998) 101-177; L'Heureaux-Dube, Claire *"Making Equality Work in Family Law"*, 14 Can. J. Fam. L. (1997) 103-127; Peter W. Hogg, and Allison A. Bushell. *"The Charter Dialogue Between Courts and Legislatures (Or Perhaps the Charter of Rights Isn't Such a Bad Thing After All)"* 35 Osgoode Hall L.J. (1997).

one year immediately preceding the commencement of the proceedings: section 3(1).

Ordinary residence of one year as the test for jurisdiction has taken the place of an over-complicated combination of domicile, ordinary and actual residence. The Court has jurisdiction when either spouse has been "ordinarily resident in the province for at least one year immediately preceding the commencement of the proceeding": section 3(1).

There is a single ground for divorce, called "breakdown of marriage" (section 8(1)), which must be established by showing one or more of only three conditions:

(1) the spouses were living separate and apart for at least one year immediately preceding the determination of the divorce proceeding and were living separate and apart at the commencement of the proceeding: section 8(2)(a),
(2) the other spouse has committed adultery: section 9(2)(b)(I), or
(3) the other spouse has been guilty of cruelty: section 8(2)(b)(ii).

(b) Separation

The breakdown of marriage ground is that the period of separation is allowed to mature after the proceeding has been commenced. The effective date for qualifying the year of separation is the date of "determination", not the date of the "commencement" of the proceedings. The time is calculated back from the time the proceeding comes before the judge for hearing or trial. The separation must exist at the time of the commencement of the proceeding. The petition for divorce cannot be issued while the spouses are still cohabiting, but the separation may have been in existence for as short a time as only one day. The petition may be issued the day after the separation begins, but cannot be disposed of by a hearing until a year has expired: section 8(2)(a).

A separation entails the mental element of an intention to separate. The intention need not be mutual in the sense that the decision to separate is jointly-made or agreed upon. The decision may be unilateral by one spouse against the will of the other spouse. In other words, a valid separation may be created by one spouse "deserting" the other. As long as the separation continues to persist for one year after the desertion, even though never accepted by the other spouse, the separation qualifies to prove the breakdown of marriage ground: section 8(3)(a). The intention to live separate and apart may be unilateral or mutual, but must be present in one of these forms. A mere physical absence of one spouse is not necessarily a separation. Spouses go on business trips by themselves, visit relatives and are posted by the armed services to another country, all without bringing about a state of living separate and apart. There must be a withdrawal from the matrimonial relationship with the intent of destroying the matrimonial consortium. Spouses are not living separate and apart unless both conditions are met.[36] Although spouses may be physically absent from one another for a long period of time, they are not living separate and apart, so long as they treat the parting as temporary and not permanent.[37]

The separation need not be in terms of place, but may exist solely in terms of attitude toward each other. A physical separation manifest to persons in the community is not required. A separation under the same roof where it can be said that there are two households, or that the spouses are living separate lives is sufficient.[38] For example, in *Rushton v. Rushton*,[39] it was held that a husband and wife living in separate rooms in the same suite were living separate and apart where it was shown that they were leading separate lives, had no sexual intercourse, performed no domestic services for one another, and simply shared the same suite because their jobs as joint caretakers of an apartment building required them to do so. The reasoning in *Rushton* was expressly agreed with by the Manitoba Court of Appeal in *Galbraith v. Galbraith*,[40] where it was held that to be living separate and apart, it is not in all cases essential to have geographical separation in the sense of different dwelling places. The evidence that a couple under the same roof are living separate and apart must be clear and convincing, but such evidence is not impossible at law to produce. A separation may exist while the spouses are still under the same roof, but great caution should be exercised in arriving at this conclusion.[41] It should be reached only after an analysis of all the available facts and circumstances prevailing in the home and, to a lesser extent, in the community. The test is not what the public believes, but what in fact all the relevant circumstances disclose the actual state of the marriage to be. In *Mayberry v. Mayberry*,[42] the Ontario Court of Appeal held that spouses may be living separate and apart under the same roof where there has been a mutual repudiation of the marital relationship producing a permanent breakdown of the marriage. An Ontario case which follows *Mayberry* is *Calder v. Calder*,[43] where in hearing the wife's petition for divorce, Mr. Justice Donnelly stated: "In 1955 the husband had a nervous breakdown and moved to a bedroom of his own. Three months later he

---

36 *Rushton v. Rushton* (1968), 66 W.W.R. 764 (B.C. S.C.).
37 *Herman v. Herman* (1969), 1 R.F.L. 41 (N.S. T.D.) and *Seminuk v. Seminuk* (1969), 68 W.W.R. 249 (Sask. Q.B.), reversed on other grounds (1970), 72 W.W.R. 304 (Sask. C.A.).
38 *B.(J.) v. B.(A.W.)*, [1958] O.R. 281 (C.A.).
39 (1968), 66 W.W.R. 764 (B.C. S.C.).
40 (1969), 69 W.W.R. 390 (Man. C.A.).
41 *Seminuk v. Seminuk* above, note 37. On the facts of the case, it was held that there was not sufficient evidence to support the finding of a separation for a required period. Following the principles stated in *Rushton v. Rushton* above, note 36 and *Seminuk*, the court found in *Rousell v. Rousell* (1969), 69 W.W.R. 568 (Sask. Q.B.) that in the circumstances the parties were living separate and apart in the same house.
42 [1971] 2 O.R. 378 (C.A.).
43 (1974), 15 R.F.L. 265 (Ont. H.C.).

returned to work and continued work until his retirement in 1956. . .".[44] He did his own shopping for food, made his own meals and usually tried to eat when his wife was not in the house. He did his own laundry, sent his own clothes to the dry cleaners. The parties would go two weeks without speaking to each other. It was only when it was essential that they communicated with as few words as possible. The parties have not slept together since 1955, and there has been no sexual intercourse since 1966. They have not been out together since that time. The husband would join the family approximately three times a year, on Christmas, Easter and Thanksgiving. On these occasions he would simply carve the turkey and then leave the table. The parties have been living separate and apart within the meaning of s. 4(1)(e)(I) of the *Divorce Act*, R.S.C. 1970, since 1966. The Court further held that a divorce should be granted on evidence, for example, which indicated there was virtually no communication between the spouses, they ate separate meals, did not share social activities, and occupied separate bedrooms. Although the cessation of sexual relations affords strong evidence of living separate and apart, it does not in itself conclusively decide the issue.

(c) **Adultery and Cruelty**

Adultery or cruelty as evidence of a breakdown marriage goes back to the old theory of matrimonial offence and characteristics of the theory are necessarily carried with it. The first characteristic is that the offence must be committed by the other spouse. It is the "wronged" spouse who sues the "guilty" party. A spouse cannot petition for a divorce on the ground that his or her own adultery produced the breakdown. It is the person "against whom the divorce is brought" who must have committed the offence: section 8(2)(b). This means, for instance that a spouse cohabiting with another person and wishing a divorce so that he or she can marry that person, cannot use the obvious adultery as proof of breakdown of marriage to obtain an immediate divorce. Instead, he or she must rely upon proving the breakdown through a separation which requires obtaining the divorce no earlier than one year from when the separation in the marriage began, or must prove the adultery or cruelty of the other spouse. Another characteristic of the offence theory is that acts of adultery or cruelty can be wiped out as actionable offences for divorce purposes. Subject to an important exception in the statute, if the offence is condoned (*i.e.* forgiven, a substantial period of cohabitation after knowledge of the offence usually implies forgiveness) or connived at (encouraged or promoted by the suing spouse), the offence is rendered inoperable and cannot be used to support a divorce proceeding.

---

44 *Ibid.*, at 265-266.

The standard of proof in a divorce case is the ordinary civil standard of establishing the allegations to meet the balance of probabilities, and not the higher criminal standard of showing proof beyond reasonable doubt.[45] Direct evidence of adultery is rarely available. What is required is proof of opportunity, and proof of facts from which it can be reasonably inferred that the opportunity was used. The kind of circumstances often relied upon are illustrated by the case of *Lemenson v. Lemenson and Draho*,[46] where a private investigator saw both respondents enter an apartment building at about midnight and the male respondent leave at about 4:00 in the morning. During this interval, the investigator heard male and female voices coming from the other side of the door. This evidence was held to be sufficient proof of adultery in the view of the failure by the respondent to deliver an answer or to testify. On the question of the inference that may be drawn from a failure on the part of the alleged guilty party to give evidence about the incident, see also *Fogel v. Fogel*,[47] where it was held that a refusal to answer questions relating to an allegation of adultery gives credulity to what otherwise might be unconvincing.

Cruelty is physical or mental treatment "of such a kind as to render intolerable the continued cohabitation of the spouses": section 8(2)(b)(ii). A spouse may be guilty of cruelty if in the marriage relationship the conduct causes wanton, malicious or unnecessary infliction of pain, or suffering upon the body, the feelings or emotions of the other, and is of such a kind as to render intolerable the continued cohabitation of the spouses.[48] Only conduct which is of a grave and weighty nature can reach this standard, and conduct which is merely trivial or which could be characterized as little more than a manifestation of incompatibility of temperament does not qualify. Cruelty occurring after the separation is within the scope of the Act and may be relied upon in support of a claim for divorce. In the phrase "of such a kind as to render intolerable the continued cohabitation of the spouses" the word "continued" is not restricted in meaning to "uninterrupted", and should also be taken as meaning "resumed after interruption".[49] Whether or not grave and weighty conduct amounts to cruelty in a particular case is measured against a subjective rather than an objective standard. It is not what the effect would be upon any reasonable minded spouse that matters. It is the effect upon the petitioner with due regard to his or her own particular temperament, sensibility and state of health. The question is whether this conduct by this man to this women, or vice versa is cruelty.

---

45 *Smith v. Smith*, [1952] 2 S.C.R. 312; and *Forster v. Forster*, [1955] 4 D.L.R. 710 (Ont. C.A.).
46 (1969), 1 R.F.L. 206 (Man. Q.B.).
47 (1976), 24 R.F.L. 18 (Ont. H.C.) affirmed (1979), 9 R.F.L. (2d) 55 (Ont. C.A.).
48 *Knoll v. Knoll*, [1970] 2 O.R. 169 (C.A.).
49 *Storr v. Storr* (1974), 14 R.F.L. 346 (N.S. C.A.) and *McMurdy v. McMurdy* (1975), 22 R.F.L. 312 (Ont. H.C.).

However, the fact that this particular petitioner finds the conduct of the respondent intolerable will not make the conduct cruelty if it falls short of being grave and weighty by objective standards.[50] Isolated acts which are not in themselves cruelty, will amount to this offence if they are part of a continued course of conduct and the cumulative effect is to make continued cohabitation intolerable.[51] Previously condoned acts of cruelty are also admissible in evidence to provide a background against which the quality of subsequent behaviour of the respondent may be assessed and determined to be cruelty.[52]

(d) Reconciliation and Condonation

The *Divorce Act* encourages attempts at reconciliation by allowing the spouses to cohabit for a single period or a total of several periods amounting to no more than 90 days without interrupting the period of separation relied upon to establish the breakdown of marriage ground and without condoning adultery or cruelty which the petitioner may be intending to prove for the same purpose.[53] This exception does not create a definition of condonation either expressly or by implication. The fact that trial cohabitation of less than 90 days is not condonation, does not mean that trial cohabitation of more than 90 days automatically is condonation. Whether or not the conduct gives rise to this bar must be determined by reference to the common law.[54] Where adultery or cruelty is used to establish the breakdown of the marriage, the court is required "to satisfy itself that there has been no condonation or connivance on the part of the spouse bringing the proceeding, and to dismiss the application for a divorce if that spouse has condoned or connived at the act or conduct complained of unless, in the opinion of the court, the public interest would be better served by granting the divorce". Three elements are necessary to constitute condonation: (1) knowledge by the innocent spouse of the matrimonial offence committed by the other spouse; (2) an intention by the innocent spouse to forgive and remit the offence; and (3) a reinstatement by the innocent spouse of the guilty spouse to his or her former marital position.[55] To amount to condonation of a matrimonial offence, there should be forgiveness to the point of a reconciliation and conduct short of this, even though involving an act of sexual intercourse, will not apply.

---

50 *Shumila v. Shumila*, [1975] 5 W.W.R. 697 (Man. C.A.).
51 *Powell v. Powell* (1971), 5 R.F.L. 194 (Sask. C.A.); and *Wittstock v. Wittstock*, [1971] 2 O.R. 472 (C.A.).
52 *Crosby v. Crosby* (1971), 6 R.F.L. 8 (Ont. H.C.); *Jaworski v. Jaworski*, [1973] 2 O.R. 420 (H.C.); and *Raney v. Raney* (1973), 1 O.R. (2d) 491 (S.C.).
53 *Divorce Act*, ss. 8(3)(b)(ii) and 11(3).
54 *Einarson v. Einarson*, [1971] 5 W.W.R. 478(B.C. S.C.).
55 *MacDougall v. MacDougall* (1970), 3 R.F.L. 175 (C.A.) at 176.

THE FAMILY   171

Under section 10(1), the duty of the Court is not to effect a reconciliation, but to determine the possibility of the parties themselves becoming reconciled, either with or without the assistance of a qualified person. The circumstances of the case may indicate that a reconciliation is not appropriate. In all cases, the Court should direct inquiries to the petitioner and, if present, to the respondent spouse, to ascertain whether a possibility exists of their reconciliation.

The *Divorce Act* changed both the grounds for a court of taking jurisdiction (section 3(1) and in section 22(1)), and the grounds for the recognition of foreign divorces. The 1985 Act expanded the court's jurisdiction by only requiring that either spouse be ordinarily resident in the province for at least one year before the commencement of proceedings. The domicile and actual residence of the petitioner are no longer relevant. The principle of reciprocity is reflected in the provision for recognition of a foreign divorce, when it is made in circumstances paralleling those in which a Canadian court would have taken jurisdiction. Accordingly, Canada will now recognize a foreign divorce if *either* spouse was ordinarily resident in the foreign jurisdiction for one year preceding the application for that divorce: section 22(1).[56]

(e) Taking Violent Conduct into Account

The existence of violence by one spouse against the other has had a direct impact on the Court's decision with respect to custody in many cases. For example, in *Stillman v. Stillman*,[57] the Court heard extensive evidence from Mrs. Stillman as to the way she had been treated throughout her 14-year marriage to Mr. Stillman. In granting Mrs. Stillman sole custody of the children, the court made some insightful comments about Mr. Stillman's behaviour and the impact that his behaviour had on his wife's life:

> The conduct of Mr. Stillman is outrageous and cannot be countenanced under any circumstances, His words were insulting and demeaning and intended to be so. They were, depending on the contest, directed to intimidate, manipulate or humiliate. His conduct and words are all the more shocking in light of the evidence that they were uttered, almost always, in the presence of young children or visitors to the house. These utterances are repugnant to any decent thinking person and have no place in any situation, least of all a home.
>
> Mrs. Stillman's reaction was to retreat, withdraw and over time come to believe that she had no value. As she put it "I didn't think I was worth the time of day". Such cowering withdrawal doesn't seem so unusual in light of the testimony

---

56 For a discussion of the meaning of "ordinarily resident", see *MacPherson v. MacPherson* (1977), 13 O.R. (2d) 233 (Ont. C.A.); *Doucet v. Doucet* (1974), 4 O.R. (2d) 27 (Co. Ct.); *Taylor v. Taylor* (1978), 6 R.F.L. (2d) 341 (Ont. U.F.C.).

57 [1991] N.S.J. No. 200, 1991 CarswellNS 407 (N.S. T.D.).

from her father that he never did anything over the years to intervene. Neither did Ms. Raymond or her husband.

In a similarly insightful decision, the court in *Burk v. Burk*[58] was asked to transfer interim custody proceedings from Hamilton to Sudbury on the basis that the wife had removed the children from the latter jurisdiction and brought them to Hamilton, Ontario without the husband's consent. After reviewing the wife's affidavit which outlined a history of very violent spousal abuse and on noting that the husband, in his material filed in support of the motion, had made only a general denial of the allegations and indicated that he had no criminal record, the Court held that the children did in fact have a substantial connection to Hamilton. His decision was based in part on the fact that the children were actually in Hamilton and in part on the fact that the husband himself did not propose a change in their care and control. The Court also indicated that the details set out in the wife's material were quite vivid and detailed and that the wife should not be exposed to the potential of further violence. A father who had been jailed for his assaults against the mother was granted access to his children in *Savidant v. MacLeod*.[59] The Court held that in all custody and access cases the Court should concentrate on the best interests of the child. The Appeal Court was satisfied that the judge who granted access had "carefully considered" the family violence.

Ontario courts have held that violence towards a partner is relevant to custody and access because it reflects the abuser's ability to be a suitable role model for children and reflects on the abuser's ability to handle stress or pressure in relationships.[60] The Court ordered that the husband exercise restricted and supervised access to his daughter who had witnessed his assaults (physical and verbal) against the wife. The husband had also continued to use profane and degrading language against the mother. He was also allowing his daughter to sleep in bed with him during access visits.

Section 46 of the *Family Law Act* provides for the making of restraining orders, as follows:

> (1) On application, a court may make an interim or final order restraining the applicant's spouse, same-sex partner or former spouse or same-sex partner from molesting, annoying or harassing the applicant or children in the applicant's lawful custody, or from communicating with the applicant or children, except as the order provides, and may require the applicant's spouse, same-sex partner or former spouse or same-sex partner to enter into the recognizance that the court considers appropriate.

---

58 [1991] O. J. No. 1443, 1991 CarswellOnt 293 (Ont. U.F.C.).
59 (1992), 40 R.F.L. (3d) 443 (P.E.I. C.A.).
60 See *Young v. Young* (1989), 19 R.F.L. (3d) 227 (Ont. H.C.), additional reasons at (1989), 19 R.F.L. (3d) 227 at 238 (Ont. H.C.); and *Renaud v. Renaud* (1989), 22 R.F.L. (2d) 366 (Ont. Dist. Ct.).

(2) A person who contravenes a restraining order is guilty of an offence and upon conviction is liable,
a. in the case of a first offence, to a fine of not more than $5,000 or to imprisonment for a term of not more than three months, or to both; and
b. in the case of a second or subsequent offence, to a fine of not more than $10,000 or to imprisonment for a term of not more than two years, or to both.
(3) A police officer may arrest without warrant a person the police officer believes on reasonable and probable grounds to have contravened a restraining order.
(4) Subsections (2) and (3) also apply in respect of contraventions, committed after this Act comes into force, of restraining orders made under Part II of the *Family Law Reform Act*.

The Court cannot restrain an individual from "annoying", "molesting" or "harassing" anybody other than a "spouse" or "former spouse" within the meaning of the legislation or the children in the applicant's lawful custody. Accordingly, a request for an order that the offending party not "annoy", "molest" or "harass" the applicant's mother, siblings, friends, neighbours, and witnesses to incidents of violence is invalid and cannot be granted. Section 46 speaks of "molesting", "annoying", "harassing" and communicating". Nowhere in the legislation are these terms defined. The Courts have therefore had to define these terms on a case-by-case basis, often in the context of a motion for contempt and for an order committing an individual to jail on account of an alleged breach of a restraining order.

Violent conduct on the part of one spouse towards the other spouse has been used by the Courts, both as a ground to reduce the quantum of support awarded to the abuser and as a reason for awarding support to a victim. For example, in *MacDonald v. MacDonald*,[61] Judge Flanigan reduced the amount of support that he would otherwise have ordered from $1,000 per month to $700 per month on the basis of the wife's violent actions towards the husband. She had slapped him across the face, boiled water on the stove and then threw it at the husband, pricked him on the back of the wrist with a knife and ultimately stabbed him in the ribs with a knife. Although he found that the relationship was not a "one-sided stormy relationship", Judge Flanigan found that almost all of the instances of violence were precipitated by the wife. Violence has been successfully used as a ground for setting aside a separation agreement. A marriage contract was set aside on the application of a wife whom the Court found had been dominated by the husband throughout the marriage and at the time the marriage contract was signed. The Court found that the wife had not been able to benefit from the independent legal advice that she had received prior to signing the contract

---

61 (May 23, 1991), Doc. Ottawa 1112-016, [1991] O.J. No. 1274 (Ont. Gen. Div.).

due to the extent of spousal abuse. The Court heard evidence from an expert who described battered woman syndrome.[62]

4. CUSTODY and ACCESS

It is important to first understand what in fact is meant by the terms *custody and access* since neither term is defined in the *Children's Law Reform Act* (CLRA) or the *Divorce Act*. A brief review of the older legislation and case law reveals that, like other areas of matrimonial law, these terms have evolved over the years, keeping pace with the overall changes in our social fabric. The CLRA makes it clear that both parents are equally entitled to the custody of the child.

There is a significant difference between custody and access. The custodial parent has the right to make all decisions regarding the child, while the access parent is entitled to information concerning the child but has no statutory right to take part in the decision-making process. Consequently, the custodial dispute involves not only where the child will reside, but who will make the decisions concerning the child. Whether the Court is addressing the issue of custody, access or incidents of custody, the best interests of the child must be its paramount consideration. The object of any proceeding is to place the child, rather than the persons applying for custody, at the crux of the decision. Due to the inherently adversarial nature of a court proceeding, coupled with the emotional anxiety that is part and parcel of a custody dispute, this central focus is often misplaced.

Case law reveals that the weight to be allotted to the child's wishes is often contingent on the child's age and level of maturity. As a child grows older, it becomes increasingly difficult to enforce a custody order inconsistent with his or her wishes. Conversely, when younger children are involved, statements about their preferences should not necessarily be taken at face value. Children who are the subject of a custody dispute may have interests that are not necessarily identical to those of either parent, even though the parents claim to be acting in the child's best interests. The children may, therefore, require separate representation.

While the Court's ability to appoint counsel for the children is without question, as is the child's ability to seek and retain independent legal representation, what is far from certain is the role that the child's solicitor is to play in the proceedings. The Children's Lawyer holds a statutory office and is thus obligated by statute to act in the best interests of the child as he or she perceives them, with perhaps little regard for the child's wishes. The wishes of the children are usually presented to the Court through the report of an assessor and sometimes by counsel for the children, being the Children's Lawyer.

---

62 See *B.(S.M.) v. B.(K.R.)* (1997), CarswellOnt. 3050 (Ont. Ct. Gen. Div.), *per* Steinberg J.

Pursuant to section 28 of the CLRA, the Court to which a custody application is made may grant the custody of or access to the child to one or more persons. Similarly, section 16 (4) of the *Divorce Act* makes provisions for a joint custodial arrangement, although that particular terminology is not used. Jurisdiction is an important preliminary procedural issue which must be examined by the Court prior to addressing the substantive issue of a custody or access application because both provincial and federal legislation address this issue. The Court may, on application by one of the spouses or on its own motion, transfer the divorce proceeding to a court in another province where: (1) an application is made for custody or access in a divorce proceeding, and (2) the child in respect of whom the order is sought is most substantially connected with the other province.

There is no statutory definition of the term "joint custody". Joint custody can have a variety of meanings due, in large part, to the situation-specific nature of the custody issue coupled with the judicial position on making such an order. Joint custody is an option available to parties who wish to separate but who both wish to continue to be actively involved with their children. In some cases, the children will reside with one parent, but both parents will have equal decision-making power. There are also cases where joint custody means that the child will share equal time with both parents and, thus, move from house to house in some form of pre-scheduled arrangement, with the decision-making ability shifting between the parents as does the child. These types of arrangements require a considerable amount of co-operation and flexibility of the part on the parents. Accordingly, perhaps it is in the best interests of both parents and children alike that such an order be made only on a consensual basis.

The Courts sometimes grant access on the condition that access be exercised in a situation that can be supervised by another person. However, supervised access will not be ordered unless there is good reason for so doing. The CLRA, s. 34, expressly gives the Court the power to give directions as to what it considers appropriate for the supervision of a custody or access order by a person, a children's aid society or another body. The Court cannot direct a third party to supervise unless the party has consented to act as supervisor.

Perhaps the most troublesome issue in the custody area is the problem that arises when the primary or custodial parent wishes to move – the "mobility" question. A custodial parent may wish to relocate as a result of meeting a new partner, obtaining a new job, or simply wanting to return to more familiar surroundings. Canadians have become more mobile in the last decade or so, with the result that the mobility question has become a significant issue in recent years. The Supreme Court of Canada, in May 1996, rendered its first decision on the effect of a custodial parent's move on custody and access. In the lengthy reasons for the majority in *Gordon v.*

Goertz,[63] Madam Justice McLachlin made it clear that the best interests of the particular child must be determined in order to resolve issues of custody and access that arise from any change in the permanent residence of the child.

The Supreme Court of Canada explained that the focus of the inquiry is not the interests and rights of the parents, but those of the child. Each case turns on its own unique circumstances and the *only* issue is the best interests of the child in those particular circumstances. Parental conduct does not enter the analysis unless it relates to the ability of the parent to meet the needs of the child. In the end, the importance of the child remaining with his or her customary custodial parent must be weighed against the continuation of full contact with the child's access parent, his or her extended family and community. The ultimate question in every case is this: what is in the best interests of the child in all of the circumstances, old as well as new?

The federal response to the most prevalent problem of parties disregarding the terms of custody and support orders or separation agreements is found in the *Family Orders and Agreements Enforcement Assistance Act.* The central purpose of this legislative scheme is twofold. First, the legislation establishes a governmental agency to assist a custodial parent or a spouse who is in receipt of child or spousal support to trace a child abducted by an access parent or to trace the payor spouse who is in breach of a provision of the Court order or agreement. This part of the legislation has been in effect since mid-1986.

At present, if a child is wrongfully removed from the jurisdiction by a parent – for example, a father removing his children from Canada contrary to an order granting custody to the mother – there is a limit as to what can be done by the other parent. Once the person and the child are located, what can the parent do? The Department of Foreign Affairs and International Trade (DFAIT) has a sub-department which deals exclusively with what it refers to as "Child-Napping". That Department will often assist a solicitor in Canada to locate a lawyer experienced in this area who resides in the jurisdiction in question. The special committee on the Civil Aspects of International Child Abduction convened by the Hague Conference on Private International Law met in the Hague in November 1979 to prepare a preliminary draft Convention on the civil aspects of international child abduction. Representatives of 22 member countries attended the sessions, which resulted in the development of a rational and practical legislative scheme designed to ensure that the factual situation which existed prior to the child's abduction is re-established as quickly as possible.

---

63 [1996] 2 S.C.R. 27, 19 R.F.L. (4th) 177, 134 D.L.R. (4th) 321.

5. DOMESTIC VIOLENCE AND SPOUSAL ABUSE

Until the 1970s, the issue of spousal abuse was largely ignored as a social and legal problem.[64] Justice system professionals were virtually all men who displayed little sensitivity to or understanding for a range of forms of violence arising in intimate contexts, such as wife abuse, sexual assault and child abuse. There was a tendency to view those cases of "domestic" violence that came to the attention of the police as "private" matters. Except in the most serious cases of wife assault, the police were unlikely to lay charges, and spousal abuse was only to be a factor in family law cases if it was "excessive". The late 1960s saw the beginnings of the modern feminist movement and the beginnings of an awareness of the serious and extensive nature of abuse of women in intimate relationships. In 1968, as part of Canada's divorce law reform, physical and mental cruelty became grounds for dissolution of marriage. In the 1970s advocates for women and various professionals began to demand government action on the issue of spousal abuse and the first shelters for battered women were established.

By the early 1980s there was a growing concern about the inadequacy of the legal responses to spousal abuse. In particular, the police practice of expecting abused wives to bring their own "private prosecutions" in criminal court was criticized; these women often lacked the psychological and financial resources to carry forward their cases, or were easily intimidated or cajoled by their abusers into withdrawing charges. There was also a growing awareness of the "cycle of wife abuse," which often resulted in abused women repeatedly going through an emotionally destructive and physically dangerous pattern of abuse and reconciliation with their partners. In the early 1980s many police forces responded by increasing training for their officers, and introducing policies requiring mandatory police charging in response to all cases of domestic violence.

In 1990, the Supreme Court of Canada ruled in *R. v. Lavellee*[65] that when a women is charged with murdering her abusive partner the Court could take account of the "battered woman syndrome". Her acts might be considered "self defence" even though at the time she faced no immediate threat to her physical safety, if taking account of her mental state as an abused woman, she had a "reasonable apprehension of death or grievous

---

64 For a history of the treatment of wife abuse in Canada, see N. Zoe Hilton, "One in Ten: The Struggle and Disempowerment of the Battered Women's Movement", 7 Can. J. Fam L. 313-336 (1989).
65 [1990] 1 S.C.R. 852, 55 C.C.C. (3d) 97; see also *R. v. M. (M.A.)*, [1998] S.C.J. No. 12, 1998 CarswellOnt 419 (S.C.C.) where the Supreme Court reaffirmed that merely because a woman had been battered, did not mean that she had a defence. Rather the jury could receive expert evidence to explain why an abused woman might stay in an abusive relationship, the effect that being in such a relationship might have on her perception of danger from her abuser, and whether she reasonably believed that her acts were necessary to protect herself from death or grievous bodily harm.

bodily harm". The jury could hear expert evidence about the mental state of abused women to determine whether this particular victim of battering was acting reasonably, taking account of all her circumstances and the context of the abusive relationship.

By the mid 1990s, the battered wife defence was being used not only to justify an attack on an abusive partner, but also in the occasional welfare fraud case to explain why a woman remains on public assistance without being eligible. In the infamous *Bernardo* case, expert testimony was called by the Crown characterizing Karla Homolka as a "battered wife" and explaining why she aided her highly abusive husband in the sexual assault and murder of three women, including Homolka's own sister. Many questioned whether Homolka was really a victim of coercion and battering, or a willing participant in these brutal perverse crimes.

(a) The Cycle of Violence

One of the most influential scholars in the field of domestic violence, American psychologist Lenore Walker, developed a descriptive model of the "cycle of violence" as well as of the concept of the "battered woman syndrome". The "cycle of violence" describes a pattern of wife abuse with three distinct phases: (1) tension building; (2) acute battering incident; and (3) loving contrition by the abuser. In the first phase, there is increasing tension and verbal abuse, with the woman attempting to placate her partner. The tension builds until there is an acute battering incident, involving verbal, physical and possibly sexual abuse; the woman may leave or call the police at this state. In the contrition phase, the batterer is remorseful, apologizes and may send flowers or "court" his partner; she may persuade herself that he will not abuse again and resumes the relationship, though without intervention it is virtually inevitable that the pattern will reoccur, sometimes with violence increasing. Understanding of this cycle of abuse is extremely important for those who work with abuse victims, since they are often called upon immediately after the abusive incident but then find themselves working in the "contrition" phase. Helping victims and abusers to understand this cycle can be a part of successful intervention strategy.

Walker also developed the concept of the "battered woman syndrome" to refer to the state of mind of a woman who has been repeatedly through cycles of violence and is suffering from lowered self esteem and perhaps "learned helplessness". She may not have disclosed the abuse to anyone and feels unable to leave the relationship, perhaps because of threats (which may have been acted on in the past) from the abuser that he will pursue her or harm the children if she leaves. She is acutely sensitive to her partner's control and tendency to violence, and can sense his building anger. In this mental state, she may "reasonably" believe that the only way to escape from the relationship is to kill her partner.

Research suggests that abused women whose children are witnesses to assaults are more likely to leave their partners than those women whose abuse "remains between the grown ups". There is a substantial and growing body of research on the negative effects on children of growing up in a home where there is inter-parental abuse, even if the children are not direct observers of the abuse. Research indicates that at least one quarter of those who physically abuse their partners also physically abuse their children. In some studies as many as three-quarters of abusive husbands also abused their children; at least some of variation in rates depends on the type of population studied, with higher degrees of spousal abuse making abuse of children more likely. An abused spouse often suffers from lowered self-esteem, depression, drug or alcohol abuse or may take out feelings of powerless by mistreating their children. A history of physical aggression in the family is "strongly associated with mother's diminished parenting, in that mothers from violent relationships are less warm and more coercive with their children. While it is clear that children suffer from the diminished parenting capacity of an abused parent, there may be difficulty for judges in deciding how to take account of this in a custody dispute. It may be argued that it is unfair for an abusive parent to be able to "hold against" the abused partner inadequacies that are caused by abuse, though a focus on the "best interests" of the child may weaken this argument.

(b) Domestic Violence Defined

Domestic violence is best defined as that combination of factors and behaviors by which a batterer forces an intimate partner to live "with a constant sense of danger and expectation of violence".[66] Why are women most often the victims of domestic violence? Researchers have found no particular personality traits in women that make them susceptible to battering; rather, the most identifiable risk factor for becoming a victim of domestic violence is being female.[67] Whether or not they grow up to become batterers or victims, children who witness domestic violence suffer from behavioral, emotional, and cognitive problems.[68]

(c) Myths about Domestic Violence

There are many myths about victims of domestic violence. Many people cannot understand a battered woman who still expresses love for her abusive

---

66 See Jeffrey L. Edleson et al., *Men Who Batter Women*, 6 J. Fam. Issues 229, 231 (1985).
67 See Gerald T. Hotaling and David B. Sugarman, *An Analysis of Risk Markers in Husband to Wife Violence: The Current State of Knowledge*, 1 Violence & Victims 101, 111, 118 (1986).
68 See Peter G. Jaffe et al., *Children of Battered Women*. (Susan K. Wilson ed. 1990); L.H. Bowker, *On the Relationship Between Wife Beating and Child Abuse*, in Feminist Perspectives on Wife Abuse 158, 162 (Kirsten Yllo & Michelle Bograd eds. 1988).

partner because they believe her response is a sign of an emotional sickness. Yet research shows that most abusers batter their victims after a strong emotional relationship has developed. Once the battering begins remaining with her batterer and supporting his behavior may be the victim's only means of survival. Understanding this real psychological dynamic and rejecting the myth of masochism allows one to respect the victim's quandary and proceed with the case in a manner that lessens emotional trauma and enhances the victim's safety. Another damaging myth is that women allege that domestic violence has occurred in divorce and child custody cases because they believe it will give them an advantage in court. Judicial experience indicates this myth is unfounded. Professionals in batterers' intervention programs report that violent men tend to rationalize, minimize, or outright deny their own very real violence against women while battered women often are excellent proxies concerning details about violent men and fairly accurate observers about violent episodes. In this sense, the reliability of female victims lends them a certain credibility as persons whose accounts of violence should be accepted. Rather than fabricating allegations of violence, victims are more likely to adopt their batterer's perception of the situation, to the point of minimizing or denying the abuse, as a survival strategy.

Victims are not always comfortable admitting to the violence in their homes. They have good reason to be mistrustful because our society has not yet shown it is willing to offer consistent support to victims of domestic violence. For instance, well-meaning friends, after hearing a victim recount her experiences, may ask in exasperation, *"Why don't you just leave?"* Family members, struggling with their own problems, may tell the victim seeking refuge for the fourth or fifth time, *"It's time for you to take responsibility for yourself"*. Finally, a lawyer irritated when a client fails to show up at a hearing or suddenly refuses to testify in court, may demand, *"Are you serious about this?"* Perhaps the more important questions to ask are: *"How can we stop the batterer from harming the victim and her children?"* and *"What resources are available to ensure that the victim and her children can live safely and independently?"*[69]

For the past three decades, in response to societal norms and values, policymakers have criminalized abusive conduct and the Courts have taken a more serious approach to domestic violence cases. The legislative and judicial branches of government have addressed domestic violence in a more interventionist and serious manner. Freedom from an assault is one of the most basic of personal liberties. Personal liberty is an important claim. Violence in families may be construed as a significant *Charter* issue. Section

---

69 Victims of domestic violence are overwhelmingly female and batterers are overwhelmingly male. See Russel Dobash, *The Myth of Sexual Symmetry in Marital Violence*, 39 Soc. Probs. 71, 74-75 (1992).

7 of the *Charter of Rights and Freedoms* clearly states that: "everyone has the right to life, liberty and security of the person and the right not be deprived thereof except in accordance with the principles of fundamental justice".

(d) Some Sobering Facts

According to a 1993 nation-wide survey, 29 per cent of all Canadian women who have ever been married or lived in a common-law relationship had been physically or sexually assaulted by their partner on at least one occasion since the age of 16.[70] In 1996, the Assaulted Women's Helpline in Metro Toronto received over 18,000 calls from abused or assaulted women. In that same year, Metro police reported 5,330 cases of domestic violence. These cases included murder (3), attempted murder (3), sexual assaults (73), assaults (4,022), harassment, threats and intimidation. Almost two of the three women who were assaulted by their partner had been assaulted on more than one occasion. Thirty-two per cent of these women were assaulted on at least 11 occasions, 9 per cent were assaulted between 6-10 times, and 22 per cent were assaulted between 2-5 times.[71] Statistics Canada now publishes a report entitled, Family Violence in Canada. It bases its findings on a number of studies including the 1993 Violence Against Women Study which was the first and largest of its kind, interviewing 12,300 women across Canada. A recent *Family Violence in Canada* report noted that in 1996, almost 22,000 cases of spousal assault were recorded; 89 per cent involved female victims and 11 per cent involved male victims. The report cautions that these figures are not nationally representative and only represent cases reported to the police. Only a minority of spousal assaults are reported to the police. Most frequently, women reported multiple acts of violence such as being pushed, grabbed, shoved, slapped or having something thrown at them. Smaller numbers reported being victims of violent acts such as sexual assault, choking, being hit with an object or having gun or knife used against them.

Long-Term Impacts of Child Abuse

- 85 per cent of runaways in Toronto have been sexually abused
- 80 per cent of female prisoners were victims of childhood physical or sexual abuse
- 80 per cent of people with eating disorders experienced some form of abuse and/or witnessed violence between parents as a child

---

70 See *Women in Canada*, Statistics Canada, August 1995. Based on the 1993 Statistics Canada *The Violence Against Women* survey. All figures are nation-wide.

71 1995 Statistics: Companion to the Annual Report, Metropolitan Toronto Police Service, 1995.

- 33 per cent of sex offenders experienced some form of sexual trauma as a child
- Suicide prevention programs report that children with a history of sexual abuse are 10 times more likely to attempt suicide
- Children with a history of sexual abuse are seven times more likely to become drug/alcohol dependent
- Child prostitution prevention programs for ages nine and up report that 99 per cent have a history of child abuse[72]

(e) Police Protocols

Early in 1994, the Solicitor General for Ontario issued Guidelines to *all* police forces in Ontario requiring every police force to have in place and follow a protocol relating to domestic violence. Generally, the protocol is designed to require *all* members of the police services,

(a) to be aware of the components of wife assault
(b) to lay criminal charges where there are "reasonable grounds" to do so
(c) to ensure broad community involvement in the establishment of police service priorities in the area of wife assault and other forms of violence against women, the creation of working groups to improve the safety of women, the development of crime prevention initiatives, the assessment of police training and the regular review of police services delivery regarding wife assault
(d) to appoint individuals to monitor police response to incidents of wife assault, ensure consistency in police service policy, liaise with community representatives and train police officers; and
(e) to put in place a policy for addressing incidents in which a police officer is charged with an offence related to wife assault. See amendments to Policing Standards Manual, Police Response to Wife Assault, Ministry of the Solicitor General and Correctional Services, Strategic Policy and Planning Division.

In 1994, the Attorney General for Ontario updated its Directive to Crown prosecutors dealing with the prosecution of cases involving spousal and partner assault. The policy deals with charges, pre-trial issues, the scheduling of cases, interviewing of complainants and witnesses, withdrawal of charges, referrals to the Criminal Injuries Compensation Board, adverse, hostile or forgetful witnesses, consent, sentencing and victim impact statements and appeals. Some jurisdictions have specialized domestic courts and special pre-trial and mediation facilities designed to deal with domestic violence.

Evidence used on motions for relief involving domestic violence is often complicated by the following factors:

---

72 Fact Sheets, Ontario Association of Children's Aid Societies.

1. There are often no witnesses to the abuse other than the victim and the alleged abuser.
2. The victims are often emotionally worn down.
3. The victims are often in complete crisis and cannot provide detailed evidence regarding the abuse.
4. Many victims are still very much afraid of the abuser.
5. Victims often do not tell people about the abuse. Their best friends, family, colleagues and neighbours have no idea about the existence of violence. They therefore have few witnesses to corroborate their stories.
6. Many victims lie to doctors, police, family members, colleagues and neighbours about the causes of visible injuries and state specifically that they have not been abused when asked directly whether they have. They therefore have "statements against interest" working against them.

School teachers can provide information about the children's progress at school, whether they are acting out or becoming aggressive, whether they have described specific incidents of abuse to their teacher(s) or classmates, whether they are afraid to go home, etc. Babysitters can also provide information about how the children function during the day, whether they suffer from apparently stress-related symptoms, whether they have described specific incidents of abuse, whether their behaviour is suddenly difficult to control or aggressive, whether they are afraid or insecure, etc. Neighbours can provide information to corroborate incidents if they have overheard incidents or witnessed them. Colleagues provide information about whether the victim is distracted at work, whether she has come into work with bruises or other visible injuries, whether they have overheard telephone conversations between the victim and the alleged abuser, whether the alleged abuser has harassed the victim at work, whether he has asked colleagues to pass on threats or vicious messages to the victim, whether the victim appeared to be afraid when taking calls or having contact with the alleged abuser, and whether the alleged abuser has sent friends to harass the victim at work. Family members may have visited the parties and witnessed violence and even confronted the abuser about his conduct. They may have seen injuries sustained by the victim and heard stories of abuse. The problem for many is that a great deal of the only evidence available is hearsay evidence.

(f) The Domestic Violence Protection Act, 2000

The class of applicant for relief under the *Domestic Violence Protection Act, 2000* (Bill 117) (which has not been proclaimed at the time of writing) is limited to persons who live or have lived in a conjugal relationship (either heterosexual or homosexual) with the respondent, or who have or have had "a dating relationship" (an undefined term) or who are "relatives" of the respondent who currently live with the respondent. The ground for any initial application is "domestic violence", term that is defined in subsection 1(2) as:

1. An assault that consists of the intentional application of force that causes the applicant to fear for his or her safety, but does not include any act committed in self-defence.
2. An intentional or reckless act or omission that causes bodily harm or damage to property.
3. An act or omission or threatened act or omission that causes the applicant to fear for his or her safety.
4. Forced physical confinement, without lawful authority.
5. Sexual assault, sexual exploitation or sexual molestation, or the threat of sexual assault, sexual exploitation or sexual molestation.
6. A series of acts which collectively causes the applicants to fear for his or her safety, including following, contacting, communicating with, observing or recording any person.

The focus of Bill 117 is clearly on "domestic violence", but the test for restraining orders under section 35 of the *Children's Law Reform Act* and section 46 of the *Family Law Act* is much broader. The current statutory provisions recognize that a person can "molest, annoy or harass" a spouse or former spouse in ways that do not involve any violence or threat to his or her safety and that, if the civilities of separation are not observed by one partner, a court should intervene. The words "molesting, annoying or harassing" in section 35 of the *Children's Law Reform Act* and section 46 of the *Family Law Act* are not defined and courts have enjoyed a certain measure of latitude in deciding what is or is not acceptable behaviour. An example of the sort of conduct that Bill 117 would miss entirely can be found in *Callon v. Callon*[73] where Justice Lee Ferrier remarked:

> In our view, letters to third parties by a spouse which contain scurrilous allegations against the other spouse, whether true or not, can constitute annoyance, harassment or both within the meaning of the section. The purpose of section 46 as it relates to interim orders is to permit both litigants the opportunity to conduct their litigation in as reasoned an atmosphere as may be possible.

(g) Effect of Family Violence upon Children

Children are affected by witnessing violence in their family. This exposure may be as an eyewitness to an incident, overhearing episodes from their bedroom or walking into the kitchen to see the aftermath of violence. Parents tend to underestimate by half (50 per cent vs 90 per cent) how much their children know. Many children report growing up in a "war-zone" where there is a climate of fear and terror even during periods of calm.

---

73 (1999), 68 C.R.R. (3d) 350, [1990] O.J. No. 3108 (Ont. Div. Ct.).

Some children suffer from multiple forms of abuse. In families where there is marital violence, children have a significant probability of suffering direct physical or sexual abuse. In fact, witnessing violence is a form of psychological or emotional abuse that can leave behind the same adjustment problems as the direct experience of physical or sexual abuse. Children who witness violence are at risk for a number of significant emotional and behavioural problems such as aggression, bullying, anxiety, destruction of property, insecurity, depression, and secretiveness. Children who witness violence are also at risk in developing inappropriate attitudes about the use of violence to resolve interpersonal conflicts – especially in "loving" relationships. In the long-term, boys who are exposed to violence are more likely to end up being an abuser in an intimate relationship.

Education is needed at all levels of our society as to the pervasiveness and complexity of the problem of domestic violence. More specifically, there must be more awareness as to the likelihood of escalated violence to the battered spouse upon or after separation. In order to combat commonly-raised allegations of reciprocal violence, education is also needed as to the fact that domestic violence is rarely mutual.

Since the law plays an important role in communicating society's values, in order to create social change with a view to reducing and eliminating domestic violence, domestic violence must be treated by society as a serious and significant crime, and the proof of its presence should have an impact on the parties' private dealings (*i.e.*, custody/access issues) as well.

6. PARENTAL AUTHORITY

(a) The Family and the Canadian Charter of Rights and Freedoms

A major concept in our laws is that of the "best interest of the child" rather than the rights of parents. In *B.(R.) v. Children's Aid Society of Metropolitan Toronto*,[74] a case decided in 1995, the appellants were Jehovah's Witness parents who had refused consent to a blood transfusion for their newborn daughter who had been born prematurely. Their refusal was on religious grounds, and the medical evidence indicated that transfusions would be necessary to protect the child's life. After the medical treatment was concluded, the child was returned to parental custody, but the parents appealed the original decision on the grounds that it had violated their constitutional rights. Mr. Justice Lamer of the Supreme Court of Canada found that the liberty interest in section 7 of the *Charter* did *not* include the right of parents to make medical decisions or to raise their children without undue state interference. Although a majority of the Court held that the parents' rights to rear their children according to their religious beliefs was a fundamental part of freedom of religion and that accordingly their section

---

74 [1995] 1 S.C.R. 315.

2(a) rights had been infringed, they went on to hold that the careful legislative scheme implemented by the state was saved by section 1.

> [. . .The common law has always, in the absence of demonstrated neglect or unsuitability, presumed that parents should make all significant choices affecting their children, and has afforded them a general liberty to do as they choose.
>
> This liberty interest is not a parental right tantamount to a right of property in children. [. . .] presumption parents should make important decisions affecting their children both because parents are more likely to appreciate the best interests of their children and because the state is ill-equipped to make such decisions itself. [. . .] This is not to say that the state cannot intervene when it considers it necessary to safeguard the child's autonomy or health. But such intervention must be justified.

B.(R.) underlines our Courts' reluctance to allow the concept of parents' rights to be in opposition to the interests or health of a child. This is consistent with the view of the family as a central social unit whose integrity should be encouraged and protected..

The *Charter* prohibits discrimination and guarantees certain fundamental rights and freedoms to all Canadians. Governments cannot interfere with these rights and freedoms, except in very limited circumstances defined in the *Charter*. The *Charter* applies to government action and government actors; it does not apply to private individuals. A broad definition of "government" is used to include all bodies that act as government agents in carrying out functions or policies. The *Charter* applies to provincial educational legislation and to school boards. The *Charter* has changed the delivery of education in two significant ways. First, it gives parents a tool for challenging school board decisions. Before the *Charter*, parents were restricted to administrative law remedies that dealt mainly with procedural irregularities. Secondly, the *Charter* has national scope, unlike the provincial education and human rights statutes. Since the *Charter* is the supreme law of Canada and applies to all Canadians, decisions of the Supreme Court of Canada are binding on all provinces, and subsequently on all school boards. The presence of the *Charter* makes it necessary for school officials to be aware of issues and conflicts in all areas of Canada. If, for example, a case involving the religious rights of a student arises in Ontario and is decided by the Supreme Court of Canada, it will dictate how students are to be treated across the nation.

With the introduction of *Charter*, the role and responsibilities of the Court were altered significantly. The Court now faces the difficult task of defining constitutionally entrenched rights and then balancing them against the social goals of elected officials. Under section 1, Courts now uphold or invalidate state action based on whether a limitation is reasonable and demonstrably justified in a free and democratic society. Established standards of review under section 1 require the Court to evaluate evidence on the importance of the state's objective and the proportionality of the means selected to achieve the desired end. The principles first enunciated in *R. v. Oakes*, have been modified so that in accordance with the nature of judicial review, section 1 could be applied with different levels of strictness in different circumstances.

The relationship between substantive equality rights in section 15 and attempts to justify discriminatory state action under section 1 becomes a discrete topic because under a contextual and flexible approach to section 1 the considerations for balancing may be different when an equality right is infringed. Our Courts have used equality rights to uphold and justify *Criminal Code* restrictions on hate propaganda in *R. v. Keegstra*,[75] obscenity in *R. v. Butler*,[76] and restrictions on an accused's access to the private records of sexual assault complaints in *R. v. Mills*.[77]

The rights revolution began before the *Charter*, and the *Charter* can be seen in some sense as its product or logical result. The revolution in question has been the explosion of rights talk and rights claims in Canadian life. Never has rights talk so monopolized the Canadian language of the public good. Rights became the key language in which women, children, and gays made claims against the family order of the 1960s; it became the way, through treaty negotiations, that aboriginal peoples advanced claims for dignity and equality and self-government, and it became the chief way in which Quebec citizens sought to protect their language. The Supreme Court's increased importance in Canadian national life is a direct result of this amazing proliferation of rights talk, and its consequent tendency to turn all conflicts of interests into conflicts of rights susceptible to judicial interpretation and adjudication. This, of course, is a global phenomenon. The passing of the Universal Declaration of Human Rights gave rights to individuals for the first time in international law, and it spawned the huge extension of international human rights instruments and institutions.

When the Supreme Court of Canada rendered its judgment in *Dolphin Delivery Ltd. v. R.W.E.S.U. Local 580*,[78] it became clear that private law areas not involving legislation or governmental connection would be immune from the scrutiny of the *Charter*. Despite the concession from the Court that the common law would be "interpreted in a manner which is consistent with "*Charter* principles", the *Charter* has not played much of a role in tort law judgments. In *Hill v. Church of Scientology of Toronto*,[79] Cory J. cautioned against amending the common law to reflect Charter

---

75 [1990] 3 S.C.R. 697.
76 [1992] 1 S.C.R. 452, reconsideration refused [1993] 2 W.W.R. lxi (S.C.C.).
77 (1999), 139 C.C.C. (3d) 321 (S.C.C.).
78 (1986), 38 C.C.L.T. 184 (S.C.C.).
79 (1995), 126 D.L.R. (4th) 129 (S.C.C.).

values, preferring instead to leave "far-reaching changes to the common law . . .to the legislature". In *Dobson (Litigation Guardian of) v. Dobson*,[80] a child disabled due to prenatal injuries caused by his pregnant mother's negligent driving sued her. The Supreme Court of Canada had many years before recognized the right of a child born with disabilities as a result of prenatal injuries to sue the party whose negligence caused the injuries. As quoted by Cory J. in *Dobson*, Lamont J.'s rationale in *Montreal Tramways Co. v. Leveille*[81], for affording the child a right of action was that it is "but natural justice that a child, if born alive and viable, should be allowed to maintain an action in court for injuries wrongfully committed upon its person while in the womb of its mother". But what if the person who wrongfully injured it was its mother?

Cory J., writing for the majority, applied the two-stage duty test. Foreseeability by a pregnant woman that her negligent acts could injure her fetus and result in post-natal disabilities was accepted virtually without question. Having determined that there was a *prima facie* duty, the majority of the Court relied on policy arguments to negate it. Although the *Dobson* case required the Court to break new ground no matter what it decided, since the issue before it was a novel one, in several respects judicial precedents and legal principles were more supportive of and consistent with the dissenting approach than with the majority's. These precedents and principles include the following considerations. First, the common law already recognizes the liability of negligent parties to children disabled as a result of prenatal accidents. Thus, the extension to mothers can be seen as a logical and incremental extension of these precedents. Secondly, the common law also recognizes the rights of children to sue their parents, including their mothers, for injuries caused to them by post-natal negligent acts, for example, negligent driving. Liability in these cases would also raise, although granted not to the same degree, some of the difficult social policy implications for mothers identified by the majority. Third, the common law, as well as legislation, is generally opposed to granting immunities based on the status of individuals.

In the last few decades, family law in Canada has risen remarkably in profile. The family has become a great subject of public discourse whose very nature, function and definition are seen as very important issues. While the notion of the family unit as one which deserves respect remains vital, the family is also seen increasingly as a social unit upon which the state depends, and which it therefore should play a role in supporting. Legislation has played an increasing role in family law, from child protection to family property. In this sense, it may be as much public as private. Family law has moved from a central preoccupation with preserving marriages to a concern

---

80 (1999), 45 C.C.L.T. (2d) 217 (S.C.C.).
81 [1933] S.C.R. 456.

with preserving parent-child relationships and the concern with protecting the vulnerable members of family units. The family is understood more in terms of a basic relationship of interdependency which may or may not involve marriage, children, heterosexual partners or even sexual affiliation at all.

Our courts have been cautious about the application of an individualistic rights discourse in family law and, apart from the "family definition" cases a few *Charter* challenges have been ultimately successful.[82] It is staggering to realize that with the exception of some changes in custody, the law of the family – and therefore the expectations of members of a family were – essentially constant until 1968. We went through two world wars, two conscription crises, votes for women, prohibition, a Depression, a quiet Revolution in Quebéc, the establishment of human rights commissions, the promulgation of a *Canadian Bill of Rights*, waves of immigration, the introduction of radio, movies, and television, and a declaration made by the Privy Council that women were persons, and yet hardly a single change was made to the law of the family. Nor is there any indication, despite seismic social changes, that in the hundred years between Confederation and the introduction of the 1968 *Divorce Act* there was any real demand for any reform of any aspect of the law of the family.[83]

By 1988, the family, starting with the pregnant woman, was seen as the focus of important social and legal issues which involved issues of rights. The Supreme Court was no longer merely "settling a dispute"; it was the final arbiter in light of the fact that social and political consensus on the issue has been impossible leaving a legislative void. As Justice Wilson had said in a 1985 speech,

> [T]he conclusion is inescapable that the scope of judicial review of legislative and executive acts has been vastly expanded under the Charter and [. . .] the Courts have become the mediators between the state and the individual.

Young v. Young[84] was a case that attracted a great deal of public attention because it was a family law case concerning the application of the *Charter*. Mrs. Young was the sole custodian of the children of the marriage. One of the contribution factors to the marriage breakdown had been Mr. Young's adoption of the Jehovah Witness faith. The trial judge had imposed significant limits on his access which included not speaking about his faith to the child, not taking them to Church and not involving them in canvassing and

---

82 See, e.g. *Miron v. Trudel* (1995), 124 D.L.R (4th) 693 (S.C.C.), and *M. v. H.*, [1999] 2 S.C.R. 3.; *Young v. Young*, [1993] 4 S.C.R. 3; *Droit de la famille - 1150*, [1993] 4 S.C.R. 141; *Thibaudeau v. R.*, [1995] 2 S.C.R. 627; *Symes v. The Queen*, [1993] 4 S.C.R. 695; and *B. (R.) v. Children's Aid Society of Metropolitan Toronto* , [1995] 1 S.C.R. 315.
83 R.S. Abella, "The Law of The family in the year of the Family", 26 Ott. L. Rev. 533 at 535.
84 [1993] 4 S.C.R. 3.

proselytizing activities. There was evidence that indicated that the children had disliked their father's religious instructions, that it was damaging their relationship with him and contributing to the stress they were experiencing in their relation to their parents' separation. The central legal issue was whether sections 16(8) and 17(5) of the *Divorce Act* relating to custody and custody variation orders respectively violated sections 2(a), (b), (d) or 15(1) of the *Charter*. Both subsections state that in making an order, "...the Court shall take into consideration only the best interests of the child". None of the judgments expressed any enthusiasm for the direct application of the *Charter* to matters involving custody or access. When *Charter* principles such as freedom of religion are in issue, the best interests standard should reflect this and require evidence of harm before restricting access. McLachlin J. held that certain limitations to access, such as those involving religious expression, should be based on evidence of harm to the child. This is predicated on the premise that maximizing access is generally a good thing and in the interests of the children, and that to rebut this one must establish harm. She was of the view that harm had not been established in this case.[85] Sopinka J. expressed general agreement with McLachlin J., but stated that while he agreed with her that the ultimate determination in deciding issues of custody and access is the "best interests of the child" test, he went on to say that it must be reconciled with the *Charter* and that it should be overridden "only if its exercise would occasion consequences that involve more than inconvenience, upset or disruption to the child and incidentally to the custodial parent.[86] Gonthier and La Forest JJ. agreed with L'Heureux-Dubé J. who went furthest in holding that the trial judge's order was not subject to the *Charter*. Cory and Iacobucci JJ. refused to express a view on this issue as it was not necessary, in their view, to the case at bar.

The Court heard and decided another very similar case, *Droit de la famille – 1150*,[87] at the same time as *Young*. There, the mother was Roman Catholic and was the custodial parent and the father a Jehovah Witness. The case differed from *Young* in two ways. First, the trial judge's order was less intrusive. While it specified that the father could not "indoctrinate" his daughter, it had also specified that he could teach his faith to her. Second, the Supreme Court (as well as the Québec Court of Appeal) emphasized the father's fanaticism" and that this was *disturbing to the child*.[88] As the parents had not married, this case did not invoke the *Divorce Act* but rather the best interests standard as articulated in the Civil Code of Québec.[89] There have

---

85 *Ibid.*, para. 129.
86 *Ibid.*, para. 107.
87 [1993] 4 S.C.R. 141.
88 *Ibid.*, at 152.
89 Civil Code of Lower Canada, article 30: In every decision concerning a child, the child's interest and the respect of his rights must be the determining factors.

been no subsequent cases arguing *Charter* rights to pre-empt the best interests at the time. It is particularly interesting to note that *Gordon v. Goertz*,[90] a case which involved, "relocation" of a custodial parent to Australia, decided in 1996, did not raise the issue of "mobility rights". This had been one of the issues discussed extensively in the academic literature in the early 1990s as potentially undermining the complex nature of families by applying unsophisticated and individualistic notions of rights.

(b) Corporal Punishment

The case of David Peterson was brought before Judge John Menzies in 1997 amidst a storm of controversy. Peterson, an Illinois family man, was vacationing in London, Ontario when he was arrested and charged with assault. An eyewitness report indicated that Peterson had spanked his five-year-old daughter on her bare bottom. Peterson testified that he had spanked his daughter to punish her for intentionally slamming the car door on her brother. Ironically, Peterson wanted to teach his daughter that wilfully hurting her brother was not acceptable. Judge Menzies ruled that in the eyes of the law a father has the right to physically discipline his children, in other words he had the authority to do so. A Québec judge ruled that a teacher who grabbed a 15-year-old boy by the hair and banged his head onto his desk had not committed an offence since section 43 of the *Criminal Code* prohibited the "excessive" use of force, not the "disgraceful" use. In Manitoba, a father who removed his shoe before kicking his son down the stairs was exonerated by the application of section 43. The judge ruled that the father had exercised restraint and reason by removing his shoe before he began kicking.[91] Several parental factors have been consistently linked to child conduct problems. Specifically, inconsistent use of discipline, failure to use positive reinforcement, and excessive use of capital punishment.[92]

Because parental involvement with their children decreases as the child approaches adolescence, a decrease in parental monitoring, supervision, and positive discipline strategies also occurs.[93] Young teens left on their own are often susceptible to falling under the influence of gangs, committing illegal acts, or becoming rebellious to all forms of authority. In the early stages of a child's development, parents play a crucial role in providing food, shelter, safety, and essential care. Appropriate discipline is a necessary element of care which may keep children free from harm and hazard.

---

90 [1996] 2 S.C.R. 27.
91 Robertson, Heather-Jane. (2000) Strike Laws not for Children. *Delta Kappan*, 81(7), 555-556.
92 P.J. Frick, R.E. Christian, and J.M. Wootton, (1999) Age Trends in the Association between Parenting Practices and Conduct Problems. *Behavior Modification*, 23(1), 106-128.
93 Henry Gleitman, (1986) *Psychology*, 2nd ed. (W.W. Norton & Company: New York).

Children have to be taught that the bright burners on a stove hurt if you touch them, coffee cups have hot liquids which scald, and vases holding pretty flowers will shatter and cut small hands if pulled from the pedestal. It is not uncommon to see mothers slapping the hands of their infants while simultaneously shouting, "No!" This is how many children are taught that some items in their surroundings are forbidden.

Research on the use of corporal punishment paints a dismal picture. Many studies which have examined the use of corporal punishment have found that it is ineffective, offensive, and may result in harmful psychological effects which last well into adulthood. Children who were spanked often become beaters themselves when they reach adulthood.[94]

The case of *Canadian Foundation for Children, Youth & the Law v. Canada (Attorney General)*,[95] concerned the extent to which parents and teachers may use force to correct children. It came before the Court in the form of a constitutional challenge to a section of the *Criminal Code*.[96] Generally, it is criminal assault to use force against another without consent. Section 43 of the *Criminal Code* is an exception to that general rule. The section provides a justification for a parent, a person in the place of a parent, or a teacher who uses force to correct a child in her or his care, where the force used is "reasonable in the circumstances". Section 43 of the *Criminal Code* became a focal point in the debate about corporal punishment in child-rearing. Section 43 does not expressly delineate the nature or limits of the force that is justified other than to require that it be "reasonable in the circumstances" and be for the purposes of "correction". Because the notion of reasonableness varies with the beholder, it is perhaps not surprising that some of the judicial decisions applying s. 43 to excuse otherwise criminal assault appear to some to be inconsistent and unreasonable.

There is a growing consensus that corporal punishment of children does more harm than good. It has been banned in virtually all Canadian school systems, and the federal Ministry of Health has mounted an educational campaign teaching that hitting children is wrong. Canadian attitudes towards corporal punishment are changing. An increasing number of Canadian adults believe that many forms of corporal punishment, at one time considered acceptable, are no longer acceptable. The right of parents and teachers to use reasonable corrective force has its roots in the British Common Law.

---

94 See Andre Imbrogno, *Corporal Punishment in America's Public Schools and the U.N. Convention on the Rights of the Child: A Case for Non-ratification.* (2000), *Journal of Law & Education*, 29(2), 125-146. and Sureshrani Paintal. *Banning Corporal Punishment* (1999), *Childhood Education*, 26(1), 36-39. Margret McFadden *Corporal Punishment: Legalized Child Abuse* (1987). *Education Canada*, 27(3), 4-7.
95 (2000), 49 O.R. (3d) 662, [2000] O.J. No. 2535, 2000 CarswellOnt 2409 (S.C.J.), additional reasons at (2000), 2001 CarswellOnt 935 (Ont. S.C.J.), affirmed (2002), 207 D.L.R. (4th) 632 (Ont. C.A.).
96 R.S.C. 1985, c. C-46.

It has been part of the *Criminal Code* since 1892. The Supreme Court of Canada considered the purpose and effect of s. 43 in the case of *R. v. Ogg-Moss*,[97] The appellant was a care worker who had used physical punishment to discipline a mentally challenged adult. The Court rejected the argument that section 43 could protect his actions. Dickson, J. noted that the effect of section 43 is to excuse one group of persons from using force that would otherwise lead to criminal liability, while at the same time removing the protection of the criminal law from another group. He also observed that its purpose is rooted in historical notions of the best interests of children. Dickson, J. referred, to Blackstone's Commentaries on the Laws of England: "He may lawfully correct his child being underage, in a reasonable manner, for this is for the benefit of his education".[98] Justice McCombs, at the trial of *Canadian Foundation for Youth v. Canada*, concluded that:

> Having regard to the history of the legislation, that Parliament's purpose in maintaining s. 43 is to recognise that parents and teachers require reasonable latitude in carrying out responsibility imposed by law to provide for their children, to nurture them and to educate them. That responsibility, Parliament has decided, cannot be carried out unless parents and teachers have a protected sphere of authority within which to fulfil their responsibilities. That sphere of authority is intended to allow a defence to assault within a limited domain of physical discipline, while at the same time ensuring that children are protected from child abuse . . .

The application to strike down section 43 of the *Criminal Code* as unconstitutional was dismissed. This decision was appealed to the Ontario Court of Appeal and that Court released its decision on January 15, 2002.[99] Speaking for the Appeal Court, Goudge J.A. saw no merit in the submission that section 43 subjects children to cruel and unusual punishment. In his view, section 43 "simply creates a criminal law defence for certain persons who apply reasonable force to children by way of correction [and] by enacting the section the state cannot be said to either inflict. . .physical punishment or be responsible for its infliction". He also rejected the submission that section 43 violates section 15 of the *Charter* by subjecting children to differential treatment on the grounds of age, because, in his opinion, differential treatment was clearly justified under section 1 of the *Charter*:

> As I have said, s. 43 implicates the child's security of the person interest. The section permits limited physical punishment of the child by a limited class of people without the punishment being a criminal assault. The section does not approve or encourage such punishment. It carefully defines the limits that must be observed if those actions are to escape criminal sanction. Those limits are

---

97 [1984] 2 S.C.R. 173, 14 C.C.C. (3d) 116.
98 *Ibid.*, at 185.
99 (2002), 207 D.L.R. (4th) 632 (Ont. C.A.).

found in the language of the section as informed by the kind of expert evidence presented in this case rather than in the reported facts of particular cases which may be incomplete or worse, wrongly decided. For exemption from the criminal law this section requires that the force be applied to the child by a parent, surrogate parent or teacher. The force must be reasonable in the circumstances which will inevitably include consideration of the age and character of the child, the circumstances of the punishment, its gravity, the misconduct of the child giving rise to it, the likely effect of the punishment on the child and whether the child suffered any injuries. Finally, the person applying the force must intend it for 'correction' and the child being 'corrected' must be capable of learning from the correction. Hence s. 43 infringes the child's security of the person only to the extent of decriminalizing the limited application of force to the child in circumstances where the risk of physical harm is modest.

On the other hand, the state interest is to avoid the harm to family life that could come with the criminalizing of this conduct. Those insulated from the criminal law by s. 43 – parents, surrogate parents and teachers – must be in close and constant contact with children to fulfil their important responsibilities to those children. As McCombs J. found, the experts agree that extending criminal sanctions so as to prosecute non-abusive physical punishment would have a negative impact upon families and hinder parental and teacher efforts to nurture children. This state interest exists in a context where the state is also vigorously pursuing educational programs to discourage and if possible eradicate physical punishment of children and where there is significant non-criminal child protection legislation designed to prevent child abuse.

Given that the infringement of the child's security of the person is carefully circumscribed, that there is an important state interest to be achieved by not criminalizing the specified conduct and that there are other mechanisms in place to significantly reduce the risk of physical harm to children, I think section 43 represents a fair balance between the interest of the state and the interest of the individual child. Hence in my opinion the section conforms to the principles of fundamental justice.

In summary, the s. 7 issue presented by section 43 is not about whether physical punishment of children is good or bad. The government has clearly and properly determined that it is bad. Rather the issue is whether section 43 infringes the child's security of the person in a way that violates the principles of fundamental justice. The appellant has not demonstrated any such violation. Indeed, in my view, section 43 fairly balances the individual and state interests at stake. This ground of appeal must therefore be dismissed.[100]

The question of whether the corporal punishment of children should be permitted in our society is, of course, controversial, and public opinion is divided now as ever. At the original five-day hearing, Justice McCombs found several areas of agreement among the experts on both sides of the issue.

---

100 Above, note 95.

1. Hitting a child under two is wrong and harmful. With very young children, even mild spanking has no value and can destroy a child's sense of security and self-esteem, essential components of a healthy nurturing environment. A child under two will not understand why he or she is being hit.
2. Corporal punishment of teenagers is not helpful and potentially harmful. There is a consensus that corporal punishment of teenagers achieves only short-term compliance and carries with it the danger of alienation from society, along with aggressive or otherwise anti-social behaviour.
3. Corporal punishment using objects such as belts, rules, etc., is potentially harmful, both physically and emotionally, and should not be tolerated.
4. Corporal punishment should never involve a slap or blow to the head.
5. Corporal punishment which causes injury is child abuse.
6. None of the experts goes so far as to advocate or recommend spanking, or other forms of corporal punishment, as a form of child discipline. They agree that other forms of discipline, such as withdrawal of privileges or removing a child from the room, are equally effective in most cases.
7. There is general agreement among the experts that the only benefit of spanking to be found in the research is short-term compliance.
8. The experts all endorsed the "time out" method as an effective and appropriate method of child discipline.
9. Most of the social science witnesses and professionals, agree that spanking (as properly defined) is not child abuse.
10. The consensus among the experts is that not every instance of physical discipline by a parent should be criminalized. Many believe that the desirable objective of changing societal attitudes regarding child discipline would be best achieved through educational incentives, rather than the use of criminal sanctions to prosecute non-abusive physical punishment. The experts agree that extending the reach of criminal law in this way would have a negative impact upon families and hinder parental and teacher efforts to nurture children.

The experts disagree about the reliability of opinions concerning the purported harmful effects of corporal punishment, including spanking. The issue of child abuse does not readily lend itself to ethical scientific research. It is not possible to conduct studies with sufficiently rigorous adherence to proper scientific method to produce statistically reliable results. The ethical impediments to empirical studies of child abuse are obvious. Consequently, there is no empirical evidence establishing a definitive, long-term causal link between corporal punishment and negative outcomes for children. It cannot be said with scientific certainty that corporal punishment causes long-term harm. Conversely, there is no reliable empirical evidence that non-abusive or mild forms of physical discipline, such as spanking, have a positive corrective effect upon children.

Despite the absence of statistically reliable empirical evidence, the experts generally agree that there is a significant body of "associational" evidence that corporal punishment is a risk factor linked to poor outcomes in children. However, the reliability of the studies is tainted by the fact that other significant variables were present in the studies, variables such as adverse social conditions and other forms of negative parental behaviour. In short, it is impossible to determine with scientific precision whether corporal punishment leads to negative outcomes or whether it is simply a factor among other negative environmental factors that cumulatively impact negatively upon a child's future. The experts disagree as to whether the existence of section 43 impairs educational efforts to discourage corporal punishment and whether the availability of the defence discourages police from laying assault charges. There was agreement that section 43 should be clarified, particularly the term "reasonable force", so as to give better guidance to parents, police and child protection workers.

It was submitted by the appellants that it is a principle of fundamental justice that laws that effect children should be interpreted and applied in a manner that reflects the "best interests of the child", and that section 43 is inconsistent with this fundamental principle because it does not consider the child's rights or best interests and has been interpreted and applied in a manner that justifies physical harm to children. Clearly, the best interests of children are of central importance in Canadian law.[101] In the context of family law, the principle of best interests of the child has been used to develop judicial guidelines concerning child access and custody issues. Justice McCoomb found that the "best interests of the child" principle is best understood as an important underlying social value that informs many legislative and policy initiatives, rather than as a principle of fundamental justice under section 7 of the Charter. The concept of children as rights holders is a relatively recent idea. The recognition of children as persons under the law is a 20th century phenomenon, prior to which children were primarily regarded as the property of their parents:[102] The contemporary children's rights movement however, questions the validity of these traditional norms. The children's rights movement, culminating in the United Nations Convention on the Rights of the Child, has progressed to the point

---

101 See, for example *Young v. Young*, [1993] 4 S.C.R. 3 at 74 and *Baker v. Canada (Minister of Citizenship & Immigration)*, [1999] 2 S.C.R. 817 at 861-62.
102 See M. Freeman, *The Rights and Wrongs of Children* (London: Francis Pinter, 1983), Chapter 1, "The Evolution of a Concept", at 6-23.

where a child is accorded not only legal personhood, but the status of individual and autonomous holder.[103]

(c) Home Schooling

In a statement to the Ontario Legislature on April 26, 2001, the Minister of Education stated that the Government will: "eliminate the institutional bias against home schooling". The *Education Act* recognizes that parents are able to teach their children at home, commonly referred to as "home schooling". The most recent statistic from Ministry of Education School September Reports indicate that in the year 1999-2000, there were close to 3,000 students being home schooled. The Ontario Federation of Teaching Parents (OFTP) reports on its web site that there are close to 20,000 children who are being home schooled. Because there are parents who do not inform their local school board that they are providing home schooling for their children, it is difficult for school boards to know the exact numbers. Section 21(2) (a) of the *Education Act* (Ontario) states that a child may be excused from attendance at school if he or she is receiving "satisfactory instruction at home or elsewhere". However, the Act does not define "satisfactory instruction". This task has generally been assigned to school boards by the Ministry. The Ontario Ministry of Education has recently issued a Policy/ Program Memorandum (No. 131) stating its policy about home schooling (dated June 17, 2002). The memorandum advises parents to notify their local school board each year that they intend to home school their children. It states that the school board "should accept the written notification of

---

103 See *Convention of the Rights of the Child (with Reservations and Statement of Understanding)*, UN doc. A/RES/44/25, November 25, 1989, entry into the force September 2, 1990; in force for Canada December 13, 1991, Can.T.S. 1992 #3 ("Convention"). On corporal punishment generally see: J. Durant, "Public Attitudes Toward Corporal Punishment in Canada" in D. Frehsee, W. Horn and K. Bussman, eds., *Family Violence Against Children* (New York: Walter de Grutyer, 1996), at 107; G.P. Rodrigues, ed., *Crankshaw's Criminal Code of Canada*, (Toronto: Carswell, 1993) at 1-326; Anne McGillvray, "'He'll Learn it on His Body': Disciplining Childhood in Canadian Law" (1997), 5 *International Journal of Children's Rights 193*, at pp. 207-08; *R. v. M. (R.W.)* (1995), 103 C.C.C. (3d) 375 (P.E.I. Prov. Ct.), Thompson C.J.: "The case law establishes that we have moved a considerable distance from the position enunciated [historically]. In my view, we are now at a point where striking a child with an object in areas of the body which can and does result in visible injury of even a relative short duration is clearly excessive."; *R. v. Atkinson*, [1994] 9 W.W.R. 485 (Man. Prov. Ct.), at para. 16: "In determining what is reasonable under the circumstances the Court must consider the standards of the contemporary Canadian community."; *The 1999 Guide to Federal Programs and Services for Children and Youth*, published by Health Canada, lists a variety of existing federal programs and services that focus on children and young people. For example, the program "Nobody's Perfect" is a parent support and education program for parents with children up to the age 5. It is accompanied by a resource called "Behaviour", which states, at 20, "No matter how angry you are it's never okay to spank children. It's a bad idea and it doesn't work.".

parents each year as evidence that the parents are providing satisfactory instruction at home." It also states that "normally, the board should not investigate the matter" but "if there are reasonable grounds to suspect that the child is not receiving satisfactory instruction at home, the board should take steps to determine whether the instruction is satisfactory". The memorandum provides guidelines for conducting an investigation. The memorandum also outlines the resources that are available to home schooling parents, including provincial testing through the Education Quality and Accountability Office. If a home schooling parent refuses to cooperate with a school board official, or if a home school feels that the local school board is trying to become too intrusive, the home schooling parent is able to obtain legal advice from the Home School Legal Defence Association. (HSLDA). This organization is committed to the belief that the parent is the primary agent responsible for providing the child with an education. HSLDA believes that the State has a minimal role to play in ensuring that a child is receiving an adequate education. HSLDA has played a useful role as an advocate for home schooling parents in preventing potential litigation with local school boards and with the Ministry of Education's Provincial School Attendance Counsellor.

(d) School Councils

In 1994 the Ontario Royal Commission on Learning released a report recommending several reforms to Ontario's education system. Among these was a recommendation that each school establish a school community council. In January 1995, the Ontario Ministry of Education and Training issued Policy/Program Memorandum No. 122 requiring each school in the province to establish a school council. Parents and guardians were to form the majority of the council and the chair of the council was to be a parent elected to the council. They were designed to provide advice to principals and sometimes to school boards on a number of issues. Trustees continued to play an active role in local school issues. More sweeping changes were brought about by the *Education Quality Improvement Act, 1997* which amended the *Education Act* to require the existence of school councils. The government mandated the Education Improvement Commission (EIC) to review the role and function of school councils. Public hearings were scheduled to consult on school councils in September and October of 1998. Following the consultation the Education Improvement Commission reported to the Ministry of Education and Training. The three key issues the EIC dealt with were: (1) whether teachers and other school board employees have the right to be elected as parent or community members to school councils; (2) whether school councils should move from being advisory to decision-making bodies; and (3) whether school councils should be autonomous independent organizations or whether they should have a direct link to the Ontario Parent Council. As we mention in Chapter 1, O. Reg. 612/00 defines the roles and responsibilities of school councils. The regulation states that the purpose of councils is "through the active participation of parents, to improve pupil achievement and to enhance the accountability of the education system to parents" (section 1(1)). The regulation states that a "primary means of achieving its purpose is by making recommendations in accordance with this Regulation to the principal of the school and the board that established the council" (section 2(2)). The regulation elaborates on the composition of the school council. While the principal, a teacher, a non-teaching staff representative and a community member are required members, the majority of positions are given to parents of children in the school. In order to sit as a parent on a council where one's child attends, one must "take reasonable steps to inform people qualified to vote in the election of parent members of that employment" (section 4 (2)(b).) Subsections 9 (1) and (2) state that the Ministry may "for the purpose of consulting and communicating directly with members of school councils, collect the names, mailing addresses, telephone numbers and e-mail addresses of the chair or co-chairs of a school council and of other members of the council". As well, the Ministry may disclose information collected under subsection (1) to the Ontario Parent Council , which may use the information for the purpose of consulting and communicating directly with members of school councils".

Other sections of the regulation outline the areas that school boards are required to solicit views of school councils. These include: conduct of persons in schools, a dress code for students, school improvement plans responding to provincial pupil testing, the process and criteria for the selection of principals and vice-principals, policies regarding board funding of school councils, fundraising activities of school councils, conflict resolution procedures for school councils and policies regarding reimbursement of expenses incurred by school council members and officers (section 19). Subsection 19(2) "does not limit the matters on which a board may solicit the views of school councils". Section 20 states that "a school council may make recommendations to the principal of the school or to the board that established the council on any matter". Section 21 of the Regulation requires the Board to respond to "each recommendation made to the Board by the council" and "advise the council of the action taken in response to the recommendation".

School councils represent a shift from the historical centralization of power within the education system to decentralization. School councils' historical foundations lie in the theory of site based management. Thus, the concept of relegating more power to parents, community members and school staffs represents a shift from the strong centralizing influences that the current wave of provincial politics has been pushing. A 1997 study by Statistics Canada and the Department of Human Resources found that only 26 per cent of schools surveyed reported that at least one in ten parents took part in school advisory committees. If a change is to occur in the traditional patterns of teacher and parent relationships parents will need to be given information from educators that they need to make informed decisions.

Parental involvement in schools has a long and distinguished history. Parents have participated in their children's education through home and school associations, parent-teacher associations, and other parent groups. Nevertheless, parental involvement in education does not necessarily mean participation in a formal organization. Parents play the first and most important roles in their children's education. By helping with homework, asking about the day's events, and expressing interest, care, and guidance, parents are the primary factors in their children's success. Parents, students, and other community members also contribute to and enhance classroom learning, by acting as mentors, classroom and library helpers, and fundraisers. It is essential to think of school councils as a means to desired educational ends, and to keep asking the question of what those particular ends should be. Even at a basic level, school council members require information sessions on school, board, and ministry procedures and priorities. This is because many committed parents and community members, especially recent immigrants, have no idea how education works in Canada. There is little doubt that parents are a crucial and largely untapped resource. On the whole parents have assets and expertise that are essential to the partnership. Parents have knowledge of their child that is not available to anyone else. They have an interest in their child's success. They have the expertise of potential partners who are paying for and experiencing a service, and they have valuable knowledge and skills by virtue of their special interests, hobbies, vocation, and community role.

There may be circumstances where school councils and their members feel strongly about the appropriateness (or lack thereof) of decisions or actions on the part of school boards or provincial Departments or Ministries of Education. In such instances, school councils or their individual members could very well attempt to initiate legal proceedings to have the decisions or actions reviewed by the Courts. School councils may be named as defendants in judicial review proceedings. They will *not* however, likely be held to have the requisite legal status to sue or be sued for damages. This, however, is not to say that the individual members of school councils will not be exposed to liability for damages. Insurers of school councils also report very few, if any, claims against the councils or their members. In most jurisdictions, school councils are purely advisory in nature. Where the school councils are functioning within their proper mandate, the potential for valid claims of the foregoing nature against their members is quite low. If school council members are guilty of misconduct in or outside (but related to) the exercise of their responsibilities, claims against them as individuals are possible. The most obvious risk management strategy for school councils is liability insurance. If school councils go beyond their statutory or agreed upon mandate, their activities may not be protected by school board liability insurance coverage. For example, if school councils use school premises for purposes similar to other community groups (e.g. fundraising events, craft sales, Christmas socials, etc.) and school board policy requires that these other community groups have their own liability insurance protection in order to make use of the school premises, school councils would likely have to obtain their own coverage separate and apart from the school board's policy (see Ontario School Boards Insurance Exchange OSBIE Bulletin #9(A) Revised, January 1997). This is due to the fact that holding craft sales or Christmas socials goes beyond the advisory mandate of most School Councils. "OSBIE" has suggested that school councils within a school district join forces to approach brokers about the possibility of a group policy for all the school councils in the district. Organizations such as Home and School Associations or Parent-Teacher Associations may also be able to add school councils to their policies, upon admission to membership in the Associations. If insurance coverage is only provided to school councils and their members for activities that are undertaken with the knowledge and consent of the superintendent, the school council should ensure that there is a written paper trail that (a) describes the nature and scope of the activities to be undertaken by the school council and, (b) confirms the superintendent's acknowledgement and consent.

4

Pupils and the Law

1. SCHOOL ATTENDANCE   204
2. DISCIPLINE   211
3. SEARCHES   214
4. SUSPENSION AND EXPULSION IN ONTARIO   221
   (a) Introduction   221
   (b) School Attendance   221
   (c) Pre-Bill 81 Provisions Respecting Suspension and Expulsion   221
   (d) The New Law: the "Bill 81" Amendments to the Education Act   222
      (i) Mandatory Grounds for Suspension   222
      (ii) Extension of a Suspension   224
      (iii) Discretionary Grounds for Suspension   225
      (iv) Suspension Reviews and Appeals   225
      (v) Additional Parties to Suspension Review or Appeal   226
      (vi) Mandatory Grounds for Expulsion   226
      (vii) Discretionary Grounds for Expulsion   228
      (viii) Appeal of Expulsion Decision   228
5. PROCEDURAL FAIRNESS   229
   (a) Nature of the Duty of Fairness   229
   (b) Factors Determining Duty of Fairness   230
   (c) Stages of Decision-Making   232
      (i) Initial Imposition of Decision-Making   232
      (ii) Post-Imposition Process   232
   (d) The Principal's Role   232
   (e) The Right to Know the School Rules   233
   (f) General Comments on Zero Tolerance   234
6. FREE SPEECH   237
   (a) Application of Constitutional Rights   237
   (b) Disciplinary Measures   238
      (i) Denial of Diploma   238
      (ii) Barring Participation in Graduation Ceremonies   238
7. ACADEMIC PENALTIES   239
   (a) As Punishment for Non-academic Misbehaviour   239
   (b) Freedom of Speech   239
8. DRESS CODES   240
9. STUDENT INTERNET USE   250

10. CONFIDENTIALITY 252
11. ADMINISTRATION OF MEDICATION TO PUPILS 257
    (a) Asthmatic or Anaphylactic Children 258
    (b) Consent to Treatment 259
12. YOUTH CRIMINAL JUSTICE IN CANADA 260
13. THE *YOUNG OFFENDERS ACT* 262
    (a) The "School Board Exception" 265
    (b) Statements Made to Persons in Authority 268
        (i) Statutory Requirements 268
        (ii) "Person in Authority" Defined 268
        (iii) "Young Person" Defined 270
        (iv) Procedure 270
14. THE YOUTH CRIMINAL JUSTICE ACT 270
15. STUDENT RECORDS 275
    (a) Types of Records 275
    (b) Confidentiality 276
    (c) Correcting Information 277
    (d) Disclosure to Parents 279

1. SCHOOL ATTENDANCE

School attendance is an experience shared by virtually all children in Canada. Almost without exception, all children aged 6 to 16 spend 5 hours per day, 9 months per year, in school. School attendance is required by law unless the child is receiving satisfactory instruction at home, or is otherwise legally excused from attendance.

Today, education is perhaps the most important function of state and local governments. Compulsory school attendance laws and the great expenditures for education both demonstrate our recognition of the importance of education to our democratic society. It is required in the performance of our most basic public responsibilities, even service in the armed forces. It is the very foundation of good citizenship. Today it is a principal instrument in awakening the child to cultural values, in preparing for later professional training, and in helping to adjust normally to his or her environment. In these days, it is doubtful that any child may reasonably be expected to succeed in life if he or she is denied the opportunity of an education.[1]

In *R. v. Jones*,[2] Pastor Jones argued that he had a God-given mandate to educate his children as he saw fit. He refused to send his children to school as required by section 142(1) of the *School Act*[3] of Alberta, or to

---

[1] *Brown v. Bd. of Education of Topeka*, 347 U.S. 483 at 493 (1954). Interestingly with respect to desegregation and the passage of more than 40 years, *(U.S. Ind. 1983), at 47*.
[2] (1983), 49 A.R. 135 (Prov. Ct.), reversed (1984), 57 A.R. 266 (C.A.), affirmed [1986] 2 S.C.R. 284.
[3] R.S.A. 1980, c. S-3.

apply for an exemption under section 143(1)(a) whereby non-attendance was permitted if the departmental authorities issued a certificate attesting that the mentioned pupils were receiving "efficient instruction" elsewhere. At trial, his section 7 *Charter* [4] defence of a deprivation of his "liberty" interest was upheld, but the Court of Appeal reversed this decision.

The Supreme Court of Canada decided that there was no deprivation of "liberty"[5] contrary to fundamental justice under section 7. The state has legitimate interest in monitoring and imposing minimum standards on private schools. The claim that it was offensive to his religious freedom to even submit his private school to inspection and certification by the state was rejected. Three judges held that the certification requirement infringed Jones' freedom but only reasonably.[6] Three other judges held that it did not infringe it at all. Madame Justice Bertha Wilson held that the certification process infringed Jones' right to "liberty and security", and the right not to be deprived thereof except in accordance with the principles of fundamental justice in section 7 of the *Charter*.[7]

This was because the legislation exposed him to penalty for truancy and provided only one defence, a certificate from a school inspector that those under his control were under "efficient" instruction. Justice Wilson also indicated that the law ought not to preclude Pastor Jones from establishing the quality of his tuition in ways *other* than a certificate.

Ontario's compulsory attendance law is typical in requiring children of compulsory school age to be sent to school for the full school year, unless legally excused. Parents can be prosecuted for failing to fulfill their legal obligations under compulsory school attendance laws; their children can be expelled for excessive truancy or be judicially ordered to return to school as well as being held in contempt of court if they defy a court order. In some instances, truant children have been made wards of children's aid societies.

Attendance at a private school can satisfy compulsory attendance legislation. The United States Supreme Court invalidated an Oregon statute requiring children between 8 and 16 years of age to attend public schools rather than private schools.[8] By restricting attendance to public schools, the

---

[4] *Canadian Charter of Rights and Freedoms* (being Part I of the *Constitution Act, 1982* [en. by the *Canada Act,* 1982 (U.K.), c. 11, s. 1.]).

[5] The term "liberty" is found in the Fourteenth Amendment to the United States Constitution which applies against the states. Freedom of religion in the First Amendment is also made applicable to the state governments by the Fourteenth Amendment.

[6] See Dale Gibson, "The Deferential Trojan Horse: A Decade of Charter Decisions" (1993), 72 Can. Bar Rev. 417, at pp. 435-442.

[7] Above, note 2 (S.C.C.), at 287-288.

[8] *Pierce v. Society of Sisters of the Holy Names of Jesus and Mary,* 268 U.S. STO (1925). See also *Wisconsin v. Yoder,* 406 U.S. 205 (1972), where the U.S. Supreme Court required the state to exempt Amish children from compulsory school attendance past the eighth grade.

state of Oregon interfered with private schools' rights to exist and with parents' rights to govern the upbringing of their children. The Court recognized that the state cannot standardize its children by forcing them to accept instruction from public school teachers only. Parents may not have the right to determine whether their children are educated, but they do have some control over where the education process takes place.

The rights of disabled and non-public school students to participate in public school athletic programs has prompted much debate and litigation. As more disabled students attend regular education programs legal challenges to enforce eligibility requirements which govern sports participation are being made. Likewise, as the number of students who are home-schooled by their parents increases, public school boards may also become subject to legal challenges brought by parents of home-schooled students, seeking enrollment of their children in the public school's extra-curricular programs.

Courts have remained consistent in acknowledging that students do not have a fundamental right to participate in extra-curricular programs, including inter-scholastic sports activities.[9]

Claims raised by disabled student athletes generally stem from the application of rules such as age requirements prohibiting students over a certain age from participation; transfer rules prohibiting students from participating for a period of time after a transfer from one school to another; academic requirements; and rules limiting sports participation to eight semesters and/or four playing seasons.

The courts which have upheld the applicable age rule have determined that this eligibility requirement is "essential" and that a student who exceeds the age limit is not "otherwise qualified" to participate.[10]

Many high school athletic associations have regulations requiring transfer students to refrain from participating in interscholastic sports for a period of time following their transfer. As a result of these transfer requirements, students who transfer from one school to another in order to address educational needs resulting from their disabling condition may be prohibited from participating in interscholastic sports programs. The courts that have addressed this issue generally require waiver of the transfer rule if the transfer is for the purpose of accommodating or serving the educational needs of the disabled student.

Legitimate physical qualifications may in fact be essential to participation in particular sports programs. Physically impaired students can be

---

9 See *Albach v. Odle*, 531 F. 2d 983 (10th Cir. 1976); *Mitchell v. Louisiana High School Athletic Assn.*, 430 F. 2d 1155 (5th Cir. 1970); *Oklahoma High School Athletic Assn. v. Bray*, 321 F. 2d 269 (10th Cir. 1963); *Kaptein v. Conrad School Dist.*, 1997 WL 51724 (U.S. Mont. 1997).

10 *Pottgen v. Missouri State High School Activities Association*, 40 F. 3d 926 (8th Cir. 1994); *Sandison v. Michigan High School Athletic Association, Inc.*, 64 F.3d 1026 (U.S. 6th Cir., 1995); *Reaves v. Mills*, 904 F. Supp. 120 (U.S. W.D. N.Y., 1995).

required to meet or pass a medical clearance in order to participate in athletic programs.

In Ontario, the Ontario Federation of School Athletic Associations regulates the eligibility of pupils to participate in OFSAA sponsored athletic competition, including eligibility in circumstances in which the student has transferred from one school to another. The OFSAA Transfer Policy states that a transfer does not render a student ineligible where,

> ... the student *has been placed* in a school by (i) an I.P.R.C. (Identification, Placement and Review Committee) decision; or (ii) a court order. The Federation's Board of Reference shall require and receive a letter from the principal of the school from which the student has transferred, stating the reason for the placement of the student by I.P.R.C., or a copy of the court order placing the student in the new school, whichever is applicable. (emphasis in original)

There are several cases in which the OFSAA transfer policy has been challenged in court. In *Johnson (Litigation Guardian of) v. Ontario Federation of School Athletic Association*[11] (which did not deal with a special education situation), the student plaintiff transferred to Ridley College in order to fast-track her completion of secondary school. The OFSAA Transfer Policy made her ineligible to participate in any OFSAA sponsored competitions for the school year. The plaintiff sought an interim injunction against the OFSAA. One of the arguments advanced in court was that the OFSAA has no jurisdiction to make rules and regulations that determine the eligibility of students attending secondary school because this constituted an improper delegation by school boards of their authority of school athletics. Granger J., held that boards had not delegated their authority to the OFSAA. The OFSAA is comprised of district associations which in turn are comprised of local athletic associations. Boards carry out their responsibility for athletics through local associations and accept the rules and regulations of the district associations and the OFSAA. If a board does not accept the rules, it can withdraw from the OFSAA. The Court held that there is nothing in the *Education Act* that mandates that students participate in particular competitions.

The Court went on to consider whether or not the plaintiff had met the test for granting of an interim injunction. Granger J. referred to other cases in which interim relief had been sought in similar circumstances, including *Warkentin v. Sault Ste. Marie Board of Education*,[12] *Smith v. Ontario Federation of School Athletic Assns.*,[13] *Milne v. Nipissing District Secondary School Athletic Association*,[14] and *MacDougall v. Ontario Federation of*

---

11 [2000] O.J. No. 4994, 2000 CarswellOnt 4986 (S.C.J.).
12 (1985), 49 C.P.C. 31 (Ont. Dist. Ct.).
13 (January 15, 1992), Flinn J. (Ont. Gen. Div.).
14 [1998] O.J. No. 4687, 1998 CarswellOnt 4377 (Div. Ct.).

School Athletic Assns.[15] and *Clark (Litigation Guardian of) v. Ontario Federation of School Athletic Assn.*[16] Granger J. stated that a court will not interfere with the rules and regulations of a club or organization, such as the OFSAA whose membership is voluntary unless the rules are patently unreasonable, and would not become involved in "minute legalistic interpretation of the rules of a properly constituted club or organization".[17] The Court held the plaintiff had failed to show that the transfer policy was patently unreasonable on its face and therefore had not established that there was a serious issue to be tried. Moreover, the decision against the plaintiff by the OFSAA's internal Board of Reference was not patently unreasonable, as it was entitled to find that the plaintiff's transfer to accelerate her education was not a "major academic need" under the transfer policy. The motion for injunctive relief was therefore denied.

In *Bradstreet v. Sobol*[18] a New York court dismissed a parent's claim that her home-schooled child was eligible to participate in the local public school's interscholastic sports program. The Court applied the rational basis test to the parent's equal protection claim, stating:

> We note that the challenged requirement does not create a classification based upon the status of plaintiff's daughter as a home-schooled student, but, rather, the classification is based upon her lack of enrollment in the public school where she seeks to participate in the interscholastic sports program, a classification which clearly includes other students, such as those who attend private or parochial schools. We see nothing irrational in requiring that a student be enrolled in a public school in order for the student to participate in the school's interscholastic sports program.[19]

The Supreme Court of Montana held that a private school student did not have a state constitutional right to participate in public school sports programs. In *Kaptein v. Conrad School District*[20] the Court upheld a board policy limiting participation in the district's sports programs to students enrolled full-time in public school. In this case Tami Kaptein, a seventh grader enrolled in the Conrad Christian School, actually participated in the Conrad Public School District program during the 1994-95 school year, but without school board approval. Her participation in the public school program was terminated upon discovery by the school board which applied its policy limiting participation in sports to students enrolled full-time in public schools. The Court analyzed applicable federal and state law from other

---

15 [1987] O.J. No. 1728, 1987 CarswellOnt 577 (Ont. Dist. Ct.), additional reasons at (April 22, 1988) Doc. 19355/87 (Ont. Dist. Ct.).
16 [1997] O.J. No. 94, 1997 CarswellOnt 397 (Gen. Div.).
17 Above, note 11, para. 21.
18 225 A.D.2d 175, 650 N.Y.S.2d 402 (U.S. N.Y. App., 1996).
19 *Ibid.,* at 403.
20 1997 WL 51724 (U.S. Mont. 1997).

jurisdictions and noted "our review of cases from other jurisdictions reveals no decisions . . . which recognize a constitutional right of a non-enrolled student to participate in a public school sports program".[21]

In *Archbishop Walsh High School v. Section VI of New York State Public High School Athletic Assn.*[22] a New York state appellate court upheld the denial of a private school's inclusion in a public school athletic league. Generally courts have upheld the exclusion of private schools from public school leagues when challenged on an equal protection constitutional basis. The decision to deny inclusion has been upheld based on a public school league's legitimate interest in minimizing or mitigating uneven or undesirable competition between public and non-public schools, especially as affected by the recruiting opportunities available to private schools but not to public schools.

In *O'Connell High School v. Virginia High School League,*[23] a parochial school sought admission to the Virginia High School League which regulates and governs all athletic, literacy and debating contests among the public high schools in the state of Virginia. The private school asserted that restricting its membership violated the equal protection clause. The Fourth Circuit Court of Appeals held that the classification rationally related to the league's policy of limiting student transfers to defined geographic areas and of discouraging recruiting for purposes of athletic competition.

In June 1997 the United States Supreme Court handed down a 5-4 decision in *Agostini v. Felton.*[24] *Agostini* involved a re-examination of the Court's decision in *Aguilar v. Felton*[25] that held it was a violation of the Establishment Clause of the First Amendment for public school teachers to provide Title I educational services inside parochial schools. The Court relied primarily on *Zobrest v. Catalina Foothills Sch. Dist.,*[26] in which the Court approved the use of a publicly employed sign language interpreter for a deaf student in a parochial school. *Zobrest* made it clear that the Establishment Clause did not absolutely bar the placement of public employees in private religious schools. In *Agostini,* the Court concluded that *Zobrest* repudiated the assumptions upon which *Aguilar* was grounded — that public school teachers may inculcate their religious beliefs more readily if they provide their services on the premises of parochial schools; that placing public teachers in parochial schools would create an impermissible "symbolic union" between church and state; that the religious mission of the parochial schools would be subsidized financially; and that the program

---

21 1997 WL 51724 at 2.
22 88 N.Y.2d 131, 666 N.E.2d 521, 643 N.Y.S.2d 928 (U.S. N.Y., 1996).
23 581 F.2d 81 (4th Cir. 1978) cert. denied, 440 U.S. 936 (1979).
24 65 U.S.L.W. 4524 (1997).
25 473 U.S. 402 (1985).
26 509 U.S. 1 (1993).

would require pervasive monitoring, resulting in an "excessive entanglement" of church and state.[27]

Some parents have failed to comply with compulsory attendance because of so-called unsafe conditions. Courts in general have rejected such claims, but query whether students' absences based on a history of physical or sexual harassment by fellow classmates warrants alternative placements or non-attendance?

Provinces have the power not only to mandate compulsory education but also to require students to comply with health legislation so as not to pose a danger to the well-being of others.[28]

Courts have upheld mandatory vaccination requirements, even when challenged on religious grounds. Parents have been convicted for indirectly violating compulsory attendance laws because they have refused to have their children vaccinated as a prerequisite to school admission. Ontario provides for a "free exercise of religion" claim — *i.e.*, conscientious objection.[29] Can a religious exemption be based on personal religious beliefs, rather than on regular attendance and good standing within a church whose membership profess such beliefs?[30]

Although school attendance may be conditional on children being vaccinated against communicable diseases, provinces cannot unilaterally refuse to educate children with such diseases. Children can be denied attendance in the regular school program if their presence poses a danger to the health of others, but an alternative educational program should be provided.

Substantial controversy has focused on school attendance by those with acquired immune deficiency syndrome (AIDS). Many board policies have been modeled after guidelines issued by the National Center for Disease Control (CDC) which mandates that students with AIDS should be allowed to attend public school unless they have open lesions, cannot control their bodily secretions, or display behaviour such as biting. The CDC has suggested that determinations of whether individual students pose a health risk to others should be made on a case-by-case basis by a team of appropriate health and educational personnel.[31]

Despite considerable evidence that AIDS is not communicated except through blood transfusions or sexual contact, some boards have attempted to bar AIDS victims from attending public school classes. In such situations, infected students have sought judicial relief, asserting a right to attend school with their classmates. Courts have found that children suffering from AIDS

---

27 65 U.S.L.W. 4524 at 4528-33.
28 See *Immunization of School Pupils Act*, R.S.O. 1990, c. I.1.
29 *Ibid.*, s. 6(2)(a)(iii).
30 *Dalli v. Bd. of Education*, 267 N.E. 2d 219 (Mass. 1971).
31 See *New York State Assn. v. Carey*, 466 F. Supp. 479 (E.D.N.Y. 1978), and see 612 F. 2d 644 (1979).

are protected by legislation barring discrimination against the handicapped. They have thus ordered schools to enroll children with AIDS upon proper proof by health officials that they pose minimal risk of infecting others.[32]

The Ontario Human Rights Commission (OHRC) has stated clearly that AIDS is considered a handicap and that persons with this are protected against discrimination in housing, contracts, and employment.[33] Employers have a duty to accommodate persons with HIV/AIDS to the point of "undue hardship". Specifically, the cost of the accommodation would need to be so significant that it would alter or threaten the existence of the position or project. Accommodation can be limited also by health and safety requirements. Undue hardship may exist if the material risks to the employee or their fellow employees cannot be removed despite attempted changes. Furthermore, according to the OHRC, "Risk to public safety shall be considered as part of the scope of the risk".[34]

2. DISCIPLINE

The issue of order and discipline has haunted educators all over the world. How do you control immature human beings? Durkheim says, "The medieval teacher addressed himself to large and impersonal audiences, among which each individual, that is to say each student was lost, drowned, and consequently abandoned to his own devices .... Hence the rowdy indiscipline of the students of the Middle Ages."[35]

The alarm today concerning the lack of discipline is not its existence but its growth. Growth implies an increase in frequency, range and seriousness which will lead to stretching the tolerance level to such a limit that a breakdown in the public school system would be inevitable. Are we heading in this direction?

As one author on the subject writes, "In 1940, the top reported offences in public schools were talking, chewing gum, making noise, running in halls, wearing improper clothing, and not putting paper in waste baskets."[36] By 1994, the offences had progressed to rape, robbery, assault, burglary, arson, bombings, murder, suicide, absenteeism, vandalism, extortion, drug abuse, alcohol abuse and gang warfare.

---

32 See *Thomas v. Atascadero Unified School Dist.*, 662 F. Supp. 376 (C.D. Cal. 1987) and *Martinez v. School Bd. of Hillsborough County Fla.*, 861 F. 2d 1502 (11th Cir. 1988), on remand, 711 F. Supp. 1066 (M.D. Fla. 1989) (plaintiff ordered admitted).
33 Ontario Human Rights Commission. Policy of HIV/AIDS-Related Discrimination, 1996.
34 Ontario Human Rights Commission. *Guidelines Policy and on Disability and the Duty to Accommodate.* November, 2001.
35 "Power and Ideology in Education", edited by J. Karabel and A.H. Halsey, in *On Education and Society,* E. Durkheim (New York: Oxford University Press, 1977), p. 102.
36 E. Gardner, "Do schools contribute to declining moral standards", *USA Today*, 114 (2484): 54-56, Sept. 1985.

We long for the time when children did not have to pass through metal detectors on their way to class, when hall monitors were other children, not armed guards, when students dressed for school without worrying about gang colors. Those were the days when sharp words, crumpled balls of paper, and, at worst, the bully's fists were the weapons of choice.

Statistics paint a compelling portrait of the rising concern for safety in schools. For example, 82 per cent of schools responding to a survey reported an increase in violence on their campuses within the previous five years."[37] Moreover, the data suggest that school violence is an issue that affects all types of schools—urban, suburban and rural.

Nationwide, teachers have expressed concern over school violence. In a 1996 national survey of teachers,[38] 71 per cent of Hispanic teachers, 61 per cent of African-American teachers and 47 per cent of white teachers said that drugs and violence were problems in their schools. For many, this concern is based on personal experience. Eleven per cent of the teachers[39] reported that they had been victims of violence in or around their schools.

Like teachers and administrators, students are unsettled by the threat of violence. Twenty-two per cent of the students indicated that they are somewhat worried or very worried about being hurt by someone else when they are in or around school. One out of five students reported that "threatening someone with a knife or gun" is a major problem in their school.

In a separate nationwide survey[40] 46 per cent of the 2,023 students surveyed indicated that they had made changes in their daily routines because of concerns about personal safety and crime. These changes included carrying a weapon and cutting class. Almost one-third (29 per cent) of these students expressed fear about being the victim of a drive-by shooting.[41]

The theme of crisis in schools has raised public consciousness regarding school discipline. An American study by Duke and Perry concluded that on the basis of available data: "American secondary schools do not seem to be bordering on being out of control . . . (but it, the data) should not conceal the existence of some schools, particularly in inner-city areas, that daily must deal with extremely serious behavior problems."[42]

A study by Kurdek and Sinclair showed that "Generally, students in two parent nuclear families had better academic performance and less prob-

---

37 *Violence in the Schools: How America's Schoolboards Are Safeguarding Your Children.* (Alexandria, VA: National School Boards Assn, 1993).
38 Steve Farkas and Jean Johnson, *Given the Circumstances: Teachers Talk about Public Education Today* (New York: Public Agenda Foundation, 1996).
39 *Violence in America's Public Schools* (New York: Harris and Associates, Inc., 1993).
40 National Crime Prevention Council, *Between Hope and Fear: Teens Speak Out on Crime and the Community. Study No. 952013* (New York: Harris and Associates, Inc., 1995).
41 *Ibid.*
42 D.L. Duke and C. Perry, "What happened to the high school discipline crisis?" (1979/80) Urban Education, Vol. 14, No. 1, at pp. 182-204.

lematic school behavior than did students in either mother-custody or stepfather families .... The results of the regression analyses indicated that family structure and family process variables were significantly related to grades, quantitative achievements, and absences from school."[43]

There is an intense social conflict today concerning the correct socialization of our children. Debates rage over permissiveness on the one hand and the need for more discipline on the other. The advocates of "parents' rights" clash with "progressive educators" over values and sex education. The antagonists are not merely quarrelling over facts, they practice in "different worlds". Lee suggests three worlds or models in which society has viewed childhood:[44]

1. In pre-industrial society, children were seen as property.
2. In the age of industrialism, children were seen as needing protection.
3. Post-industrial age children are seen as persons, as advocated by recent liberation movements.

In the pre-industrial society, children were chattels of the property-holding members of society, adult males. Unwanted children could be abandoned and exposed without criminal penalty. Children always remained firmly subordinate in status to adults, who had the right to beat them, confine them, and dispose of their labour. In the age of industrialism, children were seen as dependent on their parents for protection.

It is crucial to note a common element at the stage of transition from property to protection model: the notion that (very much in contrast to medieval society) adults were now to be viewed as a potential threat to children! Children became the emblem of moral purity and the symbol of hope for a better future. One of the roles of the new religious schools was to protect children from the morally corrupting influence of adults in general. The protection model includes children's rights, but it is important to note that these are not really "rights to", but "freedoms from".[45]

The United Nations Children's Charter provides that children have the right to freedom from cruelty, hunger, lack of shelter, lack of appropriate education and so forth. Adults, of course, decide what is appropriate. Even in a *public* library system children are often denied access to "sexual" information.

In our post-industrial era, the child is seen as a person. Age is now considered no more acceptable as a basis of discrimination than sex, race, religion or sexual orientation, for those who advocate the personal model.

---

43 L.A. Kurdek and R.J. Sinclair, "Relation of Eighth Graders Family Structure, Gender and Family Environment with Academic Performance and School Behavior" (1988) Journal of Educational Psychology, Vol. 80, No. 1, at pp. 90-94.
44 J.A. Lee, "Three Paradigms of Childhood" (1992) Review of Sociology and Anthropology, Vol. 19, No. 4, pp. 591-605.
45 *Ibid.*

In the personal model the child gains the "right to", provided that competence is demonstrated. The child has the right to travel on his or her own, to work, to leave his or her family and take up residence elsewhere, to vote, to enjoy privacy, to engage in sexual activity. In each case the test is the same as for adults — competency.

This same debate between "parents' rights" (protection model) and "progressive educators" (personal model) or between "need for more discipline" and "permissiveness" rages in the educational field under the label of "essentialism" and "progressivism". Essentialism is the back to basics movement. Its concerns are discipline, order, control and industriousness. It focuses on the three Rs and stresses strict discipline, competition, letter grades, standardized testing, ability grouping, homework and dress codes. The progressivists say that the essentialists' concept of schooling is not to educate but to indoctrinate. "The good teacher is the one who puts friendliness in place of authority, who secures enthusiasm in place of obedience . . . children will be active and engaged in self-expression . . . they will no longer be passive or merely responsive . . . children are more likely to abide by rules that they, rather than adults, make".[46]

3. SEARCHES

Local school boards have instituted "zero-tolerance" policies to demonstrate that they are dedicated to creating and maintaining safe schools. However, as we discuss below, increasingly broad interpretations of zero tolerance policies have resulted in inappropriate suspensions and expulsions. It is critical that school boards recognize that special circumstances may exist such as the age of the offender, his or her ability to understand the requirements of the policy, and the history of the offender. A code of behaviour must be displayed and clearly communicated to all stakeholders, relevant curriculum based initiatives must be implemented, and there must be training opportunities for staff.

In Ontario, the "Access to School Premises" regulation[47] states who is permitted on school property, and it allows boards and school principals to place restrictions upon access to the premises. Acts of violence that occur in schools are often instigated by outsiders, and it is evident that it is important to be able to identify trespassers easily. This is also one reason why some have suggested a dress code.

> In recent years, problems, which threaten the safety of students and the fundamentally important task of teaching, have increased in their numbers and gravity. The possession of illicit drugs and dangerous weapons in the schools

---

46 John Martin Rich, *Innovations in Education: Reformers and Their Critics*, 4th ed. (Needham Heights, Mass.: 1985).
47 O. Reg. 474/00, reproduced in Chapter 1.

has increased to the extent that they challenge the ability of school officials to fulfill their responsibility to maintain a safe and orderly environment. Current conditions make it necessary to provide teachers and school administrators with the flexibility required to deal with discipline problems in schools. They must be able to act quickly and effectively to ensure the safety of students and to prevent serious violations of school rules.[48]

From time to time, a proper investigation in school may require searching a student or his or her property. A teacher may have reason to suspect that a student is carrying a concealed weapon. A student questioned with regard to a fight may blurt out that one of the antagonists sells drugs and keeps some in his locker. A student may report that her CD player has been stolen and that it may be found in another student's knapsack. What is the proper procedure to follow in circumstances such as these?

Canadian courts have held that, in carrying out the duty to maintain order and discipline in the school, the principal may search a student. However, the courts have ruled that there must be reasonable grounds for conducting such a search. Random or arbitrary searches or searches based on groundless suspicion will likely be in contravention of the *Charter*. In undertaking an investigation on school premises, if it is apparent that a criminal offence may have been committed, the police should be contacted.

Generally, searches can be divided into three categories: (i) the personal search; (ii) the locker or desk search; and (iii) the sweep or "dragnet" search. For more than a decade, the Ontario Court of Appeal's decision in *R. v. G.(J.M.)*[49] has represented the standard in student search cases, especially since the Supreme Court refused leave to appeal in the case. The case involved a 14-year-old, Grade 7 student, who was summoned to the principal's office after the principal received information that a fellow student witnessed the accused place drugs in his socks. The fellow student informed a teacher who in turn informed the principal. The principal telephoned a police officer and a secondary school principal for advice and then in the presence of the vice-principal informed the student of his suspicion and asked that he remove his shoes and socks. The student managed to eat a rolled cigarette that he had taken out of his pant cuff, but the principal did find some tinfoil containing butts from the student's sock. The tin foil contained three butts about three-quarters of an inch in length and perhaps one-quarter of, an inch in diameter. The principal proceeded to leave the room to telephone the same police officer whom he had called earlier leaving the accused in the charge of vice principal and another teacher. The police officer appeared shortly thereafter and arrested the accused on a charge of possession of a narcotic, giving him the usual caution and informing him

---

48 *R. v. M.(M.R.)*, [1998] 2 S.C.R. 393 per Cory J.
49 (1986), 56 O.R. (2d) 705, (C.A.), leave to appeal refused (1987), 54 C.R. (3d) 380n (S.C.C.).

of his *Charter* rights. The student was subsequently charged with possession of marijuana.

At trial, the accused was convicted and fined, but on appeal he was acquitted. On further appeal to the Court of Appeal, the conviction was restored. The Court did not deal with the issue of whether section 8 of the *Charter* applied to school principals or not but assumed it did. The Court referred to the case of *New Jersey v. T.L.O.*[50] In *T.L.O.*, traces of marijuana were found in a girl's purse when it was searched by a school official after she had been seen smoking tobacco in the washroom. The Court found that the school authorities were subject to the Fourth Amendment and that students had legitimate expectations of privacy. However, weighed against that expectation was the "school's equally legitimate need to maintain an environment in which learning can take place".

Thus, given reasonable grounds for a search, school officials should have no problem engaging in a search of a student's locker without the results of the search being ruled inadmissible at trial. It is suggested that school officials conducting such searches ensure that the student and another member of the school staff be present, so that the student cannot later accuse educators of having planted something in the locker or of having stolen something from it.

Unlike personal or locker searches, which are aimed at a particular student or students, dragnet searches target a whole class or a school. For instance, a principal may wish to search all the students in a class or all the lockers on a floor. Under those circumstances, it is less likely that a court would be willing to treat the search as reasonable, given its intrusive and sweeping nature.

From jurisprudence on personal searches of students (*R. v. G.(J.M.)* the courts have recognized a duality in the legal persona of school administrators. For some purposes and under some circumstances, school principals could act as state agents for educational purposes, primarily carrying out their disciplinary and related functions under the *Education Act*. However, as Grange J. implied in *R. v. G. (J.M.)*, under other circumstances where principals' actions appear to be in the furtherance of the administration of the criminal justice system, they could be characterized as agents of the police.

The decision in *R. v. G.(J.M.)*, clarified the rights and responsibilities of principals when conducting searches but it did not directly consider the issue of whether a search of a place on school premises might interfere with a student's privacy right under the *Charter*. However, in 1998 *R. v. M.(M.R.)*, dealt with this issue. Until then, locker searches, or searches of other semi-private property used by the student to store personal items, raised the question of whether the school official can properly interfere with what the

---

50 469 U.S. 325 (U.S. N.J., 1985).

student may consider his or her "private space". The facts in *R. v. M.(M.R.)*. were that, a few weeks before a junior high school dance at a Halifax County High School, several students twice advised the school's vice-principal, Mr. Cadue that M., a 13-year-old student, was dealing drugs at the school. Cadue had reason to believe the allegations because the informants were acquaintances of M.R.M and information supplied previously by one of them about another student had proven accurate. On the day of the dance, the vice-principal was again told by one of the informants that M.R.M would be "carrying" at the dance. When Cadue saw M. arrive at the dance, he telephoned the local R.C.M.P. detachment and asked that an officer be dispatched to the school. Cadue then asked the accused and his friend to come to his office where he asked each if they were in possession of drugs and advised them that he was going to search them.

At that point, an R.C.M.P. officer entered the office. After identifying himself as a police officer, he sat down on the edge of a table and watched silently as Cadue conducted a search of the students. On request, M. turned his pants pockets inside-out but nothing was found. Cadue then asked him to roll up his pant legs. A bulge that was revealed in M.'s sock turned out to be a cellophane bag. Cadue seized the bag and handed it to the officer who identified its contents as marijuana. The officer then advised M.R.M that he was under arrest for possession of a narcotic. The constable read him the police caution and his right to counsel, and advised him that he had the right to contact a parent or adult. The accused attempted unsuccessfully to reach his mother by phone and stated that he did not wish to contact anyone else. The constable and the accused then went to the accused's locker and searched it but nothing was found there.

The trial judge found that the vice-principal was acting as an agent of the police and held that the search violated the accused's rights under section 8 of the *Charter*. He excluded the evidence found in the search. The Crown did not offer any further evidence, and the charge against the accused was dismissed. The Court of Appeal allowed the Crown's appeal and ordered a new trial. At issue was when and in what circumstances a search by an elementary or secondary school official should be considered unreasonable and therefore a violation of the student's rights under the *Charter*.

The appeal was heard by Chipman, Roscoe and Pugsley JJ.A. The appeal court rejected the Youth Court's conclusion that the *Charter* applied because Cadue was acting as an agent of the police via an "agreed strategy" between them. Nevertheless, Pugsley J.A. observed that a sufficient cogent argument could be made that Cadue, as a public school educator, was exercising a government function as an "educational state agent". Furthermore, an argument could be made that his actions therefore were subject to the *Charter*, especially insofar as the Crown relied on the statutory powers given educators under the Nova Scotia *Education Act* to justify Cadue's actions. However, no evidence was led or submission made on the application of the *Charter,* and Pugsley J.A. considered it inappropriate to rule on the matter. This ruling was reminiscent of Justice Grange's approach in *R. v. G.(J.M.),* the Nova Scotia Court merely assumed that the *Charter* did apply to Cadue's dealings with M.R.M.

Next, the appeal court examined the issue of whether M.R.M.'s section 8 right to be secure from unreasonable search and seizure had been violated. Pugsley J.A. applied the 2-step test, first enunciated by the United States Supreme Court in *New Jersey v. T.L.O.* and adopted by the Ontario Court of Appeal in *R. v. G.(J.M.).* For a search to be reasonable under the *T.L.O.* test, a school search must meet the dual requirements of being reasonable at its inception (be based on sufficient ground or "reasonable suspicion") and reasonable in its scope, that is, not overly intrusive under the circumstances. In *M.R.M.* the Court of Appeal was satisfied that both parts of the *T.L.O.* test had been met. The nature and quality of the information Cadue received from the informants, which he had reason to suspect was accurate, necessitated that he act to discover whether it was, in fact, true. Moreover, Cadue's actions were not overly intrusive and were carried out in the privacy of his office.

The Court then examined the relationship between Cadue and the R.C.M.P. officer who had been present during the search. The Court addressed three issues under this subheading: the purpose of the search, degree of involvement of the police and whether there was a pre-arranged plan with the police as to the manner in which the investigation should be carried out. The purpose of the search was to fulfill Cadue's duty as vice-principal to carry out his disciplinary obligations under the *Education Act* (N.S) and school board policies. Secondly, the Court found no evidence of direct involvement by the officer in the search conducted by Cadue. Thirdly, the evidence did not support the trial judge's conclusion that there was an agreed strategy between the police officer and the vice-principal. Having found no violation of section 8 *Charter* rights, the Court of Appeal allowed the appeal and ordered a new trial.

The Supreme Court of Canada concluded that searches by school officials must be reasonable, authorized by statute, and appropriate in the circumstances. Cory J. accepted that students attending school have a reasonable expectation of privacy so as to engage section 8 of the *Charter.* However, he reasoned:

> Students know that their teachers and other school authorities are responsible for providing a safe environment and maintaining order and discipline in the school. They must know that this may sometimes require searches of students and their personal effects and the seizure of prohibited items. It would not be reasonable for a student to expect to be free from such searches. A student's

reasonable expectation of privacy in the school environment is therefore significantly diminished.[51]

Under the general rule, established by the Court in *Canada (Director of Investigation & Research, Combines Investigation Branch) v. Southam Inc.*,[52] in order to be reasonable, a search, requires prior authorization usually in the form of a warrant from a neutral arbiter.[53] According to this rule, a search conducted without prior authorization is *prima facie* unreasonable. However, the Court recognized in *Canada (Director of Investigation & Research, Combines Investigation Branch) v. Southam Inc.*,[54] that "it may not be reasonable in every instance to insist on prior authorization". To require that a warrant or any other prior authorization be obtained for the search would be clearly impractical and unworkable in the school environment. Teachers and principals are placed in a position of trust that carry the onerous responsibilities of teaching and of caring for the children's safety and well being. Teachers and principals must be able to react quickly and effectively to problems that arise in school, to protect their students and to provide the orderly atmosphere required for learning. As stated earlier, students' expectation of privacy will be lessened while they attend school or a school function. This reduced expectation of privacy, coupled with the need to protect students and provide a positive atmosphere for learning, clearly indicates that a more lenient and flexible approach should be taken to searches conducted by teachers and principals than would apply to searches conducted by the police.

The Supreme Court was unanimous in their decision that the standard to be applied to searches by school authorities depends on whether or not the school authorities are acting as agents of the police. If the school authorities are acting as agents of the police, they must meet the same standards as the police in order to engage in a search. However, if they are not agents of the police, a different standard is applied. Nonetheless, the actual issue of whether the vice-principal acted as an agent of the police when he conducted the search of the young person was a point of contention among the Supreme Court judges and is a controversial aspect of the decision.

Cory J. summarized the approach to be taken in considering searches by teachers as follows:

1) A warrant is not essential in order to conduct a search of a student by a school authority.
2) The school authority must have reasonable grounds to believe that there has been a breach of school regulations or discipline and that a search of a student would reveal evidence of that breach.

---

51 Above, note 48, para. 33.
52 [1984] 2 S.C.R. 145.
53 *Ibid.*, at 160-162.
54 *Above*, note 54, at 161.

3) School authorities will be in the best position to assess information given to them and relate it to the situation in their school. Courts should recognize the preferred position of school authorities to determine if reasonable grounds existed for the search.
4) The following may constitute reasonable grounds in this context: information received from one student considered to be credible, information received from more than one student, a teacher's or principal's own observations, or any combination of these pieces of information which the relevant authority considers to credible. The compelling nature of the information and the credibility of these or other sources must be assessed by the school authority in the context of these circumstances existing at the particular school.[55]

The search conducted by school authorities must be reasonable, authorized by statute, and appropriate in light of the circumstances presented and the nature of the suspected breach of school regulations. The circumstances include the age and gender of the student. Cory J. summarized the factors to be considered in determining whether a search conducted by a teacher or principals in the school environment was reasonable:

1. The first step is to determine whether it can be inferred from the provisions of the relevant *Education Act* that teachers and principals are authorized to conduct searches of their students in appropriate circumstances. In the school environment such a statutory authorization would be reasonable.
2. The search itself must be carried out in a reasonable manner. It should be conducted in a sensitive manner and be minimally intrusive.
3. In order to determine whether a search was reasonable, all the surrounding circumstances will have to be considered.[56]

This standard for reasonable searches should apply to searches of students on school property conducted by teachers or school officials within the scope of their responsibility and authority to maintain order, discipline and safety within the school. Cory J. concluded that, in *R. v. M. (M.R.)*, the vice-principal was not acting as an agent of the police and the police officer himself did not carry out the search. The mere presence of the police officer was not sufficient to conclude that the officer was in fact the authority carrying out the search. The officer was at all times completely passive. The test applicable to searches conducted by teachers therefore applied. The search was authorized by inference, by the Nova Scotia *Education Act*. As a student, the accused would have a reduced expectation of privacy. The vice-principal had reasonable grounds to believe that the accused was in breach of school regulations and that a search would reveal evidence of that

---

55 Above, note 48, para. 50.
56 Above, note 48, para 54.

breach. The search was conducted in a reasonable and sensitive manner. Taking into account all the circumstances, the search was not unreasonable and did not violate the accused's *Charter* rights.

4. SUSPENSION AND EXPULSION IN ONTARIO

(a) Introduction

This section of Chapter 4 summarizes the statutory provisions that provide for the right to attend school in Ontario. It then briefly covers the suspension and expulsion provisions that existed before the amendments to the *Education Act* contained in the *Safe Schools Act, 2000* (Bill 81). The new provisions are then explained, the difficulties in interpretation or implementation are identified, and the strengths and weaknesses of the provisions are discussed.

(b) School Attendance

Residents of Ontario have the right to attend a school operated by the school board having jurisdiction in the area where they reside. Up to age 21, a "resident pupil" has the statutory right to attend elementary school. There is no age limit on the right to attend secondary school in Ontario, although persons (usually 21 years of age or over) may be directed to enrol in "continuing education" programs instead of a day school program. The *Education Act* contains special provisions in respect of the attendance rights of Roman Catholic and French-speaking persons. All children of compulsory school age[57] must attend a publicly-funded school in Ontario unless "legally excused" from attendance (for example, through home schooling or enrolment in a private school). Suspension and expulsion are a "legal excuse" for not attending school.[58]

(c) Pre-Bill 81 Provisions Respecting Suspension and Expulsion

The complexity of the "Bill 81" scheme for suspension and expulsion makes an interesting contrast with the simplicity of the pre-Bill 81 provisions, although the old and new provisions do share some features. Prior to Bill 81, section 23 of the *Education Act* prescribed the grounds upon which a student could be expelled or suspended, in a general and somewhat vague fashion. The grounds for suspension were "persistent truancy, persistent opposition to authority, habitual neglect of duty, wilful destruction of property, use of profane or improper language, conduct injurious to the moral tone of the school or to the physical or mental well-being of others in the

---

57 Prescribed in section 21 of the *Education Act* (roughly 6 to 16 years).
58 Section 21(2)(f) of the *Education Act*.

school." It is readily apparent that phrases such as "moral tone" and "habitual neglect of duty" gave principals considerable scope for interpretation.

A suspension could not exceed 20 school days (or a lesser period prescribed by board policy); nor could a suspension be imposed by a teacher. Written notice of a suspension was required to be given to the student and his or her parent or guardian, giving the reasons for the suspension and advising of the right of appeal to the school board (or to a committee of the board formed for the purpose of hearing the appeal). The "20 day" limit and the ability to use a board committee are also found in the new provisions. On appeal, or even where there was no appeal, the Board could remove, confirm, or modify the suspension and, where appropriate, expunge the student's record. The parties to a suspension appeal were the school principal and the parent or guardian (or the student if an adult). (The principal is not a specified party under the new provisions.) A suspension appeal did not automatically stay the suspension. If the suspension was served by the time the appeal was heard, the best the student could hope for was to have the record of suspension expunged.

Prior to Bill 81, a pupil could be expelled on the ground of conduct "so refractory that the pupil's presence is injurious to other pupils or persons".[59] Only a school board (or committee of the board) could expel a pupil, on the recommendation of a principal and the appropriate supervisory officer. The board or committee was required to conduct a hearing. The parties at an expulsion hearing were the parent or guardian (or adult student), the principal, and the supervisory officer. (The new provisions do not specify the principal or supervisory officer as parties to an expulsion hearing.) The procedure at a hearing of a suspension appeal or an expulsion was governed by a few specific procedural requirements in the *Education Act*, and generally by the *Statutory Powers Procedure Act*. A student had no right to appeal a board's suspension or expulsion decision.

(d) The New Law: the "Bill 81" Amendments to the Education Act

(i) *Mandatory Grounds For Suspension*

Prior to Bill 81, there were no mandatory grounds for suspension set out in statute. The *Education Act* now contains a list of infractions that constitute mandatory grounds for suspension from school and all school-related activities if committed while at school or while engaged in a school-related activity. They are mandatory in the sense that school officials and school boards are required to impose a suspension when they are satisfied that an infraction has been committed. The grounds for mandatory suspension specified in subsection 306(1) of the *Education Act* are:

---

59 Subsection 23(3), repealed by Bill 81.

- uttering a threat to inflict serious bodily harm on another person
- possessing alcohol or illegal drugs
- being under the influence of alcohol
- swearing at a teacher or another person in a position of authority
- committing an act of vandalism that causes extensive damage to school property at the pupil's school or to property located on the premises of the pupil's school
- engaging in another activity that, under a policy of a board, is one for which a suspension is mandatory.

Every school board should provide some guidance to staff as to the meaning of such terms as "threat", "serious bodily harm", "swearing", "extensive damage", and "person in a position of authority". Otherwise, there is a danger that these terms will be interpreted differently even among schools of the same board, resulting in inconsistent and possibly unfair application of the law. If students are to be treated differently, this must not be an arbitrary or accidental result but must flow from a proper exercise of administrative discretion. The Legislature must have contemplated the possibility of differences (and difficulties) in interpretation among schools, because the Minister of Education now has the power under subsection 306(11) to "issue policies and guidelines to boards to assist principals and teachers in interpreting and administering" the mandatory suspension provision; a similar provision pertains to the mandatory expulsion provisions, discussed below. Given that the Minister's policies and guidelines are merely "to assist", they are clearly not binding upon boards or courts.

The decision to add certain conduct to the list of mandatory infractions leading to suspension, removes from the board the discretion as to whether to suspend when a student is guilty of the infraction. Ontario Reg.106/01 states that a mandatory suspension is not mandatory if: (a) the pupil does not have the ability to control his or her behaviour; (b) the pupil does not have the ability to understand the foreseeable consequences of his or her behaviour; or (c) the pupil's continuing presence in the school does not create an unacceptable risk to the safety or well-being of any person. A criticism of zero tolerance laws in the United States is that local school districts have extended the application of zero tolerance to include relatively minor infractions. A board must therefore give very serious consideration as to what infractions, if any, it will add to the statutory list.

Under the new provisions, a principal has a duty to suspend a student who commits an infraction for which suspension is mandatory unless a teacher has already suspended the pupil. A principal must also suspend a student if he or she believes the student may have committed an infraction for which expulsion is mandatory. A mandatory suspension may not exceed 20 days or be for less than one day. Both the maximum and minimum duration can be varied by regulation, and different "standards" may be established for different circumstances and different classes of persons. If a teacher observes a student committing an infraction that requires a mandatory suspension, the teacher must either suspend the student or refer the matter to the principal. A suspension by a teacher cannot exceed one day (or such lesser period prescribed by regulation). It remains to be seen how teachers will exercise their discretion in choosing whether to impose a suspension or to refer the matter to the principal. Clearly, a referral will be made if the alleged infraction would justify a suspension longer than one day.

From a procedural fairness perspective, a teacher's decision whether to suspend or refer is important because, if a referral is made to the principal and a suspension of longer than one day is imposed, the pupil then has a right to a "review" and an appeal. Students who have been suspended for only one day are excluded from the "review" process and the appeal process. They have no internal recourse. Their only recourse is to apply for judicial review. Suspensions of up to one day have the advantage of permitting a teacher to deal with a disciplinary problem quickly and efficiently, but the denial of recourse to appeal is open to objection for lack of procedural fairness because a suspension of any length is a mark against a student's academic record. In our view, board policy should define a method of appealing a one-day suspension even though this is not required by the legislation. The policy should also address what protections the student should have against the prospect of facing several one-day suspensions within a short period, that are tantamount to a lengthy suspension.

(ii) *Extension of a Suspension*

A teacher may also recommend that the teacher's imposition of a mandatory suspension be extended by the principal. The consequences of the recommendation could be significant for the student. It is unclear what criteria a teacher will use in exercising discretion to recommend an extension, or how such an extension may affect the student's right to procedural fairness. As a practical matter, teachers should be informed by their board as to how the recommendation is to be conveyed to the principal, and what information must accompany it. Having obtained the recommendation and supporting background information, the principal must then make a decision as to whether or not to impose an extension. In making that decision, the principal has a duty of procedural fairness toward the student and must satisfy him or herself that appropriate grounds exist for a suspension exceeding the initial period imposed by the teacher. This may require an investigation. To ensure procedural fairness, the student and his or her parents should be notified that an extension has been recommended by a teacher and is being considered by a principal and, where possible, they should have at least an informal opportunity to be heard before the decision is made.

It appears that no extension is possible without the suspending teacher's recommendation as a condition precedent. If a teacher imposes a suspension but does not recommend an extension, query whether the matter stops there, or whether the principal may impose another suspension (or other disciplinary measure) in addition to the teacher's suspension. This situation will arise, for example, if the teacher and principal disagree about how severely the infraction should be dealt with. The absence of an "extension recommendation" arguably exposes the student to double jeopardy if the principal imposes a further disciplinary measure.[60] On appeal from the principal's decision, the student could try to use the teacher's refusal to recommend an extension as "proof" that the infraction did not merit anything more than a one-day suspension. This potential for conflict between principal and teacher can be reduced by setting out clear expectations in board policy.

(iii) *Discretionary Grounds for Suspension*

A principal may suspend a student if the student engages in an activity which board policy states is a ground for discretionary suspension. A student may be suspended from one or more classes or one or more school-related activities, or from the school entirely and from all school-related activities. The maximum duration of a suspension is 20 days, although this may be varied by regulation. The minimum duration of a discretionary suspension may be prescribed by board policy. Teachers have the power to suspend a pupil if the pupil is observed engaging in an activity for which suspension is discretionary, but the suspension cannot be for longer than the minimum period set by board policy. Alternatively, a teacher may refer the matter to the principal. As with mandatory suspensions, if the teacher believes a longer suspension is required, he or she may recommend an extension of the suspension to the principal. Written notice of any discretionary or mandatory suspension must be given to the pupil and his/her parent or guardian (if the pupil is a minor).

(iv) *Suspension Reviews and Appeals*

The Bill 81 provisions introduce the concept of suspension "review". A review may be requested by a parent or guardian (or adult pupil), or such other person as specified by board policy. A review is conducted by a person specified in board policy and in accordance with requirements established

---

60 In the U.S. the court in *Fleetwood v. Board of Educ.*, 252 N.E.2d 318 (U.S. Ohio, 1969) found that a school could punish a student twice for same offence. The student was expelled after returning from a 10-day suspension. The Court found two separate kinds of punishment — an immediate one by the principal and one by the superintendent after a thorough review.

by board policy. Following a review, the parent/guardian, adult pupil or other person specified in board policy may appeal a decision to suspend to the school board. As mentioned previously, there is no review of a suspension of one day or less, and a decision to suspend for up to one day cannot be appealed to the board. The purpose of a "review" is unclear on the face of the legislation. It appears to be intended as an opportunity for a senior administrator of the board to give the suspension another "look" and possibly to mediate a solution with the student and parents. It enables informal discussion without the greater formality and expense of an appeal. It is an opportunity to clarify expectations in respect of the student's behaviour. All participants should understand at the outset of a review whether their comments or admissions are off the record and without prejudice.

A suspension appeal must be conducted according to the "requirements" established by board policy. The school board shall "hear and determine" the appeal and for that purpose has the powers and duties set out in the board policy. The board's decision is "final". The powers and duties may be delegated to a committee of the board.

(v) *Additional Parties to Suspension Review or Appeal*

Board policy may allow another "person" to seek a review or to appeal a suspension decision. The right to be a party to a proceeding is obviously important. It is uncertain who will be allowed to participate under this provision. Possibilities include a school principal, children's aid society, non-custodial parent, and a student who is under the age of 18.

(vi) *Mandatory Grounds for Expulsion*

The mandatory expulsion provisions are where the "zero tolerance" approach has its greatest impact upon students. One might expect the provisions to be consistent with ensuring procedural protection for students. Unfortunately, this expectation is not fully met. In fact, Bill 81 permits a limited expulsion to be imposed by a principal without a hearing.

Expulsion is mandatory where a student commits any of the following infractions while at school or engaged in a school-related activity:

- Possessing a weapon, including possessing a firearm
- Using a weapon to cause or to threaten bodily harm to another person
- Committing physical assault on another person that causes bodily harm requiring treatment by a medical practitioner
- Committing sexual assault
- Trafficking in weapons or in illegal drugs
- Committing robbery
- Giving alcohol to a minor

- Engaging in another activity that, under a policy of the board, is one for which expulsion is mandatory.

Ontario Reg. 37/01 states that a mandatory expulsion is not mandatory if: (a) the pupil does not have the ability to control his or her behaviour; (b) the pupil does not have the ability to understand the foreseeable consequences of his or her behaviour; or (c) the pupil's continuing presence in the school does not create an unacceptable risk to the safety or well-being of any person.

The minimum duration of a mandatory expulsion is 21 school days. A principal is required to suspend a student where the principal believes the student has committed an infraction for which expulsion is mandatory, and upon suspending the student, the principal must either (1) refer the matter to the board, or (2) conduct an "inquiry" into the conduct of the student in order to determine if an infraction calling for mandatory expulsion has been committed. A principal's inquiry must be conducted in accordance with board policy, and the principal has the powers and duties specified in the policy.

Following an inquiry, a principal who is satisfied that an infraction has been committed may either impose a "limited expulsion" or refer the matter to the board for a determination. If an expulsion matter is referred to the board by the principal, the board (or committee of the board) must hold an expulsion hearing and for that purpose has the powers and duties specified by board policy. An expulsion hearing must be conducted according to the requirements of board policy. Following the hearing, if the board is satisfied that the pupil has committed an infraction for which expulsion is mandatory, it must either impose a limited expulsion or a full expulsion. In a *full* expulsion, the pupil is not entitled to attend any school in the province or to engage in school-related activities of any school in the province until he or she has met such requirements as may be established by regulation for returning to school.

The duration of a *limited* expulsion (which can be imposed either by a principal or a board) cannot exceed the later of (1) one year from the date the principal suspended the pupil, and (2) the date on which the pupil meets such requirements as may be established by the board for returning to school after being expelled. Presumably, if the student never meets the requirements,[61] the result is that he or she is expelled indefinitely without the benefit of a hearing. Care must be taken to avoid unreasonable conditions or those that conflict with the student's rights under another statute such as the *Health Care Consent Act*.

---

61 A condition for return might be, or example, attendance at a drug rehabilitation program. This sets up a potential conflict between the right to attend school and the right to choose whether to be treated.

Under a *limited* expulsion, a student is not entitled to attend the school he or she was attending when the infraction was committed and is not entitled to engage in school-related activities of that school. It is thus an expulsion from a specific school, not from all of the board's schools (unless, of course, the board only has one school). A limited or full expulsion must be imposed within 20 days of the time the principal first suspended the pupil, unless the parties agree to an extension. Written notice of the expulsion must be given to the pupil and parent or guardian if the pupil is a minor. As with mandatory suspensions, a board must give serious consideration as to whether it will add to the statutory list of infractions that result in mandatory expulsion.

(vii) *Discretionary Grounds for Expulsion*

A board may, by policy, designate activities for which expulsion is discretionary. Under subsection 310(3), if a principal believes that a pupil has engaged in an activity for which expulsion is discretionary, he or she may suspend the student. If the principal suspends the pupil, then most of the provisions of section 309 dealing with mandatory expulsion apply with necessary modifications. Suspension always precedes an expulsion. If the principal does not initially suspend the student, the expulsion process cannot be initiated. The principal has no duty to suspend where he or she believes a discretionary expulsion infraction has occurred, and can thus prevent the board from imposing an expulsion.[62] However, where there is a suspected infraction that could lead to a mandatory expulsion, the principal must impose a suspension, thus permitting the expulsion process to occur. If nothing else, this points to the pivotal role of the principal within the new scheme.

(viii) *Appeal of Expulsion Decision*

A parent or guardian (or the pupil if an adult), or such other person specified in board policy, may appeal a decision to expel a student. The appeal must be conducted according to requirements in board policy. An appeal of a principal's expulsion decision is made to the board (or committee of the board), and its decision is final. An appeal of a board's expulsion decision is made to the "Child and Family Services Review Board", the "entity" designated by regulation, whose decisions are "final".

A difficulty with the new provisions lies in the fact that a limited expulsion imposed by a principal following an inquiry can be appealed to the school board but not to the Review Board. It is possible that the Review Board will, over time, develop expertise about expulsions, and a student who is expelled by a principal will not have the benefit of that expertise,

---

62 Unless a supervisory officer steps in and takes over from the principal.

whereas a student expelled by a board will. This seems inherently arbitrary and, therefore, unfair.

5. PROCEDURAL FAIRNESS

(a) Nature of the Duty of Fairness

Principals and school boards have a duty of fairness when they are considering whether to suspend or expel a student. It is well-established that the duty of procedural fairness varies according to the matter before the decision-maker[63] and according to the potential gravity of the consequences to the individual, although it is not always easy to determine in any particular situation what that duty entails. For example, in some circumstances the common law right to be heard may consist only of the opportunity to make written submissions, whereas in other situations, an oral hearing may be required. Procedural fairness does not always require an oral hearing by the decision-maker.[64]

Chapter 1 contains a general discussion of the duty of fairness, and includes reference to decisions made in respect of expulsions by private schools. Those decisions, *Burke v. Yeshiva Beit Yitzchak of Hamilton*[65] and *D.(C.)(Litigation Guardian of) v. Ridley College*[66] were referred to in the case of *Gianfrancesco v. Junior Academy Inc.*[67] Unlike the other two cases, *Gianfrancesco* did not involve an application for judicial review, but rather an action in contract for damages for failure to exercise due process in an expulsion. MacDonald J. dealt with the issue of "whether or not a private school must comply with the requirement for procedural fairness when it decides to expel a student for behaviour which contravenes a zero tolerance policy with respect to violence as recommended by the Ontario Schools Code of Conduct".[68] MacDonald J. correctly takes issue with the statement by the Court in *Burke* that a private school is required to comply with the *Education Act* in respect of suspension or expulsion of pupils. However, MacDonald J. did agree, that the "drastic punishment of expulsion can only be imposed after adequate notice is provided to the parents, who should be given an opportunity to be heard".[69] MacDonald J. concluded that: "the

---

63 *Nicholson v. Haldimand-Norfolk (Regional Municipality) Commissioners of Police,* [1979] 1 S.C.R. 311.
64 *Knight v. Indian Head School Division No. 19,* [1990] 1 S.C.R. 653, a case dealing with the duty of fairness owed when a school board dismisses a director of education. See also, for example, *Baker v. Canada (Minister of Citizenship & Immigration),* [1999] 2 S.C.R. 817, at para. 33.
65 (1996), 90 O.A.C. 81 (Div. Ct.).
66 (1996), 140 D.L.R. (4th) 696 (Gen. Div.).
67 [2001] O.J. No. 2730, 2001 CarswellOnt 2383 (S.C.J.), additional reasons 2001 CarswellOnt 4536 (S.C.J.).
68 *Ibid.,* para. 1.
69 *Ibid.,* para. 35.

principle of procedural fairness can be imported into the realm of disciplinary matters involving private schools by virtue of the contract of instruction that exists between the school and the pupil's parents".[70] The Court found that, although a hearing need not be a formal oral hearing, the student and parents should have been afforded notice and the opportunity to be heard before the expulsion decision was made. We note that, by contrast, a school board has a statutory duty to hold a hearing, which is governed by the *Statutory Powers Procedure Act*.

(b) Factors Determining Duty of Fairness

In *Baker*,[71] L'Heureux-Dubé, J. outlined several factors that are relevant to determining the duty of fairness in particular circumstances. Briefly put, these factors are: the nature of the decision and the process followed in making it; the statutory scheme; the importance of the decision to the affected individual; the legitimate expectations of those affected; and the agency's choice of procedure. How do these factors apply to suspension and expulsion decisions by school boards?

(i) The nature of the decision being made and process followed in making it

> The more the process provided for, the function of the tribunal, the nature of the decision-making body, and the determinations that must be made to reach a decision resemble judicial decision making, the more likely it is that procedural protections closer to the trial model will be required by the duty of fairness.[72]

A school board is required to conduct a "hearing" to determine whether to expel a pupil. The board is also required to conduct a hearing of an appeal of a suspension or principal-imposed limited expulsion. As previously indicated, the *Statutory Powers Procedure Act* (SPPA) applies to school board expulsion hearings and appeals. (This is true even though an expulsion decision may be appealed to the Child and Family Services Review Board because the *Education Act* makes it clear that the board is to conduct a "hearing".) Under the SPPA, a party has the right to be represented by counsel, to call witnesses, to cross-examine witnesses, to a record of the proceeding, and to receive a written statement of the reasons for the decision. The procedure for hearings is also governed by the board's own "policies and guidelines" and the common law duty of procedural fairness. A board does not have the express statutory power to make policies and guidelines that conflict with the SPPA.

---

70 *Ibid.*, para. 39.
71 *Above*, note 64.
72 *Above*, note 64, para. 23.

(ii) The nature of the statutory scheme and the terms of the statute pursuant to which the body operates"

> Greater procedural protections, for example, will be required when no appeal procedure is provided within a statute, or when the decision is determinative of the issue and further requests cannot be submitted.[73]

The decision of a school board or the Child and Family Services Review Board (as the case may be) is "final" and there is no statutory right of appeal from either body. This points to the need for "greater procedural protection".

(iii) the importance of the decision to the individual or individuals affected

> The more important the decision is to the lives of those affected and the greater its impact on that person or persons, the more stringent the procedural protections that will be mandated.[74]

Here again, the need for stringent procedural protection is indicated, because of the profound impact that a suspension or expulsion may have on a student.

(iv) the legitimate expectations of the person challenging the decision.

> If the claimant has a legitimate expectation that a certain procedure will be followed, this procedure is required by the duty of fairness [case citation omitted].

> This doctrine, as applied in Canada, is based on the principle that the "circumstances" affecting procedural fairness take into account the promises or regular practices of administrative decision-makers, and that it will generally be unfair for them to act in contravention of representations as to procedure, or to backtrack on substantive promises without according significant procedural rights."[75]

The content of a board's policies and guidelines, including the Code of Conduct for each school, may give rise to legitimate expectations in respect of the procedural rights that will be accorded to students by the board.

(v) the choices of procedure made by the agency itself

A board has considerable latitude as to how an "inquiry", "review" or "hearing" will be conducted, and a board may also prescribe its own "powers and duties" in respect of hearings. A court will respect any reasonable exercise of the board's power to determine its own process, although, unlike many administrative tribunals, a school board has no particular adjudicative expertise. In law, the exact scope of the power of a board to *self-prescribe* powers and duties is uncertain. Clearly, they must relate to the "hearing",

---

73 *Above*, note 64, para. 24.
74 *Above*, note 64, para. 25.
75 *Above*, note 64, para. 27.

but that indicates very little. Taken literally, this provision would allow a board to give itself the power to issue and enforce summons to witnesses. The clause is such a broad delegation that a court is likely to infer or "read in" limits to this power.

(c) Stages of Decision-Making

The duty of fairness in a suspension or expulsion matter depends to some extent upon the stage at which the decision is made. There are at least ten different kinds of decisions that can be made with respect to an individual student:

(i) Initial Imposition of Discipline

- One-day suspension (principal or teacher)
- Extension of teacher-imposed suspension
- Short suspension over one day
- Long-term suspension to maximum of 20 days
- Limited Expulsion
- Full Expulsion

(ii) Post-Imposition Process

- Review (the powers and duties of the "reviewer" are set by board policy)
- Suspension appeal to school board
- Limited Expulsion appeal (to school board)
- Full Expulsion appeal to the Child and Family Services Review Board

Any decision to impose discipline involves a determination of (1) whether the student is actually guilty of certain conduct, (2) whether that conduct constitutes grounds for suspension, expulsion, or lesser discipline, under the *Education Act* or board policy, and (3) the severity of the discipline, if any, that should be imposed.

(d) The Principal's Role

Some aspects of the principal's role in respect of suspension and expulsion have already been discussed above. While it is reasonably clear that the *Statutory Powers Procedure Act* does not apply to a principal's decision, a principal owes what may be described as a minimal duty of fairness to a student who is being investigated, (1) to advise the student as to the possibility that he or she may face suspension or expulsion and as to the nature of the allegations, (2) to permit the student to respond to the allegations, and (3) to make an impartial decision based on the facts. A formal hearing is not required but there must be an "opportunity to be heard". However, if a student presents a continuing danger or disruption to the school, the U.S. jurisprudence indicates that a principal may suspend the student without providing notice or an opportunity to be heard, provided that the opportunity is offered as quickly as possible after the fact.[76]

The principal both investigates and decides. In the case of a possible expulsion, the principal conducts an "inquiry" which may lead to a decision to impose a limited expulsion or to make a referral to the board. However, if there is a suspension appeal hearing or an expulsion hearing before the school board, it is often the principal who is in charge of gathering information for presentation to the board. Depending upon the role assigned to a principal, he or she may be required to "prosecute" a student who is appealing a suspension or limited expulsion imposed by that principal—something in which the principal has a vested interest in terms of his or her own credibility. Whenever roles overlap, there is the potential that the circumstances may give rise to actual bias or a reasonable apprehension of bias. However, the principal's roles as investigator and decision-maker are conferred by the legislation, and the preponderance of case law indicates that where the legislation permits the same person to perform both of these functions, the Courts will not find there is a reasonable apprehension of bias merely as a result of the dual role.[77] A court may in fact conclude that there is no separation of the investigative and decision-making functions when a principal conducts an "inquiry". However, the principal's role as a prosecutor is legally more problematic because this role is not expressly sanctioned in the *Education Act*. Where a suspension appeal or expulsion hearing is conducted, the principal's role in the hearing should be that of a "witness" called to explain his or her investigation and determination. An impartial decision-maker, such as a principal, should not be called upon to prosecute his or her own decision.

(e) The Right to Know the School Rules

A student's right to procedural fairness includes the right to know the school rules, *i.e.*, what behaviour is subject to punishment. A board is required to state in policy those infractions which may result in a discretionary suspension or discretionary expulsion. It must also state in policy what additional infractions, over and above the statutory infractions, will result in a mandatory suspension or expulsion. A school's "Code of Con-

---

76 Board policy should provide guidelines as to when a parent or guardian should be called in advance of a suspension decision. (They will always be informed of an expulsion where the student is a minor.) This will likely depend on the age and circumstances of the student, and the severity of the discipline being considered. The *Education Act* requires that, after a suspension or expulsion is imposed, the student and the parent or guardian must be advised in writing, and must be provided with information about the right to appeal.

77 *Evans v. Milton* (1979), 24 O.R. (2d) 181 (C.A.), leave to appeal refused (1979), 28 N.R. 86 (note) (S.C.C.), *Centurion Investigations Ltd. v. Villemaire* (1979), 23 O.R. (2d) 371 (Div. Ct.) *Chabot v. Manitoba (Horse Racing Commission)*, [1987] 1 W.W.R. 149 (Man. C.A.), leave to appeal refused (1987), 50 Man. R. (2d) 79n (S.C.C.)).

duct" is therefore a critically important document. The United States law clearly shows that failure to state and publish a rule may enable a student to successfully challenge a suspension or expulsion that tries to enforce the rule.

(f) General Comments on Zero Tolerance

The concept of "zero tolerance" may be defined as a scheme that mandates pre-determined consequences for specific offences, regardless of the circumstances or disciplinary history of the student involved.[78] In the United States, local zero tolerance policies have resulted in harsh and discriminatory practices. Zero tolerance has come under tremendous criticism in the United States because of some of its bizarre outcomes. The criticism comes not just from disgruntled students and parents. In a recent report, the American Bar Association concluded that:

> Zero tolerance means that a school will automatically and severely punish a student for a variety of infractions. While zero tolerance began as a Congressional response to students with guns, gun cases are the smallest category of school discipline cases. Indeed, zero tolerance covers the gamut of student misbehavior, from including "threats" in student fiction to giving aspirin to a classmate. Zero tolerance has become a one-size-fits-all solution to all the problems that schools confront. It has redefined students as criminals, with unfortunate consequences.[79]

The Harvard University Civil Rights Project report, "The Devastating Consequences of Zero Tolerance and School Discipline Policies" dated June 2000, gives numerous examples of school discipline gone awry, some of which are summarized below:[80]

- A six year-old child was suspended for ten days for bringing a toenail clipper to school.
- A kindergarten boy in Pennsylvania was suspended for bringing a toy axe to school as part of his Halloween costume.
- A 14-year-old boy mistakenly left a pocketknife in his book bag after a Boy Scout camping trip. At his hearing, the boy's Scout Master testified on the boy's behalf. The student was expelled under the district's Zero Tolerance Policy, which requires expulsion for possession of knives.

---

78 Lewis, Julie, Staff Attorney, National School Boards Association, U.S. Commission on Civil Rights February 18, 2000 http://home.earthlink.net/~jhholly/zerotolerance.html.
79 American Bar Association web site.
80 "The devastating consequences of zero tolerance and school discipline policies" June 2000 Civil Rights Project, Harvard Univ. We have excluded references to the racial background of the students. The Civil Rights Project cites these cases as examples of racial discrimination but in our view they are examples of unreasonable decisions, regardless of race.

- A 9th grader was expelled for one year and sent to an alternative school because she had sparklers in her book bag. She had used them over the weekend and forgot they were in her bag.
- A four-year-old child was suspended for one day because he allegedly pushed and shoved his classmates on the playground.
- On his way to school, a male 5th grader was shown two razor blades by a classmate who stated that she planned to use the blades to hurt two girls who were bullying her. The male student took the blades from his classmate and hid them in order to prevent a potential tragedy. Another student notified school officials that the boy had hidden the blades. Although the boy took steps to ensure the safety of others, he was suspended from school for one year. The District refused a request for a due process hearing. During that year, he was provided with no alternative education. As a result, he was required to repeat the fifth grade.
- During a substitute teacher's attempts to maintain discipline in a classroom, a fifteen-year-old female told the teacher "I'm going to whip you." The child was expelled for the remainder of the school year and charged with assault.
- A high school student was referred for expulsion for assaulting a teacher. The teacher was hit accidentally while breaking up a fight between two students. (Both students were arrested.) Based on the allegation that the student assaulted the teacher, despite any evidence that it was intentional, the student remained out of school for three months.

Most of these results would offend Canadians' intuitive sense of justice. The severity of the punishment is contrary to a rational sense of proportion, particularly in view of the age of some of the students. Aside from this lack of proportionality, these boards have failed to adequately consider the individual history and background of the student, something that requires both an in-depth knowledge of the student and the ability to use that knowledge in a pedagogically meaningful way to determine the appropriate disciplinary measure. The mindset of some U.S. boards has made "safety" paramount over education, as evident from the foregoing examples. That mindset accords neither with the overall purpose of Ontario's *Education Act*, nor with the giving of proper weight to administrative law values, the fundamental values of Canadian society, or to the interests of the student. Some of the U.S. boards' decisions appear to offend a fundamental principle of the rule of law that the exercise of administrative power by a public body shall not be arbitrary. Canadian courts' notion of what is a "shocking disparity" between punishment and offence may be more compassionate than that exhibited by courts in the United States, where there has been a severe reaction to the "Columbine" school shooting and similar tragic incidents in schools.

The introduction of zero tolerance will likely increase the number of suspensions and expulsions across the province and thus exacerbate the debate between advocates of remedial discipline and those who seek merely to punish through exclusion. A discipline policy may not fetter a decision-maker's ability to consider the individual merits of each case.[81] The general principle against fettering applies to many of the "policies and guidelines" permitted or required by the Bill 81 amendments. However, the purpose of "zero tolerance" *is* to limit discretion. Therefore, when a school board in Ontario adds to the list of mandatory infractions, it has lawfully fettered its discretion. The policy has the same force, in respect of the board's pupils, as if it were expressed in the legislation itself. Because students have a right to know the school rules, it is reasonable to expect a board to determine, as a matter of policy, the general circumstances in which O. Reg.37/01 and O. Reg. 106/01 will be applied. These regulations permit a board to exercise its discretion on certain grounds not to suspend or expel even where a mandatory infraction has been committed. However, such a policy must not be applied in a manner that fetters the exercise of discretion when deciding individual cases. The existence of these regulations cannot simply be ignored because a refusal to exercise discretion can be found to be *ultra vires* where it is inconsistent with the purposes of the statute.[82]

Although courts will quash suspension and expulsion decisions when they are procedurally unfair, they are much more reluctant to intervene on the basis that the punishment itself is unduly harsh. In the United States:

> The legal standard generally is stated as prohibiting disciplinary actions that are "grossly disproportionate" to the offense or where the disparity between the offense and the punishment is "shocking." [83]

However, the Court of Appeals for the Sixth Circuit in the leading case of *Dustin W. Seal v. Knox County Board of Education*[84] was less deferential. In this case, Dustin Seal sought monetary damages to compensate him for the board's decision to expel him from high school after a friend's knife was found in the glove compartment of his car. Seal asserted that he did not know the knife was in his car. He argued that the board's action was irrational

---

81 *Capital Cities Communications Inc. v. Canada (Radio-Television & Telecommunications Commission)* [1978] 2 S.C.R. 141. The issue in each case is not whether the rule, guideline, precedent, policy or contract was a factor, or even the determining factor, in the making of the decision, but whether the decision-maker treated it as binding or conclusive, without the need to consider any other factors, including whether it should apply to the unique circumstances of the particular case. See Brown and Evans, *Judicial Review of Administrative Action* at 12-35.
82 Brown and Evans, *Judicial Review of Administrative Action*, at 14-18.
83 Civil Rights Paper, cited above.
84 Decided (October 6, 2000), 2000 U. S. App. Lexis 24939.

and violated his right to due process of law. The Court's conclusion is worth remembering:

> We would not for a minute minimize the Board's obligation to maintain the safety of its campuses, and its right to mete out appropriate discipline (including expulsion) to students who commit serious violations of its rules. But we cannot accept the Board's argument that because safety is important, and because it is often difficult to determine a student's state of mind, that it need not make any attempt to ascertain whether a student accused of carrying a weapon knew that he was in possession of the weapon before expelling him.
>
> The decision to expel a student from school is a weighty one, carrying with it serious consequences for the student. See Goss, 419 U.S. at 576 ("Education is perhaps the most important function of state and local governments, and the total exclusion from the educational process for more than a trivial period . . . is a serious event in the life of the suspended child.") (internal quotation marks and citation omitted). We understand full well that the decision not to expel a potentially dangerous student also carries very serious potential consequences for other students and teachers. Nevertheless, the Board may not absolve itself of its obligation, legal and moral, to determine whether students intentionally committed the acts for which their expulsions are sought by hiding behind a Zero Tolerance Policy that purports to make the students' knowledge a non-issue. We are also not impressed by the Board's argument that if it did not apply its Zero Tolerance Policy ruthlessly, and without regard for whether students accused of possessing a forbidden object knowingly possessed the object, this would send an inconsistent message to its students. *Consistency is not a substitute for rationality.* (Emphasis added)

6. FREE SPEECH

(a) Application of Constitutional Rights

The Supreme Court of the United States, in discussing free speech and the First Amendment in *Tinker v. Des Moines Independent Community School District*,[85] stated that students "do not shed their constitutional rights at the school-house door."[86] At the time of *Tinker*, American youth were being drafted to fight in the war in Vietnam. A group of families in Des Moines, Iowa decided to protest the war by wearing black armbands. School officials passed a regulation which banned the wearing of these armbands in the schools. When three students wore the armbands anyway, they were suspended.

The Supreme Court declared the school's regulation invalid. It further stated that schools may not restrict students' private speech, absent material and substantial interference with the operation of the school or the infringement of rights of others.

---

85 393 U.S. 503, 89 S.Ct. 733 (1969).
86 *Ibid.*

In two more recent decisions it was held that a school principal did not violate the free speech rights of students by punishing a student for using sexual innuendo in a speech during a school sponsored assembly. The Court stated that school officials can determine that a student's speech "would undermine the school's basic educational mission."[87] Shortly after this case, it was decided that schools do not violate free speech rights of students by exercising control over style and content of school sponsored student newspapers if the actions are reasonable and related to legitimate pedalogical concerns.[88]

Courts have recognized government's legitimate interests in protecting children from inappropriate materials, especially when children are in attendance at public schools.[89]

(b) Disciplinary Measures

(i) *Denial of Diploma*

What about the withholding of certificates of completion or diplomas as a disciplinary measure? If a student has completed all of his or her requirements for promotion or graduation, school officials must issue diplomas as a matter of law. In the absence of fraud in the completion of the requirements themselves, students have a right to receive the appropriate diploma.

(ii) *Barring Participation in Graduation Ceremonies*

What about school officials denying students the opportunity to participate in graduation ceremonies, as further means of discipline? Students who, for example, may not agree to wear the type of clothing that may be prescribed by those in charge of the ceremony, or who may not agree to abide by other reasonable requirements, and thus may be barred from participation. What if a student chooses to wear a Toronto Blue Jays baseball cap instead of the more traditional graduation attire?

The threat of a disruption of graduation ceremonies should be distinguished from the situation where a student is being punished for past misconduct. In one case an American court held that a student who had com-

---

87 *Bethel School Dist. No. 403 v. Fraser*, 478 U.S. 675, 106 S.Ct. 3159, 92 L.E.2d 549 (1986).
88 *Hazelwood School Dist. v. Kuhlmeier*, 484 U.S. 260, 108 S.Ct. 562, 98 L.E.2d 592 (1988).
89 See *Sable Communications v. FCC*, 492 U.S. 115, 109 S.Ct. 2829, 106 L.Ed.2d 93 (1989) (recognizing government's legitimate interest in limiting children's access to "dial-a-porn" services); *FCC v. Pacifica*, 438 U.S. 726, 98 S.Ct. 3026, 57 L.Ed.2d 1073 (1978) (recognizing government's interest in limiting indecent language in general broadcasts accessible to children); *Ginsberg v. New York*, 390 U.S. 629, 88 S.Ct. 1274, 20 L.Ed.2d 195 (1968) (upholding a conviction for distributing non-obscene but sexually explicit material to a 16-year-old).

pleted graduation requirements and did not threaten to disrupt the ceremony could not be barred from participation for misbehaviour that had occurred in the past. In this case, a final year high school student had been disciplined for her part in a disruption. Among other disciplinary measures, she was suspended for 22 school days and barred from the graduation ceremony.[90]

The Court strictly construed the power to suspend "from required attendance upon instruction" and found that graduation ceremonies, being optional, were not covered. Although a principal can discipline for educational purposes, in this case the Court felt that fairness required graduation attendance. The student in this case had completed all requirements, and had not been in trouble previously.

Therefore the authority to deprive a student of the opportunity to participate in graduation ceremonies may be valid only to the extent that it directly relates to probable disruption of the ceremony itself. When used as punishment for past behavior, it may be found to be invalid.

7. ACADEMIC PENALTIES

(a) As Punishment for Non-Academic Misbehaviour

May academic penalties, such as grade reductions or denials of credit, be imposed for misbehaviour, truancy, or non-attendance? Imposing additional penalties should be distinguished from a situation where credit is lost as a consequence of a legitimate exclusion from school for serious misbehaviour. In the latter case, no direct academic penalty has actually been imposed. In one case where a 15-year-old girl was suspended for a term because she took drugs at school and nearly died, the Court held that neither the suspension nor the eventual loss of credit violated her right to due process. There was no substantive unfairness.[91]

(b) Freedom of Speech

When a student speaks or writes as an individual, such expression cannot be restricted unless it causes substantial disruption or interferes with the rights of others. Students may not be punished for expressing their personal opinions about controversial political, social, or educational issues, even if their views are unpopular and in conflict with the ideas of most students, teachers, and administrators.

---

90 See *Ladson v. Bd. of Education Union Free Sch. Dist. #9*, 323 N.Y.S. (2d) 545 (1971).
91 See *Fisher v. Burkburnett Independent School Dist.*, 419 F. Supp. 1200 (N.D. Tex. 1976); *Campbell v. Bd. of Education of New Milford*, 475 A. 2d 289 (Conn. 1984); *Slocum v. Holton Bd. of Education*, 429 N.W. 2d 607 (Mich. Ct. App. 1988); *Knight v. Board*, 348 N.E. 2d 299 (1976) and *Homer v. Board of Education*, 383 N.E. 2d (1978).

Administrators have always had broad discretion in regulating student speech or writing that is part of the school curriculum. The key of course is the educational purpose of the program or policy of the board.

This discretion extends to student speech in school-sponsored curricular activities, even if the student's views are not disruptive or obscene and do not interfere with the rights of others. In such cases, courts will tend to presume that administrative control is valid, and it will probably be upheld unless students can prove that the school's control or punishment of the student's views was unreasonable, arbitrary, or unrelated to legitimate educational goals.

Schools generally can ban student distribution of publications because they advocate a particular religious, political, or social view.

8. DRESS CODES

In April 2000, the Ontario government released a Provincial Code of Conduct as part of an initiative to make Ontario schools safer and to promote a more respectful and responsible teaching and learning environment. The Ministry's decision to adopt a dress code policy was, in part, due to an increasing level of concern of parents, students and teachers regarding a lack of respect and responsibility in schools and the need to create a safer environment for all concerned. In light of the recent acts of violence carried out in our schools, the commitment to enforce a dress code policy is, perhaps, one way of insuring safety in our schools. All school board student dress policies are to include:

- a process that enables a majority of parents, through their school councils, to decide on what an appropriate dress policy should be for their own schools; school councils are to be involved in developing and implementing this process
- a review process that involves consultation with the school communities
- a process to address issues of affordability
- consistency with the *Human Rights Code* and the *Charter of Rights and Freedoms*
- a statement of principles, such as working towards safer and more respectful learning and teaching environments.

The U.S. courts agree that school boards have the right to create and implement dress codes, however the content, interpretation and enforcement of those codes have been debated. In order for the First Amendment to take effect, the conduct in question must demonstrate an intent to convey a specific message and there must be a real likelihood that the message will be comprehended by those who are witness to it.[92]

---
92 See Benjamin Dowling-Sendor, "A Matter of Disruption, Not Dress", The American School Board Journal, Vol. 185, No. 8, at 14-15, May 1998.

As mentioned above, the United States Supreme Court ruled in favour of students' right to freedom of expression in *Tinker v. Des Moines Independent Community School District*.[93] The case involved middle school and secondary school students suspended for wearing black armbands to protest the Vietnam War. The students argued that the school board's decision prohibited freedom of expression. The school board had not convinced the Court that the armbands disrupted the school or interfered with the students' learning and, therefore, ruled in favour of the students. Although the decision was made more than 30 years ago, the case provides precedent for other cases involving dress code and freedom of expression.

In *Bethel School Board No. 403 v. Fraser*,[94] the U.S. Supreme Court found that public schools have the jurisdiction to prohibit the use of vulgar or sexually implicit language in a speech to be delivered in front of a school assembly. The decision did not impinge on students' right to freedom of speech, but rather disciplined the use of unsuitable language. The Court distinguished between Tinker's freedom of self-expression in a political sense and Fraser's speech of a sexual nature that imposed on the rights of other students. The same distinction of the word speech can be applied to clothing, particularly T-shirts that promote violence, smoking, drugs, drinking, and messages of a sexual nature. It should also be noted that the Court distinguished between speech that is "content-based", as defined by Fraser's speech, and speech that is "content-neutral", as defined by Tinker's armbands.[95]

In *Hazelwood School District v. Kuhlmeier*[96], the United States Supreme Court dealt with a situation in which a school principal removed two pages from a student newspaper because the contents covered teen pregnancy, birth control and divorce. The students asserted that the principal's action violated their rights under the First Amendment. The Supreme Court disagreed. It held that if the school officials' actions were reasonable and limited to "legitimate pedagogical concerns", then the school could exercise control over the content of the newspaper. The Court found that the school did not have to tolerate student speech that was "inconsistent with the basic educational mission" and that the school newspaper was not a "public forum" for expression. The newspaper was produced as part of a school course on journalism, received funding from the school board, and was

---

93 393 U.S. 503, 89 S. Ct. 733 (1988).
94 478 U.S. 675 (1986).
95 See Clay Weisenberger, "Constitution or Conformity: When the Shirt Hits the Fan in Public Schools", Journal of Law and Education, Vol. 29(1) (January 2000), p. 54.
96 484 U.S. 260, 108 S. Ct. 562 (1988).

subject to review by the school principal. It was clearly school-sponsored, and therefore not a public forum.[97]

The Court of Appeals of Arizona upheld a mandatory dress code requiring students attending a particular school in the district to wear uniforms in *Phoenix Elementary Sch. Dist. No. 1 v. Green*.[98] In May 1995, the Phoenix Preparatory Academy adopted a dress code under which the boys wore white dress or polo shirts, with collars and no logos, and navy blue pants or shorts, and the girls wore white blouses or polo shirts, with no logos, and navy blue pants, shorts or skirts. The parents were authorized to purchase the white tops at any retail outlet, however, the code specifically stated that the bottoms were to be purchased at J.C. Penney Company only. By September 1995, students arriving at school without the prescribed uniform would be given a uniform for the day and their parents would be contacted. Students refusing to comply with the dress code would be transferred to another school in the district. On September 6th, 1995, one student arrived at school wearing a T-shirt that read "USA" and "I support my Country". Another student wore a T-shirt that read "Jesus, True Spirit". Neither student accepted the school's uniform for that day. The school notified the parents that their children were transferred to another school.[99] The following day, the parents and students re-entered the Phoenix Preparatory Academy uninvited, and distributed fliers criticizing the current dress code to other students. The parents sought an injunction and appealed the case after the Court ruled in favour of the school. Subsequently, the appellate court upheld the original decision of the lower court, citing *Tinker* and *Hazelwood*. The Court held that the dress code had a reasonable relation to the pedagogical purpose of the school, including the promotion of a more effective climate for learning and increased campus safety and security.

In 1992, an Oklahoma Federal District Court cited *Tinker* to argue the absence of interference or disruption within the school in the case of *McIntire v. Bethel Independent School District No. 3*.[100] Some high school students were suspended for wearing shirts with the words "The best of the nights adventures are reserved for those with nothing planned". The school

---

97 For a most informative analysis of *Hazelwood* see Nora Findlay, "Students' Rights, Freedom of Expression and Prior Restraint: The Hazelwood Decision Vol. 11, No.3, Feb. 2000, 11 ELJ 185-409. She also referred to *Lutes (Litigation Guardian of) v. Prairie View School Division No. 74* (1992), 101 Sask. R. 232 (Sask. Q.B.) in which the giving of a detention to a student for singing a school-banned song during the lunch hour was held to violate the student's *Charter* right to freedom of expression. See also David Schimmel's "Freedom of Expression" in *The Principal's Legal Handbook*, Dayton: Education Law Association, 2000.
98 943 P.2d 836, 120 Educ. L. Rep. 1170 (U.S. Ariz. Ct. App. 1997), 839 [P.2d].
99 See: Perry A. Zirkel, "Dress Codes", National Association of Secondary School Principals, NASSP Bulletin, Vol. 84 (612) (January 2000), at 79.
100 804 F.Supp. 1415 (U.S. W.D. Okla. 1992).

officials argued that the message was an advertising slogan for Bacardi Rum. However, the Court ruled in favour of the students, following *Tinker*. The case of *Stephenson v. Davenport Community School District*[101] also dealt with a regulation which had been enacted in response to increasing gang activity.[102] The restriction declared that "gang related activities such as the display of colours, symbols, signs and signals, etc. . . will not be tolerated on school grounds". A student with a small cross tattooed between her thumb and forefinger was told that she would have to have it removed or altered as the tattoo constituted a "gang symbol". The student had the tattoo removed at some cost and a scar was left as a result. She later filed suit against the school district claiming that her First Amendment rights had been violated and that the school regulation was "void for vagueness". The Court did not support the claim that the student's right to free expression had been violated but did agree that the regulation was "void for vagueness". The regulation was found to be constitutionally lacking because the use of the wording "gang-related activities" and the course of action in response to such behaviour were both open to wide interpretation.

The case of *Chalifoux v. New Cancy Independent School District*[103] also established that a dress code regulation must be clear enough that all who read it have a similar understanding of its meaning and intent.[104] The school board declared that gang-related apparel was not to be worn at school or during school-related events. Within the student handbook a few examples of prohibited apparel were listed with an addendum indicating that a complete list could be obtained from the office. When the school became aware that a local gang had adopted the wearing of rosaries and the wearing of rosaries was prohibited at school. Later on, two boys, Chalifoux and Robertson, began to wear rosaries as a sign of their Catholic faith. The Court found the wearing of rosaries to be within the boys' right to religious free speech. The school board could not prohibit the rosaries from being worn unless they could prove that the boys were at risk and that wearing the rosary resulted in disruption of the school.

The rationale for adopting uniform and dress code policies stems from an increase in school violence and a need to create a safer, more respectful and positive learning environment. About 3 million crimes a year are committed in or near the 85,000 U.S. public schools.[105] About one in nine public school teachers, and one in four public school students, report being victims

---

101 110 Fed. 1303 (U.S. 8th Cir., 1997).
102 See Benjamin Dowling-Sendor, "Watching What Students Wear", The American School Board Journal, Vol. 185, No. 1, at 12-13, January 1998.
103 976 F. Supp. 659 (S.D. Tex. 1997).
104 See Benjamin Dowling-Sendor, "Gangs and Rosaries", The American School Board Journal, Vol. 185, No. 5, at 22, 24, May 1998.
105 See: National Concerned Officers Organization on Gang Activities Inc., "Past School Shootings" at 2, April 25, 2000.

of violence. Children as young as 10 have been reported committing assorted acts of violence ranging from assault to murder.[106] According to the FBI, the arrest rate for children ages 14 to 17 for violent crimes rose 46.3% between 1989 and 1994 to become the most violent age group in the United States.

In President Clinton's 1996 State of the Union address, he recommended that public schools adopt a "uniform" policy. In support of uniforms, President Clinton remarked: "If it means that teenagers will stop killing each other for designer jackets, then our public schools should be allowed to require the students to wear school uniforms". In response to President Clinton's address, the United States Department of Education distributed a new document entitled "Manual of School Uniforms" to every school district. The literature addressed the potential benefits of school uniforms as well as necessary guidelines to enforce a uniform policy.[107]

The connection between clothing, violence and gangs, finds expression in several ways: clothing and appearance cues may be used by gang members to identify members because of their clothing or appearance, increasing their risk of becoming victims of gang violence; and expensive clothing items (e.g., athletic shoes, sports team jackets) can make their owners targets for robbery and related violence.[108]

Several guidelines are required when considering a dress code. The support of the parents and input from the community are paramount to the success of the policy. In many cases, parents initiate a uniform policy to help set the tone for a more disciplined environment that is conducive to learning. Parents are more supportive when they contribute to the decision-making process. The policies must respect and protect the religious rights of students. For example, students who traditionally wear a yarmulke must be accommodated for religious practices or beliefs in spite of a school's restriction on wearing hats or similar head coverings. Policies must not interfere with students' rights of expression, provided that there is no interference with learning. If schools adopt a mandatory policy, alternatives must be included for those parents who do not consent to the plan. Provisions are necessary for parents unable to pay for a uniform. Financial support from the parents or community may assist in solving the problem.

What happens when religious beliefs clash with existing dress codes? One case consisted of two joint complaints against the Peel Board of Edu-

---

106 See Marvin A. Zuker, "Children At Risk", Australia and New Zealand Journal of Law and Education, Vol 5 (2) (2000), at 13.
107 See: David E. Gullatt, "Rationales and Strategies for Amending the School Dress Code to Accommodate Student Uniforms," American Secondary Education, Vol. 27(4) (Summer 1999), at 42.
108 See: Beth Herbon and Jane E. Workman, "Dress and Appearance Codes in Public Secondary School Handbooks", Journal of Family and Consumer Sciences, Vol. 92(5) (2000), at 71.

cation, one by teacher Pandori claiming infringement of his rights as a practising Sikh under subsection 4(1) and section 8 of the Ontario *Human Rights Code,* 1981,[109] and the second complaint by the Ontario *Human Rights Commission* alleging that sections 1, 8, and 10 had been offended by a Peel policy restricting the religious rights of Sikh students as well as teachers. Peel denied such infringement had taken place and asserted it had legitimately exercised its rights under the *Education Act* and discharged the responsibilities arising therefrom.[110]

Peel asked to have the Supreme Court of Ontario quash the complaint pleading that the Board of Inquiry had no jurisdiction in this case because education was not one of the services covered by the *Code,* and education was under the jurisdiction of the *Education Act.* The Court rejected this plea ruling education constituted a "service" within the meaning of section 1 of the *Code* and further, that the *Code* had precedence over the *Education Act.*[111]

From the complainants' perspective, the issue was the right of Sikhs to wear full religious accoutrements which include a kirpan (an object identical to a dagger, but which in the tenets of Sikhism is a religious symbol to be worn at *all* times) and to do so at all times and anywhere including within school precincts. Proscribing the wearing of a kirpan denies Sikhs of school age a public school education, and bars those accredited as teachers from pursuing the profession of their choice. From the respondent's perspective, the issue was the right and duty of the Peel Board to maintain proper discipline in the schools, comprising the right to ban all weapons from school properties. Because a kirpan has the appearance of a dagger, it was defined by the board as a weapon and prohibited. Denying the board the right to set a weapons policy could infringe seriously upon its ability to regulate the schools in Peel Region.

Considerable testimony was heard from John W. Spellman, Ph.D., from the University of Windsor, teacher of comparative religion and renowned student of Sikhism, who described and elaborated on the tenets and accoutrements of Sikhism including the meaning of Khalsa which signifies a commitment by the individual to take on strict and clearly defined religious duties and obligations. Spellman testified that while the kirpan arose out of a particular culture and had at one time the function of a sword, it long ago lost this aspect, and has become completely spiritualized. It now speaks of law and morality, justice and order, and has become an instrument of the

---

[109] S.O. 1981, c. 53 [now R.S.O. 1990, c. H.19].

[110] *Pandori v. Peel (Bd. of Education)* (1990), 12 C.H.R.R. D/364 (Ont. Bd. of Inquiry), affirmed (1991), 47 O.A.C. 234 *(sub nom. Ontario (Human Rights Commn.) v. Peel (Bd. of Education)* (Div. Ct.), leave to appeal to Ont. C.A. refused (1991), 3 O.R. (3d) 531n (C.A.).

[111] *Peel (Bd. of Education) v. Ontario (Human Rights Commn.)* (1990), 72 O.R. (2d) 593 (Div. Ct.).

divine itself. He compared the sword-like appearance of the kirpan to the mace, which was used in times of war as a club and which from that point-of-view is a weapon, but which long ago became a symbol of power, order, and dignity.

Beyond basic Khalsa obligations, many details of religious observance, including the size of the kirpan worn, are left to the interpretation and discretion of the individual, and there appears to be considerable latitude among Sikhs regarding such details. The Shiromani Gurdwara Parbandhak Committee (considered the supreme religious instance of the Sikh faith) in Amitsrar, India has advised that:

1. No definite size of the kirpan has been fixed, though it should not be reduced to a mere formal sign. A one-foot kirpan is usual.
2. Children's kirpans will usually be smaller than those of adults.
3. No baptized Sikh may remove his/her kirpan under any circumstances.
4. There is no religious injunction that the kirpan be worn in plain view. It should be worn sensibly and not shyly, certainly without any sense of concealment.
5. The kirpan should be easily removable from the sheath. It must not be sewn, though the handle may be tied down.
6. A baptized Sikh is not to use the kirpan in anger as a weapon; a person that does so is guilty of misconduct and the *panch pyan* will summon that person, judge him/her, and pronounce the penalty. Non-appearance or insubordination may result in religious excommunication following which the observant community will likely ostracize the person concerned.

Testimony was heard regarding the institution of the Peel Board policy in 1979 (as a result of an incident which involved the death of a teacher and two students) and its development up to the prohibition of kirpans in 1988. It was shown that board agents made considerable effort to confer with representatives of the Sikh community, to acquaint themselves with the religious requirements, and to find an acceptable resolution, and that special arrangements were made to ensure the continued education of the two students involved. Any resolution was forestalled because no group within the Sikh community could lay down a universally accepted rule since the manner and strictness of observance are up to the individual. In Peel's view, the concern was solely with the hazard to safety posed by the presence of kirpans in a volatile environment which had experienced a growth in knife-related violence. Pandori saw the policy as racially motivated with intent to discriminate against Sikhs.

Comparison with policies of neighbouring school boards revealed that they had no specific kirpan policy. This, and the fact that the phrasing of the policy was not compatible with the basic objectives of the board's department on race relations, weighed very heavily against Peel. In addition,

Dr. Blackstock, chief psychologist for Peel Board, testified that, if at all possible, Peel returns students with a record of violence to school and has assigned some hundred behavioural assistant teachers to watch and counsel them. Blackstock also agreed that Sikh students present a lower risk factor because of the strong family structure of support.

Rabbi Gunther Plaut, Chair of the Board of Inquiry, acknowledged sections 1, 4, 8 and 10 of the *Code,* but based his decision on section 10(2) which requires the satisfaction "that the needs of the group of which the person is a member cannot be accommodated without undue hardship on the person responsible for accommodating those needs . . . ."[112] He rejected the complainants' contention of direct discrimination (for which there is no defence in the *Code)* because in the context of Peel's actions considerable effort had been made to find an accommodation for Sikhs in the school system. Though he criticized the phrasing of the policy, he also rejected the argument of direct discrimination because of inconsistent application on the grounds that a *weapons* policy must deal with weapons and kirpans cannot be so classified. He noted that many non-Sikhs because of lack of knowledge, consider kirpans weapons, but that even Khalsa Sikhs are not unaware that, despite its spiritual function, a kirpan has a *potential* for being used as a weapon.

Citing cases to define and clarify the intent and application of the *Code,* Plaut concluded it was "not sufficient for Peel trustees to claim that they had safety in mind when they prohibited the kirpan, they must also show that this was a necessary action, its necessity being compelling enough to override the prior right of religious freedom."[113] Peel produced no evidence of a kirpan being used as a weapon on school property anywhere in Canada despite the presence of Sikhs in this country for nearly 100 years. In response to the argument that the policy was pro-active and that the absence of a kirpan contributes to safety more than the presence of a kirpan, Plaut noted that this would be true also of eating forks and knives in the cafeteria, cutting instruments in the craft shop, and baseball bats, all of which have sometimes been misused for violent purposes. Despite statistics showing the growing use of knives in violent incidents in the schools and the claim that while a Sikh might not use a kirpan as a weapon, its presence is an invitation to violence *by others,* Peel failed to establish that the presence of kirpans constitute an unacceptable risk which would meet the qualification of "undue hardship" stipulated by section 10(2) of the *Code.*

An Alberta Board of Inquiry, in a parallel case, ruled that it "is not enough . . . in endeavouring to justify a ruling on safety grounds to rely on hypothetical and imagined circumstances".[114] Alternately, a Manitoba court

---
112 Above, note 111.
113 Above, note 112 (Bd. of Inquiry), at D/380.
114 *Tuli v. St. Albert (Protestant Bd. of Education)* (1985), 8 C.H.R.R. D/3736, at D/3745.

held that "[t]his limit on the freedom of religion was a reasonable one within the meaning of s. 1 of the Charter.... In the circumstances the public interest took precedence over the accused's desire to display his religious symbol."[115]

With regard to cases involving Sikhs who used kirpans to inflict injuries on others, Plaut concluded that they must not cast a shadow over the entire Sikh community. With respect to the rights and duties of principals, Plaut concluded, on the basis of *R. v. J.M.G.*,[116] that

> ... the maintenance of discipline, which might otherwise be deemed a diminution of civil rights and an offence under the *Charter,* may stand because of special circumstances and also because schools are special places. The fact that according to the Divisional Court the *Code* overrides the *Education Act* does not mean that thereby all provisions of the latter are set aside automatically, and especially so ss. 235 and 236.[117]

The school must preserve discipline and maximize the safety of students and staff, and it must zealously guard and maintain religious freedom. There is no merit in the argument that Khalsa Sikhs represent a particular personal risk. The argument that others might appropriate a kirpan and do harm is not persuasive given that a kirpan worn under a Sikh's clothing would be less accessible than many other potential weapons found on school properties (*e.g.,* screwdrivers, forks, baseball bats). Plaut questioned the advisability of curtailing the religious freedom of perfectly peaceable persons in order to control non-Sikhs who might be prone to violence, thereby sacrificing the rights of some of the best elements in the school to the worst. He pointed to the extraordinary measures taken by Peel to make sure that psychotic children, proven aggressors, and violent students are integrated into the system, and while not criticizing such rehabilitation efforts, suggested that to undertake such efforts while excluding a religious student creates an unacceptable imbalance.

Therefore, Plaut did not deem the Peel policy referring to Sikhs and kirpans reasonable within the meaning of section 19(1) of the *Code,* even though it was enacted in good faith. Thus, a defence of undue hardship did not avail. However, even if the policy were reasonable, thereby allowing for a defence of undue hardship, the legal remedy must fit the perceived danger, and Peel failed to prove anything more than a vague risk when kirpans are admitted into the school system. While it is logical to assert that banning kirpans will prevent their misuse for violent action, it is, then,

---

115 *Hothi v. R.,* [1985] 3 W.W.R. 256 at 256 (headnote) (Man. Q.B.), affirmed [1986] 3 W.W.R. 671 (Man. C.A.), leave to appeal to S.C.C. refused (1986), 43 Man. R. (2d) 240 (note) (S.C.C.).
116 (1986), 56 O.R. (2d) 705 (C.A.).
117 Above, note (Bd. of Inquiry), at D/383.

inconsistent to single out kirpans without also banning other potential weapons such as exacto knives and baseball bats.

Plaut recognized that when violence or potential violence reaches a certain level of danger, restrictive measures may be necessary and in the process certain conditions may be temporarily imposed on kirpan wearers, but Peel had not shown such a level of danger. However, he did not deny Peel's continued responsibility to maximize safety in its system, acknowledging that climates may differ from school to school and that the best persons to assess such climates are the principals "upon whom the direct responsibility for safety devolves by law and practice."[118] Where a particular school exhibits signs of heightened unrest or violence, it would be the right of the principal to take adequate and temporary countermeasures. In consultation with their superiors, principals have the responsibility for tailoring safety measures to the level of each school's needs. In this sense wholesale measures may not be workable, and where it touches upon a particular segment of a community, such as Sikhs, only a very clearly defined situation, best determined on an individual school level, might render special circumstances defensible.[119]

On appeal to the Divisional Court, Justice Campbell dismissed the school board application, holding that the Board of Inquiry had not erred in law or principle. More particularly, the Court found:

1. Schools were not "special places" subject to special application of the *Code*. The board had addressed itself to the particular concerns of the school environment.
2. In the absence of any concrete evidence of safety risk and having regard to the safety features built into the order, the board had not erred in principle in finding the appellant's prohibition unreasonable. The board had carefully balanced the objective of school safety against the requirements of freedom of religion.
3. The board had not erred in dismissing the appellant's arguments that it could not accommodate Khalsa Sikhs without undue hardship. In any event, its finding in this respect was an alternative conclusion.

In the case of *Islamic Schools Federation of Ontario v. Ottawa Board of Education*,[120] the Court considered the following factors in determining that the school board had made efforts at providing reasonable accommo-

---

118 Above, note 112 (Bd. of Inquiry), at D/385.
119 See also *Alabama & Coushatta Tribes v. Big Sandy School* Dist., 817 F. Supp 1319 (E.D. Tex. 1993), when Indian students successfully challenged a dress code restricting the hair length of male students.
120 (1997), 99 O.A.C. 127, 145 D.L.R. (4th) 659, (*sub nom. Islamic Federation of Ontario v. Ottawa Board of Education*) 43 C.R.R. (2d) 151 (Ont. Div. Ct.), leave to appeal refused (July 29, 1997), Doc. CA M20514 (Ont. C.A.).

dations for students and staff. (1) Students were granted a day for religious observance on holy days. (2) The Board had determined that examinations or major co-curriculum events and Board meetings not be scheduled on religious holy days of students and teachers were required to provide make up lessons and tests. (3) A multi-faith calendar was distributed to all schools. (4) A letter outlining the observance of Islamic holidays and requesting the needs of students was circulated. (5) The board had a Multiculturalism Advisory Committee, and operated heritage language classes. (6) The board had a written policy on racism and ethnic relations. (7) Schools facilitated noon prayer meetings by making facilities available and allowing for announcements in both English and Arabic.

9. STUDENT INTERNET USE

The use of technology in schools has seen a dramatic rise over the past few decades. Today, computers and technology are seen as an integral component of the academic curriculum, and certain schools have implemented laptop programs to further integrate computers across the curriculum. While educating students on the benefits and uses of information technology, administrators need to be aware that the use of computers in schools carries with it a variety of risks. Schools need to protect themselves against various liabilities that may result from student computer use and, in particular, student use of the Internet or world wide web. Schools should have policies affirming the school's right to review student browser logs to track web sites that the students have visited. Students must understand that access to school technology is a privilege contingent upon acceptable behavior and, as a result, privacy is not an issue for consideration. In addition to browser logs, school system administrators may monitor chat rooms, e-mail and access to school web sites. Disciplinary consequences for misuse of the Internet should be clearly detailed. Internet-related offences are relatively uncommon today. As a result, relevant legal precedents tend to be found in cases of American law.

The Americans view a school website which allows input from students or the community at large, as a "limited open forum." Websites are no different from a public notice board on school property. However, if the information may negatively impact the school community, school administrators may be justified in limiting these rights. Administrators face an ethical dilemma, where the right of a few individuals to exercise their freedom of speech or expression may impinge upon the rights of many to exist in a nurturing and supportive educational environment. In a school setting, administrators need to be able to control the learning environment and, as a result, will find in favour of the many. Therefore, if students post offensive or inappropriate material on a school website, school administrators have the right to remove it, without unjustly restricting the First Amendment rights of those students who posted the material. Secondly, if such postings run contrary to the behaviour outlined in the school's acceptable use policy for information technology, the students may be subject to disciplinary proceedings. A difficulty arises if students post information that affects the school on a website unrelated to that of the school. Although students would not access the material with the school website, word of an 'illegal' or gossip-ridden site would spread quickly through the student body. As a result, it can be assumed that the material would still have an effect on the school population. In such a situation, the legal principles - relating to publication of the website remain untested in Canada. The school may be able to bring libel charges against the student(s) if the, material is untrue, however it is uncertain as to whether the school would be able to remove the site altogether.

There are legal precedents with regard to written school publications such as a newspaper or yearbook which may help to predict how courts will deal with a school board that refuses to allow an offensive or inappropriate link or posting on a school website. For example, we have previously mentioned, the leading cases of *Hazelwood School District v. Kuhlmeier*,[121] and *Bethel School District No. 403 v. Fraser*,[122] in our discussion of dress codes and free expression. It will be recalled that in *Hazelwood*, the school administration deleted two pages from an issue of the school newspaper that the administration felt were objectionable. The U.S. Supreme Court held that although students still retain the right to freedom of speech within the auspices of the school, the First Amendment right of students in public schools "are not automatically coextensive with the rights of adults in other settings." The second consideration of the Supreme Court was the finding of the Court of Appeals that the school yearbook constituted a "public forum". School facilities or publications can be considered to be public forums "only if school authorities have by policy or practice, opened these facilities for indiscriminate use by the general public", as per *Perry Education Assn. v. Perry Local Educators' Assn.*[123] Because the school newspaper has a specific intended purpose, it does not represent an open forum, and school administrators are therefore entitled to impose reasonable restrictions on the material included in the publication. The newspaper may be reasonably perceived to represent the opinions and ideas of the school and its administration, and school officials are therefore entitled to regulate its contents.

Although the production and publication of school websites has not been included in case law relating to school sponsored publications, it seems likely that similar conditions and expectations would apply. In particular,

---

121 484 U.S. 260, 273 (1988).
122 478 U.S. 675, 682 (1986).
123 460 U.S. 37 (U.S. Ind. 1983), at 47.

if schools include clear expectations in their acceptable use policy, school administrators should be entitled to regulate any material which can be linked to, and reflect upon, school policies and practices. Policies should also include academic guidelines, including such requirements as adequate research and impartiality, which would likely reduce the incidence of biased or uninformed opinion pieces. Web pages and website links created by students are school sponsored publications, and therefore just as with newspapers or other "hard copy" publications, school administrators may exert editorial control over their content.

Schools now have the technological capabilities to filter or block access to Internet sites. If students are using the Internet to gather curriculum resources, the school has absolute discretion regarding appropriate material. If students are gathering information for personal interest while using school technology, the school is still able to exercise considerable discretion regarding the suitability of the material in question. Monitoring and assessment of student Internet use and content requires adequate supervision by faculty members. If a student is creating a web page, or posting information to the school website, supervision is required to ensure suitable content.

The consequences of student action may result in school liability if there is deemed insufficient supervision. A clear statement of expectations in a school policy is not sufficient. If a student is harmed in any reasonably foreseeable way while using school technology, the school board may be liable if inadequate supervision or other negligence is shown. As a result, school computer rooms must be supervised at all times, and the school is obligated to monitor student use of technology, including browser logs and e-mail transactions. Securing written permission to monitor student e-mail and Internet activity as a condition for student use of the school's electronic address helps ensure that privacy concerns do not become an issue.

10. CONFIDENTIALITY

There is a fine line between the need for patient confidentiality and the protection of public health. Needless to say, the unauthorized disclosure of confidential HIV-related information may lead to horrendous personal consequences. In Ontario, doctors are bound legally and ethically[124] to maintain patient confidentiality. Ontario legislation provides that, except in order to comply with reporting requirements, physicians cannot reveal confidential information to anyone and such revelation without a patient's consent may constitute professional misconduct.[125]

---

124 See the Canadian Medical Association Code of Ethics.
125 See the *Health Protection and Promotion Act* of Ontario, R.S.O. 1990, c. H.7, as well as s. 29 (23) of R.R.O. 1990, Reg. 548, pursuant to the *Health Disciplines Act*, R.S.O. 1990, c. H.4.

The duty to report cases of specific diseases to public health authorities is found in Part IV of the *Health Protection and Promotion Act*. The duty extends in section 28 to school principals among others. In fact all provinces and territories in Canada require reporting of AIDS cases to public health authorities. Section 39 prohibits the disclosure of identifying information received in reports subject to the exceptions set out in section 39(2)(a) to (e). Section 39(2)(e) states that subsection (1) does not apply "... to prevent the reporting of information ... in respect of the abuse or the suspected abuse of a child."[126]

All counseling sessions with adolescents are confidential along with information pertaining to the selected intervention processes which might include abortions or contraceptive prescriptions or addiction/treatment services. These services are provided under the legal authority of the *Health Protection and Promotion Act*, Part II, s. 5 and 7. It is interesting to note that included in the mandatory programs for the Ministry of Health are the sexual health education, dental health screening and hepatitis B immunization; all target grade 7 students who are generally 11 and 12 years of age. Although information and consent forms are sent home prior to students' participation in the program, a registered nurse can deem a student capable of signing their own consent form just prior to the program initiation.

As mentioned, the *Health Protection and Promotion Act* requires that physicians report certain illnesses to the Public Health Department and the *Child and Family Services Act* requires practitioners to report suspicions of child abuse to Children's Aid Societies. Staff members in the health clinics cite the *Health Care Consent Act*, common law, the *Family Services Act* and the *Charter of Human Rights* as statutes that give adolescents the right to consent to their own health care without consultation with parents and/or guardians.

> When the risk of death to a child is balance's against the burden sought to be imposed on the counselors, the scales tip overwhelmingly favor of duty. Certainly the physical component of the burden on the counselors was slight. (The parent) claims only that a telephone call, communicating information known to the counselors, would have discharged that duty here. We agree, *Eisel v. Board of Education of Montgomery County*, 324 Md. .376, 597 A.2d 447 (1991).

> Perhaps it is part of the American tragedy that we rely on courts as we do on schools, to cure almost every problem. Zirkel, Another Case of student Suicide, 77 Phi Delta Kappan 91 (1995).

As societal pressures continue to force the social problems of students into the educational setting, students often reveal matters which may affect their health and safety or the health and safety of other students. Teachers,

---

126 See the *Child and Family Services Act*, R.S.O. 1990, c. C.11, s. 72.

counselors and administrators are often seen as standing in *loco parentis*, both literally and figuratively. Students reveal facts about themselves or other students which they believe will remain confidential between themselves and teachers or others in the school setting, but which could radically affect their health, welfare and safety. These issues include potential suicide, pregnancy, drug use, criminal activity, alcohol or drug use, abuse and eating disorders. How a school and its personnel deal with these issues, particularly those which must be communicated to the parent or guardian, will often determine the success in managing the situation and, just as importantly, may determine whether any liability will attach to the individual, the school, or the school district.

In *Eisel*[127], the Court, after recognizing the traditional doctrine of in *loco parentis* focused on whether there is a duty to communicate the information possessed by the school, its teachers, counselors or administrators to the parent or guardian of the child regarding issues, such as suicide, which could impact on the health, safety or welfare of the student. The Court found that the most important variable in the determination of duty was the question of foreseeability, that is, whether Nicole Eisel's suicide was foreseeable because the defendants allegedly had direct evidence of Nicole's intention to commit suicide or otherwise participate in the murder-suicide pact. Answering in the affirmative, the Court cited a number of state, county, and school policies which instructed staff as to how they could help in a suicidal crisis.

Finding that the burden on the counselors by telling the parent was slight as compared to the overwhelming and devastating consequences if the suicide was carried out, the Court found sufficient legal ground to establish a duty in Maryland for counselors, teachers or administrators to use reasonable means to attempt to prevent a suicide when they are on notice concerning the adolescent's suicidal intent. Most critical, the Court dismissed the idea of confidentiality between student and counselor. The Court said:

> The counselors argue that there are elements of confidentiality and discretion in their relationships with students that would be destroyed by the imposition of a duty to notify parents of suicidal statements. Confidentiality does not bar the duty.. ...policy explicitly disavows confidentiality when suicide is the concern.[128]

Eisel was decided on a risk analysis weighing the minor inconvenience of a phone call and the breach of a perceived confidence as against the loss of the life of a child. Other matters which may come to the attention of teachers, counselors, administrators and or staff from perceived confidential revela-

---
127 *Eisel v. Board of Education of Montgomery* 597 A.2d 454 (1991).
128 *Ibid.*, at 455.

tions by students and which would have a potentially disastrous impact upon their health and welfare include:

A. Drug abuse
B. Alcohol abuse
C. Criminal activity
D. Pregnancy
E. Sexual Abuse
F. Eating disorders

Failure to reveal the perceived confidence could have devastating effects on the student and, in liability terms, on the teacher and the school district. It should be emphasized to teachers and other staff that they are professionals and that their professional judgment, tempered by training and common sense, can appropriately address the vast majority of these problems in order to minimize risk to the student, to themselves, and to their schools.

The notion of privacy is based on the belief in the dignity and integrity of the individual. "Invasions of privacy must be prevented, and where privacy is outweighed by other societal claims, there must be clear rules setting forth the conditions in which it can be violated."[129]

Does a school counsellor have a duty to warn if he or she becomes aware of confidential medical information that may somehow compromise the public interest by the failure to disclose? There is no equivalent in Canada to the California case of a man who, two months before he killed a particular woman, had told of his intentions to kill her to his psychologist during therapy sessions. The psychologist, Dr. Moore, had been employed by the University of California. The Court found that psychotherapist communications must yield to the extent to which disclosure is essential to avert danger to others. The protective privilege ends where the public peril begins.[130]

The Ethical Standards of the American Association for Counselling and Development states: "When the client's condition indicates that there is clear and imminent danger to the client or others, the member must take reasonable personal action or inform responsible authorities." The code of ethics of the American School Counsellor Association states that the school counsellor "informs the appropriate authorities when the counselee's condition indicates a clear and imminent danger to the counselee or others." Codes of conduct for teachers may also address the teacher's responsibility for student safety. For example, the Code of Ethics for Teachers in Minnesota states: "A teacher shall make reasonable effort to protect the student

---

129 See *R. v. Dyment*, [1988] 2 S.C.R. 417 at 430.
130 See *Tarasoff v. Regents of Univ. of California*, 551 P.2d 334 (Cal. 1976) and *R. v. Gruenke*, [1991] 3 S.C.R. 263, where the Court reviewed the issue of privilege as to the communications between a priest and penitent.

from conditions harmful to health and safety." Such statements infer an ethical duty in regard to student safety; they may also form a legal basis for duty of care.

School counsellors have a duty to use reasonable means to attempt to prevent a suicide when they are on notice of a child or adolescent student's suicidal intent.

Does a school board have a duty to train teachers to recognize suicidal behaviours as part of a suicide prevention program? Is a board liable for its negligent acts that arise out of discretionary decisions? Discretionary decisions are those that involve a consideration of the financial, political, economic, and social effects of a particular policy and include a decision to implement a suicide prevention program, including training teachers.

Guidance counsellors have no special rights relating to confidentiality. Social workers employed by school boards are held to standards of professional conduct. Provisions contained in the Code of Ethics of the Canadian Association of Social Workers regarding confidentiality apply to student records. This Code contains a declaration that social workers will protect the confidentiality of all professionally acquired information and will disclose such information only when authorized to do so.

For victims of sexual assault, the Supreme Court of Canada decision in *M. (A.) v. Ryan*[131] sets out new guidelines for the disclosure of plaintiffs' personal records in civil sexual assault cases. The majority reasons, written by Madam Justice Beverley McLachlin, established "truth finding" and fairness to defendants as the paramount considerations affecting disclosure in such cases, but also recognized a "partial privilege" for plaintiffs which could allow courts to limit disclosure on a case-by-case basis. The decision stopped short, however, of setting out strict guidelines for courts to follow in such cases, as it did for criminal sexual assault cases.[132]

The Supreme Court of Canada approved of the doctrine of partial privilege. When looking at a record for purposes of disclosure, one can assert privilege over portions of that record. The privacy interest of the plaintiff, or the person from whom records are sought, has been elevated to a constitutional level which is equal to the right of the defendant to have full production of relevant evidence. A court can now attach conditions to the disclosure of private records–allowing only defence counsel and experts, not the defendant to see the records, for example–in order to minimize the infringement of the plaintiff's privacy interests.

---

131 *M. (A.) v. Ryan* (1997), 143 D.L.R. (4th) 1 (S.C.C.).
132 *R. v. O'Connor*, [1995] 4 S.C.R. 411.

11. AMINISTRATION OF MEDICATION TO PUPILS

In Ontario, the *Education Act* does not deal specifically with the administration of medical treatment to pupils by school board employees. However, section 265(1)(j) of the *Education Act* explicitly requires principals to "give assiduous attention to the health and comfort of the pupils. . .".

Our courts have held that a person who makes a reasonable decision as to a course of action in an emergency will not be treated as having acted negligently if the course of action ultimately turns out to be wrong. What is necessary is that the decision was not unreasonable, having regard to the particular circumstances of the case. In emergency situations, the issue of consent is important. An emergency may necessitate immediate medical action, either by the supervising teacher or on the teacher's authorization. As a practical matter, acquiring parental consent in these circumstances in an emergency situation may be difficult.

At the beginning of each school year, registration forms sent home to parents should request that the parents provide information about relevant medical conditions their children may have, as well as any limitations on their activities and any treatment required. Written authorization should be provided to the school with clear instructions from the student's physician. The physician should specify the name of the medication, the reason for its use and the method of administration.

School administrators are under an obligation to assist in or manage medical treatment where doing so is in the best interests of the student, is reasonable, and can be carried out with no special training or skills. The following factors should be considered in each case to determine whether this test is met: the type of medication, the availability of qualified staff members to administer the medication, the degree to which the administering or management of medication interferes with the normal duties of staff members, the timing and locale of the administration of medication, the method of administration, potential risks associated with the management of a student's medication, and the seriousness of the student's condition.

In most schools, there will likely be more than one student who must receive medication during the school day. This fact, combined with the myriad of other duties a principal must attend to, demands that the principal delegate the responsibility of administering care and medication to other members of the staff. The question remains as to whether teachers and other school staff can be required to participate in the administration of medication and other care to students, where this duty is not undertaken by a public health or other agency.

The legislation of many provinces provides that teachers must undertake duties assigned to them, in addition to the listed statutory duties. Unless administering of medication or medical care is specifically listed in the legislation, or as a duty in the teaching contract or collective agreement of a particular staff member, any requirement to undertake such activities must form an implied obligation of the employment relationship. Generally speaking, the administration of medication in schools is in furtherance of the education of the students who require the service. Many of these students could not attend classes but for receiving medication during school hours. For the most part, the manner of administering medication does not make unreasonable demands of the designated staff member. The method is usually administering oral medication, which can be done simply and quickly. Only where the manner of administration becomes overly complex, risky or lengthy, would this assignment likely be considered unreasonable.

A valid consent to the administration of medication must be voluntarily given, informed, and by a person who is legally competent to grant it. For consent to be informed, the person consenting must understand the nature and the consequences of the act(s) which are to be performed. The consent form should detail the particular medication to be administered, the person(s) who will be responsible for its administration, where, within the school, it is to be administered, how and when the medication will be administered, and emergency procedures.

(a) **Asthmatic or Anaphylactic Children**

When an asthmatic or anaphylactic child begins school, a whole host of reasonable measures need to be in place to enable adequate care of the student so as to avoid any serious health problems and subsequent absence from school. While the onus is on the parents, as primary care givers, to inform the school of their child's medical condition, it does not necessarily release the school of responsibility.

Students with anaphylaxis should receive the Emergency Allergy Alert Form Epipen(R) Only or the Emergency Allergy Alert Form - Antihistamine/Epipen(R)/Ana-Kit to be completed. These forms describe more amply the allergy, allergens to be strictly avoided, eating rules, symptoms and action-emergency plan. The child's photograph should be included for prompt identification. High-risk students should have other means of identification such as a medical alert bracelet. A Medic Alert poster may be completed and relevant information is recorded on the Student Data Card and O.S.R. The teacher's role is to instruct the students vis-à-vis proper lunchtime and snacktime procedures, proper hygiene techniques, monitoring the at risk child for any allergic reactions, ensuring that pupils inform any teacher should they notice any health problems of any of their classmates, verifying that the Epipen(R) or medication for asthma is on the child and that a backup exists in the school. Any teacher entering the classroom should be alerted to the anaphylactic situation by a posted emergency plan on the teacher's desk. The standard of care will be higher the younger the child is as the ability to self-medicate may not be possible. Ultimately, a duty of care rests upon the parents who must disclose promptly and honestly a child's medical condition, sign required consent forms, ensure that a physician has apprised the school authorities of appropriate measures, and procured an adequate number of EpiPen(R)s or inhalers. During field trips, especially outdoor education events, additional medication may be needed if a hospital is located more than 20 minutes away. EpiPen(ROsa and inhalers both have an expiry date which will need to be checked and replacements will need to be ordered by the parents.

(b) Consent to Treatment

The Ontario *Health Care Consent Act* was proclaimed law in 1996. A person is capable of consenting with respect to a treatment, admission to a care facility or a personal assistant service if the person is able to understand the information that is relevant to making a decision about the treatment, admission or personal assistance service, as the case may be, and able to appreciate the reasonable foreseeable consequences of a decision or lack of decision. A health practitioner who proposes a treatment for a person shall not administer the treatment, and shall take reasonable steps to ensure that it is not administered, unless,

(a) he or she is of the opinion that the person is capable with respect to the treatment, and the person has given consent; or
(b) he or she is of the opinion that the person is incapable with respect to the treatment and the person's substitute decision-maker has given consent on the person's behalf in accordance with this Act.

The following are the elements required to consent to treatment:

1. The consent must relate to the treatment.
2. The consent must be informed.
3. The consent must be given voluntarily.
4. The consent must not be obtained through misrepresentation or fraud.

It is important to note that age is not a factor in the determination of capacity to give consent in Ontario. In common law there is no age of consent. A minor can consent if he or she is capable of understanding the information about treatment and of appreciating the risks and likely consequences of the treatment. An individual, regardless of age, can consult with any practitioners and if deemed capable receive a confidential diagnosis and treatment plan. A substitute decision-maker such as a parent or guardian is accessed only if the individual is deemed to be incapable. The new Act has a hierarchical list of substitute decision-makers for a person deemed incapable.

A medical consensus seems to exist with regard to consent by adolescent children. Children are often encouraged to begin having personal medical check-ups between the ages of 11 and 13 years, depending on their maturity level. Information collected during these visits is confidential. If in conversation with the doctor the child revealed experimentation with drugs, cigarettes or sex, this information would remain confidential, although the doctor might encourage the child to talk to his or her parent.

12. YOUTH CRIMINAL JUSTICE IN CANADA

Canada has one of the highest incarceration rates in the world, higher than comparative rates in most European countries, Australia and New Zealand, but lower than the United States (Canadian Centre for Justice Statistics 2000). But when only youth incarceration is considered, Canada's incarceration rate exceeds that of the United States by almost 50 per cent: 447 per 100,000 youth, compared to 311 per 100,000 youth in the United States. Over half are sentenced to custody for property offences, not crimes of violence.

The situation is even more severe for Canada's aboriginal people, as numerous studies and commissions have documented. Aboriginal people are incarcerated more than eight times the national rate. This over-representation is significantly higher in our northern territories and in the Prairie Provinces. In 1998-99, Statistics Canada provided data for a number of reporting jurisdictions where Aboriginal status was known. Aboriginal admissions accounted for 26 per cent of the total admissions to custody and 18 per cent of admissions to probation, although Aboriginal youth made up only 5 per cent of the total youth population. A U.S. Justice Department report released on March 18, 2001 referred to American Indians as more likely to be victims of violent crimes than any other group.

Aboriginal youth are complex, rooted in a history that includes lost culture, mission schools, victimization, poverty and high unemployment. In the youth justice system generally and in the north in particular, over-incarceration is driven by the absence of effective alternatives to jail.

Because crime comes from the community, the solution to it must also come from the community; we must talk with community members and leaders about how they can help the Court to better serve their community. Perhaps by reducing the formalities of sentencing proceedings, by involving community members in the sentencing process and by encouraging and welcoming oral representations from interested parties.

Canadians are *not* told (or if told, they often do not believe) that the following general trends are observed:

(1) Youth crime is *not* out of control. Rates are marginally declining, homicides have remained even or less in many years, serious assault rates are stable in number and most reported violence is minor assault. Crime rates for persons 16-17 years of age are almost the same as for the 18-19 age group. The *Young Offenders Act* is as effective as the

Criminal Code. Those 18-28 years of age commit more serious crimes. Reported rates are influenced by policy: e.g. zero tolerance policies, transfer policies and policing policy. The six-year age group 12-17 commit less crime than the young adult 18-25 age group does.

(2) One in three or four court dispositions is a custodial order. There is no statutory early release; for many, three years means three years. By comparison, an adult who served three years would likely be sentenced to eight to nine years.

(3) We incarcerate serious offenders for about twice as long as 12 years ago. Without mandated parole, many serious young offenders serve longer maximum security than similar adults do.

(4) Transfers to adult court are escalating. The Crown rarely does not prevail in transfer applications.

(5) In contrast to provincial adult offenders in Alberta, young persons serve twice as long, on average.

(6) Youth crime is not overlooked. In 1996 the average daily number of young persons in custody was 500 in Alberta and 5,000 nationally. In 1999 the average daily number in Alberta was 400. These numbers are declining as maximum sentences are found to be not indicated by the facts.

Youth Justice Issues:

(1) The goal is safe communities within the rule of law. Oppressive measures are not justified. Safety at the expense of accepted freedoms would be intolerable.

(2) The community historically in justice issues, especially youth justice, reacts in uninformed, even hysterical, cliché-driven ways – seeks simple cheap answer to complex, painful and costly issues. The *Young Offenders Act* was 20 years in the making and believed to be in contrast to the *Juvenile Delinquents Act* as "get tough", but it was misunderstood, demeaned and attacked within 20 months. Calm, dispassionate, informed debate is rare. An example of a stupid cliché is "commit adult crime, do adult time." All crime is adult. There are no youth crimes. Crimes do not change the age of the young person; he (she) is still a young person.

(3) The treatment versus punishment debate has gone on for many years and is unresolved. If more police and harsh penalties made a country safe, the U.S. would be the safest country in the world.

(4) Young offender matters are inexorably intertwined with child welfare legislation and police: e.g., response to neglect and homelessness, the out-of-control child (non-offender), the "casting out" parent, the "casting out" school. Anyone who advocates anything but a get-tougher line is derided as a "bleeding heart", "fuzzy-thinking" person. For some there is never enough punishment. Retaliation and revenge is not justice.

The confusion is promoted in that the *Young Offenders Act* encourages on one hand punitive due process and on the other informal measures such as youth justice committees and alternative measures, both with many issues of principles of fairness and due process.

Better communication among police is necessary with lawyers and social workers so that intervention will occur more rapidly after the commission of a juvenile offence, before time has erased the reality of the offence in the offender's mind. The best probation officers are parents in attendance at court and looking after their child day after day, at home and at school.

For the majority of juveniles committing an offence is an opportunity to test social norms and internalize them. The reaction of their immediate circle and society-at-large helps them absorb the norms they have violated and teaches them respect for the law. For a minority of juveniles who become more deeply involved in delinquent activity, it is necessary to show consistency, conscientiousness and skill.

The most common sentence or disposition in Youth Court is a probation order. Restrictions such as "a 6:00 p.m. curfew unless in the company of a designated adult" is tantamount to "imprisonment". The effect is quite noticeable. First, they and their parents or other caregivers are required to spend time together and this often leads to the "family" seeking professional help and counselling. Second, being at home during the evening means that the young person might as well do homework and get to bed at a reasonable hour for school the next day. Third, not being out in the evening keeps them away from the temptations of the "street". For some, hopefully many, the habit of good conduct catches on!

Community work service is a common disposition in Youth Court. If a young person acquires employment or engages in some other positive activity, such as playing or coaching a sports team these productive activities can count towards the community hours to be done. There are some new initiatives on the scene in Ontario. Restorative justice is being recognized in many communities as an alternative to a strict judicial approach. Family group conferencing and other forms of conferencing are being implemented at the pre-charge and post-charge stage. In some cases this is being supervised by a judge and in other locations by non-judicial facilitators. More training is being given to law enforcement personnel in the domain of warnings and cautions.

13. THE *YOUNG OFFENDERS ACT*[133]

The *Young Offenders Act* approaches the problem of youth crime in much the same way that the *Criminal Code*[134] approaches the problem of

---

133 R.S.C. 1985, c. Y-1.
134 R.S.C. 1985, c. C-46.

adult crime. The *Young Offenders Act,* however, has a number of specific provisions that require the consideration of the special needs and limited maturity of adolescents.

Provision is made for parents to receive notice of any proceedings. As well, parents are referred to throughout the Act and, in practice, given an opportunity to provide input. Further concessions to this age group include the ability, in respect of bail, to release a young person to a "responsible person" where, under the *Criminal Code* provisions, detention is appropriate. As well, the availability of open and secure places of custody and the restrictions on the imposition of secure custody and the length of custodial terms in general reflect Parliament's intention to modify the full effect of the criminal justice system for this age group.

Section 3 of the *Young Offenders Act* contains a "Declaration of Principles". The marginal note for section 3 states that it contains the "policy for Canada with respect to young offenders". By virtue of section 3(2), the "Act [must] be liberally construed to the end that young persons will be dealt with in accordance with the principles set out in subsection (1)".

Section 13 of the *Criminal Code* indicates that the minimum age of criminal responsibility in Canada is 12 years. Section 2(1) of the *Young Offenders Act* defines a "young person" as someone who is 12 to 17 years of age, inclusive. Similarly, "child" is defined as someone who is under 12 years of age. These age references apply to the age of the accused on the date of the alleged offence. Therefore, an adult can be proceeded with under the Act where he or she was a young person on the date that the offence was alleged to have occurred.[135]

"Parent" is given a broad interpretation in section 2(1) of the *Young Offenders Act.* In addition to the biological parent, a parent is any person who has a legal duty to care for the young person, or anyone who has custody or control over the young person, in fact or in law. Section 2(1) specifically excludes from the definition of "parent" anyone who has custody or control of the young person by reason of proceedings under the *Young Offenders Act.* Therefore, where the young person is in the care of a child protection agency, the senior official in charge of the agency is served. Where that "parent" is not available, another adult in whose care the young person is, may be notified.

The Act seeks to protect the privacy of young persons involved in the youth court process, whether by means of a publication ban of identification about the youth, restricted access to records from proceedings or a prohi-

---

135 *Cf. Juvenile Delinquents Act,* R.S.C. 1970, c. J-3, where criminal liability began at the age of 7, although children under 14 could be acquitted based on the *doli incapax* defence.

bition for employers seeking to ask whether a potential employee has ever been convicted of an offence under the Act.[136]

A very significant amendment to the *Young Offenders Act* came into force on December 1, 1995.

> (1.13) Subsection (1) does not apply in respect of the disclosure of information to any professional or other person engaged in supervision or care of a young person, including the representative of any school board or school or any other educational or training institution, by the provincial director, a youth worker, a peace officer or any other person engaged in the provision of services to young persons where the disclosure is necessary
>
> (a) to ensure compliance by the young person with an authorization pursuant to section 35 or an order of any court concerning bail, probation or conditional supervision; or
>
> (b) to ensure the safety of staff, students or other persons, as the case may be,
>
> (1.14) No person to whom information is disclosed pursuant to subsection (1.13) and (1.14) shall disclose that information to any other person unless the disclosure is necessary for a purpose referred to in that subsection.
>
> (1.15) Any person to whom information is disclosed pursuant to subsections (1.13) and (1.14) shall
>
> (a) keep the information separate from any other record of the young person to whom the information relates;
>
> (b) subject to subsection (1.14), ensure that no other person has access to the information; and
>
> (c) destroy the information when the information is no longer required for the purpose for which it was disclosed.[137]

Parliament has presumably expressed an intention that school authorities should be involved in the administration of justice.

To quote Holland, J. in *Southam Inc. v. R.*:

> The aim of ss. 38(1) and 39(1) is the protection of young people from harmful effects that publicity may have on them. The corollary to this is the protection of society since, on the evidence, most young offenders are one-time offenders only and the less harm that is caused to them from their experience with the criminal justice system, the less likely they are to commit further criminal acts. Thus, it can be said that the legislation is also aimed at rehabilitation of the young person. The aim of the Young Offenders Act as supported by the expert evidence was that the children have special needs and should be treated differ-

---

136 *Young Offenders Act*, ss. 38, 40-46. See *O. (Y.) v. Belleville (City) Chief of Police* (1993), 12 O.R. (3d) 618 (Div. Ct.), reversing (1991), 3 O.R. (3d) 261 (Gen. Div.), where the Court found that s. 44.1(1)(*i*) of the Act provided an exception to the general rule of confidentiality for youth court records.

137 *Young Offenders Act*, R.S.C. 1985, c. Y-1.

ently from adults and that the criminal justice system should in some ways operate differently for children than for adults. Thus, with respect to s. 38(1) the protection and rehabilitation of young people involved in the criminal abrogation of the fundamental freedom of expression including freedom of the press and is a reasonable limitation on that freedom. With respect of S. 39, the interests of society in the protection of rehabilitation of young people involved in youth court proceedings is a value of such superordinate importance that it justifies this discretion given to the youth court judge and is similarly a reasonable limitation.[138]

The school system is intimately involved in the protection and rehabilitation of young people as well as in their education. The school system and the Youth Court do and should, work together under the *Young Offenders Act* subject to safeguards, one of which is the prevention of disclosure of individual problems to the community at large.

(a) The "School Board Exception"

In the case of *Re N.(F.)*,[139] the Supreme Court of Canada considered whether the practice of Youth Court staff in routinely distributing its weekly Youth Court docket to local school boards contravened the non-disclosure provisions of the *Young Offenders Act*. The distribution was not limited to the one school board that was responsible for a school attended by each of the young people on the docket. A board does not have a cognizable interest in students or non-students for whom it has no responsibility whatsoever. The appellant's name was disclosed after he was charged with two counts of assault and breach of probation. His application for prohibition to the Newfoundland Supreme Court, Trial Division, and subsequent appeal to the Newfoundland Court of Appeal were both dismissed. However, the Supreme Court held that the Act did not permit this disclosure. The decision deals extensively with the rationale behind restrictions upon disclosure of information relating to young offenders, and should be read in its entirety. However, in dealing with school boards in particular, the Court stated as follows:

> School boards do have a legitimate interest in knowing of members of its student body that could present a danger to themselves or others. The schools may well desire the information for their own purposes. (The letter of the Chief Judge, supra, identified one of the objectives as the control of truancy, but this is not a purpose recognized as valid under the statutory scheme.) In my opinion, the school boards have not made a convincing case that their specific interest in the confidential information is related to the administration of justice as opposed to the administration of the schools.[140]

---

138 (1984), 48 O.R. (2d) 678 at 679.
139 [2000] 1 S.C.R. 880.
140 *Ibid.*, para. 35.

The Court then commented upon the "school board exception" in the *Young Offenders Act*, as follows:

> Section 38(1.13), referred to in argument as "the school board section", permits disclosure of information to the representative of any school board or school where disclosure is necessary either to ensure compliance by the young person with a court order or to ensure the safety of staff, students or other persons. . . .
>
> The restrictions can be summarized thus. Firstly, the disclosure under s. 38(1.13) must be by one of certain enumerated persons including the provincial director, a youth worker, a peace officer, "or any other person engaged in the provision of services to young persons". I think it is stretching a point to say that the Youth Court administrators are "engaged in the provision of services to young persons". The other persons enumerated in s. 38(1.13) do have access to the docket information, but none of these people undertook the distribution to the school boards in this case.
>
> Secondly, disclosure is limited to the school board or school engaged in the supervision or care of the young person in question. The practice of the Youth Court to send the dockets to both school boards in the St. John's area necessarily includes a school board other than the particular school board charged with the care and education of the young person in question. In fact under the present arrangement it is quite possible that none of the recipient school boards would have any responsibility for a particular young offender on the docket, e.g., the young offender could be from outside the area of St. John's, or have left school altogether.
>
> Thirdly, the limitation is directed either to ensuring compliance with a court order (in which case disclosure should not be given in respect of young offenders who are not under any relevant court order) or to ensuring safety of staff, students or other persons. With respect to compliance issues (first branch), it is quite possible that one of the St. John's School Boards could have had a role to play in ensuring compliance by the appellant with the condition of his recognizance that he keep the peace and be of good behaviour for 12 months; and that he not "initiate any contact or communication with" the alleged victims. However, there is no evidence that all or any of the school board recipients here had such a role to play in respect of the appellant, against whom all charges were ultimately dropped. With respect to safety (second branch), young persons charged with offences such as shoplifting, which ordinarily would not raise safety concerns at all, should be (but are not now) excluded from the general distribution to school boards linking specific accused with specific offences. The docket as presently distributed identifies all young persons in trouble under the Act, whether or not they are on bail, probation or conditional supervision, whether or not they are a threat to safety of the staff, students or other persons, and whether or not they attend school.
>
> Fourthly, the docket is both over-inclusive and under-inclusive in relation to the information that can legally be communicated. It is over-inclusive because it includes youong people who present no safety risk at all and who may not even be students. At the same time, it is under-inclusive because, if there is a

serious safety concern, the docket may not include enough information to alert a school to the nature of that safety concern or to enable the school to formulate in an informed way what remedial action to take. It is evident, therefore, that if the objective of the Youth Court in St. John's is to provide timely information to school boards in need of safety information, the objective can certainly be achieved through the individuals named in s. 38(1.13). The evidence is, in fact, that timely information from the Youth Court has in the past assisted schools in the St. John's area to address legitimate safety concerns, including assignment of a student assistant to monitor a student charged with arson to ensure no incidents of arson occurred; preparation of risk assessments in cases where students have been charged with serious violent offences; placement of a student in another school after an attack on a classmate to reduce the risk of further assault or confrontation; and restriction of a student's movement within a school so as to reduce the safety risk to other students.

The point, however, is that the communication will have to be more tightly tailored to comply with the non-disclosure provisions of the Act than by way of the present general distribution of all dockets to all school boards.

Once the information is lawfully in the hands of the school, of course, the school may take steps to address its safety concerns (as, of course, it is entitled to do on the basis of any information that raises safety issues). This remedial action may include, where appropriate, an expulsion hearing: F.G. v. Board of Education of Scarborough (1994), 68 O.A.C. 308 (Div. Ct.); or other restrictions even prior to trial where necessary: H. (G.) v. Shamrock School Division No. 38 (Sask.) Board of Education, [1987] 3 W.W.R. 270 (Sask. Q.B.). As stated by Smith Prov. Ct. J. in R.G. (Re), [1999] B.C.J. No. 1106 (QL) (Prov. Ct.), at para. 33, albeit he was dealing with an application under s. 38(1.5): "As important as privacy is for youth records under the YOA, there is an overriding importance, in certain circumstances, of allowing disclosure in order to protect other children".

Violent offences against people, e.g., assault, assault causing bodily harm, aggravated sexual assault, weapons offences, drugs and more serious property offences such as arson may clearly raise a sufficient safety concern for the safety of the young person as well as "staff, students or other persons" to justify notification to the board responsible for the student in question. There is nothing in the section that precludes the implementation of a general notification procedure provided the policy is properly tailored to the statutory requirements. In terms of post-disposition, the Youth Court judge would be in a very good position to know what information the school ought to receive to address any safety concerns and may, if he or she thinks fit, alert one of the officials enumerated in s. 38(1.13) to make the notification.

The scheme of s. 38(1.13) is therefore that the information should be provided not by the Youth Court as such but by the provincial director, a youth worker or peace officer, and should be directed only to the school board with which the young person is associated. Administrative arrangements may be standardized by the court's Youth Justice Concerns Committee, but the responsibility for the nature and extent of the disclosure will rest with the official identified in s. 38(1.13) who actually takes charge of the disclosure.[141]

(b) Statements Made to Persons in Authority

(i) *Statutory Requirements*

The admissibility of young persons' statements is frequently pivotal to a finding of guilt. It is therefore crucial that teachers and administrators are aware of the unique provisions of the *Young Offenders Act* if they take statements from a pupil in the context of possible criminal charges and proceedings. The case law regarding the admissibility of statements must be referred to as well as the relevant legislative provisions.[142]

Section 56(1) of the Act requires the filling out of a Statement to Person in Authority form. It imposes further obligations in respect of taking statements from young persons, including the obligation to allow the young person to consult with a parent, adult relative or other adult or a lawyer and to have that person present when making the statement. If these requirements are not met, the statement is inadmissible. There is a right of an accused to know the extent of his or her jeopardy.[143]

Section 56 of the *Young Offenders Act* reinforces the *Charter* guarantee of right to silence and to counsel, incorporates the common law requirement of voluntariness and adds statutory grounds for exclusion. The accused must have actual awareness of the consequences of waiving rights and making statements to police. There is no mandatory requirement or formula regarding what police must say. What is necessary to bring home potential jeopardy depends on the circumstances, including the accused's age, level of intelligence and sophistication.

(ii) *"Person in Authority" Defined*

The Ontario Court of Appeal, *in R. v. B. (A.)*,[144] considered the concept of the "person in authority", with reference to a parent and his or her child and a doctor and his or her patient. Justice Cory reviewed the history of the concept and lists the factors to be considered in determining the issue.

> (1) As a general rule, a person in authority is someone engaged in the arrest, detention, examination or prosecution of the accused. When the word "examination" is used, I believe it refers to interrogation by police officers, detention or security guards and members of the Crown Attorney's office.
>
> (2) In some circumstances, the complainant in a criminal prosecution may be considered to be a person in authority.

---

141 *Ibid.*, paras. 48-57.
142 *Canadian Charter of Rights and Freedoms and the Young Offenders Act.*
143 *R. v. Smith*, [1991] 1 S.C.R. 714.
144 (1986), 26 C.C.C. (3d) 17 (Ont. C.A.).

(3) The parent of an infant who is the injured party or complainant in a criminal prosecution may be a person in authority. Such a conclusion would, I suggest, depend upon the factual background.

(4) An inducement made by one who is not in authority but made in the presence of persons in authority who do not dissent from it may be deemed to have been made by a person in authority. In those circumstances, the person making the inducement can be considered as the agent of the person in authority. To put it another way, by the presence of those in authority, the person not in authority is clothed with that authority. As a result, such a statement is suspect for the same reasons that a statement being made in response to an inducement offered by a person in authority would be.

(5) The question as to whether the statement was made to a person in authority will be viewed subjectively, that is to say, from the point of view of the accused person who made the statement. The proper test is . . . to the effect that did the accused truly believe, at the time he made the declaration, that the person he dealt with had some degree of power over him? . . .

(6) A person who is to be a witness for the prosecution will not, as a general rule, be deemed to be a person in authority.

(7) As well, it has been determined that a psychiatrist, even when examining an accused to determine if he is a dangerous sexual offender, will not be considered to be a person in authority, nor will be a doctor who has examined the accused.[145]

This case involved charges of sexual assault allegedly committed by a 13-year-old boy on his stepsisters. The mother and a psychiatrist spoke with the young person about the incidents approximately one year before the charges were laid. The trial judge, in determining the admissibility of certain statements made by the young person, ruled that the parent and psychiatrist were persons in authority. On appeal, the Court ruled they were not persons in authority, and therefore ordered a new trial. Mr. Justice Cory stated:

> In my view, at the time the statement was made, A.B.'s mother was not, *in law*, a person in authority. Neither she nor her husband had any intention of calling the police or of instituting court proceedings. Rather, she wished to learn the true situation in order to help and to obtain assistance for her son. It follows that she could not in any way have affected the course of a prosecution if such a step was not even contemplated. There must be some realistic and close connection between the decision to call in the authorities and the offered inducement to a child to make a statement before a parent could be considered, in law, a person in authority. In this case, the mother was not, in February, 1984, a person in authority at common law. The words used in s. 56(2) of the *Young Offenders Act* ". . . person who is, in law, a person in authority," must be given the same meaning they had and still have at common law. This is the clear intent of the section to be gathered from the very precise wording of the subsection. It follows that even if the *Young Offenders* Act had been in force in February, 1984, A. B.'s mother would not have come within the purview of

---

145 *Ibid.*, at 26-27.

S. 56(2). To hold otherwise would be detrimental to young persons, to society and to the fabric of family life.[146]

The test in this case can be applied to any individual. In the context of a school, principals and teachers may not, in *all* instances, be persons in authority. Section 56 is a response to the declaration in section 3 of the *Young Offenders Act* that young persons "have special guarantees of their rights and freedoms" (s. 3(*e*)) and have the right "to be informed as to what those rights and freedoms are" (s. 3(g)).[147]

(iii) *"Young Person " Defined*

Section 2(1) the *Young Offenders Act* defines a young person for the purposes of the Act as "a person who is or, in the absence of evidence to the contrary, appears to be twelve years of age or more, but under eighteen years of age. . .". If you are 17 at the time of the alleged offence, but 18 when you make an inculpatory written statement to a person in authority, then section 56(2) of the Act does not apply.[148]

(iv) *Procedure*

To meet the requirement set out in subsections 56(2)(*b*) and (*c*), the appropriate procedure is to require the person taking the statement to advise the young person of the various rights described in subparagraphs (i) to (iv) of section 56(2)(*b*).

14. THE YOUTH CRIMINAL JUSTICE ACT

Bill C-7 or the *Youth Criminal Justice Act*, (the "YCJA") (assented to but not proclaimed as of the time of writing) will, once proclaimed, replace the *Young Offenders Act* ("the YOA"). It contains a significant emphasis on sanction and sentencing options, increasing the alternatives available to police, crown attorneys and judges. The Act contains a preamble and Declaration of Principle, which are further refined by "purpose and principles" sections in Parts 1, 4 and 5, related primarily to various facets of sentencing. In addition to the changes to the sentencing provisions of the YOA, the treatment of statements to the police and the publication of young offenders' identifying information, including criminal records, mark a significant departure in the YCJA. There are also numerous other changes, such as explicit recognition of victim concerns and the establishment of 'conferences'.

---

146 *R. v. B. (A.)* (1986), 26 C.C.C. (3d) 17 at 28 (Ont. C.A.).
147 See *R. v. J. (J.T.)*, [1990] 2 S.C.R. 755 for a review of s. 56.
148 *R. v. Z. (D.A.)* (1992), 76 C.C.C. (3d) 97 (S.C.C.). The Court in this instance indicated that the aim of section 56 was to protect adolescents who, by virtue of their lack of maturity, were not likely to fully appreciate their legal rights and the consequences of making a statement to the public.

The preamble and Declaration of Principle identify the primary goal of the youth criminal justice system as being the protection of the public. This goal is to be achieved through prevention, meaningful consequences for youth crime and rehabilitation (section 3). The practical effects of the YCJA are likely be felt, if they are at all, in sentencing (including extra-judicial measures and custody provisions). Extra-judicial measures replace the 'alternative measures' provisions of the YOA with some minor expansions to the diversionary scheme as it currently exists. The 'Principles' section declares that a presumption exists that extra-judicial measures are the appropriate means of holding a young person accountable where the person has committed a non-violent first offence (section 4(c)). The objectives of extra-judicial measures include encouraging young persons to take responsibility for their actions and to repair the harm that has been caused. The Act also encourages the provision of an opportunity for victims to participate in decisions related to the extra-judicial measures selected, likely through 'conferences' mentioned in Part 2 of the Act.

The YCJA provides for the consideration of the special circumstances of young persons in deciding whether to order detention prior to sentencing. First, the Act prohibits the use of pre-sentence custody as a substitute for appropriate child protection, mental health or other social measures (section 29(1)). Secondly, section 29 contains a presumption against pre-sentence detention where the young person could not, on conviction, be committed to custody on the grounds set out in section 38(1), unless there is a substantial likelihood that the young person will commit a criminal offence or interfere with the administration of justice if released.

Parts 4 and 5 of the YCJA, dealing with sentencing, custody and supervision, are the most important areas of departure from the YOA. Part 4, on sentencing, has its own statement of purpose, citing the purpose of sentencing to be to contribute to the protection of society by holding a young person accountable through just and meaningful consequences that promote rehabilitation and reintegration (section 38(1)). The principles which follow this statement of purpose require that the youth sentence imposed be the least restrictive possible for achieving the purpose set out above and be the one most likely to rehabilitate the young person while promoting a sense of responsibility (section 38(2)). These principles are subject only to the notion that the sentence must be proportionate to the seriousness of the offence and the degree of responsibility of the young person for that offence (section 38(2)(c)).

The Supreme Court of Canada considered the principles of sentencing as they applied to young offenders under the YOA in *R. v. M. (J.J.)*[149] and stated that:

---

149 [1993] 2 S.C.R. 421 at 428.

Section 3(1) attempts to balance the need to make young offenders responsible for their crimes while recognizing their vulnerability and special needs. It seeks to chart a course that avoids both the harshness of a pure criminal law approach applied to minors and the paternalistic welfare approach that was emphasized in the old [Act].

However, in the YCJA there is an apparent absence of balancing between the pure "criminal law" approach to sentencing and the recognition of young persons' particular vulnerability and needs. There is not an explicit recognition of the special circumstances inherent in being a minor that may be a significant consideration in sentencing. In that the YCJA enumerates notions of proportionality, responsibility and acknowledgment of harm caused, reparation to victims and the community, and most importantly, the protection of society as the primary goal of sentencing, its approach resembles more the principles of adult sentencing. General deterrence is not explicitly mentioned anywhere in the principles or purpose of sentencing in the YCJA. In *M.(J.J.)* the Supreme Court cautioned that general deterrence could not be discounted entirely as a principle of sentencing under the YOA because of the Act's requirement to consider the protection of society in making dispositions. There may actually be an increased emphasis on deterrence in the YCJA, given its repeated references to the purpose of "public protection".

In the YCJA, the use of custody in sentencing is circumscribed by four restrictions: (i) it must be a violent offence, (ii) the young person has failed to comply with previous non-custodial dispositions, (iii) the young person has committed an indictable offence for which an adult could be sentenced to imprisonment for more than two years and has a history of findings of guilt against them; or (iv) the circumstances of the offence make the imposition of a non-custodial disposition inconsistent with the purpose and principles of sentencing (section 39(1)). These are more precise than the YOA custody provisions, and may reduce the personal discretion of judges. The imposition of a custodial sentence is also restricted in that, as in the YOA, the youth court must consider all alternatives to custody raised at the sentencing hearing that are reasonable in the circumstances (section 39(2)). There is *no* accompanying provision in the legislation mandating that the province make alternative programming available. Section 39 also prohibits the use of custody as a substitute for appropriate child protection, mental health or other social measures (section 39(5)).

Pre-sentence reports, called "pre-disposition reports" under the YOA, are maintained in the YCJA in virtually the exact same form under the current legislation. The YCJA has a provision for the inclusion of recommendations resulting from any "conference" (section 40(2)(c)). Section 40 of the YCJA also permits the referral by a youth justice of a matter to a conference for recommendation on sentence. These conferences of course can be used as vehicles for restorative justice programming and as a means of formalizing already existing programs such as sentencing circles, subject again however to issues of political support within jurisdictions for this type of activity. A valid question is what sort of entity was the conference contemplated to be in a large, diverse, urban environment? Inclusion of such persons as victims, school officials, family members, and social service providers are likely to be relatively non-controversial, but seem unlikely to add little beyond what would already be available in a pre-sentence report. Where the young person is a member of a distinct ethnic or cultural community such community participation could be envisioned, which would apply in both a rural area as well as in an urban context. The concern that arises when issues of provincial discretion come into play is that the particular criminalization strategies and philosophy or a province may dictate the bent of such bodies.

The sentencing spectrum under the YCJA has been expanded considerably in comparison to disposition available under the YOA. The YCJA makes available to the Court a new disposition, a reprimand (section 42(2)(a)), that is separate and distinct from an absolute discharge which is still available under section 42(2)(b). A reprimand can be combined with any of the other available dispositions. Provisions for absolute discharges (section 42(2)(b)), compensation (section 42(2)(e)), restitution (section 42(2)(f)), personal service (section 42(2)(h)), and community service up to 240 hours to be completed within one year of sentencing (section 42(2)(i)), remain virtually the same as in the YOA. Fines may also be ordered with a cap of $1000, having regard to the young person's present and future means to pay (section 42(1)(d), section 54(1)). The YCJA also contains provisions similar to the YOA that allow for a fine to be discharged through a work program if the province establishes a program for that purpose (section 54(2)). A "new" disposition is available under section 42(2)(m) which allows for an order for the young person to attend a facility offering a program approved by the provincial director for a maximum of 240 hours over a period of time up to six months.

The YCJA contains sentencing provisions for a new form of custody, intensive rehabilitative custody (section 42(2)(r)). To make an order under this section four conditions must apply: (i) the young person must be found guilty of a presumptive offence; (ii) they must be suffering from a mental illness or disorder, a psychological disorder or an emotional disturbance; (iii) there are reasonable grounds to believe that a plan of care involving custodial treatment will reduce the risk of re-offending; and (iv) the provincial director consents to the young person's participation (section 42(7)). A court may order intensive rehabilitative custody for up to six years for first degree murder, four years for second degree murder, three years in the case of an offence for which an adult could be sentenced to life, and two years for all other offences (section 42(2)(q)). Given the qualifying criteria set out in section 42(7) there will, in fact, be very few young offenders who can actually be committed to rehabilitative custody.

Other questions arise about this sentence in regards to its constitutional validity. Under the section 96 division of powers, medical including psychiatric treatment, consent and capacity to treatment are within the jurisdiction of the provinces. The constitutional vulnerability of this provision of the YCJA is also an issue to consider given the section 7 guarantee that no treatment can be ordered for a capable person without their consent and the absence of such a requirement in the new provision. The Supreme Court of Canada has recognized the difference between rehabilitation and involuntary treatment, with the former being allowable in criminal sentencing, the latter not.[150]

With respect to custody issues, the distinction between open and secure custody as established in section 24.1 of the YOA is gone. Under Part 5 of the new Act, a province is required to have at least two levels of custody(section 85(1)) and it is the provincial director who decides the level of placement, not the sentencing court (section 85(3)). The province can opt to delegate this decision with respect to placement and review of placement to the youth court (section 88). Section 85(5)(a) requires that the level of custody be the least restrictive to the young person having regard to factors such as the seriousness of the offence, the needs and circumstances of the young person, the safety of the young person, and the interests of society. This section mirrors section 24.1(4) of the YOA.

Provision for review of a placement decision made by a provincial director are contained in section 87 of the Act. In section 87 there is no guarantee that the young person has a right to be represented by counsel at review hearings before the independent board constituted to hear the application. Section 87(5) indicates that the decision of the review board is final.

Under the YCJA, all custodial orders made under section 42(2)(n) must be divided into two periods: the first being a period served in custody and the second being community supervision. The second period of community supervision must be half as long as the first, or in other words, the total custodial and supervision order is divided into two-thirds custody and one-third supervision. This practice is clearly recognizable as patterned after the "statutory remission" portioning in adult sentences.

Under the YCJA, maximum sentences for first and second-degree murder are maintained as they were in the YOA (section 42(2)(q). For these two offences the strict two-thirds custody/one-third supervision calculation is relaxed. For all other offences the maximum custodial period, including supervision period, is two years, except where the offence would be punishable by life imprisonment for an adult. In that case, the maximum total custodial order is for three years (section 42(2)(o)). New to the YCJA is a

---

150 See *R. v. Swain* (1991), 63 C.C.C. (3d) 481 (S.C.C.) at 530.

sentencing provision that allows for a "deferred custody and supervision order" (section 42(2)(p)). This provision allows the Court to make an order deferring custody and supervision where the total order is for not more than six months, subjecting the young person to the same conditions as contained in a probation order under section 55. Resembling on the face of it the conditional sentence provisions for adults, the deferred sentence option in the YCJA actually contains restrictions on its application that make it much more limited than its adult equivalent. First of all, a conditional sentence is available under section 742.1 of the *Criminal Code* where the sentence imposed is of less than two years, whereas a deferred custody order is only available for sentences of less than six months. Furthermore, section 42(5) of the YCJA limits deferred custody orders to sentences for non-violent offences only, while case law has established that conditional sentences are not restricted to any particular kind of offence.[151]

Under section 62 of the YCJA adult sentences may be imposed if a young person of 14 years of age or older is found guilty of an offence for which an adult could be sentenced to more than two years of imprisonment and: (i) the offence is one of the presumptive offences of murder, attempted murder, manslaughter or aggravated sexual assault and there is no successful application under section 63 to remain in the YCJA sentencing scheme, or (ii) in the case of all other offences, including the presumptive offence defined in section 2(1) of the Act, the Attorney General makes a successful application under section 64 to have the adult sentencing scheme apply. The test for determining which sentencing scheme is to apply under the YCJA is whether the Court is of the opinion that a youth sentence would or would not be in accordance with the purpose and principles of sentencing set out in section 38 of the Act (section 73).

15. STUDENT RECORDS

(a) Types of Records

The Ontario *Education Act* requires a principal to establish, maintain, retain, transfer and dispose of a student record for each student enrolled in the school.[152] The index card remains at the school and the Ontario Student Record (OSR) is transferred when the student moves to another school. There is no express provision that prevents educators from keeping other kinds of records provided, of course, that the *Municipal Freedom of Information and Protection of Privacy Act* allows for the collection and retention of the specific information.[153]

---

151 See *R. v. W.(J.)* (1997), 5 C.R. (5th) 248, 115 C.C.C. (3d) 18 (Ont. C.A.).
152 *Education Act*, s. 265(1)(d).
153 R.S.O. 1990, c. M.56.

(b) Confidentiality

The Ontario Ministry of Education "Ontario Student Record Guideline" advises that, because subsection 266(2) of the *Education Act* states that the OSR will not be produced in the course of any legal proceedings, boards should obtain legal advice in order to deal with requests for access by law enforcement and other agencies, including advice about issues as to whether the Act prevents the production of the OSR, whether the OSR in question is relevant to the proceedings and, if the OSR is relevant, whether a copy, rather than the original, may be submitted to the Court. The OSR Guideline notes that both the municipal and provincial *Freedom of Information Acts* (FOI) permit disclosure of personal information for the purposes of law enforcement. It is not always clear whether and how the "FOI" legislation applies.

The following are excerpts from the Guidelines:

> In court proceedings, subject to an appeal, the judge's order must be followed. If a principal receives a court order requiring the release of an OSR, the principal should contact the board's legal counsel. Although court orders must be followed, the principal should obtain legal advice about the issues listed above.
>
> A principal may be served with a subpoena requiring that he or she appear in court on a particular date and bring part or all of an OSR. If a principal receives a subpoena, he or she must comply with it, but should obtain legal advice from the board's legal counsel.
>
> As a general rule, the principal should go to court with both the original OSR and a complete and exact photocopy of it, and should propose to the judge that the photocopy be submitted instead of the original. The principal should also inform the judge that the subpoena is inconsistent with subsection 266(2) of the *Education Act*. The principal must, however, relinquish the documents if ordered to do so by the judge.
>
> The *Criminal Code* is federal legislation; where there is a conflict between it and provincial legislation, it takes precedence. Therefore, if a principal is served with a search warrant under the *Criminal Code* requiring the surrender of an OSR to the police, or is served with a subpoena requiring his or her appearance at court with the OSR, he or she is obliged to comply with the search warrant or the subpoena. In both cases, the principal should obtain legal advice from the board's legal counsel.
>
> Under the *Child and Family Services Act*, it is possible for a court to order a principal of a school to produce a student's OSR for inspection and copying. A court may make such an order if it is satisfied that (a) a record contains information that may be relevant to a consideration of whether a child is suffering abuse or likely to suffer abuse, and (b) the person in control of the record has refused to permit a Children's Aid Society director to inspect it. If a principal receives a court order under the *Child and Family Services Act*, he or she should seek legal advice about how to comply with it.

A teacher could not disclose to the parent of an adult student any information contained in the student's record without the student's written consent. The Act's confidentiality provisions apply only to information that properly belongs in the OSR. In one case it was held that students' statements concerning injuries to another student should not have been included in the students' OSR, because this information was not relevant to their instruction.[154]

(c) Correcting Information

The Ontario *Education Act* provides that a parent or guardian of a pupil under the age of 18, or a pupil 18 or older, may request the correction or removal of personal information in the OSR. The *Education Act* also establishes a review mechanism for parents or pupils in the event of a dispute over a requested correction.

Subsection 36(2)(a) of the *Municipal Freedom of Information and Protection of Privacy Act* also provides individuals with a right to correct personal information records maintained by an institution – in this case a school board. Subsection 54(c) of the Act states that "any right or power conferred on an individual by this Act" may be exercised by a person in lawful custody of the individual if the individual is under the age of 16. In other words, subsection 54(c) of the Act allows a custodial parent access to a child's personal information pursuant to subsection 36(2) of the Act. If the individual is 16, a parent cannot make such a request under subsection 36(2) for correction of the child's information.

This does not mean that a parent of a pupil between the ages of 16 and 18 cannot make a request for correction or removal of personal information in an OSR pursuant to the *Education Act*. The age restriction in subsection 54(c) of the *Municipal Freedom of Information and Protection of Privacy Act* operates only for the purposes of the Act and does not derogate from the rights or powers of parents under the *Education Act*. Parents of pupils who are under the age of 18 continue to enjoy the right to request removal or correction of personal information about the pupil in the OSR when such request is made pursuant to the *Education Act*.

The relevant provincial and federal legislation with respect to the disclosure of third party records was thoroughly canvassed in the recent decision of *R. v. Keukens*.[155]

The accused, a high school teacher, was charged with sexually assaulting a student. The defence hired a private investigator who was instructed to interview with teachers and students. The principal took the position, based on section 266 of the *Education Act*, that no teachers had the right to

---

154 *Cook v. Dufferin-Peel (R.C. Separate School Bd.)* (1983), 34 C.P.C. 178 (Ont. Master).
155 (1995), 23 O.R. (3d) 582 (Gen. Div.).

discuss any information relating to the education of any of the students without the consent of their parents, or the students if they were over 18. The *Education Act* invokes a statutory privilege with respect to records to be kept by the OSR Guidelines. In addition, the *Municipal Freedom of Information and Protection and Privacy Act,* with exceptions, prohibits the voluntary release of records, containing personal information, which are in the possession, custody or control of an institution, including a school board. The latter statute provides that disclosure of recorded personal information relating, for example, to educational history, constitutes an unjustified invasion of personal privacy.[156]

On application by the accused, and on consent of the Board of Education (RA having consented to the release of his records), all records relating to RA, including his Ontario Student Record, were produced to the defence. The defence felt that the limits placed on what teachers could say to the investigator placed a "total gag" on it. The defence sought an order that the Board of Education "cease and desist from interfering with defence counsel's access to witnesses and in particular that it cease and desist from advising, instructing, and or ordering its employees in such a way so as to limit or prevent employees' participation in interviews with defence counsel or its agents".

The court dismissed the application. Regarding records under the school's control, disclosure was not required based on *Stinchcombe* as the information was not in the prosecution's possession. The school does not have a statutory protection for its records. The Board may have a confidentiality interest in the recorded information, but this can be waived by the student. The *Municipal Freedom of Information and Privacy Act* prohibits the voluntary release of records containing personal information in the possession of an institution. The Court commented that in the absence of a parent's written permission, there is no authority to implement the procedure of informally allowing the party with the subpoena access to school records. Also, the board should not counsel a subpoenaed employee to engage in an informal interview with the defence to discuss matters statutorily prohibited from disclosure except with student consent or pursuant to a court order. The Court questioned whether the materiality threshold for the issuance of a subpoena had been met, but held that production of the documents would advance the interests of justice since the complainant did not object to production, and the Board was prepared to provide the records.

To assert that less than complete access to potential witnesses constitutes an infringement of the applicant's right to full answer and defence, the

---

156 See further Judith Anderson, "Production of Student Records," The Canadian School Executive, May 1996, pp. 26-27 and Bertha Greenstein "Confidentiality of Student Records, Including Counsellor's Notes", (1996) Education and Law Journal, pp. 334-337.

applicant must establish that the infringement has been caused by a governmental actor. The applicant submitted that societal objectives for privacy issues do not inform the situation of verbal disclosure of the same information. The Court held that it is not an aspect of fundamental justice that an accused enjoys a right of unrestricted access to all information because a criminal charge has been laid. The legislation addresses the collection, use, disclosure and privacy of information held by institutions.

The purpose of the statute would be undermined by oral release of recorded information. The defence is free to interview Board employees as long as the teachers are prepared to cooperate and the interviewees do not draw upon recorded information concerning students.

It should be noted that the Supreme Court of Canada has further determined the substantive law and third-party disclosure or private records *(e.g.,* school records, private diaries, social worker records) as a result of two of its decisions released on December 14, 1995.[157]

The Court unanimously held that someone accused of sexual assault is entitled to production of the complainant's private medical and sexual assault counselling records which are in hands of third parties, such as therapists and rape crisis centres, if certain requirements are met.

Significantly, the judges split 5-4 on the precise test for production. All judges were unanimous in rejecting the positions taken by some of the parties and interveners, which advocated, at one end of the spectrum, a complete ban on disclosure of private records in sex assault cases, and at the other extreme, a virtually automatic right of production to the accused. Both the minority and majority also endorsed a two-stage test and procedure for production. At stage one, the onus was on the accused to satisfy the trial judge that the sought-after information is "likely to be relevant", which suggests that "there is a reasonable possibility that the information is logically probative to an issue at trial or the competence of the witness to testify".

(d) Disclosure to Parents

Can a school board disclose certain information about a pupil who is 16 or 17 years of age to the pupil's parents? To be more specific, in situations where a student is skipping classes, or has engaged in misconduct at the school, does subsection 54(c) of the Act implicitly prohibit the school from disclosing such information to the parent of a pupil who is 16 or 17 unless the student consents to such disclosure?

Regulation 298 authorizes a principal to "report promptly any neglect of duty or infraction of the school rules by a pupil [defined as a child up to the age of eighteen] to the parent or guardian of the pupil".[158] Subsection

---
157 *R. v. O'Connor* (1996), 103 C.C.C. (3d) 1 (S.C.C.) and *A.(L.L.) v. B.(A.)* (1995), 103 C.C.C. (3d) 92 (S.C.C.).
158 R.R.O. 1990, Reg. 298, s. 11(3)(n).

32(e) of the *Municipal Freedom of Information and Protection of Privacy Act* states that an institution may disclose personal information for the purpose of complying with an Act or an agreement or an arrangement under the Act. Regulations passed under the authority of a statute come within the meaning of subsection 32(e) and therefore can provide a school board with the necessary authority to disclose personal information under subsection 32(e). Regulation 298 establishes the authority of a school principal to contact parents about infractions of school rules by pupils under the age of 18.

The authority in the regulation is not qualified or reduced by subsection 54(c) of the Act. Subsection 54(c) merely entitles the parent to exercise the child's rights and powers on behalf of the child for any purpose under the Act. For example, under subsection 54(c) of the Act, a parent of a child under the age of 16 may request access to the child's personal information in the same way a child may access his or her own information under subsection 36(1) of the Act; a parent may provide consent on behalf of a child under 16 for various purposes in Part II of the Act; and a parent may receive a notice of collection of personal information on behalf of a child pursuant to subsection 29(2).

Where another statute (or a regulation) confers separate authority to disclose personal information about individuals over the age of 16, such authority is not qualified by subsection 54(c) of the *Municipal Freedom of Information and Protection of Privacy Act*. The Act does not require school boards to obtain consent from pupils aged 16 to 18 to disclose information to parents which may be properly revealed under subsection 11(3)(n) of Regulation 298.

Arguably a 16-year-old has the right to prevent information from being shared with his or her parents under the MFOIPPA unless the information relates to a discipline issue as set out in Regulation 298, section 11 (3)(n). See also section 32(e) of the Act. A parent of course has access to an OSR up to the student reaching 18 years of age. The student's written consent to disclosure is required if he or she is 18 years of age or over.

5

Special Education

1. INTRODUCTION 281
   (a) Different Perspectives 282
2. SPECIAL EDUCATION LAW IN ONTARIO 284
   (a) Introduction 284
   (b) Duty of the Minister of Education 285
   (c) Duty of a School Board 286
   (d) Identification and Placement Process 288
   (e) Review 290
   (f) Appeals from IPRC Decisions 290
   (g) The Special Education Tribunal 291
   (h) The Individual Education Plan 292
   (i) The Transition Plan 293
3. DISCIPLINE OF EXCEPTIONAL PUPILS 293
4. CHARTER AND HUMAN RIGHTS ISSUES 296

1. INTRODUCTION

Special education law in progressive jurisdictions follows a fairly standard set of principles. The first principle is that pupils with a disability or other condition that affects their ability to learn have a right to special education, i.e., programs and services that are designed to improve their chance of success in school. The second underlying principle is that the publicly-funded school system must provide special education programs and services. The third principle is that there must be a defined process for the identification and placement of exceptional pupils and that the process must be procedurally and substantively fair. That process is designed to do two things: ensure that children who *should* be identified as exceptional *are* identified and ensure that parents have ample opportunity to have their wishes heard.

One would have thought that the need to adhere to these principles is self-evident but they only became reflected in the law after decades of an approach to education which often did not listen to parents and which sometimes effectively shunted disabled pupils off into wholly inappropriate schools and programs and disregarded their right to be educated in an integrated setting with their peers. As societal attitudes toward the disabled and handicapped became more understanding and accommodating, so too did attitudes toward the need for special education. The first attempt at giving some protection to exceptional pupils in Ontario was in 1980 (by the *Education Law Amendment Act, 1980*) and Ontario common and statutory law has continued to evolve since then, particularly in response to the *Canadian Charter of Rights and Freedoms*, Human Rights legislation, often mirroring developments in the United States.

Despite the substantive and procedural legal protection now provided to special education pupils, "special education" remains a highly litigious area of education law. This can hardly be surprising because the ideals involved are deeply felt. The milieu in which the law must operate is highly emotional and often political. The legal and policy tensions in special education result from a multi-faceted dynamic that goes well beyond a straightforward disagreement between parent and teacher. The tensions are about whose philosophy of education is right, and about which programs work best.[1]

Conflict between parents and a school board can occur at a number of different points. They may differ as to whether or not a pupil is "exceptional" at all, or as to the particular exceptionality or exceptionalities that the pupil has. They may also disagree as to the placement of the pupil, and, more particularly, as to what supports and services should be provided. Questions abound. Should the pupil attend a neighbourhood school?[2] How much of the school day should be spent in a regular classroom versus a withdrawal setting? Is an aide required and for how long? Who will ensure that medication, suctioning and diapering are administered or provided? What guarantee is there that a pupil with behavioural difficulties will not harm himself or herself, school staff or other pupils? To what extent should the child be accommodated when taking a test mandated by a provincial body such as Ontario's Education Quality and Accountability Office? Does the placement of the pupil require special transportation arrangements?

(a) Different Perspectives

Special education gives rise to legal issues because it involves so many potentially different perspectives or "interests" that may, expressly or impliedly, influence or attempt to influence the education that is provided to

---

1 For example, see *Lewis (Next Friend of) v. York Region Board of Education* (1996) 27 C.H.R.R. D/261 (Ont. Bd. of Inquiry) (at paragraphs 33 to 39) in which a Human Rights Board of Inquiry (M. R. Gorsky) refers to the debate between the parties about integration, segregation and the "Cascade Model".
2 See *Murray v. Montrose County School District*, 51 3d Cir 921 (U.S. 10th Cir., 1995), certiori denied 116 S. Ct. 1418 (1996) in which the Tenth Circuit held that the U.S. Federal IDEA legislation does not contain a presumption that the neighbourhood school is the least restrictive environment. Moreover, in Ontario, a board has a right to determine the attendance area for each of its schools; there is no right to attend a particular school.

an exceptional pupil. Six major perspectives that readily come to mind are those of government, school board, board staff, advocacy organizations, parents, and the individual pupil whose education is under consideration.

A provincial government faces, in special education, the same challenge it faces with respect to providing other social benefits: what level of service can it provide in a fiscally responsible manner while ensuring that exceptional children receive an appropriate education? This involves weighing budgetary considerations against the ideal of providing optimal programming and services for each exceptional pupil. The provincial government also has an interest in ensuring the accountability of boards in terms of, for example, how funds are spent, the programs and services that are offered, and the qualifications of staff.[3] However, it is a frequent complaint of Ontario teachers that the paperwork required to access certain kinds of special education funding is too complex and time-consuming.

School boards often find themselves in the difficult position of having to comply with provincial regulatory, policy and funding requirements while explaining to parents and others why the program, service or placement they want is unavailable or does not meet their expectations. Boards are required to comply with a myriad set of laws that are explained in more detail in this chapter. The difficulty for a school board is that failure to adhere to all of the procedures set out in the *Education Act* and regulations exposes the board to litigation claiming that the process by which a pupil is identified or placed is materially defective or unfair. It is often easier to attack an administrative decision on procedural rather than substantive grounds (because courts are loath to enter the arena of pedagogy and education policy). Scrupulous attention must therefore be paid to giving parents (and others) proper notice of meetings and a full opportunity to participate. An Identification, Placement and Review Committee and an appeal board must only consider materials, documents and assessments that they are entitled to consider, having regard to section 266 of the *Education Act* (pupil records), the privacy legislation and the *Health Care Consent Act, 1996*. In addition, placements must not be changed without fulfilling the necessary procedures under O. Reg. 181/98.

Special education teachers and other professional staff such as psychometrists, speech language therapists and aides, draw upon their training and experience to decide, as a team, how best to deliver educational programs and services that are suited to each exceptional pupil. Their professional appraisal of the situation may differ from the parents' "lay" perspective, and where this occurs, the key is to reconcile different viewpoints

---

[3] Ontario Regulation 298 provides that teachers of special education must hold qualifications beyond their basic teaching certificate.

without resort to litigation. Indeed, the Ministry of Education recommends resort to mediation between school boards and parents where they require the assistance of a third party to resolve their differences.

Parents' wishes should clearly be the starting point for how their children are educated, and parents of exceptional pupils are no different in this regard. That being said, education of pupils with exceptionalities is often pedagogically complex, and parents may not have the training to be able to understand why one teaching approach is likely to be better than another. Parents should have the first word but not necessarily the last one. As mentioned above, it should hardly be surprising that parents should be able to participate in decision-making about their child's special education, and yet, a large part of special education law is taken up with exactly that requirement.

To the extent that a pupil has an individual perspective of his or her own, that perspective should be weighed in devising an approach to the pupil's education. Ontario law provides for formal input from a pupil who is 16 years of age or older (which we refer to as "16+") during the identification and placement process.[4]

There are numerous organizations and advocacy groups in the field of special education, and a government that fails to consult with them does so at its political peril. Ontario law in fact provides several mechanisms for these organizations to provide their input, including representation on school boards' special education advisory committees. These organizations are vocal and effective. Indeed, some of them were the impetus for existing special education laws. They often focus on ensuring that the interests of pupils within a group having a particular disability or condition are protected, and to this end, they will take up the cause of individual students.

2. SPECIAL EDUCATION LAW IN ONTARIO

(a) Introduction

Ontario special education laws and policies are built on a fairly straightforward set of components, although these are rendered complicated by the sheer number of requirements and directives aimed at school boards and their staff. The primary component is the "identification" of a pupil as "exceptional". If the pupil is exceptional, his or her "placement" must be determined. The law allows parents to appeal decisions regarding identification and placement. The law also requires that the school have an individual "plan" for each exceptional pupil. These and other legal require-

---

4 When a pupil achieves the legal age of majority at 18 years, the pupil has the legal right to make educational decisions on his or her own behalf, assuming he or she otherwise has the capacity to do so.

ments, such as the need for periodic "reviews", are discussed below. The objectives of Ontario special education law are (1) to ensure that an exceptional pupil receives an "appropriate" education and (2) to ensure that parents have a say in the decision-making process. These protections are an important exception to the general approach in the realm of publicly-funded education, inasmuch as parents of non-exceptional pupils do not have access to a legal process to force changes in the school or classroom in respect of the way their children are taught, and boards are only obligated to provide an "adequate" education to pupils in regular educational classes and programs.

From an administrative law perspective, another remarkable aspect of Ontario special education law is that the Special Education Tribunal represents an almost[5] unique area in which certain educational decision-making can be taken out of the hands of the elected trustees. Not only do parents have a say *throughout* the process, but they are able to go to a special tribunal. Other decisions of school boards about education policy and programming are within the exclusive purview of boards and are virtually unassailable in court. Aside from the narrow grounds for judicial review (mostly based on procedural fairness), there is simply no "higher body" to go to that has the statutory authority to undo what a board decides.

(b) Duty of the Minister of Education

Subsection 8(3) of the *Education Act*[6] states as follows:

> 8(3) The Minister shall ensure that all exceptional children in Ontario have available to them, in accordance with this Act and the regulations, appropriate special education programs and special education services without payment of fees by parents or guardians resident in Ontario, and shall provide for the parents and guardians to appeal the appropriateness of the special education placement, and for these purposes the Minister shall,
>
> (a) require school boards to implement procedures for early and ongoing identification of the learning abilities and needs of pupils, and shall prescribe standards in accordance with which such procedures be implemented; and
>
> (b) in respect of special education programs and services, define exceptionalities of pupils, and prescribe classes, groups or categories of exceptional pupils, and require boards to employ such definitions or use such prescriptions as established under this clause.

The term "exceptional pupil" is defined in section 1 of the *Education Act*, as follows:

---

5 Some expulsion appeals are now heard by an external entity; see Chapter 4.
6 R.S.O. 1990, c. E-2 as amended.

"exceptional pupil" means a pupil whose behavioural, communicational, intellectual, physical or multiple exceptionalities are such that he or she is considered to need placement in a special education program by a committee, established under subparagraph iii of paragraph 5 of subsection 11(1), of the board,

    (a)   of which the pupil is a resident pupil,

    (b)   that admits or enrols the pupil other than pursuant to an agreement with another board for the provision of education, or

    (c)   to which the cost of education in respect of the pupil is payable by the Minister;

The Minister of Education clarified what is meant by the five categories of exceptionality referred to in the above definition (behavioural, communicational, intellectual, physical or multiple) in a memorandum to school boards dated January 15, 1999. The clarification of these terms is also available in the Ministry's "Special Education: A Guide for Educators" dated October 2001.

"Special education program" and "special education services" are defined in section 1 of the *Education Act* as follows:

"special education program" means, in respect of an exceptional pupil, an educational program that is based on and modified by the results of continuous assessment and evaluation and that includes a plan containing specific objectives and an outline of educational services that meets the needs of the exceptional pupil;

"special education services" means facilities and resources, including support personnel and equipment, necessary for developing and implementing a special education program;

The regulations made under the *Education Act* that pertain to special education are Regulation 296 (Ontario Schools for the Blind and Deaf); sections 3(3), 11, 19, 26, 30 and 31 of Regulation 298 (Operation of Schools General); O. Reg. 181/98 (Identification and Placement of Exceptional Pupils); Regulation 306 (Special Education Programs and Services); and O. Reg. 464/97 (Special Education Advisory Committees).

(c) Duty of a School Board

A school board has a duty to provide special education programs and services to its exceptional pupils. Subsection 170(1), paragraph 7 of the *Education Act* states that a board shall:

7.   provide or enter into an agreement with another board to provide in accordance with the regulations special education programs and special education services for its exceptional pupils.

Where a board provides special education programs or services, it must establish one or more Special Education Identification, Placement and Review Committees ("IPRC"), examined in more detail below. If a board does not provide special education programs and services, it must enter into an agreement with another board to do so.[7] If a child must leave the province for medical reasons with the approval of the Ontario Health Insurance Plan, the province will pay toward the cost of his or her education. A school board is under no legal obligation to a child whose parent withdraws him or her from school in order to go to private school or to receive home schooling.

Each school board is required[8] to establish a Special Education Advisory Committee, whose duty it is: to make recommendations to the board with respect to any matter affecting the establishment, development, and delivery of special education programs and services for exceptional pupils of the board; to participate in the board's annual review of its special education plan; to participate in the board's annual budget process as it relates to special education; and to review the board's financial statements as they relate to special education.[9] Ontario Regulation 464/97 prescribes the role and composition of the Special Education Advisory Committee, whose overall purpose is to provide for input from "local associations" that further the interests and well-being of one or more groups of exceptional children or adults.

As required by the Revised Regulations of Ontario, Regulation 306, a school board must establish and maintain a "special education plan". The plan must be reviewed by the board once a year. These plans (not to be confused with Individual Education Plans) explain how the board intends to meet the needs of its exceptional pupils. The plan and any amendments must be kept on file with the Minister of Education, who can require a board to change its plan. Ontario Regulation 181/98 requires each board to prepare a guide for the use and information of parents and pupils. The required contents of the guide are listed in subsection 13(1) of the regulation and they must include, for example, an outline of IPRC procedures, an explanation of the function of an appeal board, a list of local associations, and information as to whether the board purchases special education from another board.

---

7 O. Reg. 181/98 contains several provisions that allow for the board purchasing the program or service to have input into the process at the providing school board. See, e.g., ss. 22(2) and 28(5). *Lanark, Leeds & Grenville) Roman Catholic Separate School Board) v. Ontario (Human Rights Commission)* (1987), 60 O.R. (2d) 441 (Div. Ct.) affirmed (1989), 67 O.R. (2d) 479 (C.A.) held that a Roman Catholic separate board is entitled to enter into an agreement with a public board for the provision of special education. O. Reg. 181/98 also contains provisions dealing with circumstances in which a pupil is referred to a school board from a provincially operated "demonstration" school.
8 *Education Act*, s. 57.1(1).
9 O. Reg. 464/97 ss. 11 and 12.

(d) Identification and Placement Process

The formal process by which a pupil is determined to be "exceptional" begins with the identification of the pupil's exceptionality by an Identification, Placement, and Review Committee (IPRC). Ontario Regulation 181/98 sets out the requirements for the establishment and operation of IPRC's. It is noteworthy that section 9 of O. Reg. 181/98 states that no pupil can be denied an education program pending any meeting or decision under the regulation. Pending a meeting or decision the pupil must be placed in a program appropriate to his or her strengths and needs, the placement must adhere to the principles in section 17 of the regulation, and appropriate education services must be provided to meet the pupil's apparent needs.

A school board must establish one or more IPRC's (O. Reg. 181/98 section 10). Where there is more than one, the referral of a pupil is made to the IPRC that is considered most appropriate for the pupil having regard to the jurisdiction of the committees (section 14(5)). An IPRC is composed of at least three persons, one of whom must be a principal or a supervisory officer (section 11(2)). The role of the IPRC is to decide whether or not the pupil should be identified as exceptional; to identify the pupil's exceptionality; to decide an appropriate placement for the student; and to review the identification and placement at least once in each school year. A committee may make recommendations about special education programs and special education services but it cannot make decisions about them (section 16); such decisions are within the purview of the school board. It is not always easy to distinguish between a decision about placement and one which affects the delivery of programs and services.

A referral to an IPRC may be initiated either by a principal or a parent or where applicable, a guardian (section 14(1)). A principal may refer a pupil to an IPRC on his or her own initiative, with written notice to the pupils' parents, when the principal and the pupil's teacher(s) believe that the pupil may benefit from a special education program. The principal *must* make a referral upon written request of a parent. Within 15 days of receiving such a request, or of giving a parent notice of a referral, the principal must give the parent a copy of the board's "Parents' Guide to Special Education".

Parents (and pupils 16 years of age or older) are entitled under O. Reg. 181/98 to be present at and to participate in all committee discussions about the pupil, and to be present when the committee's identification and placement decision is made. As mentioned, the IPRC must include a principal or a supervisory officer of the board. Others in attendance at an IPRC meeting will likely include resource persons such as the pupil's classroom teacher, special education teachers and support staff. The parent or pupil (16 years or older) may bring a representative with them who can provide support or speak on their behalf. An interpreter may also attend, e.g., for sign language. A parent or the principal of the pupil's school may request that others be permitted to attend the IPRC meeting. O. Reg. 181/98, section 14, provides for how the parent and pupil (16+) are to be given notice of the meeting, along with copies of information to be used at the meeting.

An IPRC is intended to be an informal meeting; it is not a hearing. The IPRC will review the relevant information about the student and to this end may consider an educational assessment of the pupil, and may also consider a health or psychological assessment of the pupil (subject to the *Health Care Consent Act, 1996*). The IPRC may interview the pupil, (with parental consent if the pupil is under 16 years), and may consider any information submitted by the parent or pupil (if 16+) (section 15). The IPRC may discuss a proposal by a parent or pupil (16+) about a special education program or special education services for the pupil (section 16).

The IPRC must provide a written statement of its decision, stating whether it has identified the pupil as exceptional (section 18). If the pupil is identified as exceptional, the decision will state the categories and definitions of any identified "exceptionalities" (as defined by the Ministry of Education), the pupil's strengths and needs, the decision as to the pupil's placement; and any recommendations regarding a special education program and special education services for the pupil. It is important to note that the committee may only make recommendations about "special education programs" and "special education services" because these remain within the jurisdiction of the school board. If the IPRC has decided that the pupil should be placed in a special education class, as opposed to a regular class, it shall provide reasons for that decision. Before considering whether the pupil should be placed in a special education class, the committee must consider whether placement in a regular class, with appropriate special education services, would meet the pupil's needs and whether this placement is consistent with the parental preferences (section 17). Placement in a regular classroom with appropriate special education services is therefore the starting point (section 17(2)). However, although parent preferences must be considered, they are not determinative of the placement issue if the pupil's needs dictate otherwise. This approach is consistent with the decision of the Supreme Court of Canada in *Eaton v. Brant (County) Board of Education*[10] discussed below.

If the parent agrees with the IPRC decision, he or she will be asked to sign the statement of decision. If the parent does not agree with either the identification or placement decision, he or she may, within 15 days of receiving of the decision, request a meeting with the committee to discuss

---

10 [1997] 1 S.C.R. 241.

the decision (section 19). The IPRC will then determine whether to make any changes to its decision and may issue an amended statement. The IPRC decision shall be implemented if the parent either consents to the IPRC decision or fails to appeal the decision (section 20).

(e) Review

Another function performed by the IPRC committee is to hold reviews of the identification or placement of pupils. A review may be conducted on written notice to the parent or at the request of a parent. Parents and pupils (16+) have the right to participate in the review process, as with the identification and placement process, and they must be given a written statement of the committee's decision either confirming the pupil's current status or making changes to the identification or placement. Here, again, the parent or pupil (16+) may request a follow-up meeting to discuss the decision, and the parent has the right to appeal a decision. A parent cannot request a review until after a placement has been in effect for at least three months (section 21(2)). A review must be held within each school year, unless an IPRC decision has already been made in the year, or the parent gives the principal notice dispensing of the need for the review (section 21(4)).

(f) Appeals from IPRC Decisions

The first stage in the appeal process prescribed in O. Reg. 181/98 provides the right of a parent to appeal to a Special Education Appeal Board in respect of an IPRC decision that a pupil is or is not exceptional, and with respect of the placement (section 26). The regulation provides for the period within which notice must be given (30 days of receipt of the decision or 15 days of receipt of a notice following a follow-up meeting to discuss the decision). These time-limits may be waived by a board. It should be noted, too, that no appeal right is given to the (non-adult) pupil or to the school board. The notice of appeal must state what the parent disagrees with and the nature of the disagreement, but cannot be rejected by the school board merely because of a deficiency in the notice or a failure to accurately indicate the subject of the disagreement (section 26(4) and (5)). Section 27 of the regulation outlines the composition of the Appeal Board. It is comprised of three persons: one selected by the school board, one selected by the parent and the third by the nominees of the school board and parent (or the Regional Office of the Ministry if no agreement). No member or employee of the school board (or purchasing board) can serve on the Appeal Board, nor can anyone who has had prior involvement in the matter.

The Appeal Board is required to conduct a "meeting" to discuss the matters under appeal, and may invite anyone who it considers may be able to contribute information. Within three days of the meeting, the Appeal Board must state whether it agrees with the IPRC and recommends implementation of the IPRC's decision, or disagrees with the IPRC. If it disagrees, it may make recommendations to the school board with respect to the identification or placement or both. It must send a statement of its recommendations to the parent, pupil (16+), chair of the IPRC, relevant principal, designated representative of the board where the pupil is placed, and designated representative of the purchasing board (where applicable). It must give reasons for its recommendations.

The Appeal Board only has the power to make recommendations. It is incumbent on the school board to consider the recommendations and decide, within 30 days of receiving the recommendations, what action to take with respect to the pupil. The school board's decision is not limited to what the Appeal Board recommended or could have recommended. When the school board advises the parent of its decision, it must also advise of the right to appeal further to a Special Education Tribunal under section 57 of the *Education Act*. The school board may implement its decision if the parent consents or fails to appeal under section 57 within 30 days of receipt of the school board's decision, or if an appeal under section 57 is either dismissed or abandoned. (O. Reg. 181/98, section 31) Therefore, if there is an appeal to a Special Education Tribunal, there is in effect a "stay" in the ability of the school board to proceed to implement the decision. This requires the school board and parent to work together to find a suitable interim solution, on the understanding that their interim agreement will not prejudice any position they may wish to take before the Tribunal. In addition, the school board and parent can (and should) "keep talking" about the school board's determination during the 30-day appeal period or during the time pending a final decision from the Tribunal, because the school is permitted to change its decision in agreement with the parent (who can nevertheless still appeal the new decision to the Tribunal).

(g) The Special Education Tribunal

The Lieutenant Governor in Council (i.e., Cabinet) may establish one or more Special Education Tribunals. Members are appointed by Order in Council, and sit in three-person panels that include the chair and two other members selected by the chair from a roster of appointees. The right to appeal a school board's decision to the Tribunal is set out in subsection 57(3) of the *Education Act*. Only a parent (or adult pupil) may appeal. Subsection 57(3) states:

> 57(3) Where a parent or guardian of a pupil has exhausted all rights of appeal under the regulations in respect of the identification or placement of the pupil as an exceptional pupil and is dissatisfied with the decision in respect of

the identification or placement, the parent or guardian may appeal to the Special Education Tribunal for a hearing in respect of the identification or placement.

A request for a hearing is made through the Secretary of the Tribunal at the Ministry of Education. The parent has 30 days to provide notice of the appeal. The Secretary will notify the school board of the request for a Tribunal, and will perform other administrative tasks in respect of setting up the date and location of the hearing. The parent will be expected to submit in advance of the hearing particulars about the grounds of the appeal and the order that he or she seeks from the Tribunal. The school board is required to file a response to the parent's submission. Both parties are required to provide an estimate of how long the hearing is expected to take, and to state how many witnesses they expect to call. They should also give notice of any preliminary issues that they wish to raise.

Subsection 57(4) of the *Education Act* states:

> 57(4) The Special Education Tribunal shall hear the appeal and may,
>
> (a) dismiss the appeal; or
>
> (b) grant the appeal and make such order as it considers necessary with respect to the identification or placement.

There is no right of the Tribunal to decide what special education programs or special education services the Board must provide, although inasmuch as the IPRC can make recommendations on these topics, it would appear that the Tribunal may also make recommendations.

A decision of the Tribunal is final and binding on the parties to the decision.[11] The practice and procedure before the Tribunal is governed by the *Statutory Powers Procedure Act*[12] because the Tribunal exercises a statutory power of decision and is required to hold a hearing. This means, among other things, witnesses may be cross-examined, that parties have a right to be represented by a lawyer or agent, that the Tribunal may issue a summons, and that the Tribunal's decision is enforceable by filing it in Superior Court.

(h) The Individual Education Plan

When a school board implements a placement decision, it must notify the principal of the school at which the special education program is to be provided of the need to develop an individual education plan (IEP) for the pupil. It must be developed within 30 days of such notification and this must be done in consultation with the parent and the pupil (16+). The IEP

---

11 *Rowett v. York Region (Bd. of Education)* (1988), 63 O.R. (2d) 767 (H.C) reversed (1989), 69 O.R. (2d) 543 (C.A.).

12 R.S.O. 1990, c. S.22 as amended.

must include (a) special education expectations for the pupil, (b) an outline of the special education program and services to be received by the pupil and (c) a statement of the methods by which the pupil's progress will be reviewed (O. Reg. 181/98, section 6(3)).

(i) The Transition Plan

Where the pupil is 14 years of age or older, the IEP must contain a plan for transition to appropriate post-secondary school activities, such as work, further education and community living (O. Reg. 181/98, section 6(4)). A pupil whose sole exceptionality is that he or she is gifted does not require a transition plan. If a pupil's placement is changed, the school board is required to review the IEP to determine if it also needs to be changed. The parent and pupil (16+) must be provided with a copy of the IEP. An IEP may also be prepared for pupils who are receiving special education, but who have not been identified as exceptional by an IPRC.

3. DISCIPLINE OF EXCEPTIONAL PUPILS

As we have mentioned, one of the most litigious areas in education law over the past 20 years has been the educational rights of "special education" students. Ontario special education law shares many features with the law in the United States, where a huge volume of litigation has been generated by the use of discipline against pupils with physical, mental or behavioural disabilities. The issue of how disciplinary practices and codes apply to these pupils has been especially challenging, particularly in an era of zero tolerance. School boards have grappled with the question of what allowances or exceptions should be made within a disciplinary policy to ensure that special education (or "exceptional") pupils are not discriminated against as a result of their exceptionality.

In the United States, the Courts have devised what is known as the "manifestation doctrine" as originally articulated in *Doe v. Koger*,[13] which states that a school district may not expel a special education pupil whose misbehaviour is caused by the pupil's disability but may expel if the misbehaviour is not related to the disability. The determination of whether the misconduct was a manifestation of the disability must be made by a specialized and knowledgeable group of persons.[14] As of 1997, this principle is enshrined in the *Individuals with Disabilities Education Act*. The U.S. courts are not consistent in their determination of "manifestation". Some have held that the relationship between the disability and the misconduct

---

13 480 F. Supp. 225 (N.d. Ind. 1979).
14 *S-1 v. Turlington*, 635 F.2d 342 (U.S. 5th Cir. 1981).

must be "direct and causal" whereas other courts have permitted an indirect connection.[15]

In Chapter 4, we discuss the provisions of the *Safe Schools Act, 2000* relating to suspension and expulsion of pupils, and we pointed out that as a result of these amendments, certain infractions result in mandatory expulsion or mandatory suspension. The legislature was obviously sensitive to the difficulties of imposing a "zero tolerance" regime upon pupils to whom the broad discipline brush should not apply. Although not expressly stated in the *Education Act*, it appears that O. Reg. 37/01 and O. Reg. 106/01 are primarily designed for "special education" situations. Ontario Regulation 106/01 states that a mandatory suspension is not mandatory if: (a) the pupil does not have the ability to control his or her behaviour; (b) the pupil does not have the ability to understand the foreseeable consequences of his or her behaviour; or (c) the pupil's continuing presence in the school does not create an unacceptable risk to the safety or well-being of any person. Ontario Regulation 37/01 states that a mandatory expulsion is not mandatory if: (a) the pupil does not have the ability to control his or her behaviour; (b) the pupil does not have the ability to understand the foreseeable consequences of his or her behaviour; or (c) the pupil's continuing presence in the school does not create an unacceptable risk to the safety or well-being of any person. However, these provisions are not limited to pupils who have been "identified" as exceptional. There are, after all, pupils with disabilities who are not formally identified, and there are still other pupils who could fall within the rather vague parameters in O. Reg. 37/01 and O. Reg. 106/01.[16] Nevertheless, the purpose of these mitigating factors is to ameliorate the effects of zero tolerance and enable a board to avoid discriminating against pupils who cannot control their behaviour or do not appreciate the consequences of their actions. Moreover, quite apart from these regulations, the *Education Act* also allows a board to establish different policies for different circumstances, locations and classes of pupils. This enables boards to ensure that policies are sensitive to the requirements of exceptional pupils or others who for educational reasons should not be subject to a policy of general application.

In the United States, the two main statutes affecting the rights of special education children are the *Individuals with Disabilities Education Act* (IDEA) and what is referred to as the "Section 504" regulation under the

---

15 See Osborne J.A. Jr., *Disciplinary Options for Students with Disabilities* (Dayton, Ohio: Education Law Association, 1997), at p. 10-11.
16 In the United States, a student may still be protected from disciplinary actions such as expulsion even if he or she has not yet been identified and provided an appropriate Individual Education Plan, if it can be shown that the school had a basis of knowledge about the child's disability before the disciplinary action occurred. In other words, a school district that does not properly identify a student as disabled and in need of services may still be held liable for improperly disciplining the student.

Americans with Disabilities Act.[17] The U.S. Department of Education states that the IDEA provides protections for students experiencing educational disabilities that adversely affect educational performance, and for which specially designed instruction is necessary. Included in these protections is the right to a due process hearing when violations of the IDEA are alleged which affect the child's right to a free and appropriate public education. The IDEA provides certain rights to identified students even when they are suspended or expelled:

> When the student's misconduct is not caused by his or her disability, the general disciplinary sanction, including suspension or expulsion, may be imposed on a student with a disability. However, even in this situation, IDEA provides students with disabilities with a right not available to all students – a free and appropriate public education. In other words, if a student with a disability is suspended or expelled, the school system still has the duty to ensure that the student is provided with an interim alternative education that fully provides the services the student needs to make effective progress.[18]

The "Section 504" regulation requires school districts that receive Federal financial assistance to provide a "free appropriate public education" (FAPE) to each qualified person with a disability in its jurisdiction, regardless of the nature or severity of the disability:

> Section 504 and the ADA [Americans with Disabilities Act] require that a school district evaluate a child believed to have a disability before making an initial placement of the child in a regular or special education program and before any subsequent, significant change in her or his placement. The permanent exclusion of a child with a disability, the exclusion of a child for an indefinite period, or the exclusion of a child for more than 10 consecutive school days constitutes a "significant change in placement" under Section 504 and the ADA. In addition, a series of suspensions each of which is 10 or fewer days in duration, but that creates a pattern of exclusions, may also constitute a "significant change in placement."[19]

Based on the United States experience, it is clear that board policies and procedures must protect students who have disabilities that affect their behaviour or their ability to understand and follow school rules, lest these students turn out to be the most vulnerable in Ontario's new zero tolerance world. If the United States experience is any indication, the discipline of

---

17 "The difference between the IDEA and s. 504 requirements is due to the underlying purpose of each statute. Section 504 was designed to prevent discrimination against individuals with disabilities whereas the IDEA imposes affirmative obligations on school districts to provide special education services": Allan G. Osborne Jr. above, note 15, at p. 19.
18 Opportunities Suspended: The Devastating Consequences of Zero Tolerance and School Discipline Policies. Report by the Advancement Project and the Civil Rights Project, June 2000, available at www.law.harvard.edu/groups/civilrights/.
19 U.S. Dept. of Education.

"special education" students is where most of the litigation will occur as a result of the *Safe Schools Act, 2000* (Bill 81). The Supreme Court of Canada has already declared in *Eaton v. Brant (County) Board of Education*[20] that the interests of the child are paramount in determining an appropriate placement of an exceptional pupil. The *Education Act* provides school boards with the means (through broad policy-making powers) of ensuring fair treatment for these students. As a purely practical matter, this policy-making exercise is probably the greatest challenge for Ontario school boards under the Bill 81 provisions.

4. CHARTER AND HUMAN RIGHTS ISSUES

The extent to which the *Canadian Charter of Rights and Freedoms* applies to the actions of school boards remains to be determined. In order for the *Charter* to apply, the action of the board must be characterized as "state action". There is little doubt that the provision of special education programs and services by school boards is a "state action" and therefore subject to scrutiny under the *Charter*. Each province provides a statutory right to receive an education, provided that certain age and residency requirements are met. In most cases it is the school board that is delegated, by the province, the responsibility of providing special education programs and services. Denial of the right to receive an education because of a disability is clearly a breach of section 15 equality rights and, arguably, section 7 (right to life, liberty and security).[21]

Exceptional pupils are entitled to special education programs and services to which other children are not entitled. For instance, they may be provided with a one-on-one instructional assistant throughout the school day. The law provides them with specific entitlements because treating people equally does not always result in equality. Some pupils must be treated differently in order to have equality:

> The treatment of a person differently from others may or may not amount to discrimination just as treating people equally is not determinative of the issue. If the effect of the treatment has adverse consequences which are incompatible with the objects of the legislation by restricting or excluding a right of full and equal recognition and exercise of those rights it will be discriminatory.[22]

---

20 *Ibid.*, at note 10.
21 In *Rowett v. York Region (Bd. of Education)* (1988), 63 O.R. (2d) 767 (H.C.), the Ontario Court of Appeal ((1989), 69 O.R. (2d) 543) refused to strike *Charter* claims from a civil statement of claim by an exceptional child, leaving it to the trial judge to decide the issue of *Charter* applicability. This case was settled out of court.
22 *Sask. Human Rights Commn. v. Cdn. Odeon Theatres Ltd.* (1985), 18 D.L.R. (4th) 93 at 115 (Sack. C.A.).

In *Eaton*,[23] the Supreme Court of Canada held that the *Charter* does not give rise to a legal presumption of a right to be integrated into a regular classroom. In *Bales v. Central Okanagan (Board of School Trustees, School District 23)*,[24] the British Columbia Supreme Court decided that the board's failure to integrate the plaintiff did not infringe his section 7 *Charter* rights. As a pre-1985 case, the child's equality rights under section 15 were not argued.

In another case, *Trofimenkoff v. Saskatchewan (Minister of Education)*,[25] the province was in the process of devolving the provision of deaf education to school boards, and the plaintiffs asked the Court to prevent the closure of the provincial school for the deaf. In other words, the plaintiffs wanted a segregated, not integrated, environment. The Court found that the requirement of boards to establish special education programs for the disabled was not discriminatory and there was no denial of the plaintiffs' right to an education.

Human rights tribunals have become a forum for disputes about special education. Their mandate is to determine whether or not discrimination on a prohibited ground has occurred in the provision of services which are covered by the pertinent human rights legislation. Although it may be subject to some specific provisions, such as the protection of denominational rights, the provision of publicly-funded education in Ontario is a service covered by the *Human Rights Code*.[26] There is little room for argument that most exceptional pupils (except the gifted) would be considered to be "disabled" under the Ontario *Human Rights Code,* which contains the following definition:

"disability" means,

(a) any degree of physical disability, infirmity, malformation or disfigurement that is caused by bodily injury, birth defect or illness and, without limiting the generality of the foregoing, including diabetes mellitus, epilepsy, a brain injury, any degree of paralysis, amputation, lack of physical coordination, blindness or visual impediment, deafness or hearing impediment, muteness or speech impediment, or physical reliance on a guide dog or other animal or on a wheelchair or other remedial appliance or device,

(b) a condition of mental impairment or a developmental disability,

---

23 Above, note 10.
24 (1984), 54 B.C.L.R. 203 (B.C.S.C.).
25 [1991] 6 W.W.R. 97 (Sask. C.A.).
26 *Human Rights Code,* R.S.O. 1990, c. H.19, s. 10(1) [previously S.O. 1981, c. 53, s. 9]. *Pandori v. Peel (Bd. of Education)* (1990), 12 C.H.R.R. D/364 (Ont. Bd. of Inquiry), affirmed (1991), 80 D.L.R. (4th) 475 (*sub nom. Peel (Bd. of Education) v. Ontario (Human Rights Commn.)*) (Ont. Div. Ct.), leave to appeal to Ont. C.A. refused (1991), 3 O.R. (3d) 531n (C.A.).

(c) a learning disability, or a dysfunction in one or more of the processes involved in understanding or using symbols or spoken language,

(d) a mental disorder, or

(e) an injury or disability for which benefits were claimed or received under the insurance plan established under the *Workplace Safety and Insurance Act, 1997.*[27]

Human rights legislation does not provide the right to attend a regular classroom or to a certain kind of placement, and it does not define the type of educational programs or services to be provided by a school board or province.[28] Special education programs and services are intended to be determined through the legislative scheme for identification and placement, leading possibly to an appeal board and a Special Education Tribunal.

Some parents and experts believe that the special treatment of exceptional pupils under the law is, by itself, an infringement of human rights. School boards are placed in a legal conundrum in which some people state that failure to provide special treatment is discriminatory and others argue that the provision of special treatment is, itself, discriminatory.

A decision of the Ontario Special Education Tribunal in *Eaton v. Brant County Board of Education*[29] dealt with the issue of the integration of an exceptional pupil into a regular class of a neighbourhood school. The child's parents appealed an IPRC decision that the child be moved to a special class where the integrated class placement was not seen to be working. The parents requested that the child be placed full-time in a regular age-appropriate class, "with full accommodation of her special needs, including provision of a full-time educational assistant, any necessary assistive devices, appropriate education materials and resources, and proper training of all staff."[30]

The Special Education Tribunal decided that the placement in a special class should be upheld. It found that, while the parents were strongly of the view that their daughter should have a regular class placement, they had not observed her in school to see for themselves whether or not she could cope in such an environment. Of the three expert witnesses who gave evidence for the parents, only one had actually observed the child in the classroom

---

27 Amended S.O. 2001, c. 32, s. 27(2).
28 For a detailed examination of the human rights legislation in the Canadian provinces in respect of special education, see: W.J. Smith and W.F. Foster, "Educational Opportunity for Students with Disabilities in Canada: A Platform of Rights to Build On" (1993) 5 E.L.J. 193, at pp. 202*ff.*
29 (November 19, 1993) Ken Weber (Chair) (Ont. Special Education Trib.).
30 *Ibid.*, p. 2.

SPECIAL EDUCATION 299

(for two and one half hours) and all three stated that they were "committed to a philosophy of full inclusion (integration)."[31]

> All three witness (sic) manifest an entirely subjective view of class placement, and in fact could not reasonably be expected to testify in any other way than strongly supportive of integration. Given the absence of clear research support and clear empirical support for the integration of exceptional children like [E.]; viz., the uncertainty in the area for which they are presented as expert, and given that they did not, except for [H.S.], observe [E.] in a school setting, we do not find their testimony significant in the specific matter of [E.'s] placement.[32]

The Tribunal accepted that it was bound by the *Canadian Charter of Rights and Freedoms* and the Ontario *Human Rights Code* and stated that consideration of the *Charter* and the *Code* was within its mandate. The tribunal did not specifically respond to, or analyze, the *Charter* or *Code* arguments made by counsel, finding instead that the case law on this issue presented to it "does not have relevance in the matter of [the child's] placement."

> It is our opinion that where a school board recommends placement of a child with special needs in a special class, contrary to the wishes of the parents, and where the school board has already made extensive and significant effort to accommodate the parents' wishes by attempting to meet that child's needs in a regular class with appropriate modifications and supports, and where empirical, objective evidence demonstrates that the child's needs are not being met in the regular class, that school board is not in violation of *The Charter* or the *[Code]*.[33]

The Tribunal's review of the body of literature on placement found that it is "seriously flawed" by: (1) "poor research methods"; (2) the "polemical stance" of many of the researchers; (3) the "inherent difficulty in controlling variables"; (4) "extrapolating conclusions that fit a hypothesis rather than the other way around"; (5) "the regular use of non-cognate cases and situations to demonstrate outcomes for other cases" and, (6) "the inexplicably wide acceptance . . . of what has come to be called 'gee whiz' literature (*e.g.*, descriptive, anecdotal, journalistic, and clearly unscientific reports on individual cases of exceptionality)."[34]

The Tribunal's closing words serve as a useful reminder to parents, school boards and legal counsel:

---

31 *Ibid.*, p. 72.
32 *Ibid.*, p. 72.
33 *Ibid.*, p. 73.
34 *Ibid.*, p. 71. The Tribunal's right to conduct its own review of the literature was upheld upon application for judicial review (see below, note 39).

> The fact that the disagreement over [E. E.'s] class placement has been allowed to continue to the level of a Special Education Tribunal hearing is a grave disservice to this child. The Tribunal has no doubt that everyone involved with [E.] has her present best interests and future well-being at heart. But we also feel that both are being put at risk by an unnecessarily rigorous adherence to principle and by the tyranny of moral certainty.
>
> Having examined the historical development of this disagreement over [E.'s] placement, is it clear to us that [E.], the child, is now at risk of becoming [E.], the symbol. It is also clear to us that engaging legal counsel, turning to judicial and quasi-judicial avenues of redress, in short, taking an adversarial approach, has pushed this disagreement away from compromise and into competition, away from accommodation and into dispute. E.'s present and future well-being will not be served by going farther down this road.[35]

The parents brought an application for judicial review of the decision of the Special Education Tribunal. The Ontario Court of Justice (General Division)[36] upheld the decision of the Tribunal. Mr. Justice Adams (for the panel of three judges) stated:

> Finally, we have great difficulty in appreciating how the *Charter of Rights and Freedoms* and the Ontario *Human Rights Code* create a presumption in favour of one pedagogical theory over another, particularly when the implementation of either theory needs the protection of the saving provisions found in s. 15 of the *Charter* and s. 14 of the *Code*. But, in this case, that issue is entirely academic because the Tribunal found the evidence clearly established that [E.'s] best interests will be better served with the recommended placement.[37]

In the final analysis, the best interests of the pupil must remain the central focus — a focus which is best attained far from the third-party intervention of courts and human rights tribunals:

> [W]e echo the Tribunal's reminder that our decision does not relieve the School Board and the parents of the obligation to collaborate creatively in a continuing effort to meet [E.'s] present and future needs.[38]

The Divisional Court decision was appealed to the Ontario Court of Appeal.[39] In that Court, Arbour J.A. looked at whether Emily Eaton's placement in a special classroom was discrimination within the meaning of section 15 of the *Charter*. Clearly, Emily was placed in a special class because of her disability; a distinction had been made on a prohibited ground. The next stage of the analysis involved the issue of whether the

---

35 *Ibid.*, p. 74.
36 (1994), 71 O.A.C. 69.
37 *Ibid.*, p. 6.
38 *Ibid.*
39 (1995), 22 O.R. (3d) 1.

distinction resulted in the imposition of a burden or disadvantage, by reason of being placed in a segregated education placement. Madam Justice Arbour found:

> When a measure is offered to a disabled person, allegedly in order to provide that person with her true equality entitlement, and that measure is one of exclusion, segregation, and isolation from the mainstream, that measure, in its broad social and historical context, is properly labelled a burden or a disadvantage.[40]

In effect, this meant that the *Charter* mandates a presumption in favour of integration. Arbour J.A. went on to find that, because section 8(3) of the *Education Act* does not provide for a presumption in favour of integration, it should be read to include a direction that, unless the parents of a disabled child consent to a segregated placement, the board must provide a placement that is the least exclusionary from the mainstream and still reasonably capable of meeting the child's special educational needs. Many school boards were understandably concerned about the implications of this decision in terms of restricting their ability to provide the best educational placement for their exceptional pupils.

The case was appealed to the Supreme Court of Canada on two grounds:

(1) The Court of Appeal had struck down a section of provincial legislation on constitutional grounds without the appellants having given notice to the Attorney General for Ontario, as required under section 109 of the *Courts of Justice Act*.
(2) The Court of Appeal had erred in finding that the decision of the Special Education Tribunal contravened section 15 of the *Charter*.

The Court found that no notice was given to the Attorney General, either in Divisional Court or the Court of Appeal, and the government had no reason to believe that the *Education Act* was under attack. In fact, the Eatons had stated expressly to the Court that they were not attacking the *Education Act*. The absence of notice and the absence of a record developed in the courts and tribunals below were not merely technical defects and the Attorney General was seriously prejudiced by the absence of notice.

The Court did not have to consider the constitutional validity of section 8(3) of the *Education Act* because it found that the Special Education Tribunal's decision was not contrary to the *Charter*. The decision written by Sopinka J., is briefly summarized below.

Before a section 15 infringement can be found, the claimant must establish that the impugned provision creates a distinction on a prohibited or analogous ground, and that it withholds an advantage or benefit from the

---

40 *Ibid.*, at 16.

claimant or imposes a disadvantage or burden on the claimant. The principles that (1) not every distinction on a prohibited ground will constitute discrimination, and (2), in general, distinctions based on presumed rather than actual characteristics, are the hallmarks of discrimination, have particular significance when applied to physical and mental disability. The purpose of section 15(1) of the *Charter* is not only to prevent discrimination by the attribution of stereotypical characteristics to individuals, but also to ameliorate the position of groups within society who have suffered disadvantage by exclusion from mainstream society. Exclusion from the mainstream of society results from the construction of society based solely on mainstream attributes to which disabled persons will never be able to gain access.

Disability, as a prohibited ground, differs from other enumerated grounds such as race or sex because there is no individual variation with respect to these grounds. However, with respect to disability, this ground means vastly different things depending upon the individual and the context. This produces the "difference dilemma": segregation can be discriminatory depending on the person and the disability.

While integration should be recognized as the norm of general application, a presumption in favour of integrated schooling would work to the disadvantage of pupils who require special education in order to achieve equality. The Special Education Tribunal balanced the various educational interests of Emily Eaton. The findings of the Tribunal made it clear that those needs would be best met in a segregated classroom. A decision reached after such an analysis could not be considered a burden or disadvantage imposed upon a child.

The decision-making body must ensure that its determination of the appropriate accommodation for an exceptional pupil be from a subjective, child-centred perspective that attempts to make equality meaningful from the child's point of view. As a means of achieving this, it must also determine that the form of accommodation is in the child's best interests. Where it is not possible to adapt an integrated setting to the child's special needs, that is, where the aspects of the integrated setting which cannot reasonably be changed interfere with meeting the child's special needs, the principle of accommodation will require a special education placement outside the integrated setting.

For older children and those who are able to communicate their wishes and needs, their views will play an important role in the determination of "best interests". For younger children and those incapable of making a choice or who have very limited means of communicating, the decision-maker must make the determination on the basis of the other evidence before it. The application of a test designed to secure what is in the best interests of a child will best achieve that objective if the test is unencumbered by a presumption.

The *Eaton* case represents an important victory for school boards and for exceptional children. As a result of the decision, boards know that they do not have to overcome a legal presumption in favour of integration that would make it very difficult for boards to segregate pupils against the wishes of their parents. Instead, boards can attempt to meet the best interests of the child by assessing his or her educational needs. However, if challenged by a pupil or parent, it must still be able to show evidence that its placement meets the "best interests" test. The board's assessment will not be accepted blindly by a tribunal or court in the absence of pedagogical and other relevant evidence.

Children benefit from the decision because it looks to their best interests as being the benchmark. The decision emphasizes that their views should be sought if at all possible. With sensitivity and insight, it analyzes the nature of discrimination based on disability. It says that, while there is no legal presumption in favour of integration, integrated settings should be the norm and that reasonable efforts must be made to accommodate exceptional pupils in integrated settings. While it is obviously not determinative of other legal issues that may arise in special education, it is hoped that this decision will guide boards and parents in seeking mutually satisfactory solutions for the benefit of special needs children, without protracted litigation in the courts and before Human Rights Tribunals.

In *Québec (Commission des droits de la personne) v. St-Jean-Sur-Richelieu (Commission scolaire)*[41] the Quebec Court of Appeal considered an appeal of the ruling of a Human Rights Tribunal on a complaint by the parents of an autistic child that a school board had discriminated against the child contrary to section 40 of the Quebec *Charter of Human Rights and Freedoms.*[42] Section 40 states that every person has the right, to the extent and according to the standards provided for by law, to free public education. The Tribunal had ordered that the child be at least partially integrated into regular classes and be provided with the necessary services for his needs.

The Court reviewed the development of special education rights in Quebec. It concluded that

> ...integration in regular classes of handicapped students and students with social maladjustments or learning disabilities was not an unfettered right prior to July 1, 1989, nor did it become so when the new *Education Act* came into force. As this court concluded in *Picard v. Prince-Daveluy, Commission scolaire,* [1992] R.J.Q. 2369, 50 Q.A.C. 128, 35 A.C.W.S. (ed) 1074, there is no provision under which a school board is required to keep all pupils in regular schools and classes.

---

41 (1994) 117 D.L.R. (4th) 67 (Que. C.A.).
42 R.S.Q., c. C-12 as amended by S.Q. 1989.

> ...
>
> The *Education Act,* while not denying the benefit of school integration to students who are handicapped or who suffer from learning disabilities, does not set such integration as a goal to be achieved for everyone. Rather, it establishes as a standard the adaptation of educational services to the needs to each such student in terms of his or her learning and his or her social integration. School boards must define for each student some arrangement of services that can help foster his or her full development.
>
> ...
>
> The duty to adapt educational services to the needs of students who are handicapped or who suffer from learning disabilities may signify, where applicable, a duty to provide such students with other than educational services, such as the physical arrangement of the premises and the provision of material assistance to ensure genuine accessibility to quality educational services."[43]

The Court found that while section 40 of the Quebec *Charter* does not guarantee the right to integration in regular classes, it does guarantee that the organization of educational services will ensure that handicapped and disabled students "are, as a priority and to the degree possible, offered methods and procedures to help integrate them into regular classes or groups, as well as support services for such integration."[44] The Court also found that the board had indirectly discriminated against the student contrary to section 10 of the Quebec *Charter.* The board could have taken action to help integrate the student when such actions did not cause undue hardship to the board. These actions included the provision of an escort for the pupil at board expense.

---

43 Above, note 41, at 88.
44 *Ibid.,* at 90.

6

Teachers

1. THE TEACHER AS ROLE MODEL   305
2. MISCONDUCT, EXPLOITATION AND HARASSMENT   313
    (a) Off-Duty Discrimination   313
    (b) Statutory Protection   323
    (c) Child Abuse   326
    (d) Sexual Harassment   330
3. THE ONTARIO COLLEGE OF TEACHERS   335
    (a) Overview of Legislation   336
    (b) Criminal Reference Checks   341
4. ACADEMIC FREEDOM   342
    (a) Vulgar Language in the Classroom   342
    (b) Criticism of Education Policy   343
    (c) Teachers' Physical Appearance   343
    (d) Lifestyle/Sexual Behaviour   344
5. EVALUATION AND COMPETENCE   344
    (a) Statutory Requirements   344
    (b) Performance Evaluation   349
    (c) TIGHT Method of Evaluation   351
    (d) De-emphasizing the Minimal Standards Approach   352
    (e) Adherence to Procedure   353
6. THE CHARTER   363
7. STRIP SEARCHES   369

1. THE TEACHER AS ROLE MODEL

Values, attitudes and acceptable behaviour in our communities often change with the times. Since teachers are supposed to be role models for their students (being, after all, substitute parents or *in loco parentis*), there has always been great debate about the moral conduct of teachers not only inside, but outside the classroom. Consider the female teacher's contract in 1915 which outlined behaviours that would constitute just cause for immediate dismissal:

> ... not to keep company with men; to be home between the hours of 8:00 p.m. and 6:00 a.m. unless in attendance at a school function; not to loiter downtown in ice cream stores; not to leave town at any time without the permission of the

chairman of the board, and not to get in a carriage or automobile with any man except her father or brother.

Today these attributes as to what makes a "good moral teacher" appear ridiculous.

The following excerpts from a teacher's contract illustrate conditions that were not uncommon in the 1920's:

> I promise to abstain from all dancing, immodest dressing and any other conduct unbecoming of a teacher and a lady.
>
> I promise not to go out with any young men except in so far as it may be necessary to stimulate Sunday-school work.
>
> I promise not to fall in love, to become engaged or secretly married.
>
> I promise to sleep at least eight hours a night, eat carefully...
>
> I promise to remember that I owe a duty to the townspeople who pay my wages . . . respect to the school board . . . and be a willing servant to the school board.[1]

Do school boards control their teachers to the extent that they can demand that teachers conduct themselves according to the board's standards outside school hours? There is a widely held expectation among the public and the education profession that teachers will model good academic standing and moral conduct for students. Most teachers are in agreement with the "role model principle" as a guide for their conduct within the classroom. However, there is considerable debate how the role model principle is applied beyond the hours of classroom duties and school responsibilities. The measure for appropriate moral conduct of teachers is often dependent upon the standards of a particular community. What standard of personal behaviour should be expected of teachers?

The role model principle assumes that any type of immoral or unprofessional behaviour that occurs within a teacher's life is detrimental to the students' learning environment. Problems occur when each school community has a different notion of what constitutes good moral conduct for teachers. Instead of the role model principle, it might be more useful if school boards established teacher discipline policies that provided a process that associates concrete direct work-related connections between a teacher's conduct off-duty and teaching performance.

The crucial element in deciding whether the teacher's conduct in his or her private life is inappropriate is a determination as to whether a private behaviour is linked causally with his or her inability or unfitness to teach. If the teacher's conduct has resulted in lost credibility among the school

---

1 Eischer & Schimmel, *The Civil Rights of Teachers* (New York: Harper and Row, 1973.)

community and the class, then this will negatively affect the teacher's ability to teach. This, in turn, will disrupt the educational process within the classroom.

Some argue that teachers' private lives and their conduct are their own business unless a teacher's private misconduct contributes to his or her ineffectiveness within the learning environment or represents a danger to students.

One area that has caused controversy involves the concept of a teacher's academic freedom. The American Association of University Teachers embraces the belief that institutions of education are conducted for the common good and not to further the interest either of the individual teacher or the institution as a whole. The common good depends upon the search for truth and its free expression.

Academic freedom does not mean that teachers can teach whatever they like, or that teachers can indoctrinate their students as a captive audience. Teachers are entitled to employ controversial materials, teaching methods and language so long as the focus is relevant to the curriculum and appropriate to the age and maturity of the students. However, the *Education Act* directs Ontario teachers to use textbooks that are either approved by the Minister of Education or the school board.[2]

Teachers are accountable to the public for their professional conduct within the classroom. Academic freedom is a powerful pedagogical tool for enabling students to learn effectively. The public must feel confident that its teachers use professional judgement in selecting relevant materials to foster student growth despite the possibilities of controversial materials, teaching methods, and questionable language in the resources.

Lifestyle choices of teachers are more closely monitored by boards and the public than most other professions. As we have stated, denominational schools established under section 93 of the *Constitution Act, 1867*[3] have special protection. Teachers accepting positions at these schools must make lifestyle choices that are compatible with denominational teaching objectives and church doctrines.

Beyond the school doors, teachers must have the same rights and freedoms as all citizens. Providing that a teacher's conduct is personal and private, immoral or illegal behaviour may not be the sole determinant for dismissal for just cause. Teachers are role models for their students but this does not mean that the teacher should be dismissed simply because the school community perceives a teacher as lacking good moral character.

In *Trinity Western University v. College of Teachers (British Columbia)*[4] the Supreme Court of Canada considered an appeal dealing with the

---

2 *Education Act*, R.R.O. 1990, Reg. 298, s. 7.
3 30 & 31 Vict., c. 3
4 [2001] 1 S.C.R. 772.

decision of the British Columbia College of Teachers not to accredit the graduates of the University. The Court provided its insight into the distinction between on-duty and off-duty conduct of teachers, as shown in the excerpt below. Trinity Western University (TWU) is a private institution associated with the Evangelical Free Church of Canada. It established a teacher training program and applied to the B.C. College of Teachers ("BCCT") for permission to assume full responsibility for the teacher education program. One of the reasons for assuming complete responsibility for the program was that it wanted the program to reflect its Christian perspective. The College considered it to be contrary to the public interest for it to approve a program offered by the university because the university's "Community Standards" for students and staff embodied discrimination against homosexuals. The College therefore declined to approve the university's request. The Court first dealt with the appropriate standard of review that should be applied to the decision of the College and held that the standard was that of "correctness" given the jurisdictional nature of the issue and the level of expertise of the College. The Court went on to consider the facts in light of the freedom of religion and the right to equality in the *Charter*. In deciding in favour of the university, the Court found that the case could be decided in a way that was consistent with its interpretation of both of these rights. Its analysis, part of which is excerpted below, provides a thought-provoking summary of how Canadian courts view these *Charter* rights.

> 25 Although the Community Standards are expressed in terms of a code of conduct rather than an article of faith, we conclude that a homosexual student would not be tempted to apply for admission, and could only sign the so-called student contract at a considerable personal cost. TWU is not for everybody; it is designed to address the needs of people who share a number of religious convictions. That said, the admissions policy of TWU alone is not in itself sufficient to establish discrimination as it is understood in our s. 15 jurisprudence. It is important to note that this is a private institution that is exempted, in part, from the British Columbia human rights legislation and to which the *Charter* does not apply. To state that the voluntary adoption of a code of conduct based on a person's own religious beliefs, in a private institution, is sufficient to engage s. 15 would be inconsistent with freedom of conscience and religion, which co-exist with the right to equality.
>
> 26 This is not to say that the BCCT erred in considering equality concerns pursuant to its public interest jurisdiction. As we have already stated, concerns about equality were appropriately considered by the BCCT under the public interest component of s. 4 of the *Teaching Profession Act*. The importance of equality in Canadian society was discussed by Cory J. for the majority of this Court in Vriend v. Alberta [1998] 1 S.C.R. 493 at para. 67:
>
>> "The rights enshrined in s. 15(1) of the *Charter* are fundamental to Canada. They reflect the fondest dreams, the highest hopes and finest aspirations

of Canadian society. When universal suffrage was granted it recognized to some extent the importance of the individual. Canada by the broad scope and fundamental fairness of the provisions of s. 15(1) has taken a further step in the recognition of the fundamental importance and the innate dignity of the individual. That it has done so is not only praiseworthy but essential to achieving the magnificent goal of equal dignity for all. It is the means of giving Canadians a sense of pride. In order to achieve equality the intrinsic worthiness and importance of every individual must be recognized regardless of the age, sex, colour, origins, or other characteristics of the person. This in turn should lead to a sense of dignity and worthiness for every Canadian and the greatest possible pride and appreciation in being a part of a great nation."

27 The equality guarantees in the *Charter* and in B.C.'s human rights legislation include protection against discrimination based on sexual orientation. In Egan v. Canada [1995] 2 S.C.R. 513, this Court unanimously affirmed that sexual orientation is an analogous ground to those enumerated in s. 15(1) of the *Charter*. In addition, a majority of this Court explicitly recognized that gays and lesbians, "whether as individuals or couples, form an identifiable minority who have suffered and continue to suffer serious social, political and economic disadvantage" (para. 175, *per* Cory J.; see also para. 89, *per* L'Heureux-Dubé J.). This statement was recently affirmed by a majority of this Court in M. v. H. [1999] 2 S.C.R 3, at para. 64. See also *Vriend, supra,* and Little Sisters Book and Art Emporium v. Canada (Minister of Justice), [2000] 2 S.C.R. 1120, 2000 SCC 69. While the BCCT was not directly applying either the *Charter* or the province's human rights legislation when making its decision, it was entitled to look to these instruments to determine whether it would be in the public interest to allow public school teachers to be trained at TWU.

28 At the same time, however, the BCCT is also required to consider issues of religious freedom. Section 15 of the *Charter* protects equally against "discrimination based on . . . religion". Similarly, s. 2(*a*) of the *Charter* guarantees that "[e]veryone has the following fundamental freedoms: . . . freedom of conscience and religion". British Columbia's human rights legislation accommodates religious freedoms by allowing religious institutions to discriminate in their admissions policies on the basis of religion. The importance of freedom of religion in Canadian society was elegantly stated by Dickson J., as he then was, writing for the majority in *Big M Drug Mart, supra,* at pp. 336-37:

"A truly free society is one which can accommodate a wide variety of beliefs, diversity of tastes and pursuits, customs and codes of conduct. A free society is one which aims at equality with respect to the enjoyment of fundamental freedoms and I say this without any reliance upon s. 15 of the *Charter*. Freedom must surely be founded in respect for the inherent dignity and the inviolable rights of the human person. The essence of the concept of freedom of religion is the right to entertain such religious beliefs as a person chooses, the right to declare religious beliefs openly and without fear of hindrance or reprisal, and the right to manifest religious belief by worship and practice or by teaching and dissemination. But the concept means more than that.

"Freedom can primarily be characterized by the absence of coercion or constraint. If a person is compelled by the state or the will of another to a course of action or inaction which he would not otherwise have chosen, he is not acting of his own volition and he cannot be said to be truly free. One of the major purposes of the *Charter* is to protect, within reason, from compulsion or restraint. Coercion includes not only such blatant forms of compulsion as direct commands to act or refrain from acting on pain of sanction, coercion includes indirect forms of control which determine or limit alternative courses of conduct available to others. Freedom in a broad sense embraces both the absence of coercion and constraint, and the right to manifest beliefs and practices. Freedom means that, subject to such limitations as are necessary to protect public safety, order, health, or morals or the fundamental rights and freedoms of others, no one is to be forced to act in a way contrary to his beliefs or his conscience.

What may appear good and true to a majoritarian religious group, or to the state acting at their behest, may not, for religious reasons, be imposed upon citizens who take a contrary view. The *Charter* safeguards religious minorities from the threat of "the tyranny of the majority"."

It is interesting to note that this passage presages the very situation which has arisen in this appeal, namely, one where the religious freedom of one individual is claimed to interfere with the fundamental rights and freedoms of another. The issue at the heart of this appeal is how to reconcile the religious freedoms of individuals wishing to attend TWU with the equality concerns of students in B.C.'s public school system, concerns that may be shared with their parents and society generally.

29 In our opinion, this is a case where any potential conflict should be resolved through the proper delineation of the rights and values involved. In essence, properly defining the scope of the rights avoids a conflict in this case. Neither freedom of religion nor the guarantee against discrimination based on sexual orientation is absolute. As L'Heureux-Dubé J. stated in P. (D) v. S.(C.)., [1993] 4 S.C.R. 141, at p. 182, writing for the majority on this point:

"As the Court has reiterated many times, freedom of religion, like any freedom, is not absolute. *It is inherently limited by the rights and freedoms of others.* Whereas parents are free to choose and practise the religion of their choice, such activities can and must be restricted when they are against the child's best interests, without thereby infringing the parents' freedom of religion." [Emphasis added.]

30 Similarly, Iacobucci and Major JJ. concluded in *B. (R.) v. Children's Aid Society of Metropolitan Toronto [1995] 1 S.C.R. 315*, at para. 226, that:

"Just as there are limits to the ambit of freedom of expression (e.g. s. 2(*b*) does not protect violent acts: R. v. Zundel [1992] 2 S.C.R. 731, at pp. 753 and 801; R. v. Keegstra [1990] 3 S.C.R. 697;, at pp. 732 and 830), so are there limits to the scope of s. 2(*a*), especially so when this provision is called upon to protect activity that threatens the physical or psychological well-being of others. In other words, *although the freedom of belief may be broad, the freedom to act upon those beliefs is considerably narrower*, and it is the latter freedom at issue in this case." [Emphasis added.]

31 In addition, the *Charter* must be read as a whole, so that one right is not privileged at the expense of another. As Lamer C.J. stated for the majority of this Court in Dagenais v. Canadian Broadcasting Corp. [1994] 3 S.C.R. 835, at p. 877:

"A hierarchical approach to rights, which places some over others, must be avoided, both when interpreting the *Charter* and when developing the common law. When the protected rights of two individuals come into conflict . . . *Charter* principles require a balance to be achieved that fully respects the importance of both sets of rights."

32 Therefore, although the BCCT was right to evaluate the impact of TWU's admission policy on the public school environment, it should have considered more. The *Human Rights Code*, R.S.B.C. 1996, c. 210, specifically provides for exceptions in the case of religious institutions, and the legislature gave recognition to TWU as an institution affiliated to a particular Church whose views were well known to it. While the BCCT says that it is not denying the right to TWU students and faculty to hold particular religious views, it has inferred without any concrete evidence that such views will limit consideration of social issues by TWU graduates and have a detrimental effect on the learning environment in public schools. There is no denying that the decision of the BCCT places a burden on members of a particular religious group and in effect, is preventing them from expressing freely their religious beliefs and associating to put them into practice. If TWU does not abandon its Community Standards, it renounces certification and full control of a teacher education program permitting access to the public school system. Students are likewise affected because the affirmation of their religious beliefs and attendance at TWU will not lead to certification as public school teachers unless they attend a public university for at least one year. These are important considerations. What the BCCT was required to do was to determine whether the rights were in conflict in reality.

33 TWU's Community Standards, which are limited to prescribing conduct of members while at TWU, are not sufficient to support the conclusion that the BCCT should anticipate intolerant behaviour in the public schools. Indeed, if TWU's Community Standards could be sufficient in themselves to justify denying accreditation, it is difficult to see how the same logic would not result in the denial of accreditation to members of a particular church. The diversity of Canadian society is partly reflected in the multiple religious organizations that mark the societal landscape and this diversity of views should be respected. The BCCT did not weigh the various rights involved in its assessment of the alleged discriminatory practices of TWU by not taking into account the impact

of its decision on the right to freedom of religion of the members of TWU. Accordingly, this Court must.

34 Consideration of human rights values in these circumstances encompasses consideration of the place of private institutions in our society and the reconciling of competing rights and values. Freedom of religion, conscience and association coexist with the right to be free of discrimination based on sexual orientation. Even though the requirement that students and faculty adopt the Community Standards creates unfavourable differential treatment since it would probably prevent homosexual students and faculty from applying, one must consider the true nature of the undertaking and the context in which this occurs. Many Canadian universities, including St. Francis Xavier University, Queen's University, McGill University and Concordia University College of Alberta, have traditions of religious affiliations. Furthermore, s. 93 of the *Constitution Act, 1867* enshrined religious public education rights into our Constitution, as part of the historic compromise which made Confederation possible. Section 17 of the *Alberta Act*, R.S.C. 1985, App. II, No. 20, and *Saskatchewan Act*, R.S.C. 1985, App. II, No. 21, s. 22 of the *Manitoba Act, 1870*, R.S.C. 1985, App. II, No. 8, and Term 17 of the Terms of Union of Newfoundland with Canada as confirmed by the *Newfoundland Act*, R.S.C. 1985, App. II, No. 32, were to the same effect. Although the constitutional protections were altered by constitutional amendment in Newfoundland in 1998 and eliminated in Quebec in 1997, they remain in effect in Ontario, Alberta, Saskatchewan and Manitoba.

35 Another part of that context is the *Human Rights Act*, S.B.C. 1984, c. 22, referred to by the Court of Appeal and the respondents (now the *Human Rights Code*), which provides, in s. 19 (now s. 41), that a religious institution is not considered to breach the Act where it prefers adherents of its religious constituency. It cannot be reasonably concluded that private institutions are protected but that their graduates are *de facto* considered unworthy of fully participating in public activities. In Ontario Human Rights Commission v. Simpsons-Sears Ltd., [1985] 2 S.C.R. 536, at p. 554, McIntyre J. observed that a "natural corollary to the recognition of a right must be the social acceptance of a general duty to respect and to act within reason to protect it". In this particular case, it can reasonably be inferred that the B.C. legislature did not consider that training with a Christian philosophy was in itself against the public interest since it passed five bills in favour of TWU between 1969 and 1985. While homosexuals may be discouraged from attending TWU, a private institution based on particular religious beliefs, they will not be prevented from becoming teachers. In addition, there is nothing in the TWU Community Standards that indicates that graduates of TWU will not treat homosexuals fairly and respectfully. Indeed, the evidence to date is that graduates from the joint TWU-SFU teacher education program have become competent public school teachers, and there is no evidence before this Court of discriminatory conduct by any graduate. Although this evidence is not conclusive, given that no students have yet graduated from a teacher education program taught exclusively at TWU, it is instructive. Students attending TWU are free to adopt personal rules of conduct based on their

religious beliefs provided they do not interfere with the rights of others. Their freedom of religion is not accommodated if the consequence of its exercise is the denial of the right of full participation in society. Clearly, the restriction on freedom of religion must be justified by evidence that the exercise of this freedom of religion will, in the circumstances of this case, have a detrimental impact on the school system.

36 Instead, the proper place to draw the line in cases like the one at bar is generally between belief and conduct. The freedom to hold beliefs is broader than the freedom to act on them. Absent concrete evidence that training teachers at TWU fosters discrimination in the public schools of B.C., the freedom of individuals to adhere to certain religious beliefs while at TWU should be respected. The BCCT, rightfully, does not require public universities with teacher education programs to screen out applicants who hold sexist, racist or homophobic beliefs. For better or for worse, tolerance of divergent beliefs is a hallmark of a democratic society.

37 Acting on those beliefs, however, is a very different matter. If a teacher in the public school system engages in discriminatory conduct, that teacher can be subject to disciplinary proceedings before the BCCT. Discriminatory conduct by a public school teacher when on duty should always be subject to disciplinary proceedings. This Court has held, however, that greater tolerance must be shown with respect to off-duty conduct. Yet disciplinary measures can still be taken when discriminatory off-duty conduct poisons the school environment. As La Forest J. stated for a unanimous Court in *Ross, supra*, at para. 45:

> "It is on the basis of the position of trust and influence that we hold the teacher to high standards both on and off duty, and it is an erosion of these standards that may lead to a loss in the community of confidence in the public school system. I do not wish to be understood as advocating an approach that subjects the entire lives of teachers to inordinate scrutiny on the basis of more onerous moral standards of behaviour. This could lead to a substantial invasion of the privacy rights and fundamental freedoms of teachers. However, where a "poisoned" environment within the school system is traceable to the off-duty conduct of a teacher that is likely to produce a corresponding loss of confidence in the teacher and the system as a whole, then the off-duty conduct of the teacher is relevant."

In this way, the scope of the freedom of religion and equality rights that have come into conflict in this appeal can be circumscribed and thereby reconciled.

2. MISCONDUCT, EXPLOITATION AND HARASSMENT

(a) Off-duty Discrimination

For several years, Malcolm Ross, a teacher, publicly made racist and discriminatory comments against Jews during his off-duty time. His writings and statements communicating his anti-Semitic views included four books or pamphlets, letters to a local newspaper, and a local television interview.

A Jewish parent filed a complaint with the New Brunswick Human Rights Commission, alleging that the School Board, which employed Ross as a teacher, violated section 5(1) of the *Human Rights Act* by discriminating against him and his children in the provision of accommodation, services or facilities on the basis of religion and ancestry.

A Board of Inquiry found that Ross's off-duty comments denigrated the faith and belief of Jews. The Inquiry further found that the school board was in breach of section 5(1), concluding that it discriminated by failing to discipline Ross meaningfully in that, by its almost indifferent response to the complaints and by continuing his employment, it endorsed his out-of-school activities and writings.

The Inquiry directed the school board to comply with the following: (a) place Ross on leave of absence without pay for a period of 18 months; (b) appoint him to a nonteaching position, if one became available during that period; (c) terminate his employment at the end of that period if, in the interim, he had not been offered and accepted a non-teaching position; and (d) terminate his employment with the school board immediately if he published or wrote anti-Semitic materials or sold his previous publications any time during the leave of absence period or at any time during his employment in a non-teaching position.

The Court of Queen's Bench allowed Ross' application for judicial review in part, ordering that clause (d) of the order be quashed on the ground that it was in excess of jurisdiction. The Court also concluded that the four parts of the order violated sections 2(a) and 2(b) of the *Canadian Charter of Rights and Freedoms* but that, with the exception of clause (d), they could be saved by section 1 of the *Charter*. The Court of Appeal dismissed the cross-appeals with respect to (d) and allowed Ross's appeal, holding that clauses (a), (b) and (c) of the order infringed Ross' freedom of expression and freedom of religion and could not be justified under section 1.

The Supreme Court overturned the Court of Appeal's ruling and restored clauses (a), (b) and (c) of the order. Mr. Justice LaForest, writing for the Supreme Court of Canada in *Ross v. New Brunswick District No. 15*,[5] stated that,

> The school is an arena for the exchange of ideas and must, therefore, be premised upon principles of tolerance and impartiality so that all persons within the school environment feel equally free to participate. Young children are especially vulnerable to the messages conveyed by their teachers. They are less likely to make an intellectual distinction between comments a teacher makes in the school and those the teachers make outside the school. They are therefore,

---

5 [1996] 1 S.C.R. 825.

more likely to be threatened and isolated by a teacher who makes comments that denigrate personal characteristics of a group to which they belong.

The Board of Inquiry, was correct in finding that Ross' continued employment as a teacher constituted discrimination under section 5(1) of the Act, with respect to educational services available to the public.

"Public school teachers assume a position of influence and trust over their students and must be seen to be impartial and tolerant. By their conduct, teachers, as 'medium' of the educational message (the values, beliefs and knowledge sought to be transmitted by the school system), must be perceived as upholding that message. A teacher's conduct is evaluated on the basis of his or her position, rather than whether the conduct occurs within or outside the classroom," said the Court.[6]

The Board's order did infringe Ross' freedom of expression. The order also infringed his freedom of religion. However, the educational context must be considered when balancing Ross' freedom to make discriminatory statements against the right of the children in the school board to be educated in a school system that is free from bias, prejudice and intolerance. Ross' religious belief, which denigrates and defames the religious beliefs of others, erodes the very basis of the guarantee in section 2(a) of the *Charter*.

Ross' removal from his teaching position was necessary to ensure that no influence of this kind is exerted by him upon his students and to ensure that the educational services are discrimination-free. Accordingly, clauses (a), (b) and (c) of the order were carefully tailored to accomplish this objective and minimally impair Ross's constitutional freedoms. Clauses (a), (b) and (c) of the order were justified under section 1 of the *Charter* and were properly made within the board's jurisdiction.

In *Toronto (City) Board of Education v. O.S.S.T.F., District 15*[7] (the "*Bhadauria*" case), the Supreme Court of Canada considered an appeal of a decision of the Ontario Court of Appeal that upheld the award of a board of arbitration conditionally reinstating a teacher. The teacher had written abusive letters to the board, containing what could be perceived as threats to the lives of certain senior officials and members of the board. The teacher was complaining about the fact that he had been consistently turned down for a promotion. After obtaining psychiatric reports stating that Bhadauria was not suffering from a psychiatric illness, the Board ultimately passed a resolution terminating the teacher's employment. The matter was grieved and the board of arbitration held that the teacher should be conditionally

---

6 See also *Kraychy v. Edmonton Public School District No. 7* (1990), 73 Alta. L.R. (2d) 69 (Q. Bd. of Reference under the School Act) and *Greenway v. Seven Oaks School Division No. 10* (1990), 70 Man. R. (2d) 2 (C.A.), leave to appeal refused [1991] 1 S.C.R. ix.
7 (1997), 144 D.L.R. (4th) 385 (S.C.C.).

reinstated. The award was unanimously quashed by the Ontario Divisional Court.[8] This decision was appealed by the grievor's union.

The Ontario Court of Appeal restored the arbitration award, stating that the lower court had permitted itself to review the merits of the arbitration award to a greater extent than is appropriate under the definition of "patently unreasonable".

The issue in this case, therefore, was whether or not the decision of the board of arbitration to overturn the employer's dismissal of the grievor was patently unreasonable. The court stated that there was no doubt that Mr. Bhadauria was guilty of misconduct. The standard of conduct that applied to the teacher was set out in the *Education Act*, section 264 (1)(c):

> 264(1) It is the duty of a teacher and a temporary teacher,
>
> (a) to teach diligently and faithfully the classes or subjects assigned to the teacher by the principal;
> (b) to encourage the pupils in the pursuit of learning;
> (c) to inculcate by precept and example respect for religion and the principles of Judaeo-Christian morality and the highest regard for truth, justice, loyalty, love of country, humanity, benevolence, sobriety, industry, frugality, purity, temperance and all other virtues;

The Court (Cory J.) stated:

> The language is that of another era. The requirements it sets for teachers reflect the ideal and not the minimal standard. They are so idealistically high that even the most conscientious, earnest and diligent teacher could not meet all of them at all times. Angels might comply but not mere mortals. It follows that every breach of the section cannot be considered to infringe upon the values that are essential to the make-up of a good teacher. However, the section does indicate that teachers are very properly expected to maintain a higher standard of conduct than other employees because they occupy such an extremely important position in society.[9]

The Court found that Bhadauria's conduct in respect of his letters to the board, constituted,

> ... very significant if not extreme misconduct. The letters did not simply express dissatisfaction with working conditions; they were threats of violence. The fact that they may have been written outside the hours of teaching duty cannot either excuse or alleviate the seriousness of the misconduct.
>
> ...
>
> In their position of trust, teachers must teach by example as well as by lesson, and that example is set just as much by their conduct outside the classroom as

---

8 (1991), 52 O.A.C. 8, 83 D.L.R. (4th) 552.
9 Above, note 7, at 401.

by their performance within it. The misconduct which occurs outside regular teaching hours can be the basis for discipline proceedings.[10]

The Court cited *Ross v. New Brunswick School District No. 15*,[11] and *R. v. Audet*,[12] as affirming the responsibility of teachers in respect of their conduct outside the school.

Although concurring with the majority, Madam Justice L'Heureux-Dubé differed as to the questions that an arbitration board should be asking itself in deciding whether there was "just cause". She found that the conduct of the teacher was,

> ... *per se* sufficient evidence for a finding that the grievor has seriously prejudiced his status as a role model, and for the consequential finding of just cause for discharge. Accordingly the subsidiary question as to whether this kind of aberrant behaviour was temporary or permanent is irrelevant in this case. Failure on the part of the arbitration board to formulate the questions properly, to address the primary legal issues, and to make the findings of just cause on the two letters *per se,* was not merely incorrect, it was patently unreasonable.[13]

In her view,

> If a single offence, standing alone, is serious enough to constitute just cause for discharge under any circumstances whatsoever, then an employee's past record or his potential for future rehabilitation cannot turn that just cause into an unjust one ... There can be some cases where an offence is so grave that no factor would be sufficient to mitigate the discharge, and other circumstances where an offence is so critical to the employment relationship that mitigation simply cannot come into play.[14]

In a British Columbia case where husband and wife teachers were suspended for misconduct after the husband submitted three semi-nude photographs of his wife to *Gallery* magazine (both were suspended by the school board for six weeks, ultimately reduced to four weeks), the Court of Appeal found in part that "the publication of such a photograph of a teacher in such a magazine will have an adverse effect upon the educational system to which the teacher owes a duty to act responsibly."[15]

Should a teacher be dismissed if convicted of a criminal offence? Proponents of the role model principle would argue yes to this inquiry unless the teacher showed reforming behaviour and actually discouraged students from committing a similar offence. Could a rehabilitated cocaine addict or dealer serve as a teacher and role model for students if he or she discouraged

---

10 *Ibid.*, at 402.
11 [1996] 1 S.C.R. 825.
12 [1996] 2 S.C.R. 171.
13 *Ibid.*, at 414.
14 *Ibid.*, at 413.
15 *Abbotsford School Dist. 34 v. Shewan* (1987), 21 B.C.L.R. (2d) 93 at 97 (C.A.), affirming (1986), 70 B.C.L.R. 40 (S.C.).

students from experiencing illegal drugs? Boards and courts perceive illegal activity by teachers as a deliberate undermining of respect for the educational profession and a diminished respect for the teacher's credibility. Teachers have been terminated for encouraging students to partake in alcohol and illegal drugs. The basis for dismissal relates not only to the role model principle, but also the effectiveness of a teacher in a classroom where credibility has been diminished among students and the school.

Factors considered for determining dismissal may include:

1. the likelihood of recurrence of the questioned conduct
2. the extenuating or aggravating circumstances
3. the effect of notoriety and publicity
4. impairment of teachers' and students' relationships
5. disruption to the educational process
6. motive; and
7. proximity or remoteness at the time of conduct.

The overriding consideration is whether the behaviour relates to one's effectiveness as a teacher. Each case must be judged on its own merits.

To illustrate the utility of guidelines, consider the California teacher who was convicted of six counts of driving under the influence of alcohol. The teacher's dismissal was upheld because his use of alcohol was obviously uncontrollable and therefore was likely to reoccur. He had shown repeated disregard for the law. His behaviour occurred in a public area, and finally his conviction was highly publicized within the community and subsequently damaged his credibility as a teacher in the eyes of both teachers and students.[16]

The *Criminal Code of Canada*[17] addresses offences by persons in positions of trust. A person in a position of trust is in a particular position in relation to another which imposes upon him or her a duty of care in relation to that other person. That relationship is often accompanied by an authority of the dominant person over the other. It is the existence of this trust relationship that frequently results in a position of dependency. The offence created by section 153 can be established whether or not the accused uses the position of authority or trust to gain the sexual purpose or contact referred to in the section.[18]

In a case of sexual assault the accused, a school principal, was acquitted after the trial judge found that the touching incident in question was not an assault because there was no "environmental of hostility". The touching was not sexual because buttocks were not a sexual attribute and the touching was trifling. It was alleged that accused had approached the student in the

---

16 *Watson v. State Bd. of Education*, 99 Cal. Rptr. 468 (1971).
17 R.S.C. 1985, c. C-46, ss. 151 and 153.
18 *R. v. G. (T.F.)* (1992), 11 C.R. (4th) 211 (Ont. C.A.).

gym, and "placed his cupped hand against her buttocks, closer to the bottom than to the top, and in the area of the center, over the crack in her bum". When the student looked at him, he asked whether she wanted to help clean the room. The principal admitted to the touching.

On appeal[19] the Court found that in order to prove assault, the Crown need not prove that there was an atmosphere of hostility, or that the touching was done with anger or violence, but rather whether there was a deliberate touching without consent. There was no requirement that the part of the body touched be part of the genitalia in order to constitute a sexual assault. The test whether the impugned conduct had the requisite sexual nature was an objective one to a reasonable observer. Although there may have been uncertainty as to whether the criminal law was concerned with trifles, the touching here was not trifling. It was touching, on school premises, by a principal on a student, where there was a great imbalance in power, age and emotional maturity.

A New Brunswick physical education teacher who had oral sex with a 14-year-old female student while on summer vacation was guilty of sexual exploitation because he remained in a position of trust and authority, according to the Supreme Court of Canada in *R. v. Audet*.[20] It is irrelevant that the accused did not abuse or exploit his position of trust or authority as a teacher to obtain the student's consent, stated the Court in a 5-2 decision:

> In my view no evidence is required to prove that teachers play a key role in our society that places them in a direct position of trust and authority towards their students. Parents delegate their parental authority to teachers and entrust them with the responsibility of instilling in their children a large part of the store of learning they will acquire during their development," stated Mr. Justice Gerard La Forest for the majority.

The case provided the first opportunity for the Court to review the scope of section 153 of the *Criminal Code* which makes it a crime for a person in a position of trust or authority to touch a young person for a sexual purpose. At issue was the scope of the terms "position of authority" and "position of trust", and the elements which the Crown must prove to make out the offence.

The offence took place on the night of July 8, 1992 when the accused and a friend went to a club in Campbellton, New Brunswick. The accused met the complainant, who he had taught during the previous year, at the club. The complainant, who had just turned 14, had arrived at the club with two cousins who were in their 20s. The five spent the evening at the bar but, at the suggestion of the accused's friend, later went to a cottage. The

---

19 *R. v. Lasecki* (1994), 163 A.R. 354 (Q.B.).
20 [1996] 2 S.C.R. 171.

complainant's teacher developed a headache and lay down in an adjoining bedroom.

Actual abuse or exploitation is not relevant because consent is not a defence, explained Mr. Justice La Forest. "Clearly Parliament wanted to afford greater protection to young persons. It chose harsher means by criminalizing the activity itself, regardless of whether it is consensual (s. 150.1(1) of the *Code*), in so far as it involves a person who is in a position or relationship referred to in s. 153(1) with respect to the young person."

The majority found that the trial judge must determine as a matter of fact that a position of trust or authority existed before a conviction can be entered. This must be done by an examination of the nature of the relationship. The status of the accused is not determinative of the issue, noted Mr. Justice La Forest, but "it would be excessively formalistic to refuse to recognize that certain persons, by reason of the role entrusted to them by society, will in fact and in the vast majority of cases come within the ambit of s. 153(1) by reason of their status vis-a-vis the young person and, in particular, the relationship they are engaged in with that young person as a consequence of such status." Teachers fall into this category, the Court stated. "I am of the view that in the vast majority of cases teachers will indeed be in a position of trust and authority towards their students," wrote Mr. Justice La Forest.

He rejected the minority opinion that his interpretation of "position of trust" creates a presumption against teachers that makes the crime of sexual exploitation an absolute liability offence which undermines the presumption of innocence:

> "My analysis indicates that in the absence of evidence raising a reasonable doubt on this point, teachers are necessarily in a position of trust and authority towards their students."

As mentioned, the integrity of the educational process depends upon adherence to sexual boundaries in the teacher-student relationship. The essential features of this relationship involve trust, dependency, and authority. In *R. v. Leon*[21] Judge Proulx of the Quebec Court of Appeal discussed the findings of the Badgely Report, a report of the committee on "Sexual Offences Against Children and Youths",[22] which sought to study sexual offences against children and young persons. The intent of the committee was to enhance the prevention of sexual exploitation by persons in position of trust or authority against dependent persons. Judge Proulx considered "position of authority" to entail:

---

21 (1992), 44 Q.A.C. 143.
22 Committee on Sexual Offences Against Children and Youth, *Sexual Offences Against Children in Canada* (Ottawa: Supply and Services Canada, 1984).

far more than a legal right over the young person, but also a lawful or unlawful power to command which the adult may acquire in the circumstances.

Dependence, according to Judge Proulx, relates to the status of an individual whose relationship to another is such that his or her independence or freedom of action is deprived.

The "trust" element of the teacher-student relationship is one with its inner source in the parent-child relationship. The teacher and parent share a number of common features in the eyes of the impressionable student. Professional ethics, which assert that the interest of the student must be upheld uppermost, encourage students to perceive the teacher as worthy of their trust and to be certain that this trust will never be betrayed.[23]

Cases occurring in the United States support the need to protect the vulnerable student. In *Hegener v. Bd of Ed. of the City of Chicago*,[24] the Court recognized the numerous roles required by teachers with students "entrusted" to them. The case involved a high school teacher who used her position to develop an intense relationship with one current and one former student. The Court acknowledged the need to spend

> ... additional time with particular students to help them with their learning. Nonetheless, a teacher must be able to draw the line between conduct which is necessary for the proper performance of her educative function and that which denigrates into one which is primarily for her own emotional gratification.

Based on this, the teacher was dismissed from her position.

In the case of *Sauter v. Mount Vernon School District*,[25] a Washington appellate court rejected a dismissed teacher's contention that his alleged misconduct, involving soliciting a sexual relationship with a student, was outside his teaching duties and had no impact on the quality and effectiveness of his teaching. The court stated:

> ... we are not faced with conduct involving a teacher's private life unrelated to school activities. The appellant's conduct was sexually exploitive and was directly related to his duties of a teacher.

As persons considered "not yet fully mature", high school students are deemed extremely vulnerable to a teacher's misuse of authority and to lack the capacity to fully appreciate the nature of their actions. However, unlike in the case of children under the age of 14, greater consideration is given to the circumstances of the teacher-student relationship when dealing with cases involving "young adults".

---

23 See *Carruthers v. College of Nurses of Ontario* (1996), 31 O.R. (3d) 377 (Div. Ct.), where a nurse was suspended for three months for kissing a psychiatric patient.
24 (1991), 567 N.E. 2d 566.
25 (1990), 791 P. 2d 549.

In the course of learning, emotional bonding between teachers and students is critical. The most effective teaching comes about "when a student develops admiration and even affection for a teacher".[26]

Once sexual relations begin between a teacher and a student, the effectiveness of teaching and learning deteriorates. Neither the learner's nor the listener's mind is fully engaged with the material to be learned anymore, but is entangled instead in the relationship. The teacher-mentor transforms from someone the student trusts to teach her what she wants to know into someone she fears, or hates, or loves, or feels equal or superior to. The title of "teacher" may hold questionable relevance as professional respect declines. Similarly, the student's due honour within her official status is misplaced or entirely lost. Thus, the trust between teacher and student, essential to the learning process within the classroom, ends.

A trust relationship involves special responsibilities which help define it. The teacher who is in a position of trust has a duty to act in the interest of the beneficiary of that trust (the student), and he or she cannot use his or her authority or influence over a child for sexual gratification.[27] Sexual assault represents an unacceptable intrusion upon, or violation of, a victim's sexual privacy or integrity. It is an act of power, aggression and control.[28] It has been further held that sexual assault is not an included offence of sexual exploitation.[29]

It is certainly clear that where a teacher has been terminated on the grounds of immorality the conduct referred to has some connection to the occupation as a teacher, and unlike other forms of inappropriate conduct, such conduct in these instances is usually considered irremediable.[30]

It should also be noted that in terms of character evidence of those working in an educational setting who are sentenced for sexual assault, the value of character evidence as to morality in respect of the propensity to commit the offence is of diminished value.[31]

---

26 Wayne C. Booth, "Beyond Knowledge and Inquiry to Love, Or: Who Mentors the Mentors?" (1994) Aacademe, Vol. 80, No. 6, pp. 29-38, at p. 30.
27 *R. v. Hann (No. 2)* (1990), 86 Nfld. & P.E.I.R. 33, 268 A.P.R. 33 (Nfld.T.D.), affirmed (1992), 15 C.R. (4th) 355 (Nfld. C.A.).
28 See *R. v. V. (K.B.)* (1992), 71 C.C.C. (3d) 65 (Ont. C.A.), affirmed [1993] 2 S.C.R. 857; *R. v. G. (T.F.)* (1992), 11 C.R. (4th) 221 (Ont. C.A.). Leave to appeal to S.C.C. refused (1992), 145 N.R. 391 (note) (S.C.C.). See also *R. v. N. (R.O.)* (1986), 6 B.C.L.R. (2d) 306 (S.C.), which dealt with a dangerous offender application relating to N., a known child molester, affirmed (1987), 22 B.C.L.R. (2d) 45 (*sub nom. R. v. N.*) (C.A.). Leave to appeal to S.C.C. refused (1988), 27 B.C.L.R. (2d) xxxv (note) (S.C.C.).
29 *R. v. Nelson* (1989), 51 C.C.C. (3d) 150 (Ont. N.C.).
30 *Bd. of Education of City of Chicago v. Box*, 547 N.E. 2d 627 (Ill. App. Dist. 1989).
31 *R. v. Profit* (1993), 85 C.C.C. (3d) 232 (S.C.C.).

(b) Statutory Protection

There exists a plethora of legislation, regulatory provisions, policies, protocols and programs designed to address the maintenance of safe learning environments and the protection of students. Section 151 *et seq.* of the *Criminal Code* identifies a number of offences which criminalize sexual abuse by teachers against students — sexual interference, invitation to sexual touching, sexual exploitation, indecent acts, exposure and sexual assault. The *Code* provides for the sentencing judge to make an order prohibiting an accused found guilty of certain sexual offences respecting a child under the age of 14, "from seeking, obtaining or continuing any employment or becoming or being a volunteer in a capacity that involves being in a position of trust of authority towards children under 14". This section has the potential to further enhance student security and public safety.

The *Charter* recognizes that, "Everyone has the right to life, liberty and security of the person" (section 7) and "the right not to be subjected to any cruel and unusual treatment" (section 12). The *Ontario Human Rights Code* addresses sexual discrimination, harassment, solicitation and reprisals. Although highly sexualized comments and suggestions may not constitute harassment under the *Code*, they clearly do not fall within the understanding of the conduct expected of a teacher. Article 19(1) of the Convention on the Rights of the Child, 1989, states that:

> State parties shall take all appropriate legislative, administrative, social and educational measures to protect the child from all forms of physical or mental violence, injury or abuse, neglect or negligent treatment, maltreatment or exploitation, including sexual abuse while in the care of parent(s), legal guardian(s) or any other person who has care of the child [including teachers].

Section 18.4 of the Ontario *Evidence Act* proposes measures be taken to protect the best interest of child witnesses (so as not to re-victimize). The basic rule of evidence is the (sworn) oral account of facts of which the witness has personal knowledge. The witness is available in person in court to have his or her account tested by cross-examination. Two subsidiary rules of evidence apply to documentary evidence. The first is the "best evidence" rule: to prove something in court, you must use the best evidence that can be produced. "Best" means closest to direct sworn oral evidence. This produces a hierarchy of documents judged on such criteria as when they were made, by whom they were made, and their status as "original" documents or copies.

The *Child and Family Services Amendment Act (Child Welfare Reform) 1999*, section 72, which came into force on March 31, 2000, set the stage for the most significant changes to Ontario's child protection laws in over a decade. These amendments make up one very important part of an overall reform to the child protection system that includes changes to funding, a new information system, training, monitoring, and the provision of better tools for assessing when a child is at risk. Professionals *and the public* are now required to report if there are reasonable grounds to suspect that a child is or may be in need of protection. Penalties for failing to report have been extended to all grounds for protection; not just abuse. The Act also clarifies that professionals and the public cannot delegate the duty to report to another individual and that the duty to report is an ongoing obligation. They must also report additional suspicions even if they already reported a previous incident.

Ontario Regulation 437/97 made under the *Ontario College of Teachers Act, 1996*, defines professional misconduct for the purposes of subsection 30(2) of the Act as including:

> 7. Abusing a child physically, sexually, verbally, psychologically or emotionally. Any such abuse of a student is a failure to comply with the member's duties under the Act.

Section 27 of O. Reg. 437/97 also defines, "failing to comply with the member's duties under the *Child and Family Services Amendment Act, 1999*" as professional misconduct also.

Section 14 of the Regulation made under the *Teaching Profession Act* (Ontario) states that a member shall:

> (a) regard as his first duty the effective education of his pupils and the maintenance of a high degree of professional competence in his teaching; and
>
> . . .
>
> (f) concern himself with the welfare of his pupils while they are under his care.

The *Education Act* section 265(1)(j) states that it is the duty of a principal, in addition to his or her duties as a teacher, "to give assiduous attention to the health and comfort of the pupils". Regulation 298 under this Act, section 11(3) identifies that, in addition to the duties under the Act, the principal shall,"(k) provide for the instruction of pupils in the care the school premises". Ontario Ministry of Education Policy/Program Memorandum No. 9, *Child in Need of Protection - Child Abuse Reporting Requirements*, identifies that it is the responsibility of the Directors of Education to ensure that all staff members are aware of, and understand, the relevant sections of the *Child and Family Services Act*, particularly the requirement to report cases of children in need of protection and that board policies and procedures conform with the provisions of the Act. Policy/Program Memorandum No. 22, *Trespass, Property Protection and Providing a Safe Environment*, sets out a working guide for establishing and maintaining a safe school environment. As mentioned in Chapter 1, the *Trespass to Property Act* can assist school personnel in the designation and maintenance of school sites as unique, safe and special places. This Act also facilitates in the charging of offenders.

April 7, 2001 marked the first anniversary of the release of a report by the Attorney General of Ontario entitled, *Protecting Our Students: A Review to Identify and Prevent Sexual Misconduct in Ontario Schools*. On May 5, 1999, the Lieutenant Governor in Council (LGIC) appointed the Honourable Sydney Robins to carry out a review of the incidents of sexual misconduct which occurred in a school system and to make recommendations regarding protocols, policies and procedures to effectively identify and even prevent sexual assault, harassment and violence in Ontario schools. The LGIC, as part of the Order in Council, directed that all ministries, boards, agencies and commissions of the Government of Ontario assist to the fullest extent in the review.

The Robins Report contains 101 recommendations, approximately 90 per cent of which involve the education system, specifically the Ontario College of Teachers (OCT) and district school boards. The general themes of the recommendations are:

- strengthening the College of Teachers' discipline and fitness to practice processes, policies and regulations;
- improvements to district school board policies and procedures as they relate to hiring, screening and reporting between schools and boards and agencies, police and parents;
- better professional development and training for all individuals at all steps in the process - identification, reporting and tribunal; and
- to combat sexual misconduct effectively, education and training needs to be directed to prospective teachers, current teachers, volunteers and other school staff; as well as students and parents.

The legislation resulting from the Robins Report (the *Student Protection Act, 2002*) is summarized in Chapter 2.

Meanwhile, the problem has not diminished. A teacher was convicted of sexually abusing a former student on several counts including a firearms charge and was sentenced to four years. (October 2000) A Barrie, Ontario teacher who wrote inappropriate letters to a 13-year old student and returned to the classroom in the fall after a 30-month suspension has been removed again following being charged by the South Simcoe Police Services. The teacher had received an indefinite suspension and was ordered to undergo counseling by the Ontario College of Teachers in April 1998. The Ontario College of Teachers found a Toronto teacher who had a romantic relationship with a student, guilty of professional misconduct. The student was a 14 year old boy. Their relationship involved several clandestine meetings and sexually explicit e-mails. (February 2001) Toronto Police Services laid criminal charges against an English Department head with respect to the making, distribution and possession of child pornography. (March, 2001)

Three teachers were disciplined by the College for inappropriate conduct with students. Charges included sexual touching with a young woman, inappropriate conduct with a young male student and the third for his involvement in the journal entries of a female student. (March 2001) A Leamington, Ontario elementary school teacher was charged in connection with videotaping young girls during after-school hours, following two months of investigation. The 31-year-old teacher was arraigned on two counts of invitation to sexual touching. He was released under several conditions - that he have no contact with the 27 witnesses or alleged victims involved in the case and that he report to police every Sunday and not be in contact with children under 14 unless accompanied by an adult. (March 2001) to face charges of invitation to sexual touching and performing indecent acts.

(c) Child Abuse

As mentioned above, the *Child and Family Services Act* as amended in 1999, made the promotion of a child's best interests, protection and well being "paramount". Children's lives and health override parental rights to freedom from state intervention. The state is not required to wait until a child has been seriously harmed before intervening. An emergency threshold for apprehending a child without prior judicial authorization was inappropriate, given the seriousness of the interests at stake and the difficulty in distinguishing emergency from non-emergency child protection situations. Serious harm, or risk of serious harm, was the appropriate threshold. While parents' and children's rights and responsibilities must be balanced together with children's right to life and health and the state's responsibility to protect children, the underlying philosophy and policy of legislation must be kept in mind when interpreting it and determining its constitutional validity.[32]

The sexual abuse of children is a problem that is not unique to our society let alone our schools. In recent years, sex abuse scandals have struck schools everywhere as well as churches, mentoring organizations, and day care centres: in short, all organizations that provide services for children. These organizations, with long traditions of providing essential services to children, have understandably been thunderstruck when child sexual abuse emerged in their ranks. Reactions have ranged from full disclosure to denial to cover-up, but rarely has there been a proactive, comprehensive effort to prevent sexual abuse or to prepare an effective response before abuse occurs.

After a child has disclosed an incident of sexual abuse, he or she is surprised to learn that the details must be repeated numerous times to various strangers. Victims of child sexual abuse are often subjected to multiple

---

32 See *Winnipeg Child & Family Services (Central Area) v. W. (K.L.)* (2000), 10 R.F.L. (5th) 122 (S.C.C.).

interviews by investigators, medical personnel, social workers, and lawyers. Thus, in the course of the investigation, the child victim is traumatized a second time - by the very individuals who are trying to help. In some cases, a child will become so confused or grow so tired of the questions that he or she will change the details, which decreases the chance that offenders will be caught and punished.

It is vital for children that everyone who works in the school system be obligated to at least meet a minimum standard, so that if a child reports an allegation of abuse to anyone in the school, that person is at least prepared to bring the child to someone who can provide the help and support the child is seeking. As the Supreme Court of Canada reiterated in the case of *R. v. D.(D.)*,[33] the doctrine of recent complaint in sexual assault cases as a principle of law no longer exists in Canada and a failure to make a timely complaint must not be the subject of an adverse inference based upon rejected stereotypical assumptions of how persons react to sexual abuse. There is no rule about how people, who are victims of trauma like a sexual assault, will behave. In this case the complainant alleged that she was sexually assaulted when she was five to six years old. She told no one for two and a half years. She was cross-examined about delay and fabrications. The evidence of a child psychologist was found to be neither relevant nor necessary.

Principals, as the chief administrators in their schools, have the ability as well as the responsibility to set the tone in their schools on a number of issues. Their efforts are critical to creating an environment in the school community where everyone knows that allegations of sexual harassment and abuse will be handled very seriously. The leaders of the local school districts must work together to send a strong message that sexual harassment and abuse of students will absolutely not be tolerated.

Section 79(2) of the *Child and Family Services Act*, as amended, makes it an offence for someone having charge of a child to inflict abuse on that child, by failing to care and provide for or supervise and protect the child adequately, or to permit the child to suffer abuse. Abuse herein means "a state or condition of being physically harmed, sexually molested or sexually exploited". A person who contravenes section 79(2), and a director, officer or employee of a corporation who authorizes, permits or concurs in such a contravention by the corporation, is guilty of an offence and, on conviction, is liable to a fine of not more than $2,000 or to imprisonment for a term of not more than two years, or to both. A child is defined as a person under the age of 16 years.

If found to have had charge of the child at the material time, a teacher who sexually abuses his or her student, has committed a section 79(2) offence. Section 72 imposes a statutory duty on every person to report certain

---

33 [2000] 2 S.C.R. 275.

suspicions of child abuse, and the information upon which those suspicions are based, to a children's aid society. Also, section 72 makes it an offence for certain professionals to fail to so report. Section 72(1) creates the statutory duty to report. In part:

> 72 (1) Despite the provisions of any other Act, if a person, including a person who performs professional or official duties with respect to children, has reasonable grounds to suspect one of the following, the person shall forthwith report the suspicion and the information on which it is based to a society.

Section 72, prior to recent amendments, imposed a duty upon any person to report. However, the threshold test involved a belief, on reasonable grounds. The lower threshold of reasonable grounds to suspect applied to professionals only. The legislation, as amended, continues to impose liability on professionals only, but imposes the same threshold test for everyone.

The duty to report is ongoing:

> 72 (2) A person who has additional reasonable grounds to suspect one of the matters set out in subsection (1) shall make a further report under subsection (1) even if he or she has made previous reports with respect to the same child.

The person who has a duty to report must do so directly to a children's aid society:

> 72 (3) A person who has a duty to report a matter under subsection (1) or (2) shall make the report directly to the society and shall not rely on any other person to report on his or her behalf.

Information which a party would otherwise keep in confidence, such as the content of sessions with a guidance counselor, must nonetheless be reported:

> 72 (7) This section applies although the information reported may be confidential or privileged, and no action for making the report shall be instituted against a person who acts in accordance with this section unless the person acts maliciously or without reasonable grounds for the suspicion.

The protection contained in section 72(7) is not limited to civil proceedings, but applies to professional disciplinary proceedings as well. See *Ontario (Police Complaints Commissioner) v. Dunlop*.[34]

Section 72(4) and (5) create the offence of "failing to report" applicable to persons who perform professional or official duties respecting children. Every school official, supervisory officer and employee and, indeed, a school volunteer, has the duty to report. The legislation puts the best interests of the child first. A standard of "reasonable grounds to suspect", a requirement that reporting be done "forthwith" and that there need only be reason-

---

34 (1995), 26 O.R. (3d) 582 (Div. Ct.)

able grounds to suspect that "there is a risk" of future sexual abuse all support early intervention. The term "forthwith" may mean "immediately" or "within a reasonable time", depending upon the legal context and the factual circumstances.[35]

Where there are reasonable grounds to suspect that a teacher's conduct, as described by a student or fellow teacher, does not constitute, in and of itself, sexual molestation or exploitation, but evidences that it is taking place or is intended to facilitate such abuse in the future, then such conduct may well be reportable either under section 72(1) 3 or under 72(1) 4.

There is only a duty to report suspected abuse which is at the hands of a person having charge of the child or by another person where the person having charge of the child knows or should know of the possibility of abuse but fails to protect the child. Again, teachers and principals are likely characterized as persons having charge of a child for the purposes of section 72. Section 72(5)(b) expressly provides that teachers and principals are persons who perform professional or official duties with respect to children.

In *Ontario (Police Complaints Commissioner) v. Dunlop*[36], a police officer overheard other officers discussing allegations of abuse that a person had made in a statement to police. The Divisional Court held that the officer had obtained the information in the statement "in the course of his professional or official duties", even though he was not the officer assigned to the case in which the statement was taken. The Court stated that "all police officers have a primary duty to prevent the commission of crime". Similarly, a teacher who overhears a conversation at school giving rise to a suspicion of abuse, or who is approached by a member of the community and given information regarding possible abuse by reason of his or her status as a teacher, will likely be found to have obtained this information "in the course of his or her professional or official duties".

A teacher's statutory duty pursuant to the *Education Act* requires that a teacher intervene to protect a student from being victimized by any sexual misconduct in the school environment. That duty might involve various forms of intervention, including reporting to a principal or a supervisory officer. A teacher's failure to comply with his or her duties constitutes professional misconduct before the Ontario College of Teachers. Members of the College include principals, vice-principals and supervisory officers, all of whom are teachers. A failure to comply might form the basis for disciplinary action by the employer. Any school employee (not just teachers) could be disciplined by a school board for a failure to comply with his or her duty. A principal or supervisory officer who fails to fulfill his or her

---

35 See *R. v. Grant* (1991), 67 C.C.C. (3d) 268 (S.C.C.); and *R. v. Bernshaw* (1993), 85 C.C.C. (3d) 404 (B.C. C.A.), reversed (1994), 8 M.V.R. (3d) 75 (S.C.C.).
36 Above, note 34.

duties under the *Education Act* may be disciplined by his or her employer or by the College.

(d) Sexual Harassment

Sexual harassment is a form of sex discrimination. Sexual harassment in the workplace is unwelcome conduct of a sexual nature that detrimentally affects the work environment or leads to adverse job-related consequences for the victims of the harassment. Requiring an employee, male or female, to contend with unwelcome sexual actions or explicit sexual demands in the workplace attacks the dignity and self-respect of the victim both as an employee and as a human being.

> The fact that only some, and not all, female employees at the restaurant were subject to sexual harassment is not a valid reason to conclude that sexual harassment could not amount to discrimination on the basis of sex. Sex discrimination does not exist only where gender is the sole ingredient in the discriminatory action and where, therefore, all members of the affected gender are mistreated identically.[37]

Reports of sexual harassment of students by teachers in high school settings are appalling. In a study conducted by Corbett *et al.*[38] that surveyed 185 university students (51% male and 49% female) to recall instances of sexual harassment by high school teachers, half cited instances where they felt another student had been treated inappropriately by a teacher.

Most incidents consisted of unwanted sexual remarks or touching. Examples were "an offer to stay after school and go over 'hand techniques'", "just got too close for me", "made lewd suggestive remarks", and "he'd walk up and put his arm around my waist—he thought he was complimenting me but I took it differently". Most of these students discussed the incidents with their friends, but did not report the behaviour to authorities.

In another study, conducted by Wishnietsky,[39] a survey of teacher-student relationships was sent to 200 recent female graduates and 100 recent male graduates of North Carolina high schools. Results indicate that, of the 148 students who responded, 61% believed they experienced some form of sexual harassment during their high school years. Only 4.7% of these students reported the harassment to school officials and, in 86% of these reported cases, nothing was done.

As with students in elementary school, high school students are also often incapable of either comprehending or manifesting the unwelcomeness

---

37 *Janzen v. Platy Enterprises Ltd.*, [1989] 1.S.C.R. 1252 at 1254 (quoted from headnote).
38 Kelly Corbett, Cynthia S. Gentry, and Willie Pearson, Jr., "Sexual Harassment In High School," Youth & Society 25 (September 1993):97. See also Cynthia Lutz Kelly, "Harassment and the First Amendment: Inquiry and Analysis", January 1996 at 1.
39 Dan H. Wishnietsky, "Reported and Unreported Teacher-Student Sexual Harassment," Journal of Educational Research 84 (January/February 1991): 166.

of a teacher's behaviour. Many young adults ascribe exaggerated notions of superior experience, maturity, wisdom, and sophistication to their teachers and often accept everything that the teachers espouse as true or correct. It is not surprising that many students would be initially thrilled or flattered to be chosen as the objects of a teacher's unusual attentions. Thus, most high school students who are sexually harassed by their teachers often do not realize that they have been victimized until considerable time has passed. As a result, as the above studies indicate, incidents of sexual harassment often go unreported.

In *Graesser v. Porto*, Chairperson Zemans, in the difficult role of decision-maker in an inquiry pursuant to the *Code*, determining an issue of sexual harassment, stated:

> When dealing with matters involving sexual harassment . . . one rarely encounters the situation where the offence or alleged offence takes place in the open, and therefore can be proven through eye witness testimony. That is, rarely will one sexually harass another in full public view. Rather, these events usually take place behind closed doors or with no witnesses present. Such being the case, if similar fact evidence were excluded, the trier of fact would be faced with having to decide an issue based solely on the evidence of the parties before him.[40]

The earliest case of sexual harassment in Ontario is *Bell v. Ladas*,[41] a decision of O.B. Shime, Q.C., in which he recognized not only the obvious and overt forms of discrimination on the basis of sex but indicated that there could be more subtle forms of conduct which would fall within the prohibited category:

> *The forms of prohibited conduct that, in my view, are discriminatory run the gamut from overt gender based activity, such as coerced intercourse to unsolicited physical contact to persistent propositions to more subtle conduct such as gender based insults and taunting, which may reasonably be perceived to create a negative psychological and emotional work environment.*[42]

He also raised the caution that the normal social contact between employer and employee is not and should not be prohibited.

That caution was affirmed in *Aragona v. Elegant Lamp Co.* when Professor Ed Ratushny stated:

> . . . sexual references which are crude or in bad taste, are not necessarily sufficient to constitute a contravention of section 4 of the Code on the basis of sex. *The line of sexual harassment is crossed only where the conduct may be reasonably construed to create, as a condition of employment, a work environ-*

---

40 (1983), 4 C.H.R.R. D/1569 at D/1572 (Bd. of Inquiry).
41 (1980), 1 C.H.R.R. D/155 at D/156 (Bd. of Inquiry).
42 *Ibid.*

ment which demands an unwarranted intrusion upon the employee's sexual dignity as a man or women. The line will seldom be easy to draw.... [*Emphasis added.*]⁴³

The concept of an affront to dignity was confirmed in *Howard v. Lemoignan*:

> This Board also agrees ... that an affront to the dignity of an individual resulting from different treatment because of that individual's sex constitutes discrimination.⁴⁴

The "negative psychological and emotional work environment" concept of the *Bell* case was further developed in *Dhillon v. F.W. Woolworth Co.*⁴⁵ Professor Cumming in that decision discussed in detail both the *Bell* case and that of *Bundy v. Jackson.*⁴⁶ He drew an analogy between racial and sexual harassment with respect to the work environment and concluded:

> The atmosphere of the workplace is a "term or condition of employment" just as much as more visible terms or conditions, such as hours of work or rate of pay. The words "term or condition of employment" are broad enough to include the emotional and psychological circumstances in the workplace.⁴⁷

Bundy v. Jackson discussed the concept of a poisoned work environment and suggested that no tangible actions need to be taken against an employee for that employee to have suffered harassment. Nor is it always necessary to show resistance to the harassing conduct. Professor Cumming in *Giouvanoudis v. Golden Fleece Restaurant* concluded:

> ... sexual harassment that does not otherwise adversely affect the woman's employment may nonetheless be discrimination on the basis of sex, if it simply makes the work environment unpleasant.⁴⁸

The Supreme Court of Canada has indicated that *Human Rights Codes* are civil, not criminal or penal in nature. McIntyre J., in *Ontario (Human Rights Commission) v. Simpsons Sears Ltd.,* stated:

> To begin with, experience has shown that in the resolution of disputes by the employment of the judicial process, the assignment of a burden of proof to one party or the other is an essential element. The burden need not in all cases be heavy — it will vary with particular cases — and it may not apply to one party on all issues in the case; it may shift from one to the other. But as a practical expedient it has been found necessary, in order to insure a clear result in any judicial proceeding, to have available as a "tie-breaker" the concept of

---

43 (1982), 3 C.H.R.R. D/1109 at D/1110 (Bd. of Inquiry).
44 (1982), 3 C.H.R.R. D/1150 at D/1153 (Bd. of Inquiry).
45 (1982), 3 C.H.R.R. D/743 (Bd. of Inquiry).
46 641 F.2d 934 (1981).
47 Above, note 45, at D/763.
48 (1984), 5 C.H.R.R. D/1967 at D/1978 (Ont. Bd. of Inquiry).

the onus of proof. I agree then with the Board of Inquiry that each case will come down to a question of proof, and therefore there must be a clearly-recognized and clearly-assigned burden of proof in these cases as in all civil proceedings. To whom should it be assigned? Following the well-settled rule in civil cases, the plaintiff bears the burden. He who alleges must prove. . . . The complainant in proceedings before human rights tribunals must show a *prima facie* case of discrimination. A *prima facie* case in this context is one which covers the allegations made and which, if they are believed, is complete and sufficient to justify a verdict in the complainant's favour in the absence of an answer from the respondent-employer.[49]

The development of human rights jurisprudence regarding sexual harassment has been an inventive exercise undertaken to bring such conduct within the reach of prohibitions against discrimination, especially in order to provide a remedy for such conduct in the workplace. As stated by Professor Cumming in *Torres v. Royalty Kitchenware Ltd.*:

> There is no doubt that Boards of Inquiry, by their creative interpretations of the *Human Rights Code,* have made a substantial penetration into the workplace in order to eradicate an insidious form of discrimination.[50]

In expressing its view as to the meaning of sexual harassment, the Supreme Court in *Janzen*,[51] would appear to have espoused that liberal course. It seems to have provided a larger definition than might otherwise have been attached to that phrase, thereby making it easier to eradicate from the workplace other insidious forms of discrimination and harassment not as readily seen to fall within the legislation as conduct of a kind already dealt with by the courts.

As to the taking of a broad view of the meanings of "sexual harassment" it should be stressed that the *Code is* to be interpreted liberally in the light of its preamble, which makes it the public policy of Ontario to "recognize the dignity and worth of every person" and to create "a climate of understanding and mutual respect . . . so that each person feels a part of the community and able to contribute fully to [its] development and wellbeing".[52]

In *Ontario (Human Rights Commission) v. Simpson-Sears Ltd.*, McIntyre J. said such legislation must be given "an interpretation which will advance its broad purposes. Legislation of this type is of a special nature,

---

49 (1986), 7 C.H.R.R. D/3102 at D/3108 (S.C.C.).
50 (1982), 3 C.H.R.R. D/858 at D/862 (Bd. of Inquiry).
51 Above, note 37.
52 R.S.O. 1990, c. H.19. Support for this view is found, *inter alia,* in *Janzen,* above, note 37, and *Cashin v. C.B.C. (No. 2)* (1990), 12 C.H.R.R. D/222 (Cdn. Human Rights Trib). The Supreme Court of Canada has expressed such views in *Robichaud v. Canada (Treasury Bd.)* (1987), 8 C.H.R.R. D/4326; *Ontario (Human Rights Commn.) v. Simpsons-Sears Ltd.,* above, note 49; *Cdn. National Ry. Co. v. Canada (Cdn. Human Rights Commn.)* (1987), 8 C.H.R.R. D/4210.

not quite constitutional but certainly more than the ordinary — and it is for the courts to seek out its purpose and give it effect."[53]

In *Canadian National Railway Co. v. Canada (Canadian Human Rights Commission)*, Chief Justice Dickson stated:

> Human rights legislation is intended to give rise, amongst other things, to individual rights of vital importance, rights capable of enforcement, in the final analysis, in a court of law. I recognize that in the construction of such legislation the words of the Act must be given their plain meaning, but it is equally important that the rights enunciated be given their full recognition and effect. We should not search for ways and means to minimize these rights and to enfeeble their proper impact.[54]

Janzen v. Platy Enterprises Ltd.[55] seems to indicate that the broad definition of sexual harassment laid down in that case extends to some of the behaviour that occurred. According to the guidelines established by the American Equal Employment Opportunity Commission, verbal conduct of a sexual nature will constitute sexual harassment when such conduct has the effect of creating an offensive working environment. After citing that guideline with approval, Chief Justice Dickson went on to say that sexual harassment may take a variety of forms and that it encompasses inappropriate comments.

The Supreme Court of Canada's *dicta* in *Janzen* appear to take a broader approach to sexual harassment than the provisions under section 6 of the *Human Rights Code:*

> ... discrimination on the basis of sex may be defined as practices or attitudes which have the effect of limiting the conditions of employment of, or the employment opportunities available to, employees on the basis of a characteristic related to gender.[56]

The Supreme Court specifically stated that sexual harassment

> ... may be broadly defined as unwelcome conduct of a sexual nature that detrimentally affects the work environment or leads to adverse job-related consequences for the victims of the harassment.[57]

The Chief Justice, writing for the Court, played down the distinction made by some Canadian courts and human rights tribunals between "*quid pro quo*" and "hostile environment" sexual harassment. Instead, he noted:

---

53 Above, note 49, at D/3105.
54 Above, note 52, at D/4224.
55 Above, note 37.
56 Above, note 37, at 1279.
57 Above, note 37, at 1284.

> The main point in allegations of sexual harassment is that unwelcome sexual conduct has invaded the workplace. . . . [58]

The Court made no mention of a requirement of reasonable knowledge by the perpetrator of unwelcome conduct.

Sections 7(2) and (3)(b) [previously s. 6(2), (3)(b)] of the *Code* read as follows:

> (2) Every person who is an employee has a right to freedom from harassment in the workplace because of sex by his or her employer or agent of the employer or by another employee.
>
> (3) Every person has a right to be free from,
>
> . . . .
>
> (b) a reprisal or a threat of reprisal for the rejection of a sexual solicitation or advance where the reprisal is made or threatened by a person in position to confer, grant or deny a benefit or advancement to the person.

It should be noted that "harassment" is not defined in section 7 of the *Code*. It is defined in section 10(1) of the *Code* as "engaging in a course of vexatious comment or conduct that is known or ought reasonably to be known to be unwelcome".

The present *Human Rights Code* expressly makes freedom from sexual harassment a human right. The legislative articulation of a new human right ought to be viewed as an especially significant innovation in public policy. It is arrived at only through a process which includes considerable human suffering, governmental agonizing over the imposition of new legal duties, and an ultimate determination that the injustice suffered is of such magnitude that legal prohibitions are justified.

In interpreting the new provisions, it is important to note Mr. Justice Lamer's statement that laws such as the Ontario *Human Rights Code* are "fundamental law."[59]

3. THE ONTARIO COLLEGE OF TEACHERS

On June 27, 1996, the *Ontario College of Teachers Act, 1996*, received Royal Assent. Some sections of the Act were proclaimed on July 5, 1996. Sections 62 and 63 were proclaimed on April 4, 1997 and the remaining sections were proclaimed on May 20, 1997. The first proclamation permitted the Minister to appoint a Registrar and permitted the holding of elections to the first governing Council; these were completed in early 1997 and the council had its first meeting on May 1 and 2, 1997.

---

58 Above, note 37, at 1283.
59 *Ins. Corp. of B.C. v. Heerspink*, [1982] 2 S.C.R. 145.

(a) Overview of Legislation

The Act establishes the Ontario College of Teachers as a body corporate without share capital, and with all the powers of a natural person. It is a self-governing body for persons who hold teaching qualifications in Ontario. The College has responsibilities similar to other professional bodies, including setting standards of practice for teachers, coordinating and monitoring initial and ongoing professional learning, disciplining members for professional misconduct or incompetence, and regulating teachers' qualifications.

Membership in the College is mandatory for any person employed by a publicly-funded school board whose employment requires teaching qualifications. This includes teachers, principals, consultants, academic supervisory officers, and directors of education.

In carrying out its objects, the College must serve and protect the public interest. The council of the College includes lay-members who represent the broader public.

The revenues of the College are from fees collected from members (as set out in the by-laws). Its annual membership fees are still low in comparison to other similar bodies. New registrants are charged registration fees.

There is a provision for the government to exercise some control over the College by requiring it to make, amend or revoke its regulations.

The membership includes academic supervisory officers because they are required to hold teaching qualifications. Academic supervisory officers are those persons responsible for the development, implementation, operation and supervision of educational programs in the schools. The College does not grant the "Supervisory Officer's Certificate" referred to in the *Education Act*. Candidates for the academic "Supervisory Officer's Certificate" can obtain the certificate from the Ministry of Education upon providing evidence that they have completed a supervisory officer's qualification program accredited by the College. The College grants an "additional qualification" to academic supervisory officers, that appears on their Certificate of Qualification. The College has no legal jurisdiction to determine qualifications requirements for Business Supervisory Officers.

Ontario Regulation 184/97 prescribes how a person may qualify as a teacher in Ontario. Each member will receive a Certificate of Registration and a Certificate of Qualification, which together comprise the "Certificate of Qualification and Registration." The College has extensive latitude to determine what certificates and qualifications it will issue. A person who was qualified to teach under the *Education Act* on May 20, 1997, is deemed by law to be a member of the College and will automatically receive a certificate of qualification and registration denoting qualifications similar to those previously held. Regulation 297 was repealed by O.Reg. 183/97. Letters of Permission are granted to school boards that are unable to find a qualified teacher to fill a regular position. The granting of these Letters remains the responsibility of the Ministry of Education under O. Reg. 183/97.

Under O. Reg. 184/97, the Ontario Teacher's Certificate and Ontario Teacher's Qualifications Record Card have "become" the "Certificate of Qualification". A Temporary Letter of Standing is now an "Interim Certificate of Qualification". A Permanent Letter of Standing is now called a "Certificate of Qualification (Restricted)". A Provisional Letter of Standing that is not restricted to a particular subject is a "Certificate of Qualification (Limited)". A Provisional Letter of Standing that is time-limited and restricted to a particular subject (e.g. Native as a Second Language) is a "Certificate of Qualification (Limited, Restricted)".

It should be noted that under Regulation 298, the Minister of Education and Training remains responsible for determining if a teaching position actually requires specialized qualifications. It is the College that determines how the teacher may obtain the qualifications that are required by the *Education Act* and Regulation 298.

The College also has the power to prescribe by regulation what its members must do to maintain their qualifications, i.e. on-going education requirements and professional development. The College is working with faculties of education and other bodies in respect of teacher education programs and has the power to accredit their programs.

The College has the power to make by-laws prescribing professional and ethical standards for its members. It also has the duty to receive complaints against members and has the power to discipline them for incompetence and misconduct. The College's "Fitness to Practise" committee can find a member unfit to practise.

The College is governed by a Council consisting of 31 persons. Seventeen persons are members of the College who are elected by their fellow members. Fourteen persons are appointed by the Lieutenant Governor in Council (see O.Reg. 345/96). The Council serves for a three year term, and members may be re-elected or re-appointed. The details of the election process are prescribed by regulation.

The Council must meet at least four times a year. Meetings are open to the public. An annual report to the Minister of Education and Training is required, and must be tabled in the Legislature. The chief executive officer of the College is the Registrar.

Six committees are required by the legislation: Executive Committee, Registration Appeals Committee, Investigation Committee, Discipline Committee, Fitness to Practise Committee and Professional Learning Committee. Other committees may be established by the College.

A person who wishes to be a member of the College may apply to the Registrar for membership in accordance with the academic and other requirements set out in the regulations. If registration is refused, the person may appeal to the Registration Appeals Committee. A process is prescribed for the Registration Appeals Committee to conduct hearings by means of written submissions.

If a complaint is made to the College about a member, the matter is referred to an Investigation Committee for a determination of whether the complaint should be referred to the Discipline Committee or Fitness to Practise Committee. The Registrar, the Minister, any member of the public, or a member of the College may make a complaint about a member. Procedures are prescribed in the Act to ensure procedural fairness to the parties.

The Discipline Committee deals with complaints referred to it by the Investigation Committee, the Council, or the Executive Committee pertaining to professional misconduct (as defined in the regulations) and incompetence. A finding of incompetence may be made if the Discipline Committee forms the opinion that the member has displayed in his or her professional responsibilities a lack of knowledge, skill or judgment or disregard for the welfare of a student of a nature or extent that demonstrates that the member is unfit to continue to carry out his or her professional responsibilities or that a certificate held by the member under the Act should be made subject to terms, conditions or limitations. (See section 30(3) of the Act.)

The Council or Executive Committee may order an interim suspension in cases where there is urgency because the member may be a danger to students (section 27).

A member who is the subject of a complaint is entitled to an oral hearing by the Committee. The hearing is open to the public, unless it is closed for one of the reasons specified in the Act.

After hearing the matter, the Committee may make an order, which can include revocation of membership, suspension, payment of a fine, or the imposition of terms and conditions on the member's certificate of qualification and registration. The Committee's decision can be appealed to Divisional Court.

The Fitness to Practise Committee does not discipline members. Its duty is to determine if a member is incapacitated, i.e., suffering from a physical or mental condition or disorder such that the member is unfit to continue to carry out his or her professional responsibilities. After a hearing, this Committee may revoke a member's certificate, suspend the certificate for up to 24 months, impose terms, conditions or limitations on the certificate, or direct that imposition of a penalty be postponed for a specified period under certain terms.

A person may apply for reinstatement of his or her certificate of qualification and registration, or for variation of the terms, conditions or limitations that have been placed on the certificate. The Discipline Committee must hold a hearing and decide upon the applicant's request for reinstatement or variation. The Council and the Executive Committee have the power to reinstate a person's membership without a hearing.

With the approval of the Executive Committee, the Registrar may, for certain specified reasons, order an investigator to obtain information from any member's place of work. The purpose of the investigation is to inquire into and examine the conduct of the member to be investigated by gathering information that is relevant to allegations of misconduct, incompetence or incapacity.

The investigator can examine and copy documents or anything else relevant to the investigation. He or she can seek a warrant from a Justice of the Peace enabling the entry and search of a place for the purpose of an investigation.

The Council has the power to make regulations with prior review of the Minister and with the approval of the Lieutenant Governor in Council, on a wide range of matters, including:

- elections, nominations, voting and representation
- prescribing quorums of the Council and statutory committees (see O.Reg. 72/97)
- establishing committees
- defining "professional misconduct"
- issuing certificates of qualification and registration to members and the requirements for becoming qualified as a member (see O.Reg. 184/97).

According to O. Reg. 437/97, the following acts are defined as professional misconduct for the purposes of subsection 30(2) of the *Ontario College of Teachers Act, 1996*:

1. Providing false information or documents to the College or any other person with respect to the member's professional qualifications.
2. Inappropriately using a term, title or designation indicating a specialization in the profession which is not specified on the member's certificate of qualification and registration.
3. Permitting, counselling or assisting any person who is not a member to represent himself or herself as a member of the College.
4. Using a name other than the member's name, as set out in the register, in the course of his or her professional duties.
5. Failing to maintain the standards of the profession.
6. Releasing or disclosing information about a student to a person other than the student or, if the student is a minor, the student's parent or guardian. The release or disclosure of information is not an act of professional misconduct if,
    i. the student (or if the student is a minor, the student's parent or guardian) consents to the release or disclosure, or
    ii. if the release or disclosure is required or allowed by law.

7. Abusing a student physically, sexually, verbally, psychologically or emotionally.
8. Practising or purporting to practise the profession while under the influence of any substance or while adversely affected by any dysfunction,
    i. which the member knows or ought to know impairs the member's ability to practise, and
    ii. in respect of which treatment has previously been recommended, ordered or prescribed but the member has failed to follow the treatment.
9. Contravening a term, condition or limitation imposed on the member's certificate of qualification and registration.
10. Failing to keep records as required by his or her professional duties.
11. Failing to supervise adequately a person who is under the professional supervision of the member.
12. Signing or issuing, in the member's professional capacity, a document that the member knows or ought to know contains a false, improper or misleading statement.
13. Falsifying a record relating to the member's professional responsibilities.
14. Failing to comply with the Act or the regulations or the by-laws.
15. Failing to comply with the *Education Act* or the regulations made under that Act, if the member is subject to that Act.
16. Contravening a law if the contravention is relevant to the member's suitability to hold a certificate of qualification and registration.
17. Contravening a law if the contravention has caused or may cause a student who is under the member's professional supervision to be put at or to remain at risk.
18. An act or omission that, having regard to all the circumstances, would reasonably be regarded by members as disgraceful, dishonourable or unprofessional.
19. Conduct unbecoming a member.
20. Failing to appear before a panel of the Investigation Committee to be cautioned or admonished, if the Investigation Committee has required the member to appear under clause 26(5)(c) of the Act.
21. Failing to comply with an order of a panel of the Discipline Committee or an order of a panel of the Fitness to Practise Committee.
22. Failing to co-operate in a College investigation.
23. Failing to take reasonable steps to ensure that the requested information is provided in a complete and accurate manner if the member is required to provide information to the College under the Act and the regulations.
24. Failing to abide by a written undertaking given by the member to the College or by an agreement entered into by the member with the College.
25. Failing to respond adequately or within a reasonable time to a written inquiry from the College.
26. Practising the profession while the member is in a conflict of interest.
27. Failing to comply with the member's duties under the *Child and Family Services Act*.

According to section 2 of the Regulation, "a finding of incompetence, professional misconduct or a similar finding against a member by a governing authority of the teaching profession in a jurisdiction other than Ontario that is based on facts that would, in the opinion of the Discipline Committee, constitute professional misconduct as defined in section 1, is defined as professional misconduct for the purposes of subsection 30 (2) of the Act."

In all, there are 31 by-law powers, dealing with the administrative and domestic affairs of the College. The Lieutenant Governor in Council has the power to make regulations on some matters including professional learning requirements. These also include prescribing the composition of the appointed portion of the governing Council (O. Reg. 345/96) and any other matter deemed necessary or advisable in connection with the College, including transitional matters.

There are provisions pertaining to the service of documents, the exchange of personal information between the Ministry and the College, the confidentiality of information obtained by the College, immunity for Council members, officers and employees, and the use of the French language in dealings with the College.

An employer must, upon request, provide a paid leave of absence to a Council or committee member to attend meetings or other proceedings of the Council or a committee during work hours. The College will reimburse the employer for the salary expense of replacing the member.

It is an offence to obtain a certificate from the College by making a false representation, or to assist another person to do so.

(b) Criminal Reference Checks

Ontario Regulation 521/01, made under the *Education Act*, sets out requirements for school boards to collect a "personal criminal history" of every employee and service provider of the board. Under the Regulation, "personal criminal history" means, in respect of an individual, "information on criminal offences of which the individual has been convicted under the *Criminal Code* (Canada) and for which a pardon under section 4.1 of the *Criminal Records Act* (Canada) has not been issued or granted to the individual." The Regulation requires the school board to collect a criminal background check through the police, from the Canadian Police Information Centre (CPIC) e.g., in respect of all employees and service providers. The implementation for obtaining this information is phased-in according to when the individual commences employment or first becomes a service provider with the board. The Regulation also prescribes when an "offence declaration" must be provided. The declaration provides information regarding any criminal offence convictions that occurred since the initial criminal background check. The declaration is also required when the employee or provider moves to another school site within the same school board.

According to section 1 of the Regulation, "service provider" means,

an individual who comes into direct contact with pupils on a regular basis,

   (a) at a school site of a board in the normal course of,

      (i) providing goods or services under contract with the board,

      (ii) carrying out his or her employment functions as an employee of a person who provides goods or services under contract with the board, or

      (iii) providing services to a person who provides goods or services under contract with the board, or

   (b) at a school under the jurisdiction of the Minister in the normal course of,

      (i) providing goods or services under contract with the Minister,

      (ii) carrying out his or her employment functions as an employee of a person who provides goods or services under contract with the Minister, or

      (iii) providing services to a person who provides goods or services under contract with the Minister.

School boards are also required to collect an annual "offence declaration" from all individuals covered by the Regulation. An "offence declaration" is defined in the Regulation as,

a written declaration signed by an individual, listing all of the individual's convictions for offences under the *Criminal Code* (Canada) up to the date of the declaration,

   (a) that are not included in a criminal background check collected by the Ontario College of Teachers after December 31, 1998 or in the last criminal background check collected by the board under this Regulation, and

   (b) for which a pardon under section 4.1 of the *Criminal Records Act* (Canada) has not been issued or granted;

4. ACADEMIC FREEDOM

(a) Vulgar Language in the Classroom

The case of *Keefe v. Geanakos*[60] illustrates the principle that vulgar language can be protected within the umbrella of academic freedom. In his

---

[60] 418 F. 2d 359 (1st Cir. 1969). *Silano v. Sag Harbour Union Free School District Board*, 42 F. 3d 719 (2d Cir. 1994) provides a lengthly discussion of the restrictions on teachers' in-class speech, at pp. 722-273

grade 11 English class, Keefe distributed an article entitled "The Young and the Old" from *Atlantic* magazine which used the word "motherfucker" several times. Despite protests from the community and parents, a U.S. federal appeals court ruled that the article's purpose, and the word itself, was not harmful to the students.

(b) Criticism of Education Policy

Outside the classroom, teachers can voice their opinions about educational concerns. Warren Pickering publicly criticized the educational policies within his school and board as a method of informing the public of these educational concerns. The Court noted that school policies are public policies.[61] Statements made that are not true, malicious, or in breach of confidentiality raise other concerns.

A government tax audit manager[62] was dismissed for creating doubt about the ability and impartiality of public servants. The manager criticized the conversion to the metric system and the implementation of the *Charter of Rights*. Similarly, a teacher's contract was terminated for insubordination.[63] The insubordination included openly criticising school administration in front of students.

(c) Teachers' Physical Appearance

Freedom of expression may involve the physical appearance of teachers. Can boards regulate their teachers' physical appearance? Some argue that this violates the freedom of expression as granted in the *Canadian Charter* and *American Constitution*. A Court upheld a state's interests in maintaining neutrality by forbidding a teacher from wearing her religious garb in the classroom. Courts have provided boards with the right to demand that their teachers dress in a professional manner including restrictions that may be perceived as infringing upon religious, racial or ethnic freedom.

In one case the Court found a right to grow a beard because "wearing a beard is a form of expression of an individual's personality as long as it did not interfere with the teacher's effectiveness in the classroom."[64] What if a board policy dictates wearing neckties and jackets? Would refusal be wilful neglect of duty? In another case a teacher was unsuccessful when the board insisted that she not wear skirts that in their opinion "overexposed herself to the students."[65]

---

61 *Pickering v. Bd. of Education*, 391 U.S. 563 (1968). See also *Metropolitan Toronto Separate School Board v. O.E.C.T.A.* ((1994), 41 L.A.C. (4th) 353 (Ont.).
62 *Fraser v. Canada (Public Service Staff Relations Board)*, [1985] 2 S.C.R. 455.
63 *Whaton v. Flin Flon School Division No. 46* (1980), 4 Man. R. (2d) 420 (C.A.).
64 *Finot v. Pasadena City Bd. of Education*, 58 Cal. Rptr. 520 (1967).
65 *Tardif v. Quinn*, 545 F. 2d 761 (1976).

(d) Lifestyle/Sexual Behaviour

Denominational cause may override individual guarantees of equality under section 15.[66] Cases involving the termination of teachers in denominational schools reflect a denominational school board's right to mandate that its teachers practise the lifestyle outlined by the church's doctrine. In the case of *Casagrande v. Hinton (Roman Catholic Separate School District No. 155)*, Casagrande became pregnant out of wedlock, but was not dismissed for this reason. The reason stated was that she violated the Roman Catholic's doctrine against pre-marital sexual intercourse. In a public school context, teachers may not be dismissed for contravening specific religious practices.[67]

Teachers marrying outside the Roman Catholic church have also been dismissed, as reflected by the cases of *Essex County (Roman Catholic Separate School Board) v. Tremblay-Webster*[68] and *Caldwell v. Stuart*[69] Teachers' lifestyle choices within a denominational school are certainly more closely scrutinized than those in the public school. When teachers accept a job at a denominational school, they must realize that cause for dismissal may include violations against religious doctrine.[70]

Teachers today actively make lifestyle choices which could affect their teaching careers. It should, however, be noted that unmarried heterosexual couples receive express protection in the Ontario *Human Rights Code,* which prohibits marital-status discrimination.[71]

5. EVALUATION AND COMPETENCE

(a) Statutory Requirements

The *Quality in the Classroom Act, 2001*, which received Royal Assent on December 12, 2001, is, according to a government press release, intended

---

66 *Casagrande v. Hinton (R.C. Separate School Dist. No. 155)* (1987), 51 Alta. L.R. (2d) 349 (Q.B.).
67 *Eckman v. Bd. of Education of Hawthorne School Dist.*, 636 F. Supp. 1214 (1986) and *Avery v. Homewood City Bd. of Education*, 674 F. 2d 337 (1982).
68 (1984), 45 O.R. (2d) 83 (C.A.).
69 [1984] 2 S.C.R. 603 (S.C.C.). See also *Essex (County) Roman Catholic Separate School Board v. Porter* (1977), 78 D.L.R. (3d) 417 (Ont. Div. Ct.).
70 See *Essex County (R.C. Separate School Bd.) v. Porter* (1977), 16 O.R. (2d) 433 (H.C.), affirmed (1978), 21 O.R. (2d) 255 (C.A.); *Stack v. St. John's (R.C. School Bd.)* (1979), 99 D.L.R. (3d) 278 (Nfld. T.D.); and *Walsh v. Newfoundland (Treasury Bd.)* (1988), 71 Nfld. & P.E.I.R. 21, 220 A.P.R. 21 (Nfld. C.A.); leave to appeal to S.C.C. refused (1989), 39 C.P.R. 188n (S.C.C.). See also *Black v. Metropolitan Separate School Bd.* (1988), 52 D.L.R. (4th) 736 (Ont. Div. Ct.) re separate school taxes.
71 R.S.O. 1990, c. H.19, s. 1 and see definition of "marital status" in s. 10. Discrimination on this ground is also prohibited by human rights legislation in every other Canadian jurisdiction.

to establish clear and fair standards for measuring teachers' skills in the classroom. The Act sets standards for the appraisal of teachers' classroom performance, establishes a qualifying test for new teachers, and requires school administrators to review teacher performance on a regular basis. The performance appraisal system, which is expected to be fully implemented by September 2004, is intended to ensure that teachers are evaluated in a consistent manner across Ontario. Principals or vice-principals will do the performance appraisals. Supervisory officers may do the appraisal in agreement with the principal or if the principal is unable to do so. Supervisory Officers also become involved if an evaluation results in an unsatisfactory rating.

Teachers are required to be evaluated on a three-year cycle, with two evaluations in the year in which their performance is appraised. However, teachers new to the profession will be evaluated two times in each of their first two years, and teachers new to an employer will be evaluated two times in each of their first two years with the new employer. A principal may perform additional appraisals if he or she considers it advisable. Moreover, a teacher may request additional appraisals. Ontario Regulation 99/02 sets out the standards and methods for performance appraisal. It provides for such matters as:

- the giving of notice to a teacher that he or she will be evaluated
- a rating scale of teacher "competencies" (exemplary, good, satisfactory, unsatisfactory)
- the areas of competency that must be evaluated (set out in a Schedule to the regulation)
- the establishment of guidelines and policies by the Minister and school board
- the requirement of a meeting with the teacher to discuss the appraisal, complete a post-observation report and finalize the teacher's learning plan
- the opportunity for the teacher to respond in respect of parental and student input. The principal must "consider" the teacher's response
- preparation by the principal of a summative report of the performance appraisal in the form prescribed by the Minister and which includes the evaluation, the overall rating and an explanation for the rating. A copy must be given to the teacher within 20 days after the evaluation. The regulation purports to require the teacher to sign the evaluation indicating receipt. The Board is to receive a copy of the evaluation
- how to calculate the three-year evaluation cycle and how to deal with secondments (sections 7 and 8).

Each school board is required to conduct an annual parent survey and pupil survey "in consultation with the school councils and principals for the schools governed by the board, the special education advisory committee and those parents, pupils and teachers who are interested" (subsection 5(1)). The survey will ask for parental input "on each teacher of each child of the parent and the parent's level of satisfaction with communication between the parent and the teacher about the child's learning and progress" (subsection 5(2)). The Regulation also prescribes the content of the survey of pupils in the senior division, in subsection 5(3). According to subsection 5(4) the responses in a parent or pupil survey are not to be disclosed to anyone other than the principal, the appropriate supervisory officer and the appropriate board, except as permitted by the Regulation. It is not abundantly clear whether the completed survey itself can be disclosed to the teacher who is being evaluated, because section 4(1)[5] of the Regulation only provides that the teacher shall have "an opportunity to review and respond to the principal in respect of the parental input, pupil input or both". This refers to "input" rather than the "responses given in a parent survey and a pupil survey" as per subsection 5(4) of the Regulation. As mentioned above, a teacher must be evaluated in respect of certain "competencies" as set out in the Schedule to the Regulation. These fall into five broad categories: commitment to pupils and pupil learning; professional learning; teaching practice; leadership and community; and ongoing professional learning.

The specific requirements of the "qualifying test" are set out in O. Reg. 100/02. Passing the qualifying test (first implemented on a trial basis in Spring 2002) is a requirement for obtaining a certification of qualification and registration from the Ontario College of Teachers. The test must be taken by new graduates from Ontario's faculties of education and by teachers from other jurisdictions new to Ontario. Each test is to contain "general components" and, in addition, components related to the divisions (primary/junior, junior/intermediate or intermediate/senior) for which the teacher seeks to be certified by the Ontario College of Teachers. No qualifying test is required to obtain certain limited or restricted certificates issued by the College, as listed in section 3 of the regulation. The test may be deferred for one year in the case of some interim certificates (section 4). The administrator of the test must provide "accommodation" for candidates who identify needs that they consider need to be accommodated. A person requires accommodation "if completing the qualifying test in the usual time, on the usual date, or in the usual manner would impose an undue hardship on the person because of an attribute of the person mentioned in section 1 of the *Human Rights Code*" (section 5). Section 1 of the Code states:

1. Every person has a right to equal treatment with respect to services, goods and facilities, without discrimination because of race, ancestry, place of origin, colour, ethnic origin, citizenship, creed, sex, sexual orientation, age, marital status, same-sex partnership status, family status or disability.

The *Education Act* requires teachers to have learning plans for their professional growth, commencing in the 2002 school year. According to

O. Reg. 98/02, the learning plan is to include the teacher's "professional growth objectives, proposed action plan and time lines for achieving those objectives" (section 2). The learning plan is to be prepared by the teacher in consultation with the principal.

The *Ontario College of Teachers Act, 1996* was amended in 2001 to create "professional learning requirements" and a new committee of the College, namely, the "Professional Learning Committee" in what is referred to as "Part III.1" of the Act. The committee is comprised of up to five persons appointed by the Minister (if the Minister chooses to make appointments), two persons elected to the Council of the College, two persons appointed to the Council, and two persons who are not members of the College (section 24.1). The duties of the committee are, for the purposes of professional learning requirements, to:

(a) approve persons or entities as providers of professional learning courses;
(b) approve courses as professional learning courses;
(c) establish the procedure for applying for approval as a provider and for approval for a professional learning course
(d) conduct regular reviews of providers and professional learning courses to ensure that providers and professional learning courses continue to meet the current criteria for approval; and
(e) perform such additional duties as are prescribed by regulation (subsection 24.1(8)).

Certain additional powers of the committee are outlined in subsection 24.1(12), including the power to establish "standards for measuring outcomes expected of members who take a professional learning course as proposed by the provider applying for approval for that course." The College is to record each course successfully completed by a member. Section 24.6 sets out the course requirements. Each member must successfully complete, every five years, (a) seven core courses, one from each of the seven categories of professional learning courses established by regulation, and (b) seven elective courses. The Registrar shall suspend or cancel a member's certificate if the member does not comply with the Act and regulations respecting professional learning requirements. The relevant provisions regarding suspension and expulsion are set forth in sections 24.6(4), 24.9 and 24.10 of the *Ontario College of Teachers Act, 1996*. It should be noted, as well, that although the College has extensive regulatory powers in respect of the operation of its *other* committees, it was not given similar powers in respect of the Professional Learning Committee. Instead, the Lieutenant Governor in Council has power to make regulations concerning virtually all aspects of the Committee's structure, operation, and mandate as set forth in section 42.1. In addition, the Minister of Education may make "policy directives with respect to matters relating to professional learning course content and curriculum" that must be followed by the Committee (section 42.2).

Ontario Regulation 270/01 (as amended by O. Reg. 79/02) provides some details as to the Professional Learning Committee, including the appointment of a chair and vice-chair, quorum, filling of vacancies, and frequency of meetings. Section 6 provides that any person or entity may apply to be approved by the Professional Learning Committee as a provider, including but not limited to the following persons or entities:

1. A faculty of education of a post-secondary educational institution or of any other body.
2. A board as defined in subsection 1 (1) of the *Education Act*.
3. A teacher federation.
4. A person or entity in the private sector.

According to section 7, the minimum course criteria in order to be approved as a professional learning course are:

1. The course content and outcomes expected of members who take the professional learning course as proposed by the provider applying for approval for that course match,
    i. the skills and knowledge reflected in the professional standards approved and issued by the College, and
    ii. the standards established by the Professional Learning Committee or by the regulations for measuring the outcomes expected of members who take the professional learning course as proposed by the provider applying for approval for that course.
2. The course will contribute to student achievement.
3. The course includes a formal testing or assessment mechanism to confirm that the member has passed the course requirements.

Section 8 of O. Reg 270/01 provides that, for the purposes of clause 24.6(2)(a) of the Act, the seven categories of professional learning courses are the following:

1. Curriculum
2. Student assessment
3. Special education
4. Teaching strategies
5. Classroom management and leadership
6. Use of technology
7. Communication with parents and students.

Section 9 of the Regulation was amended by O. Reg. 79/02, and provides for the crediting of courses completed during a certain window prior to the commencement of the member's "five-year" period (as per section 24.6 of the Act) during which the course requirements must be completed. Section

10 and 11 of the Regulation provide for certain exemptions from the requirement to complete the courses required by section 24.6 of the Act.

(b) Performance Evaluation

It is most important that a teacher's personnel file contain documented evidence that the teacher has been given direction as to how to improve performance, has been assisted in areas requiring improvement, and that a reasonable time for remediation has been provided. It should be shown that the behaviour resulting in the recommendation for dismissal is not remediable. Incidents that are subject to discipline and the complaints of a third party should be carefully documented, as should the meetings with the teacher to resolve the issues arising from the incident. Progressive discipline can be well-documented by periodic summaries of incidents, meetings, and recommendations that have been made. The teacher should be given the chance to respond in writing, and should be asked to acknowledge receipt of all documentation and that copies will be kept in the teacher's personnel file.

Before a teacher's termination is recommended to the board, the teacher should be given the opportunity to present his or her side, and any misunderstandings can be eliminated at this time.

Once a recommendation of dismissal or termination has been made to the board, the board must give the teacher an opportunity to make submissions as to the proposed dismissal or termination. As we discuss in Chapter 1, the board is well-advised to offer the teacher the opportunity to appear in person to respond to the allegations against him or her. The teacher should be permitted to bring legal counsel. Adequate advance notice to the teacher is essential to give time to prepare submissions. After a teacher has been dismissed or terminated, he or she must be provided with written notice to that effect, along with reasons.

Evaluation of teacher performance is an important part of the documentation process. It is expected that the teacher has been measured against the standard used for other teachers, not against some hypothetical standard of perfection. While a broad interpretation of "just cause" has been allowed, boards of reference, boards of arbitration, and courts have required that an employer's findings be supported by substantial evidence and that they conform with employees' rights. Teachers have the right to grieve termination or dismissal through arbitration, as permitted by the collective agreement.

Many boards have policies which do not allow, e.g., the voluntary transfer of probationary teachers, except under compelling circumstances, so that evaluations must be carried out fairly, consistently, and thoroughly. It is often board policy that a written evaluation of probationary teachers be provided in November and March of each of the two probationary years, while other evaluations may be provided as deemed necessary by the principal and a board superintendent.

Dismissal of teachers because of incompetence, according to Edwin Bridges[72] may be due to one or more of five types of failure:

1. *Technical Failure* occurs when the teacher is deficient in one or more of the following: discipline, teaching methods, knowledge of subject-matter, explanation of concepts, evaluation of pupil performance, organization, planning, lesson plans, and homework assignments.
2. *Bureaucratic Failure* is indicated when the teacher fails to comply with school/district rules and regulations or directives of superiors. Failure to follow suggestions to adhere to the content of curriculum or allow supervisors into the classroom to supervise constitutes bureaucratic failure.
3. *Ethical Failure* results when the teacher fails to conform to standards of conduct applicable to the teaching profession. Physical or psychological abuse of students, negative attitudes toward students and neglect or indifferent performance of the teacher's instructional duties demonstrate ethical failure.
4. *Productive Failure* is indicated by the academic progress of students, the interest of students in what is being taught, the attitudes of students toward school, the respect of students for the teacher, and the climate of the classroom.
5. *Personal Failure* occurs when the teacher lacks certain cognitive, affective, or physical attributes perceived to be necessary for the teaching profession. Poor judgment, emotional instability, lack of self-control, and insufficient strength to withstand the rigours of teaching demonstrate personal deficiencies.

Bridges suggests that there are often multiple areas of failure in the majority of cases when tenured teachers are dismissed. Dismissal is rarely based on a single occurrence; rather, termination results from a series of events persisting over periods ranging from several months to several years.[73]

Incompetency is one of the main reasons for teacher termination. It is difficult to dismiss a teacher for incompetency because it is argued that certification may well suggest competency. Challenges to provide a more specific definition of incompetency have proven unsuccessful. The incom-

---

[72] "It's Time to Get in Touch With the Turkeys", *Principal*, 64, pp. 19-21 (1985). See also E.M. Bridges, *The Incompetent Teacher: The Challenge and the Response* (Philadelphia: The Falmer Press, 1986). See *Mongitore v. Regas*, 520 N.Y.S. 2d 194 (1987); *Hayes v. Phoenix-Talent School Dist.*, 893 F. 2d 235 (1990) and *Davidson v. Winston-Salem, 303* S.E. 2d 202.

[73] *Ibid.*, at p. 20.

petent teacher is one the courts find incompetent after having been warned, counselled and helped.[74]

Dismissal for insubordination is possible where a teacher has had wilful disregard for school policies or administrative directives.

In *Re Termination of James E. Johnson*,[75] Johnson was a tenured teacher who was charged with insubordination warranting discharge when,

> he made no effort to comply with specific directive that he improve his relationship and rapport with students and parents, and specifically that he provide worksheets containing assigned problems instead of having students copy them off the board, and furnish each student with copies of tests and materials used to supplement the textbook.

(c) TIGHT Method of Evaluation

Randklev and Lemon have identified a series of skills for consideration when a principal is involved with improving a teacher's performance.[76] Known by the acronym TIGHT, Randklev and Lemon emphasize that the principal must communicate the following skills clearly and carefully with the teacher:

Tell the teacher the area requiring improvement; be honest, direct and clear.

Interpret your concerns and expectations clearly and completely to the teacher. Be prepared to provide data that supports your position, and to answer the questions:

1. What are you using to measure this inadequacy?
2. How will we both know if there is improvement?

Gather data on how to assist the teacher to overcome deficiencies. Sources for the data will include: senior administration, local board of education consultants, other principals, teachers, faculty of education personnel and professional literature. Throughout the improvement process, comprehensive data must be gathered about the teacher's performance.

Help the teacher make the needed improvements by establishing a plan, addressing specific concerns. The plan should describe the assistance to be provided, identifying individuals, i.e., principal, other professionals within the board or outside, and specifying the expected outcomes.

Time must be provided for improvement, with a reasonable amount of time prescribed for each area of improvement. At the end of the time period, the principal should meet with the teacher, providing documentation to describe the performance in the targeted area. If the problem has been

---

74 *Eshome v. Board of Education of School District of the State of Nebraska*, 364 N.W. (2d) 7 (1985).
75 451 N.W. 2d 343 (Minn. 1990).
76 Beth Randklev and Ronald K. Lemon, "When Tenured Teachers Fail", *Principal*, 70, pp. 44-45 (1990).

addressed, the principal should applaud the improvement before proceeding with the next area of concern.[77]

Proceeding through the stages of the "review process", and arriving at the decision of termination will be difficult for a principal. Although staff members may be fully cognizant of a teacher's incompetence, they may still criticize the principal's decision to terminate their colleague's teaching position. The dismissed teacher may attempt to enlist support from his or her colleagues by claiming that adequate assistance was not provided by the principal.

If the principal can demonstrate that due process procedures have been evident throughout the "review process", the decision to terminate the incompetent teacher will be made easier. Repeated evaluations by multiple observers may identify deficiencies related to on-the-job performance, and along with this is giving the teacher regular and periodic notice of these deficiencies and an opportunity to improve performance. Principals have a responsibility to students, parents, senior administrators and the school board to recommend the dismissal of incompetent teachers.

(d) De-emphasizing the Minimal Standards Approach

Any method of evaluation is accompanied by a concept of what teaching is and a definition of what good and effective teaching is. In the process of evaluating teachers one immediately is confronted by the source of the problem – defining teaching itself. This means that effective evaluation necessarily must emphasize judgmental factors.

Two major initiatives — teacher professionalism and school restructuring — are the major "watchwords" of the 1990's.[78] These initiatives have been gaining momentum aiming to improve education by recruiting, preparing and retaining competent teachers so that they can better utilize their knowledge and talents to focus more on learners' needs. With these new initiatives have come more standardized evaluation instruments developed by school boards and teachers' federations. These evaluative systems may be used to deny promotion or justify dismissal of teachers. These types of decisions, often based in part on teachers' performance appraisals, may lead to court cases.

Michael Fullan, in *The New Meaning of Educational Change*,[79] suggests that many districts' appraisal systems tend to identify minimum competencies of teachers and do not have procedures in place to help change teaching behaviour. In a 1986 study, Lawton and Associates examined appraisal

---

77 *Ibid.*, at pp. 44-45.
78 Jason Millman and Linda Darling-Hammond, eds., *The New Handbook of Teacher Evaluation: Assessing Elementary & Secondary School Teachers* (Newbury Park, California: Corwin Press, 1991).
79 2nd ed. (New York: Teachers College Press, 1991).

systems in 30 Ontario school boards. They found that "84 per cent of the over 3,000 teachers surveyed indicated little or no improvement as a result of the appraisal process".[80] However, teacher evaluation systems in various forms have been used since the late nineteenth century. Why then are evaluation systems that focus on inspecting minimal performance to identify incompetent teachers still being used by many school boards? The answer, it seems, lies in the fact that rating and evaluation systems were developed primarily by people external to education to demonstrate to the public that students were receiving appropriate instruction and that teachers were competent. These systems focused on assessing the minimal competencies of teachers, and none of these systems were used to help teachers improve instruction. The contemporary view of teacher evaluation is that its primary purpose should be for teacher development and that there should be separate procedures for decisions concerning employment, termination, promotion, *etc.* This approach makes sense because making personnel decisions about individuals is usually more crucial and the criteria more rigorous than decisions about how to improve teaching.

(e) Adherence to Procedure

In *Kudasik v. Board of Directors, Port Alleghany School*,[81] Karen Kudasik, a temporary teacher hired to replace a teacher who had been transferred, received an unsatisfactory rating at the end of the year. As a result of the rating the board decided to terminate her. The teacher challenged the rating and termination decision. The Court's decision to uphold the board's dismissal of the teacher was based on the fact that the board adhered to statutory procedures and "satisfied their proof of procedural burden concerning the rating and dismissal of Karen Kudasik".[82]

In another case regarding the dismissal of a tenured teacher in Michigan, the Court upheld the school board's decision to terminate the teacher because "substantial, material, and competent evidence supported the State Tenure Commission's findings in support of discharge of the tenured teacher".[83]

In *Eston-Elrose (School Division No. 33) v. Stoneouse*,[84] the school board was found to have acted in bad faith in the way in which it dismissed a tenured teacher. The school board appealed. The Court referred the case back to the Board of Reference which again upheld the previous decision

---

80 S. Lawton, E. Hickcox, K. Leithwood, D. Musella, *The Development and Use of Performance Appraisal of Certified Education Staff in Ontario School Boards* (Toronto: Ministry of Education, 1986).
81 455 A. 2d 261 (Pa. 1983).
82 *Ibid.*, 264.
83 *Hagerty v. State Tenure Commn.*, 445 N.W. 2d 178 (Mich. App. 1989).
84 (1988), 65 Sask. R. 216 (Q.B.).

based on two reasons. The reasons centred on the failure of the school board to follow its supervision and evaluation policies "to the letter". The Board of Reference concluded that the school board did not follow its policies in this case because before the evaluation process was even concluded the teacher was "being asked, even coerced, into resigning in order that the report not be written in a negative way".[85] In addition, the evaluators did not present to the Board of Reference all of the teacher's records, which "clearly indicates bad faith".[86]

In the above-mentioned cases the courts did not question the validity of the evaluation instrument, the criteria used to evaluate teachers, or the qualifications of the evaluators. Instead they focused on evidentiary standards and the adherence to procedural rules. It is important, therefore, that school subjective and objective evaluation techniques be used.

School boards sometimes fail to comply with the regulatory requirements, in particular, the requirements of Reg. 298, under the *Education Act*, which provides as follows:

> 11(3) In addition to the duties under the Act and those assigned by the board, the principal of a school shall, except where the principal has arranged otherwise under subsection 26(3),
>
> (j) make recommendations to the board with respect to,
>
>   (ii) the demotion or dismissal of teachers whose work or attitude is unsatisfactory;
>
> (4) A principal shall only make a recommendation to the board under subclause 3(j)(ii) after warning the teacher in writing, giving the teacher assistance and allowing the teacher a reasonable time to improve.

In several cases, arbitration boards have found that the school boards violated their collective agreements when they failed to provide procedural fairness to the grievors.

In *Re Kirkland Lake Board of Education and O.S.S.T.F.*[87] the school board terminated the contract of a probationary teacher who had been absent from work for much of her probationary period as the result of a compensable injury. The arbitrator found that the school board had failed to comply with its obligations under Reg. 298 and that it had failed because of the grievor's absence due to her injury. He therefore found that her termination was contrary to the *Human Rights Code* and perforce without just cause.

Many of the duties of teachers are set out in the *Education Act*. Principals also have statutory duties imposed upon them. Many of these duties

---

85 *Ibid*, at 217.
86 Ibid., at 218.
87 September 13, 1994 (Burkett), E.R.C. #543.

are quite specific and relate to the carrying out of specific assignments or functions. Others are more general in nature and relate to moral and ethical conduct. One of the statutory duties most prominently featured in the case law is the duty imposed upon Ontario teachers to inculcate by precept and example respect for religion and the principles of Judaeo-Christian morality and the highest regard for truth, justice, loyalty, love of country, humanity, benevolence, sobriety, industry, frugality, purity, temperance and all other virtues.

Other statutory duties also suggest that the conduct of teachers should be judged against a more stringent set of moral standards than would be applied in industrial settings. Teachers do not necessarily check their teaching hats at the school yard gate and may be perceived to be wearing their teaching jobs even off duty.[88]

Penalties short of discharge have also been upheld for violation of statutory duties of this type. In *Re City of Hamilton Board of Education and O.P.S.T.F.*,[89] an arbitration board upheld a 19 1/2-day suspension imposed because the teacher refused to obey directives from the discipline of a particular student. The arbitration board found the teacher's conduct contrary to section 264(1)(a) and (e) of the *Education Act*.

Arbitrators have consistently found that teaching requires particularly high standards of morality and probity and that they have not hesitated to enforce such standards in their decisions. For example, in *Re Durham Board of Education and O.S.S.T.F.*,[90] the arbitration board found the teacher's misrepresentation of qualifications to constitute "moral turpitude" within the meaning of the collective agreement. It specifically invoked section 264(1)(c) of the *Education Act* for the proposition that teachers are held to a "high standard of probity and honesty". In *Re Lincoln County Roman Catholic Separate School Board and O.E.C.T.A.*,[91] the discharge of a teacher of "pre-Kindergarten" students was upheld for involving students in a fraudulent book ordering scheme. In *Re Windsor Roman Catholic Separate School Board and O.E.C.T.A.*,[92] the arbitration board, in upholding the discharge of a teacher who had written sexually explicit letters to students, referred to the fact that the teacher's conduct was in violation of his statutory duties, among other things. In *Re Hornepayne Board of Education and O.S.S.T.F.*,[93] a case involving a three-day suspension for the use of profane language among other offences, the arbitration board specifically distinguished private sector cases on profanity as inapplicable in this professional

---

88 *Cromer v. B.C.T.F.* (1986), 29 D.L.R. (4th) 641 (B.C. C.A.).
89 December 3, 1985 (Saltman), E.R.C. #260. See also *Cox v. Dardenelle*, 790 F. 2d 668 (1986) and *Miles v. Denver Public Schools*, 944 F. 2d 773 (1991).
90 May 24, 1990 (Hunter), E.R.C. #118.
91 1981 (Tammi), E.R.C. #118.
92 January 11, 1993 (Brandt), E.R.C. #488 at p. 108.
93 July 30, 1992 (Marcotte), E.R.C. #456.

context. It accepted the argument that section 264(1)(c) of the *Education Act* establishes a standard of conduct for teachers which is higher than "that which can be legitimately expected of employees outside the teaching profession".

The use of physical force by teachers against students has emerged as an issue in a number of arbitration cases. Generally, arbitration boards have taken a stringent approach to the use of force. In *Board of Education for the City of London and O.S.S.T.F.*[94] the arbitration board commented that:

> Striking a student is never an appropriate response and therefore the defence of provocation is not one that can be accepted in the circumstances. Thus absent any other factors I would have no difficulty in finding that the employer had just cause to dismiss the grievor.

The issue of whether a criminal conviction constitutes just cause for discharge was first considered at length in *Etobicoke Board of Education v. O.S.S.T.F.*[95] a case involving a teacher convicted of conspiracy to possess stolen property. The school board took the position that conviction for an indictable offence violated the duty imposed by section 264(1)(c) of the *Education* Act. The arbitration board did not take issue with this proposition. Indeed, by implication, it accepted it. It found, however, that section 264(1)(c) "cannot be enforced to the letter by use of disciplinary sanctions".

In *Roman Catholic Separate School Board of Sudbury and A.E.F.O.*[96] an arbitration board reinstated a teacher who had pleaded guilty to eight counts of common assault against students. The grievor had originally been charged with several additional offences, including sexual assault. All these additional charges were subsequently withdrawn.

The arbitration board in this case was influenced by two features of the offences in minimizing their significance. First of all, it emphasized that the assaults were not sexual. It found that there was no element of violence. The board relied on factors personal to the grievor: long service (approximately 32 years' seniority) and a clean disciplinary record. As a result, the arbitration board reinstated the grievor with a three-month suspension.

The appropriate standards of proof are stringent in sexual misconduct cases, but there is also no doubt that it is appropriate for school boards to hold teachers to stringent codes of behaviour in sexual matters involving students. In *Provincial Schools Authority and Provincial Schools Authority Teachers*[97] an arbitration board considered the case of a teacher discharged

---

94 February 15, 1993 (Keller), E.R.C. #504.
95 (1981), 2 L.A.C. (3d) 265 (Ont.). See also *Wellington Board of Education v. O.S.S.T.F.* (1991), 24 L.A.C. (4th) 110, and *Board of Education for the City of London v. O.S.S.T.F.*, October 7, 1986, (Tepitsky) E. R. C. #305.
96 February 4, 1993, (Bendel) E.R.C. #477.
97 November 22, 1984 (Burkett), E.R.C. #228.

as a result of a number of allegations of impropriety, including sexual harassment. The arbitration board held:

> It goes without saying that the boundaries which divide sexual harassment from acceptable social interchange between male and female employees in the work setting do not apply as between those in authority and those over whom authority is exercised in an institutional setting. There is no room for any type of sexually oriented social interchange between those in authority and those over whom authority is exercised in an institutional setting and where it is proven that such has been instigated by the person in authority a union would be hard pressed to establish that the penalty of discharge is unreasonable.

As professional educators, teachers must be accorded a degree of discretion in the manner in which they carry out their duties and responsibilities. The difficulty identifying insubordination in the context of employment often lies in identifying the boundaries of this "reasonable latitude".

One U.S. federal court held that "a student should have the same protection in school that an employee has in the workplace." Specifically, the Court reasoned:

> Indeed, where there are distinctions between the school environment and the workplace, they "serve only to emphasize the need for zealous protection against sex discrimination in the school." The ability to control and influence behaviour exists to an even greater extent in the classroom than in the workplace, as students look to their teachers for guidance as well as for protection. The damage caused by sexual harassment also is arguably greater in the classroom than in the workplace, because the harassment has a greater and longer lasting impact on its young victims, and institutionalizes sexual harassment as accepted behaviour. Moreover, as economically difficult as it may be for adults to leave a hostile workplace, it is virtually impossible for children to leave their assigned school. Finally, "[a] nondiscriminatory environment is essential to maximum intellectual growth and is therefore an integral part of the educational benefits that a student receives. A sexually abusive environment inhibits, if not prevents, the harassed student from developing her full intellectual potential and receiving the most from the academic program."[98]

It is imperative for boards to adopt and enforce strict policies prohibiting sexual harassment in schools. When thoughtfully developed, a school sexual harassment policy becomes the foundation on which a board can build its anti-sexual harassment platform to improve the health, safety, and welfare of students and staff.

In *Nevels v. Board of Education*,[99] the appellant, Nevels, argued that the school board violated its own policy that the termination of a tenured teacher must be based on the teacher's performance-based evaluations. He argued that his two evaluation reports showed him to be competent and

---

98 *Davis v. Munroe County Bd. of Education*, 74 F.3d 118 Cat 1193 (U.S. 11th Cir., 1996).
99 822 S.W. 2d 898 (Mo. App. 1991).

efficient. The principal conducted two evaluations and several formative observations of Nevels' classroom teaching. Although the evaluations indicated that he met all performance levels, the principal made notations regarding several concerns he had about Nevels' performance in the classroom. In fact, Nevels received a series of "job target sheets, defined as 'measurable, precise objectives stated in terms [to] assist in attainment of goals', identifying and eliminating weaknesses in teaching skills".[100] The superintendent testified that many different tools can be used to evaluate a teacher's performance. The performance evaluations, the handwritten notes and other relevant factors were used as a framework for decision-making in this case.

The Court determined that neither the school guidelines nor the *Teacher Tenure Act* required the school board to make its decision based solely on the performance evaluations. The Court held that such information "may" serve as a basis for decision-making and, in fact, the school board did consider the evaluation reports in reaching its decision concerning the teacher's dismissal. This case supports the notion that classroom observation should constitute only one facet in the evaluation of a teacher's overall performance and that other factors can be used to make a decision to dismiss a teacher.

It is important for principals to accumulate numerous examples of a teacher's weaknesses and not make a decision based on one classroom visit. The Court in *Board of Education v. Ingels* stated very clearly that:

> [P]roof of momentary lapses in discipline and order or of a single day's lesson gone awry is not sufficient to show cause for dismissal of a tenured teacher.... Yet, where brief instances and isolated lapses occur repeatedly, there emerges a pattern of behaviour which, if deficient, will support the dismissal of a tenured teacher. Where the School Board fails ... to show that the examples of conduct constitute a pattern of deficiency, then dismissal cannot be permitted.[101]

Some boards have developed an appraisal system that encourages the professional growth of its teachers. In combination with this philosophy of professional growth, the appraisal system's goal is to enhance the learning environment of the students. The procedure specifies the process of teacher appraisal in a "consistent, system-wide manner". The performance appraisal criteria includes the planning abilities of the teacher, the instructional skills and strategies used by the teacher, classroom management skills, evaluation methods used, and the professionalism of the teacher.

A five-step appraisal system may include:

1. notification to the teacher of the appraisal;
2. pre-observation conference to determine the time, nature, and criteria

---

100 *Ibid.*, at 905.
101 394 N.E. 2d 69 (1979).

to be used for the visit, to review the characteristics of the class to be visited, and the data gathering techniques to be used by the evaluator;
3. the observation of the class;
4. post conference to discuss the teacher's performance;
5. the written report.

Time lines for conducting the appraisal and the number of observations should be clearly stated.

It is important that performance appraisal principles clearly state that the standards to be applied by an evaluator in classroom visits will be those held by a particular evaluator. This statement assumes, what several courts have determined, that the evaluators' training and qualifications make them capable of making these evaluative decisions.

There is no doubt that performance evaluation systems geared toward improving teachers and teaching are far more effective than systems which focus on assessing the minimal competencies of teachers. Standard evaluation criteria and methods, and strict adherence to these policies and procedures by principals and board officials, attempt to guard against teachers having to resort to legal avenues to resolve conflicts related to the use of performance appraisal data in hiring, promotion, or dismissal cases.

As we have discussed, performance appraisals serve two distinct purposes. On the one hand, evaluation policies are geared toward the improvement and development of teachers through remediation. On the other hand, evaluations can be used as a means to justify the dismissal or demotion of a teacher. At the heart of this dual-natured evaluation process is a system of documentation. The documentation system is designed to improve communication and to protect both parties involved in the evaluation process.

Beckham, in *Legal Aspects of Teacher Evaluation*,[102] outlines four fundamental aspects of what is referred to in the United States as "due process". First, the employee must be made aware of the criteria being used to evaluate his or her performance. Second, after the evaluation period, the employee must be made aware of any deficiencies with his or her performance. If the problems are serious, the employer may contemplate termination. In this case, the employee must also be made aware of that possibility. Third, the employee must be given a chance to improve his or her performance. The nature of the contract also assumes that the board will provide the necessary assistance to reach the stated goals. Finally, a reasonable amount of time must be allotted for the employee to improve. "If a teacher's performance does not improve, the system is designed to provide an incentive for voluntary resignation or provide the necessary documentation for the principal recommending termination to the Board."[103]

---

102 (Topeka, Kansas: NOLPE, 1981).
103 Marvin A. Zuker, *The Legal Context of Education* (Toronto: OISE Press, 1988), at p. 127.

In *Hyde v. Wellpinit School District No. 495*,[104] a dismissed school principal brought action against the school district, its superintendent and its board of directors, challenging the non-renewal of his contract. Hyde was a teacher and administrator for 18 years and employed as a principal for Wellpinit in 1977-78. In November of 1977, Hyde was reported to be working well in all areas. In April of 1978, the superintendent approached him about his salary for the following year and indicated that he would recommend the renewal of his contract. A week and a half later, Mr. Hyde received a letter from the superintendent indicating 15 negative items regarding his performance as principal and a request for his dismissal was attached.

The Court reinstated Mr. Hyde on the basis that there was no evaluative criteria evident. As a result, Mr. Hyde was at "the whim and pleasure" of the superintendent. Moreover, the principal had no guidelines to measure his performance and therefore could not have been given a legitimate chance to improve.

In a further case, the defendant, Dr. Jones,[105] sent a memo to all principals and teachers informing them that the scores attained by their students on the California Achievement Test (CAT), in the specific areas of reading, language and math, would be used to evaluate teacher performance. After the scores were documented, Dr. Jones required principals to observe the classrooms of teachers who received an unsatisfactory rating in order to document other deficiencies. The teachers claimed that the evaluation process failed to provide them with equal protection of the law and due process.

The Court found that specific use of the CAT scores for English and math, and the continued evaluation of those teachers who received an unsatisfactory rating, did not create an arbitrary or capricious classification among the teachers and therefore their claim of a violation of liberty interests was denied. Claims that the plaintiffs suffered damage to their reputation within the community and were denied salary advancement were also dismissed because a link of the evaluation process to these actions could not be drawn. The allegation that the plaintiffs were placed in jeopardy of termination was not able to be determined and the judge instructed the plaintiffs to file a more definite statement of their claim. The judge also found that the defendants' adoption and implementation of these new guidelines violated various provisions of the policy statement.[106]

Procedural fairness relating to teacher competency was canvassed in the case of *Orth v. Phoenix Union High School System*.[107] The appellant,

---

104 611 P. 2d 1388 (Wash. Ct. App 1980), cert. denied 648 P. 2d 892 (1982).
105 *St. Louis Teacher's Union, Loc. 420 v. St. Louis Bd. of Education*, 652 F. Supp. 425 (E.D. Mo. 1987).
106 See also S.E. Phillips, "Legal Issues in Performance Assessment", 79 Ed. Law Rep. 709 (March 11, 1993).
107 613 P. 2d 311 (Ariz. App. 1980).

Carl Orth, had been a tenured teacher at the Phoenix Union High School since 1965. In June of 1977 the district adopted a new evaluation program. Orth was evaluated in the fall of 1977 and received unsatisfactory ratings in some teaching areas. In December of the same year more extensive evaluations were given. Orth received 15 unsatisfactory ratings of the 85 monitored, resulting in an overall unsatisfactory rating. A list of objectives for improvement were given with a target date of March 14, 1978. No notice of future employment was given at this time. In January of 1978 he received a letter from the principal which reminded him of the events and the offering of assistance. Orth was evaluated in March and was served with notice to dismiss in April due to classroom inadequacy.

Orth requested a hearing. The hearing commission recommended dismissal. The appellant filed suit in the Superior Court seeking reinstatement based on the contention that the district did not comply with ARS 15-265 (provision of a preliminary notice of inadequacy). The board argued that the evaluation letter in December and the letter from the principal served this purpose. The Court disagreed, saying the letter did not specifically state inadequacies and therefore an opportunity to remediate was not given. The preliminary notice had to be issued by the board.

Trimboli v. Board of Education of Wayne County involved an appeal by the Wayne County Board of Education of a circuit court decision to reinstate Don Trimboli to his position as Director of Federal programs for four county schools.[108] Initially, when the case came to Court, it was held that members of a board of education are not qualified to make teacher evaluations. No administrator had ever evaluated the Director's performance. The Court held that professionally trained teachers, principals and superintendents shall have exclusive control over matters such as evaluation.

Iven v. Hazelwood School District[109] reflects the importance of all aspects of the evaluation process being completed properly. Leo Iven was a permanent math teacher, who, when evaluated, received an unsatisfactory rating. The evaluation listed 12 areas for improvement. In February, the superintendent issued a letter warning Iven of the possibility of termination if remediation did not occur. The letter also indicated that D.C. Huff would continue in the place of the superintendent and a conference date was set.

Huff visited Iven's classroom four times but none of the visits were scheduled and pre-conferences were not held. No mention was made as to how Iven could improve. Huff held a discussion with Iven and extended his evaluation period for the next school year. He did not evaluate or observe Iven until November when formal charges were outlined in a letter. Fall evaluations were conducted by the head of the math department, Carmen,

---

108 280 S.E. 2d 686 (1981).
109 710 S.W. 2d 462 (Mo. App. 1986).

who was not a designate of the superintendent. Carmen told Iven that he had made the necessary improvements.

In May, Huff wrote a memorandum to be placed in Iven's personnel file which stated that efforts to improve were being made and deficiencies were outlined. The letter of November was deficient because it stated that letters of May 1983 and February 2, 1984 stated charges, but they did not. Moreover, the letter indicated that Huff and Carmen were working with the teacher to improve, a statement that was not supported by evidence. The Court found that it was not possible for Iven to know from the letter of November 21, 1984 what specific grounds were to be tried at the termination hearing.

A case with a bit of a twist involved a teacher who argued that her dismissal and her poor evaluations were linked to her union activities and a personality conflict with her supervisor.[110] After teaching for nine years, Hickman moved to the Valley School District where she taught for three-and-a-half years. During that time she was an active member of the union. She published a newsletter, negotiated a contract on behalf of her membership and alienated her principal and superintendent by not dealing with them specifically when problems in the school arose.

During her first year with the board she was given an excellent rating. Second-year performance appraisal indicated excellent teaching but poor interpersonal relationships. During the final year, after three 15-30 minute observations, declines in teaching performance and professionalism appeared on her review. Also attached were a list of infractions and a recommendation not to renew her contract. The superintendent supported the request for termination based on the evaluations presented by the principal. The Court found that Hickman's evaluations indicated that her union activities had led to her poor evaluations and the board was unable to prove otherwise.

Teacher termination cases reveal that teacher evaluations are presented in the courts as a form of evidence. A review of these cases reveals that procedural due process and accurate documentation must be proven in the courts for a teacher termination decision to be upheld.

In his book, *The Incompetent Teacher*,[111] E.M. Briggs notes several problems faced by administrators. First, evaluation and the possibility of termination is an emotional ordeal. "Accordingly, administrators are inclined to suffer other people's shortcomings in silence and to 'manage by guilt'."[112] Management by guilt includes avoiding the disappointment of the employee, failure to confront individuals about realistic problems with job behaviour and the choice to avoid dealing with the problem by transferring

---

110 *Hickman v. Valley Local School Dist. Bd. of Education*, 619 F. 2d 606 (1980).
111 (Philadelphia: Falmer Press, 1986).
112 *Ibid.*, at p. 25.

the teacher to another location or position. Administrators are also aware of the time constraints placed upon them by their job and are often hesitant to form critical judgements based on limited time in another teacher's classroom. According to Briggs, transfer is a favourite escape hatch, with nearly 70 per cent of the 141 California schools he studied reported using this practice.

In recent years, boards have spent a great deal of time and energy creating new performance appraisal policies and support documents. In one recent study of performance appraisals in Ontario, the authors found that the problems inherent in the process are not going to go away by simply recombining and reshuffling the value and activity of different elements of the procedure. They maintain that it is still vitally important to follow the legal notions of due process and documentation. In addition, however, they state that it is important to stop viewing performance appraisals as an "isolated system within the organization".[113] Instead, a broader performance management system should be used. To do this, there must be a fundamental understanding of the nature of the work done by teachers and at least an attempt to develop consistent and appropriate policies for management and evaluation.

The relationship between school boards and their employees is very complicated and often disputed. Although the development of an ideal performance appraisal has not occurred, administrators can avoid or reduce litigation by making themselves aware of the issues brought forth by the courts and teachers. The goal of teacher growth and improvement, while at the same time removing individuals unable to perform satisfactorily, is best achieved by ensuring that the two most essential components, procedural fairness and proper documentation, occur.

6. THE CHARTER

The application of the *Charter* is found in section 32(1), which reads:

32. (1) This Charter applies

- (*a*) to the Parliament and government of Canada in respect of all matters within the authority of Parliament including all matters relating to the Yukon Territory and Northwest Territories; and
- (*b*) to the legislature and government of each province in respect of all matters within the authority of the legislature of each province.

---

113 Edward S. Hickcox, *et al.*, *Making a Difference Through Performance Appraisal* (Toronto: OISE Press, 1988).

Section 32 has been interpreted to apply only to government or governmental action and not to private actors engaged in private activities.[114] However, this interpretation by the courts has proved difficult in determining what constitutes "government" for *Charter* purposes.

R.W.D.S.U. Dolphin Delivery Ltd., the first Supreme Court case to consider this issue at length, stated that the *Charter* applies only to government and governmental action and not to private actors engaged in private actions. However, the Court failed to specify what constitutes governmental action and how that determination ought to take place.

As stated in *Dolphin Delivery Ltd.*, the *Charter* does not apply to actions between private parties that are "divorced completely from any connection with Government."[115]

Drawing the line between public and private parties is not always easy to determine. This is evident from an examination of the Supreme Court's elaboration of section 32 in *McKinney v. University of Guelph*,[116] *Stoffman v. Vancouver General Hospital*,[117] *Harrison v. University of British Columbia*,[118] and *Douglas/Kwantlen Faculty Association v. Douglas College*,[119] four cases in which the mandatory retirement policies of various institutions were challenged.

In these cases, the Supreme Court divided on the issue of the appropriate test to be applied to section 32 of the *Charter*. The majority decision in each of the four cases on this issue was written by Mr. Justice La Forest. Rather than articulate a broad test to be applied in each particular case, La Forest J.'s approach was to focus on the relationship of each institution to the government, critically described by Wilson J. as "an *ad hoc* approach to the status of each entity brought before the Court".[120]

McKinney v. University of Guelph involved the mandatory retirement policies of four Ontario universities. Eight professors and a librarian applied for declarations that the universities' policies of mandatory retirement at age 65 violate section 15 of the *Canadian Charter of Rights and Freedoms*, and that section 9(a) of the Ontario *Human Rights Code, 1981*,[121] by not treating persons who attain the age of 65 equally with others, also violates section 15. They also requested an interlocutory and permanent injunction and sought reinstatement and damages. Mandatory retirement policies had been established through various combinations of resolutions of the board,

---

114 *R.W.D.S.U. v. Dolphin Delivery Ltd.*, [1986] 2 S.C.R. 573 (hereinafter referred to as *Dolphin Delivery Ltd.*
115 *Ibid.*, at 593. See also *Stoffman v. Vancouver Gen. Hospital*, [1990] 3 S.C.R. 483.
116 [1990] 3 S.C.R. 229.
117 Above, note 115.
118 [1990] 3 S.C.R. 451.
119 [1990] 3 S.C.R. 570.
120 *Lavigne v. O.P.S.E.U.*, [1991] 2 S.C.R. 211 at 239.
121 S.O. 1981, c. 53 [now R.S.O. 1990, c. H.19]

by-laws, pension plan provisions and collective agreements, depending on the university.

Several of the individuals had filed complaints with the Ontario Human Rights Commission but the Commission refused to deal with the complaints because its jurisdiction was confined to persons between 18 and 65 years of age. It advised the appellants that it would review its position when their application concerning the constitutional validity of section 9(a) was decided. The High Court dismissed the appellants' application and a majority of the Court of Appeal of Ontario upheld that decision. Five constitutional questions were considered: (1) whether section 9(a) of the *Human Rights Code, 1981* violated the rights guaranteed by section 15(1) of the *Charter;* (2) if so, whether it was justified by section 1 of the *Charter;* (3) whether the *Charter* applied to the mandatory retirement provisions of the respondent universities; (4) if applicable, infringed section 15(1); and finally, (5) if section 15(1) is infringed, whether the respective mandatory retirement provisions are demonstrably justified by section 1. The Attorneys General of Canada, Nova Scotia and Saskatchewan intervened. It was held by the Supreme Court of Canada (Wilson and L'Heureux-Dubé JJ. dissenting), that the appeal should be dismissed.

The Court held that the mere fact that an institution has been created by statute does not necessarily imply that it is governed by the *Charter*. Private corporations, for example, are not subject to the *Charter*. Although the majority acknowledged that a distinction may be made between a private corporation and a corporation serving the public interest, it stated that a public purpose test should not be relied upon with respect to the application of the *Charter*. Entities such as railroads, airlines and symphonies all perform public services, yet they do not form part of the government for the purposes of the application of the *Charter*.[122] In the Court's opinion, it is not sufficient, for the purposes of section *32*, for a party to prove that an entity engages in activities that are subject to the legislative jurisdiction of the federal or provincial government.

In *McKinney*, the Court examined the relationship of the university to the government. La Forest J. stressed that although universities are highly dependent on the government, they do not in fact constitute organs of the government. As the Court stated, universities are independent in the management of their affairs and this is certainly the case with regard to the universities' mandatory retirement policies. Thus, the Supreme Court held that universities do *not form part of the government* within the meaning of section 32 and therefore, the *Charter* provisions have no application to the mandatory retirement policies of the university.[123]

---

122 See above, note 116, at 265-269.
123 The Court in *Harrison*, above, note 118, adopted the reasoning in *McKinney*.

In *Stoffman v. Vancouver General Hospital*,[124] the respondents held admitting privileges at the Vancouver General Hospital. Medical Staff Regulation 5.04 at the hospital required physicians to retire when they reached 65 years of age, unless it could be shown that they "had something unique to offer the hospital". The Regulation was approved by the hospital's Board of Trustees and the Minister of Health as required by statute. In May of 1985, the Board decided not to renew the admitting privileges of most of the respondents – all of whom had turned 65. As the doctors were not employees of the Vancouver General, but rather were retained by their patients and paid through the provincial medicare plan, they did not fall within the protection provision against age-based discrimination found in the *Human Rights Act*. That protection is limited to employment situations.

The Minister's power with respect to the by-laws of the Vancouver General extended beyond the negative power of veto set out in the *Vancouver General Hospital Act*[125] to the positive power under the *Hospital Act*[126] to require the Board to adopt new by-laws or change existing by-laws.

The intention of the proceedings was to set aside the board's decision and to obtain a declaration that Regulation 5.04, either by its terms or by the manner of its application, violated sections 7 and 15 of the *Charter*, as well as the *Human Rights Act*. The Court of Appeal upheld the issuance of the interim injunction. The British Columbia Supreme Court then granted the respondents' application and the Court of Appeal also upheld that decision.

The constitutional questions were:

1. whether the *Charter* applied to the hospital's establishing and administering Regulation 5.04; if so,
2. whether the Regulation or its administration contravened section 15(1) of the *Charter;* and
3. given an affirmative answer to either part of question 2, whether the Regulation or the manner of its administration was nevertheless justified under section 1 of the *Charter*.

The Attorneys General of Canada, Ontario and British Columbia intervened. It was held by the Supreme Court of Canada (Wilson, L'Heureux-Dubé and Cory JJ. dissenting) that the appeal should be allowed and the plaintiffs' action dismissed.

The Court came to the conclusion that *Charter* principles had no application to the hospital's mandatory retirement policy. The Court stressed that the hospital by-laws are *the internal management of the hospital*. The by-laws in issue had not been imposed on the hospital by the Ministry of

---

124 [1990] 3 S.C.R. 483.
125 S.B.C. 1970, c. 55.
126 R.S.B.C. 1979, c. 176.

Health. La Forest J. stated that a distinction must be made between ultimate control and routine control, and, that in *Stoffman,* the hospital had routine control of its affairs. The Court reiterated that it is not determinative for section 32 of the *Charter* that the institution perform an important public service. Hospitals are not part of the "government" and thus the *Charter* provisions have no application to the mandatory retirement policy of the Vancouver General Hospital.

In *Douglas/Kwantlen Faculty Association v. Douglas College,*[127] Douglas College was one of the colleges in a system of post-secondary education operated by British Columbia through the *College and Institute Act.*[128] A college, once designated under the Act, became a corporation and was for all purposes an agent of the Crown and could only exercise its powers as such. It was subject to direct and substantial control by the Minister. Its board was appointed by the Lieutenant-Governor in Council at pleasure and its annual budget was submitted to the Minister for approval. The Minister was empowered to establish policy training, to provide services considered necessary, to approve all by-laws of the board and to provide the necessary funding.

The collective agreement, which was governed by the *Labour code,*[129] and came into effect after the commencement of the *Charter,* provided for mandatory retirement at age 65 (Article 4.04). Two faculty members who were about to be retired filed a grievance challenging Article 4.04 as violating section 15(1) of the *Charter.* The arbitrator appointed pursuant to the collective agreement, held, in a preliminary award, that the college was a Crown agency subject to the *Charter* and that any action taken by it, including the collective agreement, constituted a "law" within the meaning of section 15(1) of the *Charter.* This preliminary award did not deal with whether Article 4.04 of the collective agreement was justified under section 1, or whether the association was estopped from claiming the benefits of the *Charter.*

The constitutional questions before the Court were:

1. whether the *Charter* applied to the negotiation and administration of the retirement provision in the collective agreement;
2. whether that provision or its application was "law" as that term is used in section 15(1) of the *Charter;*
3. whether the arbitration board appointed to resolve a grievance disputing the constitutionality of that provision was a court of competent jurisdiction under section 24(1) of the *Charter;* and
4. whether the arbitration board had jurisdiction to hear and determine such a grievance.

---

[127] Above, note 119.
[128] R.S.B.C. 1979, c. 53.
[129] R.S.B.C. 1979, c. 212.

Interventions were filed by the Attorneys General of Canada and Saskatchewan. The appeal to the Supreme Court of Canada was dismissed.

The Court stated that colleges are agents of the Crown pursuant to a statute and can only exercise powers as defined in the legislation. The Minister retains direct and substantial control over the college. The college is a delegate of the government and performs acts of the government. Consequently, any dealings which the college has with its employees constitute government action within the meaning of section 32 of the *Charter*.[130]

In *Lavigne v. O.P.S.E.U.*[131] Mervyn Lavigne, a community college teacher in Ontario was required to pay dues to the respondent union under a mandatory check-off clause in the collective agreement between the union and the Council of Regents (the bargaining agent for college employees). Such clauses are permitted by section 53 of the *Colleges Collective Bargaining Act*.[132] Lavigne objected to certain expenditures made by the union, such as contributions to the New Democratic Party and disarmament campaigns, and applied for declaratory relief. The trial judge declared that sections 51, 52 and 53 of the *Colleges Collective Bargaining Act*, and the provisions of the collective agreement, were of no force and effect in so far as they compelled the appellant to pay dues to the union for any purpose not directly related to collective bargaining. The trial judge found that the *Canadian Charter of Rights and Freedoms* applied, that the appellant's freedom of association guaranteed by section *2(d)* had been infringed and that the infringement was not justified under section 1. There was no infringement of appellant's freedom of expression.

The Ontario Court of Appeal reversed the judgment. It found that the use of the dues by the union was a private activity by a private organization and hence beyond the reach of the *Charter*. In any event there had been no infringement of the appellant's freedom of association, since he remained free to associate with others and oppose the union. The Court agreed with the trial judge's finding that the appellant's freedom of expression was not infringed. An appeal to the Supreme Court of Canada was dismissed.[133]

In *Tomen v. F.W.T.A.O.*,[134] wherein Margaret Tomen applied to the courts on the basis that being forced to belong to a particular affiliate of the Ontario Teachers' Federation was discriminatory, the Court found that the *Charter* did *not* apply to the issue, as the by-law respecting membership in the provincial teachers' affiliates was enacted pursuant to the provisions of

---

130 Above, note 119, at 584-585.
131 [1991] 2 S.C.R. 211.
132 R.S.O. 1990, c. C.15 [previously R.S.O. 1980, c. 74].
133 Above, note 120.
134 (1987), 29 Admin. L.R. 1 (Ont. H.C.).

Part III of the *Corporations Act*[135] and thus the by-law governed internal matters.[136]

The Supreme Court decisions dealing with section 32 demonstrate that the majority's approach to the *Charter* application issues is *ad hoc*. This is in contrast to the principled approach of Wilson J., set out at length in her dissent in *McKinney*.[137] Wilson J. delineated a three part test to be used to determine whether a body constitutes "government" for the purposes of section 32 of the *Charter*:

1. whether the institution performs a function pursuant to statutory authority on behalf of the government in furtherance of a governmental purpose;
2. whether there is government control of the institution as for example, in governing structure, its policies, its funding; and
3. whether the institution performs a government function.[138]

7. STRIP SEARCHES

On occasion, it is necessary for principals or teachers to ascertain whether or not a pupil is in possession of a weapon, illegal drugs or other contraband. This raises the issue of when it is appropriate and lawful to conduct a search of the student's person. Sections 8 and 24 of the *Charter* state as follows:

> 8. Everyone has the right to be secure against unreasonable search or seizure.
>
> . . .
>
> 24. (1) Anyone whose rights or freedoms as guaranteed by this Charter, have been infringed or denied may apply to a court of competent jurisdiction to obtain such remedy as the court considers appropriate and just in the circumstances.
>
> (2) Where, in proceedings under subsection (1), a court concludes that evidence was obtained in a manner that infringed or denied any rights or freedoms guaranteed by this Charter, the evidence shall be excluded if it is established that, having regard to all the circumstances, the admission of it in the proceedings would bring the administration of justice into disrepute.

A search will be reasonable within the meaning of section 8 of the *Canadian Charter of Rights and Freedoms* where (1) it is authorized by law; (2) the law itself is reasonable; and (3) the search is conducted in a reasonable

---

135 R.S.O. 1980, c. 95 [now R.S.O. 1990, c. C.38].
136 (1987), 61 O.R. (2d) 489 (H.C.), affirmed (1989), 70 O.R. (2d) 48 (C.A.); leave to appeal to S.C.C. refused (1991), 3 O.R. (3d) xiii (note) (S.C.C.).
137 Above, note 116.
138 Above, note 116, at 359-371.

manner.[139] An appropriate balance must be achieved between the interest of citizens to be free from unjustified, excessive and humiliating strip searches upon arrest, and the interests of the police in finding and preserving relevant evidence and ensuring that persons who are arrested are not armed with weapons.[140]

The term "strip search" may be defined as the removal or rearrangement of some or all of the clothing of a person so as to permit a visual inspection of a person's private areas, namely genitals, buttocks, breasts (in the case of a female), or undergarments. This reflects the definition of a strip search that has been adopted in various statutory materials and policy manuals in Canada and other jurisdictions (see for example Toronto Police Service Policy & Procedure Manual: Search of Persons.) This definition distinguishes strip searches from less intrusive "frisk" or "pat down" searches, which do not involve the removal of clothing, and from more intrusive body cavity searches, which involve a physical inspection of the detainee's genital or anal regions. While the mouth is a body cavity, it is not encompassed by the term "body cavity search". Searches of the mouth do not involve the same privacy concerns, although they may raise other health concerns for both the detainee and for those conducting the search.

The case of *R. v. Laporte*[141] represents the high water mark in Canadian law as far as the degree of intrusiveness of searches of the person. In that case, the police sought a search warrant authorizing them to conduct a search of the body of Mr. Laporte for one or more bullets which were alleged to have been fired by police into Laporte's body during a hold-up that occurred a year and a half earlier. The warrant issued authorized surgery upon Laporte to have the bullets removed and seized. Upon an application by Laporte to quash the search warrant, Hugessen J. concluded that the warrant could not be justified under either the common law power of search incident to arrest or any of the statutory provisions of the *Criminal Code*. Accordingly, he set aside the warrant in order to prevent what he described as "a grotesque perversion of the machinery of justice and an unwarranted invasion upon the basic inviolability of the human person".[142]

Another pre-Charter case dealing with a highly intrusive personal search is *Reynen v. Antonenko*.[143] In that case, the plaintiff brought a civil action for assault and battery and exemplary damages arising out of a body cavity search carried out on the plaintiff to search for drugs secreted in his rectum. The search was carried out by a doctor at a hospital on the basis of

---

139 *R. v. Collins*, [1987] 1 S.C.R. 265; *R. v. Debot*, [1989] 2 S.C.R. 1140; *Cloutier c. Lasglois*, [1990] 1 S.C.R. 158 and *R. v. Stillman*, [1997] 1 S.C.R. 607.
140 *R. v. Araujo*, [2000] 2 S.C.R. 992, 2000 SCC 65.
141 (1972), 8 C.C.C. (2d) 343 (Que. Q.B.).
142 Laporte, at p. 354.
143 (1975), 20 C.C.C. (2d) 342 (Alta. T.D.).

the common law authority to search incident to arrest. MacDonald J. dismissed the plaintiff's action and concluded that

> [T]he police in this case has not only the right but also a duty to conduct a search of the plaintiff for drugs, and to seize any drugs found as evidence to be presented to the Court. In making this search and seizure the police are clearly authorized to use such force as is reasonable, proper and necessary to carryout their duty, providing that no wanton or unnecessary violence is imposed.[144]

At the trial level, there are many cases involving strip searches performed as an incident to arrest, although there is inconsistency in court decisions as to when strip searches are reasonable and when they are unreasonable under section 8. In *R. v. Stott* (1997),[145] a strip search of an individual arrested for impaired driving carried out as a matter of routine police policy was held not to violate section 8. Similarly, in *R. v. S. (K.D.)*,[146] the strip search of a young offender at the police station as part of normal police procedure following his arrest for possession of a stolen licence plate was held not to be a violation of section 8. Strip searches accompanied by the threat of a subsequent body cavity search as an incident to arrest have also been found not to infringe section 8. In *R. v. Miller*,[147] on the other hand, a routine strip search of a female accused arrested for theft and possession of stolen property was held not to be authorized by the common law of search incident to arrest in *R. v. King*.[148] In *R. v. Kalin*,[149] a routine strip search conducted at the police station following an arrest for impaired driving was held to be unreasonable under section 8.

A "frisk" or "pat down" search at the point of arrest will generally suffice for the purposes of determining if the accused (e.g., a student) has secreted weapons on his or her person. Only if the frisk search reveals a possible weapon secreted on the detainee's person or if the particular circumstances of the case raise the risk that a weapon is concealed on the detainee's person will a strip search be justified. Whether searching for evidence or for weapons, the mere possibility that an individual may be concealing evidence or weapons is not sufficient cause to justify a strip search.

School administrators should be aware that strip searches should generally be conducted at the police station except where there are circumstances requiring that the detainee be searched prior to being transported to the police station. Strip searches conducted in the field can only be justified

---

144 *Ibid.*, at 348.
145 [1997] O.J. No. 5449, 1997 CarswellOnt 5443 (Prov. Div.).
146 (1990), 65 Man. R. (2d) 301 (Q.B.).
147 (June 14, 1993), Doc. Victoria 69465-C2, [1993] B.C.J. No. 1613 (B.C. S.C.).
148 (January 7, 1999), MacDougall J., [1999] O.J. No. 565 (Ont. Gen. Div.).
149 (October 5, 1987), Doc. Vancouver CC870602, [1987] B.C.J. No. 2580 (B.C. Co. Ct.).

where there is a demonstrated necessity and urgency to search for weapons or objects that could be used to threaten the safety of the accused, the arresting officers or other individuals. The police would have to show why it would have been unsafe to wait and conduct the strip search at the police station. Strip searches conducted in the field represent a much greater invitation of privacy and pose a greater threat to the detainee's bodily integrity and, for this reason, field strip searches can only be justified in exigent circumstances.

Appendix

CANADIAN CHARTER OF RIGHTS AND FREEDOMS*

Whereas Canada is founded upon principles that recognize the supremacy of God and the rule of law:

Guarantee of Rights and Freedoms

Rights and freedoms in Canada.

1. The *Canadian Charter of Rights and Freedoms* guarantees the rights and freedoms set out in it subject only to such reasonable limits prescribed by law as can be demonstrably justified in a free and democratic society.

Fundamental Freedoms

Fundamental freedoms.

2. Everyone has the following fundamental freedoms:
   (*a*) freedom of conscience and religion;
   (*b*) freedom of thought, belief, opinion and expression, including freedom of the press and other media of communication;
   (*c*) freedom of peaceful assembly; and
   (*d*) freedom of association.

Democratic Rights

Democratic rights of citizens.

3. Every citizen of Canada has the right to vote in an election of members of the House of Commons or of a legislative assembly and to be qualified for membership therein.

---

* Being Part I of the *Constitution Act, 1982*, R.S.C. 1985, Appendix II, No. 44 [en. by the *Canada Act*, 1982 (U.K.), c. 11, s. 1].

Maximum duration of legislative bodies -Continuation in special circumstances.

4. (1) No House of Commons and no legislative assembly shall continue for longer than five years from the date fixed for the return of the writs of a general election of its members.

(2) In time of real or apprehended war, invasion or insurrection, a House of Commons may be continued by Parliament and a legislative assembly may be continued by the legislature beyond five years if such continuation is not opposed by the votes of more than one-third of the members of the House of Commons or the legislative assembly, as the case may be.

Annual sitting of legislative bodies.

5. There shall be a sitting of Parliament and of each legislature at least once every twelve months.

Mobility Rights

Mobility of citizens—Rights to move and gain livelihood—Limitation - Affirmative action programs.

6. (1) Every citizen of Canada has the right to enter, remain in and leave Canada.

(2) Every citizen of Canada and every person who has the status of a permanent resident of Canada has the right

(*a*) to move to and take up residence in any province; and
(*b*) to pursue the gaining of a livelihood in any province.

(3) The rights specified in subsection (2) are subject to

(*a*) any laws or practices of general application in force in a province other than those that discriminate among persons primarily on the basis of province of present or previous residence; and
(*b*) any laws providing for reasonable residency requirements as a qualification for the receipt of publicly provided social services.

(4) Subsections (2) and (3) do not preclude any law, program or activity that has as its object the amelioration in a province of conditions of individuals in that province who are socially or economically disadvantaged if the rate of employment in that province is below the rate of employment in Canada.

Legal Rights

Life, liberty and security of person.

7. Everyone has the right to life, liberty and security of the person and the right not to be deprived thereof except in accordance with the principles of fundamental justice.

Search or seizure.

8. Everyone has the right to be secure against unreasonable search or seizure.

Detention or imprisonment.

9. Everyone has the right not to be arbitrarily detained or imprisoned.

Arrest or detention.

10. Everyone has the right on arrest or detention
    (*a*) to be informed promptly of the reasons therefor;
    (*b*) to retain and instruct counsel without delay and to be informed of that right; and
    (*c*) to have the validity of the detention determined by way of *habeas corpus* and to be released if the detention is not lawful.

Proceedings in criminal and penal matters.

11. Any person charged with an offence has the right
    (*a*) to be informed without unreasonable delay of the specific offence;
    (*b*) to be tried within a reasonable time;
    (*c*) not to be compelled to be a witness in proceedings against that person in respect of the offence;
    (*d*) to be presumed innocent until proven guilty according to law in a fair and public hearing by an independent and impartial tribunal;
    (*e*) not to be denied reasonable bail without just cause;
    (*f*) except in the case of an offence under military law tried before a military tribunal, to the benefit of trial by jury where the maximum punishment for the offence is imprisonment for five years or a more severe punishment;
    (*g*) not to be found guilty on account of any act or omission unless, at the time of the act or omission, it constituted an offence under Canadian or international law or was criminal according to the general principles of law recognized by the community of nations;
    (*h*) if finally acquitted of the offence, not to be tried for it again and, if finally found guilty and punished for the offence, not to be tried or punished for it again; and

(*i*) if found guilty of the offence and if the punishment for the offence has been varied between the time of commission and the time of sentencing, to the benefit of the lesser punishment.

Treatment or punishment.

12. Everyone has the right not to be subjected to any cruel and unusual treatment or punishment.

Self-crimination.

13. A witness who testified in any proceedings has the right not to have any incriminating evidence so given used to incriminate that witness in any other proceedings, except in a prosecution for perjury or for the giving of contradictory evidence.

Interpreter.

14. A party or witness in any proceedings who does not understand or speak the language in which the proceedings are conducted or who is deaf has the right to the assistance of an interpreter.

Equality Rights

Equality before and under law and equal protection and benefit of law—Affirmative action programs.

15. (1) Every individual is equal before and under the law and has the right to the equal protection and equal benefit of the law without discrimination and, in particular, without discrimination based on race, national or ethnic origin, colour, religion, sex, age or mental or physical disability.

(2) Subsection (1) does not preclude any law, program or activity that has as its object the amelioration of conditions of disadvantaged individuals or groups including those that are disadvantaged because of race, national or ethnic origin, colour, religion, sex, age or mental or physical disability.

Official Languages of Canada

Official languages of Canada—Official languages of New Brunswick - Advancement of status and use.

16. (1) English and French are the official languages of Canada and have equality of status and equal rights and privileges as to their use in all institutions of the Parliament and government of Canada.

(2) English and French are the official languages of New Brunswick and have equality of status and equal rights and privileges as to their use in all institutions of the legislature and government of New Brunswick.

(3) Nothing in this Charter limits the authority of Parliament or a legislature to advance the equality of status or use of English and French.

English and French linguistic communities in New Brunswick-Role of the legislature and government of New Brunswick.

16.1 (1) The English linguistic community and the French linguistic community in New Brunswick have equality of status and equal rights and privileges, including the right to distinct educational institutions and such distinct cultural institutions as are necessary for the preservation and promotion of those communities.

(2) The role of the legislature and government of New Brunswick to preserve and promote the status, rights and privileges referred to in subsection (1) is affirmed. SI/TR93-54.

Proceedings of Parliament—Proceedings of New Brunswick legislature.

17. (1) Everyone has the right to use English or French in any debates and other proceedings of Parliament.

(2) Everyone has the right to use English or French in any debates and other proceedings of the legislature of New Brunswick.

Parliamentary statutes and records—New Brunswick statutes and records.

18. (1) The statutes, records and journals of Parliament shall be printed and published in English and French and both language versions are equally authoritative.

(2) The statutes, records and journals of the legislature of New Brunswick shall be printed and published in English and French and both language versions are equally authoritative.

Proceedings in court established by Parliament—Proceedings in New Brunswick courts.

19. (1) Either English or French may be used by any person in, or in any pleading in or process issuing from, any court established by Parliament.

(2) Either English or French may be used by any person in, or in any pleading in or process issuing from, any court of New Brunswick.

Communications by public with federal institutions—Communications by public with New Brunswick institutions.

20. (1) Any member of the public in Canada has the right to communicate with, and to receive available services from, any head or central office of an institution of the Parliament or government of Canada in English or French, and has the same right with respect to any other office of any such institution where

(a) there is a significant demand for communications with and services from that office in such language; or
(b) due to the nature of the office, it is reasonable that communications with and services from that office be available in both English and French.

(2) Any member of the public in New Brunswick has the right to communicate with, and to receive available services from, any office of an institution of the legislature or government of New Brunswick in English or French.

Continuation of existing constitutional provisions.

21. Nothing in sections 16 to 20 abrogates or derogates from any right, privilege or obligation with respect to the English and French languages, or either of them, that exists or is continued by virtue of any other provision of the Constitution of Canada.

Rights and privileges preserved.

22. Nothing in sections 16 to 20 abrogates or derogates from any legal or customary right or privilege acquired or enjoyed either before or after the coming into force of this Charter with respect to any language that is not English or French.

Minority Language Educational Rights

Language of instruction—Continuity of language instruction -Application where numbers warrant.

23. (1) Citizens of Canada

(a) whose first language learned and still understood is that of the English or French linguistic minority population of the province in which they reside, or
(b) who have received their primary school instruction in Canada in English or French and reside in a province where the language in which they received that instruction is the language of the English or French linguistic minority population of the province,

have the right to have their children receive primary and secondary school instruction in that language in that province.

(2) Citizens of Canada of whom any child has received or is receiving primary or secondary school instruction in English or French in Canada,

have the right to have all their children receive primary and secondary school instruction in the same language.

(3) The right of citizens of Canada under subsections (1) and (2) to have their children receive primary and secondary school instruction in the language of the English or French linguistic minority population of a province

> (a) applies wherever in the province the number of children of citizens who have such a right is sufficient to warrant the provision to them out of public funds of minority language instruction; and
>
> (b) includes, where the number of those children so warrants, the right to have them receive that instruction in minority language educational facilities provided out of public funds.

Enforcement

Enforcement of guaranteed rights and freedoms—Exclusion of evidence bringing administration of justice into disrepute.

24. (1) Anyone whose rights or freedoms, as guaranteed by this Charter, have been infringed or denied may apply to a court of competent jurisdiction to obtain such remedy as the court considers appropriate and just in the circumstances.

(2) Where, in proceedings under subsection (1), a court concludes that evidence was obtained in a manner that infringed or denied any rights or freedoms guaranteed by this Charter, the evidence shall be excluded if it is established that, having regard to all the circumstances, the admission of it in the proceedings would bring the administration of justice into disrepute.

General

Aboriginal rights and freedoms not affected by Charter.

25. The guarantee in this Charter of certain rights and freedoms shall not be construed so as to abrogate or derogate from any aboriginal treaty or other rights or freedoms that pertain to the aboriginal peoples of Canada including

> (a) any rights or freedoms that have been recognized by the Royal Proclamation of October 7, 1763; and
>
> (b) any rights or freedoms that now exist by way of land claims agreements or may be so acquired.

Other rights and freedoms not affected by Charter.

26. The guarantee in this Charter of certain rights and freedoms shall not be construed as denying the existence of any other rights or freedoms that exist in Canada.

Multicultural heritage.

27. This Charter shall be interpreted in a manner consistent with the preservation and enhancement of the multicultural heritage of Canadians.

Rights guaranteed equally to both sexes.

28. Notwithstanding anything in this Charter, the rights and freedoms referred to in it are guaranteed equally to male and female persons.

Rights respecting certain schools preserved.

29. Nothing in this Charter abrogates or derogates from any rights or privileges guaranteed by or under the Constitution of Canada in respect of denominational, separate or dissentient schools.

Application to territories and territorial authorities.

30. A reference in this Charter to a province or to the legislative assembly or legislature of a province shall be deemed to include a reference to the Yukon Territory and the Northwest Territories, or to the appropriate legislative authority thereof, as the case may be.

Legislative powers not extended.

31. Nothing in this Charter extends the legislative powers of any body or authority.

Application of Charter

Application of Charter- Exception.

32. (1) This Charter applies

(*a*) to the Parliament and government of Canada in respect of all matters within the authority of Parliament including all matters relating to the Yukon Territory and Northwest Territories; and
(*b*) to the legislature and government of each province in respect of all matters within the authority of the legislature of each province.

(2) Notwithstanding subsection (1), section 15 shall not have effect until three years after this section comes into force.

Exception where express declaration—Operation of exceptions -Five year limitation—Re-enactment—Five year limitation.

33. (1) Parliament or the legislature of a province may expressly declare in an Act of Parliament or of the legislature, as the case may be, that the Act or a provision thereof shall operate notwithstanding a provision included in section 2 or sections 7 to 15 of this Charter.

(2) An Act or a provision of an Act in respect of which a declaration made under this section is in effect shall have such operation as it would have but for the provision of this Charter referred to in the declaration.

(3) A declaration made under subsection (1) shall cease to have effect five years after it comes into force or on such earlier date as may be specified in the declaration.

(4) Parliament or a legislature of a province may re-enact a declaration made under subsection (1).

(5) Subsection (3) applies in respect of a re-enactment made under subsection (4).

Citation

Citation.

34. This Part may be cited as the *Canadian Charter of Rights and Freedoms*.

YOUNG OFFENDERS ACT*

DECLARATION OF PRINCIPLE

Policy for Canada with respect to young offenders-Act to be liberally construed.

3. (1) It is hereby recognized and declared that

(*a*) crime prevention is essential to the long-term protection of society and requires addressing the underlying causes of crime by young persons and developing multi-disciplinary approaches to identifying and effectively responding to children and young persons at risk of committing offending behaviour in the future;

(*a*.1) while young persons should not in all instances be held accountable in the same manner or suffer the same consequences for their behaviour as adults, young persons who commit offences should nonetheless bear responsibility for their contraventions;

(*b*) society must, although it has the responsibility to take reasonable measures to prevent criminal conduct by young persons, be afforded the necessary protection from illegal behaviour;

(*c*) young persons who commit offences require supervision, discipline and control, but, because of their state of dependency and level of development and maturity, they also have special needs and require guidance and assistance;

(*c*.1) the protection of society, which is a primary objective of the criminal law applicable to youth, is best served by rehabilitation, wherever possible, of young persons who commit offences, and rehabilitation is best achieved by addressing the needs and circumstances of a young person that are relevant to the young person's offending behaviour;

(*d*) where it is not inconsistent with the protection of society, taking no measures or taking measures other than judicial proceedings under this Act should be considered for dealing with young persons who have committed offences;

(*e*) young persons have rights and freedoms in their own right, including those stated in the *Canadian Charter of Rights and Freedoms* or in the *Canadian Bill of Rights,* and in particular a right to be heard in the course of, and to participate in, the processes that lead to decisions that affect them, and young persons should have special guarantees of their rights and freedoms;

---

* R.S.C 1985, c. Y-1 [ss. 3, 14, 38 and 56 reprinted in this Appendix].

(f) in the application of this Act, the rights and freedoms of young persons include a right to the least possible interference with freedom that is consistent with the protection of society, having regard to the needs of young persons and the interests of their families;

(g) young persons have the right, in every instance where they have rights or freedoms that may be affected by this Act, to be informed as to what those rights and freedoms are; and

(h) parents have responsibility for the care and supervision of their children, and for that reason, young persons should be removed from parental supervision either partly or entirely only when measures that provide for continuing parental supervision are inappropriate.

(2) This Act shall be liberally construed to the end that young persons will be dealt with in accordance with the principles set out in subsection (1). 1995, c. 19, s. 1.

PRE-DISPOSITION REPORT

Pre-disposition report—Contents of report—Oral report with leave—Report to form part of record—Copies of pre-disposition report—Cross-examination—Report may be withheld from private prosecutor—Report disclosed to other persons—Disclosure by the provincial director-Inadmissibility of statements.

14. (1) Where a youth court deems it advisable before making a disposition under section 20 in respect of a young person who is found guilty of an offence it may, and where a youth court is required under this Act to consider a pre-disposition report before making an order or a disposition in respect of a young person it shall, require the provincial director to cause to be prepared a pre-disposition report in respect of the young person and to submit the report to the court.

(2) A pre-disposition report made in respect of a young person shall, subject to subsection (3), be in writing and shall include,

(a) the results of an interview with

(i) the young person,
(ii) where reasonably possible, the parents of the young person and,
(iii) where appropriate and reasonably possible, members of the young person's extended family;

(b) the results of an interview with the victim in the case, where applicable and where reasonably possible;

(c) such information as is applicable to the case including, where applicable,

(i) the age, maturity, character, behaviour and attitude of the young person and his willingness to make amends,
(ii) any plans put forward by the young person to change his conduct or to participate in activities or undertake measures to improve himself,
(iii) the history of previous findings of delinquency under the *Juvenile Delinquents Act,* chapter J-3 of the Revised Statues of Canada, 1970, or previous findings of guilt under this Act or any other Act of Parliament or any regulation made thereunder or under an Act of the legislature of a province or any regulation made thereunder or a by-law or ordinance of a municipality, the history of community or other services rendered to the young person with respect to those findings and the response of the young person to previous sentences of dispositions and to services rendered to him,
(iv) the history of alternative measures used to deal with the young person and the response of the young person thereto,
(v) the availability of community services and facilities for young persons and the willingness of the young person to avail himself or herself of those services or facilities,
(vi) the relationship between the young person and the young person's parents and the degree of control and influence of the parents over the young person, and where appropriate and reasonably possible, the relationship between the young person and the young person's extended family and the degree of control and influence of the young person's extended family over the young person;
(vii) the school attendance and performance record and the employment record of the young person; and

(*d*) such information as the provincial director considers relevant, including any recommendation that the provincial director considers appropriate.

(3) Where a pre-disposition report cannot reasonably be committed to writing, it may, with leave of the youth court, be submitted orally in court.

(4) A pre-disposition report shall form part of the record of the case in respect of which it was requested.

(5) Where a pre-disposition report made in respect of a young person is submitted to a youth court in writing, the court

(*a*) shall, subject to subsection (7), cause a copy of the report to be given to

(i) the young person,

(ii) a parent of the young person, if the parent is in attendance at the proceedings against the young person,
(iii) counsel, if any, representing the young person, and
(iv) the prosecutor; and

(b) may cause a copy of the report to be given to a parent of the young person not in attendance at the proceedings against the young person if the parent is, in the opinion of the court, taking an active interest in the proceedings.

(6) Where a pre-disposition report made in respect of a young person is submitted to a youth court, the young person, his counsel or the adult assisting him pursuant to subsection 11(7) and the prosecutor shall, subject to subsection (7), on application to the youth court, be given the opportunity to cross-examine the person who made the report.

(7) Where a pre-disposition report made in respect of a young person is submitted to a youth court, the court may, where the prosecutor is a private prosecutor and disclosure of the report or any part thereof to the prosecutor might, in the opinion of the court, be prejudicial to the young person and is not, in the opinion of the court, necessary for the prosecution of the case against the young person,

(a) withhold the report or part thereof from the prosecutor, if the report is submitted in writing; or

(b) exclude the prosecutor from the court during the submission of the report or part thereof, if the report is submitted orally in court.

(8) Where a pre-disposition report made in respect of a young person is submitted to a youth court, the court

(a) shall, on request, cause a copy or a transcript of the report to be supplied to

(i) any court that is dealing with matters relating to the young person, and
(ii) any youth worker to whom the young person's case has been assigned; and

(b) may, on request, cause a copy or a transcript of the report, or a part thereof, to be supplied to any person not otherwise authorized under this section to receive a copy or transcript of the report if, in the opinion of the court, the person has a valid interest in the proceedings.

(9) A provincial director who submits a pre-disposition report made in respect of a young person to a youth court may make the report, or any part thereof, available to any person in whose custody or under whose supervision the young person is placed or to any other person who is directly assisting in the care or treatment of the young person.

(10) No statement made by a young person in the course of the preparation of a pre-disposition report in respect of the young person is admissible in evidence against him in any civil or criminal proceedings except in proceedings under section 16 or 20 or sections 28 to 32. R.S.C. 1985, c. 24 (2nd Supp.), s. 11; 1995, c. 19, s. 6.

PROTECTION OF PRIVACY OF YOUNG PERSONS

Identity not to be published—Limitation—Preparation of reports -No subsequent disclosure—Schools and others—No subsequent disclosure—Information to be kept separate—Ex parte application for leave to publish—Order ceases to have effect—Application for leave to publish—Disclosure with court order—Opportunity to be heard—Ex parte application—Time limit—Contravention—Provincial court judge has absolute jurisdiction on indictment.

38. (1) Subject to this section, no person shall publish by any means any report

(*a*) of an offence committed or alleged to have been committed by a young person, unless an order has been made under section 16 with respect thereto, or

(*b*) of any hearing, adjudication, disposition or appeal concerning a young person who committed or is alleged to have committed an offence

in which the name of the young person, a child or a young person who is a victim of the offence or a child or a young person who appeared as a witness in connection with the offence, or in which any information serving to identify the young person or child, is disclosed.

(1.1) Subsection (1) does not apply in respect of the disclosure of information in the course of the administration of justice including, for greater certainty, the disclosure of information for the purposes of the *Firearms Act* and part III of the *Criminal Code*, where it is not the purpose of the disclosure to make the information known in the community.

(1.11) Subsection (1) does not apply in respect of the disclosure of information by the provincial director or a youth worker where the disclosure is necessary for procuring information that relates to the preparation of any report required by this Act.

(1.12) No person to whom information is disclosed pursuant to subsection (1.11) shall disclose that information to any other person unless the disclosure is necessary for the purpose of preparing the report for which the information was disclosed.

(1.13) Subsection (1) does not apply in respect of the disclosure of information to any professional or other person engaged in the supervision or care of a young person, including the representative of any school board or school or any other educational or training institution, by the provincial director, a youth worker, a peace officer or any other person engaged in the provision of services to young persons where the disclosure is necessary

> (*a*) to ensure compliance by the young person with an authorization pursuant to section 35 or an order of any court concerning bail, probation or conditional supervision; or
> (*b*) to ensure the safety of staff, students or other persons, as the case may be.

(1.14) No person to whom information is disclosed pursuant to subsection (1.13) shall disclose that information to any other person unless the disclosure is necessary for a purpose referred to in that subsection.

(1.15) Any person to whom information is disclosed pursuant to subsections (1.13) and (1.14) shall

> (*a*) keep the information separate from any other record of the young person to whom the information relates;
> (*b*) subject to subsection (1.14), ensure that no other person has access to the information; and
> (*c*) destroy the information when the information is no longer required for the purpose for which it was disclosed.

(1.2) A youth court judge shall, on the *ex parte* application of a peace officer, make an order permitting any person to publish a report described in subsection (1) that contains the name of a young person, or information serving to identify a young person, who has committed or is alleged to have committed an indictable offence, if the judge is satisfied that

> (*a*) there is reason to believe that the young person is dangerous to others; and
> (*b*) publication of the report is necessary to assist in apprehending the young person.

(1.3) An order made under subsection (1.2) shall cease to have effect two days after it is made.

(1.4) The youth court may, on the application of any person referred to in subsection (1), make an order permitting any person to publish a report in which the name of that person, or information serving to identify that person, would be disclosed, if the court is satisfied that the publication of the report would not be contrary to the best interests of that person.

(1.5) The youth court may, on the application of the provincial director, the Attorney General or an agent of the Attorney General or a peace officer, make an order permitting the applicant to disclose to such person or persons as are specified by the court such information about a young person as is specified if the court is satisfied that the disclosure is necessary, having regard to the following:

(a) the young person has been found guilty of an offence involving serious personal injury;
(b) the young person poses a risk of serious harm to persons; and
(c) the disclosure of the information is relevant to the avoidance of that risk.

(1.6) Subject to subsection (1.7), before making an order under subsection (1.5), the youth court shall afford the young person, the young person's parents, the Attorney General or an agent of the Attorney General an opportunity to be heard.

(1.7) An application under subsection (1.5) may be made *ex parte* by the Attorney General or an agent of the Attorney General where the youth court is satisfied that reasonable efforts have been made to locate the young person and that those efforts have not been successful.

(1.8) No information may be disclosed pursuant to subsection (1.5) after the record to which the information relates ceases to be available for inspection under subsection 45(1).

(2) Every one who contravenes subsection (1), (1.12), (1.14) or (1.15)

(a) is guilty of an indictable offence and liable to imprisonment for a term not exceeding two years; or
(b) is guilty of an offence punishable on summary conviction.

(3) Where an accused is charged with an offence under paragraph 2(a), a provincial court judge has absolute jurisdiction to try the case and his jurisdiction does not depend on the consent of the accused. R.S.C. 1985, c. 27 (1st Supp.), s. 203; R.S.C. 1985, c. 24 (2nd Supp.), s. 29; 1995, c. 19, s. 27; 1995, c. 39, s. 184.

EVIDENCE

General law on admissibility of statements to apply—When statements are admissible—Exception in certain cases for oral statements—Waiver of right to consult—Statements given under duress are inadmissible—Misrepresentation of age—Parent, etc. not a person in authority.

56. (1) Subject to this section, the law relating to the admissibility of statements made by persons accused of committing offences applies in respect of young persons.

(2) No oral or written statement given by a young person to a peace officer or to any other person who is, in law, a person in authority on the

arrest or detention of the young person or in circumstances where the peace officer or other person has reasonable grounds for believing that the young person has committed an offence is admissible against the young person unless

    (*a*) the statement was voluntary;
    (*b*) the person to whom the statement was given has, before the statement was made, clearly explained to the young person, in language appropriate to his age and understanding, that

        (i) the young person is under no obligation to give a statement,
        (ii) any statement given by him may be used as evidence in proceedings against him,
        (iii) the young person has the right to consult counsel and a parent or other person in accordance with paragraph (*c*), and
        (iv) any statement made by the young person is required to be made in the presence of counsel and any other person consulted in accordance with paragraph (*c*), if any, unless the young person desires otherwise;

    (*c*) the young person has, before the statement was made, been given a reasonable opportunity to consult

        (i) with counsel, and
        (ii) a parent, or in the absence of a parent, an adult relative, or in the absence of a parent and an adult relative, any other appropriate adult chosen by the young person; and

    (*d*) where the young person consults any person pursuant to paragraph (*c*) the young person has been given a reasonable opportunity to make the statement in the presence of that person.

(3) The requirements set out in paragraphs (2)(*b*),(*c*) and (*d*) do not apply in respect of oral statements where they are made spontaneously by the young person to a peace officer or other person in authority before that person has had a reasonable opportunity to comply with those requirements.

(4) A young person may waive the rights under paragraph (2)(*c*) or (*d*) but any such waiver shall be videotaped or be in writing, and where it is in writing it shall contain a statement signed by the young person that the young person has been apprised of the right being waived.

(5) A youth court judge may rule inadmissible in any proceedings under this Act a statement given by the young person in respect of whom the proceedings are taken if the young person satisfies the judge that the statement was given under duress imposed by any person who is not, in law, a person in authority.

(5.1) A youth court judge may in any proceedings under this Act rule admissible any statement or waiver by a young person where, at the time of the making of the statement or waiver;

>   (*a*) the young person held himself or herself to be eighteen years of age or older;
>   (*b*) the person to whom the statement or waiver was made conducted reasonable inquiries as to the age of the young person and had reasonable grounds for believing that the young person was eighteen years of age or older; and
>   (*c*) in all other circumstances the statement or waiver would otherwise be admissible.

(6) For the purposes of this section, an adult consulted pursuant to paragraph 56(2)(*c*) shall, in the absence of evidence to the contrary, be deemed not to be a person in authority. R.S.C. 1985, c. 24 (2nd Supp.), s. 38; 1995, c. 19, s. 35.

Index

Abuse. *See also* Intentional torts; Negligence; Teachers.
confidentiality 255
reporting abuse 328-330
sexual 326-327

Academic freedom
criticism of policy 343
physical appearance 343
vulgar language and 342-343

Academic penalties. *See* Pupils.

Access. *See* Custody and Access.

Acquired Immune Deficiency Syndrome (AIDS)
compulsory attendance and 210
confidentiality 252-257
removal from classroom 210-211

Appearance codes. *See* Pupils - dress codes; Teachers.

Assault. *See* Intentional torts.

Asthma. 256

Athletic transfer policy 206-207

Attendance. *See* Compulsory attendance.

Battery. *See* Intentional torts.

Boards. *See* School Boards.

Charter of Rights. See also Constitution.
application
generally 363-364
to families 185-191
community colleges 367-368
denominational rights 6-12, 15-22
freedom of expression 237-241, 250-252, 314-315
freedom of religion 245-250, 308-313
hospitals 366-367
minority language education 22-28
Section 1 test 186
special education 296-304
unions
choice of union 358
mandatory dues 368
universities 364-365

Child abuse. *See* Abuse.

Child and Family Services Act (Ont.) 235, 324, 326-329

Children
troubled, reasons for 260-262

Closure of school 58-64

Communicable diseases 210

Compulsory attendance
Charter of Rights and Freedoms 204-205
generally 205, 221
health issues 210
home schooling 197-198
non-compliance 205
private schools 71-74

Confidentiality
counsellor 255
medical records 252-257
student records 276-277
Young Offenders Act 263-266

Conflict of interest 46-51, 69

Consent to medical treatment 259-260

Constitution
native education 28-30
denominational rights 6-12, 15-22
division of powers 2
French-language rights 22-28
running for election 66

Corporal punishment 132, 191-197

Cree-Naskapi 29

Criminal Reference Checks 341-342

Custody and access rights 163-165, 174-176

Delegation of power 31-36

Denominational rights 6-12, 15-22

Discipline of pupils. *See* Corporal punishment; Pupils.

Dismissal. *See* Teachers.

Divorce Act (Canada) 165-174

Domestic violence 177-185

Dress codes. *See* Pupils.

Due process
    expulsion and suspension hearings 229-234
    generally 38-42
    teacher evaluation 353

Evaluation. *See* Teachers.

Exceptional pupil. *See* Special education.

Expulsion. *See Pupils.*

Fairness. *See* Procedural fairness.

Family
    changes in 150-151
    same sex relationships 157-158
    spousal rights 154-156

Fiduciary duty 134-141

Freedom of information
    exemptions 51-52
    generally 51-53
    inspection of board records 51
    personal information, defined 52-53
    record, defined 52
    student records 53

French-language minority education 22-28

Gays and lesbians 158-165

Graduation
    banned from ceremony 238

Health Protection and Promotion Act 253

Hearings. *See* Procedural fairness

Home schooling 197-198, 221

Human rights. *See also* Kirpans.
    marital status 158-160
    racism 313-315
    sexual harassment 330-335, 356-357
    special education 297

Identification. *See* Special education.

Immunization 210

Indian Act 29

Intentional torts
    assault and battery 123-124
    consent 133
    corporal punishment 132
    defamation 121-123
    defences 133-134
    false imprisonment 123
    generally 121
    of minors 124
    sexual assault 124-131

Internet 250-252

Kirpans 242-249

Limitation periods 110-116

Malpractice 141-145

Mandatory retirement 365-367

Marriage 150-153

Medical treatment
    administration of medication 257-259
    consent to treatment 259-260

Meetings of board
    access to 42-46
    exclusion from 43
    in camera 43
    procedures 67-68
    retreats and workshops 43-45

Minority language education 22-28

Minors' liability. *See* Intentional torts; Negligence.

Municipal Conflict of Interest Act (Ont.) 46-48

Municipal Freedom of Information and Protection of Privacy Act (Ont.) 51-53

Native education 28-30

Natural justice. *See* Procedural fairness.

Negligence. *See also* Fiduciary duty; Intentional torts; Risk management.
    abuse 104-105
    assumption of risk 107, 120
    burden of proof 79
    commentary on 109-110
    consent 88, 108
    contributory 106-107
    customs 109-110
    defences 105-107
    duty of care 80-84

INDEX 395

Negligence — *Cont'd.*
   football 88-90
   foreseeability 99-100
   generally 79-80
   gymnasium 85-87, 91, 95
   limitation periods 110-116
   malpractice 141-145
   occupiers' liability 116-121
   of minors 107-108
   outside school hours 102-103
   proximate cause 99-100
   public authorities 111-116
   rock climbing 90
   science class 85
   sewing class 97
   sexual misconduct 103-105
   snow and ice 116
   standard of care generally 84-95
   standard of care modified 95-99
   statutory duty 80-83
   supervision of pupils 92-95
   swimming 98, 99
   transportation 100-102
   vicarious liability 79, 124-132
   woodworking class 94, 98
   wrongful reference 105

Occupiers' liability 116-121

Ontario College of Teachers
   complaints process 338
   Council 337
   membership 336
   professional learning 345, 347-348
   qualification 336-337, 346
   registration 337
   reporting misconduct 104-105
   statute 336

Parents
   access to student records 53, 276-280
   influence and control 150
   involvement, need for 6-7
   rights (access parent) 163-165, 174-176
   school councils 198-201

Personal information 52-53

Persons in authority 268-270

Placement. *See* Special education.

Private schools
   funding 12-15
   generally 71-74, 229
   inspection 72

Procedural fairness
   employee dismissal 39-42
   expulsions and suspensions
      generally 229-234
      private schools 72-74
   generally 38-42
   hearings 41, 230
   school closure 58-64

Property. *See* School board; Occupier's liability

Provincial jurisdiction
   native education 28-30
   delegation 31-36
   denominational rights 6-12
   exercise of power 31
   minority language education rights 22-28

Public Schools Act, 1891 60

Pupils
   academic penalties 239-240
   AIDS. *See* Acquired Immune Deficiency Syndrome
   attendance. *See* Compulsory attendance.
   civil liability. *See* Negligence; Intentional torts.
   corporal punishment. *See* Corporal punishment.
   disciplinary problems 239
   discipline of 211-214
   dress codes 240-244
   exclusion from school 56-57
   expulsion from school 221-229
   freedom of speech 237-241
   graduation 238
   health and comfort 82
   home schooling 197-198
   immunization. *See* Immunization.
   locker searches 216
   medical records 252-257
   medication. *See* Medication.
   records. *See* Student records
   representation 30
   restraint of 132
   safety 81-83, 104
   search of 214-221
   suspension from school 221-229
   vaccination. *See* Immunization.
   violence 211-214

Quality in the Classroom Act 344-349

Religion
    freedom of 12-15, 307-313
    kirpans 242-249

Retreats 43-45

Risk management 145-148

Role model. *See* Teachers.

Satisfactory instruction 72

School boards. *See also* Meetings of board; Trustees.
    books, inspection of 51
    chair 67
    conflict of interest 46-51
    decisions, nature of 31-33
    exercise of delegated power by 3-6, 31-36
    first meeting 67
    judicial review of resolutions 32
    liability *See also* Negligence
        corporate 78, 104
        generally 78
        personal 70-71
        sexual abuse, for 104-105
        vicarious 79, 124-132
    meetings 42-46
    members. *See* Trustees.
    powers 3-6, 31-36
    procedures 67-68
    public access to property 53-58
    quorum 68
    records 51
    school closure 58-64
    secretary-treasurer 68
    security bond 69
    tie vote 68
    vacancies 67
    vice-chair 68

School councils 30, 198-201

School lockers 216

Searches
    of personal property 216
    of pupils 216-230
    of school lockers 216
    reasonableness 220
    Strip searches 369-372

Sechelt Band 29

Separate schools 71-74

Sexual harassment 330-335, 356-357

Special education
    appeals 290-291
    Charter rights 296-304
    discipline 293-296
    entitlement to 286-287, 296
    exceptional pupil 286
    generally 281-284
    human rights 296-304
    identification 288-290
    individual education plan 292
    integration 298, 302-303
    litigation 296-304
    Minister 285
    placement 288-290
    review 290
    statutory duty 285-287
    transition plan 293
    tribunal 285
    United States model 294-295

Speech. *See* Freedom of expression.

Student records
    confidentiality 53, 276
    correction of 277
    generally 276-280
    protection of privacy 279
    types of 275

Students. *See Pupils*.

Supervision of pupils. *See* Negligence.

Suspension. *See Pupils*.

Teachers. *See also* Arbitration, Ontario College of Teachers
    academic freedom 307
    appearance 343
    conduct
        generally 305-326, 330-335, 342-344
        sexual behaviour 319-322
    denominational cause 15-22, 344
    dismissal
        incompetence 350
        making threats 315-317
        sexual harassment 330
    evaluation and performance
        contemporary view 358-359
        documentation/evidence 347

Teachers. — *Cont'd.*
    minimum standards approach 352
    performance management system,
        need for 349
    statutory requirements 344-349
    "TIGHT" method 351
    freedom of expression
        conduct outside classroom
        discrimination 313-315
    incompetence
        procedure for handling 349
        types of 350
    negligence. See Negligence.
    qualification 336-337
    reporting abuse 328-330
    Robins Report 325
    role model 305-307, 317-318
    sexual exploitation of pupils 318-323
    sexual harassment 330-335, 356-357

Trespass 55-58

Trespass to Property Act (Ont.) 55-57

Torts. See also Fiduciary duty; Intentional torts; Malpractice; Negligence; Occupiers' liability; Risk management
    burden of proof 79
    defined 78

Truancy. *See* Compulsory attendance.

Trustees
    cannot be employee of same board 64
    capacity 31-36
    conflict of interest 46-51
    conviction 67
    discretion 36
    election 64
    interaction with staff 32
    native 28-30
    offences 69-70
    personal liability 70-71
    qualification 64-67
    retreats and workshops 43-45
    vacancy 67

Vaccination. *See* Immunization.

Violence in schools 212

Visitors 56, 57

Young Offenders Act
    age 263, 270
    confidentiality 263-268
    parental involvement 263
    persons in authority 268-270
    school board exception 265-268

Youth Criminal Justice 260-268

Youth Criminal Justice Act 270-275

Zero Tolerance 234-237